COMMISSION OF THE EUROPEAN COMMUNITIES

The finances
of Europe

by Daniel STRASSER

Director-General for Budgets
Commission of the European Communities

Revised and enlarged edition

THE EUROPEAN PERSPECTIVES SERIES
BRUSSELS

This publication is also available in

GR ISBN 92-825-2073-0
PT ISBN 92-825-2081-1

Cataloguing data can be found at the end of this publication

Luxembourg: Office for Official Publications of the European Communities, 1981

ISBN 92-825-2072-2

Catalogue number: CB-30-80-980-EN-C

This book is a translation of Les Finances de l'Europe *published in 1980 by Labor, Brussels.*

It is the second edition—recast, enlarged and updated—of the book published in 1975 by Presses Universitaires de France, Paris.

This is the third time that the original book has been updated. It was first updated for publication in English by Praeger, New York, and in Spanish by the Institute for Fiscal Studies, Madrid, in 1978, and subsequently for publication in German by Europa Union Verlag for the Institut für Europäische Politik, Bonn, in 1979 and in Italian by le Monnier for the review L'Italia e l'Europa, *Florence, in 1980.*

The translation of the first English edition was made by David Wyllie, Head of Division in the Directorate-General for Budgets.

Preface

It gives me great pleasure to introduce 'The finances of Europe' by Daniel Strasser to an English-speaking readership. For most of the four years that I have been the Commissioner responsible for the Budgets of the European Communities he has been the Director-General. I have relied greatly on his wise counsel, great experience and dedication to the European cause. Before assuming his present post in 1977, he was for four years Director of the Budgets. He has therefore been at the centre of events for much of the time during which the Communities' budgets have assumed their present form. His experience of the Community goes back a great deal further, as he entered the service of the Commission from the French civil service in 1958.

For many years he has written extensively about the issues and problems with which he deals in his professional life in learned journals and in books.
Indeed this book is already a classic.

It was first published in 1975 by the University Press of France. An updated English language edition was produced by Praeger (New York) in 1977 and a Spanish edition by the Institute of Fiscal Studies (Madrid) in 1978. In 1979 after further updating a German language edition was published by the Europa Union Verlag for the Institute of European Politics (Bonn) and an Italian one by Le Monnier for the periodical 'Italy and Europe' in 1980. Meanwhile Monsieur Strasser was undertaking a complete revision of the whole work to produce what amounted almost to a new book which was published in French by Labor Publications in Brussels in 1980. This volume is an English translation of that.

Its canvas is enormous. The history of the development of the Communities' finances is comprehensively covered. The legal texts are closely analysed. The different policies which have gradually been worked out since the Communities' inception are described in a wealth of detail. The reader will also learn how the annual budget procedure works and what are the roles of the Council of Ministers, the European Parliament the Commission, and the Court of Auditors. The principal focus is on the main budget of the European Communities and on the budget of the European Coal and Steel Community but other aspects of the Community's finances, including the work of the European Investment Bank, are dealt with as well.

The frequency of the changes reflects in part the growth and dynamism of the European Communities. It also reflects, however, the increasing importance of budgetary matters in the life of Europe. In recent years the budget has moved from the periphery of Community affairs to the centre. It has become the point where national interests meet and where the responsibilities of the different Community institutions—the Council, the Parliament, the Commission and the Court of Auditors—come together. Tensions and sometimes even clashes are bound to occur but they must always be reconciled. The process by which agree-

ment is reached and progress achieved is complex and often difficult for the uninitiated to follow. But all who wish to know how the Community works need to understand it.

The issues discussed and the procedures described in this book are certain to remain in the forefront of Community affairs for some time to come. The Community is approaching the limits of its own financial resources. While the principles of what has been achieved will be respected, every aspect of its income and expenditure will need to be examined. New ideas will be considered and no doubt certain initiatives will be taken. The European Council, which brings together the Heads of State or Government, has already found itself drawn more and more deeply into budgetary matters. This trend will continue and in addition to the Council of Ministers, the European Parliament and the Commission, national parliaments too will have to be involved in any decision to increase or alter the Communities' own resources.

Daniel Strasser's book provides an indispensable contribution to understanding the events which will unfold and the developments that will take place in the next few years. After participating in them I hope he will continue to find the time to write about them as well. By virtue of his experience and the position he holds he is uniquely well-qualified to do so.

Christopher Tugendhat

Foreword

Four of the ten highest gross national products in the world. Two members of the nuclear weapons club. Two permanent members of the Security Council. Four of the seven richest countries in the western world. Four of the International Monetary Fund 'Group of Ten'. Two of the seven space powers. The strongest commercial power in the world. These are some of the essential features which mark the Europe of the Communities. Fascinating distinctions, but deceptive.

For the Europe of the Communities is more impressive seen from the outside than experienced from the inside. We must realize that Europe is in the middle of a process of change and that opposing forces—sometimes in open conflict—are active there. This book deals with the Community's finances, which clearly exemplifies this situation.

The finances of Europe—or to be more precise the finances of the European Communities, i.e. the two budgets, the European Development Fund, and the banking activities carried on by the three Communities and by the European Investment Bank—are involved either openly or just below the surface in a good many of the major events in the history of Community Europe. The 1965 crisis was partly centred on financial matters, while the Summits and European Councils have often dealt with finances, sometimes in great depth. But since the enlargement of the Community from six to nine Member States, Europe's finances have become a constant topic of speeches and concern, and many claims have been made in relation to them. They have a bearing on the major problems of today: the European Monetary System, convergence of the Member States' economies, solidarity among—and financial transfers between—Member States, not to mention the common agricultural policy or the powers of the European Parliament.

Of what then do the European Communities' finances, now so often the subject of controversy, consist? To answer this question, we must first consider the nature of the European Communities themselves.

The *European Communities* are not international organizations and, in view of the original quality of the relations between their Member States, would indeed reject any such title. Several unique features should be noted: the responsibilities attributed to the Member States, the way the Community institutions operate (in particular, the parallel existence of Commission and Council), the pre-eminence of European law over national law, and the financing of the budgets. However, as Walter Hallstein, President of the European Economic Community (EEC) Commission for nearly ten years, wrote in his book *Der Unvollendete Bundesstaat*—meaning 'the uncompleted federal State' but translated under the title *Europe in the making*—'Europe is as yet neither a federation nor a State. It does however unite some elements of sovereignty which are common to the Member States and have been detached from them.' This Europe has been well named a 'community'. Since then, matters have hardly changed at all.

In fact, the European Communities already form a political superstructure, superimposed in certain fields on the administrative structures within the Member States. In the Federal Republic of Germany, for instance, as in other non-centralized States, a fourth level has been added, supplementing those of municipality, *Land* and *Bund*. In France, the European Communities constitute as it were, a third level. This superstructure functions in a subtle but democratic balancing process (described in Annex 1), to which we shall often return. Legally, it comprises three Communities, as the three Treaties which brought these into being are still in force, despite the occasionally-expressed desire that the three Communities should be merged into one. One must, therefore, speak of the European Communities in the plural; politically, it is more appropriate—as Parliament recommended in its Resolution of 16 February 1978—to use the expression 'the European Community' when referring to 'all the institutions created pursuant to the Treaties establishing the three European Communities and the grouping of the Member States'. In this book we shall use the singular where possible. At this point it is worth summarizing the historico-legal context of the different Communities.

By the *Treaty signed in Paris on 18 April 1951*, which came into force in January 1952, Belgium, the Federal Republic of Germany, France, Italy, Luxembourg, and the Netherlands declared that they established among themselves 'a European Coal and Steel Community (ECSC) founded upon a common market, common objectives, and common institutions'. Article 2 of the Treaty, *inter alia,* states that 'the ECSC shall have as its task to contribute, in harmony with the general economy of the Member States and through the establishment of a common market, to economic expansion, growth of employment, and a rising standard of living in the Member States'. This Treaty is very elaborate, not to say exhaustive; the subjects dealt with are covered in great detail.

By a *Treaty signed in Rome on 25 March 1957,* which came into force on 1 January 1958, the same six States declared the establishment of a European Economic Community (EEC). Article 2 of this Treaty states that 'the Community shall have as its task, by establishing a common market and progressively approximating the economic policies of Member States, to promote throughout the Community a harmonious development of economic activities, a continuous and balanced expansion, an increase in stability, an accelerated raising of the standard of living, and closer relations between the States belonging to it'. Unlike the first, this Treaty could be described as procedural: it defines objectives and powers but does not set out the substance in detail.

In other words, we are here concerned with the difference, familiar to lawyers, between a treaty containing rules and a 'framework' treaty.

By a *second Treaty signed in Rome on the same day*, which came into force on 1 January 1958, the same six States declared the establishment among themselves of a European Atomic Energy Community (EAEC or Euratom), 'whose task it is to contribute to the raising of the standard of living in the Member States and to the development of relations with the other countries by creating the conditions necessary for the speedy establishment and growth of nuclear industries', as stated in Article 1 of the Treaty.

In order to realize these objectives, the three Treaties created a unique organization. Article 7 of the Treaty establishing the ECSC states that the institutions of the Community shall be a High Authority, assisted by a Consultative Committee, a Common Assembly, a Special Council of Ministers, and a Court of Justice. Article 4 of the Treaty establishing the EEC lays down that the tasks entrusted to the Community shall be carried out by an Assembly, a Council, a Commission, and a Court of Justice, and that the Council and the Commission shall be assisted by an Economic and Social Committee. Finally, Article 3 of the

Treaty establishing the EAEC stipulates a similar organization. The same four institutions were thus reproduced in each of the three European Communities. Two of them, the Assembly and the Court, were common to all the Communities by virtue of the 'Convention on certain institutions common to the European Communities' signed in Rome on 25 March 1957 at the same time as the EEC and EAEC Treaties. Subsequently, a treaty signed in Brussels on 8 April 1965, which came into force on 1 July 1967 (the 'Merger Treaty'), combined the three Councils into a single Council and merged the High Authority of the ECSC, the Commission of the EEC and the Euratom Commission into a single Commission. It should be noted that the order of precedence used in the Merger Treaty of 1965 follows that used in the EEC and EAEC Treaties and gives official sanction to the relegation of the Commission, the 'supranational body', from first to third place among the Community institutions.

Since the Merger Treaty there have thus been only four institutions. In all four cases:

(i) they possess particular powers conferred on them by the Treaties to enable them to carry out the tasks devolving on the Communities (Articles 3 and 7 of the ECSC Treaty, Articles 2, 3 and 4 of the EEC Treaty and Articles 1, 2 and 3 of the EAEC Treaty). In order to carry out their tasks, they have the power to defend their own position against the other Community institutions in law;

(ii) their members are appointed directly by the authorities of the Member States;

(iii) they enjoy a certain degree of legal, administrative, and financial autonomy.

Let us now examine these four institutions.

The *Commission* is the guardian of the Treaties, the initiator of Community policy, and the executive organ of the Community. It is composed of 13 members appointed by common agreement of the governments of the Member States (Article 11 of the Merger Treaty), who must, in the general interest of the Communities, be completely independent in the performance of their duties (Article 10(2) of the same Treaty). The Commission is a highly original element in the institutional interplay of the Community, whose overriding interests it has to represent. It plays the role of mediator.

The *Council* is the legislative organ of the Community. It is composed of nine members, one from each State, who are delegated by the governments of the Member States (Article 2 of the Merger Treaty), and are either the foreign ministers, or, in the case of meetings on specific subjects, ministers of finance, agriculture, budgetary affairs, and so on. The Council is the scene of the delicate and often impossible task of reconciling the Community's interests and those of the Member States. The Council takes decisions either on a unanimous vote, or by a majority of its members, or by a 'qualified' majority on the basis of the weighting shown in Annex 2.

On the initiative of President Giscard d'Estaing, it was decided at the Paris Summit of 10 December 1974 that there should be meetings of the Council at head of government level three times a year instead of the previous system of summit meetings, which had tended to support the idea of cooperation among States to the detriment of a Community approach.

Since that time the *European Council* has met at the prearranged intervals and has become the supreme decision-making body in the Community. It has addressed itself to Europe's financial problems many times, as Annex 3 shows.

The *Assembly*, known (by a custom adopted by itself on 30 March 1962 but not recognized by the Council) as the *European Parliament*, has a generally consultative role. In Decision No 76/787/ECSC, EEC, Euratom of 20 September 1976 the Council adopted an act, the first article of which reads: 'The representatives, in the Assembly, of the peoples of the Member States of the Community shall be elected by direct universal suffrage'. The text was adopted by the Member States in accordance with their respective constitutional rules, and the first elections were held between 7 and 10 June 1979. The number of representatives for each State has changed and now corresponds more closely with their population, although it is not strictly proportionate thereto. The distribution of seats is as follows: France, the Federal Republic of Germany, Italy and the United Kingdom 81 each; the Netherlands 25; Belgium 24; Denmark 16; Ireland 15 and Luxembourg 6. The grand total of 410 is more than twice the previous one of 198. The institution does not possess all the attributes of a parliament in a democratic State, as its powers are very limited, except in budgetary matters. Parliament may, however, pass a vote of censure on the Commission, in which circumstances the members of the latter would be required to resign. Election by direct universal suffrage has not altered Parliament's powers, but some fear (and others hope) that it will try to obtain greater legislative power by revising the Treaties. However that may be, Parliament's election has strengthened the Community's democratic legitimacy and given it a new dynamism.

The planned enlargement of the Community to 12 countries will inevitably raise some tricky political problems (see Annex 16, p. 407). Two questions are enough to demonstrate the extent of the problems: will the Commission be able to function properly with 17 members? Will the Council be able to reach unanimity with 12 members? For the other institutions the problems posed by enlargement are totally different.

The *Court of Justice* consists of nine judges and four advocates-general appointed by agreement of the governments of the Member States (Articles 32b of the ECSC Treaty, 167 of the EEC Treaty and 134 of the EAEC Treaty). It has managed to build up a body of law that considerably strengthens the legal powers of the Community.

In addition to these four institutions, there is a further quasi-institutional body, set up by the Treaty of 22 July 1975, namely, the *Court of Auditors*, charged with the function of auditing Community accounts. This has nine members appointed for six years by the Council, acting unanimously, after consultation with Parliament; the feature distinguishing this body from the four previously mentioned is the fact that its members are appointed by other Community institutions (see Article 78e of the ECSC Treaty, 206 of the EEC Treaty and 180 of the EAEC Treaty). The Court of Auditors inherits the functions of the EEC/EAEC Audit Board and of the ECSC Auditor. It has the duty of checking the legal basis and regularity of receipts and expenditure and satisfying itself that the quality of financial management is satisfactory.

The European Communities also possess certain other 'organs' (although they are not called this in the Treaties). Two of them do, in fact, appear in the institutional part of the Treaties and have already been referred to: the ECSC Consultative Committee and the Economic and Social Committee. Others are the subject of a title or a chapter in the EEC Treaty: the European Investment Bank (EIB), which has legal personality, and the European Social Fund, which, by contrast, is merely a department of the Commission and does not really deserve to be called an organ. We shall have frequent occasion to describe the position and characteristics of these institutions.

Where budgetary matters are concerned, two Community institutions, and not the Member States, constitute the Budgetary Authority. Under the ECSC Treaty, and by virtue of established practice, the High Authority/Commission and Parliament are the holders of budgetary powers in the case of the ECSC. Under the Treaties of 21 April 1970 and 22 July 1975, Council and Parliament are the holders of budgetary powers in the case of the general budget.

The Commission, together with the other institutions for their respective administrative expenditure, carries the responsibility for proposing the budget and implementing it within the limit of the funds made available. When examined from the budgetary standpoint, the originality of the European Communities is in fact quite remarkable, for whereas international organizations are generally financed by contributions from the member countries, the European Communities have their own direct revenue. Similarly, whereas the expenditure of international organizations is most often just administrative expenditure, the principal outlay of the European Communities—almost 90%—consists of grants designed to contribute to the realization of the aims of the Treaties transferred to them by the Member States, without any idea of 'a just return', which means that certain States may, as a result of the action of this system, be net contributors. Europe's finances, then, resemble those of a State and have their own consistencies, constraints and drawbacks. In addition, the three European Communities have enjoyed the right—either from the beginning or more recently—to finance certain activities by means of loans rather than non-recoverable grants, thus diversifying the means available to the Community.

In 1980 the funds to be spent in the form of non-returnable grants amounted to 16 556 m EUA and the funds made available in the form of loans to probably some 4 000 m EUA, making a total of over 20 000 m EUA. The tables given in the annexes bear witness to the dynamism of Europe's finances. Thus the non-repayable expenditure of the European Communities has increased 190-fold since 1953-54 (the year of inception of the ECSC), 13-fold since 1967 (the year the common agricultural policy started) and by a factor of nearly 3.5 since 1973 (the year of enlargement to a Community of Nine).

It is a good moment, at this early stage, to explain the significance of 'm EUA'. The initials stand for 'millions of European units of account' and constitute the unit of measurement of Europe's finances. They will be met with continually in this book. As will be explained later, there have been several different definitions of the unit of account in the Community's history, with the result that its equivalent in national currencies has often varied. However, we shall henceforth aggregate units of account without updating them to the last known rate. We shall not therefore be using 'constant units of account'. This solution has been adopted in order to avoid having to keep revising the figures and above all to ensure concordance with the financial documents drawn up each year by the Communities, which, obviously, are based on 'current units of account'. On 1 September 1980 one European unit of account (EUA) was equivalent to UKL 0.60 or IRL 0.67. The ECU, the new name for the EUA, has the same value as the EUA.

In Part One of this book we shall attempt to analyse the budgetary legislation in the European Economic Community, in Part Two to describe the Community's financial resources and in Part Three to analyse the measures financed from these resources. These three parts are followed by annexes giving information about the past or contributing to an understanding of the present situation. Reference will frequently be made to other parts of the book in order to avoid repetition and to make the explanations as concise as possible as required by the constraints on the length of the book.

But before closing this foreword we should like to draw attention to one fundamental, if obvious, fact and that is that the Communities' public finances give one of the best pictures of what is happening on the small cape that the European Economic Community constitutes on the vast Euro-Asian land-mass. The budget crisis of December 1978 to April 1979 and the rejection of the budget in December 1979, to mention two recent events falling within the scope of this study, are only superficially budgetary phenomena. In essence they are manifestations of the confrontation between Parliament and the Council in the struggle for budgetary power, that is to say, in the struggle to wield political power in the Community. By the same token, the agreement on a solution to the budgetary aspect of the British problem for 1980, 1981 and 1982, reached with difficulty on 30 May 1980, reflects the malaise felt by the Community in trying to continue to live by the principles that have been its *raison d'être* for nearly thirty years.

Contents

xvi

General introduction:
The struggle for budgetary power

Like every organized society, the European Community is the scene of a struggle for control among the forces constituting it. Securing budgetary power is incontestably one way of exercising such control.

In the course of the Community's history, the struggle for budgetary power has been waged on two levels, very often at the same time. First, the Member States and the Community as such have been in dispute about whether the latter should or should not have its own financial resources. Second, the Community institutions have been in conflict over which of them should possess the power: the High Authority/Commission, the Council, or the Parliament. An account of the tenure of budgetary power is therefore a kind of condensed history of European integration itself. At the time when the supranational principle was dominant, budgetary power was conferred on the institution that embodied it, the High Authority of the ECSC. Later, with the retreat from supranationality, the notion prevailed that this power should be entrusted to the Council, the organ of national governments. Today, the contest is between this latter institution and that expression of the people of Europe, the European Parliament, within a Community which has gradually acquired complete financial independence.

If we try to establish its scope, the exercise of budgetary power essentially comprises four rights: to create revenue, to authorize expenditure, to fix the budget, and to audit the implementation of the budget. Let us now very briefly describe where these four capabilities have rested, and how their holders have changed, during the history of the struggle for budgetary power. The story is really quite short, covering hardly more than a quarter of a century. We can consider it as falling into four partly overlapping periods. We shall supplement this account with a few thoughts on the exercise of regulatory power in the financial sphere, because this is a power that comes very close to being budgetary power.

1. The Treaty of Paris of 18 April 1951
(from 1952 to date)

The Treaty of Paris, which established the ECSC, contains three Articles dealing with budgetary matters: Articles 49, 50, and 78.

Article 49 states that the High Authority is empowered to procure the funds it requires to carry out its tasks by imposing levies on the production of coal and steel and by con-

1

tracting loans. Article 50, which states what expenditure the levies are intended to cover, stipulates in its second paragraph that these levies shall be assessed annually on the various products according to their average value, but that their rate shall not exceed 1% unless this is previously authorized by the Council, acting by a two-thirds majority, the mode of assessment and collection being determined by a general decision of the High Authority taken after consulting the Council.

The original Article 78 provided that each of the four Community institutions should draw up an estimate of its administrative expenditure and that the four estimates should be consolidated in a 'general estimate' to be adopted, not by the High Authority, but by a 'Committee of the Four Presidents', consisting of the President of the Court of Justice, who acted as chairman, the President of the High Authority, the President of the Parliament, and the President of the Council. Article 78, paragraph 3, subparagraph 4 of the ECSC Treaty stipulates that the adoption of the general estimate was to have the effect of authorizing and directing the High Authority to collect the corresponding revenue, as provided in Article 49.

These laconic provisions bear witness to the simplicity and likewise to the originality of the budgetary system of this Community, which Mr Cheysson—the Commissioner for the budget from 1973 to 1976—characterized as 'exemplary' to Parliament on 11 December 1973. The High Authority, a supranational body, can authorize revenue because the Member States have surrendered to it the sovereign power of raising a tax, the 'levy'. Expenditure is authorized by the High Authority in the case of operational expenditure, the most significant category, leaving only administrative expenditure to be authorized by the Committee of the Four Presidents, a rather hybrid body, which has now disappeared. There is therefore no need for the adoption of a budget since there is no budget as such, but rather an operational activity covered by non-reimbursable payments. Audit of the implementation of the budget is carried out by the Community Auditor, whose report is 'laid before' Parliament.

It should also be noted that in practice it has never been necessary to exceed a levy rate of 1% and so the Council has never had to discuss the question. On the other hand, Parliament obtained from the High Authority in 1957 a procedure associating it in decisions about the rate of the levies and in the preparation of the ECSC's estimates of revenue and expenditure. This procedure has acquired real significance since the Commission abandoned its resolve to fix a rate of 0.30% for the financial year 1973, and again for the financial year 1974, after Parliament expressed an unfavourable opinion, and reverted to the existing rate of 0.29%; the Commission was accordingly obliged to revise its estimates of operational expenditure.

In practice, therefore, Parliament plays a dominant, if not exclusive, role in fixing the rate of the levy. The Commission, in its 1973 proposal for the revision of the Treaties (see p. 8), suggested that the Treaty should be amended in this respect. In the end the proposal was withdrawn, as it was considered that practice in this instance was equivalent to law and that a problematical constitutional amendment was not called for.

Today the administrative expenditure of the ECSC is incorporated in the general budget of the Communities; only the 'ECSC operational budget' covering this Community's grant expenditure still preserves its independent and unique character.

2. The Treaties of Rome
of 25 March 1957 (1958-70)

A—The budgetary machinery of the Treaties of Rome

The Treaty establishing the EEC and the Treaty establishing the EAEC devote much more space to the budgets of those Communities and are much more precise on the subject of their budgets than was the Treaty of Paris in the case of the ECSC. Both Treaties devote. an entire title to the subject (Title 2 of Part 5 of the EEC Treaty and Title 4 of the EAEC Treaty), under the heading 'Financial provisions', which takes up 11 articles in the EEC Treaty (Articles 199 to 209) and 13 articles in the EAEC Treaty (Articles 171 to 183). For our present purposes, namely definition of the Budget Authority, the budgetary machinery is exactly the same, *mutatis mutandis*, in both Treaties.

The powers in this sphere are determined by Article 203 of the EEC Treaty (Article 177 of the EAEC Treaty). Under this article each of the Community institutions has to draw up estimates of its own expenditure. The Commission then consolidates them in a 'preliminary draft budget', adding its own views, which may include alternative estimates, and places it before the Council not later than 30 September of the year before that in which the funds are to be spent. The Council consults the Commission, and, as appropriate, the other institutions concerned wherever it intends to depart from the preliminary draft budget. Then, acting by a qualified majority, it adopts the draft budget, which it has to place before Parliament not later than 31 October. Parliament has the right to propose amendments to the draft budget (technically known as modifications) to the Council. If, within one month of the document being placed before it, Parliament gives its approval or fails to give its opinion to the Council, the draft budget is deemed to be finally adopted. If within this period Parliament has proposed modifications, the draft budget so revised is forwarded to the Council. The Council has to discuss it with the Commission and, where appropriate, with the other institutions concerned, and finally to adopt the budget, acting by a qualified majority in respect of each of the modifications proposed by Parliament.

Since the budget must balance and the revenue consists of the contributions of the Member States, the amount of the revenue is adjusted to match the amount of expenditure approved.

Since the Treaties of Rome are less supranational than the Treaty of Paris, budgetary power was not conferred on the supranational institution, the Commission, but on the Council, the body that represents the Member States. In practice, the machinery of Article 203 of the EEC Treaty, which seemed to give certain guarantees to each institution, particularly the Commission, since they must be consulted, actually ensures the complete preeminence for the Council. For 12 years the Council was the sole budgetary authority. Parliament, it is true, made use of its opportunity to propose modifications each year, but generally speaking the Council confirmed at its second reading what it had decided at its first. The final budget was always virtually the same as the draft budget. It should be emphasized that in this matter the Treaties stipulated that the Council shall act by a 'qualified majority' (see Annex 2, p. 347) and not, as so often, unanimously, and that practice has preserved the intention of the two Treaties. In fact the budget has generally been voted by a qualified majority rather than unanimously, thus enabling some national representatives to register their disapproval of this or that detail by voting against it, without provoking a lengthy debate likely to end in cutting the Community's budgetary resources in order to have unanimous agreement on the amount thereof.

In contrast to this, it should be noted that the old Euratom research budget was, like the research programmes, decided by unanimous vote, although under Article 177(5) of the EAEC Treaty, the research and investment budget itself could have been adopted ,by a special qualified majority (see Annex 2, p. 347). The political forces in play on the European chess-board did not permit this.

Thus a financially independent Community, whose budgetary authority was essentially the High Authority itself, was operating in Luxembourg, but at the same time, the two Communities developing in Brussels were essentially without financial independence, since it was the Council that determined revenue and expenditure, adopted the budget, and formally approved the Commission's implementation thereof.

In addition, the EEC Treaty had set up the European Investment Bank, an autonomous body monitored only by the Member States, and had created the European Development Fund, another body operating outside the Community's budget machinery.

B—The reforms proposed by the Commission of the EEC in 1965

Council Regulation No 25 of 14 January 1962 made the Community responsible for financing the common agricultural policy (CAP) through the medium of the European Agricultural Guidance and Guarantee Fund (EAGGF). However, this Regulation only laid down concrete provisions for carrying the joint financing arrangements into effect for the three years 1962-63, 1963-64 and 1964-65. It was therefore necessary to decide what method of financing should be used from 1965-66 onward. The Council accordingly asked the Commission, in its Decision of 15 December 1964, to submit proposals before 1 April 1965. So, on 31 March 1965, the Commission made proposals to the Council on the financing of the common agricultural policy, the provision of independent revenue—'own resources'—for the EEC, and a strengthening of the powers of the European Parliament, which was to be elected by universal suffrage. Owing, however, to determined opposition, particularly from France, these proposals failed and the Council was forced to acknowledge, on 30 June 1965, that agreement could not be reached. This affair caused a serious crisis in the Community; for seven months, until the agreement of 29 January 1966, France pursued the policy of the 'empty chair'. The Conference of Heads of State or Government in the Hague on 1 and 2 December 1969 represented a change of ideas and provided a decisive stimulus, materializing in the Treaty of Luxembourg of 21 April 1970 (see Annex 3, p. 350).

3. The Luxembourg agreements of 21 April 1970

The Treaty of Luxembourg of 21 April 1970 alters the distribution of budgetary power in certain respects (expenditure, adoption of the budget, discharge), while the Decision of 21 April 1970 grants the European Communities eventual financial independence by endowing them with their own resources. Three resolutions recorded in the minutes of the Council meeting of 21 April 1970 also deserve attention. These texts taken together mark an important date not only in the history of the financing of Europe but in the history of Europe itself.

A—The Decision of 21 April 1970 on the replacement of financial contributions from the Member States by the European Communities' own resources

The Decision of 21 April 1970, taken by the Council pursuant to Articles 201 of the EEC Treaty and 173 of the EAEC Treaty,[1] for the first time gives the European Communities genuine resources of their own intended to permit them progressively to cover all their expenditure. This decision was subsequently ratified by the Member States in accordance with their respective constitutional requirements; this had to be done because it involved a transfer of resources from the Member States to the Community, with all that that implied in loss of sovereignty by the States and loss of parliamentary control by their legislative bodies.

The Decision was based on two ideas:
(a) to grant the European Communities genuine fiscal revenue—agricultural levies, customs duties, value-added tax (VAT)—even if this revenue was collected by national authorities; and
(b) following a well-established Community tradition, to establish this new system in stages, at first transferring in full only the revenue from agricultural levies, and bringing in the VAT percentages only at the end of the transitional period.

This decision by the Council marks an important stage in the European Community's progress forward toward financial independence, by assigning certain types of revenue to pay for its expenditure. The momentous step of transferring financial resources from the Member States to the Community carried the implication that the European Parliament's powers in the budgetary field should be strengthened. That was the object of the Treaty of Luxembourg.

B—The Treaty of Luxembourg of 21 April 1970

The Treaty of Luxembourg made significant changes in Articles 78 of the ECSC Treaty, 203 of the EEC Treaty and 177 of the EAEC Treaty and marked a new phase in the broadening of budgetary power. The Treaty fixed two phases, the first ending with the budget for the financial year 1974, the second beginning with the budget for the financial year 1975, corresponding to the stages by which the Community was to acquire its own resources (see Annex 10, p. 379).

1971-74 (interim period)—The Treaty was signed in Luxembourg on 21 April 1970[2] and entered into force on 1 January 1971, the time taken by each State to ratify it being remarkably short. Its main novelty was to give Parliament a degree of influence over expenditure that it had not hitherto enjoyed, through new provisions set out in the fourth and fifth paragraphs of Article 203a (a transitional article intended to lapse on 1 January 1975).

Under these provisions the European Parliament could, as before, put proposed modifications to the draft budget to the Council, but where a given modification involved no net increase in an institution's expenditure (in particular because the increase in expenditure involved was specifically balanced by offsetting cuts contained in one or more additional modifications), the Council, acting by a qualified majority, had power to reject the proposed modification; in the absence of a decision to reject it, the proposed modification was accepted. On the other hand, where a modification proposed by Parliament involved a net increase in an institution's expenditure, its acceptance required positive endorsement by the Council, again acting by a qualified majority.

Thus these provisions only amounted to a modest step forward by Parliament on the way to becoming a true budgetary authority. The right to propose modifications was nothing new; the Treaties of Rome already gave it this right. But from now on it became more difficult for the Council to exercise its supremacy since it needed a qualified majority to decide against any proposed modification not involving an increase in total expenditure. This is what has been called 'the reversed majority', a vivid but inaccurate phrase, for what was really 'reversed' was not the majority but the question put. To adopt the budget or an item of expenditure, the normal rule was that a qualified majority of the Council had to vote in favour of it—in other words, a positive vote was needed. Now, however, in order to reject an increase in one item of expenditure which was compensated for by a reduction in another item of expenditure, a similar qualified majority had to oppose it; so what was needed now was a negative vote. In practice this system has enabled Parliament to play a role of some significance by getting some of its priorities accepted.

When the procedure had been completed, it was still the task of the President of the Council to 'declare the budget finally adopted'; but it is worth noting that at the time of the preparatory work before the signature of the Treaty of Luxembourg there was discussion of the right of Parliament to reject a budget *in toto*. Although such a right was not explicit in the Treaty, Parliament in fact held that it had the right to reject a budget in its entirety, and the Commission agreed with this view. In practice this right was never invoked; although Parliament invariably proposed modifications during the discussions on the draft budgets for the financial years 1971, 1972, 1973 and 1974, it never actually dreamed of rejecting the draft budget in its entirety.

The Treaty of Luxembourg also changed the articles in the three Treaties dealing with formal acceptance of the accounts. The provisions of Articles 206 of the EEC Treaty, 180 of the EAEC Treaty and 78d of the ECSC Treaty were worded in virtually identical form, stating that both the Council and Parliament should approve the Commission's final accounts dealing with the implementation of the budget. To this end, the report of the Audit Board was to be examined first by the Council, which decided on its position by a qualified majority, and then by Parliament, the Commission being given discharges only after both the Council and Parliament had so determined. In this field of supervision and implementation of the budget, Parliament thus gained a right of co-decision, which represents a not inconsiderable element of budgetary power.

From the 1975 budget onward—For the preparation and adoption of the budget for the financial year 1975, i.e. in 1974, the Treaty of Luxembourg laid down new rules that strengthened the European Parliament in its new role of Budgetary Authority. Paragraphs 1, 2 and 3 of Articles 203 of the EEC Treaty, 177 of the EAEC Treaty and 78 of the ECSC Treaty were not changed, but paragraphs 4 and 5 were radically altered and some new paragraphs were added. The new provisions may be summarized as follows:[3] on the first reading of the draft budget, Parliament, acting by an absolute majority of the votes cast, now has power to propose 'modifications' to the draft budget in respect of expenditure the Community is obliged to incur under the Treaty or under acts adopted in accordance with it, but that it can propose—by a majority of its members—'amendments' in respect of the so-called non-compulsory items of expenditure in the draft budget. Its power thus varies according to whether or not the expenditure is 'compulsory' or not. This distinction is one of the major budgetary innovations introduced by the Luxembourg Treaty and will be discussed below (see p. 40).

If Parliament proposes a modification to an item of compulsory expenditure, the Council must act by a qualified majority. If the Council rejects the proposed modification, it must inform Parliament of the result of its discussions, but its decision is final. On the other hand, while Parliament may propose an amendment with regard to non-compulsory expenditure, the Council may either reject that amendment by qualified majority or adopt it under one of the following three procedures: acceptance by a qualified majority, amendment by a qualified majority, or finding itself unable to reject it because a 'minority for acceptance' is present.[4] If the amendment is not accepted *in toto* by the Council, it is returned for a second reading to Parliament, which then decides by a majority of its members and three-fifths of the votes expressed (see Annex 2, p. 347). Parliament, then, has the last word, unless the subject of the consultation is the adoption of a new rate (see p. 123).

In addition to this strengthening of Parliament's powers, a new clause stipulates that it is the President of Parliament (rather than the President of the Council) who now 'declares' that the budget has been finally adopted.

C—The three resolutions recorded in the minutes of the Council meeting of 21 April 1970

In the minutes to its meeting of 21 April 1970, the Council recorded three resolutions which we ought to mention here in view of their significance.

'1. Resolution with regard to the section of the budget concerning the European Parliament for the period referred to in Article 78a of the ECSC Treaty, Article 203a of the EEC Treaty, and Article 177a of the EAEC Treaty'.

By this resolution the Council undertakes to make no amendments to the estimate of Parliament's expenditure, provided such an undertaking involves no conflict with Community enactments, in particular with regard to the Staff Regulations of Officials, the Conditions of Employment of Other Servants, and the siting of the institutions.

Parliament thus gained sole responsibility for its own budget. The Council has, since then, strictly observed this undertaking.[5] The Parliament, in return, has in practice refrained from amending the Council's expenditure estimates; thus, each of the joint holders of the power of decision on the budget has complete independence as far as its own budget is concerned.

'2. Resolution regarding Community acts which have financial implications and collaboration between the Council and the Assembly'.

In this resolution the Council invites the Commission to include financial estimates with every financially significant proposal sent by it to Parliament so that the latter has the full information needed to give its views on all such Community acts. Currently, this resolution is fully implemented. The Council also undertook to collaborate very closely indeed with Parliament in the examination of these acts, and, if it took a different view from the latter, to explain its reasons.

Originally the procedure was fairly informal, but it has since become a proper 'legislative' consultation, as we shall see at the end of this chapter.

'3. Resolution regarding cooperation between the Council and the European Parliament in the framework of the budgetary procedure'.

Under this resolution, by agreement between the Council and Parliament, everything possible should be and has been done to ensure close cooperation at all levels between the two institutions, with regard to the processing of the budget, notably by having the President-in-Office or another member of the Council attend Parliament's discussions on the draft budget.

This resolution has not, however, given rise to a genuine dialogue between the two institutions, except perhaps from 1974 onward. We shall often have occasion to mention inter-institutional cooperation of this kind and shall henceforth refer to it as 'budgetary concilia-tion'.

4. The Treaty of 22 July 1975

In Declaration No 4, embodied in the minutes of the Council meeting of 21 April 1970, the Commission had stated its intention of submitting proposals, not more than two years after th ratification of the Treaty of Luxembourg, for further progress along the road opened up by the Treaty and by the Decision of 21 April 1970 towards reinforcement of Parliament's budgetary powers. After some delay owing to reorganization consequent upon the enlargement of the Community, the Commission put its proposals to the Council on 8 June 1973.[6] The Commission subsequently amended these proposals in the light of an opinion produced by Parliament on 5 October 1973 in order to take account of various observations Parliament had made. The Commission's definitive proposals, dated 10 October 1973, gave rise to lengthy discussions in the Council which ended only on 4 June 1974, despite the interest shown by the Copenhagen Summit of 15 December 1973 (see Annex 3, p. 351). In reply to Parliament's wish, the Council supplied the texts on which it had based its guidelines. Two meetings then took place between the Council and a Parliamentary delegation, with Commission representatives in attendance, which enabled a compromise to be reached on several points at issue, so that, on 22 July 1975, a new treaty could be signed amending certain financial provisions in the previous treaties. The political circumstances in some Member States have meant that ratification has often long been delayed. This Treaty did not therefore come into force until 1 June 1977, i.e. 22 months later.

As before, we shall analyse its provisions from the standpoint of the four rights that make up budgetary power.

Raising of revenue—In order to underpin the financial autonomy of the European Communities and to enable Community resources to keep pace with the needs of Community policies, the Commission had proposed the establishment of a special Community procedure to procure new forms of independent revenue or alter the existing level of Community revenue (notably the 1% of VAT). The procedure proposed was a decision of Parliament, to be taken by a majority of its members and three-fifths of the votes cast on a proposal from the Commission that had first to be unanimously agreed upon by the Council; this last stipulation would permit governments to bring the matter before the national parliaments if necessary. Knowing that it would meet with difficulties in the Council, the Commission had put forward this extremely important change in a separate draft treaty so

8

that non-acceptance thereof would not compromise the approval of its other proposals; in fact, the Council refused to enhance the Communities' financial independence in this way. It was tacitly understood that the question could be reopened in the context of discussions on the establishment of a European Union.

Moreover, on a similar topic, the Commission had also proposed that the Community should be able to raise loans as part of the budgetary procedure, on the strength of a decision by the Council acting by qualified majority after assent from Parliament acting by a majority of its members and an absolute majority of the votes cast (proposed new Articles: 203b of the EEC Treaty and 172(4) of the EAEC Treaty). The Council refused to accept this innovation too, which means that it entirely rejected the Commission's proposals with regard to the raising of revenue, despite the fact that Parliament supported them. Accordingly the Treaty of 22 July 1975 is silent on this point and does not in any way alter the former situation. By contrast, the borrowings of the ECSC and EIB continue to escape the control of the Budgetary Authority.

Acceptance of expenditure under the budgetary procedure—The Treaty of 22 July 1975 amends the fifth paragraph of Article 203 of the EEC Treaty. It accepts the 'reversed majority' rule for the adoption of modifications proposed by Parliament when these do not increase overall expenditure. But it does not incorporate the Commission's proposal to use the reversed majority for proposed changes that do involve increasing total expenditure. However, there is no change to the order of the budgetary procedure, and Parliament still has the last word on non-compulsory expenditure, provided it keeps within the maximum rate of increase for such expenditure. To exceed this rate, a joint decision by Council and Parliament is necessary (see p. 123).

A word must now be said about what in the jargon of the Communities is called 'the Parliament's room for manoeuvre'. This refers to a sum in units of account that the Parliament has gained the right to assign as it wishes over and above the amounts put into the draft budget by the Council. What this means is that in the field of non-compulsory expenditure, Parliament may have the last word on a proposed increase or even the creation of a new item of expenditure, provided the money is found within the limit of this sum. Here the Treaties have been interpreted with flexibility—up to the budget for the financial year 1978— since there has been no official invocation of the 'observed rate of increase for non-compulsory expenditure' or of the 'new rate'. But the spirit of the law is not infringed. This procedure has given Parliament a significant power to endorse or even initiate expenditure. New activities have been started that would not otherwise have existed. The progress of the Communities has gained a further impulse from this innovation, but at the same time, serious conflicts of views have arisen (see pp. 56 and 57).

The budget crisis of December 1978 to April 1979, on the other hand, was settled by applying Article 203 of the EEC Treaty in a more legalistic fashion, which we shall examine below.

Adoption or rejection of the budget—The new Treaty states that Parliament, acting by a majority of members and two-thirds of the votes cast, should have power, for reasons of major importance, to reject the draft budget and to ask for a new draft to be submitted. This is no more than the confirmation of a right that Parliament and the Commission considered to have existed since the Treaty of 21 April 1970. The provision is now, however, covered in the Treaty (new Article 203(8) of the EEC Treaty, *inter alia*).

Right from its first dealings with the budget, the newly-elected Parliament has made use of the power given it by the Treaty. On 13 December 1979, it rejected the draft budget for

1980 by 288 votes to 64, holding that its conditions for the budget's adoption had not been fulfilled. These conditions, announced on 7 November 1979 on the occasion of the first reading of the draft budget, were four in number: action to control agricultural expenditure; an increase in some items of non-compulsory expenditure; bringing the EDF into the budget; and bringing borrowing and lending operations into the budget. Rejection of the draft budget had the effect of triggering off, as from 1 January 1980, the system of 'provisional twelfths' provided for by Article 204 of the EEC Treaty (see p. 75). By rejecting the budget, Parliament was trying to prod the Council into adopting certain regulations and was thereby also endeavouring to gain a firmer foothold in the legislative process.

Auditing the budget—The proposal made by the Commission, and approved by Parliament, that the power to give discharge in respect of the audited accounts should be given to the latter—acting on a recommendation from the Council to be adopted by qualified majority—was accepted (new Article 206b of the EEC Treaty). Agreement was also given to the Commission's proposal, approved by Parliament, to set up a European Court of Auditors (see p. 93). Thus, the Treaty of 22 July 1975 is highly innovative in this respect, but in this respect alone.

5. The exercise of power to make regulations; conciliation in respect of legislative measures

The Treaties, the only legislation to which we have referred up to this point, confine themselves to laying down basic principles, leaving the task of drawing up the rules for their implementation to the regulations. As far as budgetary and financial matters are concerned, the basic text—Articles 209 of the EEC Treaty and 183 of the EAEC Treaty—read as follows in its 1957 version:
'The Council shall, acting unanimously on a proposal from the Commission:
(a) make Financial Regulations specifying in particular the procedure to be adopted for establishing and implementing the budget and for presenting and auditing accounts;
(b) determine the methods and procedure whereby the contributions of Member States shall be made available to the Commission;
(c) lay down rules concerning the responsibility of authorizing officers and accounting officers and concerning appropriate arrangements for inspection'.

These provisions thus establish the principle that budgetary law is made by the Council taking unanimous decisions on proposals put forward by the Commission; in other words each Member State has a right of veto and Parliament is not even consulted.[7] The system lasted 15 years. In its proposed amendment to the Treaties, dated 8 June 1973, the Commission had recommended that henceforth the Council should take its decisions 'in agreement' with Parliament, taking the view that this would give Parliament its rightful power in connection with preparation and inspection of the budget; in the Commission's definitive proposal of 10 October 1973 the formula became 'with the assent' of Parliament. In fact the Council, well aware of the crucial importance of this power, refused to share it.

However, the Treaty of 22 July 1975 did amend Articles 209 of the EEC Treaty, 183 of the EAEC Treaty and 78f of the ECSC Treaty by stipulating *inter alia* that the Council should act 'after consulting' Parliament and after obtaining the opinion of the Court of Auditors. This is a meagre consolation from Parliament's point of view; yet the latter has been accorded a certain degree of participation by means of the conciliation procedure, in consideration of the fact that the increase in Parliament's budgetary powers had to be accompanied by its effective participation in the processes of preparing and adopting the decisions giving rise to substantial items of expenditure or revenue in the budgets of the European Communities.

In fact, conciliation was not then really a new phenomenon in interinstitutional relationships, having already been in existence for some years (see the third resolution recorded in the minutes of the Council meeting of 21 April 1970 (pp. 8 and 44)) thanks to the systematic establishment of contacts between Council and Parliament. But Parliament's demand, in its resolution of 5 October 1973, was for a more formal conciliation procedure. After lengthy discussions within each of the three institutions and after two meetings, agreement was finally reached by the institutions on 4 March 1975 on the text of a 'joint declaration' establishing a conciliation procedure. This procedure may be used for 'Community acts of general application which have far-reaching financial implications and whose adoption is not required by existing acts' and also for the adoption of the Financial Regulations themselves.[8] Under this procedure the Commission, when it submits a proposal, must state whether the act in question falls within the scope of the procedure. Operation of the procedure may be requested both by Parliament, when delivering its opinion, and by the Council; the procedure is initiated when the conditions just outlined are met and the Council intends not to follow the opinion adopted by Parliament. It is then the task of a conciliation committee, bringing together the Council and representatives of Parliament—with the Commission in attendance and actively participating—to seek a conciliation of views. This process must normally be completed within three months. When the positions of the two institutions are sufficiently close, Parliament may give a fresh opinion and the Council then gives its definitive verdict.[9]

This formula has achieved varying degrees of success (see Annex 5, p. 363). Nevertheless, conciliation—which in this case may be called 'legislative conciliation'—is a very important innovation. It makes possible a genuine dialogue between the institutions and to some extent brings to an end the practice of the Council's working behind closed doors. Admittedly, there is no precisely-defined procedure to ensure that conciliation will lead to agreement, but the new procedure substantially alters the climate of relations among the Community institutions and gives Parliament an additional means of action in the form of a certain degree of participation in legislative power.

*
**

All the Community's constitutional amendments to date have to a greater or lesser extent been connected with the budget. The Treaty of Brussels of 8 April 1965—the so-called Merger Treaty—merged the Communities' budgets. The Treaty of Luxembourg of 21 April 1970 and the Treaty of Brussels of 22 July 1975 came into being solely to change 'certain budgetary provisions' of the basic Treaties. Juridical development within the Community has thus been concentrated mainly on the budget and on Parliament's budgetary powers. This is worth emphasizing. The result has been a redistribution of powers between the Member States and the Community and also between the Community institutions themselves.[10]

With the introduction of the new Article 203 of the EEC Treaty by the Treaty of 21 April 1970, that is, as from the preparation of the 1975 budget, Parliament came of age as an institution concerned with the budget. In dealing with that budget, Parliament showed itself ready to make use of a procedure that it had itself described as dubious by raising the majorities needed to vote a number of amendments of a definitely political character to items of non-compulsory expenditure—no easy or self-evident matter, since the agreement of all the major political groups had to be obtained (see Annex 2, p. 347). The Council, while yielding no ground as regards the fixing of compulsory expenditure, was obliged to acknowledge the fullness of Parliament's powers over non-compulsory expenditure, within the limits of its 'room for manoeuvre'. The Council has remained on the defensive and a real diarchy has thus come into being in the field of budgetary power. The procedural conflict over adoption of the 1979 budget and in particular over the appropriations for the Regional Fund is proof of this,[11] repeated the following year by the rejection of the 1980 budget.

The basis of this legal and political development is such that this development is limited by factors internal to itself. The exercise of a budgetary power does not make it possible to acquire legislative power. Parliament has of course managed to use its budgetary responsibilities with great skill and to obtain the maximum advantage from them; it is, however, continually coming up against the political fact that it does not possess legislative power, even when it allies itself with the Council. But this is another battle, which the directly-elected Parliament is sure to fight.

It is interesting to observe, however, that although Parliament was granted budgetary powers, they were essentially concerned with monitoring revenue, own resources being attributed to the European Communities as a whole; in practice, however, Parliament has exercised its powers in connection with expenditure rather than revenue, and has often managed to impose its own wishes; this is an astute use of its powers.

The position occupied by the Commission in this conflict is highly uncomfortable. It is the Commission which puts forward drafts and compromises, but—placed as it is between two institutions whose points of view are both traditionally and actually very far apart—it is simultaneously charged with timidity and temerity, pragmatism and idealism. It has several times been threatened with motions of censure, a threat never made except in the budgetary field. It has more than once been the target of scathing criticism from the Member States. Such is the strange law of this novel interinstitutional interplay that takes place within the European Communities.[12] It is interesting to note that despite criticisms from one side or the other the Communities are developing along the lines of the middle course that the Commission has steered.

Footnotes to the General introduction

[1] Articles 201 of the EEC Treaty and 173 of the EAEC Treaty read as follows:
Article 201 of the EEC Treaty: The Commission shall examine the conditions under which the financial contributions of Member States provided for in Article 200 could be replaced by the Community's own resources, in particular by revenue accruing from the common customs tariff when it has been finally introduced. To this end, the Commission shall submit proposals to the Council.
After consulting the Assembly on these proposals the Council may, acting unanimously, lay down the appropriate provisions, which it shall recommend to the Member States for adoption in accordance with their respective constitutional requirements.
Article 173 of the EAEC Treaty: The financial contributions of Member States provided for in Article 172 may be replaced in whole or in part by the proceeds of levies collected by the Community in Member States. To this end, the Commission shall submit to the Council proposals concerning the assessment of such levies, the method of fixing their rate and the procedure for their collection.
After consulting the Assembly on these proposals, the Council may, acting unanimously, lay down the appropriate provisions, which it shall recommend to the Member States for adoption in accordance with their respective constitutional requirements.

[2] On 14 December 1976 the Italian Foreign Minister, the Depositary of the Treaty, corrected an error as to the date of this Treaty: the date of 22 April 1970, previously quoted, was replaced by the correct date of 21 April 1970.

[3] For further details, see my article in *La Revue du marché commun*: 'La nouvelle procédure budgétaire des Communautés européennes et son application à l'établissement du budget pour l'exercice 1975' (February 1975).

[4] A 'minority for acceptance' is formed by 18 votes in the Council (see p. 347 for the system of vote-weighting). To obtain 18 votes it is necessary to secure the votes either of two 'big' Member States (10 + 10), or of one big State plus Belgium and the Netherlands (10 + 5 + 5), or of one big State plus Belgium or the Netherlands and Ireland or Denmark (10 + 5 + 3), or one big State plus Ireland, Denmark and Luxembourg (10 + 3 + 3 + 2) or of all the Member States other than the 'big four' (5 + 5 + 3 + 3 + 2).

The machinery of the 'minority for acceptance', surprising as its consequences may seem, has played a role in every budget cycle. In connection with the adoption of the 1979 budget it had the notable effect of triggering the crisis of November 1978 to April 1979. (See also footnote 11 below). On that occasion the minority for acceptance was made up of the votes of Italy and the United Kingdom. To date, the machinery has operated in favour of Parliament's views.

[5] In the course of adoption of the second supplementary budget for 1979, the Council seemed to show a desire to question the validity of the agreement, arguing that it had become obsolete since Parliament could in the last resort take a decision on its administrative expenditure—this being non-compulsory expenditure, on which it has the last word. Eventually, however, the agreement was held to be still valid.

[6] The Commission had undertaken to put forward a new treaty as a result of Parliament's dissatisfaction with the 1970 Treaty. The two-year period set for the introduction of the amendments ran out at the end of 1972. In November 1972 a censure motion against the Commission was tabled. Although subsequently withdrawn, the motion acted as a spur to the new Commission taking office in January 1973 to act speedily on this matter (see Supplement 9/73—Bull. EC).

[7] In practice Parliament succeeded in ensuring that it was consulted on the proposed revision of the Financial Regulation which was to take final form as the Regulation of 25 April 1973. Parliament had delivered an opinion on 19 January 1971, then again on 14 February 1973 on the Commission's revised proposal. A procedure had thus to a certain extent been established, set in motion by Resolution No 3 of 21 April 1970 (see p. 8).

[8] This latter provision was written into the minutes of the Council meeting of 10 and 11 February 1975.

[9] See OJ C 89 of 22.4.1975, pp. 1 and 2.

[10] The distinction between the transfer of powers from national to Community level and the distribution of powers between Community institutions is not always clearly perceived. This was especially the case in the campaign leading up to the elections of 10 June 1979 with regard to Parliament's powers. It is perfectly possible to increase Parliament's powers without any increase in the powers of the Community as a whole.

[11] For further details, see my article in *La Revue du marché commun*: 'Le budget 1979, bilan d'une procédure, difficultés politiques et juridiques, perspectives pour une nouvelle année' (June 1979).

[12] For a good appreciation of all the subtleties of 'interinstitutional interplay', see the article in the same issue of the above periodical by Mr Emile Noël, Secretary-General of the Commission of the European Communities: 'Les rouages de l'Europe'.

PART ONE

The budget legislation of the European Community

We have now examined the Community budgets in the light of the exercise of the budget power by the Budgetary Authority over a period of more than 25 years. Limitations of space preclude a similar historical description of the development of the two Community budgets as legal and financial instruments throughout this period. For the most part we shall seek, in Part One, to describe the Community budgets as they were at the end of 1980.

The document that brings together the rules applying to the general budget is known as the 'Financial Regulation'. The revised Articles 209 of the EEC Treaty and 183 of the EAEC Treaty state that:

'The Council, acting unanimously on a proposal from the Commission, and after consulting the Assembly and obtaining the opinion of the Court of Auditors shall:
(a) make Financial Regulations specifying in particular the procedure to be adopted for establishing and implementing the budget and for presenting and auditing accounts;
(b) determine the methods and procedure whereby the budget revenue provided under the arrangements relating to the Communities' own resources shall be made available to the Commission, and determine the steps to be taken, if need be, to meet the need for cash in hand;
(c) lay down rules concerning the responsibility of authorizing officers and accounting officers and concerning appropriate arrangements for inspection.'

The new Article 78h of the ECSC Treaty, as is appropriate to the ECSC Treaty, contains only items (a) and (c).

Pursuant to Article 209 of the EEC Treaty and Article 183 of the EAEC Treaty the Council has adopted several financial regulations; the most recent general one was enacted on 21 December 1977 and came into force on 1 January 1978.[1] It contains six general titles (85 articles), four special titles (18 articles), and one further title (7 articles comprising the transitional and definitive provisions. The four special titles concern: research and investment appropriations (Title VII), the EAGGF Guarantee Section (Title VIII), food aid (Title IX) and the Office for Official Publications of the European Communities (Title X). Still to be determined are the implementation procedures,[2] which are to be issued by the Commission in the form of a Regulation—an interesting delegation of legislative power to the Commission.

Finally, it should be noted that Article 107 of the Financial Regulation expressly states that it shall be examined every three years, and allows for recourse to the conciliation procedure regarding the text of any amendments.

The rules governing the ECSC operational budget derive very often from custom, since. strictly speaking, this particular Community has neither a budget nor a financial regulation. Whereas the budgetary legislation of the ECSC has remained somewhat static, that of the other two Communities is continually evolving.[3]

Chapter I:
The budgetary rules of the
European Community

A reading of the Treaty of Rome, specifically of the section entitled 'Financial provisions', and the current Financial Regulation shows the degree to which the general budget complies with conventional budgetary principles. In examining each of these, we shall attempt to make clear what the current ECSC practice amounts to. At the outset, however, we should emphasize the Community's desire to make its budgets transparent and precise so that meaningful democratic control can be exercised.

In addition to the classical budgetary rules, the two budgets of the European Community observe the unit of account principle; if they did not, the multitude of national currencies would render their preparation impossible.

1. The Community budgets and the classic rules of budget theory

Traditional budgetary theory envisages five 'rules' or basic principles: those of unity, universality, annuality, specification, and budgetary equilibrium; these we shall now examine.

A—The rule of unity

The rule of budgetary unity (comprehensiveness) requires any official public body to bring together all the financial transactions which concern it—i.e. its income and expenditure—in a single document generally known as its budget; this document is put to the vote in Parliament.[4] The European Communities did not at first accept this principle but were subsequently converted to it. It will be worth summarizing this process of conversion.

The word 'budget' is not mentioned in the 1951 Treaty of Paris, nor does it evoke any procedure resembling a budget. It merely refers to an 'overall forecast' of administrative expenditure (Article 78, paragraph 3, subparagraph 4 of the ECSC Treaty), a forecast that, in fact, lapsed at the time of the merger of the executives; oddly enough, at this point it was designated the 'administrative budget of the ECSC' (Article 20, paragraph 1 of the Merger Treaty). On the other hand, the great bulk of the ECSC's expenditure and virtually all its revenue are not included in the 'overall forecast' but are summarized in a different document currently known as the 'ECSC operational budget'. As can be seen from this title, the term 'budget' thus was, and still is, also used, for ease of understanding to refer to the income and expenditure of the ECSC, although this has no legal significance.

This budget remains very different from the general budget of the Communities. ECSC borrowing and lending operations are not included, though this omission is perfectly in accordance with the special nature of this particular budget.

Between 1958, the year of the inception of the Brussels Communities, and the end of 1968 there were four parallel budgets: the EEC budget (Article 199 of the EEC Treaty), the EAEC operational budget, the EAEC research and investment budget (Article 171 of the EAEC Treaty), and the ECSC administrative budget. To complete the picture, one should also add the ECSC operational budget.

The Treaty of Brussels dated 8 April 1965 (known as the Merger Treaty) merged three of these budgets into a single budget, the exception being the research and investment budget, which was only integrated with the others by the Treaty of Luxembourg of 21 April 1970. This combined budget is known, in practice, as the 'general budget of the European Communities'. The principle of comprehensiveness found statutory sanction in Article 20 of the Merger Treaty as amended by Article 10 of the Treaty of Luxembourg. This reads as follows:

'1. The administrative expenditure of the European Coal and Steel Community and the revenue relating thereto, the revenue and expenditure of the European Economic Community, and the revenue and expenditure of the European Atomic Energy Community, with the exception of that of the Supply Agency and the Joint Undertakings, shall be shown in the budget of the European Communities in accordance with the appropriate provisions of the Treaties establishing the three Communities. This budget, which shall be in balance as to revenue and expenditure, shall take the place of the administrative budget of the European Coal and Steel Community, the budget of the European Economic Community, and the operating budget and research and investment budget of the European Atomic Energy Community.'

Thus dispersion gave way to unification. Three legally distinct bodies now share a single general budget, although one of them, the ECSC, retains a quasi-budget of its own in its operational budget. It is still, however, incorrect to refer to 'the budget of the European Communities'; it has to be their 'budgets'.

The 'general budget of the European Communities' takes the form of a document published in the *Official Journal of the European Communities*, normally some time after the date of its approval. For example, the 1979 budget, approved on 14 December 1978, was published on 31 January 1979[5] and distributed in the middle of February. The sheer bulk of the document (657 pages) and the requirement to publish it simultaneously in the six official languages of the Community account for this delay in producing the published version. The ECSC operational budget is also published in the *Official Journal of the European Communities* in the six official languages, but in a very brief form. In the case of the 1979 budget, 'Commission Decision No 3097/78/ECSC of 22 December 1978 fixing the rate of the levies for the 1979 financial year and amending Decision No 3/52/ECSC of 23 December 1952 on the subject of the amounts and implementation of the levies described in Articles 49 and 50 of the ECSC Treaty'—this being the way the ECSC budget is described—occupied three pages, published in the *Official Journal* on 29 December 1978.[6]

The peculiar status of the ECSC operational budget is well justified and does not impair the principle of comprehensiveness. Its basis is in fact its separate financial regime, founded on the levies on the production of the coal and steel industries, which are used to grant financial aids to these industries. If it became politically imperative to combine the two budgets without amending the Treaties, it would be necessary to set this expenditure against the corresponding receipts, in violation of another budgetary principle: the rule of non-assignment of revenue. Such a move could also place in jeopardy the ECSC's ingenious and well-devised financial system.

There are four much more serious infringements of the principle of comprehensiveness. First, the activities of the EIB are not shown in the budget. This omission is understandable, given that the Bank enjoys independent status and financial autonomy. Second, there is the case of the EAEC Supply Agency, whose activities are covered in a 'special account' (Article 171(2) of the EAEC Treaty). Since, however, in practice the Agency is a department of the Commission and not an independent body, and since the 'charge on transactions' relating to fissile material provided for in Article 54, paragraph 5 of the EAEC Treaty has never come into being, its supposed budgetary independence has remained a fiction. Although the funds to meet the running costs of the Agency are separately identified in the general budget, they are an integral element of it.

The third exception is the European Development Fund. This really does infringe the principle of comprehensiveness since it is not the case that the totality of the EEC's revenue and expenditure appears in the budget (as required by Article 199 of the EEC Treaty and Article 3(1) of the Financial Regulation) because of the treatment of the EDF. The receipts of this fund (contributions paid in by the Member States) and its expenditure (aid granted to associated countries) are authorized and implemented outside the budgetary framework. The reasons for this exception are explained below (see p. 280). The same view was advanced with regard to financial aid granted to certain non-Communist States (countries in the Mediterranean area) but did not in the end predominate since this item was entered in the 1977 budget.

The last exception is to be found in the field of capital operations (borrowing/lending). Those of the EIB and the ECSC do not need to be given particular mention, in view of the explanations that have just been given. On the other hand, as will be explained below (see p. 62), entry in the budget of the capital operations carried out since 1976 by the EEC and since 1977 by the EAEC has been somewhat defective.

So the Community does observe the principle of comprehensiveness (i.e. of budgetary unity), but with two major exceptions—which the Commission proposes to remove.[7] Parliament is staunchly supporting the Commission on this issue and, since the Council refuses to agree, the former has brought into play its most effective weapon: rejection of the budget. It is interesting to note that among the four 'major reasons' for rejection of the budget on 13 December 1979 are to be found these two instances of failure to include important groups of revenue and expenditure.

B—The rule of universality

The principle of universality, which has the same objective as that of budgetary unity, states that budgetary revenue may not be allocated to particular items of expenditure in advance (rule of non-assignment) and that no adjustments between revenue and expenditure may take place (gross budget principle). The Member States of the Community are familiar with these rules, which have much in common with that of budgetary unity:[8] they have their origin in the political desire to make the budget more flexible, easier to follow and easier to monitor. What has been the Community's attitude to these principles?

This rule against correlating individual items of income and expenditure was not at first accepted by the European Communities. In the case of the ECSC, as already explained, the levies are applied to specified types of expenditure (Article 50(1) of the ECSC Treaty). The EEC and EAEC likewise, at the beginning, established a system of 'political' scales for the sharing of particular sorts of expenditure (see the scales for the Social Fund, atomic-research expenditure, and the agricultural policy, given in Annex 9, p. 377). But, except in the case of the ECSC operational budget, this approach was brought to an end with the introduction of the 'own-resources' system of Community revenue when it was laid down that 'revenue . . . shall be used without distinction to finance all expenditure entered in the budget of the Communities, in accordance with Article 20' of the Merger Treaty (Article 5 of the Decision of 21 April 1970). None the less, Articles 3(4) and 4(6) of this Decision allow an exception for supplementary research programmes that interest and are financed by only some of the Member States (see p. 261). In addition, Article 3(2) of the Financial Regulation allows certain receipts with a tied object, such as receipts from foundations, grants, gifts, and legacies, to keep their intended destinations; this is a purely theoretical exception since the Community has never been given money in this way. Laying aside these two cases, it should be noted that the general budget of the Communities does in fact observe the principle of non-assignment. Thus, the agricultural receipts (levies) of the EAGGF are not set against the expenditure from the Fund, nor is the contribution for sugar appropriated in aid of the Community's operations on the sugar market.

Netting-off is formally prohibited (Article 199 of the EEC Treaty, Article 171 of the EAEC Treaty). The injunction is repeated in Article 3(1) of the Financial Regulation, the first subparagraph of which reads: 'Subject to Article 22, all estimated revenue and all estimated expenditure shall be entered in full in the budget and in the accounts without any adjustment against each other'. However, Article 22(1) lays down that fines imposed, adjustments of amounts paid in error and the value of scientific and technical equipment may be deducted from all bills, invoices and statements. Similarly, Article 22(2) provides for revenue arising from the refund of amounts paid in error, insurance payments received and refunds of taxes incorporated in prices in cases where the Communities are exempt—to be re-used. If provision is made therefor in the budget, the proceeds from the supply of goods and services (interpreting services) to other institutions or for payment, the sale of publications and the replacement of certain equipment may also be re-used. The 1980 budget authorized the re-use of funds in the case of 16 different headings covering a total of 8 965 250 EUA. Finally, Article 22(4) of the Financial Regulation allows losses and gains to be adjusted. Although by no means negligible, these exceptions do not prejudice application of the principle of universality in any fundamental way.

The ECSC operational budget follows the same approach and indeed uses the term 'gross appropriations' in order to make it clear that there is no question of adjustment between particular items of income and expenditure.

None the less, there is no doubt that the temptation exists to use a process of netting-off in order to avoid increasing the size of the Community budget and to escape criticism from the Member States. There is evidence of this in the sphere of agricultural policy (see p. 185) and in connection with the practice of refunding the cost of collecting Community revenues (see p. 306). The rule prohibiting assignment of revenues is thus under pressure in the European Communities. However, in the stage of development it has now reached, the continuity and effectiveness of the Community budget stems from a punctilious application of the system of own resources.

C—The rule of annuality

The principle of covering a single and complete financial year by the budget is reflected in the setting of time limits for preparation, adoption and implementation of the budget. The principle is a rule of order.

The principle of annuality is observed by the general budget of the European Communities, as it is in the Member States.[9] It is in fact laid down in the Treaties establishing the Communities. Articles 202(1) of the EEC Treaty, 175(1) of the EAEC Treaty and 78a(2) of the ECSC Treaty prescribe that 'expenditure shown in the budget shall be authorized for one financial year, unless the Financial Regulation made pursuant to Articles (209 of the EEC Treaty, 183 of the EAEC Treaty and 78f of the ECSC Treaty) provide otherwise'.

Articles 203(1) of the EEC Treaty, 177(1) of the EAEC Treaty and 78(1) of the ECSC Treaty lay down that 'the financial year shall run from 1 January to 31 December', repeating the words of the Financial Regulation, Article 5(1). The first sentence of Article 1(2) of this regulation states that 'the appropriations entered in the budget shall be authorized for the duration of one financial year'. Article 5(2) states that 'the revenue of a financial year shall be entered in the accounts for that financial year on the basis of the amounts collected during the financial year', while the third subparagraph declares that 'the allotted appropriations shall be used solely to cover expenditure properly entered into and paid in the financial year for which they were granted'. There are, however, some very considerable exceptions (to which we will return later) to this body of rules, namely: the making available of 'differentiated' appropriations comprising both commitments and payments (see p. 60), possible carry-overs from one year to another (see p. 74) and the exceptions granted by the EAGGF Guidance Section (see p. 217). In short, the European Community has had to admit that observing adherence to the principle of annuality has become archaic and, since 1975, it has abolished this restriction in respect of operations which run over several years.

As for the ECSC operational budget, this is on the face of it an annual budget, prepared and adopted each year, but its implementation is generally based on the use of 'provisions of resources' over a period of time which can be as long as eight or ten years. Observation of the principle of annuality here is thus only a formality.

D—The rule of specification

The purpose of this rule is to ensure that the appropriations made available are not aggregated but allocated to the various budgetary headings and subheadings. The rule therefore resembles the principle of annuality, which constitutes a specification in time whereas the action of the principle of specification itself is 'material', i.e. it specifies the destination of the funds. For the budgetary authority, application of this rule is the condition for the exercise of its power. For the budgetary executive, it constitutes a legitimate constraint in a democratic system.

The rule is applied in the Community (i.e. in the general budget and the ECSC operational budget) as in the Member States,[10] but with certain exceptions. With regard to the general budget, the principle is incorporated in the Treaties in the third sentence of Article 202 of the EEC Treaty, the third sentence of Article 175 of the EAEC Treaty and the fourth sentence of Article 78a of the ECSC Treaty, which read: 'Appropriations shall be classified under different chapters grouping items of expenditure according to their nature or purpose and subdivided, as far as may be necessary, in accordance with the regulations made pursuant to Article (209 of the EEC Treaty and others)'.

Article 21(1) of the Financial Regulation stipulates that 'Appropriations shall be classified by chapter and by article'. But the appropriations are not kept in completely watertight compartments. Numerous exceptions are provided for and made use of when it comes to implementation of the budget (see p. 72). Necessity has thus proved stronger than principle. Moreover, the Commission intends that this necessity shall be confirmed, recommending, for example, the creation of a 'global operational reserve' in the budget.[11]

The ECSC operational budget acknowledges the principle of specification, but only formally.

E—The principle of equilibrium between revenue and expenditure

This principle has long been the golden rule of budgetary legislation, although it is not applied in the Member States.[12] It is, however, enshrined in the second paragraph of Article 199 of the EEC Treaty, the second paragraph of Article 171(1) of the EAEC Treaty and Article 20(1) of the Merger Treaty, which state that 'The revenue and expenditure shown in the budget shall be in balance'. In using this wording, the Member States—most prudently, no doubt—wished to avoid offering the Community the temptation of an easy solution, as they would have done had they authorized it to borrow to cover its expenditure. However, the rule is not observed by the ECSC operational budget, which allows balance over several years, thus recognizing the possibility of years which show a deficit, this being covered by the gross profits of the financial activities.

This brief commentary[13] on the application of traditional budgetary principles to the budgets of the Community demonstrates that the general budget is perfectly orthodox, but that the ECSC operational budget does not heed the rules relating to annuality or to the balancing of revenue and expenditure. This conclusion testifies to the unique characteristics of this Community instrument, a fact which will emerge again many times in the course of this work.

2. The unit of account

The notion of an accounting currency is very old. It was known to the Egyptians and Babylonians and was used by them as much as 1 500 years before the appearance of commercial currencies. So it was nothing original when the European Communities instituted, as they did right from the start, their own unit of account (u.a.). The ECSC High Authority, in fact, in its Decision 2/52 of 23 December 1952, defined it by adopting for this purpose something that already existed, 'the unit of account of the European Payments Union'. The two Treaties of Rome went a stage further and solemnly and expressly prescribed the establishment of a unit of account (Articles 207 of the EEC Treaty and 181 of the EAEC Treaty). In broad terms, it can be said that the European Communities have made use in succession of two species of unit of account: first, the parity unit of account; then, when this broke down, a basket unit of account.

A—The parity unit of account

Article 10 of the Financial Regulation applicable to the general budget until 31 December 1977 laid down that:

'1. The value of the unit of account in which the budget shall be established shall be 0.88867088 grams of fine gold' (weight equivalent to that of the US dollar from 1934 to 1972).

'2. In case of change in the parity of the currency of one or more Member States in relation to the unit of account, the Commission may submit to the Council within two months of such change in parity a rectifying preliminary draft budget adjusting the appropriations expressed in units of account and the revenue so that the volume of services provided for in the budget remains unchanged.'

This system provided the Community with an exchange guarantee, since all currency conversions took place on the basis of the gold parities officially declared by each country to the IMF (International Monetary Fund). Devaluation produced a writing-up of items denominated in the currency concerned, while revaluation meant that the corresponding sums were written down in the currency in question. Since, however, such adjustments were likely to produce a net change in the real amount of the Community's resources, an amending budget could be drawn up in order to maintain their real value.

This unit of account system, therefore, depended on the prior existence of parities declared to the IMF and there was no serious random fluctuation in Community exchange parities. The margin of variation of some 0.75% on either side of the declared parity did not interfere with the smooth operation of the unit-of-account system. Broadly speaking, real exchange rates remained stable up to the year 1971 apart from the devaluation of the French franc and the revaluation of the German mark in 1969 (neither of which was declared to the IMF). On the other hand, the very wide divergences in exchange rates that developed after 1971 have wrought havoc with this system.

The Smithsonian Agreement of 19 December 1971 led the Community to decide on 7 March 1972 that, by reference to the official parity relationship, Member States should limit the maximum market variation between the strongest and the weakest of Community currencies to 2.25%, this being what was colourfully known as the 'snake in the tunnel' or 'monetary snake', system. In practice, only some Member States found it possible to apply this system continuously: the Federal Republic of Germany, the three Benelux countries and Denmark. The other countries left the snake at some time or another, with the outcome that the gap between 'strong' and 'weak' currencies has become more and more pronounced. The system was terminated on 31 December 1978.[14]

The discrepancy between official exchange rates (those declared to the IMF and used to convert units of account into currencies for general budget operations) and the real exchange rate (used on the market) had reached the point of causing distortions that were prejudicial to the good order of European finance and damaging to the Community's economy.

It may be recalled that the principal consequences of the parity unit of account's obsolescence were inequity in the payment of 'own resources', the application of the monetary compensatory amounts and the double exchange rate in the common agricultural policy (see, footnote 8, p. 195), and exchange losses or gains for the budget.[15]

Meanwhile the ECSC operational budget was beset with the same problems and those concerned had sought to overcome them in 1974 and 1975 by using an updated parity unit-of-account system.[16]

Escape from this impasse had become a vital necessity for the Community.

B—The basket unit of account (EUA)

Definition of the basket unit of account (EUA)

The event that led to the change in the unit-of-account system was the negotiation of the Lomé Convention, the aim being to achieve greater stability in the financing of aid to the associated developing countries. At this juncture, the Commission took up a proposal put forward by the French to adopt a new definition of the unit of account, the basket unit of account.

The Commission's view was that this 'basket' should represent an average of the value of all Community currencies but should not include any other currencies. It therefore rejected the idea of adopting the 'special drawing rights (SDR) basket' established by the International Monetary Fund, since this would have involved applying for Community purposes a unit of account whose value would depend as to 45% on the future strength of Community currencies and as to 55% on that of non-Community currencies (the dollar accounting for 33% of this latter figure). It would hardly have been possible to accept that there should be an impact on internal Community relationships arising simply from a change in value of the dollar. Apart from this, as an economic group, the Community was sufficiently large and uniform for the currencies of its Member States to constitute an independent basket, the value of which would follow the monetary trends in this zone. It was certainly right and proper for the Community to be the master of the unit of account used for its own operations; the SDR 'basket', in contrast, could in fact be changed even if the Community was opposed to doing so.

The starting value of this basket unit of account was established on 28 June 1974, this being also the introduction date for the basket SDR, then valued at USD 1.20635. This date was selected to provide a link not only with the value of the SDR but also with that of the old Community unit of account, defined as equivalent to 0.88867088 grams of fine gold, since this also was worth USD 1.20635. The factors used to determine the weights to be given to the different Community currencies within the new unit of account (see Annex 6, p. 372) were based on a five-year average (over the period 1969-73) of the GNP and intra-European trade of the Member States, adjusted for their participation in short-term monetary support. The resulting percentage weightings were: DM = 27.3 + FF = 19.5 + UKL = 17.5 + LIT = 14 + HFL = 9 + BFR = 7.9 + DKR = 3 + IRL = 1.5 + LFR = 0.3, making 100%.

The basket unit of account is therefore made up of the following amounts of Community currencies: DM 0.828 + FF 1.15 + UKL 0.0885 + LIT 109 + HFL 0.286 + BFR 3.66 + DKR 0.217 + IRL 0.00759 + LFR 0.14.

To determine the basket's conversion rate against a given currency, the sum is taken of the equivalents in that currency of the nine amounts of national currency on the basis of the daily rate of exchange of Community currencies (the data being taken from the Brussels market, for ease of calculation). The 'basket' value is thus first calculated in Belgian francs and then, from that figure, in other currencies. These include the dollar and other major currencies, for which use is likewise made of the Brussels exchange rate, or, failing that, the London or the Frankfurt rate, in that order. The value of the basket thus varies from day to day according to the exchange rates prevailing on the foreign exchange market (see Annex 6, p. 370).

On 21 April 1975 the Council recorded its agreement to the use of the basket unit of account, denoted the European unit of account (EUA), to express the European Development

Fund aid quotas under the Lomé Convention, signed on 28 February 1975 by the Community and 46 African, Caribbean and Pacific countries. The EUA has also been used by the European Investment Bank since 31 December 1974 under the terms of a decision approved by its Board of Governors on 18 March 1975. The High Authority/Commission, with the agreement of the Council, likewise introduced it in the ECSC with effect from 1 January 1976. In its amendment to the Financial Regulation of 21 December 1977, the Council confined itself to providing, in Article 10, a new definition of the unit of account, which thereby also became applicable to the general budget and to the accounting procedure applicable thereto.[17]

Proposal for a regulation applying the basket unit of account (EUA) to the acts adopted by the institutions of the European Communities

The Commission had to examine the practical impact of the adoption of this new unit of account on the denomination of Community claims and obligations and on the arrangements for accounting for Community financial transactions. On 6 October 1976 the Commission put forward a proposal on this matter,[18] but despite Parliament's support the proposal had not yet been adopted by the Council four years later.[19] The content of this proposal is as follows.

Denomination of claims and obligations in EUA—All claims and obligations of the European Communities are fixed in EUA. Exceptions are none the less allowed both for Community revenues which, in the nature of things, can only at present be calculated and collected in national currency (customs dues and agricultural levies) and for certain fields of expenditure (the common agricultural policy and staff pay) where considerable turmoil would be produced if Community obligations were fixed in EUA. However, all other Community obligations (the Social Fund, the Regional Fund, the Guidance Sector of the EAGGF, financial assistance in the energy field) are—both at the commitments and at the payments stage—denominated and paid in EUA with effect from 1 January 1978. Since the conversion rates between each national currency and the EUA alter daily, there is an exchange risk in either direction carried by the Community's creditor. This is a big change, but it is entirely in agreement with the old-established principle whereby any financially significant transaction that crosses national boundaries naturally involves a risk arising from the variations in relative values of national currencies. In the current situation, with its floating exchange rates, the application of the EUA to Community commitments thus involves two different concepts of their maximum limit—first the commitment ceiling in terms of EUA, and second, the actual expenditure in national currency converted to EUA at that stage. In a concrete example, this will mean that a creditor in a country whose currency is on a downward trend may receive more in national currency when his claim is paid off than was foreseen when it was first contracted (when the Community took on the EUA commitment). Conversely, a creditor in a country whose money is following an upward trend will find himself receiving less in national currency since the commitment contracted by the Community (in EUA) represents, in principle, a limit that cannot be exceeded.

Under Commission Decision 3289/75/ECSC of 18 December 1975, this rule is applied in all its rigour to the operational expenditure of the ECSC. In contrast to this, in its proposal for a regulation of 6 October 1976, the Commission accepted that for expenditure items charged to the general budget (representing the claims of its contractors and other beneficiaries), it would be possible to agree to a supplementary commitment when the time came to pay off its obligations in order to ensure that, at least, the recipient did not receive a smaller sum in national currency than that represented by the original commitment. In fact, if the recipient is a private person, and not a Member State or public authority, as arises with those aided under individual EAGGF Guidance Section projects, the Commission even proposes that it should be automatically obliged to supplement its original commitment.

Accounting arrangements for Community financial transactions—Community financial transactions (commitments and payments) are accounted for on the basis of the EUA conversion rate of the day that precedes the accounting operation with a few exceptions: receipts of Community revenues (reference date the 15th of the month) and expenditure in the field of the common agricultural policy (reference date 20th of the month).

Results of the Commission's proposal of 6 October 1976

The Commission's proposal was very well received by the European Parliament at its session of 14 December 1976. The Council examined the proposal at length. On 21 December 1977 the Council introduced the EUA in Article 10 of the Financial Regulation, as we have already said. By a declaration written into the minutes of that day's meeting, the Council stipulated that until the Regulation came into force the conversion rates of the EUA into the various national currencies for budget implementation purposes would be based on the rates of the first working day of each month. Despite the Council's pledge to adopt the proposed Regulation by 31 March 1978 at the latest, the provisional system—namely application of the EUA to the accounting system only—is still in force. On 24 July 1978 the Council adopted a 'common position' affirming the principle that the EUA should be used for the Community institutions' financial transactions but allowing exceptions which had the effect of postponing application of the principle. The common position was the subject of conciliation with Parliament but the end result was merely a statement of disagreement (see Annex 5, p. 365).

C—The ECU

The ECU came into being on 1 January 1979.

Presentation of the ECU

The way was prepared for the appearance of the ECU by the work of two European Councils, that of Bremen on 6 and 7 July 1978, and that of Brussels on 4 and 5 December 1978, and especially by the resolution on the establishment of the European Monetary System adopted at that time (see Annex 3, pp. 353 and 354).

The ECU's official 'birth certificate' is a Regulation (EEC 3180/78 of 18 December 1978),[20] Article 1 of which states that the transactions of the European Monetary Cooperation Fund (EMCF), up to that time expressed in EMUA (European monetary units of account) based on the central exchange rates of the 'snake' currencies, would thenceforth be denominated in 'ECU', a unit of account defined in the same way as the EUA.

The name 'ECU' as well as being the name of a famous medieval currency, is also an acronym for 'European currency unit'.

Unlike the EUA, which was designed as a fixed unit to remain unchanged at least until the Community was enlarged to a membership of twelve, the ECU can be changed if desired. Article 2 of the Regulation provides that the Council, acting unanimously on a proposal from the Commission after obtaining the opinion of the monetary committee and board of governors of the EMCF, shall determine the circumstances under which the ECU's composition may be changed. It was agreed in practice that six months after the European monetary system had come into operation, i.e. on 13 September 1979, and after that every five years or on demand if the weight of one of the currencies had altered by 25%, the composition of the ECU should be reviewed and if necessary revised. Revisions of this kind would not by themselves have the effect of changing the external value of the ECU. On 17 September 1979 the Council noted that the system had been working satisfactorily. Since then,[21] the Community authorities have been investigating whether they will be in a position to 'consolidate' the system in March 1981, i.e. two years after the inception of the EMS, as they had agreed. The consolidation was intended to take the form of extension of the role of the ECU and creation of a genuine European Monetary Fund (EMF). The European Council, meeting in Luxembourg on 27 and 28 April 1980, confirmed its determination that the Community should make progress along the road to monetary integration (see Annex 3, p. 357).

Introduction of the ECU
into the Community's public finances

The new unit of account thus created was introduced provisionally into the agricultural field by Council Regulation EEC 652/79 of 29 March 1979 concerning the consequences of the European Monetary System for the common agricultural policy.[22] So as to make progress, the Commission considered it essential to harmonize the units of account used for the Community's finances and that such harmonization should take place before the values of the different units of account had started to diverge. Use of a single unit of account for all activities of the European Communities would have obvious advantages from the accounting, legal and even political points of view. Against this background, on 10 December 1979, the Commission presented a group of texts designed to allow simultaneous adoption of the ECU for the general budget of the European Communities, the ECSC operational budget, the activities of the European Development Fund, and all transactions under Community law in which there was any mention of units of account. The first objective could only be attained by altering Article 10 of the Financial Regulation.

The proposal put forward by the Commission, which received a favourable opinion from Parliament on 23 May 1980,[23] goes back to Council Regulation EEC 3180/78 of 18 December 1978 which changed the value of the unit of account used by the European Monetary Cooperation Fund. The composition of the ECU 'basket', at present the same as the composition of the EUA basket fixed by the Financial Regulation currently in force should henceforth be given simply as a footnote rather than in the body of the Regulation, so as not to invalidate the text if the ECU has to be revised. On the latter point the new text also states that all changes in the definition of the ECU shall be decided upon by the Council within the framework of the European Monetary System. In this way the Financial Regulation will ensure that there will still be a single unit of account despite any revisions that may be made, once the Council has so decided.

The European Community is undergoing very rapid legal and political change in the budgetary field. This chapter shows that graphically. As the struggle for budgetary power develops, so budgetary legislation evolves. The major revision of the Financial Regulation at the end of 1977 is but a stage in this process of continuous creation. Politicization of the budget, modernization of the budget, diversification of the budget—these are the themes the Community bodies are thinking about and acting on. On the Commission's initiative and with determined support from Parliament, the Council has thus taken important decisions.

The dominating event of recent years will prove to have been the change in the definition of the unit of account used not only in the two Community budgets but for the whole range of Community financial activities. Slowly but surely the use of the EUA has spread. The character of this unit of account makes it the forerunner of a European currency. It is already possible to hold a bank account in EUA and thus, on the strength of a claim on the Communities denominated in EUA, obtain payment in any national currency desired. Gradually, the various accounting systems of the European Communities and of those who have dealings with the Communities are being switched to EUA. There is thus every reason to suppose that step by step the point will be reached when conditions will be ripe for a European currency to take its place alongside the national currencies. This development, which started three years ago, will certainly be speeded up by the introduction of the ECU.

The inclusion of all the Community's financial resources in the budget still remains to be completed, the aim being to make the public finances of the Community consistent and transparent. The political will for this must be unanimous, but it has so far not materialized.

Footnotes to the Introduction to Part One and Chapter I

[1] See OJ L 356 of 31.12.1977.

[2] The current implementing rules are contained in the Commission Regulation (75/375/Euratom/ECSC/EEC) of 30 June 1975. They run to 88 articles (see OJ L 170 of 1.7.1975).
On 22 July 1980, the Commission adopted a draft set of new rules which it passed on to the European Parliament and the Council for consultation purposes and to the Court of Auditors, the Court of Justice and the Economic and Social Committee for their opinions.

[3] On 15 June 1978, the Commission had proposed a new amendment to the Financial Regulation (see OJ C 160 of 6.7.1978) on the following three points, listed in order of importance: bringing borrowing and lending operations into the budget (see p. 63), simplifying the presentation of research and investment appropriations (see p. 264), and extending the time-limit for approval of carry-overs (see p. 75). The proposal was referred for conciliation (see Annex 5, p. 365), the outcome being adoption by the Council of Regulation (ECSC, EEC, Euratom) No 1252/79 of 25 June 1979 (see OJ L 160 of 28.6.1979). This Regulation only deals with the last two points listed above.
On 23 April 1979, the Commission put forward another amendment to the Financial Regulation (see OJ C 116 of 9.5.1979), relating to the additional period for the EAGGF (see p. 186). It withdrew the proposal on 15 February 1980 (see OJ C 55 of 3.5.1980).
On 10 December 1979, the Commission proposed that the ECU should be introduced in the Financial Regulation.

[4] *The rule of budgetary unity* (comprehensiveness) is observed by all Community members except the United Kingdom and Ireland where there are two laws governing the national finances, one for revenue and one for expenditure, and where a large part of both revenue and expenditure escapes parliamentary control. In four countries, Belgium, the Federal Republic of Germany, Luxembourg and the Netherlands, the rule is actually written into the constitution.

[5] See OJ L 23 of 31.1.1979.

[6] See OJ L 344 of 31.12.1979.

[7] On 10 January 1979, the Commission again proposed that the EDF should be brought into the budget. On 15 June 1978, it proposed that borrowing and lending operations should be brought into the budget (see footnote 3 above).

[8] *The rule against netting-off of revenue and expenditure* (principle of the gross budget) is respected by all Member States almost completely. In France the only exception is the 'comptes spéciaux du Trésor' (Treasury special accounts).
The rule of non-assignment of revenue, by contrast, is departed from in many instances by all countries. France, for example, has its 'comptes d'affectation spéciale' (special assignment accounts) and Belgium its 'section particulière' (special section) of the budget.

[9] *The rule of annuality* is observed by all Member States except the United Kingdom. However, coincidence of the fiscal year and the civil year is only a fairly recent innovation in the Federal Republic of Germany (1 April until 1960), Italy (1 July until 1964), Ireland (1 April until 1974) and Denmark (1 April until 1978).

[10] *The rule of specification* is applied by all the Member States but with some important possibilities of departing from the rule. France, for example, has a very elaborate system of transfers, distinguishing between 'virement' and 'transfert' of appropriations.

[11] In its preliminary draft budget for 1979, the Commission proposed the setting-up of an overall operational reserve which would be entered in Chapter 103 of the budget to finance expenditure that might become necessary in the course of the year in connection with new or further developments in energy policy, industrial policy or aid to countries wishing to join the Community. This innovation was rejected by the Council in its draft budget. Parliament put forward an amendment designed to reinstate the proposal but the amendment became a casualty of the budget crisis and fell by the wayside (see p. 45).
In its preliminary draft budget for 1980 the Commission again proposed an overall operational reserve, in particular for energy policy. This was rejected by the Budgetary Authority. Because of the current budgetary constraints, the Commission did not repeat the proposal in the preliminary draft budget for 1981.

[12] *The rule that revenue and expenditure must balance* is enshrined in the constitution of the Federal Republic of Germany; this is the only example we were able to find.

[13] For details, see Professor Guy Isaac's analysis, published on 30 April 1975 in 'Notes et études documentaires' (Documentary notes and studies) under the title 'Les systèmes budgétaires européens' (European budgetary systems).

[14] The history of the system known as the currency snake is as follows:
(a) 1972, 24 March: the snake came into being for the Six; 1 May: Denmark, the United Kingdom and Ireland joined the system; 23 May: Norway joined; 23 June: the United Kingdom, Ireland and Denmark left; 12 October: Denmark rejoined.
(b) 1973, 14 February: Italy left the system; 16 March: the Deutschmark was revalued by 3%; Sweden joined the system; 29 June: Deutschmark revalued by 5.5%; 15 September: Dutch guilder revalued by 5%; 15 November: Norwegian krone revalued by 5%.
(c) 1974, 19 January: France left the system.
(d) 1975, 10 July: France rejoined the system with no change in parity.
(e) 1976, 15 March: France again left the system; 17 October: Deutschmark revalued by 2%; Swedish krona and Norwegian krone devalued by 1%; Danish krone devalued by 4%.
(f) 1977, 4 April: Danish and Norwegian kroner devalued by 3%; Swedish krona devalued by 6%; 29 August: Norwegian and Danish kroner devalued by 5%; Sweden left the system.
(g) 1978, 10 February: Norwegian krone devalued by 8%; 16 October: Deutschmark revalued by 4% against Danish and Norwegian kroner and by 2% against Belgian and Luxembourg francs and Dutch guilder; latter three currencies revalued by 2% against Danish and Norwegian kroner; 12 December: Norway left the system; 31 December: the system came to an end.

[15] The author has analysed the distorting effects of the parity unit of account's obsolescence in the four translations published after his book 'Les finances de l'Europe' appeared: in English by Praeger (New York, 1977); in Spanish by the Spanish Institute of Fiscal Studies (Madrid, 1978); in German by the Institute for European Integration (Europa Union Verlag, Bonn, 1979) and in Italian by Le Monnier (Florence, 1980).

[16] See Decision No 3542/73/ECSC of 19 December 1973, published in OJ L 361 of 29.12.1973.
An analysis of this system is given in the first, French, edition of 'Les finances de l'Europe', published by Presses universitaires de France (Paris, 1975).

[17] It took the Council more than two years to introduce the EUA into the general budget. As long ago as 16 November 1975, and again on 24 March 1976, the Commission had proposed that the EUA should be adopted for the general budget with effect from 1 January 1978. The Commission had put the proposal into

concrete form in its draft amendment to the Financial Regulation, introduced on 19 May 1976 (a new Article 10), and formulated it again in a proposal dated 6 October 1976. Although the European Council meeting in Rome on 2 December 1975 showed an interest in the Commission's proposals (see Annex 3, p. 352), it was necessary to wait until the European Council of 5 and 6 December 1977 (see Annex 3, p. 353) for acceptance of the introduction of the EUA for use in the general budget and until 21 December 1977 for the Council of Ministers to adopt the relevant Regulation.

The texts for the application of the EUA were published in the OJ as follows: Lomé Convention (L 104 of 24.4.1975), ECSC (L 327 of 19.12.1975), general budget (L 356 of 31.12.1977).

[18] See OJ C 271 of 17.11.1976.

[19] For urgent technical reasons, however, one aspect of the matter had to be dealt with separately. Regulation (EEC) No 2779/78 introducing the EUA for transactions in the customs field was adopted by the Council on 23 November 1978 (see OJ L 333 of 30.11.1978).

[20] See OJ L 379 of 30.12.1978. With regard to this Regulation, the Greek Accession Treaty of 28 May 1979 states that: 'The effective inclusion of the drachma in the basket will be realized before 31 December 1985 if, before that date, a revision of the basket has been undertaken pursuant to the procedures and under the conditions laid down in the Resolution of the European Council of 5 December 1978 on the European Monetary System. In any event, the inclusion of the drachma in the basket will be realized at the latest on 31 December 1985.'

[21] By 13 March 1980, the European Monetary System had been functioning satisfactorily for one year, despite inflation, gold speculation and international conflicts. President Giscard d'Estaing declared: 'In accordance with the role assigned to it by those who had proposed its creation, the European Monetary System now constitutes a pole of stability within the international monetary system. The ECU is a factor making for monetary stability, and the franc has performed particularly well within the European Monetary System.'

[22] OJ L 84 of 4.4.1979 and L 161 of 29.6.1979.

[23] By virtue of this text, Article 10 of the Financial Regulation would be amended as follows:

'1. The budget shall be drawn up in ECU.

The ECU shall be defined by reference to the sum of specified amounts of the currencies of the Member States as set out in Council Regulation (EEC) No 3180/78 of 18 December 1978 changing the value of the unit of account used by the European Monetary Cooperation Fund.[a, b]

Any change in the definition of the ECU decided on by the Council in the context of the European Monetary System shall automatically apply to this provision.

2. The value of the ECU in any given currency shall be equal to the sum of the equivalents in that currency of the amounts of the currencies making up the ECU. It shall be determined by the Commission on the basis of the rates recorded each day on the exchange markets.

The daily rates for the purpose of conversion into the various national currencies shall be available each day and shall be published in the Official Journal of the European Communities.

3. Where appropriate, conversions between the ECU and national currencies shall be effected at the rate of the day, without prejudice to the special provisions laid down in Article 108(7).'[c]

Notes relating to the Regulation:

[a] *OJ L 379 of 30.12.1978, p. 1.*

[b] *On the entry into force of this Regulation, these amounts were as follows: DM 0.828 ..., etc., as stated on p. 26.*

[c] *This Article stipulates that the conditions for application of the EUA to revenue and expenditure shall be determined by implementing rules drawn up by the Commission (see p. 17).*

Chapter II:
Preparation and adoption of the Community budgets

On 1 January 1975, when the Communities started relying entirely on their own resources to finance the expenditure entered in the general budget, the character of the budget was in theory transformed. Before then it was expenditure-determined; since then it has been on the way to becoming income-determined. This is a shorthand way of indicating that for 17 years the Budgetary Authority, on a proposal from the Commission, has first determined expenditure and then adjusted revenue to match, whereas with effect from 1975 the first thing to be done by the Commission and the Budgetary Authority in turn has been to consider the overall limit imposed by the Community's revenue entitlements under the Decision of 21 April 1970, in order to ensure that expenditure is kept within that limit. This, incidentally, has always been the way the ECSC operational budget has worked.

So today more than ever the budgets must be strictly and accurately prepared and the inevitable 'trade-offs' between competing claims carefully decided at the right moment. We shall examine the methods the Commission has adopted to do this and then go on to describe the procedure for drawing up and approving both budgets.

1. The preparation of estimates by the Commission of the European Communities

The preparation of budget estimates has two aspects, annual (for the year ahead) and long-term (projections extending to later years). For the ECSC operational budget estimates, however, things have not yet reached this degree of sophistication.

A—Estimates for the general budget

The general budget forecasts are based on economic indicators and are expressed in the form of financial data in the light of the political options.

Estimates for the next year's budget

Since the 1971 budget, budget estimates have had to cover both expenditure and revenue. Their degree of accuracy affects both subsequent budgetary procedure, and, above all, the implementation of the budget.

Estimates of revenue and expenditure—Estimates of revenue are based on a range of macro-economic forecasts suited to the type of revenue concerned:
(a) the rate of increase in the yield of a percentage of VAT, the basis of which depends essentially on the trend of private consumption;
(b) estimates of export duties and levies. These respectively depend on the trend in exports and imports in the agricultural sector, which in turn depend partly on demand on world markets and on world prices, and partly on domestic prices, present or revised (since the agricultural year straddles two financial years);
(c) the trend in customs revenue. This depends on the trade-liberalization policy pursued by the Communities and on import quantities of non-zero-rated products, that is, essentially, of manufactured goods.

The expenditure estimates are also based on a number of macro-economic forecasts:
(a) the forecast rate of inflation; this factor is in fact a crucial one but is difficult to calculate, as much for political as for economic reasons: the forecasts the Member States draw up of their future rates of price increase are more political than economic. The rate of inflation assumed enters into the calculation of every class of estimated Community expenditure (social policy, energy policy, research policy, and so on);
(b) the rise in agricultural prices; this must be distinguished from the general price-increase forecast, because the criteria involved are different. The aim in this case is to predict relative prices which differ from those calculated using a forecast rate of inflation;
(c) the trend of exports in the agricultural sector; this is needed to enable estimates of refunds to be prepared;
(d) the trend of agricultural production, itself largely dependent on the weather, which conditions the estimates for intervention operations.

Risks of error in the estimates—The revenue estimates are generally made with a small, but not insignificant margin of error as far as customs duties and agricultural levies are concerned (see Annex 10, p. 387). As regards estimates for the yield from the VAT percentage, there is as yet no experience to go on.

For unavoidable expenditure, on the other hand, that is, agricultural expenditure on the 'guarantee' side and also for agricultural receipts, errors in forecasting may be substantial. When one realizes that agricultural spending accounts for 70% of all Community expenditure, the formidable consequences of estimating errors can be imagined. Indeed, one of the main characteristics of agriculture is the significance of chance factors. For the Community of the Nine these have to do with variations in Community production and consumption, developments in trade between the old and the new Member States, variations in world prices, and the trend in the monetary situation. An analysis of expenditure over recent years shows that for a budget of 10 000 m EUA (roughly the 1976 appropriations) there are 68 chances out of 100 that real expenditure will fall within a bracket of 15% on either side of the trend curve (that is, 1 500 m EUA over or under). Admittedly, the trend curve for real expenditure is not known until after the event, but it is nevertheless true that a budget planner who wished to balance his budget without having recourse to a supplementary budget would have to set aside a substantial reserve, of the order of 30%, which would be quite unacceptable.

Adjustment of the preliminary draft budget by 'letter(s) of amendment'—The Commission can still introduce a letter of amendment amending its preliminary draft budget after the budget process has been initiated, in order to bring into the reckoning elements not known at the time of the original estimate. In fact, these letters of amendment have become standard procedure, and the changes that have been made to the budget timetable (see p. 42) have merely underlined the need for this procedure to meet the need to update forecasts that have been brought forward even further. Specifically, what is needed is to make adjustments in September to the forecast financial requirements of the 'guarantee' side of agricultural expenditure to take account of harvest yields reported for the summer of the year before that to which the estimated appropriations relate, and of the most reliable forecasts of world prices.

Constraints arising from macro-economic indicators specified in the Treaties—It should be noted that the indicators prescribed by statute for budget purposes inevitably belong to the past. Thus the GNP-based contributions to Community revenues relate to data for years n−3, n−4, and n−5 (see Annex 10, p. 379). For calculating the maximum rate of increase of non-compulsory expenditure, the reference year is n−2 (see p. 122). Revision of pay scales is based on the year n−1 (see p. 308).

All this means that budget policy is out of step with reality, since it is based on indicators belonging to the past whose use will lead to objections or at least to bewilderment. Thus, a period when the Member States ran budget deficits can only have an impact on the options for the Community budget two years later, when the figures appear extravagant and, at all events, unacceptable.

Budget policy options—The Commission comes up against two constraints in preparing its budget estimates, that is, when it decides on the preliminary draft budget: the revenue ceiling and the maximum acceptable level of expenditure estimates to present.

The adequacy of budgetary receipts is in fact taken for granted, at least for estimating purposes. Currently, by reason of the budgetary funds placed at the disposal of the European Communities through the Decision on the Community's 'own resources', the revenues to which they are entitled (see p. 122) are invariably greater than the forecast expenditure required to cover politically agreed outlays.

In respect of these items of expenditure,[1] the Commission is in fact faced with four virtually invariable tasks. The first is to estimate unavoidable expenditure (not to be confused with so-called compulsory expenditure, which is determined (see p. 40) on the basis of political criteria)—that is, the expenditure it will be obliged to meet regardless of the amount of budgetary revenue available, since this expenditure flows necessarily from the economic situation and the application of Regulations that relate thereto. What is involved here is agricultural 'guarantee' expenditure, the forecasting problems for which have already been explained, administrative expenditure, payment appropriations required to honour commitments entered into, and any other expenditure which, for political reasons, is unavoidable.

The Commission's second task is to work out figures of budgetary expenditure to meet the cost of present policies; three types of policy are involved. First—to take the class where the Commission has the greatest power of initiative—there is the energy policy (aid to hydrocarbon and uranium exploration projects, etc.) and the policy of cooperation in the development of non-member countries, for which the Commission can specify the amount of funding desirable without any special constraint. Second, there are policies embodied in programmes: research policy (direct activities of the Joint Research Centre and indirect activities pursued in conjunction with national research institutes), and the agricultural struc-

35

tures policy which are both covered by a multi-year programme fixed in advance determining the overall amount of funds. Here the Commission can only make proposals at the time when a programme is drawn up, since the amount of annual funding (for commitments or for payments) is just read off from the programme concerned. The third class of expenditure is represented by the appropriations for the Social Fund and the Regional Fund, where the preparation of the estimate consists essentially of checking on the amount of funds that each Member State is likely to spend on the operations concerned, which are in part to be financed from national resources, and in part from Community funds, the ultimate aim being to provide an allocation.

The third task the Commission has always felt bound to pursue is to advocate new activities. Each year it makes a number of proposals designed, among other things, to promote savings, to avoid duplication of effort and to achieve greater convergence of the economies. Such policies amount to a very modest proportion of the total funds requested but they represent the spark of life in the Community and an act of faith in its future. The amount of expenditure estimated under this heading depends on a judgment of what is politically possible. This is the appropriate juncture to point out (preferably in a humorous tone) that the Commission often has to exercise discretion and refuse to adopt the budget proposals put forward by its Members or departments, when they are motivated merely by what might be called their 'EAGGF complex'. The agricultural policy and the considerable budget appropriations allotted to it every year are the object of some envy. Some folk even go so far as to think that, in order to merit interest and esteem in the Community, they should conduct or recommend measures, or even a policy, only if Community finance (and the more the better) is involved. The complex will probably persist for a long time yet.

The fourth and last task the Commission faces in preparing its budget is to see that the costs of its administrative machine (staff and running costs) increase at a reasonable rate, i.e. at a rate such that the Community's functions may be satisfactorily carried out without letting the growth of the Community administration get out of hand.

It should be noted here that the Commission has the responsibility for estimating its own administrative expenditure, but exercises virtually no influence over that of the other Community institutions.

Programming of Community decisions—In October 1970, the Commission decided in principle to introduce PPBS ('planning-programming-budgeting system') into its departments by stages. Progress was blocked, however, by a number of fundamental and inherent difficulties: the partial and incomplete character of common policies, and the Community's peculiar machinery for making decisions. In addition, the task of quantifying Community policies involving financial assistance on a comparable basis proved rather difficult. Almost every analysis revealed an unquantifiable element that was generally of predominant importance. The most notable of these was the factor of 'European independence', a political concept brought to bear by certain people, which it is virtually impossible to quantify in money terms. The same goes for the 'well-being of the people', which, although not included in so many words among the aims of the three European Communities, was an idea underlying their creation and remains a goal of their development. The day will come, perhaps quite soon, when the European Communities face hard decisions and are called on to rise tenaciously above the difficulties in a spirit of Community solidarity. It will then be a task for the politicians to identify this unquantifiable conception and they may succeed or fail in their assessments of priorities. Then Europe will truly be a State.

The Commission is, none the less, running two experiments in programming, although these clearly do not aim to act out all the stages of PPBS. The first, already in operation for some time, relates to the programming of nuclear-research activities and has resulted in production of a programme budget with classification of expenditure by purpose, the possibility of trade-offs between programmes, and an analytic accounting system. The second experiment consists in the preparation of a programme structure—drawn up, it is true, after the event—for activities connected with the dissemination of information.

The multiannual estimates

When it was decided to finance Community expenditure from independent Community revenue, it was deemed necessary to estimate revenue and expenditure over a longer period than one year. Thus the Council, in its Decision of 21 April 1970 (70/244/ ECSC/EEC/Euratom) laid down that the Commission should each year—after receiving an opinion from the Budgetary Policy Committee, which has since become the Economic Policy Committee—'draw up a financial forecast for the three subsequent financial years, showing the financial implications for the Community resulting from regulations and decisions in force and from proposals submitted by the Commission to the Council'. Since that time, the Commission has prepared estimates for three years, that for the first year corresponding to the preliminary draft budget for the year to come. The first long-term (or multiannual) estimates prepared were for 1971-73. Those prepared for the period 1974-76 and the subsequent periods were revised at the request of the Budgetary Policy Committee and the European Parliament's Committee on Budgets so as to include, in addition to the material prescribed by the Council Decision of 1970, expenditure resulting from the possible future development of Community activities.[2]

Errors in the multiannual forecasts have to date, however, been a far less serious matter than those in the actual budget. For the long-term projections are estimates and nothing else, whereas errors in the budget estimates could upset its implementation.

Up to 1979 the Commission's estimates were of little interest to Parliament and of little more to the Council. Only the Economic Policy Committee examined them in depth. This situation will probably change as the source of independent Community revenue made available under the Decision of 21 April 1970 will very soon run out. It will then become necessary to forecast and plan more carefully for the future. Annex 15 (p. 404) gives the Commission's assumptions for 1981-83 and shows that the present independent revenue ('own resources') system will fall short of requirements in 1982.

Amendment of the budget estimates and of the multiannual estimates

The budget forecasts have to be revised during the year. The most noteworthy development that can occur is a revision leading to a supplementary budget. Article 1, paragraph 5, of the Financial Regulation lays down that the Commission may submit preliminary draft supplementary or amending budgets 'in the event of unavoidable, exceptional or unforeseen circumstances'. When the Financial Regulation was being revised in 1977 Parliament tried to secure that a supplementary budget should only be admissible if all three 'circumstances' were present at the same time. The Council succeeded in preventing this modification from being made and the three circumstances remain alternatives (see Annex 5, p. 363). In the event, the Commission has frequently had to resort to supplementary budgets in circumstances not meeting any of the three abovementioned criteria, because the budgetary authority, the Council, has refused to sanction appropriations to finance decisions (e.g. on farm prices) which it knows full well will have to be taken some time early in the fiscal year whose budget it is discussing. The only thing that can be said in justification of the attitude is that forecasting the required appropriations is, and always will be, an extremely difficult and chancy business. Faced with this attitude on the part of the Council, the Commission itself appears to have given up making proposals in the field of agricultural 'guarantee' expenditure and to have accepted the situation. In the case of the remaining expenditure, on the other hand, it has recommended—since the 1979 budget—that an overall operational reserve, i.e. one that is not earmarked in advance, should be set up (see footnote 11, p. 31). It must be emphasized, moreover, that there is very little possibility of transferring appropriations from one operation to another during the year. To suppose that the European Communities could withdraw substantial appropriations from, let us say, the EAGGF in order to allocate them to the Social Fund or for exploration for oil and gas in the Channel would be quite unrealistic. The legal rules, political pressures and psychological attitudes encountered preclude any idea that a change of this kind is to be expected.

The multiannual forecasts are not updated, much as this is desired in some quarters.

The role of the Budget Commissioner

At the beginning of 1974 the Commission of the European Communities came to feel that the position of the Member of the Commission entrusted with budget matters needed special recognition. It took the view that this Member should devote himself to his particular responsibilities and that these could not be combined with those of authorizing a particular class of expenditure. On the occasion of its Rome meeting on 1 and 2 December 1975 (see Annex 3, p. 352) the European Council took note of the intention of the Commission to strengthen the role of the 'Commissioner for the Budget' without thereby impairing the collegial responsibility of the Members of the Commission under the Treaties. *De facto*, the Budget Commissioner does enjoy powers of some importance. He can request the Commission to put off until a later meeting its consideration of any measure with financial implications; he also has an important say in deciding what requests for funds should be included in the Commission's expenditure estimates. The way things have gone, the Budget Commissioner has in practice played a key part in the preparation of budget estimates. A hope that a few years ago seemed Utopian has now been fulfilled. The Member of the Commission responsible for budget affairs has become its budgetary conscience and its counsellor and spokesman in budgetary matters. Mr Claude Cheysson (Socialist, France) occupied the office from 1973 to 1976, being at the same time the Commissioner responsible for development policy; he was succeeded in January 1977 by Mr Christopher Tugendhat (Conservative, United Kingdom), who likewise had other duties but none which made him in any major way an authorizer of expenditure.

B—Estimates for the ECSC operational budget

The annual estimates for the ECSC operational budget are also based on economic indicators, in this case relating to the coal and steel sector, and dealing with trends in the volume of production. The percentage levy is based on average values for production in a period beginning on 1 July and ending on 30 June of the year before that to which it relates (see p. 111). So this budget, no less than the general budget (see p. 35) can get out of step with the economic cycle and thus run into controversy. Arguments that arose in connection with the 1976 budget in fact induced the Commission, at the Parliament's instigation, to add to the ground rules a provision (Decision 2239/76/ECSC of 15 September 1976) allowing it to hold back an increase in the level of average values employed for one financial year if the development of the economy gave cause to expect a significant reduction in these values during the following year.

The ECSC's annual budget estimates are not, however, supplemented by longer-term forecasts. On the contrary, the annual budgets often have to be revised during the second half of the year to take account of unexpected fluctuations in levy revenue (see Annex 8, p. 376). It must be emphasized that since the ECSC operational budget is a truly 'revenue-determined budget', that is to say a document in which expenditure must match revenue as closely as possible, it may be necessary to correct it to take account of unforeseen expenditure—which is rare—or the failure of forecast revenue to materialize—which is more common—a characteristic which is not at present shared by the general budget.

2. Adoption of the Community budgets by the Budgetary Authority

The adoption procedure for the Community budgets is governed by the Treaties establishing the European Communities, which lay down the budgetary procedure, that is, the whole body of rules and time-limits that must be observed in connection with the budget. Here again we must distinguish between the general budget and the ECSC operational budget; the procedure relating to the former is laid down in the Treaties, whereas that relating to the latter is merely the outcome of 30 years' practice.

A—The procedure for adopting the general budget

Articles 203 of the EEC Treaty, 78 of the ECSC Treaty and 177 of the EAEC Treaty lay down the budgetary process with great precision, although they only once actually use the term 'budgetary procedure' (3rd subparagraph of paragraph 9). Under these Articles the procedure starts on 1 May when the Commission communicates the maximum rate of increase for non-compulsory expenditure to all the institutions of the Community, but in actual fact the procedure for preparing the budget begins before this.

The preparation of the budget within each institution

On 28 November 1973 the Commission of the European Communities adopted some new guidelines for preparing and implementing the budget, in which it lays down rules which are more stringent, and procedures which are more refined, than those applied in the past. The internal budgetary stage begins on 1 February, when the Directorate-General for Budgets issues a circular to all the departments involved asking them to state their precise needs for the coming financial year. Within the Budget Directorate-General, budget officers assess the projects drawn up by the spending departments, their compatibility with other projects and their economic effectiveness. Each budget heading (chapter, or article, if there are articles in a chapter, or item if there are items in an article) is provided with a financial record sheet setting out the justification, in economic terms, for the financial operation to be continued or initiated, along with the consequential budgetary effects and staff requirements.

This preparatory work is examined at various levels so that competing claims may be settled (by the Director-General for Budgets, the Commissioner for the Budget, and the President of the Commission) before being placed before the Commission for final decision and adoption in the form of an expenditure estimate. This is in fact the budget estimate, drawn up in the light of the various factors and considerations explained in the first part of this chapter. In order to facilitate the study and comprehension of the budget—and starting with the 1977 financial year—the Commission has made the general introduction to the preliminary draft budget into a highly comprehensive document, providing *inter alia* a detailed analysis of each budget heading (Paragraph 1: legal basis for and description of the operation in question; Paragraph 2: nature of the expenditure; Paragraph 3: method of calculation and justification).[3]

Before 1 May the Commission determines the maximum rate of increase for non-compulsory Community expenditure (see p. 122). The other institutions of the European Communities prepare their estimates in complete independence and forward them to the Commission which combines them in the preliminary draft budget; examination of this document then initiates the 'budgetary procedure'. Before going on to discuss what is involved, it is essential to go deeper into the question of compulsory and non-compulsory expenditure since this is a distinction which keeps cropping up throughout the budgetary procedure.

Classification of expenditure into compulsory and non-compulsory items

Since the coming into force of Articles 203 of the EEC Treaty, 177 of the Euratom Treaty and 78 of the ECSC Treaty (see p. 6), it has been possible to divide the various financial outlays of the European Communities into those that do and those that do not necessarily result from the Treaties or acts adopted in accordance with the Treaties. In rather simpler jargon, expenditure can be compulsory or non-compulsory. This distinction has a twofold significance: non-compulsory expenditure is limited to a maximum annual rate of increase and the last word on this class of expenditure belongs to Parliament.

When preparing the budget for 1975, in which this distinction figured for the first time, the Commission sought to avoid a doctrinal debate and approached the question pragmatically. It therefore simply attached a list of budget headings to the preliminary draft budget showing how it proposed to classify each heading as between compulsory expenditure (CE) and non-compulsory expenditure (NCE). To do this, the Commission must clearly have had certain criteria in mind; it may well have considered an item of expenditure as compulsory when the principle and the amount (either a figure or a precise mechanism for arriving at it) of the expenditure were statutorily prescribed in the Treaties establishing the Communities, secondary legislation, international conventions and treaties, or private-law contracts. In drawing up the list, the Commission was guided by an earlier document, the so-called Harmel list, named after the Belgian Foreign Minister who was President of the Council when it was prepared. This list dates from 1970 and was the first attempt to distinguish the two types of expenditure. For its part, the Council, when adopting the draft budget for 1975, regarded as compulsory all expenditure 'in respect of which, by virtue of existing enactments, no budgetary authority, be it the Council or the European Parliament, has the right freely to determine the appropriations'. In the end, the two bodies competent to decide on the budget, i.e. the Council and Parliament, reached a provisional agreement for the purposes of adopting the 1975 budget and hence on the distinction between compulsory and non-compulsory expenditure.

Later on, when two supplementary budgets for 1975 were drawn up—one of them to provide appropriations for the Regional Fund and the other for the second instalment of the Community's contribution to emergency aid for certain developing countries severely hit by recent changes in international prices for energy and raw materials (the Cheysson Fund)— the tone of the discussion sharpened, though still without reaching a state of open conflict. The argument might have flared up again during preparation of the 1976, 1977 and 1978 budgets, but the two holders of budgetary power—the Council and Parliament—were wise enough to avoid a full-scale dispute. They simply agreed on the amount of the increase in budget expenditure without resolving the question of classification. The budget crisis of 1979, which we will come to later, did not centre on this question but on other provisions of Article 203 of the EEC Treaty. Similarly, the budget was rejected on 13 December 1979 partly because of the amount of non-compulsory expenditure to be entered in the 1980 budget, but this had nothing to do with the question of classification. In the 1980 budget compulsory expenditure (CE) amounted to 75.9% of the total (EAGGF Guarantee Section, EAGGF Guidance Section, interest rebates on loans granted under the EMS, food aid, Mediterranean financial protocols, repayment to Member States of 10% of the own resources paid over, remuneration of Members of the Commission, and pensions and severance grants for retired officials) and non-compulsory expenditure (NCE) to 24.1% (other intervention and running cost expenditure). The designation 'compulsory' or 'non-compulsory' does not appear in the budget, only in the preparatory documents.[4] This proportion of 24.1% is fairly modest of course, but it is growing—it was only 13.9% in 1974, the year before the new machinery came into force (see Annex 4, p. 359). In absolute terms, non-compulsory expenditure, in the form of appropriations for commitments, rose from 728 m u.a. in 1974 to 4 170 m EUA in 1979, i.e. in the course of five budget cycles it more than quadrupled while the budget itself tripled. In the budgetary field, non-compulsory expenditure could be said to be the catalyst in the process of European integration.

This machinery remains ambiguous and a source of conflict, however, because it conditions the exercise of budgetary power by the two authorities who wield it. Now that the matter of the classification of the appropriations for the Regional Fund has been cleared up, the point at issue is classification of the EAGGF Guidance Section appropriations, appropriations for aid to non-member countries, interest rebates on loans to the less prosperous Community countries who are members of the European Monetary System, and payments to the United Kingdom to solve its budget contribution problem, Parliament asking that all these appropriations should be classified as being for non-compulsory expenditure. For its part, the Commission has already proposed to classify part of the EAGGF Guidance Section (appropriations not limited by Regulation) and part of food aid (non-contractual aid) in this way. Nevertheless, a principle of sorts is beginning to emerge: the main criterion for classification is taken to be the existence or otherwise of third-party rights. If a third party, whether a corporate body or a private individual, has a right to payment by the Community by virtue of the application of the Treaties, secondary legislation or international treaties, the resultant expenditure is regarded as compulsory. But the real problem lies in the

41

fact that while fixing the amount of the non-compulsory expenditure is beset with serious problems (see p. 45) on account of the rivalry between Council and Parliament, fixing the compulsory expenditure raises no difficulties because this spending is not subject to any maximum rate of increase. When it comes to 'unavoidable expenditure' (see p. 35) such as spending on agricultural market guarantees—spending from the 'bottomless purse'—there is a definite imbalance in the exercise of budgetary power.

Budgetary procedure

In practice, the timetable for budgetary procedure is more flexible than the official schedule would lead one to suppose. The three Treaties lay down the budgetary procedure with great precision and the dates and time-limits they specify—in Articles 203 of the EEC Treaty, 177 of the Euratom Treaty and 78 of the ECSC Treaty—are in many cases very tight. The present powers of the two authorities competent to make decisions on the budget were explained above (see p. 6); it remains to specify the official procedure, which falls into five stages:
— *Stage 1*: 1 July to 1 September: the Commission adopts a preliminary draft budget (an aggregate of the estimates prepared by each of the institutions) and forwards it to the Council. The transmission of the preliminary draft initiates the procedure.[5]
— *Stage 2*: 1 September to 5 October: the Council examines the preliminary draft budget and adopts a draft budget which it forwards to Parliament. The Council Decision, which confirms that the Commission's preliminary draft budget is not just a budget proposal, is the cue for an automatic procedure to start.
— *Stage 3*: 5 October to 19 November: Parliament examines the draft budget and has 45 days to propose changes to the Council.
— *Stage 4*: 20 November to 4 December: the Council has 15 days to examine Parliament's proposals and determine the provision for compulsory expenditure.
— *Stage 5*: 5 to 19 December: Parliament in turn has 15 days to determine the provision for non-compulsory expenditure and formally adopt the budget. A complication may arise, however, if the Council and Parliament have to agree on a revised rate of increase for this expenditure.

The budget cycle[6] is thus dictated by the dates when the Commission must decide on the preliminary draft and the Council on the draft, and by the fixed intervals within which the two holders of the budget authority must exercise their rights. If the latter do not do so, the budget passes without amendment. During the early months of 1976, pressure of time led the Commission to propose and the Council and Parliament to agree to a new budgetary timetable accepted by all three institutions involved, that is to say without any change in the Treaties. The stages in the new timetable are as follows:
— *Stage 1*: 15 June: the Commission submits the preliminary draft budget.
— *Stage 2*: 15 June to 31 July: the Council examines the preliminary draft and adopts the draft budget.
— *Stage 3*: September to mid-October: Parliament examines the draft budget and makes proposals for changes.
— *Stage 4*: Mid-October to mid-November: 'second reading' by the Council of Parliament's proposals and decision on compulsory expenditure.
— *Stage 5*: Mid-November to mid-December: 'second reading' by Parliament of the views taken by the Council and decision on non-compulsory expenditure.

The new timetable allotted more time for Parliament's first reading, doubled the time allowed for each of the two second readings, and left free the traditional holiday period, the month of August. If the institutions failed to agree, they could always revert to the legally correct dates laid down by the Treaties. The new timetable was used in 1976 for the approval of the 1977 budget, but not in 1979 because the Council was unable to reach a decision on the draft budget before the August holidays. The official calendar was thus observed anew for the 1980 budget and for that for 1981 as well. Not wanting the two budgetary procedures to overlap, the Commission waited for the 1980 budget to be adopted on 9 July before submitting its preliminary draft budget for 1981, which made it impossible to apply the pragmatic timetable.

The practical rearrangement of the budget timetable, and above all the desire of the three bodies concerned to improve the quality of their dialogue on the budget, have made the budget debates worthwhile and valuable in recent years; this was not so in the past. Fortified both by the powers they enjoy and by their desire to work together, the Community's institutions have accorded to the general budget an important and unique place in the life of the Community.[7]

The actors in the budget drama

The Council, the Parliament and the Commission are the three institutions fully involved in the budgetary procedure. Others only play a part to the extent that they must put forward and justify their demands before the two first-named institutions, the holders of budgetary authority.

Within the three institutions there are some committees we must mention. In the Council the first body to be involved is the Budget Committee, composed of experts from the Offices of the Permanent Representatives of the Members States to the European Communities. The basis of the existence of this committee is to be found in Article 104 of the Financial Regulation which stipulates that it is 'set up within the framework of the Permanent Representatives Committee'. Its task is to examine all budgetary matters brought before the Council and to report to the Permanent Representatives Committee (COREPER) which in turn is required by Article 4 of the Merger Treaty of 8 April 1965 to be responsible for 'preparing the work of the Council and for carrying out the tasks assigned to it by the Council'. A few years ago the committee split into two to form COREPER/I, functioning at the level of Deputy Permanent Representatives (usually with full ministerial status), and COREPER/II, functioning at ambassador level. Budgetary matters are dealt with by COREPER/I. The Permanent Representatives Committee and the Budget Committee, like the Council, are presided over by each Member State in turn at six-monthly intervals in alphabetical order of countries (see p. 343). Thus on 1 July 1980 the presidency fell to Luxembourg. The Council votes on the budget by a qualified majority.[8] In practice, the Budget Committee, although it is the first body to be involved, plays a fairly important role because it is here that future majorities take shape.

Within the Parliament the body that does the preparatory work on the budget is the Committee on Budgets. It has 37 members (see Annex 2, p. 348). Its Bureau consists of a chairman and three vice-chairmen, elected each year but re-electable, which is good for continuity.

Unlike the Council and its committees, Parliament works by the 'rapporteur' method; this means that one of its members is made responsible for reporting on every matter submitted to it, in this case on the budget. In practice two rapporteurs are appointed, one for revenue and the Commission's appropriations (often called the General Rapporteur) and one for the other institutions' appropriations.

Within the Commission, the Budget Commissioner and the Directorate-General for Budgets have the task of justifying the preliminary draft budget to the committees of Council and Parliament. Only the Budget Commissioner may speak on the budget before the Council itself, and before Parliament in plenary session. The budgetary hierarchy is often assisted by representatives of the spending departments.

The procedural machinery

Operating the budgetary procedure—apart from matters connected with the timetable, which we have already discussed—has obviously caused a great many problems.[9, 10, 11, 12, 13] The relevant texts had to be—and were—modified considerably. We shall pick out six problems together with their solutions, namely: Parliament's 'margin for manoeuvre', the absence of systematic contacts between the two holders of budgetary power, the ambiguity of Article 203 of the EEC Treaty and other Articles, the entry in the budget of two-part ('differentiated') appropriations following a procedure which was not designed for this purpose, procedural anomalies, and finally the division of areas of responsibility as between the legislative authority and the budgetary authority.

Parliament's margin for manoeuvre—As noted above (see p. 9), Parliament has succeeded in winning for itself a 'margin for manoeuvre', that is to say a sum of money which it can use to increase expenditure. This involves a completely unique mechanism, specific to Community budget legislation because it is not the practice of Member States to grant their own parliaments this right. Historically, parliaments have effectively grasped this power by ensuring that the ruler granted them the authority to levy taxes but not that of increasing expenditure; this the ruler was perfectly able to do on his own.

The European Parliament's margin for manoeuvre is at all times equal to half the 'maximum rate of increase in non-compulsory expenditure' calculated by the Commission according to the rules laid down by Article 203, paragraph 9 of the EEC Treaty (see p. 122). If the Council uses less than half of this rate, the balance is at Parliament's complete disposal. Moreover the granting of a margin for manoeuvre to Parliament may result in the initial maximum rate being exceeded without a decision on a new rate becoming necessary (see p. 123). For if the Council uses all the maximum rate, as is its right, and if Parliament uses all its margin for manoeuvre, as is *its* right, the rate will automatically be exceeded by half, without any need for co-decision. So in this respect the Treaty may be said to be self-contradictory.

It must be emphasized that this margin for manoeuvre, whether enlarged or not, has enabled Parliament to reinforce its traditional political instruments; it has opened and funded some new budget headings, thus initiating Community measures.

Budgetary conciliation—As a result of the third Resolution written into the minutes of the Council meeting of 21 April 1970 concerning cooperation between Council and Parliament within the framework of the budgetary procedure (see p. 8), a form of contact now called 'budgetary conciliation' to distinguish it from 'legislative conciliation' (see p. 10) has gradually emerged and developed. Thus it has become established practice for the Council, before taking any decisions on its first or second reading of the budget, to receive a parliamentary delegation, very often headed by the President of Parliament. Similarly, it has become the practice for the President of the Council to take part in Parliament's work on the budget and to attend at least one meeting of the Committee on Budgets. Since 1976 there has actually been a third and final conciliation meeting between, on one side, the under-secretaries responsible for the budget in the governments of the Nine (in 1976), the

President of the Council on his own (in 1977) and the Council itself (in 1978 and 1979) and, on the other side, Parliament's delegation at the time of that assembly's second reading. These meetings make the budgetary procedure a good deal more cumbersome but undeniably help it to reach a satisfactory conclusion because although Article 203 of the EEC Treaty and other articles lay down the details of a complicated procedure, they say nothing about how the views of the two wings of the Budgetary Authority should be reconciled if they differ. It can be said that starting with the preparation of the 1975 budget, i.e. from 1974 onwards, budgetary conciliation has played a very helpful role, without however completely obviating interinstitutional conflict—witness Parliament's rejection of the budget on 13 December 1979.

Ambiguity of Article 203 of the EEC Treaty and other articles—Up to 1977, that is to say the time of preparation of the 1978 budget, the institutions had managed to follow the spirit of the law enshrined in Article 203 and other articles if not its letter. Council and Parliament succeeded in reaching agreement within the specified time. But in 1978 the 'budget war' broke out—over adoption of the 1979 budget.[13] To summarize as briefly as possible, the course of the conflict was as follows: at first reading Parliament made two amendments—among others—increasing the money voted to the Regional Fund from 620 to 1 100 m EUA; the Council, at its second reading, could not muster a qualified majority to reject or modify these amendments—because a 'minority for acceptance (see p. 7) approved them—but was also unable to fix a new rate of increase for non-compulsory expenditure; Parliament, on its second reading, confined itself to stating that its two amendments had been accepted, withdrew its other amendments, and its President duly adopted the budget; the Commission and six Council delegations then took the view that the budget had been adopted and ought to be implemented; but three delegations (Denmark, France and the United Kingdom) took the view that the budgetary procedure had not been completed and that the system of 'provisional twelfths' was now operative (see p. 75); the Commission therefore had to introduce a supplementary and amending budget as a compromise; this was accepted by the two holders of budgetary power and put an end to the conflict on 25 April 1979.

To avoid finding itself in a similar situation in future, the Council—or rather, eight delegations, the Dutch delegation opposing—made a declaration on 22 March 1979 about the internal procedure it intended to follow when examining Parliament's amendments to the draft budget and fixing a new rate of increase for non-compulsory expenditure. The main point about this procedure is that there must be correspondence between the amendments accepted and the maximum rate of increase that may be applied, the motive being to secure a proportionate reduction in the amendments under discussion so that they can be accommodated within the limit of the agreed maximum rate of increase. In 1979, at the time of preparation of the 1980 budget, the Council used this internal procedure, without however making use of the technique of proportionate reduction.

Budgetary power and two-part ('differentiated') appropriations—Article 203 of the EEC Treaty and other articles were drafted at a time when the budget did not contain appropriations separated into commitment appropriations and payment appropriations (see p. 60) apart from the research and investment appropriations of the European Atomic Energy Community (EAEC or Euratom). The 1975, 1976 and 1977 budgets were thus drawn up on the basis of appropriations which, by definition, were simple ('non-differentiated') appropriations, and, in the case of Euratom appropriations, were for payments rather than commitments. Parliament made use of the uncertainty, in connection with the 1976 budget, to exercise its rights freely with regard to Euratom commitment appropriations by reinstating those rejected by the Council, which led to the Commission being asked to give its interpretation of Article 203 of the EEC Treaty in view of the widespread introduction of two-part appropriations. The Commission's 'reflections', issued on 14 March 1977, concluded with a recommendation that for the application of Article 203 (maximum rate of increase, calculation of the basis of assessment for non-compulsory expenditure, Parliament's margin for manoeuvre) the appropriations to be considered should be the simple appropriations plus commitment appropriations if there was differentiation of appropriations. For the Commission the commitment appropriations are vital—they are the only sort of commitments with significance for the future, whereas the payment appropriations are merely the inevitable consequence of the commitment appropriations.[14] The Commission's interpretation was upheld by the Council but rejected by Parliament,[11] so that the affair had to be referred to a conciliation committee, at which it was agreed that the provisions of Article 203 of the EEC Treaty would thenceforth apply to 'appropriations for payments' (i.e. simple appropriations plus payment appropriations where there was differentiation of appropriations) as well as to 'appropriations for commitments' (i.e. to the same simple appropriations plus commitment appropriations where there was differentiation of appropriations) (see Annex 5, p. 363).

Procedural anomalies—As seen by the Treaties the progress of the budget cycle is majestic, inexorable, complete. But a closer look reveals that some bodies which officially have no role in the procedure in fact play an important part in it. Thus in the sector of compulsory expenditure ultimately authorized by the Council, the budget proposals drawn up by the Commission departments in respect of EAGGF Guarantee Section expenditure are submitted to the EAGGF Committee for an opinion (see Annex 7, p. 374). The figures contained in this opinion are in practice taken over by the Commission without alteration for inclusion in its preliminary draft budget, by the Council bodies (Budget Committee and Permanent Representatives Committee) and by the Council itself which confirms it at first reading, then adopts it definitively. The EAGGF Committee's opinion generally differs little, it is true, from the quantified proposals of the Commission departments, which have the best forecasting facilities. It should also be mentioned in connection with this EAGGF Guarantee Section expenditure that the participation of the 'Budget' Council is mainly a formality, the real decisions being taken by the 'Agriculture' Council.[15]

Similarly, the opinions of the Scientific and Technical Research Committee (CREST) (see Annex 7, p. 374) are also followed and acted upon, with the slight difference that they are not so often in accord with the Commission department's proposals and that the expenditure is ultimately sanctioned by Parliament. Finally, in the field of 'own resources' the opinions of the specialist Advisory Committee are followed completely (see Annex 7, p. 374).

These three examples (others could be adduced) are a good illustration of the Community's technical character and of the transfer of power to technocratic organs comprising representatives of ten entities: the nine Member States and the Commission.

The budget: an accounting document or a policy document?—The preparation of the annual budget gives rise to fresh debate every year between those who consider it 'an accounting and recording instrument' and those who view it as 'an instrument of policy and planning'. From the beginning, regardless of the Commission's views, it has been the wish and practice of the Council to fix the level of the budget on the basis of the financial implications of decisions already made (see p. 57): The Council has even succeeded in limiting the budgetary consequences of some of its acts, namely its 'Resolutions', which are in fact novel instruments and receive no mention in the Treaties. Accordingly, the 'Budget' Council has come to regard any resolution by a 'Technical' Council (social affairs, research and technology, and so on) as being devoid of budgetary relevance even if the financial implications of the resolution are clearly established, holding the only valid legal basis to be the Treaties or the Council's own regulations and directives. It is now time to define the notions of regulation and directive: a regulation, like a law, gives rise to rights and duties which apply directly and immediately to every citizen of the Community; a directive, on the other hand, is a sort of outline law addressed only to the Member States and restricted to defining the objective to be attained, the Member States usually being responsible for defining the method and the requisite instruments for attainment of the objective. Before it can be implemented therefore, a directive entails detailed legislation by the Member States. Both the Commission, which makes proposals, and the Council, which takes decisions, use both types of instrument, but especially directives—which, as we shall see, causes considerable delays in the attainment of the goal the Community had set itself. Several layers of legislation thus came into being: the primary legislation of the Treaties, the secondary legislation of regulations and directives enacted in pursuance of the Treaties, and sometimes a tertiary legislation, consisting of regulations—enacted in application of the foregoing regulations and directives—which may be necessary for implementation of the budget.[16]

Because of this attitude on the part of the Council the budget, until 1975, contained only appropriations for expenditure the implementation of which was known and certain at the moment the budget was adopted. By contrast the budgets for 1976, 1977 and 1978 contained, at Parliament's behest, budget headings which sometimes included appropriations for which no basic regulation had yet been enacted. This stance by the Council generally prevented it from playing the role of initiator in the budget cycle. Whilst the Commission makes proposals, it is Parliament which innovates, while the Council—or a qualified majority within it—prefers to proceed with great caution.

Another, but still very important, aspect of this conflict is the dispute regarding *limits to expenditure*. The results of the annual budgetary procedure are sometimes predetermined by the fixing of the multiannual programmes. From a historical point of view, the first multiannual programmes were those of the European Atomic Energy Community, implemented under Article 7 of the Euratom Treaty (see p. 263). This budgetary technique involves an overall allocation covering several years, called a 'tranche', which is made available for each research objective. The sums authorized each year under the budget are divided into differentiated appropriations (commitment appropriations and payment appropriations). The Budgetary Authority is bound therefore by the decisions of the legislative authority. Multiannual programmes are adopted by the Council acting unanimously, and the Treaty does not even state that Parliament's opinion must be sought; Parliament's budgetary powers are consequently diminished, since the programme decision will indicate the sums (and the staff) allocated. In its proposal of 15 June 1978 to amend the Financial Regulation, the Commission therefore introduced a provision which stressed that the sums and numbers of staff specified in the programme decisions were to be taken as guidelines only. In so doing, it shared the view often expressed by Parliament, namely that the quantified statements of the resources required for implementing the relevant programme decisions and stated therein can be only estimates and do not bind the Budgetary Authority when it comes to prepare the budgets. This gave rise to difficult discussion between the Community institutions, especially as the Council has long been trying to extend this technique to other fields. The budgetary allocation of the Regional Fund, for instance, was fixed for three years by the Regulation of 21 March 1975 which established the Fund, after the Paris Summit of 10 December 1974 (see Annex 3, p. 351). The allocation for the second three-year period was also fixed, this time by the European Council of 5 and 6 December 1977 in

Brussels (see Annex 3, p. 353), sparking off the budget crisis which we have just analysed. Similarly, with regard to the agricultural structures policy (see p. 212) and the energy policy (see p. 250), the Council has also acquired the habit of fixing ceilings for the multiannual programmes. This approach can only make a nonsense of the budgetary procedure and will certainly give rise to serious differences between the institutions, reintroducing the matter of demarcation between the legislative and budgetary authorities.[17]

B—The procedure for adopting the ECSC operational budget

The procedure for the ECSC budget is much more flexible. There are three stages:
— *Stage 1*: June to October: the Commission's departments, under the responsibility of the Directorate-General for Budgets, prepare a draft ECSC operational budget. Towards mid-October the High Authority/Commission adopts the draft and forwards it to Parliament.
— *Stage 2*: October to December: Parliament entrusts to four of its committees (the Committee on Budgets, the Committee on Social Affairs, Employment, and Education, the Committee on Economic and Monetary Affairs, and the Committee on Energy, Research and Technology) the task of examining the draft budget. The four committees, which for practical reasons can be convened only in conjunction with a plenary session, meet in mid-November. The Committee on Budgets draws up a report. Parliament, at its December plenary session, delivers an opinion.
— *Stage 3*: End of December: the Commission/High Authority adopts the ECSC operational budget before the end of the year.

This procedure is thus quite satisfactory as far as the time allowed is concerned, but on the political side one must acknowledge that the most important element in this budget, the fixing of the rate of levies, is no longer accorded detailed discussion, since Parliament strongly objects to any increase.

3. Periodical reflections on the budget

We would not wish to end this chapter without some reference to two very interesting events which although not implicit in the budgetary procedure are nevertheless connected with it in that they consist of reflections about budget problems and about how the budget might develop in future. They consist firstly of the discussions in the Council and in Parliament on the Commission's overall assessment of Community budget problems, and secondly of the interinstitutional dialogue organized by Parliament.

A—The overall assessment of Community budget problems

The European Council meeting in Rome on 1 and 2 December 1975 took note of the need to hold every year a joint meeting of Foreign Affairs and Finance Ministers to carry out an overall assessment of Community budget problems (see Annex 3, p. 352). This approach, which is not provided for in Articles 203 of the EEC Treaty, 177 of the Euratom Treaty and 78 of the ECSC Treaty, was considered acceptable provided it paid due respect to the powers of the Commission, which has the right of 'budgetary initiative', and to the powers of the two holders of budgetary authority: the Council and, not least, Parliament. Possible fears on this score proved groundless and those who, like the Federal German Government, hoped that the outcome would be a rigid budget ceiling which would then be imposed throughout the budget cycle, were disappointed. In the event, a Joint Council meeting took place in April of 1976, 1977, 1978 and 1979. The Commission prepared a major paper[18] each year as a basis for the discussions in each Joint Council. However, in 1980, because of the special difficulties confronting the Community (the 'British problem', agricultural prices for 1980/81, rejection of the draft budget for 1980)—which have been touched on elsewhere in this book—it did not prepare such a paper. Unfortunately the results of the Joint Council's deliberations were generally not satisfactory, and have done little to help the Community define and solve its budget problems. In 1977, and above all in 1978, Parliament made its own parallel assessment of the situation and, in the last analysis, achieved quite good results.

The exercise is not without its uses, however, as it gives the Community institutions an opportunity to discuss budget problems freely and to a certain extent academically, that is, without necessarily having to arrive at a positive and practical result.

B—The interinstitutional dialogue

The 'interinstitutional dialogue on certain budgetary questions'—or 'trialogue'[19]—was born of the agreement reached between the Council and Parliament during the preparation of the 1976 budget. Parliament's Resolution on the draft general budget of the European Communities for 1976, adopted on 18 December 1975, noted that during the first quarter of 1976 a joint examination of various questions relating to budgetary procedure would be undertaken, with the assistance of the Commission.

As early as 18 November 1975, Parliament's Committee on Budgets had decided to create its own *ad hoc* working party on certain budgetary questions composed of specialists including in particular former budget rapporteurs. Each year from 1976 to 1978, the working party's efforts resulted in a report which was ratified by a resolution of Parliament in which the latter put forward solutions to the problems raised, e.g. inclusion of borrowing operations in the budget, inclusion of financial cooperation appropriations in the budget, the utilization of commitment appropriations, recourse to supplementary budgets, nomenclature, budget clarity, budgetary timetable, questions of implementation and financial planning.

Adoption of the report gave the occasion for a debate in plenary session[19] and for the passing of a Resolution in which Parliament greatly hoped that this dialogue would enable the institutions concerned to reach agreement on the main questions in time to be of use in the procedure for the next year's budget. Whereas the Commission played a full part in the dialogue both by written reply[20] and by participating in the debate in the Chamber, the Council was less keen on the procedure, as it has no legal foundation.

Although the dialogue cannot by itself smooth out all the differences of opinion between the institutions, it is not without its benefits. Precisely because it takes place outside any formal procedure, it helps clarify the respective positions of the institutions on all the problems involved, thus paving the way for the institutionalized discussions that will take place later. This is why progress has been made during successive budget cycles on a number of issues and why 'conciliation' on the subject of the Financial Regulation of 21 December 1977 was particularly fruitful. The directly-elected Parliament has, however, not resumed this dialogue.

*
**

The new Financial Regulation of 21 December 1977 introduced major innovations in the field of budget estimating both on the expenditure side and on the receipts side. Thus, the possibility of introducing two-part appropriations—showing separate figures for commitment and payment—is a step towards making the general budget a 'commitment budget', whose main role is to fix the commitments the Commission is empowered to undertake each year, leaving the consequential payments to follow automatically depending on the rate at which the actions concerned are implemented. Budget estimates must therefore be very accurate, both for commitments and for payments. The Member States pay great attention to the estimates, for obvious reasons. The 'paymaster' States keep a watch on the estimates of payments. The others worry about what possibilities of action will be given to the Commission and call for larger commitment estimates.

But the root of the problem lies elsewhere, in the quality of the dialogue between the budget institutions: between the Commission which makes proposals, and the Council and Parliament which take decisions. The Community budget must be credible, useful, modern. It must be flexible, not rigidly fixed. It must be the product of a joint operation.

The budget procedure has also provided unexpected opportunities to examine certain financial aid proposals that would not otherwise have seen the light of day. In this way, during the budget discussions, the Commission confirmed that certain Community grants were envisaged in a case where only the principle of such aid had so far been proposed. By proceeding to establish corresponding headings in the budget and appropriating funds to them, Parliament had led the Commission to implement specific actions despite the absence of legal authority for the expenditure. Thus the budget provided the spark. Accordingly, the budget has assumed fundamental importance. But the two-headed nature of the Budgetary Authority makes it difficult for a genuinely new policy to come into being in this way: one of the twin powers—the Council, in fact—only has to refuse to approve what the other power has decided in order to frustrate implementation of the adopted policy.

Footnotes to Chapter II

[1] In Part Three of this book, in each of the five chapters dealing with specific Community policies, we shall describe *how the budget estimates are made*. See EAGGF guarantee (p. 184), EAGGF guidance (p. 215), social policy (p. 209), regional policy (p. 225), energy policy (p. 253), industrial policy (p. 257), cooperation with developing countries and non-member countries (pp. 291 and 296), and administrative policy (p. 322).

[2] The three-year estimates for 1980-82 are the ninth not the tenth to be published, those for 1975-77 having not reached the publication stage owing to technical problems.

[3] For the 1980 budget the general introduction (also called Volume 7) runs to 1015 roneoed pages. It includes a policy report and summary tables.

[4] In Part Three of this book, in each of the five chapters dealing with specific Community policies, we shall indicate *whether an outlay is compulsory or non-compulsory and what the consequences of this are*. See

EAGGF guarantee (p. 184), EAGGF guidance (p. 215), social policy (p. 209), regional policy (p. 225), environmental policy (p. 231), energy policy (p. 253), industrial policy (p. 257), cooperation with developing countries and non-member countries (pp. 292 and 296), and administrative policy (p. 322).

[5] After rejecting the draft budget for 1980 on 13 December 1979, Parliament asked the Commission to produce a new preliminary draft budget; this went against Article 203(8) of the EEC Treaty, *inter alia*, which stipulates that Parliament 'may ... reject the draft budget and ask for a new draft to be submitted to it'. Since the 'major reasons' adduced by Parliament (see p. 9) for its rejection of the budget related not to the preliminary draft budget but to the draft budget—which differed from the preliminary draft precisely on the four points mentioned—the Commission considered that it was not bound to produce a fresh preliminary draft budget. However, to set the budget cycle in motion again the Commission introduced a new budget proposal on 29 February 1980, without going right back to the start of the budgetary procedure. The Commission's budget proposal was thus a unique document designed to meet the needs of an exceptional situation arising for the first time.

[6] The reader wishing to gain an overall view of the progress of the work and procedures relating to the budget should turn to p. 101 and read what is said about the discharge procedure.

[7] In Part Three of this book, in each of the five chapters dealing with specific Community policies, we shall indicate *how the budget is prepared*. See EAGGF guarantee (p. 184), EAGGF guidance (p. 215), social policy (p. 209), regional policy (p. 225), energy policy (p. 253), industrial policy (p. 257), cooperation with developing countries and non-member countries (pp. 292 and 296), and administrative policy (p. 322).

[8] The work of preparing the budget can, to a certain extent, be paralysed, despite the fact that the Council can take decisions by a qualified majority rather than unanimously. Thus it may happen that because of the weighting of the votes no qualified majority can be obtained (see footnote 4 on p. 13). If a new budget heading has to be created the consequences are tiresome rather than dramatic. On the other hand if it is a matter of voting money for a heading opened in the traditional way, the result may be catastrophic. The Council can only escape from the impasse by obtaining a qualified majority on the lowest possible common denominator.

[9] For details, see my article (in French) in *La Revue du marché commun*: 'Le bilan des procédures budgétaires: pour l'exercice 1975' (February 1975, pp. 79 to 87).

[10] *Idem* re 1976 (January 1976, pp. 10 to 19).

[11] *Idem* re 1977 (March 1977, pp. 128 to 137).

[12] *Idem* re 1978 (January 1978, pp. 13 to 29).

[13] *Idem* re 1979 (June 1979, pp. 240 to 262). Also, in the same periodical, the article by Mr Bangemann: 'La procédure budgétaire de 1979: l'équilibre nécessaire de la répartition des pouvoirs entre le Conseil et le Parlement' (April-May 1979, pp. 169 to 184).

[14] On 14 March 1977 the Commission wrote in its 'reflections' on the interpretation of Article 203 of the EEC Treaty, *inter alia*:
'... The commitment appropriation is the true budgetary instrument, enabling an action to be initiated and the corresponding legal obligation to be entered into. The attention of the Budgetary Authority and those responsible for audit should therefore quite naturally be directed first of all to the commitment appropriation, which expresses the financial dimensions of the action in question ...
The payment appropriation is an inevitable corollary to the commitment appropriation. This is not to say, of course, that the Budgetary Authority should no longer pay attention to payment appropriations; quite the contrary, the payment appropriations—which, under the principle of budgetary balance, correspond in total to the total estimated revenue—influence the determination of the commitment appropriations. Consequently the Budgetary Authority, before fixing a commitment appropriation, will have due regard to its financial implications, i.e. to the timing of the payment appropriations. Once the commitment appropriation has been authorized, however, the payment appropriation becomes an inevitable consequence.
The commitment appropriation is thus the cause, the payment appropriation is its effect.'

[15] The Commission wrote as follows in the policy section of its general introduction to the preliminary draft budget for 1979: 'The Commission considers it essential to stress once again that the impact of EAGGF guarantee expenditure is not determined by budgetary authorization, that is to say by the allocation of budget appropriations, but by the whole body of regulations governing the various common market organizations. The budget is only a reflection of these regulations; it is the instrument of implementation and management, but it is not an instrument for influencing the causes of the expenditure. This is where the problem lies, in the Commission's view, and it is thus in the sphere of basic regulations that it proposes measures and adjustments to bring agricultural spending under better control.'

[16] Later in this book we shall give a few examples of cases where tertiary law has to be adopted if the budget is to be implemented: a typical example is the Regional Fund (see p. 221).

[17] Parliament has always shown itself opposed to any kind of imposition of ceilings by regulation. This has sometimes led to confusion, as in the case of the Regulation on the appropriation of funds to the EAGGF Guidance Section: in a Resolution on the budgetary aspects of this legislation Parliament opposed—and in a Resolution on the agricultural aspects supported—the idea of a five-yearly ceiling (OJ C 6 of 8.1.1979, p. 76).

[18] The Commission, in its overall assessment of Community budget problems, emphasized the following themes, which we give here in very summarized form:
(a) in 1976: 6th VAT Directive, inclusion of Mediterranean financial protocols in the budget;
(b) in 1977: introduction of the EUA, ratification of the Treaty of 22 July 1975, new Financial Regulation;
(c) in 1978: the budget as an instrument of redistribution, transfer of powers at Community level, recourse to borrowing and lending;
(d) in 1979: new independent revenues (own resources), control of agricultural expenditure, structural expenditure and the EMS, inclusion of the EDF in the budget, development of borrowing and lending activities.

[19] In 1976, on 13 May (OJ C 125 of 8.6.1976, p. 30); in 1977, on 15 June (OJ C 163 of 11.7.1977, p. 39) and in 1978 on 15 June (OJ C 163 of 10.7.1978, p. 47). There was no debate in 1979 or 1980.

[20] Letters of 26 April 1976, 3 October 1977 and 8 August 1978.

Chapter III:
The structure of the Community budgets

The extent to which the Community budgets respect—or depart from—classical budgetary principles has been determined by a mixture of political and technical constraints, and the structure of the budget bears the marks of the same imperative constraints.

In examining the structure of the budgets we shall look first at the general budget and then at the ECSC operational budget.

1. The structure of the general budget of the European Communities

This rather general term of 'structure' covers a multitude of different aspects, often of great political and legal significance. We have grouped them into three sections: the statement of expenditure, the statement of revenue and the entry in the budget of borrowing and lending operations. Before considering them in detail we shall examine the general principles which apply.

A—Basic principles governing the structure of the general budget

The structure of the general budget is determined by Article 15 of the Financial Regulation.[1] Rather than paraphrase it, we quote it as it stands:

'1. The budget shall consist of:
   - a general statement of the revenue of the Communities, and
   - separate sections subdivided into statements of revenue and expenditure of the European Parliament, the Council, the Commission, the Court of Justice and the Court of Auditors. The revenue and expenditure of the Economic and Social Committee shall be entered in the section dealing with the Council and presented in the form of a statement of revenue and expenditure, subdivided in the same way as the sections of the budget and subject to the same rules.

2. Within each section, the items of revenue and expenditure shall be classified according to their type or the use to which they are assigned under titles, chapters, articles and items.

3. The budgetary nomenclature shall be decided, in respect of the apportionment of the revenue and expenditure under separate titles, chapters and articles during the budgetary procedure.'

The form in which the budget should be presented is laid down in Article 16 of the Financial Regulation:

'The budget shall show:

1. In the general statement of revenue:
   - the estimated revenue of the Communities for the financial year in question, divided into titles, chapters, articles and items,
   - the revenue for the preceding financial year, divided into titles, chapters, articles and items,
   - appropriate remarks on each subdivision.

2. In the section for each institution:
   (a) as regards the statement of revenue:
       - the estimated revenue for each institution for the financial year in question, divided into titles, chapters, articles and items, following a decimal classification system,
       - the revenue entered in the budget for the preceding financial year and the revenue established for the last financial year for which accounts have been closed, using the same decimal classification,
       - appropriate remarks on each revenue heading;
   (b) as regards the statement of expenditure:
       (ba) in the case of the various items, articles, chapters and titles:
            - the appropriations made available for the financial year in question, these appropriations being the payment appropriations for the budget headings for which the distinction between commitment appropriations and payment appropriations has been agreed,
            - the appropriations made available for the preceding financial year,
            - the actual expenditure in the last financial year for which the accounts have been closed;
       (bb) in the case of the appropriations intended for the implementation of multiannual activities and consisting of commitment appropriations: in the remarks column, an indicative schedule of the payments relating to the financial year concerned and subsequent financial years;
       (bc) appropriate remarks on each subdivision;
   (c) as regards total staff:
       - in an annex to the budget, a list of posts fixing the number of posts for each grade in each category and in each service,
       - annexed to the Commission Section, a list of posts in respect of officials, established staff of the Joint Research Centre and temporary staff occupying permanent posts, classified by categories and grades, whose employment is authorized within the limits of the budget appropriations. However, as regards scientific and technical staff, the classification may be based on groups of grades, in accordance with the conditions laid down in each budget. The list of posts must specify the number of highly qualified technical or scientific personnel who are accorded special advantages under the Staff Regulations applicable to these officials.

The list of posts shall constitute an absolute limit for each institution; no appointment may be made in excess of the limit set.

3. As regards borrowing and lending operations:

    (a) in the Commission Section:
    — the budget headings relating to the categories of operation accorded a token entry, so long as no effective charge which has to be covered by specific resources has appeared thereunder,
    — remarks giving a reference to the legal basis, where appropriate the volume of the operations envisaged, and the financial guarantee given by the Communities in respect of these operations;

    (b) in a document annexed to the Commission Section, as an indication:
    — current capital operations and current debt management,
    — the capital operations and debt management for the financial year in question.'

Although it has a rather forbidding appearance, the budget is easy to read. Once the reader has assimilated the contents of Articles 15 and 16 of the Financial Regulation, he or she can penetrate the mysteries of European budgetary policy with comparative ease.

B—The Commission's statement of expenditure

Each institution has its own statement of expenditure. To save time we shall only analyse the Commission's here; it accounts for 98% of Community expenditure. We shall concentrate on the following five aspects: criteria for inclusion of Community expenditure in the budget, budget nomenclature, criteria for entry in the budget, classification of expenditure according to type or use, and the differentiation of appropriations.

Criteria for inclusion in the budget of Community expenditure (and revenue)

Articles 199, first paragraph of the EEC Treaty and 171(1), first subparagraph of the Euratom Treaty stipulate that: 'all items of revenue and expenditure of the Community . . . shall be included in estimates to be drawn up for each financial year and shall be shown in the budget'. As we have already seen, there are some instances where the general budget ignores this rule of comprehensiveness (budgetary unity) and these often stem from actual Treaty provisions.

The most spectacular exclusion of expenditure and revenue from the budget in recent years has certainly been the exclusion of the fourth EDF in 1975. By contrast, in 1976 the Council eventually agreed that aid under the financial protocols with the Mediterranean countries should form part of the budget, having opposed this for some months for reasons connected with the financing of the general budget and the European unit of account; some Member States had advocated the use of 'political scales' for the payment of financial contributions, as is done in the case of the EDF. On 18 September 1979 the Council decided not to include the fifth EDF in the budget.

Budget nomenclature

It will be recalled that Articles 202, third paragraph of the EEC Treaty, 175, third paragraph of the Euratom Treaty (referring to administrative appropriations), and 78a, fourth paragraph of the ECSC Treaty stipulate that 'appropriations shall be classified under different chapters grouping items of expenditure according to their nature or purpose and subdivided, as far as may be necessary, in accordance with [financial] regulations'. The Financial Regulation repeats and amplifies this provision in Article 21(1), requiring that 'appropriations shall be classified by chapter and article'. In the same way Article 4, first paragraph, provides that no revenue may be collected and no expenditure effected unless charged to an article in the budget. The *article* is thus the basic unit to which revenue and expenditure must be assigned, the chapters and titles being added merely to produce an orderly and self-consistent arrangement of the articles. We shall see in due course that a fairly strict logic governs this classification system. In practice the articles are subdivided into '*items*' at the time the budget is drawn up; new items may be created either by the Commission, if they merely represent a more refined subdivision of the content of the arti cle concerned, or by the Budgetary Authority, as and when required.

Ultimately, the budget nomenclature will grow only if the budget itself develops. This in turn depends on the progress achieved in building Europe. Adoption of a new policy, if it is one with financial consequences, will be registered by the creation of one or more new chapters or at least some new articles, since the budget itself is just the reflection of Europe in development. In the past few years budget nomenclature has developed and changed in a remarkable way.

The budget nomenclature was set out in the Annex to the Financial Regulation of 25 April 1973 and accounted for 44 pages in the Official Journal. However, the Budget Authority amended the nomenclature, at the Commission's proposal, when drawing up each new budget and did not amend the Annex itself; the latter therefore eventually became completely obsolete. The new Financial Regulation of 21 December 1977, in Article 15, paragraph 3, quoted above (see p. 54), brought the law into line with reality by stipulating that the budget nomenclature should thenceforth be decided 'during the budgetary procedure'. This provision, proposed by the Commission and initially rejected by the Council, was finally accepted by the latter in a legislative 'conciliation committee' at the end of 1977 (see Annex 5, p. 363). It is of more than mere formal significance to Parliament, since it enables that institution to make the budget an act of policy-forecasting rather than simply a snapshot of the existing situation.

A further point to be mentioned is that alongside each budget heading and amount (on the left-hand side of each page of the budget) there is a 'remarks column' (on the right-hand side) which is there by virtue of Article 16 (2) (bc) of the Financial Regulation (see p. 54). The 'remarks column' states the basis for the appropriation and sometimes gives further explanation; in the case of two-part appropriations, a schedule of payments for the financial year in question and for subsequent years appears (see p. 60). On occasions the Budgetary Authority enters comments addressed to the authorizing officer, sometimes with mandatory force. When the Financial Regulation of 25 April 1973 was being revised, Parliament tried—unsuccessfully—to have the remarks made mandatory, hoping, in this indirect way, to be able to play a regulatory or even legislative role by making the implementation of budget appropriations subject to certain rules (see Annex 5, p. 363). During the preparation of the 1979 budget, Parliament tried to use the remarks as a means of initiating new actions in the absence of Council regulations.

Criteria for entry in the budget
of appropriations for new policies or actions
with financial consequences

As long as the Council, the Community's legislative body, was the sole holder of budgetary power, a convention grew up that expenditure could be authorized only if based on a Council Decision or on a requirement absolutely necessary to the functioning of the Community institutions. In practice this meant that the Council, as the Budgetary Authority—without disputing the possibility of applying Article 199 of the EEC Treaty, etc.—always refused to create a heading in the budget for an item of expenditure that had not yet been agreed in principle, arguing that the budget cannot be an instrument for policy-making but only the quantified expression of policy that is already determined.

It should be mentioned, however, that the Council has broken the rule which it imposed on at least two occasions: aid to the Sahel and industrial restructuring and conversion in the Community.[2]

In this connection attention must be drawn to the importance of Articles 235 of the EEC Treaty and 203 of the Euratom Treaty. Article 235 was invoked some 150 times between 1 January 1973 and 31 December 1979, in accordance with the wishes of the Paris Summit of 19 to 21 October 1972 (see Annex 3, p. 351). It has been used as a legal basis for new Community measures carrying financial implications. These Articles read as follows: 'If action by the Community should prove necessary to attain, in the course of the operation of the common market, one of the objectives of the Community and this Treaty has not provided the necessary powers, the Council shall, acting unanimously on a proposal from the Commission and after consulting the European Parliament, take the appropriate measures'. A similar provision is to be found in Article 95 of the ECSC Treaty.

With the acquisition of budgetary powers by the European Parliament there has arisen a conflict stemming from the fact that Parliament has taken the view that the Budgetary Authority, by the mere fact of creating a budget heading and voting appropriations to it, can authorize a measure. Relying on this reasoning Parliament has created many new budget headings[3] since the 1976 budget without the dispute being really settled, since it is not enough for the Commission—the Budgetary Executive—to have appropriations made available to it: it must also be placed in a position to use them, and this has not always been the case. However that may be, it must be emphasized that Parliament, thanks to its position as co-holder of budgetary power, has several times enabled new measures to be initiated, e.g. aid to non-associated developing countries (see p. 289), aid to non-governmental organizations carrying out measures to assist developing countries (see p. 288), and aid for uranium prospecting (see p. 249), without any decision having been taken on the overall policy of which these measures are to form a part.

But to enable it to implement the budget without coming into conflict with the Council or Parliament, the Commission has sought to make the best possible use of the opportunities provided by the Financial Regulation, particularly the 'token entry' and the Chapter 100 reserve. There are in fact two clever budget devices, the 'dash' and the 'token entry'. They work in this way. A heading may be entered in the budget with its complete title but with the amount of the appropriation replaced by a dash (—). This means that the principle of this expenditure is recognized through the budget, but no actual funds can be committed as there are no corresponding appropriations. There are also limitations on transferring funds to such a heading from elsewhere in the budget since funds may only be appropriated to it on the occasion of an ordinary budget or a supplementary budget. By contrast, when a

57

budget heading is accompanied by the words 'token entry', this means that in addition to the fact that the item of expenditure is recognized in principle, appropriations may be allocated to it by the transfer procedure (Article 21(5) of the Financial Regulation). This procedure will be explained later. The dash is not provided for in the Financial Regulation.

As for Chapter 100, this is not an ordinary budget heading against which expenditure may be charged, but a reserve made up of a number of amounts which are to be assigned to certain purposes. For example, in the case of the 1980 budget there were 24 appropriations covering payments totalling 51.7 m EUA. For these appropriations to be used it is necessary for them to be transferred by the Budgetary Authority under the provisions of Article 21(2), second, third, fourth and fifth subparagraphs, of the Financial Regulation.

For the 1979, 1980 and 1981 budgets the Commission proposed in the general introduction to the preliminary draft budget that the Council and Parliament should lay down criteria to govern the question of the entry in the budget of new policies or measures. The Commission proposed three principal criteria, to the extent that the legal basis has to be fixed beforehand by the Council if an item of expenditure is to be implemented:[4]

— *First criterion*: appropriations should be entered against the budget heading when the Commission's proposal for new measures or policies carrying financial implications has been accepted or, provided it has been made before 15 June, when it has every chance of being accepted before 31 December in view of what is known of the state of discussions in the relevant Community bodies.
— *Second criterion*: a heading should be entered at the requisite place in the Commission Section of the budget and accompanied by the words 'token entry', and appropriations should be entered in Chapter 100 if the Commission's proposal, although not yet accepted, has every likelihood of being accepted in the next financial year; the amount of appropriations to be entered will depend on the presumed date of entry into force of the policy in question.
— *Third criterion*: a heading should be entered and merely marked 'token entry' when a new policy is being framed in the responsible quarters of the Community but has not yet been the subject of a formal proposal for a regulation by the Commission or when, although a proposal has been made, it is impossible for the time being to estimate the financial cost of the policy and there is therefore no point in voting appropriations and increasing the amount of own resources to be collected.

The institutions concerned have not yet started to discuss this matter in earnest; this is highly regrettable.

Classification of expenditure by type and by objective

As provided by the Treaties (Article 202 of the EEC Treaty, *inter alia*) and the Financial Regulation, items of revenue and expenditure must be classified 'according to their nature or purpose'. The Commission has sought to develop the general budget's structure on this basis. After amendments every year, the nomenclature of the 1979 budget, on the expenditure side, comes very close to achieving the end sought—that is, a completely transparent presentation enabling the Budgetary Authority and public opinion to see clearly and precisely what resources have been sought and obtained for the objectives pursued.

For expenditure, the Commission's Section of the budget for 1980 includes ten titles comprising a total of 75 chapters. To avoid repetition, we shall not at this stage analyse the contents of these chapters; this will be done in the last five chapters of the book under the heading 'budgetary and legal framework':[5]

— *Title 1*: Expenditure relating to persons working with the institution (6 chapters).
— *Title 2*: Buildings, equipment and miscellaneous administrative expenditure (10 chapters).
— *Title 3*: Community policies relating in particular to research, technology, industry, the social order, the environment and the supply of energy and raw materials (9 chapters).
— *Title 4*: Repayments and aid to Member States and other aid (5 chapters).
— *Title 5*: Social and Regional Funds (10 chapters).
— *Titles 6 and 7*: EAGGF Guarantee Section (17 chapters).
— *Title 8*: EAGGF Guidance Section and fisheries policy (8 chapters).
— *Title 9*: Cooperation with developing countries and other non-member countries (7 chapters).
— *Title 10*: Provisional appropriations, contingency reserve, EUA reserve (3 chapters).

Thus the appropriations for Titles 3 to 9 are grouped according to their purpose, i.e. by 'intervention policy', while those for Titles 1 and 2 are classified according to their nature; Title 10 consists solely of reserves which require a transfer before they can be used.

The quest for transparency encourages the endless generation of new headings, and the development of large numbers of subdivisions, to use the word employed in Article 202(3) of the EEC Treaty. The danger of this is that appropriations will be widely scattered, producing an apparent reduction in the volume of certain types of expenditure. Thus, appropriations for studies are found under 41 different headings and those for publishing under 21. Furthermore, this scattering arouses the apprehensions of the Budgetary Authority, and the particular department responsible for authorizing expenditure also faces problems of coordination. A number of appropriations are in any case classified according to their nature and will remain so as long as the budget keeps its present broad shape. These are the appropriations for Titles 1 and 2. They cover appropriations for staff, regardless of their duties (Title 1) (except, in fact, staff assigned to research activities at the Joint Research Centre or in respect of 'indirect' action projects (Chapter 33)), and appropriations for administrative expenditure divided into its major categories: buildings, equipment, and so on, to enable the staff to do their work (Title 2). The distinction between appropriations classified by nature and those classified by purpose is not, however, watertight; some appropriations in Title 2 are put there for a specific purpose indicated either by the title or in the remarks column opposite the heading concerned.

This account would not be complete without some reference to the research and investment appropriations of the European Atomic Energy Community. Article 10 of the Treaty of Luxembourg of 21 April 1970 brought Euratom's separate research and investment budget to an end by merging it into the general budget, as required by the principle of financing Community expenditure entirely from Community revenue. In the general budget the appropriations were grouped according to purpose in Chapter 33, supplemented by an annex which constituted a genuine budget on which implementation was based. This system, based on the *ad hoc* Financial Regulation of 28 September 1971 and restated in Articles 93 to 103 of the Financial Regulation of 25 April 1973, was in force from 1971 to 1977. Transparency was poor in this functional budget owing to its complexity (see p. 264) and the sheer volume of data it contained (45% of its pages covered 1.8% of its appropriations). The presentation was simplified by the Financial Regulation of 21 December 1977, the first budget affected being that for 1978. At Parliament's instigation the Commission, on 15 June 1978, proposed a fresh modification of the Financial Regulation on this point, to make the 1979 budget even clearer. To put it briefly, the research and investment appropriations are set out in Chapter 33 according to their purpose, that is to say that in principle each item within the Chapter represents a research objective. A new budget annex contains a table of equivalence analysing the expenditure both by objective (i.e. by purpose) and by nature. A recommended timetable giving the entire funding of each objective, the 'tranches' of appropriations allocated and a schedule of estimated dates for the use of the commitment and payment appropriations throughout the duration of the programme appears in the same annex. The new method of presentation, although not covered by the Financial Regulation, since the 21 December 1977 Regulation was not amended until 25 June 1979,[6] was nevertheless used in the 1979 budget, adopted on 14 December 1978. This is an interesting legal peculiarity. However that may be, the number of pages devoted to these appropriations has been cut by two-thirds, without any prejudice to clarity, indeed very much the reverse.

Differentiation between commitment appropriations and payment appropriations

The Community gradually came to feel the need to reconcile the constraint of the principle of annuality with the requirements of managing multiannual measures which were steadily gaining in importance as a part of Community expenditure. The Financial Regulation of 21 December 1977, which came into force on 1 January 1978, provides in Article 1, paragraph 3, fifth subparagraph, that 'multiannual activities in respect of which a distinction is to be made between commitment appropriations and payment appropriations shall be decided on during the budgetary procedure'. Up to that time the creation of 'differentiated appropriations' of this kind had been effected either by treaty: research and investment appropriations (Article 176(1) of the Euratom Treaty and its application in Article 88(3), third subparagraph, of the Financial Regulation) or by regulation: the Regional Development Fund (Regulation of 18 March 1975) and seven other sectors in the 1977 budget (Regulations of 21 October, 1977 and 21 December 1977). There were also some other multiannual activities covered by individual sets of rules (commitment authorizations for the Social Fund, five-year carry-overs for the EAGGF Guidance Section). Thenceforth the Budgetary Authority was able to create two-part appropriations in the course of the budget procedure using the powers conferred on it by the Treaties. This represents a considerable change: financial regulations are adopted by the Council acting unanimously after consulting Parliament and with referral to the conciliation committee to reconcile divergent points of view, whereas the budget is adopted by the Budgetary Authority, of which the Council forms only one part and moreover votes by a qualified majority. Commitment appropriations not committed in the financial year for which they were created continue to be available for the following year. Payment appropriations, on the other hand, obey the normal rules.

The appropriations entered in the budget are thus of two types: simple (officially: 'non-differentiated') appropriations, which allow commitments to be entered into during the financial year in question and the corresponding payments to be made within a period of two years (that is, for one year with automatic carry-over to the following financial year), and two-part (officially: 'differentiated') appropriations, which specify both an appropriation for commitment which is the upper limit of the commitments which can be entered into during that financial year, and an appropriation for payment, for disbursements to be made in fulfilment of commitments undertaken either during the current financial year or in previous years.[7]

In the 1980 budget many headings in Titles 3 and 9 and most headings in Titles 5 and 8 have two-part appropriations. Only the payment appropriations have to be covered by revenue, which removes a burden from the budget at the time of preparation and makes it easier to keep implementation in line with the estimates.

C—The Community's statement of revenue

The general statement of revenue can be described far more briefly than the statement of expenditure. One aspect, the inclusion of revenue in the budget, has already been dealt with. Two other aspects do not apply, the distinctions between nature and purpose and between commitment and payment. But something must be said about nomenclature.

The general statement of revenue has six titles; in the 1979 budget these ran to 19 chapters. As with expenditure, we shall avoid repetition by not analysing the contents of these chapters at this stage.
— *Title 1*: Own resources (4 chapters).
— *Title 2*: Surpluses available (2 chapters).
— *Title 3*: Portion of proceeds of ECSC levies paid in pursuance of Article 20 of the Treaty of 8 April 1965 (1 chapter).
— *Title 4*: Deductions from staff pay (2 chapters).
— *Title 5*: Financial contributions (2 chapters).
— *Title 9*: Miscellaneous revenue (8 chapters).

Each institution's section contains some 'own receipts' attributable to that institution. These are the receipts entered under Titles 4 and 9, which are totalled in the general statement of revenue.

Revenue nomenclature is less varied and less changing than that of the expenditure, but is no less significant for all that. The creation of Title 1 was a historical event, as was the creation of its various chapters. Similarly, the virtual elimination of Title 5 reflects the final attainment of financial autonomy by the European Communities.

D—Inclusion of borrowing and lending operations in the budget

Euratom and the EEC undertake four types of borrowing and lending operation; in chronological order they are: Eximbank borrowings; Community borrowings in connection with aid to Member States in balance-of-payments difficulties as a result of the rise in price of petroleum products (called Community loans); Community borrowings to finance nuclear power stations (called Euratom loans); and the New Community Instrument (NCI). The ways in which these loans are treated for budget purposes differ considerably, but the end result is the same.

Inclusion of Euratom's borrowing and lending operations (Eximbank loans) in the budget from 1963 to 1977

When Euratom was granted a loan by the Export-Import Bank of Washington (Eximbank) on 10 August 1959, the Budgetary Authority decided that the operation should be wholly included in the budget. The amounts paid on behalf of the recipients (interest and repayments of principal) came out of Community revenue and corresponded exactly to the expenditure flowing from the Community's obligations to Eximbank. From 1978 these operations were treated like the other borrowing and lending operations.

Inclusion of borrowing and lending operations in the 1976 and 1977 budgets

As a result of a decision by Parliament, borrowing and lending operations were included in the 1976 budget, but in a highly rudimentary form: one expenditure heading and one revenue heading were created ('Community loans'[8] and 'Euratom loans'[9]), and assigned a 'token entry'; the entry in the remarks column merely stated 'this Article was entered by the European Parliament when it adopted the general budget on 18 December 1975'. In the 1977 budget some comments with legislative force appeared in the remarks column, envisaging, in particular, 'performance guarantees'. In addition, an Annex 2 to the Commission Section of the budget gave the full account of the capital operations and related debt management.

Inclusion of borrowing and lending operations in the 1978, 1979 and 1980 budgets

In the 1978 budget, the budgetary and accounting presentation of the four types of borrowing and lending operation obeys the following six principles, as laid down in the new Financial Regulation which came into force on 1 January 1978:
(a) to avoid artificially inflating the budget, the proceeds of borrowings are not treated as revenue and loans granted are not treated as expenditure;
(b) to meet any expenditure the Commission might incur as a result of its legal obligation to the providers of the funds if the recipients of the corresponding loans became insolvent a budget heading is created in the Commission's statement of expenditure and accorded a token entry. This potential liability is the result of the performance guarantee[10] mentioned in the remarks column; the remarks in this column must also, under the provisions of Article 16(3), of the Financial Regulation, indicate the volume of the operations envisaged (see p. 55). These remarks are mandatory in character;
(c) to accommodate revenue stemming from the Community's right of recourse against borrowers in respect of expense which it has had to incur by reason of its 'financial responsibility', a budget heading is created in the Commission's statement of revenue and accorded a token entry;
(d) borrowing and lending operations do not entail any financial charge on the budget, the expenses incurred by the Community for arranging and implementing each operation being borne by the recipients;
(e) a document annexed to the Commission section of the budget gives a full account of the capital operations and related debt management;
(f) an annex, forming an integral part of the Community's annual revenue and expenditure account, indicates the operations carried out during the year.

62

The proposed inclusion of borrowing and lending operations in the budget

At Parliament's suggestion, the Commission proposed, on 15 June 1978, that the borrowing and lending operations should be more fully integrated into the budget (see footnote 3, p. 30).[3] Specifically, the Commission proposed that a Part II of the general budget should be created, in application of Article 199 of the Treaty, etc., which stipulates that 'all items of revenue and expenditure of the Community ... shall be shown in the budget', the proceeds of borrowings being treated as revenue and the loans as expenditure. For each budget heading, for both borrowings and lendings, there would be shown, for the reference year, the current year and the preceding year:

(1) the annual amounts for the borrowings and of the related lendings;
(2) the annual amounts of repayments of principal both to the Community and by the Community to the providers of the funds;
(3) the annual amounts of interest payable to the Community and paid by the Community to the providers of the funds; and
(4) the annual amounts of expenses of a 'one-off' nature for arranging the borrowings, and the annual amounts to be paid to the Community to cover the administrative expenses of the same borrowings and of the lendings, and, on the expenditure side, payment of the same expenses by the Community.

Entering the annual amounts estimated for the borrowing and lending operations and the expected annual repayments of principal and payments of interest in Part II of the general budget would mean that the Commission would be authorized, within the limits set by the basic regulations, to borrow money, to lend the money received in this way and to make the necessary repayments of principal and payments of interest and expenses each year. The recipients of the loans granted would have to make their repayments to the Community in good time for the Community in turn to make the payments due to the providers of the funds. However, if a debtor was unable to pay in good time, the Commission would be authorized to make immediate payment of the sums due. A payment of this kind could involve the making of a transfer or the introduction of a supplementary budget; for this reason it is proposed that Part I should include—on both the expenditure and the revenue sides—budget headings which, when accorded a token entry, could accommodate any expenditure not covered by payments from the recipients of the loans granted and any receipts resulting from the Community's exercise of its right of recourse against defaulting debtors.

The above principles, together with the entry in Part II of the budget of the amounts constituting the Commission's authorization to borrow and repay money, and together with the obligation imposed by Article 1, paragraph 4, of the Financial Regulation (as modified by the Commission's proposal) to enter the necessary appropriations in successive budgets, would furnish a clearer and more convincing guarantee for the providers of funds. Finally, to cover the possibility of non-fulfilment of the authorized operations before the end of the financial year, the Commission proposes that authorizations entered in Part II of the budget which have not been used should automatically be carried forward to the following year.

The Commission's preliminary draft budget for 1979 was based on this proposed amendment to the Financial Regulation. On 10 October 1978 Parliament gave a favourable opinion on the Commission's proposal, but on 18 July and 20 November 1978 the Council implicitly rejected the new structure in its draft budget for 1979. The subject was discussed during conciliation on the New Community Instrument and contributed to making the proceedings rather acrimonious (see Annex 5, p. 364). In the definitive budget for 1979, the presentation therefore remained the same as for 1978 because the proposed amendment to the Financial Regulation had not been accepted by the Council. In its preliminary draft budget for 1980 the Commission again used the modified form of presentation and the Council again rejected it implicitly when adopting its draft budget on 11 September and 23 November 1979. This time round Parliament did not yield and made the matter one of its four 'major reasons' for rejecting the draft budget on 13 December 1979 (see p. 9).

Faced with the impossibility of reaching agreement with the Council, it refused, however, to alter the presentation in the 1980 budget. In its preliminary draft budget for 1981, the Commission—for the third time—has introduced a Part II devoted to borrowing and lending activities. The debate, which has far-reaching political implications, thus remains open.

2. The structure of the ECSC operational budget

For many years, the form and layout of the ECSC operational budget did not reflect firmly established rules but merely long-standing practice in the drawing-up of the annual budget documents. The conventions evolved in this way were made binding by a Commission decision of 2 August 1976 setting out rules of procedure.

A—The ECSC's resources and requirements

The ECSC operational budget contains the two traditional parts of a budget, a revenue side and an expenditure side, the former being called 'resources' and the latter 'requirements'.

For 1980 the requirements side is divided into six chapters:
Operations to be financed from resources for the financial year (non-repayable):
— *Chapter 1*: Administrative expenditure,[11]
— *Chapter 2*: Aid to redeployment (Article 56),
— *Chapter 3*: Aid to research (Article 55),
— *Chapter 4*: Interest rebates,
— *Chapter 5*: Aid to coking coal and coke for the steel industry.
Operations financed with loans granted out of non-borrowed funds:
— *Chapter 6*: Subsidized housing.
The resources side is divided into seven chapters:
— *Chapter 1*: Current resources,
— *Chapter 2*: Cancellation of commitments which will probably not be implemented,
— *Chapter 3*: Revaluation of assets and liabilities,
— *Chapter 4*: Receipts for 1979 not utilized,
— *Chapter 5*: Extraordinary receipts,
— *Chapter 6*: Repayments on loans for subsidized housing,
— *Chapter 7*: Special reserve and former ECSC Pension Fund.

The notable feature of this budget is the fact that it contains 'below-the-line' expenditure financed from the special reserve. The expenditure in question goes to subsidized housing for workers in the coal and steel industries. It is a genuine case of lending from own resources.

The budget authority—The High Authority/Commission acting after advice from Parliament (see p. 2)—has always made sure that all financing requirements of the ECSC representing a call on the Community's resources are included in its budget.

B—Inclusion of borrowing and lending operations in the budget

The ECSC's borrowing and lending operations do not appear as such in the ECSC operational budget. No form of budget entry such as practised or provided for by the EEC has ever been used. However, Article 50, paragraph 1, third item of the ECSC Treaty stipulated that the levies, and hence the ECSC operational budget, must cover any deficit on Community borrowing and lending transactions, although in practice no such deficit has ever arisen.

For its part Parliament implicitly requires ECSC borrowings and lendings to be included in the budget. In paragraph 13 of its Resolution of 13 December 1978 on the ECSC operational budget for 1979, Parliament 'points in this connection once again to the need for control by Parliament of all the financial activities of the ECSC and declares its intention of exercising control over the ECSC's "investment budget"; is accordingly of the opinion that the Commission should submit appropriate proposals to Parliament as rapidly as possible to ensure that this control can be applied with effect from the 1979 financial year'.

*
* *

The structure of its budgets is one of the most important facets of the Community's image, at least on the financial plane. This image has been subject to a process of continuous change throughout the past ten years. Anyone reading the budget for 1968, the year when the executives were merged, will find that it contains 49 chapters, 18 of them for staff appropriations and 31 for agricultural and other policies. In 1979 the corresponding figures were 68, 16 and 52 respectively. At the same time, in terms of current units of account, budget resources have grown sixfold. We have thus seen a broadening and a deepening of the budget's structure and resources through the inclusion in it—against continual opposition, it is true, of the financing of Community activities.[12]

Footnotes to Chapter III

[1] See OJ L 356 of 31.12.1977.

[2] When the 1974 budget was drawn up, the Council provided substantial appropriations (35 m u.a.) against a heading for Community aid to disaster victims for reconstruction projects in the drought-afflicted countries of the Sahel, without any previous agreement in principle on the matter. Here, therefore, the budget acted as a policy-making instrument.

Further, in the course of preparing the 1978 budget, the Council created an Article 375 for Community aid for restructuring and conversion operations in certain crisis-hit industrial sectors and made payment appropriations of 17 m u.a. available for it.

Whereas the first action proceeded normally, it had been possible only to make a partial start with the second by the end of 1979 because the Council had not sanctioned the legal basis for the new policy.

[3] See footnotes 9, 10 and 11 to Chapter II.

[4] In the Commission's preliminary draft budget for 1979—the first illustration of the criteria which the Commission proposed for adoption—72 budget headings were assigned a 'token entry', as follows:
(a) in application of the second criterion mentioned: 6;
(b) in application of the third criterion: 20;
(c) where an item of expenditure is small and only potential, and the amount is uncertain: 17;
(d) where an item of expenditure is completely a matter of chance or where it relates to a measure which is nearly at an end and for which moreover any funds that might become necessary could easily be made available by means of a transfer: 24;
(e) where a measure has come to an end but a residual balance could still become payable, thus requiring a budget heading to be kept in existence in order to accommodate the resultant expenditure: 5.

[5] In Part Three of the book, in each of the five chapters dealing with specific Community policies, we shall describe the *relevant budgetary structures*. The policies in question are: EAGGF guarantee (see p. 185), EAGGF guidance (see p. 216), social policy (see p. 210), regional policy (see p. 226), energy policy (see p. 254), research policy (see p. 264), cooperation with developing countries and non-member countries (see pp. 292 and 296), and administrative policy (see p. 303).

[6] See OJ L 160 of 28.6.1979.

[7] In the remarks column (see p. 56) alongside headings carrying two-part appropriations there is an indicative schedule of payment appropriations for the financial year and subsequent years (see e.g. p. 209—Social Fund—or p. 225—Regional Fund).

[8] 'Community loans' were thus only included in the budget in any way in one year: 1975.

[9] The Euratom loans were thus included in the budget for 1976 before they had even been authorized by regulation.

[10] The Community's performance guarantee reads as follows: 'If the other operations provided for by the financial machinery applying to these loans cannot be implemented in time, bearing in mind the due dates fixed, the Commission will temporarily undertake to service the debt contracted by the Community, on the basis of its direct legal commitment *vis-à-vis* the lenders, out of its own cash resources.
Any expenditure which the Community may have to bear definitively shall be charged to this chapter and the Community shall then exercise its right to bring proceedings against defaulting debtors.'

[11] Under the heading of administrative expenditure the ECSC budget showed only a lump sum paid from this budget to the general budget pursuant to Article 20 of the Merger Treaty. Thus the administrative expenditure of the ECSC is not distinguished from that of the other institutions in the general budget, except for a few specific headings in the Commission Section (ECSC committees and commissions; the Mines Safety and Health Commission; conferences, congresses and meetings connected with the ECSC; economic and social studies as provided for in Article 46 of the ECSC Treaty.

[12] A fascinating problem of inclusion or non-inclusion in the budget is facing the Community at this moment. In a request for an opinion submitted to the Court of Justice on 13 November 1978 under the provisions of Article 228, paragraph 1, second subparagraph of the EEC Treaty, the Commission asked to what extent the International Agreement on Natural Rubber negotiated within the framework of the United Nations Conference on Trade and Development (Unctad) was compatible with the Treaty. The main point of the request was to ascertain the Court's opinion as to whether or not the Community had the power to conclude this arrangement and, if so, whether or not such power was exclusive.
In its Recommendation of October 1978 to the Council, the Commission had proposed that the contributions to the financing of the buffer stock of 400 000 tonnes prescribed by the International Agreement should be charged to the Communities' budget. In its request for an opinion the Commission drew attention to this proposal without maintaining that charging the contributions to financing the buffer stock to the Communities' budget was the sole legally correct solution. It confined itself to pointing out the logic of this solution and indicating that the Community would have the necessary powers to undertake commitments at international level to pay the contributions.
In Opinion 1/78 given on 4 October 1979, the Court of Justice declared as follows:
'1.   The Community's powers relating to commercial policy within the meaning of Article 113 of the Treaty establishing the European Economic Community extend to the International Agreement on Natural Rubber which is in the course of negotiation within the United Nations Conference on Trade and Development (Unctad).
2.   The question of the exclusive nature of the Community's powers depends in this case on the arrangements for financing the operations of the buffer stock which it is proposed to set up under that Agreement. If the burden of financing the stock falls upon the Community budget the Community will have exclusive powers.

If on the other hand the charges are to be borne directly by the Member States that will imply the participation of those States in the Agreement together with the Community.

3.   As long as that question has not been settled by the competent Community authorities the Member States must be allowed to participate in the negotiation of the Agreement.'

The Member States subsequently decided that the financing should be national rather than via the Community budget. The refusal to include it in the budget was admittedly likely after the Court's Opinion, but it was no less regrettable for that. The Court nevertheless indicated the crucial importance of the Budget Authority's decision.

Chapter IV:
Implementing the Community
budgets

Implementation of the budget goes on throughout the financial year, which runs from 1 January to 31 December (Articles 203(1) of the EEC Treaty, 177(1) of the Euratom Treaty, and 78(1) of the ECSC Treaty). The ECSC's financial year, however, only came into line with these dates on 1 January 1969 (Article 21 of the Merger Treaty of 8 April 1965). Before then it ran from 1 July to 30 June (former Article 78(1) of the ECSC Treaty).

The Treaties give a pre-eminent role in this field to the Commission, which is the budget-implementing organ of the Community; it performs this function on its own responsibility. The Commission decides all transfers within chapters and requests permission from the Budgetary Authority to transfer appropriations between chapters. The Commission, regardless of which section of the budget is involved, asks the Budgetary Authority to carry funds over from one year to the next. The Commission, too, draws up the revenue and expenditure account and is granted discharge for the implementation of the budget. It is the Commission that has the right to make proposals in connection with the Financial Regulation, and the Commission, too, draws up the detailed rules for implementing the Financial Regulation. As regards implementation of the budget, these various powers correspond, but with greater scope, to the powers the Commission enjoys in regard to preparation of the budget, which have already been discussed in the previous chapter. But in reality each institution has a large measure of autonomy. Thus, since 1970, the implementation of Parliament's budget has escaped control by the Commission. Parliament considers that it should be its own sole budgetary authority and that it alone should approve its transfers and carry-overs.

In this, as in the previous chapters, a distinction must be drawn between the general budget and the ECSC operational budget. The rules for implementing the latter are less elaborate.

1. Implementing the general budget of the European Communities

Implementation should be examined in terms of expenditure, on the one hand, and revenue, on the other.

A—Implementation of the expenditure side of the general budget

Analysing implementation of the expenditure side of the budget is a highly complicated matter.[1] To keep the description as brief as possible, we shall examine in turn the rules and procedures governing implementation, the argument about the Commission's executive powers in respect of the budget, the persons responsible for implementing the budget and the reports produced about this Community activity.

Rules and procedures concerning the implementation of the expenditure contained in the general budget

A number of rules and procedures have become established in law and custom in the now very wide field of financial implementation of Community policies and measures.

Rules governing the implementation of the expenditure side of the general budget

The basic text concerning the implementation of the budget is to be found in the first paragraph of Article 205 of the EEC Treaty, with equivalent passages in the first paragraph of Article 179 of the Euratom Treaty and the first paragraph of Article 78c of the ECSC Treaty; the wording is as follows: 'The Commission shall implement the budget in accordance with the provisions of the regulations made pursuant to Article 209, in its own responsibility and within the limits of the appropriations'.

Another rule is that no expenditure may be effected unless charged against an 'article' in the budget nomenclature (Article 4 of the Financial Regulation); as we have already explained (p. 56), the article is the basic unit to which appropriations are assigned and is itself divisible into 'items' in order to simplify and clarify preparation and implementation of the budget. It may happen that the appropriations assigned to an Article prove inadequate for the Community's purposes and that they have to be increased. This can be done in several ways: by transfer within a budget chapter, by transfer between chapters, by transfer from Chapter 100, or by supplementary budget. Yet another rule states that appropriations granted may only be used to meet items of expenditure properly committed and paid in the financial year for which they were accorded. There are some exceptions to this rule and we shall deal with them in due course.

The golden rule for the implementation of the budget is that the principles of sound financial management should be applied, (as stated in Article 206a(2) of the EEC Treaty, *inter alia*). The authorizing officer must be guided by these principles when exercising his powers, and the internal controller and external auditor must then make sure that he has observed them. But when it comes to defining these principles, opinions differ and traditions conflict. At the time of the debate on the Financial Regulation that finally came into force on 1 May 1973, the budget experts discussed them at length but without success. The German experts claimed that it was all a matter of *Wirtschaftlichkeit*, i.e. 'good housekeeping', while others claimed that sound financial management meant making sure that expenditure was apposite. In the end they managed to agree that 'sound financial management' was that of a 'responsible family man'.

Problems concerning the implementation
of the expenditure side of the general budget

In approving the 1976 budget, the European Parliament, using the funds available through its discretionary margin, introduced a number of new headings and appropriated sums to these headings. It was then a matter of life or death for Parliament whether or not these expenditure items were implemented. The Commission had to choose between committing the expenditure or waiting for the Council to make a decision of principle authorizing such action—the Council being the body possessing the necessary legislative power. The Commission, acting on its own authority, then defined a new doctrine to determine how to handle cases of this sort. It deemed itself entitled, under Article 205(1) of the EEC Treaty and other provisions already referred to, to commit expenditure authorized by the Treaties (grants to aid uranium prospecting under Article 70 of the Euratom Treaty, or for specific operations (aid for non-government organizations cooperating in the development of non-member countries, aid to non-associated developing countries, grant of building loans to Community officials, and so on). However, the Commission feels that if the introduction of a new policy is at stake, then it must found its action on a proper statutory basis properly decided before any grant of funds can be made (aid for off-shore hydrocarbon prospecting, aid to research in the aeronautics sector, aids to the coal industry, etc.). As early as 16 June 1976, Parliament adopted a Resolution stating that the budget 'must be implemented, even in the event of new measures being introduced', thus making the issue a bone of contention between the Community's institutions. Let it be recalled that Parliament considers it an affront that no use should be made of appropriations created by the use of its discretionary margin. It has made the implementation of parliamentary decisions on the budget by the Commission into a fundamental issue of principle.

In a debate on the same subject on 11 October 1977 Mr Tugendhat, speaking as Commissioner for the budget, said: 'I can confirm that we do consider that the budget, as approved, provides a requisite legal basis for the use and expenditure of appropriations. In the absence of such a basis no expenditure or receipts can be incurred. However, this basis is not sufficient in every circumstance to allow the expenditure . . .'. This declaration was used as a basic document for the conciliation meetings on the Financial Regulation at the end of 1977 (see Annex 5, p. 363). Mr Tugendhat took up the argument again on 23 October 1979, in Parliament's annual debate on the implementation of the budget (see footnote 12 on p. 105), when he said: 'To the Commission the budget, as adopted, constitutes the legal basis indispensable to the use and expenditure of appropriations. Without the appropriate budgetary entry, there can be neither expenditure nor receipts. However, this basis is not always alone sufficient. There are cases where the legal basis constituted by the budget has to be underpinned by separate legislative bases. The two instruments are complementary; one authorizes the allocation of appropriations, the other establishes the conditions under which they may be used. If one is lacking, the operation cannot legally be carried out. Now, clearly, there are also cases where the appropriations are for the implementation of well-defined and specified actions of a limited nature, and in these cases, which our French colleagues refer to as *actions ponctuelles*, the Commission uses the appropriations and incurs the expenditure in accordance with budgetary rules alone. Mr Bangemann, the rapporteur last year, sought to distinguish in the budget commentary between these two categories. The Commission welcomes this sort of constructive thinking on what is admittedly a difficult and contentious area.'

To surmount these difficulties Parliament had followed the advice of its general rapporteur, Mr Bangemann (Liberal, Federal Republic of Germany), in the course of the budgetary procedure for 1979 and had proposed in its amendments that the remarks columns in the budget should contain a 'magic formula' enabling the Commission to use the appropriations entered under a budget heading if the Commission had been expressly authorized to do so. With the help of this formula the Commission, it was thought, would be able to implement the budget more easily. The attempt failed owing to the conditions of crisis in which the 1979 budget was adopted (see p. 45), but it is very likely that the idea will be revived.[2]

Increases in appropriations during the financial year

During the financial year it may prove necessary to amend an estimate so that the item concerned may be properly implemented in accordance with the actual funding requirements. Several different options are available to the Community institutions to achieve this. But it must be stressed at the outset that the intention enshrined in the Treaties has been distorted in the Financial Regulations enacted pursuant to those Treaties. Articles 205, third paragraph, of the EEC Treaty, 179, third paragraph, of the Euratom Treaty and 78c, third paragraph, of the ECSC Treaty provide that 'the Commission may, subject to the limits and conditions laid down in the (Financial) Regulation . . ., transfer appropriations from one chapter to another or from one subdivision to another'. But the Financial Regulation, as we shall see, has greatly curtailed the Commission's powers.

Transfers within a chapter—These transfers are authorized by the Commission for all the institutions by virtue of Article 21(3) of the Financial Regulation. They enable the appropriations against different headings of a chapter (articles or items) to be adjusted in order to meet expenditure that could not have been foreseen when the budget was being prepared. Transfers of this type are frequent and very necessary; they produce no particular problems.

Transfers between chapters—Article 21(1) of the Financial Regulation states that appropriations granted for one chapter or article may not be transferred to another, but Article 21(2) provides that the Commission may propose such transfers to the Council. Since the Commission is obliged automatically to send on to the Budgetary Authority the proposals made by other institutions for transfers from one chapter to another, the most it can do in such cases is to append its own opinion, though it does not in fact do so. The Financial Regulation of 21 December 1977 considerably altered the division of responsibility between the two wings of the Budgetary Authority, in the light of the new equilibrium created by the Treaties of 1970 and 1975. The current legal position, which is very complex, is as follows. When proposals for transfers are made regarding compulsory expenditure, the Council, after consulting Parliament, decides by a qualified majority within six weeks (except in an emergency), Parliament having delivered its opinion in good time for the Council to take note of it and reach its decision accordingly within the required time limit. If the Council does not take a decision within that time, the proposals are deemed to be approved.

When, however, the proposals for transfers concern non-compulsory expenditure, it is Parliament, after consulting the Council, which decides within six weeks (except in an emergency), and the Council which must have prepared its opinion in good time for Parliament to decide within the required time limit. Here too, if no decision is taken, the transfer proposals are deemed to be approved.

Proposed transfers in respect of both CE and NCE are deemed to have been approved if neither Council nor Parliament has taken a contrary decision within six weeks from the date of receipt of the proposals. If, however, Parliament and Council reduce the amount of a proposed transfer by different amounts, the lowest amount accepted by one of the two institutions is deemed to be approved. If one of the two institutions refuses to accept the transfer in principle, the transfer cannot be made.

There are many transfers, particularly for the Commission's appropriations. In the case of the budget allocation to the EAGGF Guarantee Section, a large number of transfers is in fact essential because it is so difficult to forecast expenditure accurately.

Each for their own section of the budget, Parliament and the Council may each make transfers from one chapter or article to another, and in such cases they simply inform the Commission that they intend to do so. The Commission itself may, in respect of its own section, make transfers between chapters in respect of the titles covering staff and administrative expenditure, but must inform the Budgetary Authority two weeks in advance. By this provision the Council acknowledges that the Commission does have a certain amount of administrative autonomy.

Transfers from Chapter 100—The Budgetary Authority enters appropriations in Chapter 100 (under the heading 'provisional appropriations') when it thinks that an institution will have to incur expenditure on a given operation but where the operation in question has not yet been fully approved in principle or where there is uncertainty as to the amount involved. To release them from this 'safe deposit' it is necessary to go through the lengthy procedure just described, in order to enter them against the appropriate heading (chapter, article, or item).

In similar fashion, in 1976 Parliament brought in a new practice modelled upon transfers from Chapter 100. This involves entering an appropriation against the correct heading, but making its implementation subject to 'unblocking' by the Budgetary Authority. The fact that the transfers are blocked or frozen is brought out in the remarks relating to the budget heading concerned which thus assume mandatory force (see p. 56). Parliament introduced this practice to bolster its own powers because, under the Financial Regulation in force until 31 December 1977, it only had the right to be consulted in the case of transfer from Chapter 100, and was not consulted at all on transfers between chapters. This procedure, which has no basis in Community law—and has now become unnecessary because Parliament has been granted the powers it wished to have—was nevertheless, surprisingly, retained by Parliament in the 1978 and 1979 budgets, despite hostility from the Commission and opposition from the Council. There are no blocked transfers in the 1980 budget.

Open transfers—When it became apparent at the end of a year that an unavoidable item of expenditure had to be committed but the appropriate budget heading contained insufficient funds or was marked 'token entry', the Commission asked the Budgetary Authority (at that time the Council) for permission to transfer appropriations from chapter to chapter on its own sole authority—in a given order—in order to increase the funds allocated to the heading in question by as much as was necessary. The last examples of this were the open transfers sanctioned in 1973 and 1974 to cover expenditure resulting from exchange losses, and in 1975, to cover EAGGF Guarantee Section spending. We have here an interesting extension of the rule of specification.

Amending and/or supplementary budgets—The Community institutions, especially the Commission, have to resort to amending budgets—which do not affect the overall size of the budget but merely the distribution of expenditure and/or revenue—or supplementary budgets—which alter the aggregate amount of expenditure and revenue—to cope with unforeseeable events or to implement financially significant decisions that could not be provided for in the original budget because of insufficient knowledge at the time the budget was drafted. Although the Commission has been anxious to introduce as few supplementary budgets as possible and the Budgetary Authority—Council and Parliament—has never liked to be presented with them, there have been considerable numbers of such budgets. In 1973, for example, there were four supplementary budgets, in 1974 one, in 1975 three, in 1976 two, in 1977, in 1978 and in 1979, three.

Extensions of and exemptions to the annuality principle

As we have already said, the principle of annuality is not always strictly adhered to. The chief extensions and exemptions are as follows.

Carry-over of appropriations for one year—In theory there are two possible approaches to the idea of a budget: the 'year of origin' approach and the 'year of payment' approach. The latter takes in all payments and receipts transacted from day to day throughout the year, without regard to the date of origin of the underlying obligation. The year of origin approach, on the other hand, holds that expenditure and revenue may be booked to a given year's budget regardless of the date of the operation, the attribution being determined solely by the time of origin of the obligation or right involved. A financial year on this basis embraces all payments and receipts authorized by the budget for that year, whether paid during or after the 12 months of the year concerned. The European Communities have traditionally chosen the year of origin system but now seem to be moving towards a mixed system.

Articles 202, second paragraph of the EEC Treaty, 175, second paragraph of the Euratom Treaty and 78a, third paragraph of the ECSC Treaty stipulate that any appropriations, other than those relating to staff expenditure, that are unexpended at the end of the financial year may be carried forward to the next financial year only, in accordance with the conditions laid down by the Financial Regulation. The latter has in fact introduced two types of carry-over, the 'automatic' and the 'non-automatic', the system differing depending on whether the appropriations concerned are differentiated or not (i.e. whether they are two-part or simple). For budget headings which make no distinction between commitment appropriations and payment appropriations, i.e. principally staff and administrative and agricultural guarantee appropriations, the formula is as follows: staff appropriations cannot be carried forward, but the other appropriations, if they relate to payments still outstanding at 31 December in respect of commitments entered into after 15 December for the supply of goods and services, and also the portion of appropriations still not committed by 31 December, may be the subject of a carry-over, known as a non-automatic carry-over, to the next financial year only. Appropriations corresponding to payments still outstanding in respect of commitments properly contracted between 1 January and 31 December, apart from commitments contracted after 15 December for the supply of goods and services, are the subject of a carry-over known as an automatic carry-over, which is limited to the next financial year (Article 6(1) of the Financial Regulation).

In the case of budget headings distinguishing between commitment and payment appropriations, i.e. headings for multiannual operations, the commitment appropriations remaining uncommitted at the end of the financial year for which they were entered in the budget are still available for the following year. The payment appropriations unused at the end of the year for which they were created are carried forward automatically but not beyond the end of the following year (Article 6(2)).

Under Article 6(3) of the Financial Regulation of 21 December 1977, as amended on 25 June 1979, non-automatic carry-overs must be submitted by the Commission for approval not later than 21 April and approved (or otherwise) by the Council, after consulting Parliament, which has four weeks at its disposal for this purpose. If the Council, acting by a qualified majority, has taken no decision to reject the application for carry-over within six weeks, the carry-overs are deemed to have been approved.[3] This is tantamount to increasing budget appropriations without going through the proper procedure involving a supplementary budget, a clear violation of the rule of annuality.

In fact, the appropriations carried forward automatically to the next year to cover the payment of commitments properly entered into are quite sizeable, since the rule of budget annuality is not easy to observe. This extension of the rule makes it possible to implement about 90% of commitments undertaken, a not unreasonable percentage. As to appropriations carried forward non-automatically, these are not easy to implement. It calls for a real administrative *tour de force* to commit and meet the expenditure concerned in the period of a few months between the carry-forward decision (often made in September in the past) and the end of the financial year to which the expenditure is carried forward. So it is quite common for these carried-over appropriations to lapse.

The Commission therefore proposed in its draft amendments to the Financial Regulation, submitted on 26 May 1976, that unspent payment appropriations should remain *en bloc* at the Commission's disposal until the commitments had been met. This would have meant the end of the system of automatic one-year carry-overs. The Commission also proposed that the use of non-automatic carry-overs should be abandoned. But the Council did not agree, taking the view that the time was not ripe for such a change even though it would have amounted to a simplification.

Extension of the financial year; additional period—As an exception to the rule mentioned above, under which staff appropriations must be committed and paid by 31 December if they are not to lapse, the Commission has sometimes asked the Council to make a special Financial Regulation departing from Article 5 of the Financial Regulation to enable expenditure resulting from decisions made in December to be charged against the appropriations for the financial year even when it cannot be implemented before 31 December. This special Financial Regulation made by the Council allows expenditure in the form of payments of this kind up to, say, 15 February to be charged against the previous financial year.

Similarly, Article 98 of the Financial Regulation allows the charging of EAGGF Guarantee Section payments made as late as 31 March of the year after the financial year in question, thus delaying the presentation of the revenue and expenditure account to 1 June. On 23 April 1979 the Commission submitted a proposed amendment to the Financial Regulation which would have the effect of reducing this period.[4]

The system of provisional twelfths

We must also deal with the very special—and happily rare situation[5]—in which the Community may find itself when there is no budget. Under the Treaties this situation can occur if Parliament rejects the budget or if for procedural reasons the budget is not adopted.[6] To cope with such an eventuality Community law provides for a holding operation similar to the conventional mechanism of provisional twelfths but fairly flexible as regards the implementation of appropriations. Thus Articles 204 of the EEC Treaty, 178 of the Euratom Treaty and 78b of the ECSC Treaty, which incidentally are among those Articles amended by the Treaty of 22 July 1975, stipulate that 'a sum equivalent to not more than one-twelfth of the budget appropriations for the preceding financial year may be spent each month . . . (but) this arrangement shall not . . . have the effect of placing at the disposal of the Commission appropriations in excess of one-twelfth of those provided for in the draft budget in course of preparation'. Article 8 of the Financial Regulation relates implementation to chapters, avoiding the additional straightjacket which implementation by twelfths within the framework of budget articles or items would have imposed. This flexibility is a violation of the principle of specification.

This legislation thus introduces the rule of the so-called 'double limit' into the system of twelfths. What it means is that within every chapter expenditure must not exceed one-twelfth of the appropriations allocated under the previous budget or one-twelfth of the appropriations provided for in the draft budget in course of preparation for the year in question, whichever is the lower.

Article 204 of the EEC Treaty and others also provides that the Budgetary Authority may authorize expenditure in excess of the 'twelfths'. By analogy with the provisions governing preparation of the budget—and it was on precisely this point that the Treaty of 22 July 1975 amended the existing legislation—the Council has the power to take decisions on 'compulsory' expenditure while the European Parliament has the last word on 'non-compulsory' expenditure.

To these rather general provisions Article 8 of the Financial Regulation adds some specific instructions, the most important of which differentiates between commitments and payments: commitments may be entered into initially within the more flexible limit of one-quarter of the total appropriations of the preceding year increased by one-twelfth for each completed month.

The system of 'twelfths' is of course a temporary system designed to deal with a wholly exceptional situation. It enables business to go on as usual, it ensures continuity of the public service, but it rules out any possibility of development or evolution in the Community's affairs.[7]

Nature of the expenditure side of the general budget

The expenditure charged to the various headings in the general budget is essentially non-recoverable, taking the form either of administrative expenses (costs of staff, administration, meetings, studies, publishing, and so on) or of conditional grants (that is, sums of money which are only paid if the conditions for their granting are fulfilled—e.g. grants for the purpose of executing Community policies or measures) or of interest subsidies on loans granted for the purpose of executing a Community policy.

It does happen sometimes, however, that budget appropriations are used to make loans which may be repayable, as is the case with energy policy (see p. 254) or building loans for Community officials (although the latter has occurred only once, in 1976).

We should also mention that peculiar item the 'negative expense', to be found in the chapter of the budget on the common organization of the market in milk and milk products. It is an item of revenue collected under the head of 'co-responsibility levies' (see p. 185).

Finally, we should say something about the 'guarantees' given by the Community budget. These can be of two kinds. First, there are the guarantees given directly to lenders when the Community floats a loan itself, as in the case of Community loans (see p. 144), Euratom loans (see p. 143) and the New Community Instrument (see p. 144). Second, there are the guarantees given by the European Investment Bank in respect of the loans it grants, as in the case of the Mediterranean protocols (see p. 294), Turkey (see. p. 295), Portugal (see p. 295) and Yugoslavia (see p. 295). In the first case the guarantee given by the budget adds nothing, since the Community has undertaken a commitment in any case, as have the Member States. In the second case the Community would be called upon, where necessary, to pay the lender the sums he is owed, although here the guarantee covers only 75% of the total amount lent. In the budget the two types of guarantee are given token entries (mentioned elsewhere in this book: see pp. 62 and 296). In 1979 guarantees in respect of Community loans amounted to 538.5 m EUA and in respect of EIB loans to 365 m EUA. In some quarters consideration is being given to the possibility of making the budget guarantee cover loans granted by any financial institution to borrowers desiring to carry out investment projects relevant to Community policies.

The argument about the Commission's executive powers in respect of the budget

The Treaties (Article 205, first paragraph of the EEC Treaty, *inter alia*) stipulate that the Commission shall implement the budget on its own responsibility and within the limits of the appropriations. The Commission is thus certainly seen by the Treaties as the Community's 'Budgetary Executive'. But the way in which these provisions have been applied in practice is far from being so simple, particularly because the 'financing committees' which were created to assist the Commission have not restricted themselves to an advisory role.

Attempts to solve the problem of Article 205 of the EEC Treaty, etc.

Describing the successive formulas that have been used to define the Commission's powers as Budgetary Executive is no easy matter. We can perhaps do it best by breaking the developments down into four periods.

The solutions of 1958—The Treaty establishing the EEC has itself laid down the formula as far as the Social Fund is concerned. Article 124 states: 'the Fund (the European Social Fund) shall be administered by the Commission. The Commission shall be assisted in this task by a Committee . . .'. This Committee is purely advisory. The Commission can exercise its powers as Budgetary Executive to the full; if it does not wish to take the Committee's advice, all it has to do is to inform it to that effect within six weeks.

At the same time, however, the Member States instituted a quite different system for the European Development Fund (EDF). Under Article 5 of the Implementing Convention on the Association of the Overseas Countries and Territories with the Community, signed on the same date as the Treaties of Rome, the Commission is required to submit its financing proposals to the Council for examination if one of the Member States so requests. The Council must then act within two months. This formula substitutes the Council for the Commission as Budgetary Executive.

The ascendancy of the Council of Ministers was further strengthened later when an 'EDF Committee' was set up under the terms of the First Yaoundé Convention of 1964. Under this new procedure, if the Commission does not wish to follow the EDF Committee's opinion or if the Committee does not deliver an opinion, the matter is referred to the Council which must take a decision but in this case without any time limit.

This astonishing divergence of solutions may be explained, if not justified, by the fact that whereas the Social Fund appropriations formed part of the budget, those of the EDF did not. The Member States were thus more anxious to be able to control EDF appropriations than Social Fund appropriations. At that time, admittedly, the resources for both the EEC budget and the EDF operations came from Member States' financial contributions (see Annex 9, p. 377).

The management committee solution in agriculture—Establishment of the common agricultural policy led to the creation of so-called management committees. The first in time was the Standing Committee on Agricultural Structures, set up on 4 December 1962, followed by the EAGGF Committee on 5 February 1964 (see Annex 7, p. 374), then a great many management committees for the various agricultural markets. The Commission has to refer its draft decisions to these committees. It then takes its decisions, which come into force immediately; however, if the Commission's decision is not in line with the committee's opinion, the Commission must submit the decision to the Council and postpone application for one month. During that month the Council may take a different decision. This formula is thus more viable than the EDF Committee formula because there is as it were a safety net, in that the Council must take a decision within one month or be debarred from action. It should further be noted that these committees—with the exception of the first-named—seldom have to deliver an opinion on decisions which are purely a matter of budget implementation; the usual cases are Commission decisions entailing the making of regulations or the enacting of legislation. These committees are but rarely 'financing committees'.

Contradictory solutions (1973-79)—Later solutions applied by the Council have been frankly contradictory. On 9 November 1973, for instance, the Council withdrew all Commission decision-making powers on assistance to Community projects for technological development relating to hydrocarbons and took to itself the sole right to take decisions on every grant. On 18 March 1975, on the other hand, the Council applied the management committee formula to aids to be granted by the Commission under the head of the Regional Fund, extending the 'safety net' to two months. But on 12 June 1978 it withheld from the Commission the power to take decisions on grants in aid under the Community energy-saving programme and the programme to develop new energy sources. Yet on 11 September 1979 it applied the EDF Committee formula, that is to say without any 'safety net', to deal with Community assistance in the data-processing field.

The present position (1980)—Since this last decision, a deadlock has arisen as a result of the impossibility of reaching agreement within the Council or between the institutions involved. Ten or so regulations were held up in this way as of spring 1980.[8]

On 17 June 1980, however, the Council decided on joint guidelines on the Regulation concerning financial and technical aid to the non-associated developing countries by deciding to accept the 'ERDF Committee' formula. Similarly, in July the Council adopted the Regulation on the non-quota section of the Regional Fund by deciding that the special programmes would be adopted after consulting the ERDF Committee and in using its own formula, rather than merely on the basis of the Regional Policy Committee's opinion, as the Commission had suggested.

*The cases put forward by the individual
Community institutions with regard to the application
of Article 205 of the EEC Treaty, etc.*

The Council's case is based firstly on Article 155 of the EEC Treaty which states: 'In order to ensure the proper functioning and development of the common market, the Commission shall: ... (fourth indent) exercise the powers conferred on it by the Council for the implementation of the rules laid down by the latter'. Article 124 of the Euratom Treaty says the same thing except that it is 'in order to ensure the development of nuclear energy within the Community'. Hence the Council considers that where a prior act on its part is indispensable for implementation of the budget, it is free either to confer on—or to withhold from—the Commission the power to take implementing decisions, the Council thus reserving to itself the right to take decisions on individual measures granting financial aid if it so desires. This is what the Council has in fact done—by a number of different methods, notably by setting up certain types of committee (under various different names) whose contrary opinion (contrary to that of the Commission, that is) can in principle force the Commission to submit a budget implementation decision to the Council itself.

It must be pointed out that the Council has been self-contradictory in its attitudes, witness the declaration at Heads of State or Government level (see the communiqué on the Paris Summit of 9 and 10 December 1974 in Annex 3, p. 351) in which the latter stated that they 'agree on the advantage of making use of the provisions of the Treaty of Rome whereby the powers of implementation and management arising out of Community rules may be conferred on the Commission'. This has remained a pious hope.

Parliament's case and the Commission's case are initially very similar, being based on Article 205 of the EEC Treaty which in the view of both institutions is sufficient unto itself and allows of no restrictions or exceptions. They diverge, however, in that Parliament, while conceding that consultation with a committee may be useful, rejects all procedures which carry any risk of the Commission's decision being replaced by a decision of the Council, even in exceptional circumstances,[9] whereas the Commission is more flexible. On 24 May 1978 it adopted the position that it would endeavour in future—in all cases where it had to be helped by committees when implementing policies—only to give such committees a purely advisory status. For the proposals currently pending before the Council and the European Parliament[8] the Commission has instructed its departments to accept no solution which would give the Council greater powers than those conferred on it by the Regional Development Fund formula. This stance is official and has on occasions been made public.[10] Parliament's stance is inspired by the desire to defend its own powers, without which the new provisions of Article 206b of the EEC Treaty—under which it henceforth becomes the sole authority competent to give a discharge to the Commission in respect of the implementation of the budget—are liable to lose their force. In fact, it is clear that this power of control is only fully valid if the Commission alone executes the budget and if it is allowed an adequate discretionary margin in doing so. The proposition that the Council should implement the budget or that the Commission should implement it following strict instructions from the Council would make Parliament's power of control absolutely meaningless. The debate is on: the newly-elected Parliament is engaged in defending its rights.

Those responsible for implementing expenditure and their functions

We shall first examine the conditions under which the powers of the Commission as 'Authorizing Agent'[11] are exercised, then look at the division of powers between 'Authorizing Officer', 'Controller' and 'Accounting Officer'. It should be noted that pursuant to the Treaties (Article 205, second paragraph of the EEC Treaty, Article 179, second paragraph of the Euratom Treaty, and Article 78c, second paragraph of the ECSC Treaty and the Financial Regulation (Article 18(2)) the powers needed for implementation of the sections of the budget relating to the other institutions are to be conferred by the Commission upon each of those institutions, which means that each institution is the Authorizing Agent for its own administrative expenditure. The description that follows is an attempted summary rather than an exhaustive analysis.

Exercise by the Commission of its power
as Authorizing Agent

The exercise by the Commission of the power of Authorizing Agent for appropriations in its own part of the budget is a highly complex matter, and at times highly circumscribed. In outline, the Commission's power as Authorizing Agent, that is to say the power of the public agency (in this case the Commission itself) or of natural persons (in this case the persons to whom the Commission has delegated its powers—the Commissioners or heads of department) to 'commit' an item of expenditure, can take four possible forms:

(i) full authorizing power,
(ii) authorizing power after seeking the opinion of a consultative committee which is not part of the Commission,
(iii) authorizing power subject to possible blocking by the Council, and
(iv) subordinate authorizing power. This breakdown into different types of authorizing power must not blind us to the fact that the power is exercised 'within the limits of the appropriations' and within the framework of the regulations enacted or the programmes adopted.

Full authorizing power—The Commission exercises to the full its power to commit administrative expenditure (passing items for payment and issuing payment orders); the same applies to expenditure on specific tasks (Title 3 of the general budget), one of which is particularly important—the management of the Joint Research Centre and of indirect research activities.

Authorizing power subject to the opinion of a consultative committee—In one sole instance, that of the Social Fund, already mentioned, the Commission has full authorizing power after seeking the opinion of a consultative committee, and in this case the power is based on the EEC Treaty itself.

Authorizing power subject to possible blocking—The Commission's authorizing power may be contested where, after a committee which is required to be consulted has given a contrary opinion or has not stated an opinion at all, the Council is allowed to take different commitment decisions from those taken by the Commission; the committees in this case are:

(a) the Standing Committee on Agricultural Structures;
(b) the Standing Committee for the Fishing Industry;
(c) the European Regional Development Fund Committee;
(d) the Advisory Committee on the Management of Demonstration Projects in the Field of Energy Saving;
(e) the Advisory Committee on the Management of Projects to Exploit Alternative Energy Sources; and
(f) the Advisory Committee for the Management and Coordination of Data-Processing Programmes (see Annex 7, pp. 373-374).

In practice, the referral system has never been used. From the legal point of view, however, it is very much to be regretted, since it is capable of making the Council the 'Budgetary Executive', an executive moreover which is free of constraints as it escapes the scrutiny of the authority which grants discharge. We should also mention here that the management committees set up in connection with the various agricultural market organizations and the EAGGF Committee operate along the same lines, but if the draft regulations on which they are consulted are liable to have any financial implications these bodies do not normally intervene in the course of adoption of commitment decisions taken under the provisions of the

Financial Regulation. They nevertheless belong under this heading of our study by analogy.

Subordinate authorizing power—The Commission has had its authorizing power taken away by the Council in the case of aid to Community hydrocarbon exploration projects and food aid to developing countries.

For these types of aid the Commission is still officially the Authorizing Agent, but the power of decision rests with the Council. This is an abuse of the rules laid down by the Treaties. The excuse that emergent or embryonic Community intervention policies are involved is not valid because the provisions in question are of a permanent nature. They make the Commission merely the Community cashier.

The Authorizing Officer's duties are to commit expenditure, to pass items for payment and to issue payment orders: this implies a form of control, the Authorizing Officer's control. The Authorizing Officer has to travel to the relevant locations to check that the recipients of Community aid have in fact used it in the way they claim. This control is of vital importance in the present system which involves very close association with the national administrations in executing the budget.

Powers of the Budget Commissioner and of the Directorate-General for Budgets

The role of the Commissioner for the Budget and his special powers during the drawing up of the budget have already been discussed (see p. 38). At the stage of implementation his role is similar; he can request deferment and further study of any proposals put to the Commission by any Commissioner responsible for authorizing expenditure. In addition, the Directorate-General for Budgets, which comes under his authority, has the right to put its own opinion—which may be a critical one—to the Commission on any proposed decision that has an impact on the budget. These two provisions are not devoid of interest.

Exercise of the functions of Financial Controller and Accounting Officer

Article 17 of the Financial Regulation stipulates that execution of the budget is to be carried out in accordance with the principle of the separation of Authorizing Officer and Accounting Officer. Appropriations are to be administered by the Authorizing Officer, who is the sole person empowered to enter into commitments regarding expenditure and to issue instructions for payment; payments themselves are to be made by the Accounting Officer. The whole administrative and budgetary organization of the Community institutions, particularly the Commission, is based on this Article 17.[12]

The *Financial Controller*, for his part, has the task—by virtue of Article 19 of the same Regulation—of checking all proposed commitments and all payment orders. He is an official of the Commission and works under the authority of the Budget Commissioner but enjoys a guaranteed independence entrenched in the Financial Regulation. His powers cover revenue (Article 23), expenditure commitments (Articles 32 to 34) and approval of payment orders (Article 43). His control is exercised before the event and relates mainly to ensuring that appropriations are available, that expenditure accords with the current regulations and that there is sound financial management. If the Financial Controller 'vetoes' any aspect of the transactions coming under his scrutiny—apart from matters connected with the availability of appropriations—the Commission has the right to override his veto provided it states its reasons, and this usually happens several times a year. The Commission must inform the Court of Auditors every three months of all such decisions (Articles 35 and 44 of the Financial Regulation).

Since the executives were merged the Commission has been endeavouring to adapt its internal control procedures and methods to the growing demands of a continually expanding budget. Its Decision of 25 July 1979 on financial control represented a change of approach in the direction of greater emphasis on sound financial management. It must be pointed out, however, that the bulk of Community expenditure is effected on the spot by the Member States themselves and that consequently any improvement in Community control depends first on strengthening control on the spot and secondly on improving collaboration with the national authorities and audit bodies.[12]

The *Accounting Officer's* role is to see that expenditure is paid out, up to the limit of the funds available. He has sole power to handle Community funds and assets. He comes under the authority of the Director-General for Budgets.

Incidentally, it is worth noting that the Commission undertakes approximately 30 000 commitments a year, represented by about 600 000 pages of documents.

The reports on the implementation of the general budget

Annual reports

The annual report, which the Commission has to publish every year under Article 18 of the Merger Treaty of 8 April 1965, deals only incidentally with the budget and its implementation. Parliament, in its Resolution of 14 May 1974 on the Seventh General Report, expressed regret that owing to its (the General Report's) essentially descriptive nature it is not possible to form a more coherent idea of overall policy in the financial and budgetary sphere. There has been little or no improvement since then.

However, Articles 74 and 75 of the Financial Regulation require the Commission to draw up an account of Community revenue and expenditure by 1 June. This document is prefaced by an analysis of financial management during the year in question, and must include all revenue and expenditure transactions relating to that year for each institution, presented in the same form and with the same subdivisions as the budget. In addition, under Article 76 of the Financial Regulation, the Commission must also not later than 1 June draw up a balance sheet of the Communities' assets and liabilities as of 31 December of the preceding year, attaching to it a statement showing the movements and balances of the accounts, drawn up on the same date.

Each institution must therefore, by 1 April at the latest, send the Commission the information it needs to prepare the three documents just mentioned, which are then forwarded by the Commission to Parliament, the Council and the Court of Auditors not later than 1 June, so initiating the discharge procedure.

Quarterly reports

Article 29 of the Financial Regulation states that four times a year the Commission shall present a report to Parliament and the Council on the financial situation of the Communities covering both revenue and expenditure. A detailed statement showing the sums carried over from previous financial years and any change resulting from the adoption of supplementary or amending budgets is attached to these reports. The fourth quarterly report, which is in practice an annual report, is published after the accounts are closed on 31 March and becomes the analysis of financial management just mentioned.[13]

Monitoring the budget

The Commission has placed increasing emphasis on more effective monitoring of the budget; since 1973 it has paid increasing attention to the implementation of the budget. The Member of the Commission with responsibility for the budget keeps the Commission itself informed at regular intervals of the observations and suggestions of the Directorate-General for Budgets. Parliament, too, takes considerable interest in, and holds debates and passes resolutions on, matters affecting the implementation of the budget.

B—Implementation of the revenue side of the general budget

The revenue of the general budget is first and foremost (to the extent of 99.8% in fact) independent Community revenue (the 'own resources'), namely agricultural levies, sugar levies, customs duties and a percentage of value-added tax (VAT), the latter item being markedly different from the others.

Implementation of the own resources of the European Communities

Rules governing own resources other than VAT

It is important in this connection to distinguish between the establishment, entry in the accounts, making available, payment and internal control of own resources.

Establishment and accounting—Council Regulation (EEC, Euratom, ECSC) No 2891/77 of 19 December 1977[14] lays down the rules governing implementation of the Decision of 21 April 1970 on the replacement of financial contributions from Member States by the Communities' own resources. Under the system adopted, collection of the revenue is delegated to the Member States themselves. There is thus no Community tax-collecting authority. The Commission department responsible for own resources is the Directorate-General for Budgets.

Article 1 of the Regulation provides that own resources other than VAT shall be 'established' by the Member States in accordance with their own provisions laid down by law, regulation or administrative action; entitlement to the revenue is deemed to exist—states Article 2—as soon as the corresponding claim has been duly confirmed by the competent authority in the Member State. Accounts for the own resources are kept—under the provisions of Article 7—with the Treasury of each Member State, the validated claims being entered in these accounts not later than the 20th of the second month following that in which they were first 'established'.

Making available and payment of own resources—The amount of own resources established is credited by each Member State to an account opened for this purpose with its Treasury in the name of the Commission, as provided by Article 9.

By virtue of Article 12, the Commission has at its disposal the amounts credited to its accounts to the extent necessary to cover its cash requirements for implementing the budget. If the budget requirements exceed the balances on the accounts, the Commission is empowered to make drawings beyond the total available from the aforesaid accounts, but it must inform the Member States of foreseeable overruns in advance. This possibility can be used only in very exceptional cases and goes much further than the bringing forward by one month of the entry of own resources other than VAT resources allowed by Article 10(2) of Council Regulation No 2891/77 of 19 December 1977. It shows that the Member States are prepared to accept some responsibility despite the fact that the Commission is considered to enjoy financial independence. The situation referred to in Article 12 has not yet arisen, although the reverse situation has occurred whereby the Community had a surplus of more than 1 000 m u.a. In any event, the difference between the total balances on the accounts and the total cash requirements is spread among the Member States in proportion to the amounts of estimated budget revenue each provides.

Article 17 of Council Regulation No 2891/77 of 19 December 1977 requires the Member States to take all requisite measures to ensure that the amounts corresponding to the established entitlements are made available to the Commission. They are only exempted from this rule if the amounts could not be collected for 'reasons of *force majeure*'.

Internal control of own resources—Article 18 stipulates that the Member States shall carry out the verifications and inquiries concerning the establishment and making available of own resources and shall carry out any additional measures of control the Commission may ask for in a reasoned request. If the Commission so requests, they must associate the Commission with the control measures they are carrying out. On this particular point the judgment of the Court of Justice of 10 January 1980 in the Como case (267/78) contains some interesting comments on the Commission's right to ask for additional measures of control to be carried out and to be associated with the measures of control carried out by the Member States themselves, from the moment at which establishment should have taken place.[15] We may also mention Council Regulation (EEC, Euratom, ECSC) No 165/74 which determines the powers and obligations of the officials appointed by the Commission. These texts demonstrate that the Council has refused to allow inspection to take place upstream of the establishment phase, i.e. at taxpayer level. And the Commission cannot institute an audit of its own accord. To sum up, the Commission's control is imperfect owing to the unwillingness of the Member States to relinquish any of their prerogatives, and this despite the fact that the resources in question belong to the European Communities. It is true that the existence of the Advisory Committee on the Own Resources (see Annex 7, p. 373) facilitates cooperation and an exchange of information between the Member States and the Commission. It cannot be asked to do more.

On 19 March 1979 the Commission submitted to the Council a proposal for a Regulation on measures to be taken in the event of irregularities in connection with own resources, which also envisaged the creation of an information system to help the Commission in this area. To date the Council has not taken any action on the proposal.[16]

The responsibility for these control measures lies with the authorizing agent for own resources, namely the Directorate-General for Budgets, and the Commission's internal controller, namely the Financial Controller.

Rules on VAT

These rules are laid down in Council Regulation (EEC, Euratom, ECSC) No 2892/77 of 19 December 1977.[14]

Payment of VAT—The Member States are obliged to pay to the Commission each month one-twelfth of the amount entered in the budget for the financial year in question, by virtue of Article 10(3) of Regulation No 2891/77.

Accounting for and availability of VAT—Pursuant to Article 10 of this Regulation, Member States must forward to the Commission before 1 July a summary account indicating the total final amount of the basis relating to transactions for which tax has become chargeable during the previous calendar year. The balance from each financial year, calculated in accordance with Regulation (EEC, Euratom, ECSC) No 2891/77 is entered as revenue or expenditure—depending on whether it is a surplus or a deficit—in the budget for the following financial year in an amending budget.[17]

Internal control of VAT—Pursuant to Article 12 of the aforementioned regulation, the Commission's audits take place at the offices of the competent authorities of the Member States. Within the framework of these audits the Commission checks, in particular, the correctness of the operations to centralize the assessment basis and the determination of the weighted average rate as well as the total amount of net revenue collected from VAT. Council Regulation No 165/74 of 21 January 1974, setting out the rights and duties of the officials appointed by the Commission, applies to control of VAT revenue. The departments responsible for controlling VAT are the same as those responsible for controlling other Community revenues.

Transfer of Community holdings from one national currency to another

We have already seen that the Commission holds funds that have been credited to its account in the Treasury or other designated authority in each Member State to the extent necessary to cover the cash needs of the budget (Article 9(1) of Council Regulation No 2891/77).

Article 208 of the EEC Treaty empowers the Commission to transfer its holdings in the currency of one Member State into the currency of another Member State as needed for use, provided it notifies the competent authorities of the Member States concerned. But the Commission is enjoined to avoid making such transfers as far as possible if it possesses cash or liquid assets in the currencies which it needs. Article 31 of the Financial Regulation requires the Commission to send each Member State, every three months, a statement indicating the transfers effected from that Member State's national currency into another currency and vice versa. Article 208 of the EEC Treaty also stipulates that the Commission must deal with each Member State through the authority designated by the State concerned. In carrying out financial operations the Commission must employ the services of the central bank of the Member State concerned or of any other financial institution approved by that State.

Methods of collecting miscellaneous revenue

Miscellaneous revenue under the Communities' budget has been classified into six categories (see p. 130) to give a grouping by nature; when it comes to the method of implementation, however, there are only two groups.

Collection at fixed intervals

The first group consists of items of revenue collected at regular intervals at dates fixed in advance by regulation. The most important of these have been the contributions based on

GNP (Article 4(2) or (3) of the Decision of 21 April 1970). These contributions are paid on the first working day of the month and are immediately entered in the Commission's accounts.

At present the amounts derived from ECSC levies are paid into the Commission's accounts quarterly, whilst contributions due under the complementary programme (Article 3(3) and Article 4(6) of the above Decision) are paid in two annual instalments (January and July) of 7/12ths and 5/12ths respectively.

The proceeds of the tax on salaries and pensions is collected directly and entered automatically as an item of Community revenue.

All this revenue is thus made available to the Commission automatically without the authorizing agent having to claim it from the taxpaying persons or authorities.

Variable collection rates

The second group consists of miscellaneous revenue with widely varying collection procedures, each depending on the specific nature of the item of revenue in question, for example proceeds of sale of movable assets, gains on exchange, and so on.

The Commission's accounts are credited with these receipts as and when the corresponding payment is implemented. Mention should also be made of the category 'other miscellaneous revenue'—often unforeseen—the legal basis of which is fixed individually; this category includes fines on firms in breach of the competition rules.

Mention of collection of fines raises an interesting point. A dispute arose between the Commission and certain sugar firms liable to such payments who had initially refused to pay them. In December 1975 the Court of Justice had fixed the fines to be paid. In the Court's findings the amount payable was stated in EUA, with the amount in national currency added in parentheses. All the firms except one paid their fines in Italian lire, the parity at that time standing at 6.25 lire to the unit of account. As the lira's value on the exchange markets on the date in question was some 40% lower than parity the Commission suffered a considerable loss; it referred the matter to the Court of Justice again in March 1977. The Court laid down that the amount of the debts brought into being by the fines was to be determined by the amounts fixed in each firm's national currency, the Commission being free, however, to accept payment in another Community national currency, conversion in that case to be made on the basis of the free rate of exchange ruling on the date of payment.

2. Implementation of the ECSC operational budget

As with the general budget, we must distinguish between expenditure and revenue.

A—Implementation of the expenditure side of the ECSC operational budget

The implementation of the ECSC's administrative expenditure will not be discussed here, since it lost its special character with the Merger Treaty of 8 April 1965 and was incorporated into the general administrative expenditure of the European Communities. We shall confine our attention to the ECSC's operational expenditure, following the same plan as for the expenditure of the general budget.

Rules and procedures for implementing ECSC expenditure

The High Authority/Commission's internal regulations of 2 August 1976, while duly respecting the procedures peculiar to the ECSC operational budget, lay down implementing procedures corresponding to those applying to the general budget. If it appears likely during the year that resources will fall short of actual and planned commitments, the Commission adopts a revised operational budget adjusting its estimates for the remaining months of the year. There are no transfers in the statutory sense, nor any carrying forward of appropriations or extension of the financial year.

It should be remembered that commitments of ECSC expenditure are fully covered by provisions. This unique mechanism stems from the fact that the ECSC was created for only 50 years (Article 97 of the ECSC Treaty); as a guarantee of implementation of the commitments their full amount is entered as a liability of the Community. Until they are used for payment, the sums involved are invested and earn interest that supplements the levy revenue. However, when the accounts for each operation are cleared, or when clearance can be forecast with sufficient precision, unwanted provisions are cancelled and the corresponding sums can then be used for new commitments.

In short, the ECSC operational budget is very different from the general budget, being much more like a private-sector management budget than the budget of a public authority subject to the traditional budgetary rules.

Agents responsible for implementation of expenditure and their powers

The dominant role in implementing the expenditure belongs to the High Authority/Commission. Its internal management procedures are very flexible. We shall come across both these characteristics throughout this section of the book. All the same, the Commission must take proper account of the responsibilities given to the Council and to the consultative committees constituted either by the Treaty or by the Commission itself (see Annex 7, p. 374).

Exercise of the power of Authorizing Agent

The Commission/High Authority—Under the terms of various articles of the ECSC Treaty, the power of authorizing agency belongs to the High Authority. For some types of expenditure it enjoys a considerable freedom of assessment and choice, now exercised by the Commission. This applies to aid to research, interest subsidies, and aid to housing construction. On the other hand, in the case of resettlement aid the expenditure derives from an obligation in Article 56 of the ECSC Treaty requiring the High Authority to provide non-repayable aid if a Member State so requests,[18] and in the case of aid for coking coal, from a Council regulation. These are thus both non-discretionary items of expenditure that the High Authority/Commission is bound to implement.

Role of the Council—In fact, even where discretionary expenditure is involved, the High Authority/Commission has to consult the Council. Thus, it must obtain the Council's assent if it wishes to grant:

(i) non-repayable aid to research, financed from the levy (Article 55(2) (b) of the ECSC Treaty);

(ii) loans with interest subsidies to non-ECSC undertakings for programmes intended to create new and economically sound activities capable of reabsorbing redundant workers into productive employment (Article 56(1) (b) and (2) (a) of the ECSC Treaty);

(iii) similar loans for investments contributing directly and primarily to increasing the production, reducing the production costs, or facilitating the marketing of coal and steel products (Article 54, second paragraph of the ECSC Treaty).

In the latter case (loans to promote technical progress), the Council's assent must actually be given unanimously. Note in contrast that interest subsidies on 'internal' loans, i.e. for conversion operations within the industry itself, are the sole competence of the High Authority/Commission.

Separation of functions of Authorizing Agent, Controller and Accounting Officer

On 2 August 1976, the Commission adopted a series of internal rules defining the roles of Authorizing Agent, Controller, and Accountant for the implementation of the ECSC operational budget. The Authorizing Agent is the Commission itself. and the Controller and Accountant are identical with those for the general budget.

Reports on the implementation of ECSC expenditure

Under past practice the implementation of ECSC expenditure has also been the subject of reports. Although the Treaty of Paris does not require it, the High Authority/Commission has drawn up a balance sheet every year since the beginning. What happened was that when the ECSC's first public loan was being negotiated the banks, particularly those on the other side of the Atlantic, advised the first President of the ECSC, Mr Jean Monnet, to give the public, and especially the lenders, some information about the ECSC's financial position in the form of a balance sheet. This was done.

Balance sheet—The ECSC's final accounts for the year are summed up in a balance sheet showing the assets and liabilities arising from all that Community's transactions. Far from being limited to budgetary transactions, the document also sets out the figures for the ECSC's banking operations. An ECSC revenue and expenditure account is also drawn up for the period 1 January to 31 December.

Both documents are submitted to the ECSC Auditor, since 1977 the Court of Auditors. Traditionally the balance sheet is signed by the ECSC Auditor.

General statement on the European Coal and Steel Community's finances—Starting with the financial year 1954/55 the High Authority adopted the custom of preparing a general statement on the Community's finances that distinguished the implementation of the budget from this Community's banking activities. This statement was appended to the General Report dealing with the financial year concerned. The last general statement covered the period 1 July 1967 to 31 December 1968; after that date the Commission ceased to prepare a general statement, confining itself to the balance sheet alone.

Since the 1977 budget, however, the Commission has organized another form of reporting. It prepares a long list of explanations for its draft budget, in order to provide the European Parliament with as much information as possible.

B—Implementation of the revenue side of the ECSC operational budget

The current revenue (resources) of the operational budget consists firstly of levy revenue and secondly of interest on the ECSC's invested funds plus a number of receipts which are merely book entries. Mention should also be made of some exceptional items of revenue such as payments by new members in respect of their share of ECSC reserves and *ad hoc* contributions by Member States to meet exceptional costs arising from the recent crisis in the Community steel industry.

The rules governing ECSC levies

Under Article 4 of Decision No 2-52 of 23 December 1952, levies are payable by each undertaking on the tonnage of its chargeable production, which must be declared monthly. To this end, the High Authority sends each undertaking a form each month that it must fill in to show its production during the previous month. The payments in respect of this production fall due on the 25th of each month and are made directly to an account maintained by the High Authority/Commission for that purpose in the Member State in whose territory the undertaking in question is operating. Thus the system of collection here is quite different from that for collecting the own resources assigned to the European Communities, in that collection takes place directly without passing through the national authorities. As a consequence, the High Authority/Commission must itself arrange to audit the calculation and payment of the levies. This it does through a specially created inspectorate.

The administrative structure created by the High Authority/Commission is very slim, consisting of only 12 persons (6 Category A officials, 2 Category B and 4 Category C), but then the number of taxable firms is small; there are only 433, of which 403 are in the steel sector and 30 in the coal sector. Their geographical distribution is interesting: there are 175 Italian (175+0), 82 German (71+11), 74 British (68+6), 62 French (59+3), 24 Belgian (20+4), 6 Dutch (5+1), 6 Irish (1+5), 2 Danish (2+0) and 2 Luxembourg firms (2+0).

The procedure with other ECSC revenue

The other items of revenue are dealt with solely by the departments of the High Authority/Commission.

Interest on invested funds

The ECSC's own funds are invested by the High Authority/Commission departments—specifically by its Directorate-General for Credit and Investments—in accordance with their nature and with due regard to market conditions. The net interest received on these investments is available for financing the ECSC's operational budget and is credited as a provision at the end of the financial year; this provision is then used the following year to cover expenditure.

Receipts which are merely book entries

The payments to be made in implementation of earlier decisions by the High Authority/Commission come out of the provisions created at the time the legal commitment was entered into. When the commitments are fulfilled, the amounts which had been credited as provisions are adjusted on the basis of the actual expenditure and the sums thus released as no longer required for the original purpose are then entered as revenue in the ECSC operational budget.

Payments by acceding States and ad hoc contributions by Member States

These exceptional receipts are entered as revenue in the operational budget for the year in which they were approved and are collected as and when received.[19]

*
* *

In the matter of implementation a major debate between the institutions is under way. Although the Heads of State or Government like to declare that they ought to follow the provisions of the Treaties—whereby executive and management responsibility under Community enactments may be entrusted to the Commission—the Council, not content with exercising legislative power but desirous of exercising executive power as well, particularly in the budgetary field, makes it difficult to honour the terms of this declaration. What is at stake is no less than the virtual recasting of the Community's decision-making machinery.

The controversy probably has a historic dimension. Enlargement of the Community to twelve will only emphasize it.

Footnotes to Chapter IV

[1] In Part Three of this book, in the five chapters dealing with specific Community policies, we shall say something about the problems involved in *implementing the budget*. See EAGGF Guarantee Section (p. 186), EAGGF Guidance Section (p. 216), social policy (p. 210), regional policy (p. 226), energy policy (p. 254), research policy (p. 264), cooperation with developing countries and other non-member countries (pp. 292 and 297), and administrative policy (p. 323).

[2] Parliament's attitude has been slightly ambivalent. Thus on 26 April 1979 it passed a resolution containing the following passage: '10. Although the Commission is authorized in accordance with Article 205 of the Treaty establishing the European Economic Community to utilize on its own responsibility the appropriations allocated to it within the budget, Parliament considers it advisable to provide the Community with a regulation defining the permanent legal basis for operations for the financing of which it is not enough to enter a certain sum in each year's budget'.

[3] In 1978 the Commission had found that adherence to the one-month time-limit for carry-overs laid down by Article 6(3) of the Financial Regulation of 21 December 1977 (as also in the previous Financial Regulation of 25 April 1973) caused practical difficulties. In fact, the time allowed for the Council to reach a decision on carry-over applications is very hard to comply with, since the Council also has to consult the European Parliament during this brief period. Parliament will have to debate the matter in plenary session, basing its deliberations on the report of the Committee on Budgets, which for its part must hold a meeting to examine the carry-over applications. The Commission therefore proposed, on 15 June 1978. to extend the time-limit, adopting that fixed for transfers of appropriations, namely six weeks.

[4] See footnote 3 to the Introduction to Part One.

[5] It occurred in 1964 with the EEC and Euratom budgets and in 1968 with the budget of the Communities.

[6] In practice, rejection of the budget is the only event which can cause the system of provisional twelfths to be applied. Clearly the authors of the Treaty had no wish to envisage a situation in which the institutions should fail to meet their obligations in the course of the budget cycle (see p. 42).

[7] The 1980 budget year did in fact start with a period of 'provisional twelfths' owing to Parliament's rejection of the draft budget on 13 December 1979 (see p. 9). Application of Article 204 of the EEC Treaty etc. in conjunction with Article 8 of the Financial Regulation gave rise to numerous interpretational difficulties, quite apart from differences of opinion on how the budget cycle should be restarted (see footnote 5 on p. 51). The majority view emerging in both Council and Parliament—though for different reasons and with different objectives—was that the draft budget and even the preliminary draft budget had been cancelled by the vote in Parliament. The upshot of this opinion, from the legal point of view, was to consider that the double limit laid down by the Treaty had become a single limit, namely that of the previous year's budget (the 1979 budget). From the time of submission of the Commission's new budget proposal this limit was sometimes regarded by the Budgetary Authority as the second limit.

The first recourse to the system of provisional twelfths has thus demonstrated that the system as it stands at present contains a number of ambiguities. Clarification is called for, preferably when emotions have cooled. It must be admitted, however, that the Community institutions have been as one in following the law as scrupulously as possible in the matter of using several provisional twelfths. Bitter reflections have followed.

[8] Regulations involving financial intervention by the Community held up as a result of the dispute over application of Article 205 of the EEC Treaty: aid to non-associated developing countries; financial protocols with Mediterranean countries (financing projects); management procedure for food aid; assistance to joint hydrocarbon exploration projects; Community grants for industrial restructuring and conversion; research and development programme in the clothing and textiles field; system of Community financial aid to finance coal stocks; Community financial measures in connection with trade in power-station coal; Community financial aid to promote the use of coal for electricity generation.

[9] Parliament's attitude is sometimes more obscure. Thus on 12 May 1978 it agreed, in connection with a proposed regulation specifying how certain EAGGF Guarantee Section grants should be financed, that the Council should be able to take a different decision from the Commission, recommending: 'however, if the measure has significant budgetary consequences, the Council shall act only in agreement with the European Parliament'.

[10] The Commission has been able to make its position publicly known through three replies to written questions from Euro-MPs: replies No 485/78 of 17 July 1978 (OJ C 227 of 25.9.1978), No 193/78 of 12 September 1978 (OJ C 238 of 9.10.1978) and No 155/79 of 6 July 1979 (OJ C 192 of 30.7.1979). The Commission's President confirmed the position at the plenary session of Parliament on 16 April 1980.

In addition, on the occasion of adoption of the Regulation on a four-year programme for the development of data-processing, the Commission declared that it considered that this programme entailed a decision-making procedure (for the choice of projects) which diverged from the Commission's general position in that in the event of the committee delivering an adverse opinion the Commission could not commence implementation of the proposed project or grant the funds entered in the budget unless the Council, acting by a qualified majority and with no time-limit, had first reached a favourable decision on the matter.

[11] In the Commission of the European Communities the function of delegated Authorizing Agent is assumed by the responsible officials of the Directorates-General and spending departments (see Annex 14, p. 402), that of Accounting Officer by the responsible officials of the Directorate-General for Budgets, and that of the 'Financial Controller' by the Director-General for Financial Control.

[12] In Part Three of this book, in each of the five chapters dealing with specific Community policies, we shall describe how *control of budget implementation* is exercised. See EAGGF guarantee (p. 188), EAGGF guidance (p. 217) social policy (p. 211), regional policy (p. 227), energy policy (p. 254), research policy (p. 265), cooperation with developing countries and other non-member countries (p. 293) and administrative policy (p. 323).

[13] These reports are very substantial documents. For instance, the report for the fourth quarter of 1978, i.e. the annual report for 1978, runs to 141 pages, the fourth quarterly report for 1979 to 169 pages.

[14] See OJ L 336 of 27.12.1977 (and corrigendum in OJ L 15 of 19.1.1978).

[15] The Como case is crucial for an understanding of the limits within which the Commission exercises its right of control over own resources. In 1976 about 7 000 tonnes of butter from outside the Community stored in the Netherlands was exported to Italy in several shipments. The operation was fraudulent because during transit forged Community T2 documents purporting to show that the butter was of Community origin were substituted for the genuine T1 documents, attesting to the non-Community origin of the goods and issued properly by the Rotterdam customs. The clearance copies of the T1s had been submitted to the customs of origin with false Italian seals purporting to demonstrate that the butter had been released for consumption in the proper way as though it had been subject to agricultural levies.

The Guardia di Finanza were asked to investigate and criminal proceedings were subsequently instituted by the Turin court. As soon as the Commission heard about the transactions it took part in a first associated audit starting in October 1976, by examining the customs documents. But Italy contested the Commission's right to audit, claiming that this operation could only take place before the establishment of the entitlements, so the audit was restricted to actual customs matters alone. No contact with the judicial authority responsible for bringing the criminal prosecution was possible owing to the secrecy surrounding judicial investigation in a criminal matter. Consequently the Italians were unable to supply any information about the facts of the case or even about what had been done by the Guardia di Finanza, who were working on behalf of the judge. The Commission brought an action before the Court of Justice on 21 December 1978, seeking to have the Court declare that the Republic of Italy, by refusing to let the Commission take part in control measures relating to the establishment and making available of Community own resources and to inform it of the results of those control measures had failed to fulfil the obligations arising out of Article 5 of the Treaty and Article 14 of Council Regulation No 2/71 (replaced by Article 18 of Regulation No 2891/77).

So the point at issue was the extent of the Commission's powers. The Commission maintained in the first place that it had the right to exercise its powers from the moment when an operative event had given rise to a liability to tax or duty. On 10 January 1980, the Court ruled that the Commission's right to exercise its control starting at the stage of establishment of own resources by the Member State's agency was incontestable. Also at issue were the objects that the Commission had the right to examine. The Republic of Italy claimed that the Commission ought only to examine the documents in the Member States's file on establishment of the revenue. But the Court's judgment of 10 January 1980 rejected this claim, stating that the Commission did have the right to be associated with the control measures carried out by Member States in the course of the establishment process. All restrictions on examination of the file documents were rejected; the inspections by the Commission, like those of the Member States, could cover all material facts and documents relevant to the operative event giving rise to the own resource and to its proper administrative and financial appreciation.

Finally the Commission claimed that its power of control could not be impeded by national provisions on the secrecy of investigations carried out in the course of criminal proceedings. Here the Court ruled against the Commission. The judgment of 10 January 1980 states that the rules in national criminal legislation preventing communication to certain persons of records used in criminal proceedings could be invoked against the Commission to the same extent as they could be invoked against the authorities of the country concerned.

[16] The proposed system (see OJ C 88 of 4.4.1979) would mean that the Commission was informed automatically of any irregularities in connection with the various categories of revenue provided for by the Decision of 21 April 1970. The information given would furnish the material for additional audits to determine the financial repercussions of the irregularities; Community interests would thereby be defended because correct application of the own resources system would be ensured. The proposed Regulation is in line with Parliament's desire for a system to curb own resource irregularities similar to that introduced for the EAGGF by Regulation (EEC) No 283/72. Moreover, the proposal would in some measure provide a way round the obstacle of secrecy of criminal investigations whenever a Member State was explicitly required to furnish certain specific items of information. Parliament expressed a favourable opinion on 11 May 1979 and the Court of Auditors stated its opinion on 17 May 1979; the Council has not yet started to examine the proposal.

[17] The first amending budget of this kind was for an amount of 40 m EUA—against the revenue needed to cover the expenditure of amending and supplementary budget 3/79; the second for a total of 459 m EUA, was incorporated in the ordinary budget for 1980, established on 9 July 1980.

[18] Only Article 56(1) of the ECSC Treaty actually obliges the Commission to take action, but apparently it has never been invoked. In practice it has been pursuant to Article 56(2)(b) of the same Treaty that the High Authority/Commission has signed bilateral agreements with Member States' governments. The High Authority/Commission has thus voluntarily created an obligation for itself.

[19] See footnote 3 to Chapter VI.

Chapter V:
External and parliamentary audit of the European Communities' budgets

The European Communities have gradually developed a system of audit, both external and parliamentary, of the implementation of their budgets. The activities of the European Investment Bank (EIB) are, however, outside the scope of these arrangements. In this chapter, we shall look at the institutions responsible for these two stages of audit over and above the internal audit arrangements already described (see p. 81). We shall then outline the nature of the legal or political acts carried out by virtue of these powers of audit.

1. Bodies responsible for external and parliamentary audit

Until the Treaty of 22 July 1975,[1] the authorities responsible for external audit had been twofold—the Audit Board and the ECSC Auditor. Their functions are now carried out by a European Court of Auditors. By contrast, the process of monitoring by Parliament has developed slowly and only found its mature form in 1976.

A—The Court of Auditors of the European Communities

In the proposals formulated on 10 October 1973 for strengthening the Parliament's budgetary powers, the Commission saw fit to suggest the creation of a European Court of Auditors. In a preamble 'Principles taken as a basis by the Commission', the Commission declared: 'Control over the use of public money by the institutions of the Community is insufficient and must be strengthened. In this connection, Parliament has a key role to play: in this role it will have both the means and the opportunity to exercise control over the whole range of activities.'

Simultaneously, in a set of papers entitled *The case for a European Audit Office*, published by Parliament in September 1973, Heinrich Aigner, vice-chairman of the European Parliament's Committee on Budgets, recorded the following criticism: 'While parliamentary control over public finance in the Member States is well supported by the professional services of the national public audit bodies and their various ancillary staffs, members of the European Parliament have to rely on a body which, to judge from its present charter, can hardly be considered a suitable instrument for proper and effective audit, let alone parliamentary audit, i.e. the European Communities' Audit Board'.

At the same time the Copenhagen Summit of 15 December 1973 showed an interest in the creation of a Court of Auditors (see Annex 3, p. 351).

This convergence of ideas gave birth to the Court of Auditors of the European Communities established by the Treaty of 22 July 1975. The Court actually commenced operation on 25 October 1977.

The European Court of Auditors' inheritance from previous audit bodies

The European Court of Auditors has inherited the functions both of the ECSC Auditor and of the Audit Board.

The ECSC Auditor was originally instituted by Article 78(6) first subparagraph of the ECSC Treaty, which stated: 'The Council shall appoint an auditor for a term of three years, which shall be renewable. He shall be completely independent in the performance of his duties. The office of auditor shall be incompatible with any other office in any institution or service of the Community.'

Article 21 of the Merger Treaty of 8 April 1965 repealed the foregoing provisions. It distinguished two external audit authorities: first, an Audit Board, which examined the accounts for all ECSC administrative expenditure incorporated in the general budget (new Article 78d of the ECSC Treaty); second, an auditor whose audit only extended to the operational expenditure and revenue of the ECSC (new Article 78e of the same Treaty), although his original terms of appointment were otherwise preserved.

The Commission, in its proposed amendments of 8 June 1973—and subsequently of 5 October 1973—to the Treaties, had not envisaged the abolition of the ECSC Auditor. The Council took the initiative and did so and the Commission had no reason to oppose it.

As for the Audit Board itself, it had been created by Article 206 of the EEC Treaty, which stipulated that 'the accounts of all revenue and expenditure shown in the budget shall be examined by an Audit Board consisting of auditors whose independence is beyond doubt, one of whom shall be chairman'. The Council, acting unanimously, determined the number of the auditors and appointed the auditors and the chairman of the Audit Board for a period of five years. Article 180 of the Euratom Treaty repeated these provisions, but in fact only one Audit Board was set up for the two Communities. Article 22 of the Merger Treaty of 8 April 1965 had then created the 'Audit Board of the European Communities' to take the place of the 'Audit Boards of the ECSC |sic|, the EEC and Euratom' and 'exercise, under the conditions laid down in the Treaties establishing the three Communities, the powers and jurisdiction conferred on those bodies by these Treaties'.

The constitution of the European Court of Auditors

The Treaty of 22 July 1975 amends Article 22 of the Merger Treaty of 8 April 1965 and adopts the revised articles numbered as 206 of the EEC Treaty, 78e of the ECSC Treaty and 180 of the Euratom Treaty laying down that the Court of Auditors is composed of nine members chosen from among persons who belong or have belonged to external audit bodies in their respective countries, or who are especially qualified for the task and whose independence is beyond doubt.[2]

Nine auditors is a small number; it will certainly have to be increased if the pattern of work of the Court is to follow that found in some national audit institutions. Members of the Court of Auditors are appointed for six years by unanimous decision of the Council, after consultation with Parliament. This last provision is an innovation, but does not go as far as the Commission suggested in proposing that the appointments should be approved by Parliament. When the initial appointments were made, four members of the Court chosen by lot had their tenure fixed at only four years. The members of the Court of Auditors can be reappointed. They select the President of the Court from among themselves for a period of office of three years, this appointment being renewable.

This system of appointment marks a distinction between the Court of Auditors and the Commission or the Court of Justice, since the members of the latter are 'appointed by a common accord of the governments of Member States', whereas members of the Court of Auditors are appointed by the Council, in common with members of the Economic and Social Committee and the ECSC Consultative Committee. None the less, the Financial Regulation of 21 December 1977 places the Court of Auditors in the same class of administratively independent bodies as the four Community institutions set up by the basic Treaties (see p. x).

The members of the Court of Auditors pursue their functions in complete independence and in the general interest of the Communities. In carrying out their tasks, they neither seek nor accept instructions from any government or other body. They avoid all activity inconsistent with the nature of their roles. During their tenure of office the members of the Court of Auditors may not assume any other paid or unpaid professional activity. This brings to an end the previous system whereby part-time appointments were allowed. They may not be relieved of office or declared ineligible for their pension rights or other alternative benefits, unless, at the request of the Court of Auditors itself, the Court of Justice rules that they either no longer satisfy the qualifications laid down, or do not measure up to the obligations of their role.

The organization of the European Court of Auditors

The Court of Auditors has inherited the former staff of the Audit Board and the ECSC Auditor. However, unlike these two bodies, it is administratively and financially independent, having its own financial estimates and staff establishment and its own powers of internal management. In 1977 the staff of the Audit Board and the ECSC Auditor amounted to 35 officials (17 Category A, 14 Category B and 4 Category C) and their budget to 1.6 m EUA. The resources of the Court of Auditors are already far more substantial. In 1980, its staff establishment comprised 231 permanent posts (74 A, 54 B, 60 C, 21 D and 22 LA) and 28 temporary posts (22 A and 6 C) and its budget amounted to 13 m EUA.

The powers of the European Court of Auditors under paragraphs 1, 2, 3 and 4 of the new Articles 206a of the EEC Treaty, 78f of the ECSC Treaty and 180a of the Euratom Treaty

The Court of Auditors has been given no decision-making power and no judicial role. It has, however, been given the task of examining the accounts for all Community revenue and expenditure. It also looks at EDF operations and at the complete revenue and expenditure accounts of every institution created by the Communities, unless this is specifically ruled out in the act constituting such a body. The Treaty of 22 July 1975 has removed an ambiguity with regard to the responsibility for auditing non-budgetary accounts (e.g. suspense accounts). Whereas the Audit Board had the task of scrutinizing all the revenue and expenditure of the budget of the Communities, the powers of the Court of Auditors cover all the revenue and expenditure of the Communities.[3] The Treaty of 22 July 1975 thus broadens the power of the audit body, since the Court of Auditors' jurisdiction extends to all bodies set up by the Communities. Greater importance is thus attached to the general principle which up to then had figured only in the Financial Regulation: 'The granting of subsidies to bodies outside the Community institutions shall be subject to their agreement to an audit being carried out by the Court of Auditors'.

Like the Audit Board before it, the Court of Auditors has the task of examining the legality and correctness of receipts and expenditure and the observance of good financial management. Two refinements are, however, specified. Audit of revenue is based on verification of entitlements as well as of actual Community receipts, while that of expenditure considers commitments as well as payments, and audits may take place before the accounts of the financial year concerned are closed. A further innovation is that audits may be carried out either on the basis of documents, or, if need be, on the spot,[4] and not only in the Communities' institutions[5] but also in Member States. In the latter case the audit takes place in cooperation with national audit institutions or other suitably qualified national agencies if the official audit bodies do not consider themselves qualified to act. These organizations let the Court of Auditors know if they desire to take part in its audit. All documents or other information the Court of Auditors needs to fulfil its task are provided, on demand, by the Community institutions or national audit organizations, or, if these latter do not consider themselves competent to act, by the competent national bodies. These measures provide a uniform and effective external audit system which keeps Parliament and the Council fully informed.[6]

In addition, the Court of Auditors may raise observations on particular matters at any time, acting on its own initiative, and give an opinion at the request of one of the institutions—in most cases Parliament. There is an innovation here in that these various reports are no longer restricted to a financial year that has ended (Article 83 of the Financial Regulation) and hence actions in the course of implementation may be commented on and discussed. As soon as it took office the Court made determined use of this new right.

After the accounts for each financial year have been closed, the Court of Auditors draws up an annual report which is accompanied by the replies of the Community institutions to the Court's observations. The Court also draws up an annual report on the accounts of the ECSC as prescribed in Article 78f(5) of the ECSC Treaty. The Court's annual reports and opinions are adopted by a majority vote of its members.

The Court's first report was on the financial year 1977.[7] It gave rise to a disagreement between itself and the Commission. The Court thought that it had the right to prepare and publish some sort of comment if it considered that the reply given to it by the institution being audited was unsatisfactory. The Commission contested this new right.

The Court of Auditors' reports and opinions are published in the *Official Journal of the European Communities*.[8]

Powers of the European Court of Auditors under paragraph 5 of the new Article 78f of the ECSC Treaty

Under the provisions of this Article, the Court of Auditors must 'draw up a separate annual report stating whether the accounting other than that for the expenditure and revenue referred to in paragraph 1 and the financial management by the High Authority relating thereto have been effected in a regular manner'. This means that the Court of Auditors must draw up a report on the activities of the High Authority/Commission under the head of the ECSC operational budget—a term, it should be noted, which does not occur in the Treaty of Paris—and on that institution's financial activities—we might also say 'banking activities'. The wording of the new Article 78f(5) of the ECSC Treaty does not differ from the old Article 78(6), second subparagraph of the same Treaty in regard to these two areas.

Although Article 78f(5) of the ECSC Treaty only applies the criterion that the revenue, expenditure and financial management should have been effected in a regular manner, the powers of the Court of Auditors are no different in practice from what they are in connection with the general budget,[9] except for one very important point, namely that it is empowered to carry out independent checks. The ECSC Auditor does not have this power, as indeed was emphasized by the Court of Auditors and by Parliament with regard to the discharge for the financial year 1977.

The old Article 78(6), third subparagraph of the ECSC Treaty, like the new Article 78f(5), last two sentences thereof, requires that the report shall be drawn up within six months of the end of the financial year to which the 'account' refers. The Court of Auditors must submit it to the High Authority/Commission and to the Council; the High Authority/Commission must forward it to Parliament.

The Court of Auditors' first report was that for the year 1977. But it was not submitted to the High Authority/Commission until 28 September 1979, i.e. nearly 15 months late. It was a brief document and was followed a few days later by a report entitled 'Comments and observations on the ECSC's financial activities—1977'. The High Authority/Commission forwarded it to Parliament with its own observations.[10]

The Court of Auditors' right to give an opinion

Finally we must mention that Article 209 of the EEC Treaty, etc. gives the Court of Auditors the task of stating its opinion to the Council when the latter wishes to adopt a Financial Regulation. An apparently insignificant right, it is important in practice, and the Court of Auditors has been trying to extend it to include consultation on other proposed regulations which would significantly amend the Communities' financial and/or budgetary mechanisms.

B—Parliamentary audit

Since 11 April 1973 Parliament has possessed a body responsible for 'control'. At the instigation of the European Council held in Rome on 1 and 2 December 1975, Parliament was led to confirm and specify the powers of this body.[11] There is thus another form of scrutiny of the Community's accounts, external to the Commission and complementing the audit made by the European Court of Auditors; it is an audit with a political dimension. The body in question was the 'Control Subcommittee' of the Committee on Budgets until the election of Parliament by universal suffrage, when it became a full committee in its own right, called the Budgetary Control Committee.

The European Parliament's Control Subcommittee (1973-79)

We give below some details of the constitution, terms of reference and work of this body.

Constitution of the Control Subcommittee—Under the terms of a Resolution approved by Parliament on 15 June 1976, this subcommittee, appointed by Parliament itself, comprised nine members taken from the members of the Committee on Budgets. Its balance as between political groups followed the same pattern as this latter committee (see Annex 2, p. 349). The quorum of this subcommittee was three members.

Terms of reference of the Control Subcommittee—In the terms of the Resolution on the role and function of parliamentary control of Community resources and expenditure just referred to, Parliament authorized the Committee on Budgets and the Control Subcommittee to contact the Council and the Commission in order to consider the legal and practical problems of exercising its powers of control. The Resolution very precisely defined the following tasks:
(a) to carry out an on-going post-audit of all Community revenue and expenditure;
(b) to consider the combined results of internal and external audit activities and draw any necessary conclusions in the political sphere;
(c) to undertake direct responsibility for the audit of the implementation of the European Parliament's budget;
(d) to apply Article 92 of the Financial Regulation which provides that 'the institutions shall take all appropriate steps to take action on the comments appearing in the decisions giving discharge'.

The Resolution of 15 June 1976 stipulates that the Subcommittee should act through:
(i) close and permanent assistance from the Court of Auditors and help provided by Community and national authorities;
(ii) access to all documents relating to the implementation of Community expenditure from Community institutions and national governments;
(iii) taking oral evidence from officials or experts from the Community institutions and Member States responsible for matters connected with the implementation of Community expenditure;
(iv) making inspection visits to Community institutions and national bodies whose activities have to do with the implementation of Community expenditure.

Work of the parliamentary Control Subcommittee—The Subcommittee was asked to prepare the ground firstly for decisions required of Parliament, notably granting of discharge, and secondly for any kind of draft resolution on budget implementation that it felt it should lay before the plenary session.

There was a steady growth in the Subcommittee's activities; it met 11 times in 1976, 14 in 1977, 15 in 1978 and 6 during the first half of 1979. It allocated the major budget sections (both revenue and expenditure) among its members, each member reporting, in the context of the Commission's work on discharge in respect of budget implementation, on the section for which he was responsible and monitoring budget implementation throughout the year on the basis of quarterly implementation reports submitted by the Commission. In addition, any topical matter—for example, fraud in respect of the EAGGF as reported in the press, or the use of appropriations for the information campaign about the election of the European Parliament by universal suffrage—could be made the subject of an immediate debate on the free initiative of a member of the Subcommittee, followed if necessary by an investigation to ascertain whether the Commission had shown due diligence.

Parliament's Budgetary Control Committee (since July 1979)

The directly-elected Parliament replaced the Control Subcommittee which came under the Committee on Budgets by a fully-fledged committee of 27 members (see Annex 2, p. 349) called the Committee on Budgetary Control. Between its inception in September 1979 and July 1980 it held 19 meetings, devoting a major part of its work to preparing the discharges to give to the Commission regarding the implementation of the budget (procedure for the 1977 discharge to be completed; entire discharge procedure for the 1978 budget). For the latter it not only appointed a General Rapporteur but also instructed 13 of its members to examine one major sphere of Community activity each.

In addition to the annual report of the Court of Auditors which provided the basis for the work on the discharge granted to the Commission, the Committee on Budgetary Control has examined special reports by the Court of Auditors on particular activities of the Community—e.g. the operation of Stabex (see p. 277). On the financial side, it has also examined the—generally annual—reports prepared by the Commission on each of its major spheres of action—the EAGGF Guidance and Guarantee Sections, the Regional Fund, financial and technical cooperation under the Lomé Convention, and borrowing and lending operations. Fraud and irregularities, especially in the agricultural sector, have been one of the Committee's constant concerns. Thus, by its continuing and painstaking examination of all Community financial matters, even though its powers are not very precisely defined, the Committee on Budgetary Control certainly constitutes a particularly active instrument for Parliament in its search for more democratic control of the Community's finances.

Debates on the implementation of the budget

From 1976 onwards, Parliament, at the instigation of its Control Subcommittee, has organized a debate each year[12] on the implementation of the budget for the current year on the basis of an oral question with debate. The debates have often produced a wide-ranging exchange of views and some very interesting opinions, especially from the Commission (see p. 71).

It is worth noting that this control activity by Parliament has already caused a crisis between that institution and the Commission on the extent of this control and the methods used. This was the 'malt affair',[13] which nearly led to a motion of censure against the Commission.

2. Exercise of the power of discharge

The last stage in the life-cycle of a Community budget is the 'discharge', the first stage being its preparation and adoption (see Chapter II) and the second its implementation (see Chapter IV). The purpose of the discharge decision is to endorse the actual outturn of revenue and expenditure for the financial year involved. As usual, we need to distinguish between the accounts of the general budget and those of the ECSC budget.

A—Endorsement of the general budget accounts

We shall examine in turn the authority competent to grant discharge, the process followed, the actual granting of the discharge, and the effects of discharge.

The authority competent to grant discharge

The procedure for the grant of discharge was laid down in the Treaties of Rome. Article 206, last paragraph of the EEC Treaty and Article 180, second paragraph of the Euratom Treaty stated that: 'The Council shall, acting by a qualified majority, give a discharge to the Commission in respect of the implementation of the budget. It shall communicate its decision to the Assembly'. Articles 3, 6 and 9 of the Treaty of Luxembourg of 21 April 1970 amended the first-mentioned two Articles and also Article 78d of the ECSC Treaty. The new provisions were that: 'The Council and the Assembly shall give a discharge to the Commission in respect of the implementation of the budget. To this end, the report of the Audit Board shall be examined in turn by the Council which shall act by a qualified majority, and by the Assembly. The Commission shall stand discharged only after the Council and the Assembly have acted'. The Treaty of 22 July 1975 amends the three Articles yet again. They now read: 'The Assembly, acting on a recommendation from the Council which shall act by a qualified majority, shall give discharge to the Commission in respect of the implementation of the budget. To this end, the Council and the Assembly in turn shall examine the accounts and the financial statement ... and the annual report by the Court of Auditors together with the replies of the institutions under audit to the observations of the Court of Auditors'. The way the law has evolved with regard to the power to grant discharge is extremely significant: it was first given to the Council (1958-70), then shared equally between the Council and Parliament (1971-76), and then assumed by Parliament alone. Thus the end of the road has been reached with the complete transfer of power. On this point, Parliament has triumphed. The political implications of this transfer are not inconsiderable: Parliament has gained the chief power—in practice virtually exclusive power— in the matter of scrutiny of implementation of the budget, and the Commission, the budgetary executive, has been given even greater responsibility, since Parliament, if it disagrees, can vote a motion of censure on that institution.

Process for granting discharge

The Treaty of 22 July 1975 and the Financial Regulation applicable to the general budget fix the stages in the discharge procedure.

On 23 April 1979, the Commission proposed an amendment to the Financial Regulation which, *inter alia*, would change the dates of the various stages by partially abolishing the EAGGF additional period.[14] We show the proposed dates below in brackets after the currently valid dates. The chief landmarks are:

(a) not later than 1 June (1 April) the Commission must prepare a revenue and expenditure account for the Communities for the preceding financial year (Article 73 of the Financial Regulation), together with a balance sheet showing the assets and liabilities of the Communities as at 31 December and an analysis of the financial management (Articles 75 and 76). Not later than 1 April (15 February) the other institutions must forward to the Commission the information required for drawing up these three documents (Article 74);

(b) not later than 1 June (1 April) the Commission must forward the three documents to Parliament, the Council and the Court of Auditors (Article 77);

(c) not later than 15 July (15 June) the Court of Auditors must transmit to the Commission and the other institutions concerned any comments which in its opinion ought to appear in its report (Article 83(1));

(d) not later than 31 October each institution must submit its replies to the Court of Auditors. The institutions other than the Commission must forward their replies at the same time as the Commission (Article 83(1));

(e) not later than 30 November the Court of Auditors must transmit to the authorities responsible for giving discharge and to the other institutions its annual report accompanied by the replies and must arrange publication in the *Official Journal of the European Communities* (Article 84);

(f) before 30 April of the next year Parliament gives a discharge to the Commission in respect of the implementation of the budget, following the procedures already described (Article 85, paragraph 1).

On 15 February 1980 the Commission withdrew its proposal of 23 April 1979 for technical reasons, but will need to put it forward again sooner or later.

Joint discharge by the Council and Parliament

Practice hitherto shows that joint action has been taken long after the time-limits fixed by the Financial Regulation. Thus the Council's decision for the financial year 1971 was only taken on 20 February 1973 and the Parliament's on 9 May 1973. Discharge of the accounts for 1972, 1973 and 1974, which were (sensibly, in the circumstances) considered together, was granted on 1 June 1976 by the Council and on 14 December 1976 by the Parliament, and for the accounts for 1975 on 25 April 1977 by the Council and on 7 July 1977 by the Parliament.

Discharge by Parliament alone

The first discharge granted by Parliament on its own, in respect of the accounts for 1976, did not take place until 13 December 1978,[15] the Council's opinion having been given only on 19 September 1978. Parliament itself had in fact been ready to grant discharge in July. As for discharge in respect of the accounts for 1977, this had not been granted owing to Parliament's need to bring its work to an end before its re-election by universal suffrage, but was granted by the newly-elected Parliament on 16 November 1979. The latter also granted the discharge for the financial year 1978 on 23 May 1980, after some very intensive preparation and a fairly lively debate in plenary session.

At this juncture we must mention one extremely tricky point which is not dealt with in the legislation, namely what happens if discharge is refused. On 7 July 1977, Mr Tugendhat, speaking as Commissioner responsible for the budget, declared: 'Thus, logically it is a general sanction which the Treaties confer upon Parliament, that is, a political sanction which would be the normal consequence of a refusal to give discharge. Such refusal would hence be extremely serious; the Commission thus censured would, I think, have to be replaced. Without a shadow of doubt we shall never reach that point.'

Effects of discharge

Article 85, third paragraph of the Financial Regulation provides that the institutions shall take all appropriate steps to take action on the comments appearing in decisions giving discharge. At the request of the European Parliament or the Council, the institutions must report the measures taken as a result of such observations, and, in particular, the instructions issued in consequence to the departments responsible for implementing the budget.[16] Such reports must also be sent to the Court of Auditors. The internal Financial Controller of each institution must take account of the observations featuring in the discharge decision. This monitoring of the discharge, which has hardly aroused any interest hitherto, is beginning to assume particular importance by virtue of the emphasis which the directly-elected Parliament is giving to the implementation of the budget.

B—Endorsement of the ECSC accounts

The ECSC Treaty did not establish a discharge procedure, just as it did not provide for the drawing up of a balance sheet. Nevertheless, since the inception of this Community the High Authority has drawn up a balance sheet which is signed by the Auditor to certify that it shows the financial position correctly.

Furthermore, despite the lack of any formal need to examine the Auditor's report (all that is formally stated is the requirement in Article 78f(5) of the ECSC Treaty for the Auditor to submit his annual report to the Commission and the Council and for the Commission to send it on to Parliament), Parliament has formed the practice of holding a debate on the subject. On receipt of the Auditor's report, Parliament now places it before its Committee on Budgets, which designates a rapporteur. His report is considered by the committee in the presence of representatives of the Commission, and, since 1973, of the Auditor himself. After approval by the Committee on Budgets, the report is placed before Parliament, which examines it in plenary session. The Commission again takes part in the debate. Finally, Parliament votes a resolution in which it gives a discharge to the Commission. This wording dates from December 1977 and reflects Parliament's desire to extend the rules of the two other Communities to the ECSC.[17] This is quite understandable: in the first Community the Treaty gives Parliament very little importance; in the other two it possesses genuine budgetary power.

The European Communities' budgetary legislation is in continuous evolution. A number of successive layers have accumulated, one on top of another. In the field of audit, after the period marked by the straightforward and flexible attitude of the ECSC, the Communities acquired a pre-audit (internal control) system modelled on French practice. Then gradually a system of post-audit (external control) grew up, unable to obstruct action by the executive it is true, but gaining in authority with the creation of the Court of Auditors; this system reproduces the German approach. Finally, the influence of the British tradition has produced a system of parliamentary audit (political control). With the legal and procedural framework as it now is, the part to be played by these various forms of audit is still far from clear. In its Communication of 5 April 1976 to the Joint Council of Foreign Affairs and Finance Ministers, the Commission sounded a warning to the Community institutions on the risks inherent in this accumulation of procedures. 'These three forms of control must be reconciled and combined and not simply strung together', it stated, 'if we are to avoid the risk of seeing the monitoring of actions impede their execution'. This question remains to be settled.[18] Both Parliament and the Council accept the force of the Commission's words of warning, but they are still considering how to react. What will be the ultimate position of the European Court of Auditors? There are strong grounds for believing that Parliament will seek to make this body its servant, and that the dialogue will be between the Commission as spending authority and Parliament, as holder of budgetary authority partly responsible for adopting the budget and responsible for monitoring its execution, drawing its authority from its election by universal suffrage. If things work out this way, the basis of the constitutional machinery of the European Communities—of the European Community— will be assured in accordance with the best traditions of democratic government.

Conclusion to Part One

We may contrast the way the ECSC's originality—compounded of dogged pragmatism, a simple and uncomplicated legal structure, and practical effectiveness in action—has been conserved down the years with little alteration, with the continual sequence of changes through which the two other Communities have passed and continue to pass to this day. For them, the merger of their budgets, the creation of the system of own resources, and the 1973 Financial Regulation ushered in a new era. But the Commission very soon sketched out a further advance, proposing that the Communities' financial instruments should be modernized, stressing the need to recognize that their operations carry financial implications for several years ahead, making a case for wider use of borrowing powers, and bringing up to date the yardstick of the Communities' finances, the unit of account. For its part, Parliament has intelligently and tenaciously pursued its role in the budgetary and legislative sphere. The claiming of budgetary power, or at least a share in this power, by the Parliament is an event of the utmost significance from all points of view. From the standpoint of the present study, the effect is to convert the budget from little more than an accounting operation into a genuine political exercise. Gradually, it is becoming a Community instrument embracing all the expenditure and all the revenues that arise because of the existence of the European Communities. The trend towards a comprehensive budget is progressing and becoming more and more firmly entrenched. Audit activity is also developing both in depth and in scope. In sum, what we are witnessing is the transformation of the task of financing Europe into a broader and more democratic operation. In all this the Commission has an essential indispensable role to play in seeking—often successfully—ways of avoiding conflict between the Council and Parliament.[19] It has its own stock of wisdom to offer in trying to settle differences. In continues to be the source of new ideas and innovations.

At the same time the Commission has had difficulty holding on to—and still greater difficulty therefore in extending—the powers attributed to it by the Treaties, and especially Article 205 of the EEC Treaty, as budgetary and financial executive. The suspicion with which it is regarded by the Council has often resulted in its being denied the exercise of its historic role. History will decide how wise it was to strip it of its birthright in this way.

It is natural to turn from the contemplation of this considerable constitutional change now going on in the legislative framework, and which we have just sought to depict, to consider how this alteration has affected the resources assigned to the European Communities.

Footnotes to Chapter V and to the Conclusion to Part One

[1] The Treaty of 22 July 1975 did not come into force until 1 June 1977. In December 1975 the European Council had called for a speedy conclusion to the ratification procedures so that the Court of Auditors could start operation during 1976 (see Annex 3, p. 352). The Court was not finally sworn in until 25 October 1977. The Treaty of 22 July 1975 thus took three times as long to ratify as that of 21 April 1970 (see p. 5).

[2] See also Claus-Dieter Ehlermann: *The European Court of Auditors, budgetary audit in the Community,* published in German by Nomos, 1976.

[3] The only difference from the original Article 206 of the EEC Treaty is the deletion of the words 'shown in the budget', to indicate that the Court of Auditors may examine all non-budget accounts. To avoid any possibility of misunderstanding, a declaration annexed to the Treaty states that the Court is empowered 'to audit the operations of the EDF'.

[4] A declaration annexed to the Treaty places a limit upon the right of audit of own resources 'established' by Member States: 'the audit shall not cover substantive transactions properly so called shown in the supporting documents which relate to establishment; accordingly, the audit on the spot shall not be carried out by recourse to the debtor'.

[5] On 1 February 1978 the Commission Member with responsibility for the budget sent a memorandum to the Commission departments, outlining the attitude they should adopt to the Court of Auditors. This memorandum is noteworthy as a remarkably open attitude by a body subject to audit, the Commission, to the body responsible for auditing it.

[6] In Part Three of this book, in each of the five chapters dealing with specific Community policies, we shall indicate how *the implementation of the budget is audited.* See EAGGF guarantee (p. 188), EAGGF guidance (p. 217), social policy (p. 211), regional policy (p. 227), energy policy (p. 254), cooperation with developing and other non-member countries (p. 293) and administrative policy (p. 323).

[7] This report covered 154 pages of text and a further 80 pages of annexes, all printed in two columns. It was published in the Official Journal (C 313 of 30.12.1978, distributed at the end of January 1979). Some of the Commission's replies are incorporated in the body of the report, together with the Court's 'answers' if any; they also appear in full in the annexes. The reports prepared by the old Audit Board were less voluminous: its last report, like its report for 1976, consisted of 185 pages of typescript.
The Court of Auditors second report, relating to 1978, was published in OJ C 326 of 31.12.1979 (distributed at the end of January 1980).

[8] The Court of Auditors first opinion was dated 2 December 1977. It delivered several opinions in 1978 (OJ C 139 of 5.6.1979) and issued its first special reports in 1979 (OJ C 221 of 3.9.1979).

[9] Article 78f of the ECSC Treaty groups together firstly the new provisions strengthening audit of administrative management (paragraphs 1 to 4 of the Article) and secondly the provisions—little changed—of the old Article 78e (Article 21 of the Merger Treaty) concerning the High Authority's accounting and financial management. Application of this old Article 78e gave rise to an accepted practice whereby very wide powers were conferred on the external audit body. Thus in practice the Commission/High Authority, the Parliament and the former ECSC Auditor were of one mind in considering that financial management could only be effected in a regular manner if:
(1) it had a basis in law (a regulation or a decision)—the principle of legality;
(2) it complied with internal procedural rules—the principle of regularity; and
(3) it obeyed the principle—found in all democratic institutions—of sound financial management of public funds.
By contrast, the Court of Auditors has no power to undertake an independent audit in the Member States concerning the High Authority/Commission's implementation of the operational budget or its financial activities. In this respect the Treaty of 22 July 1975 is following the wishes of the parties to the ECSC Treaty that monitoring of the management of the ECSC—an organization half-way between a public authority and a bank—should be modelled more on private-sector business practices than on the methods of public financial institutions. Experience has shown that this limitation has not detracted from the efficacity of external control. In the debate on the ECSC's financial and budgetary activities in 1976, on 14 December 1977, the rapporteur, Mr Bangemann, stated: 'it is also gratifying to note that the external audit in this field has cooperated exceptionally well with the Commission. There are no complaints from the Auditor about any lack of cooperation with the Commission's offices; everything seems to have gone very well.'

[10] Up to 1976, the Auditor's report was a weighty document of around 200 printed pages. In addition to very detailed annexes, it contained two sections: the first presented the balance sheet, the income and expenditure account and an account of the allocation of surplus receipts, supplemented by analytical comments; the second, observations on the main fields of ECSC activity. The 1977 report covered five pages. It was followed by a 110-page document containing comments and observations, consisting of a descriptive section, a critical section and substantial annexes.

[11] Reading the Conclusions of the Presidency of the European Council (see Annex 3, p. 352), one gets the impression it was not realized that Parliament had already had a Control Subcommittee for over two years.

[12] See in the OJ the debates of the European Parliament of 16 June 1976, 11 October 1977, 9 October 1978 and 23 October 1979. See also p. 71 of this book.

[13] The 'malt affair' illustrates the difficulty of reconciling wide-ranging and effective external political control and the independence of the institution being monitored.

Basically, an investigation by the Commission's Financial Controller in 1976 had revealed that owing to special circumstances on the malt market the system of export refunds for this product had led, in 1975 and 1976, to speculative transactions. Appropriate steps were immediately taken to modify the system.

As soon as it was appointed, the European Parliament's Control Subcommittee, alerted by the press, took the matter up and asked to see the Financial Controller's report. Since the document was for internal circulation only and had been drawn up by an official on behalf of his own institution, and since moreover the independence of the Financial Controller in carrying out his specific duties was at stake, the Commission expressed very strong reservations about divulging the contents of the report. It did however give Parliament all the relevant information, either in the form of working documents or through interviews with officials.

This did not prevent the principle involved from becoming a bone of interinstitutional contention. Parliament devoted a long debate to the matter, on 12, 13 and 16 December 1976, and a motion of censure was actually tabled against the outgoing Commission (it was later withdrawn). A compromise was reached at the beginning of the following year: the Commission agreed to forward to the parliamentary Control Subcommittee the internal reports which it made available to the Audit Board (and later to the Court of Auditors) on condition that the information was treated as strictly confidential by the parliamentary bodies using it.

[14] See footnote 3 to Chapter I.

[15] See OJ L 18 of 25.1.1979. Parliament approved: a decision on discharge in respect of the implementation of the budget for 1976; a resolution containing 68 observations; and a decision on discharge in respect of implementation of the EDF for 1976.

[16] The action taken by the Commission in response to the observations contained in the discharge decision in respect of implementation of the 1976 budget is described in an annex to the revenue and expenditure account for 1978. It is a document of 21 pages of typescript. Similarly, for the following year, 1977, the report (19 pages) was annexed to the 1979 accounts.

[17] The way the concluding words of Parliament's Resolution have developed over the past few years has been significant. Thus:
(a) on 7 November 1973, in connection with the accounts for 1971 and 1972, Parliament approves the ECSC accounts;
(b) on 16 June 1975, in connection with the 1973 accounts, and on 8 March 1976, in connection with the 1974 accounts, Parliament notes the ECSC's expenditure and revenue;
(c) on 28 February 1977, in connection with the 1975 accounts, Parliament uses the same wording but adds that it considers that it can give a discharge to the Commission of the European Communities;
(d) finally, on 14 December 1977, in connection with the 1976 accounts, Parliament gives a discharge; this formula was repeated on 22 May 1980, in respect of the 1977 accounts.

[18] The danger of an excess of control—leading to an excess of criticism—arose in July 1980. Thus, even before the European Court of Auditors had presented its report on the accounts for 1979, a resolution was tabled in Parliament criticizing not only the Council, but also the Commission, in respect of certain aspects of the latter's implementation of the budget. The resolution was approved, despite the Commission's protests, which in particular stressed that the time had not yet come for a discussion of the discharge.

[19] One of the Member States of the Community also plays a very original role in the 'interinstitutional interplay'. In this country a continuous conciliation process operates between the government and the national parliament, between its MPs and its MEPs (even before the election of the European Parliament by universal suffrage), and between the office of its Permanent Representative in Brussels and those involved in the interinstitutional interplay in the Community.

PART TWO

The financial resources
of the European Communities

Resources determine policy options. Giving the Communities substantial financial resources must imply granting them liberty to pursue the sort of policies needed to foster harmonious economic development on a large scale. Conversely, limiting their resources has the effect of restricting the Communities to insignificant executive tasks. Which of these approaches have the governments of Member States chosen to follow?

There is no doubt that those who drafted the Treaties wished to endow the Communities with independent revenue, but the governments later on were very reluctant to give real effect to the relevant clauses in the Treaties establishing the two Brussels Communities, Euratom and the EEC. So long as they enjoyed no independent revenue, the European Communities were able to balance their budgets thanks to the financial contributions paid in by Member States. This system has now come to an end; all that is left is their contributions to the EDF. Considerations of space rule out a detailed treatment of the mechanism of financial contributions to the budget, which are now part of history; a summary account will be found in Annex 9 (see p. 377). Contributions to EDF finance will be dealt with in Chapter XIV. The aim of this part of the book, however, is to set out the present policies of Member States and of the European Communities with regard to the financial ways and means the Communities should possess—that is, Community tax revenue and Community borrowing. Both will be dealt with in chronological order.

The three Treaties establishing the European Communities do provide them with the possibility of borrowing. Articles 49 and 51 of the first Treaty in time, that of the ECSC, give borrowing a prominent place, empowering the High Authority to procure the funds it requires to carry out its tasks by imposing levies and contracting loans (Article 49). Likewise Article 172(4) of the Euratom Treaty empowers the Community to raise loans to finance research and investment.

For the EEC, Article 130 authorizes borrowing, but only by the European Investment Bank (EIB), a financial institution whose task is to grant loans and give guarantees to facilitate investment in all sectors of the economy, mainly out of resources borrowed on the capital market. Subsequently, Article 235 of the EEC Treaty was invoked to give the EEC power to borrow in order to grant certain types of loan.

Chapter VI:
The budget revenue of the
European Coal
and Steel Community

The first Community tax was the ECSC levy, or, more precisely, the ECSC's levies on the production of coal and steel. Nearly 20 years went by before the next Community taxes were created by the Decision of 21 April 1970.

These levies are not the only source of revenue for the ECSC's budget: there are some other receipts, which we shall be analysing.

1. ECSC levies since 1952-53

We shall examine in turn the basis of assessment and the proceeds of the ECSC levies.

A—Basis of assessment of ECSC levies

The High Authority/Commission is empowered by Article 49 of the ECSC Treaty to procure the funds it requires to carry out its tasks by imposing levies on the production of coal and steel. Its fiscal power is substantial, since it decides both the base and the amount of the tax. Its dependence is almost total and its freedom of action complete, since it possesses its own tax administration.

However, the High Authority/Commission must obtain the agreement of Parliament before fixing the rate of the levy. It also informs the ECSC Consultative Committee (see Annex 7, p. 374) of its intentions with regard to the rate of the levy.

The levies are assessed annually on coal and steel products according to their average value. The method of assessment and collection is determined by a general decision of the High Authority after consultation with the Council and must so far as possible avoid 'double taxation'. The relevant Decision of the High Authority was No 2-52 of 23 December 1952; Article 1 of this Decision lists the categories of product liable to the levy while Article 2 stipulates that the average value per tonne of each product shall be determined by dividing the overall value of Community production, estimated on the basis of the net price per tonne ex works, by the tonnage produced. To avoid double taxation, the average value actually used for purposes of assessment is a net figure in which the gross value per tonne is abated by the value of the products subject to levy normally consumed in producing a tonne of the product concerned. The system devised by the High Authority is thus similar to the VAT system.

Under the Decision of 23 December 1952, the categories of products liable to the levy were six in number, as follows:
(1) brown coal briquettes and semi-coke derived from brown coal;
(2) hard coal, all grades;
(3) pig iron other than that intended for ingot production;
(4) Bessemer steel ingots;
(5) non-Bessemer steel ingots;
(6) finished products and end products as designated in Annex I to the Treaty.

In order to keep pace with technical progress, the Commission Decision No 1761/75/ECSC of 2 July 1975 combined two of the categories of steel ingots (Bessemer and non-Bessemer steel) into a single category.

B—Proceeds of ECSC levies

The rate of the levy has varied little since 1956 and for the past few years has been running at a fairly low level (see Annex 8, p. 376). Apart from the first four years (1953-56) when the levy varied from 0.30% to as much as 0.90% in order to finance the creation of the guarantee fund (100 m u.a.), the rate has been fixed at a level sufficient only for the current requirements of the High Authority. From 1 January 1972 to 31 December 1979 it was 0.29%, although the High Authority/Commission would have liked it to be higher.

All attempts to raise the levy had come up against fierce hostility from Parliament even in the boom period of high profits in the steel industry. The Commission accepted defeat in connection with the 1973 and 1974 budgets despite its theoretical power to override Parliament's negative attitude (see p. 2) and thereafter, up to 1978, it did not ask for any rise in the rate. In 1979, i.e. for the 1980 budget,[1] it succeeded in securing Parliament's approval for a rise from 0.29% to 0.31%, to enable the two industries in question to support the financial effort that the governments were making in the form of financial contributions (see p. 116).

It should be noted that the High Authority/Commission has never had to ask the Council for authority to exceed the 1% limit laid down by the Treaty of Paris.

Although there is no requirement for an exact balance of receipts and expenditure in the ECSC operational budget, the High Authority/Commission draws up a detailed estimate of levy revenue every year; these estimates sometimes prove wrong. Since the receipts are based on the average value of coal and steel output, they are essentially sectoral and liable to fluctuate in keeping with changes in the economic situation. Thus in 1971, 1973, 1975 and 1977, outturn was lower than the estimates, while in 1972, 1974, 1976, 1978 and 1979 it was higher (see Annex 8, p. 376).

Since 1954, the steel industry's contribution to the levies, which originally came almost equally from the coal and steel sectors (coal: 48%, steel: 52%), have increasingly predominated, so that by 1972, in the Community of the Six, the steel sector accounted for 84.1% of levies paid. In 1973, however, British accession raised the coal industry's share from 15.9% to 19.2%. In 1974 and 1975, the coal industry's share again went down, to 16.5%, though it climbed to 19% in 1976, 22% in 1977 and 1978 and 23% in 1979. Within the steel industry, the proportion of levies derived from finished products and end products remained more or less constant during this period (at around 21-22%), as did the amount coming from pig iron (5% to 2%). By contrast, the levy drawn from basic Bessemer steel fell from 35% to 3% in 1975, with an offsetting increase for steels and ingots made by other processes, in particular steel made by the basic oxygen process. This explains why since 1976, basic Bessemer steel has been combined into a single category with steel made by other processes.

The increasing disparity between the amounts contributed by the coal and steel industries to the ECSC's resources has caused problems within the ECSC's various institutions, because in fact the Community has spent more money on the coal than on the steel sector. This transfer of resources, although strictly speaking totally in order, given the principle of Community solidarity, does not fail to evoke constant recrimination from the steelmakers.

A breakdown of levy payments by Member States is given in Annex 8 (p. 376). The breakdown for 1979 and 1980 is shown in the table below. We have added columns showing Community GDP broken down over countries and also customs duties on coal and steel, on which we shall have something to say by way of explanation later.

Clearly, the amount Member States contribute to the ECSC operational budget is an exact reflection of the size of the coal and steel sectors in relation to their economies. The sectors are important in Belgium, the Federal Republic of Germany, Luxembourg and the United Kingdom, average in Italy, of less than average significance in France and insignificant in Denmark, Ireland and the Netherlands.

It is also interesting to compare the pattern of levy payments with that of payments of own resources (see p. 128). The comparison shows that for four States (Belgium, France, Italy and the United Kingdom) the share is roughly the same in the two cases. In three countries the proportion of levy is less (Denmark, Ireland and the Netherlands) and in two, more (the

ECSC budget revenue in 1979 (revenue collected) and 1980 (estimated revenue)

	Steel levies		Coal levies		Total levies		ECSC customs duties	GDP (estimates)	
	1979	1980	1979	1980	1979	1980	1979	1979	1980
Belgium	9.4	9.4	2.7	2.5	7.8	7.8	8.8	4.6	4.4
Denmark	0.6	0.6	0	0	0.4	0.5	2.6	2.8	2.5
Federal Republic of Germany	32.3	32.4	42.1	42.5	34.6	34.8	45.8	31.7	30.5
France	17.8	18.0	8.1	8.0	15.6	15.6	5.2	23.9	24.1
Ireland	0.1	0.1	0	0	0.1	0.1	0.6	0.6	0.6
Italy	18.0	18.0	0	0	13.8	13.7	14.0	13.5	14.0
Luxembourg	3.5	3.5	0	0	2.7	2.7	0.03	0.2	0.2
Netherlands	4.1	4.0	0	0	3.1	3.0	4.3	6.3	6.0
United Kingdom	14.2	14.0	47.1	47.0	21.9	21.8	18.6	16.4	17.8
%	100	100	100	100	100	100	100	100	100
% of levies	76.7	76.2	23.3	23.8	100	100			
in m EUA, 1979	79.37		23.87		103.24				
in m EUA, 1980 (estimates)	89.10		27.90		117.00				

Federal Republic of Germany and Luxembourg), again reflecting the different importance of the coal and steel industries in the overall economy of each country. Similarly, the analysis between steel and coal levies tells us about the respective situations of the two industries in each Member State. Levy revenue from 1952 to 1978 amounted to 1 256.1 m u.a. (323.2 m u.a. in respect of coal levies and 932.9 m u.a. in respect of steel levies). Under Article 50 of the ECSC Treaty the levy is intended to cover administrative expenditure, aid to resettlement (see p. 207) and aid to research (see pp. 259 and 260) and to make good any deficit arising from the Community's borrowing and lending activity.

2. Proposed new own resources for the ECSC

The crisis, together with restriction of the levy rate, prompted the High Authority/Commission to propose new own resources for the ECSC.

A—Reasons for the proposed new own resources

The serious economic and social problems facing the members of the Community in the wake of the crisis of 1973 led to a search for solutions at Community level. Several of the solutions put forward carried financial implications; this was the case with the ECSC and the question of the funds available arose. The same question arose with the EEC and Euratom, but here for reasons inherent in the general and, especially, financial development of the Community. So for the ECSC the problem of new own resources has a short-term economic cause whereas for the EEC and Euratom the cause is to some extent structural.

The Commission's draft operational budget for the ECSC for 1978, prepared on 8 November 1977, contained requirements totalling 152 m EUA, mainly as a result of the need—in view of the crisis—to increase the funds available for interest rebates on loans granted by the ECSC itself. With non-levy resources estimated at 20 m EUA, this would have entailed raising the rate of levy to 0.38%. It was impossible to propose a rate as high as this because, as we have already said, the rate had been politically frozen at 0.29% since 1972 and moreover any rise at this time would have been counter-productive, given the disastrous state of the steel industry.

B—The solutions proposed

The Commission therefore suggested two novel measures. First, it proposed, in application of Article 20 of the Merger Treaty, that the ECSC's contribution to the Commission's administrative expenditure, fixed by the Treaty at 18 m EUA, should be reduced to 5 m EUA. This would amount to transferring a charge of 13 m EUA from the ECSC budget to the general budget to enable operations based on the Treaty of Paris to be financed. The Council accepted this proposal in Decision No 77/729/ECSC of 21 November 1977 and put the practical consequences into effect on 22 November 1977 on its second reading of the general budget for 1978 when it fixed the amount in the revenue statement of that budget at 5 m EUA.

Secondly, the Commission proposed paying off the deficit, which still stood at 32 m EUA, by allocating to the ECSC part of the customs duties levied on ECSC products. For it is a peculiar feature of Community law that—although by virtue of the Decision of 21 April 1970 on own resources, duties under the Common Customs Tariff are assigned to the EEC and Euratom as own resources as from 1 January 1971—this arrangement does not extend to customs duties on coal and steel products covered by the ECSC Treaty since the Common Customs Tariff adopted on the basis of Article 9 of the EEC Treaty does not apply to products covered by the ECSC Treaty. It is true that customs duties on ECSC products have been harmonized in application of decisions taken pursuant to Article 72 of the Treaty of Paris, but they have remained the revenue of each Member State which collects the duty when the goods are imported into its territory. The Council did not accept this proposal to transfer customs duties to the Community; instead, on 21 December 1977, it approved an *ad hoc* solution whereby the Member States would pay a contribution to the Community calculated according to a scale to be agreed upon in 1978.

In 1978 the Commission returned to this matter, proposing, on 16 May, that revenue derived from customs duties collected by the Member States in trade with non-member countries on products falling within the scope of the Treaty establishing the European Coal and Steel Community should be allocated to the ECSC. Moreover, on 26 October 1978, the Commission included the total of such revenue, which is estimated at 60 m EUA, in its draft operational budget for 1979. Similarly, it again entered only 5 m EUA for administrative expenditure. The Council accepted the second proposal but rejected the first, as we shall see later. The table on p. 113 shows that customs duties break down in a different way from the levies and that to give customs duties to the Community would have the effect of changing the members' respective contributions to ECSC finance. This is the basic reason why the Commission's plan failed to gain acceptance.

It is now very unlikely that the Council will transfer customs duties on coal and steel to the ECSC. If, however, the Council did accept this proposal the ECSC budget would be radically altered. The fact that customs receipts are about two-thirds the amount of levy receipts would probably mean that during a boom period, when requirements were low, the levy rate would be reduced and it would then be very difficult to raise again if that became necessary. There would thus be a risk that the ECSC budget, despite gaining these new own resources, would not acquire more scope and flexibility but would merely undergo a substitution, with customs duties replacing the levy.

3. The other resources of the ECSC

The ECSC's other substantial resources consist of income from investment of its own funds, which it has always had, and, since 1978, financial contributions from Member States.

A—Income from investment of ECSC funds

Between 1952 and 1956 the High Authority accumulated a 'guarantee fund' from levy receipts, which had been increased for the purpose during this time. The guarantee fund remained unchanged at 100 m EUA from 30 June 1956 until additions, mainly owing to the capital contributions paid by the three acceding States, raised it to 150 m EUA at 31 December 1975. The purpose of the guarantee fund is to meet any part of the interest payable on the Community's borrowings that cannot be met from interest on its loans. The annual interest earned by this fund constitutes a budgetary resource additional to the levy. At 31 December 1979 the fund stood at 230 m EUA.

In addition, a special reserve fund has been built up from income other than the levy (derived from investments, fines and surcharges for delayed payment of levies, and interest on loans granted out of ECSC funds). On 31 December 1975 this reserve stood at 103 m EUA, thanks in part to an allocation from the capital contributions made by the three acceding States in 1973. The fund has served in the past to finance industrial redevelopment operations and is at present being used for loans to finance the construction of subsidized housing. The interest earned on special reserve moneys is another additional budgetary resource. At 31 December 1979 the reserve amounted to 140 m EUA.

All other Community funds derived from the levy and other sources are allocated to finance expenditure commitments and invested until such time as they are used for payments. At 31 December 1979 overall liquid assets amounted to 827 m EUA. During the year 1979 they produced interest totalling 36.4 m EUA.

B—Financial contributions by the Member States

As we explained just now, the Council refused to allow the ECSC to be given customs duties on steel and coal but gave consideration to this Community's financial difficulties by sanctioning the payment to it of financial contributions by the Member States. The High Authority/Commission was able to accept this because Article 49, second paragraph of the ECSC Treaty states: 'It (i.e. the High Authority) may receive gifts'.

As far as the 1978 budget was concerned, it was not until 17 October 1978 that the Council, after lengthy discussions, reached agreement on a figure of 28 m EUA, the High Authority/Commission having asked for 32 m EUA. The contributions were to be calculated according to a highly political scale based in essence on the philosophy behind the negotiations over Article 131 of the Treaty of Accession (see p. 381) and consisting of a mixture of a GNP scale, an ECSC levy scale and an ECSC customs duty scale. The percentages were: Belgium 5.50%, Denmark 2.75%, Federal Republic of Germany 33.08%, France 21.27%, Ireland 0.62%, Luxembourg 0.14%, Netherlands 6.38%, United Kingdom 17.42%.[2]

For the 1979 budget the High Authority/Commission, in the absence of permission to allocate customs duties, requested financial contributions totalling 60 m EUA. On 19 December 1978 the Council reduced this to 32 m EUA, with one delegation expressing a reservation even so. So the High Authority/Commission, on 22 December 1978, presented a budget totalling 152 m EUA (98 m EUA from the levy, 22 m EUA from miscellaneous revenue and 32 m EUA from Member States' contributions). To secure withdrawal of the reservation the Member States' contribution was cut to 28 m EUA on 9 April 1979, the same figure as in the previous year's budget and calculated according to the same scale.[2] For 1980 the High Authority/Commission adopted a budget total of 188 m EUA on 19 December 1979, consisting of 117 m EUA from the levy, 28 m EUA from miscellaneous revenue and 43 m EUA from extraordinary receipts. Thus 1980 is the third financial year for which this strange procedure of *ad hoc* financial subsidies from Member States has been followed. The contributions were reduced to 28 m EUA by a Council Decision of 18 March 1980 and the High Authority/Commission will have to revise its budget in consequence.

C—Miscellaneous revenue

The revenue side of the ECSC operational budget also contains an item for the cancellation of commitments which will probably not be implemented. These cancellations are not properly speaking part of the resources of the financial year but unused resources from an earlier financial year or years which, under the ECSC's unique budgetary system, remain available for later use. Unlike the EEC and Euratom, the ECSC can keep all the tax revenue it collects for good; it does not have to make refunds to the taxpayer.

Like unused revenue from earlier years, the item 'revaluation of assets and liabilities' is not a true resource of the financial year in question, but represents funds becoming available as a result of the drawing up of the balance sheet. There is no creating of new Community resources in these cases.

On the other hand, the item 'fines and late payment surcharges' is a genuine additional resource, though a very small one in practice.

D—The contribution to the general budget

The Commission has proposed that an exceptional, non-recurring contribution of 100 m EUA should be paid from the general budget to the ECSC operational budget in 1980 to finance exceptional measures to assist workers in the steel industry (see p. 208).

(see p. 208)

*
* *

The ECSC levy is an almost perfect Community tax. Its only fault is that the rate is too inflexible; it has been impossible to raise the rate during good years to build up a cyclical reserve which would have been invaluable just now.

Despite this, the ECSC levy has been adequate to cover the expenditure prescribed for it by the Treaty of Paris (resettlement, research and administration). On the other hand, expenditure in the form of interest subsidies, not provided for in the Treaty, has completely unbalanced the ECSC operational budget and has caused the Council to become involved in the budgetary procedure therefor.

Nevertheless—and this cannot be stressed enough—the levy remains the true guarantor of the High Authority's borrowing and lending activities. Obviously the ECSC's reserves of 411.5 m EUA are no reassurance to lenders aware that the total loans outstanding amount to 4 675 m EUA. So paradoxically the levy has hitherto fulfilled its banking role even better than it has fulfilled its budgetary task.

[1] A list of the levy rates for 1971-80 is given in Annex 8 (see p. 376). For 1952/53 to 1970 the rates are given in an article by the author entitled 'Histoire budgétaire de la CECA' (Budgetary history of the ECSC) in the *Revue du marché commun* for December 1976 (pp. 560 and 561).

The levy for 1980 was fixed by Commission Decision No 3059/79/ECSC of 19 December 1979 (OJ L 344 of 31.12.1979).

[2] Although the Council Decision of 17 October 1978 stipulated that each Member State's contribution was due on 1 December 1978, the money was not actually made available until each had gone through its own parliamentary procedures; for this reason none of the contributions was paid up on time. For eight countries the lateness ranged from a fortnight to 13 months, the payments having been made on 14, 15 and 31 December 1978, 20 January 1979, 30 March 1979, 31 July 1979, 1 August 1979 and 25 January 1980. At 1 July 1980, 19 months after the due date, one country had still not paid up.

The due date for the second contribution, approved on 9 April 1979, was 1 October 1979. For the same procedural reasons mentioned above, only one country paid its contribution on time. Seven countries were between one and four months late, payments by them having been made on 22 October 1979, 6, 20 and 28 December 1979, 2, 16 and 25 January 1980. At 1 July 1980, six months after the due date, one country (still the same one) had still not paid up.

Although Member States have always been punctual in paying their financial contributions to the general budget (see p. 377), they have been remiss in the timing of their *ad hoc* contributions to the ECSC operational budget. The explanation lies in large part in the exceptional nature of this type of financing.

Chapter VII:
The European Communities' budget revenue

For 17 years, from 1958 to 1974, the Brussels Communities (EEC and Euratom) were financed by a system of financial contributions (see Annex 9, p. 377). The scales were 'political scales', that is to say, based on agreements between States and not on objective macroeconomic data such as the respective GDPs. Since 1 January 1978, after the seven-year transition period, they have been financed entirely, in theory at least, from their own independent resources (see Annex 10, p. 379). After analysing what 'own resources' mean, we shall briefly examine the Communities' other revenue and conclude by discussing the question of new 'own resources'.

1. Own resources allocated to the European Communities by the Decision of 21 April 1970

This analysis will cover the basis of assessment, limits and compensations.

A—Basis of assessment of own resources

Under Articles 201 of the EEC Treaty and 173 of the Euratom Treaty, the Community could propose to the Member States the conditions under which their 'financial contributions' could be replaced by 'own resources'.[1] After years of hesitation, in 1970[2] the Council took action on the Commission's most recent proposal under pressure of the need to find a way of financing the agricultural policy. Its Decision of 21 April lists the own resources allocated to the Communities in order to ensure a balanced budget and lays down the rules of allocation.

Pursuant to the Decision of 21 April 1970, the resources of the European Communities derive from the following fiscal revenue:
(a) levies, premiums, additional or compensatory amounts, additional amounts or factors and other duties established or to be established by the institutions of the Communities in respect of trade with non-member countries within the framework of the common agricultural policy, and also contributions and other duties provided for within the framework of the organization of the markets in sugar. These resources are 'Community by nature' since they result from the operation of the common agricultural policy;

(b) Common Customs Tariff duties and other duties established or to be established by the institutions of the Communities in respect of trade with non-member countries. These resources are also Community by nature and in federal systems are traditionally assigned to the central government;

(c) resources accruing from value-added tax and obtained by applying a rate not exceeding 1% to an assessment basis determined in a uniform manner for Member States according to Community rules. This is basically a national fiscal revenue, but has been subjected to Community harmonization measures;

(d) revenue accruing from other charges introduced within the framework of a common policy in accordance with the provisions of the Treaties establishing the EEC and Euratom.

While agricultural levies were made over to the European Communities from the outset, Common Customs Tariff revenue was only assigned gradually, on the basis of a special system (see Annex 10, p. 379).

VAT has been collected only since 1 January 1979. In fact there are two different types of own resources: traditional own resources (customs duties and agricultural levies) and VAT. The former are inherent to the Community and untouchable, as recognized by the financial mechanism of which we will speak later (see p. 124). The VAT percentage, however, is less sacred.

Agricultural levies—These are variable levies imposed on imports of agricultural products subject to the common organization of markets (COM) originating in third countries, in order to compensate for the difference between world prices and the level of Community prices. The establishment of these levies is one of the basic characteristics of the common agricultural policy, namely the Community preference system.

Apart from these levies, the common agricultural policy derives its revenue from *contributions and other duties levied within the framework of the common organization of the market in the sectors of sugar and isoglucose.* The common organization of the market in sugar lays down that sugar undertakings must pay production levies to cover expenditure on support of the market.[3] Moreover, in order to ensure regular sugar sales throughout the marketing years, a system has been introduced to equalize storage costs; the financial balance is ensured, in accounting terms, by trade contributions called 'storage levies', which are entered in full in the Community budget.

Lastly, the levy on isoglucose production is to be treated in the same way as the sugar production levy and therefore forms a Community own resource within the meaning of the Council Decision of 21 April 1970.[4]

Agricultural levies were thus introduced at the same time as the common agricultural policy. On 1 July 1967 they were taken into account in calculating the Member States' contributions (Regulation No 130/66/EEC, Article 11), but it is only since the 1971 budget that they have become own resources made over to the European Communities (see Annex 10, p. 383).

Customs duties—Revenue from customs duties derives from applying the Common Customs Tariff to the customs valuation of imported goods. Their allocation to the financing of common expenditure—a possibility merely provided for in Article 201 of the Treaty of Rome—is nevertheless a logical result of the free movement of goods in the EEC. Indeed, it would be inconceivable for some Member States, better endowed with large maritime ports, to collect for their own national budgets customs duties pertaining to goods which can move freely within the Community (see Annex 10, p. 385).

Value-added tax (VAT)—With the adoption of the Sixth Council Directive of 17 May 1977, VAT became the first harmonized tax system in the Community of Nine, and implementation of the Directive made it possible to assign this resource to the Community budget.[5] This Directive was due to enter into force on 1 January 1978, but since only one Member State (Belgium) observed the deadline, an amending budget had to be drawn up reintroducing financial contributions based on GDP. VAT became a genuine own resource in 1979, although not all Member States applied the Sixth Directive.[6] The two implementing regulations are Council Regulations Nos 2891/77 and 2892/77 of 19 December 1977.[7] In fact, VAT only looks like an own resource, for three reasons. First, the rate the Community can collect—a maximum of 1%—under the harmonized common basis of assessment is not added to the rate(s) fixed nationally. In a sense each Member State 'deducts' it from its national VAT revenue and then reassigns it to the Community.[8] Secondly, alternative rules exist for determining the collection of revenue for a transitional period of five years. A State may choose either the returns method, i.e. the 'base on base' method, which is the only way of assessing VAT exactly but involves certain administrative (and psychological) constraints, or the revenue method which is in fact a statistical method. The choice was left to the Member States because the Council found it impossible to adopt the first and only solution proposed by the Commission. In practice, only two countries chose the first method (Denmark and Ireland), the remainder the second, which accentuates the financial contribution character of VAT levies. VAT contributions are paid each month in twelfths of the budget estimates adopted for the current financial year, which is further confirmation of the predetermined nature of these payments which bear no relation to day-to-day economic reality, unlike agricultural levies and customs duties. On the other hand, it should be noted that the VAT percentage made over to the Community is an own resource in the sense that the Member States pay it to the Community each month automatically and it is therefore no longer available to them. True, the VAT percentage helps balance the revenue side of the budget of the Communities, as Member States' financial contributions had done, but unlike these, it is paid regularly in twelfths and not as and when needed for Community financing.

A further criticism one could make of VAT as an own resource is its 'regressive effect', i.e. that it sometimes imposes a heavier burden than financial contributions based on GDP. With regard to the budget for 1979 (OJ L 41 of 18.2.1980) the regressive effect, indicated by a plus sign, was as follows: Ireland (+30.79%), United Kingdom (+11.13%), Federal Republic of Germany (+2.32%), Netherlands (+1.93%), Luxembourg (−1%), Belgium (−1.14%), France (−1.18%), Denmark (−7.21%) and Italy (−18.12%). The percentages show that there is a regressive effect in four Member States, a more or less neutral one in three (Belgium, France and Luxembourg) and a positive one in two. In the country where the progressive effect is most obvious, Italy, the calculations must be interpreted in the light of major tax evasions, since the VAT assessment basis is greater *de facto* than *de jure*. In the case of the Federal Republic of Germany, the regressive effect cannot be explained and will no doubt be corrected when the Community has the correct statistics before it. The regressive effect is most marked in the least-rich countries (Ireland—in a way which calls for analysis—and the United Kingdom). There the effect is due mainly to the following three factors:
(1) the VAT assessment basis is relatively higher than the GDP, since the share of investment—which is not subject to VAT—is smaller;
(2) imports are higher than exports; VAT is charged on imports but not on exports;
(3) public expenditure is relatively lower than in other countries; often VAT is not charged on this expenditure (no doubt this third factor has only a limited effect).

121

B—Limits imposed on own resources

The Treaty and the Decision of 21 April 1970 lay down certain limits to the increase in Community resources.

Maximum level—The Decision of 21 April 1970 sets a ceiling on the Community's resources, since these are drawn from two specific sources: agricultural levies, sugar levies and customs duties on the one hand, and a maximum of 1% of the uniform VAT assessment basis on the other.

Thus in 1980 the maximum resources available to the Community could have been:

Agricultural levies	1 719.2 m EUA
Sugar levies	504.5 m EUA
Customs duties	5 667.8 m EUA
1% VAT	9 910.0 m EUA

17 801.5 m EUA

In its proposal for the strengthening of Parliament's budgetary powers of 10 October 1973, the Commission did in fact propose to set up a purely 'Community' procedure for creating new own resources (see p. 8). But for the present, the procedure is national; Article 201 of the EEC Treaty remains unamended and paragraph 9 thereof still stipulates that the Council may lay down the appropriate provisions on own resources but that these provisions must be adopted by the Member States in accordance with their respective constitutional requirements, thus bestowing on the decision the status of a treaty.

Temporal limits—Besides this maximum limit, the EEC Treaty provides for a further limit to be calculated year by year. Article 203(8) of the Treaty lays down that non-compulsory expenditure (see p. 40), i.e. expenditure not resulting from the Treaties or secondary legislation, must be restricted each year to a maximum rate of increase. That rate is 'established' by the Council, after consulting the Economic Policy Committee, and then notified to all the institutions before 1 May.

To enable it to draw up the budget for the 1975 financial year according to the new provisions of the Treaty of 21 April 1970, the Commission worked out a method in 1974 of determining the maximum rate of increase of non-compulsory expenditure based on three factors specified by the Treaties and matched the appropriate macroeconomic indicator to each of them, as follows:
- (a) 'the trend, in terms of volume, of the gross national product within the Community', to be calculated according to the indicator of GNP in terms of volume, subsequently converted to value terms;
- (b) 'the average variation in the budgets of the Member States', to be calculated from central government expenditure, an indicator in value terms;
- (c) 'the trend of the cost of living', as measured by an indicator converting GNP in terms of volume to GNP by value; this is, of necessity, the GNP deflator and not that of private consumption since the latter represents only a part of GNP.

In order that the three indicators should refer to the same period and be mutually consistent, they had to relate to the same year in all cases. In view of the specific wording of the Treaty and the fact that the rate had to be objectively determined, the most suitable year to choose was the financial year n−2, since for this year it was possible to have firm estimates rather than forecasts. So for the 1975 budget, the reference year was 1973 and the calculations were as follows: trend of GNP by volume: 5.7%; average variation in Member States' budgets: 15.4%; trend of GNP deflator: 7.7%. These three factors give a bracket of 15.4% (central government expenditure) to 13.8% (105.7 × 107.7; GNP by value) and thus an average increase of 14.6% (15.4 + 13.8 ÷ 2), which was duly adopted as the maximum established rate. For the 1976 budget, the rate was 15.3%; for 1977, 17.3%; for 1978, 13.6%; for 1979, 11.4%; and for 1980, 13.3%.

Apart from being highly complicated, this system of a maximum rate of increase for non-compulsory expenditure is a major obstacle to growth of the Community budget, since it subjects it to the growth limits imposed on the Member States' own budgets two years previously. The system does not therefore take any account of the Communities' main problem, which derives both from the constraints of their limited budget (with its extremely limited scope for transferring appropriations between major budget categories) and from the new or expanding character of much of the expenditure, which may call for considerable increases in budgetary resources in some years. It must be noted, however, that Article 203(9) of the EEC Treaty provides for exceptions to the system of a maximum rate of increase, since it states that 'another rate' may be fixed by decision of the Council and Parliament, 'where the activities of the Communities so require'. This most fortunate provision has been used for every budget since that of 1975, whether at the time of adoption of the initial budget or for supplementary budgets.[9] The maximum rate may under certain conditions also be exceeded without this requiring the adoption of a new rate (see p. 44).

At any rate, the two-year time-lag between the indicators used for the calculation and the financial year in question can mean that the Community budget develops in a way ill-suited to the current trend of Member States' budgetary policies and gives rise to unproductive disputes.

C—Compensations under the own resources system

Hitherto, the own resources system has always been regarded as a Community right which cannot be encroached upon. Besides the traditional measures laid down in the 1972 Act of Accession, three types of compensation have, however, been invented to deal with unacceptable situations arising from full application of the system. They are the financial mechanism, the transitional measures adopted with a view to the accession of Greece, and financial compensation for non-participation in the EMS. All these provisions are designed to comply with Community principles, and at the same time ensure that they are maintained without dispute. Whilst they therefore comply with the spirit of the Community, they do have a serious drawback in that they do not make the use of 'recovered funds' subject to the objectives laid down by the Community. These funds become anonymous receipts, at the discretion of national governments.

Transitional measures laid down at the time of the first enlargement

The special provisions adopted for the three States which joined the European Communities in 1973 did not depart from this system since it did not exist at the time. They were designed to ensure parallelism between the founding States and the acceding States in this very sensitive area (see Annex 10, p. 380). On 1 January 1978, the system of own resources was therefore applied fully both to the six founding States and to the three new Member States.

As for the provisions of Article 131 of the Act of Accession of 22 January 1972 for the years 1978 and 1979, they only had an impact outside the Community budget, which means that the amounts involved did not affect the Community accounts—this is rather difficult to understand—although they appear in the revenue and expenditure account as a point of information.

The financial mechanism

On 4 June 1974, speaking before the Council, Mr Wilson described the system of own resources as unfair and called for an equitable balance between revenue and expenditure. On the same day, the Council asked the Commission to look into the situation. The Commission accordingly produced an 'Inventory of the Community's economic and financial situation', and a 'Survey of future developments'[10] which it forwarded to the Council on 27 October 1974. It found that the distribution of Member States' contributions to Community expenditure could indeed produce problems in future. At the Paris Summit on 10 December 1974, the Heads of State or Government accepted in principle the British request. The Council and the Commission were therefore invited 'to set up as soon as possible a correcting mechanism of a general application which . . . could prevent during the period of convergence of the economies of the Member States the possible development of situations unacceptable for a Member State and incompatible with the smooth working of the Community' (see Annex 3, p. 351). After this, events moved swiftly. On 30 January 1975 the Commission completed its proposal. On 11 March 1975, the 'European Council', meeting in Dublin, agreed on the correcting mechanism (see Annex 3, p. 352) and Mr Wilson declared the renegotiation over. On 18 March 1975 he announced to the House of Commons that his government would recommend a 'yes' vote for the forthcoming referendum on whether the United Kingdom should remain in the Community. The regulation setting up the mechanism, henceforth known as the 'financial mechanism', was adopted on 17 May 1976 (Regulation (EEC) 1172/76), pursuant to Article 235 of the EEC Treaty, for a trial period of seven years.

Operation of the financial mechanism

The financial mechanism is triggered off when an unacceptable situation arises in a Member State. This involves a particular combination of readings from an indicator of national wealth (*per capita* GNP falling below 85% of the Community mean) and an indicator of economic progress (real rate of growth of GNP falling below 120% of the Community mean). This unacceptable economic situation must be accompanied by a disproportionate contribution to Community financing—that is to say, too high a contribution to Community revenue in the sense of a share of more than 110% of the amount needed to bring the Member State's contribution into line with its share in Community GNP.

Where it is found that a Member State has contributed too much, the amount to be repaid is calculated on the basis of a progressive system of stages so that the payment increases in step with the percentage of the State's GNP represented by the excess payment.[11] However, the payment may not exceed the lowest of the amounts below:

(1) the amount of the deficit balance for the Member State concerned between its transfers of funds to the Community budget and the transfers received from that budget. If a Member State has an excess balance this mechanism becomes inapplicable. The balance is established irrespective of payments made in application of this mechanism. The payments received by a Member State include, however, payments to it by other Member States in the form of monetary compensatory amounts;

(2) the amount of payment by the Member State to the budget of the current financial year in the form of VAT or on the basis of GNP.

The total payment (or payments if several Member States are eligible) may not exceed the higher of the following amounts: 250 m EUA or 3% of expenditure chargeable to the current financial year. If the total payments exceed this limit, they are reduced to the proportional limit for each Member State.

However, where the balance of current payments of the Member State (average balance of payments over the three years preceding the current financial year, at current market exchange rates) is positive, the overall payments by that Member State are not taken into account (total of customs duties, agricultural levies and VAT resources or GNP contributions), but only the VAT or GNP payments. So the condition for this payment is that these latter payments must exceed 10% of the amount which the Member State would have had to pay (to finance expenditure not covered by customs duties and agricultural levies) on the basis of the proportion of its GNP to the total GNP of the Nine, the figures being estimates for the current financial year.

At the request of an interested Member State, a part payment of 75% of the provisional amount of the total payment can be paid at the beginning of the following year. The Commission then calculates the final amount on the basis of the final figures.

Why the financial mechanism was not used

The financial mechanism was a very complex system which could work in favour of any Member State. The first deadline for application was 30 June 1976. Not one State applied in 1976, 1977, 1978 or 1979.[11] Yet for those financial years a budget heading was provided for the purpose in Title 4 (Miscellaneous repayments and aid to Member States).

Why was this mechanism not used? Three conditions had to be satisfied.

The first was that *per capita* GNP in the Member State had to be below 85% of average *per capita* GNP in the Community. The three poorest Community States satisfied this condition in 1976, 1977 and 1978: Ireland (51, 49 and 48%), Italy (64, 63 and 62%), and the United Kingdom (77, 75 and 73%).

The second condition was that the rate of growth by volume of *per capita* GNP in the Member State must not exceed 120% of the average rate in the Community. In a sense this reflected the non-convergence between Member States. Of the Member States mentioned above, two satisfied this condition in 1976, 1977 and 1978: the United Kingdom (44.2 and 51%) and Ireland (55, 48 and 99%) while Italy remained apart with very high rates (278, 234 and 171%). These first two conditions must be established by means of indicators calculated on the basis of the three years preceding the current financial year, while the third condition we are about to examine relates to the current financial year, i.e. to estimates.

The third condition was that a Member State's contribution to the Community budget must exceed by more than 10% the amount it would have had to pay if the contribution had been based on the share of its GNP in the Community GNP. It was difficult for the United Kingdom or Ireland to satisfy that condition because of the terms of the Act of Accession which limited the payments by new Member States until 1977 and even up to and including 1979 (see Annex 10, p. 380).

Yet on 4 May 1979, for the first time, a government, the British Government, called for application of the mechanism.[11] The Commission, having accepted the soundness of the request since the above three conditions had been satisfied, entered an amount of 68 m EUA in its preliminary draft budget. But some months later, on 11 September 1979, when the 1980 draft budget was adopted, the British Government withdrew its request, which led to removal of this appropriation. In the initial calculations, the conversion rate adopted for the pound sterling had been that of 1 February 1978, used for the 1979 budget (i.e. 1 EUA = UKL 0.629926). With the revaluation to 1 EUA = UKL 0.644686, the value of the parameters changed and the United Kingdom's total contributions no longer exceeded by more than 10% the payments it would have had to make on the basis of its GNP.

Italy did not satisfy this condition either although it came close in 1978: −14.42% in 1976, −23.03% in 1977 and + 9.97% in 1978.

Review of the financial mechanism

In summer 1979 the United Kingdom protested again that it had become a net payer in 1978. Mrs Thatcher called for a review of the current budgetary system in order to produce a 'broad balance' between her country's payments into the Community budget and the expenditure which such payments are used to finance or in order at least to secure that her country had to bear no more than an equitable burden, as the British Chancellor of the Exchequer put it at one Council meeting. At the European Council in Strasbourg on 21 and 22 June 1979, the situation was reviewed and the Commission was asked to undertake studies and produce proposals (see Annex 3, p. 356). The European Council in Dublin, in November 1979, and then in Luxembourg, in April 1980 could not agree on a solution to what has been called the 'British problem'.

In fact, it was not the reform of the financial mechanism as such which was the problem, because a certain consensus already existed among the Nine as to the fact that the Regulation of 17 May 1976 needed amendment on three points: abolition of the limit based on balances of payments, abolition of the system of reimbursement in stages and abolition of the ceiling of 3% of the budget total.

Finally, in the Brussels Compromise of 30 May 1980 the Council was able to find a way out of the crisis which had been afflicting the Community for over a year with a solution to the British problem which at the same time made it possible to fix farm prices for 1980/81 and consequently to adopt a draft budget on 20 June 1979.

In its proposed amendment submitted on 11 June 1980, the Commission confined itself to proposing the three 'amendments' just mentioned and making a few technical adjustments such as the use of GDP instead of GNP.

The Council's agreement has already laid down the amounts of the repayments (see footnote 7 on p. 340). The modified financial mechanism would authorize—instead of 187 m EUA—a gross payment of 469 m EUA, i.e. barely one-third of the sums repaid, the other two-thirds being used to finance specific items called 'supplementary measures' (see p. 222).

Transitional measures adopted for the accession of Greece

These measures were laid down in Articles 124 to 127 of the Act of Accession for Greece signed in Athens on 28 May 1979. After noting that the Decision of 21 April 1970 is applicable from 1 January 1981, these articles provide that the Community will refund to Greece every month a proportion of its VAT contributions (or financial contributions based on its GNP) as follows: 70% in 1981, 50% in 1982, 30% in 1983, 20% in 1984 and 10% in 1985. The degressive feature of these arrangements takes its inspiration from Article 131 of the 1972 Accession Treaty, although it differs therefrom in that all Community own resources are paid over—which was not the case with the first enlargement—and a part is later refunded, without any conditions being attached to how they are used. In this respect, the transitional measures in the Greek proposal are similar to those in the financial mechanism.

The financial provisions of the Act of Accession provide for a transitional period during which, under special rules, the customs duties levied in Greece will be paid over up to the limits of the customs duties that survive after the transitional period in accordance with full application of the Common Customs Tariff. Agricultural levies will be paid in full from 1 January 1981.

Financial compensation for non-participation in the European Monetary System

At its meeting in Brussels on 4 and 5 December 1978, the European Council (see Annex 3, p. 354) provided for interest rebates on loans granted to the less-prosperous Member States which effectively and fully participated in the European Monetary System. It was also agreed that Member States which did not take part in this system would not contribute to its financing. Since it was decided that these interest rebates would be included in the budget, appropriations relating to interest rebates introduced by the Council Regulation of 3 August 1979 would be financed from own resources pursuant to the Council Decision of 21 April 1970. Since the United Kingdom does not take part in the European Monetary System, it receives a financial compensation which is entered as expenditure under Title 5 of the Commission budget. As and when appropriations for interest rebates are used, the Commission pays the United Kingdom financial compensation at quarterly intervals. This compensation is calculated on the basis of the United Kingdom's share in financing the budget by VAT contributions, since all marginal expenditure is financed out of VAT revenue.

D—Revenue from own resources

Annex 10 (p. 379) analyses the progressive application of the system of own resources made over to the European Communities from 1971 to 1980 inclusive. Since 1978, the Communities have applied the own resources system in full.

In 1980, the three traditional sources of Community funds in the budget as voted provided budget revenue amounting to 7 891.5 m EUA, as follows: customs duties 5 667.8 m EUA, agricultural levies 1 719.2 m EUA, and sugar levies 504.5 m EUA. The new source of Community funds, VAT, should bring in 7 151 m EUA (with a rate of 0.7216%). The Community's own resources therefore account for 98.8% of the total figure of 15 683 m EUA, 50.3% coming from traditional resources and 48.5% from VAT, disregarding the surplus available from the financial year 1979, which was 458.6 m EUA and would diminish the amount to be called for from the VAT source accordingly.

It must be made quite clear here that in budgetary terms the agricultural levies and customs duties have a major drawback, since they are not designed as fiscal revenue nor are they administered to serve this end. Customs duties are designed to protect the market. Their amount is fixed at international meetings—especially in GATT—which do not take the Community's financing problems into account. There can even be conflicts between the Community's commercial policy and its financial policy. The same applies to agricultural levies which are introduced to safeguard the 'Community preference' and depend mainly on world prices. So almost half the Community's financial resources are not determined for reasons of profitability, which is surely a risky situation. Moreover, VAT has two serious drawbacks: firstly, it grows less quickly than GDP; secondly it allows tax evasion, which in some countries reaches considerable proportions.

Annex 10 (p. 387) shows the divergences between estimates and actual payments of traditional own resources. They are often considerable in the case of agricultural levies and sugar levies, but less so for customs duties. In all, the divergences for 1971 to 1979 inclusive came to 5% more or less, except in 1977 (+10%). Clearly the Community has no experience as regards VAT. Divergences were observed in 1980 for the financial year 1979. This prospect is not surprising, however, although it is disquieting since VAT represents more than half of the budget resources.

Annex 10 also shows the annual distribution of payments broken down by Member State from 1971 to 1980 for each of the three traditional own resources. The table below shows the percentage distribution for 1979 and 1980.

Financing of the general budget in 1979 (resources collected) and in 1980 (estimated resources)

	Agricultural levies		Customs duties		VAT		Total		GDP (estimates)	
	1979	1980	1979	1980	1979[1]	1980	1979[2]	1980	1979	1980
Belgium	12.2	10.4	6.5	6.5	4.7	4.5	6.7	6.1	4.6	4.4
Denmark	1.4	1.6	2.4	2.4	2.6	2.6	2.3	2.4	2.8	2.5
Federal Republic of Germany	19.1	19.4	30.6	30.2	31.9	32.8	30.7	29.8	31.7	30.5
France	11.6	12.9	14.5	14.6	24.4	24.7	20.1	19.1	23.9	24.1
Ireland	0.4	0.4	1.1	1.1	0.6	0.9	0.7	0.9	0.6	0.6
Italy	21.3	21.0	9.6	9.7	10.6	10.9	12.5	12.0	13.5	14.0
Luxembourg	.	.	0.1	0.1	0.2	0.2	0.1	0.1	0.2	0.2
Netherlands	16.4	14.7	9.4	9.5	6.4	6.1	9.4	8.6	6.3	6.0
United Kingdom	17.7	19.6	25.9	26.0	18.5	17.4	17.5	20.9	16.4	17.8
%	100	100	100	100	100	100	100	100	100	100
% of own resources	14.9	14.8	36.1	37.7	49.0	47.5	100	100		
In m EUA in 1979	2 143.5		5 189.1		7 039.8		14 372.4			
In m EUA in 1980	2 223.7		5 667.8		7 151.0		15 042.5			

[1] Financial contributions for the Federal Republic of Germany, Ireland and Luxembourg.
[2] Taking account of the implementation of Article 131 of the Treaty of Accession (see p. 381), i.e. an adjustment between States.

On the basis of this table, one can try to define the structure of the Community's own resources, i.e. the revenue structure of the 'budgetary system' of the Community, to adopt the expression used by the European Council on 22 June 1979.

Customs duties are the most important of the two traditional elements of the own resources, since they amount to more than twice the agricultural levies. The two main importing countries (Federal Republic of Germany and the United Kingdom) collect 56.2% of the total customs duties. Some countries are large importers for structural reasons, such as the United Kingdom and the three Benelux countries. For example, the Netherlands collects as much in customs duties as Italy. Taking the simplest indicator of national wealth, GDP, one can see that the percentages of customs duties collected by the United Kingdom, Benelux and Ireland are far higher than their respective percentage of the Community's GDP. The reverse applies to France and Italy, while the percentages for the Federal Republic of Germany and Denmark are more or less the same.

It is not so easy to analyse the *agricultural levies,* although basically they are similar to customs duties. No importing State stands out by the volume of its transactions, although it is interesting to note that Italy, the United Kingdom and the Federal Republic of Germany record the same level of transactions. Comparing their percentage of GDP and their percentage of contributions from agricultural levies in the Community, we find that the three Benelux countries diverge widely; Italy remains a major collector of agricultural levies; while Denmark, the Federal Republic of Germany and in particular France are very little involved here. The United Kingdom and Ireland have comparable percentages.

It is certainly interesting to analyse these different percentages, but one must remember that the amounts collected are not necessarily finally paid by the consumers of the Member State in which the levies are imposed. The most widely quoted example is the port of Rotterdam, where substantial customs duties are imposed on goods very often consumed outside the Netherlands. The conclusion to be drawn from this is that payments by one State do not necessarily reflect the real financial burden it bears as regards traditional own resources.

VAT payments, calculated from a harmonized assessment basis, give results that deserve some explanation (see p. 128) if one compares these percentages with the Member States' shares of Community GDP.

In overall terms, if one adds up the percentage values of these various payments, one finds that in the present situation of the 'budgetary system', i.e. before the exhaustion of own resources and the full use of VAT resources, the system introduced by the Decision of 21 April 1970 has had a 'regressive effect' for Belgium and the Netherlands and to some extent also for the United Kingdom and Ireland, a 'progressive effect' for Italy, France, Denmark and Luxembourg, and a virtually nil effect for the Federal Republic of Germany.

It should be noted, however, that in 1980, with the ending of the special system set up pursuant to Article 131 of the Accession Treaty (see p. 380) for the three new Member States, some effects are becoming accentuated. For example, the regressive effect will intensify for the United Kingdom and Ireland and weaken for Belgium and the Netherlands. The progressive effect will diminish in the case of Denmark and increase in that of the Federal Republic of Germany, Luxembourg, France and Italy. For the last two States, however, the progressive effect should be roughly similar to what it was in 1979, if one disregards the influence of Article 131 of the 1972 Accession Treaty. In times of trouble such as we are now experiencing, the structure of Community revenue may therefore give rise to tensions. This structure is developing only slowly, faced with a structure of expenditure which is rather more mobile.

This state of affairs provoked violent reactions by the United Kingdom which, referring back to the 'reference paper' drafted by the Commission on 12 September 1979, pointed out that in 1980 it would have to finance a 20.5% share of the budget, which would cost it 650 m EUA more than it would have had to pay if the budget had been financed according to a system of contributions based on GDP; on the basis of the 1980 budget, as at July 1980, the amount will be 593 m EUA. Even if these figures are correct, they must still be examined in the light of two considerations. First of all it is likely, or at least to be hoped, that the United Kingdom's imports from other Community countries will increase in future. In this connection, it should be mentioned that since its accession to the Community, the United Kingdom's imports from the Community have risen by 10% in relation to its overall imports. Its partners are therefore calling on it to accelerate this transfer, which would proportionately reduce the customs duties and agricultural levies it collects from non-Community imports and as a result of which it contributes to the general budget more heavily than other countries under this heading. The second consideration is that the United Kingdom's share of VAT is fairly close to its GDP share and therefore, the more it resorts to VAT to finance the budget, the closer its share of financing will approach its share of the Community GDP. A proposed solution to the British problem was discussed earlier (see p. 126).

Lastly, it should be stressed that in 1980 two-thirds of the Community's financial resources will be paid by three countries: the Federal Republic of Germany (29.8%), the United Kingdom (20.9%) and France (19.1%), but that if one considers only VAT payments—which for the time being are the only ones to produce any financial dynamism in the Community—the Federal Republic of Germany (32.8%) and France (24.7%) alone would account for more than half the contributions (57.5%), or, with the United Kingdom (17.4%), three-quarters (75.9%). So the Community's financial future depends largely on the attitude the governments of these three countries will take.

2. The other revenue of the European Communities

The European Communities have other revenue in addition to own resources:
(1) the share of the proceeds of the ECSC levies paid pursuant to Article 20 of the Merger Treaty of 8 April 1965, which is a flat-rate payment to cover the ECSC's administrative expenditure; this amount, which used to be 18 m EUA, was reduced to 5 m EUA in 1978 (see p. 114);
(2) the proceeds of the tax on staff salaries and staff contributions to their pension scheme; in 1980 this came to 121.9 m EUA;
(3) the Member States' financial contributions to balance the budget (these were financial contributions in the strict sense of the term until 1974, GNP-based contributions from 1974 to 1979 inclusive);
(4) Member States' financial contributions for their participation in 'complementary' research programmes (see p. 261); this involved two contributions in 1980: 6.4 m EUA by the Federal Republic of Germany and 6.4 m EUA by the Netherlands;
(5) any surplus left over from the preceding financial year; in 1980, 458 m EUA was entered as surplus revenue over expenditure for the financial year 1979;
(6) miscellaneous receipts (bank interests, sale of furniture, sale of publications, reimbursements from other institutions, and so on), which came to 42.2 m EUA in 1980. In fact,

this last category is a complete miscellany, for it can include, for instance, reimbursements of aid to support Community projects in the hydrocarbon sector (see p. 254), a point which is of great interest in doctrinal terms; moreover, in some years substantial exchange-rate gains were entered under this heading when the unit of account was the IMF parity unit of account.

3. Ideas for new own resources for the EEC and Euratom

The problem of financing the budget on the basis of the system provided for in the Decision of 21 April 1970 is a medium-term one, since the available margin is liable to be exhausted at the beginning of the 1980s. This was one of the considerations stressed by the Commission in its Communication of 27 February 1978 to the Joint Council of Foreign and Finance Ministers and to the European Parliament. On the following 15 June the Commission stated in its three-yearly financial estimates for 1979-1980-1981 that there was a real possibility that the 1% VAT ceiling would be exceeded in 1981.

A—Justification of the need for new own resources

The Commission based these statements on the following evidence and forecasts: First, it drew up its estimates on the basis of a forecast for the following three years (1979-81) which showed that in 1981, depending on how effectively the trend of agricultural expenditure was controlled, the VAT percentage would be between 0.99% and 1.12%, with a Community GDP growth rate of 3.5%. Second, in the longer term, the Commission found that inclusion of the EDF in the budget and the enlargement of the Community would inevitably lead to an increase in Community expenditure. Moreover, since the Commission was in favour of an increased transfer of expenditure from the national level to the Community level and of progress towards economic and monetary union, it had to call for new own resources to be assigned to the Community.

In 1979, both at the Joint Council of Foreign and Finance Ministers in April and at the November European Council, the Commission intensified its warnings.

B—The possible solutions

On 21 November 1978 the Commission forwarded a reference document to the Council and Parliament entitled 'Financing the Community budget: the way ahead'.[12] In this 'green paper', the Commission proposed no solutions but merely listed possibilities. This leads us to make some comments on the matter.

Comments on the possible solutions

The question that arises for the Community institutions, and especially the Commission because of its right of initiative, is just what these new financial resources could be. The first answer that springs to mind is certainly to increase the Community share of VAT, since its assessment basis is harmonized and its practical implementation familiar. However, as we explained earlier (see p. 121), the system of VAT allocations is still very similar to the system of Member States' financial contributions towards financing the Community. Now, politically it is most important that a new own resources should look like a genuine tax collected in full or in part for the benefit of the Community, in order to highlight the responsibility of the Budgetary Executive and the Budgetary Authority, and to make public opinion more aware of the problems involved in European union.

If, temporarily at least, we must dismiss the VAT solution, what criteria must a new own resource satisfy? We know it must be a Community resource, collected on a Community-wide basis. In our view, the second requisite feature is that it must not require the organization of a major and complex tax administration system. So it must be a tax that is already levied, or a new tax that could be levied by the existing national tax administrations, or, preferably, by the Commission without the need for any substantial increase in staff. In this respect, we may repeat that the system set up for the ECSC levies seems exemplary (see p. 111) in its simplicity and efficiency, although it is true that there are only 433 payers involved.

The third criterion should be that the assessment basis of this tax must be harmonized, and be so by a simple and rapid procedure. It is most advisable to avoid the lengthy and difficult discussions which preceded the adoption of the Sixth VAT Directive and its implementing rules. There must be no mixing of the two systems: a tax harmonization system introduced for purposes of economic integration and a supplementary tax resources system required for budgetary reasons.

The fourth and last criterion is purely financial and would involve seeking a tax with a very wide basis of assessment so that, as appropriate, it could guarantee high receipts which, moreover, would have to increase in real terms at least as fast as the economic growth of the Community.

Combining these four criteria would be rather like trying to square the circle. So we must briefly consider the yields from the various possible taxes. It should be pointed out that customs duties and agricultural levies represent about 0.43% of the Community GDP and 1 percentage point of VAT 0.50%, which places the Community's financial autonomy at less than 1% of its GDP. Moreover, a 1% tax on *per capita* taxable income, for example, would account for 0.75% of GDP and the total of company taxation[13] as currently levied by the nine Member States would represent 1.65% (it would be difficult and indeed risky to harmonize the latter two taxes); a tax of 3 EUA per tonne of oil equivalent on total energy consumption would represent 0.23% of Community GDP (this tax has not yet been introduced). For the sake of illustration, we may point out that although it does not seem advisable to tamper with the Finance Ministers' 'pocket money' receipts, the sum of the product of tobacco taxes would represent 0.82% of GDP. The conclusion to be drawn from these few figures is that not just one but several taxes would have to be transferred in part or even in full to the Community in order to obtain the required Community GDP percentage, i.e. 5 to 7%, for the Community's general budget, a percentage which some consider the realistic threshold for any federal system (see p. 335). Here necessity is linked to appropriateness. For it would seem more consistent and more feasible for the Community to have a range of possible taxes at its disposal so that it could vary the taxes collected in line with the economic or political situation. As for the idea of creating tax receipts payable to the Community, for the time being at least it must be dismissed since it would be dangerous at this stage to question the gross budget principle. The Community has not yet become sufficiently mature to tolerate that kind of dismembering of its finances.

There is, in addition, a matter which runs alongside the question of new own resources, i.e. the transfer of resources between Member States of the Community, with the payment of tax receipts undoubtedly one of the two methods of achieving it. But if it is possible to make the rich pay out, it is also possible to help the less rich. If a policy of transfers were systematized, one could envisage a system of progressive payments on the basis of the capacity of each Member State, or a general system of expenditure quotas in favour of the less prosperous.

The technique of quotas is familiar to Community public finance, but that of progressive payments is unknown and must be approached very circumspectly. Suffice it to say that with a coefficient of average progressivity, the percentage of financing imposed on the Netherlands, for instance, could be higher than for Italy.

How the Commission's comments were received

At the Joint Council of Foreign and Finance Ministers held in Luxembourg on 2 April 1979, a clear trend emerged in favour of increasing the VAT percentage if it became necessary to assign new own resources to the Community, a need contested by several Member States. Subsequently, the opposition increased, as shown on various occasions which were, in their time, considered very significant: negative vote in the Bundestag on 27 June 1979,[14] rejection at the Franco-German Summit in Bonn on 2 October 1979 and rejection at the Council of Finance Ministers on 11 February 1980.[15]

The European Parliament did not concern itself seriously with this question until the end of December 1979, when a subcommittee on own resources, created by the Committee on Budgets on 28 November 1979, started work on behalf of that committee. The subcommittee delivered its report on 5 May 1980.

$$*\atop{*\,*}$$

The system of own resources is both threatened by the adjustments to it to accommodate United Kingdom and Greek interests and enhanced by the growing need for it to be developed; the creation of new own resources has now become one of the major issues of the financing of Europe. There is every reason to believe that it will be essential to increase own resources in the near future, otherwise the Community will inevitably stagnate.

For the Commission, it has become an absolutely vital question. At its first budgetary debate on 20 July 1979, the newly-elected Parliament expressed the same concern. Mrs Simone Veil herself, in her inaugural speech the previous day, declared: 'The first task on the programme of this Parliament will be to take the first reading of the preliminary draft budget for 1980, which we are to examine very shortly.

In a more general appraisal of the exercise of the budgetary powers of the directly-elected Parliament, it seems to me that one point deserves emphasis. A responsible Parliament should not confine itself, when drawing up the budget, to the adoption of a given volume of expenditure, but must also examine the collection of revenue. This is perfectly consistent with the democratic calling of this Parliament. History teaches us that the world's first parliaments stemmed from the authorization to levy taxes.

The urgency of this consideration is heightened by the fact that, during the life of this Parliament, the European Community budget will reach the ceiling of 1% of VAT revenue laid down in the Treaties, for the collection of own resources. In the years to come, the problem of revenue must thus remain in the forefront of our minds, and this Parliament, representing as it does all the citizens and thus all the taxpayers of the Community, will necessarily be called upon to make a leading contribution to the solution of this problem.'

Basically this matter is perhaps the most delicate of all those affecting the financing of Europe. It has a symbolic significance, involving as it does the transfer of powers and resources from the States to the Community—a transfer to which everyone is highly sensitive.[16]

Footnotes to Chapter VII

[1] Article 201 of the EEC Treaty reads as follows: 'The Commission shall examine the conditions under which the financial contributions of Member States provided for in Article 200 could be replaced by the Community's own resources, in particular by revenue accruing from the Common Customs Tariff when it has been finally introduced. To this end, the Commission shall submit proposals to the Council. After consulting the Assembly on these proposals the Council may, acting unanimously, lay down the appropriate provisions, which it shall recommend to the Member States for adoption in accordance with their respective constitutional requirements.'
The first two paragraphs of Article 173 of the Euratom Treaty read as follows, the third being the same as that of Article 201 of the EEC Treaty: 'The financial contributions of Member States provided for in Article 172 may be replaced in whole or in part by the proceeds of levies collected by the Community in Member States.
To this end, the Commission shall submit to the Council proposals concerning the assessment of such levies, the method of fixing their rate and the procedure for their collection.'

[2] At the Hague Summit in December 1969 (see Annex 3, p. 350), the Heads of State or Government gave a new impetus to solving the question of own resources to be allocated to the Communities.

[3] More specifically, the common organization of the market in sugar distinguishes three stages in total production:
(1) Category A, which corresponds to direct sales on the domestic market at a guaranteed basic price;
(2) Category B, with a price guarantee but subject to levies (undertakings are guaranteed the basic price but contribute towards the cost of market support (mainly expenditure on refunds following sales on the world market);
(3) Category C, with no guarantees.

[4] A judgment of the Court of Justice of the European Communities, issued on 25 October 1978, concluded that Regulation (EEC) No 1111/77 of 13 January 1977, introducing a levy on the production of isoglucose, was illegal (see Annex 10, p. 383 for further details). Regulation (EEC) No 1293/79 therefore repealed some provisions of the Regulation on 25 June 1979 and laid down other rules.

[5] The history of the Sixth VAT Directive is recounted in Annex 10, p. 385. It thus took more than nine years for the Decision of 21 April 1970 on the replacement of financial contributions by the Communities' own resources to be implemented. Moreover, its partial entry into force will be four years late. By the time it becomes fully operational, the system created by the Decision of 21 April 1970 will have nearly exhausted its effectiveness (see p. 379).

[6] Only one country, Belgium, implemented the Sixth Directive on the proper date, 1 January 1978. In these circumstances, the Commission proposed—and the Council agreed to—the postponement, by means of the Ninth Directive, of the date of entry into force to 1 January 1979. The actual implementing dates were as follows: 1 April 1978 in the United Kingdom, 1 October 1978 in Denmark, 1 January 1979 in France and the Netherlands, 1 March 1979 in Ireland, 1 April and 1 July 1979 in Italy and 1 January 1980 in Luxembourg and the Federal Republic of Germany.
In January 1979 the Commission started proceedings against the Federal Republic of Germany, Ireland, Italy and Luxembourg, under Article 169 of the EEC Treaty, for infringement of the Sixth Directive, but subsequently abandoned them.

Comments on the French position: Strong emotion was expressed in the Assemblée nationale. On 30 October 1978 it rejected the bill adapting VAT legislation to the Sixth Directive by 333 votes to 132. One argument was that this Directive was too specific and left the national legislature no choice. In the end, the text was adopted on 7 December 1978 by the entire Assembly by 279 votes to 200.

Comments on the Italian position: In spite of major internal political difficulties, the Italian Government successfully concluded the approval procedure. In terms of the 1979 Community budget, this had a considerable effect, for had Italy remained in the group of States paying financial contributions, this would have cost it 140 m EUA more.

Comments on the Federal German position: The delay in parliamentary ratification was not due to divergent views on the substance of the directive but to the CDU/CSU opposition who demanded that the definition of the field of application must not prejudice the possible reunification of Germany. Since the opposition had a majority in the Bundesrat, the two chambers had to find a compromise—which was laboriously worked out in the coordinating committee.

[7] See OJ L 336 of 27.12.1977.

[8] The VAT rates in force at the end of 1979 in the Nine Member States were: Belgium (normal rate 16%, increased rate 25%, reduced rate 6%); Denmark (normal rates 20%, 25%); Federal Republic of Germany (normal rate 13%, reduced rate 6.5%); France (normal rate 17.6%, increased rate 33.33%, reduced rate 7%); Ireland (normal rate 20%, reduced rate 10%); Italy (normal rate 14%, increased rate 35%, reduced rates 1, 3, 6, 9 and 12%; there is also an 'intermediate' rate of 18%); Luxembourg (normal rate 10%, reduced rates 2% and 5%); Netherlands (normal rate 18%, reduced rate 4%); United Kingdom (normal rate 15%. 15%).

[9] The author has analysed this mechanism in his article in *La revue du marché commun*: 'Le budget pour 1978, bilan d'une procédure, innovations juridiques, perspectives pour une année nouvelle' (January 1978, p. 16).

[10] See Supplement 7/74—Bull. EC.

[11] At the time when the United Kingdom thought the financial mechanism would operate in its favour in the 1979 budget, the figures were as follows: surplus 237 m EUA, or 11.2%; the UK share of Community GNP was 2 119 m EUA; so one 5% tranche came to 106 m EUA.
No payment is made for the tranche from 0 to 5%. So for the tranche from 5 to 10%, which allows for payment of 50% of the amount, the figure is 53 m EUA. That leaves only 25 m EUA for the tranche from 10 to 15% which gives an entitlement to payment of 60% of that amount, i.e. 15 m EUA. So the total amount repaid would have been 68 m EUA (53+15 m EUA).
It should also be noted that the tranche above 30%, which gives rise to a 100% payment of the corresponding surplus, represents an extremely high percentage of surplus.

[12] See Supplement 8/78—Bull. EC.

[13] A few words may be said here about the question of federal income tax. In the United States, in 1913, the 16th amendment gave the federal government the right to levy income tax. We do not think the time has come in Europe for such an innovation, for the already inequitably distributed and necessary burden of direct taxes makes it politically unadvisable further to increase the load by introducing a European levy. Since it is difficult to imagine that as things stand the Member States would surrender part of the proceeds of such different direct taxes, there only remains the possibility of introducing a new direct tax. Some ideas have been put forward, such as a tax on the profits of the multinationals, but they are sensational rather than realistic.

[14] On 27 June 1979 the Bundestag adopted a resolution calling on the Federal Government to draw the attention of the Commission of the European Communities to the fact that in the short and medium term the federal budget could not tolerate heavier burdens than those resulting from the existing own resources system. The Bundestag feels that the principle that the volume of expenditure should be determined by the volume of revenue should also be applied to the Community budget. New projects should be financed by reducing expenditure in other fields, in particular the EAGGF.

[15] In its conclusion, the Council of Finance Ministers of 11 February 1980 stated that 'An improvement of the common agricultural policy with the aim of considerably reducing the growth rate of agricultural expenditure was absolutely essential also in order to ensure that the 1% own resources limit was not exceeded, having regard to the resources required for other policies'. This statement was recalled by the Council of Foreign Affairs Ministers which arrived at a solution to the 'British problem' on 30 May 1980.

[16] It is interesting to note how each Member State treats the revenues which were formerly its own but now go to the European Community. In 1980 the situation was like this:
(a) five States do not show revenue destined for the Community in their budgets proper but disclose them in an appendix, Belgium in an 'Exposé général du Budget', the Federal Republic of Germany in an 'Anlage E zu Kap. 6006', France in an 'Evaluation des recettes (Voies et Moyens)', Luxembourg in a 'Budget

pour ordre' and the Netherlands in a 'Miljoenen nota'. These revenues are thus segregated from fiscal revenues;

(b) the other four States include revenue destined for the Community in their budgets, but use different methods of accounting for it:

    (i) Ireland and the United Kingdom still show customs duties and agricultural levies among fiscal revenue; on the expenditure side the full amount of Community 'own resources', including the Community's portion of VAT, is treated as a transfer to the Community;

    (ii) Italy shows Community 'own resources' separately from fiscal revenues under the heading 'revenue to be transferred'; on the expenditure side it shows them as a transfer to the Community;

    (iii) Denmark shows Community 'own resources' on the revenue side of the budget only, as a negative item deducted from fiscal revenue.

Chapter VIII:
The ECSC's financial activity

Seen from the point of view taken in this chapter, the High Authority of the European Coal and Steel Community carries out activities similar to those of a financial institution, without however being a bank. Article 51(4) of the ECSC Treaty stipulates that 'The High Authority shall not itself engage in the banking operations which its financial tasks entail'. We shall therefore successively describe the tasks and operations, resources, rules of intervention and, lastly, the financing of the High Authority/Commission.

1. Tasks and operations of the ECSC as a financial institution

The financial activity of the ECSC is based on Articles 49 and 51 of the Treaty. From the outset it has organized its activity in a very original fashion.

A—Tasks of the ECSC

Pursuant to Article 49 of the ECSC Treaty, the High Authority/Commission 'is empowered to procure the funds it requires to carry out its tasks: ... by contracting loans'. The first subparagraph of Article 51(1) of the Treaty adds that it 'may not use the funds obtained by borrowing except to grant loans'.

Pursuant to Article 54, paragraphs 1 and 2 and Article 56(1)(b) and (2)(a) of the ECSC Treaty loans granted from borrowed funds must be used to finance:

(a) the carrying out of investment programmes drawn up by coal and steel undertakings;
(b) works and installations which contribute directly and primarily to increasing the production, reducing the production costs or facilitating the marketing of products within the ECSC's jurisdiction;
(c) programmes for the creation of new and economically sound activities capable of reabsorbing the redundant workers into productive employment following the introduction of new technical processes or equipment in the industries under the ECSC's jurisdiction; or, with the assent of the Council, and after obtaining the opinion of the Consultative Committee, in any other industry;
(d) programmes to create new and economically sound activities or for the conversion of existing undertakings capable of reabsorbing the redundant workers into productive

137

employment, following fundamental changes in market conditions for the coal and steel industry under the ECSC's jurisdiction or, with the assent of the Council, in any other industry.

The ECSC thus became the first financial institution in the coal and steel sector.

B—Operation of the ECSC

The High Authority/Commission entrusted one of its departments with the management of this financial activity. At present the responsible department is the Directorate-General for Credit and Investments. This department is located in Luxembourg, pursuant to Article 7 of the Decision of 8 April 1965, adopted on the same date as the Merger Treaty, of the representatives of the governments of the Member States on the provisional location of certain institutions and departments of the Communities. The capital of the Grand Duchy was thus given a recognized financial task by the Community. That explains why the EMCF and the EIB also have their 'provisional' seat in Luxembourg.

The administrative organization of the Directorate-General for Credit and Investments differs from the organization of the EIB in its very simplicity.

It has a small staff and a very lightweight structure (see Annex 14, p. 402). It is headed by a Director-General under the authority of a Vice-President of the Commission who is normally also responsible for the Directorate-General for Economic and Financial Affairs.

2. The ECSC's resources

Apart from the proceeds of levies, which are clearly specified by the Treaty, interest on investment of its own funds and resources from unexpended levies, the ECSC's only resources are the proceeds of borrowing.

A—The ECSC's own resources

Unlike the EIB, the ECSC did not obtain any capital from the Member States. So the High Authority created a guarantee fund out of the levies which, in the early years, were fixed at a higher level for this purpose. Thanks, *inter alia,* to the funds paid by the three new Member States under Protocol 24 to the Treaty of Accession (57.7 m u.a. to be paid in three equal annual instalments) and the regular allocation of appropriations to maintain a balance between the guarantee fund and the borrowings incurred, this fund amounted to 230 m EUA on 31 December 1979. A special reserve of 140 m EUA was also set up. But the guarantee fund can only be used after recourse to all the other reserves. Lastly, there is the former pension fund (for staff) of 41.5 m EUA.

So the ECSC's total reserves were 411.5 m EUA on 31 December 1979.

138

B—ECSC borrowing

Since it had no capital, the ECSC began to borrow in 1954. The history of its borrowing falls into two periods. From 1954 to 1971, the amount borrowed each year only exceeded 100 m u.a. twice (in 1964 and in 1968), and the average number of loans raised per year was four (in 1955 and 1959 there was no borrowing at all). From 1972, i.e. even before enlargement, the amount borrowed each year increased markedly and reached nearly 1 068.7 m EUA in 1978 (when 51 loans were floated). During this second period, loans were raised on the American market, a practice in abeyance since 1962. It should also be pointed out that the ECSC's American dollar loans are 'AAA rated', which gives considerable advantages in that it facilitates investment and offers lower interest rates (approximately 1 to 1.5%), because of the guarantee provided by the ECSC's fiscal power and reserves.

From 1952 to 1979, it borrowed 6 583.3 m EUA (see survey of loans by year, Annex 13, p. 400). Of loans raised 41.7% were in US dollars, 25.7% in German marks, 10.6% in Swiss francs, 8.5% in French francs, and the remainder (12.9%) in Luxembourg francs, guilders, lire, Belgian francs, and so on. By 31 December 1979, 1 908.2 m EUA had been repaid, leaving 4 675.1 m EUA still due.

The diversity of this borrowing in terms of currencies and markets is explained by the increase in the annual volume needed to meet the growth of financing requirements. A flexible policy of exploiting the various supply sources was also necessary because of the international monetary situation. Until the beginning of the 1970s, borrowed Community and other currencies could be exchanged on the money market at rates very similar to the fixed parity rates set by the International Monetary Fund and offered on the capital markets at very similar interest rates. The same no longer applies now that the monetary system based on fixed exchange rates has been abandoned and a generalized system of floating exchange rates introduced. The divergent economic performances of various countries in recent years has produced wider differences between the exchange rates of the various currencies and a wider range of repayment timetables and has also narrowed the access to various capital markets.

3. Rules governing ECSC intervention

A—The ECSC's decision-making mechanism

Decisions to borrow or lend are taken by the Commission. The Council does not intervene except for certain borrowings in connection with employment problems which it must approve (Article 56 of the ECSC Treaty, quoted on p. 137; Article 54 of the Treaty was not applied in this case).

Under Article 51(1) of the ECSC Treaty, Member States may be required by the High Authority/Commission to provide a guarantee when it contracts certain loans. The High Authority then consults the Council and the interested government(s) who are in no way

obliged to give this guarantee. In fact, the High Authority/Commission has never asked for this guarantee, since the lenders have felt that its fiscal power and reserves constituted sufficient guarantee.

In practice, the Vice-President responsible for this sector is authorized, on behalf of and under the responsibility of the Commission, to take decisions on contracting borrowings and granting loans.

B—Assessment of applications for ECSC aid and the criteria used

Applications for loans and guarantees are sent to the Commission. The documents, on the basis of which the Commission arrives at its decisions, are examined by the Directorate-General for Credit and Investments. Each dossier includes an economic and financial assessment of the project submitted and of the borrower, the assessment being carried out in accordance with the general objectives of the Community and based on normal financial criteria.

C—ECSC interest rates

Since the ECSC has no profit-making goals, the rate of interest it charges on its loans depends on the cost of obtaining funds, which varies in the different capital markets resorted to.

In some cases the rate of interest may be reduced by 3% during the first five years and, in the case of loans for subsidized housing (see p. 208), may even be as low as 1%.

In 1979, the normal rate for loans was between 7.2% and 12.2%, depending on the currency used.

Certain priority projects may qualify for a three point interest subsidy from the ECSC's own resources.

4. ECSC financing operations

The loans granted by the ECSC are of two kinds, depending on the origin of the funds lent: loans from borrowed funds and loans from Community funds.

A—Loans granted from borrowed funds

The golden rule of the ECSC is to borrow only in order to on-lend and to borrow in the currency required by the party seeking the loan. Such loans may be used, however, to finance only part of the cost of the projects (generally 50%). From 1952 to 1979 loans granted amounted to 5 848.27 m EUA. At any one moment therefore, the amounts lent and the amounts borrowed are not exactly equivalent, the latter most often being temporarily greater than the former. So far we have been primarily concerned with the figure for borrowing operations, since these in our opinion give a better indication of how these activities have developed over a period of time.

From the start of the High Authority/Commission's activities until 31 December 1979, the 5 848.27 m EUA of loans from borrowed funds (reduced to 4 628.47 m EUA after repayments) can be divided up as follows:

Industrial investment	5 151.59 m EUA (88.1%)
Conversion	623.41 m EUA (10.7%)
Subsidized housing	69.54 m EUA (1.2%)

B—Loans granted from Community funds

There are three sources of Community funds used for loans: the levy itself, the special reserve and the former ECSC Pension Fund. They serve, or have served, to grant loans totalling 227.41 m EUA in respect of the following:
(i) financing up to 60% of the cost of building social housing, from the special reserve: 206.03 m EUA, and if necessary from the former ECSC Pension Fund;
(ii) financing conversion through the special reserve: 3.79 m EUA;
(iii) financing industrial investment from the former Pension Fund (for the Friuli operation, see p. 235): 3.89 m EUA, and
(iv) financing various loans: 13.70 m EUA.

In all, ECSC loans amounted to 6 075.68 m EUA from 1952 to 1979. This figure breaks down as follows: loans from borrowed funds (5 899.49 m EUA)—conversion changes (51.22 m EUA) = 5 848.27 m EUA; loans from Community funds (229.40 m EUA)—conversion changes (1.99 m EUA) = 227.41 m EUA. Guarantees amounting to 64.97 m EUA should be added to these loans, giving a total figure of 6 139.75 m EUA.

ECSC loans were allocated as follows: 58.1% to the steel industry, 25.2% to the coal industry, 10.3% to industrial conversion, 4.6% to workers' housing, 1.6% to iron ore mines and 0.3% to miscellaneous recipients. As far as the Member States were concerned, the main beneficiary was the Federal Republic of Germany with 32.2%, followed by the United Kingdom with 22.8%, France with 19.3%, Italy with 14.9% and Ireland, Denmark and the Benelux countries with 10.8% between them.

*
**

With very slender means at its disposal, the ECSC has played a fundamental role in providing funds for the coal and steel industries. In this respect, it has been the most important Community, since nearly all investment undertaken includes an ECSC loan. In all, between 18 and 25% on average of the financial requirements of Community coal and steel undertakings are covered by the ECSC. Despite the crisis, its credit has remained good, thanks essentially to the tax-raising power which the High Authority possesses.

Chapter IX:
EEC and Euratom borrowing/
lending operations

EEC borrowing/lending operations have been authorized only since 1976. Euratom operations, however, have their basis in the Treaty of Rome, but have only acquired significant proportions since 1977. We shall first examine the working rules for these two Communities and then the financing procedures.

1. The EEC and Euratom working rules

As it is the older of the two, we shall begin with Euratom.

A—The financial activity of the European Atomic Energy Community

Article 172(4) of the Euratom Treaty empowers Euratom to borrow on the capital markets to finance research and investment. Pursuant to that Article and the Cooperation Agreement of 8 November 1958 between Euratom and the United States, Euratom received a loan on 10 August 1959 of USD 135 000 000 from the Export-Import Bank of Washington ('Eximbank') enabling it in turn to finance the granting of Community loans for the construction of nuclear power stations. Little in fact has been made of this facility.

On 29 March 1977, after a very long investigation, the Council decided to authorize the Commission to grant loans up to a maximum amount of 500 m EUA, the proceeds to be applied to *financing investment projects aimed at producing electricity from nuclear energy* and the installations required to supply them with fuel.[1]

On 30 July 1979 the Commission asked the Council to raise this ceiling from 500 to 1 500 m EUA, basing its proposal on three considerations, namely:
 (i) the general political and economic situation, as it had evolved over the previous few months, in particular in the light of oil price increases;
 (ii) the position adopted by the European Council on 21 and 22 June 1979, whereby 'a strong fresh impetus must be given to nuclear programmes';
 (iii) the applications submitted by the proposers.

In Decision 80/29 of 20 December 1979, the Council approved an increase but only of 500 m EUA, thus raising the maximum amount authorized for Euratom loans to 1 000 m EUA.

The Commission, more specifically the Directorate-General for Credit and Investments, raises and on-lends these funds. However, special cooperation arrangements between the Commission and the EIB ensure that the activities of the two institutions regarding the financing of power stations and other nuclear installations are coordinated (the EIB having significantly increased its assistance from its own funds); these arrangements also give the EIB the task of carrying out the lending operations. In practice, the Bank has been authorized to review applications for loans, to act as agent for the conclusion of finance contracts, to administer the loans thereafter and to monitor projects on behalf of Euratom.

B—The financial activity of the European Economic Community

In 1973 the Commission proposed that a special procedure for authorizing the raising of loans by the EEC should be set up. The draft of a second Treaty, put forward by the Commission on 10 October 1973 amending certain budgetary provisions of the Treaties establishing the European Communities and of the Treaty establishing a Single Council and a Single Commission (see p. 8) laid down in Article 2 that 'recourse to the raising of loans shall be decided during the budgetary procedure by the Council acting on a qualified majority and with the agreement of the Assembly acting by a majority of its members and an absolute majority of the votes cast'. The Member States' representatives did not endorse this proposal, arguing, with some justice, that the present system of Community revenues provided enough to cover foreseeable expenditure in the next few years.

Community borrowing operations

In February 1974, however, the Commission put forward a further proposal for raising *Community loans to help Member States in balance of payments difficulties* and in this way recycle some of the unemployed capital of the oil-producing countries (these loans are also known as the Haferkamp Facility, after one of the Vice-Presidents of the Commission). On 21 October 1974 the Council decided, after consulting Parliament, to empower the Community, pursuant to Article 235 of the EEC Treaty, to borrow in cases of this kind.

Rules for raising these loans are laid down in Regulations (EEC) Nos 397/75 and 398/75 of 17 February 1975 and can be summarized as:
 (i) the EEC may engage in fund-raising operations either by direct arrangement with non-member countries and lending institutions, or on the capital market;
 (ii) borrowings are subject to an upper limit equivalent in EUA to USD 3 000 million, with a minimum average loan period of five years;
 (iii) the loan to a Member State is contingent on the latter's adoption of economic policy measures designed to correct its balance of payments situation;
 (iv) Member States shall provide guarantee arrangements enabling them to pay to the EEC the sums needed to cover debt-servicing requirements with regard to both interest and capital. (This is an additional guarantee which is not required for Euratom loans.)

The New Community Instrument

The New Community Instrument which came into being with some difficulty on 16 October 1978 was again in the headlines barely two months later.

The Decision of 16 October 1978—After considerable pressure from the Commission, in particular Mr Ortoli, a Vice-President at the time, and thanks to the impetus given in December 1977 and April 1978 by the European Council (see Annex 3, p. 353)—despite a disagreement with Parliament (see Annex 5, p. 364)—the Council introduced a new financial mechanism in Decision No 78/870/EEC of 16 October 1978, to be known as the *New Community Instrument* (NCI); this supplemented existing Community mechanisms, and was designed to make a further contribution to the investment effort in the Community.[2] The Commission was thereby empowered to contract loans on behalf of the EEC which were not to exceed the equivalent of 1 000 million EUA in principal. The proceeds of these borrowing operations were to be made available, in the form of loans, to finance investment projects which contribute to greater convergence and integration of the economic policies of the Member States. These projects must help attain the priority Community objectives in the energy, industry and infrastructure sectors, taking account, *inter alia,* of the regional impact of the projects and the need to combat unemployment. As a result, a first tranche of borrowing operations and loans, amounting to 500 m EUA, was authorized by the Council on 14 May 1979. On 24 January 1980, the Commission, realizing that the total for loans already granted or in an advanced state of preparation stood at 498 m EUA, proposed that the Council should release a second tranche of 500 m EUA, to be used especially for urban renovation, housing and advance factory construction projects. It was not until 15 July 1980 that the Council, pursuant to Decision No 78/870, approved the second tranche, or rather 80% of it (400 m EUA), stipulating in fact that it should be used for the same type of operations as its predecessor. It was however agreed that the Council would examine at a later stage whether the balance of 100 m EUA could not be used for the new objectives proposed by the Commission, which were of particular interest to Italy.

The working procedure is very complicated, since it is the Council, deciding unanimously on a proposal from the Commission and after consulting Parliament, which authorizes the borrowing tranche and lays down guidelines for project eligibility, while the Commission actually decides whether the projects comply with those guidelines. Within the limits authorized for the tranche, the Commission proceeds to borrow on the capital markets, but the funds acquired are in fact made over to the EIB, to be invested on a temporary basis if necessary.

The decision-making process is no less complicated: a mandate is given to the Bank to grant the loans.[3] The Bank carries out transactions under this mandate on behalf of, for and at the risk of the Community. Applications for a loan are forwarded to the Bank either directly or through the Commission or a Member State. After the Commission has decided whether a project is eligible, the Bank, in accordance with the procedures laid down in its Statute and applying its usual criteria in turn, examines the application. The granting of a loan and the conditions attaching thereto are decided jointly by the Bank and the Commission, the Bank being responsible for actually managing the loan.

It has been agreed that the mechanism of the New Community Instrument would be reviewed as soon as 800 m EUA had been committed, or a two-year period had expired, whichever was the sooner.

The policy statement of 5 December 1978—At the European Council in Brussels on 4 and 5 December 1978 it was agreed that the Community's institutions should use the NCI and the EIB to make loans—carrying interest subsidies—with a ceiling of 1 000 m EUA a year for five years (see Annex 3, p. 355) to the less-prosperous States taking part fully and effectively in the European Monetary System (Ireland and Italy).

145

Interest subsidies

The practice of granting interest subsidies, which the ECSC has used for several years, is being increasingly used by the EEC. Provision was made in the 1979 budget for several headings to incorporate interest subsidies, so that EIB loans were made more attractive (see p. 158).

Interest subsidies on loans granted by the EIB under the 1980 budget—In the 1980 budget there are 11 headings against which the notes in the 'remarks' column clearly state that interest subsidies are available. The appropriations concerned are primarily for financial cooperation with the Mediterranean countries (see p. 294). In addition, the Regulation establishing the European Regional Development Fund (ERDF) provides that in the case of infrastructure investment within the eligible zones, assistance from the Fund may take the form, either wholly or in part, of three point interest subsidies on the loans granted by the EIB pursuant to Article 130(a) and (b) of the EEC Treaty.

Interest subsidies under the European Monetary System—The European Monetary System arrangements include interest subsidies among the measures designed to strengthen the economies of the less-prosperous Member States participating in the system.

For this reason, the European Council in its Resolution of 4 and 5 December 1978 (referred to above) invited the Community's institutions and the EIB to grant interest subsidies to those countries for a five-year period. On 12 February 1979 the Commission accordingly put forward a proposal for a Council Regulation enabling a three point interest subsidy to be granted on loans made under the New Community Instrument and on certain EIB loans from its own funds. The total cost of the measure was 1 000 m EUA, i.e. 200 m EUA for each of the five years. The loans carrying interest subsidies were to be 'assigned primarily to financing selected infrastructure projects and programmes, on the understanding that any direct or indirect distortion of the competitive position of specific industries in the Member States should be avoided'.

Parliament, which delivered a favourable opinion on 24 April 1979, had asked that this text should be the subject of a conciliation procedure. On 3 August 1979,[4] the Council adopted the Regulation in question, but informed Parliament that it was not a general implementing regulation, and could not therefore be the subject of a conciliation procedure (see Annex 5, p. 366). One of the two points in dispute between Parliament and the Council was the question as to whether this expenditure should be classified as compulsory or non-compulsory: the Council took the view it should be regarded as compulsory expenditure, since it derived from an agreement between the Member States establishing the European monetary arrangement. The other difference of view was whether the figures should be regarded as indicative or not.

As far as the budget is concerned, the resources have been available since the supplementary and amending budget No 1/79, which emerged from the budget crisis of December 1979 (see p. 45). In point of fact, the inclusion of these interest subsidies in the budget has never been contested, although it is true that some of them have acquired a 'bilateral' character, between a 'more prosperous' and a 'less prosperous' Member State, so that they do not figure in the Community budget.

On 3 August 1979 the Council confirmed the arrangement made at the European Council, namely that two-thirds of such interest subsidies should be given to Italy and one-third to Ireland.

On 17 September 1979 the Commission and the EIB signed a Cooperation Agreement, under which the Bank would examine the projects in accordance with its usual procedures, while the Commission would decide which projects were eligible for interest subsidies, the Bank having the final say on the loans granted under such arrangements.

Hitherto, interest subsidies have been granted in the form of a number of percentage points. As a general rule, three percentage points are allowed over a five-year period. Another formula is currently being considered, however, which consists in calculating the subsidy as a percentage of the interest rate to which the loan itself is subject.

C—Loans granted from non-borrowed funds

There are two categories of loans from non-borrowed funds besides those granted by the ECSC to finance *subsidized housing*: loans charged to the Commission's statement of expenditure and loans from the European Development Fund's resources.

The first category includes loans *to promote technological development in the energy sector and special loans to certain non-member countries*. The Commission may use the budget appropriations to help (a) promote technological development projects directly connected with oil and gas exploration, exploitation, storage and transport (Regulation (EEC) No 3056/73 of 9 November 1973) and (b) demonstration projects in the field of energy saving and new sources of energy (Regulation (EEC) No 1302/78 and Regulation (EEC) No 1303/78 of 12 June 1978). If the results of these projects are commercially exploited the loans must be repaid. The Community may not contribute more that 49% of the costs; in practice its contribution for oil and gas projects lies between 25% and 40%. Repayments are entered under a heading in the Commission's statement of revenue. Special loans may be granted from budget funds under the financial protocols to the agreements signed with the Mediterranean countries. Repayments by these countries are also entered under a special heading in the Commission's statement of revenue.

The second category of loans are loans *from the EDF's funds,* i.e. from the financial contributions paid by Member States.

2. EEC and Euratom financing operations

Here too, we shall begin with Euratom, as it is the older of the two.

A—Euratom financing operations

Eximbank loans

The only use which the Euratom Commission has made of this facility was to lend 40.4 m u.a., 28 m EUA at the December 1979 rate (see Annex 13, p. 400), to two firms in 1963.

The sums paid by them (interest and repayments) are Community revenue and cover the expenditure under the Community's commitments to Eximbank. By 31 December 1979, a total of 23.2 m EUA had already been repaid at the December 1979 rate. Basically, Euratom offers a form of guarantee.

Euratom loans

Pursuant to its Decision of 29 March 1977, the Council agreed a first tranche of loans with a ceiling of 500 m EUA which the Commission was authorized to contract. As at 31 December 1978, the Commission had borrowed 146 and paid out 142 m u.a. for financing nuclear power stations in France, Italy and the Federal Republic of Germany. As at 31 December 1979, it had borrowed and on-lent 321 m u.a. for the same purpose, 111 m u.a. thereof going to the Federal Republic of Germany, 89 to France, 70 to Italy and 51 to Belgium.

B—EEC financing operations

The EEC's borrowing/lending activities began only in 1976, but from the beginning represented a significant proportion of Europe's finances. On 15 March 1976, for instance, the Council in Decision 76/322/EEC authorized the Commission to conclude on behalf of the European Economic Community a number of agreements which led to borrowing operations contracted on 22 March 1976 (USD 1 100 million and DM 500 million) and loans granted on 23 March 1976 (782 m u.a. to Italy and 235 m u.a. to Ireland, or a total of 1 017 m u.a.).

The Commission likewise consolidated some of these borrowing operations in order to replace variable interest rates by a fixed rate; in 1977 it also carried out a second borrowing/lending operation whereby Italy received 484 m u.a. and Ireland 34 m u.a.

In all, the sums borrowed by the EEC in 1976 and 1977 amounted to 1 535 m u.a. The details are given in Annex 13 on p. 400.

On 9 March 1979, the Commission proposed that the Council should release a tranche of 500 m EUA under the New Community Instrument, so as to on-lend them on favourable terms to Community undertakings to finance investment projects in infrastructure (transport, telecommunications, agricultural developments, water engineering and environmental protection schemes) and energy (development, exploitation, transport and storage of energy resources, and especially of alternative sources of energy). On 14 May 1979, the Council authorized the first tranche of 500 m EUA to be used for financing projects in the Community complying with the Community's priority objectives in the infrastructure and energy fields. Investment of this kind is required to make a contribution towards solving the main structural problems of the Community, in particular the reduction of regional disparities and of energy dependence. As at 31 December 1979, two borrowing operations had been initiated, one amounting to 86.5 m EUA and the other to 91 m EUA. The corresponding loans amounted to 81 m EUA in the case of the United Kingdom, 54 m EUA in the case of Ireland and 39 m EUA in the case of Italy.

* * *

The launching and development of EEC and Euratom borrowing and lending activities have been among the most significant events in the public finances of the Community during the last few years. It is clear that increasing emphasis should be given to this type of Community intervention, especially as the system of Community own resources will soon reach its peak.

Footnotes to Chapter IX

[1] The Commission put forward its proposal on 24 January 1975, and Parliament delivered its Opinion on 19 June 1975. Council Decision 77/270 was adopted on 29 March 1977, authorizing the Commission to contract Euratom loans to help finance nuclear power stations. This Decision was supplemented by implementing Decision 77/271 of 29 March 1977 (OJ L 88 of 6.4.1977). It should be noted that the Council, in the preamble to the Decision, added Article 203 of the Euratom Treaty to the only citation given by the Commission, namely Article 172(4) of the Euratom Treaty, since it felt that the latter did not authorize the Community to borrow on the international capital markets or make loans to finance investment in the nuclear industry.

We should remember that no conciliation procedure was followed with regard to this legislation, as Parliament had agreed with the Council as to the substance. The only difficulty arose over the inclusion of the borrowing/lending operations in the budget. A provisional solution was reached in the Financial Regulation of 21 December 1977, but discussions on the matter have still not been closed.

[2] Having defended this idea since June 1977, the Commission put forward an official proposal on 30 January 1978; in the light of Parliament's Opinion of 12 April, the Commission subsequently amended its proposal on 8 May. The Council Decision dates from 16 October 1978 (OJ L 298 of 25.10.1978).

[3] The Bank's mandate was the subject of a Cooperation Agreement between the Commission and the EIB signed on 27 November 1978.

[4] See OJ L 200 of 8.8.1979.

Chapter X:
The European Investment Bank

The European Investment Bank (EIB), whose shareholders are the EEC Member States, was established in 1958 by Article 129 of the Treaty of Rome.

This chapter concentrates on the following four aspects: the Bank's tasks and operation, its resources, its rules of intervention and its financing.

1. Tasks and operation of the EIB

The EIB is a genuine banking establishment. In that respect it differs from the ECSC.

A—Tasks of the EIB

As a Community banking establishment, the task of the Bank is as follows: by having recourse to the capital market and utilizing its own resources, to contribute to the balanced and steady development of the common market in the interest of the European Economic Community. For this purpose, the Bank, operating on a non-profit-making basis, grants loans and gives guarantees[1] which facilitate the financing of projects in all sectors of the economy. Article 130 of the EEC Treaty and the directives of its Board of Governors define the economic policy aims with which investments financed by the Bank must comply. The Statute of the Bank, which is an integral part of the Treaty, defines the criteria for granting finance, the Bank's decision-making procedures and, more generally, its internal organization.

It can finance the following within the Community:
(a) projects for developing less-developed regions (Article 130(a) of the EEC Treaty);
(b) projects of common interest to several Member States or to the Community as a whole (Article 130(c) of the EEC Treaty):
   (i) either because they contribute to the economic integration of Europe (infrastructure and communications: motorways, railways and shipping lines, telecommunications, etc; projects resulting from close technical and economic cooperation between the undertakings of various Member States, etc);
   (ii) or because they contribute to the achievement of objectives of recognized Community interest, such as the search for improved energy supplies, protection of the environment or the introduction of advanced technology;

151

(c) projects for modernizing or converting undertakings or for developing fresh activities called for by the progressive establishment of the common market, where these projects are of such a size or nature that they cannot be entirely financed by the various means available in the individual Member States (or, in practice, because of the structural difficulties encountered in certain sectors (Article 130(b) of the EEC Treaty).

Article 20 of the Statute stipulates that the Bank shall ensure that its funds are employed as rationally as possible in the interests of the Community and that it may grant loans or guarantees only where the execution of the project contributes to an increase in economic productivity in general and promotes the attainment of the common market. In fact, this is a difficult situation because the Bank's borrowing policy must reconcile two demands: as a public financing institution of the Community, the Bank must ensure the economic effectiveness of the projects it finances and their contribution to the establishment of the Community policies; as a banking establishment it cannot lend funds which it has itself borrowed from public sources unless it is sure that the transaction is financially sound and that its subscribers can be reimbursed at the required date.

The EIB was established mainly in order to finance investment projects situated in the EEC Member States. However, the second subparagraph of Article 18(1) of its Statute provides that, by way of derogation authorized by the Board of Governors, acting unanimously on a proposal from the Board of Directors, the Bank may grant loans for investment projects to be carried out, in whole or in part, outside the European territories of Member States.

B—The operation of the EIB

The EIB has its own Statute which makes it autonomous within the Community with its own decision-making and supervisory bodies: the Board of Governors, Board of Directors, Management Committee and Audit Committee.

The *Board of Governors* consists of ministers designated by each of the Member States, generally the Finance Minister. It lays down general directives on the Bank's credit policy and approves the balance sheet, the profit and loss account and the annual report. It decides whether to increase the subscribed capital, fixes the percentage to be paid up and authorizes loans for projects to be carried out outside the Community territory. It appoints the members of the Board of Directors, Management Committee and Audit Committee. The presidency rotates among its members on an annual basis. Where decisions are taken by a majority of its members, this majority must represent at least 40% of the subscribed capital.

The *Board of Directors* consists of 18 directors appointed by the Board of Governors for a five-year period, 17 designated by the Member States[2] and 1 by the Commission of the European Communities, and of 10 alternates, of whom 9 are designated by the Member States[2] and 1 by the Commission. They are chosen from persons whose independence and competence are beyond doubt and are responsible only to the Bank.

The Board of Directors meets periodically under the presidency of the *President of the Bank*. It has sole power to take decisions in respect of granting loans and guarantees and raising loans. It fixes the interest rates on loans granted. It ensures that the Bank is managed in accordance with the provisions of the Treaty of Rome and of its Statute and with the general directives laid down by the Board of Governors. Its decisions are normally taken by a simple majority of its members.

The *Management Committee* consists of the President of the Bank and four Vice-Presidents appointed for six years by the Board of Governors on a proposal from the Board of Directors. It prepares and ensures the implementation of the decisions of the Board of Directors and is responsible for the current business of the Bank.

The *Audit Committee* consists of three members appointed for a period of three years by the Board of Governors and is responsible for annually verifying that the operations of the Bank have been conducted and its books kept in a proper manner.

Initially the Bank was located in Brussels, but since 1968 its seat has been in Luxembourg, pursuant to Article 5 of the Decision by the representatives of the Member States on the provisional seat of the Community institutions, which was adopted at the same time as the Merger Treaty on 8 April 1965.

2. The EIB's resources

The Bank's resources consist of its own resources, including borrowings and the resources of the special section.

A—The EIB's own resources

The Bank's own resources are made up of its own funds, i.e. the called-up part of its capital, reserves and funds, and the resources from borrowing, with which we will deal separately.

At the time of its creation, the Bank was endowed with a *capital* of 1 000 m u.a.[3] subscribed by the six founding Member States, of which 250 m u.a. was paid up. Since the aggregate outstanding amount of loans and guarantees granted by the Bank may not exceed 250% of its subscribed capital (Article 18(5) of its Statute), several increases in capital accompanied the growth of its financing activities. At the 1973 enlargement of the Community, the United Kingdom, Denmark and Ireland subscribed capital shares in line with their economic and political strength.

Since 19 June 1978, when the most recent increase was made, the subscribed capital has been 7 087.5 m u.a. The amount of capital paid and to be paid gradually rose to 911.25 m u.a. (Annex 13, p. 401). The statutory limit to the amount of loans and guarantees outstanding is 17 718.75 m u.a. On 31 December 1979, this figure was 10 325.9 m u.a.

The difference between the subscribed capital and the part that has been or is to be paid constitutes a *guarantee capital* in respect of which the Board of Directors may require payment 'to such an extent as may be required for the Bank to meet its obligations towards those who have made loans to it' (Article 5(3) of the Statute). In fact this is a very hypothetical situation, given the quality of the Bank's loan and guarantee system and the existence of its reserves and funds. Article 24 of the Statute provides that 'a reserve fund of up to 10% of the subscribed capital shall be built up progressively. If the state of the liabilities of the Bank should so justify, the Board of Directors may decide to set aside ad-

153

ditional reserves'. Over the years, the administrative surpluses have regularly been incorporated in the reserves and funds; at the end of the 1979 financial year, they came to about 785 m EUA.

The Bank's own capital, i.e. capital called up, together with the reserves and provisions, came to nearly 1 700 m at the end of 1979. In part these funds help to finance loan operations.

Nevertheless, it is clear that the collection and subsequent employment of resources from borrowing raised on the capital markets constitute the Bank's *raison d'être* and that the principal function of its own funds is to underpin its credit on these markets. So borrowed resources progressively came to constitute the nucleus of its means of financing.

B—The EIB's borrowings

Article 22 of the Statute provides that 'The Bank shall borrow on the international capital markets the funds necessary for the performance of its tasks' and specifies that it 'may borrow on the capital market of a Member State ... in accordance with the legal provisions applying to internal issues ... The competent authorities in the Member State concerned may refuse to give their assent only if there is reason to fear serious disturbances on the capital market of that State'.

In 1961 the Bank raised its first loans, amounting to 21.4 m u.a. Since then the annual amount of resources, raised on most of the world's financial markets, has risen rapidly, reaching 2 481.2 m EUA in 1979 (see Annex 13, p. 400). The aggregate amount of funds borrowed since its origins came to 10 600 m EUA at the end of 1979, and at that same date the net amount of borrowing outstanding, after deducting repayments and taking account of exchange-rate adjustments, came to 8 547 000 m EUA.

After drawing mainly on Member States' national markets, the Bank has turned to the national markets of non-Member countries: Switzerland, the United States since 1975 (foreign issues market), Japan, then Austria. Parallel to this it floats loans on the international capital markets: Eurobond markets in various currencies, Middle Eastern markets and Asian dollar markets of Hong Kong and Singapore.

The Bank's borrowings in the currencies of the EEC Member States, which originally accounted for most of its financing resources, fell sharply over the period 1974-77 when the currencies of non-Member countries made up 65% of its borrowed funds, the US dollar alone accounting for more than 50%; in 1978 and 1979, however, the funds borrowed in Community currencies came to nearly half the total.[4]

The breakdown of borrowings as of 31 December 1979 shows the dominant place of the American dollar (41.2%) and—among Community currencies—of the German mark (23.4%), while the guilder (9.0%), French franc (5.5%), Belgian franc (4.5%), Luxembourg franc (2.0%), Italian lira (1.5%) and pound sterling (1.6%) each accounted for only a small share of the total resources from borrowing.

What we said earlier (p. 139) about the terms of access to financial markets in recent years applies fully here too.

C—Operations from special section resources

In 1963 it was decided to expand the Bank's activities outside the Community to various developing countries by granting loans, some of which could not be provided from the Bank's own resources but were required to carry more favourable terms; these loans came from special budget resources which the Bank had been instructed to administer on behalf of the Member States or of the Community. The Board of Governors therefore set up a special section for the non-balance-sheet accounting of operations effected from budget resources on behalf of the Member States or the Community as development aid.

More recently, its mandated operations have extended to granting loans from funds borrowed in the Member States in the name of and on behalf of the Community: Euratom (see p. 143) and NCI (see p. 144) borrowings.

3. Rules governing EIB intervention

A—The EIB's decision-making machinery

The Board of Directors, the composition of which we described earlier, has sole authority to decide on granting loans and guarantees. This decision is preceded by the delivery of an opinion on all applications for loans or guarantees addressed to the EIB: before granting them, the Bank must obtain the assent of the Member State on whose territory the project will be carried out and the opinion of the Commission. Where the Member State concerned delivers an unfavourable opinion, the application is refused. Where the Commission gives an unfavourable opinion, the project can be approved only subject to the unanimous vote of the Board of Directors, the director nominated by the Commission abstaining. This procedure enables the Commission to ensure that the project in respect of which the Bank intervenes complies with the provisions of the Treaty and of secondary legislation and, where appropriate, to make comments on the particular objectives or economic policy problems. In addition to the Commission's opinion, decisions to finance projects outside the Community are subject to the opinion of the specialized committees of Member States' representatives.

The organizational links with the Commission provided for in the Bank's Statute are supplemented by a number of informal contacts and working sessions during which views and information are exchanged on each institution's activities and concerns and, where appropriate, actual cases of coordination are considered. Such contacts tend to develop naturally given the diversity of Community policies and the financial mechanisms administered by the Commission, and also the increase in the mandated operations and administrative tasks the Bank performs on the Community's behalf.

B—Examination of applications and criteria for EIB financing

Pursuant to Article 21 of the Bank's Statute, applications for financing may be made to the Bank direct, or through the Member State concerned, or through the Commission of the

European Communities. In practice, initial direct contacts between the applicant and the Bank are the rule, in the interests of both parties, so that a preliminary idea can be gained of the possibility of Bank intervention.

The EIB must ensure that:
(a) the projects to be financed comply with the provisions of Article 130 of the EEC Treaty and fully satisfy the intervention criteria laid down in the Statute and the Board of Governors' directives,[5] that they are technically feasible, that the sales or utilization prospects are satisfactory and that they are of general economic interest and, in the case of projects in the production sector, sufficiently profitable;
(b) the undertaking is financially sound and its financing plan is so adjusted as to ensure that the achievement of the proposed projects will not prejudice its financial balance;
(c) the interest and repayment arrangements appear secure.

The Bank may finance only part of the cost of the projects, supplementing the own funds or means derived from other sources. At present Bank loans are limited to 50% of the capital cost of the project and in fact this ceiling is not always reached; in the 1979 financial year, EIB financing on average covered about 32% of the cost of the projects (36% if one includes loans from NCI resources).

C—EIB interest rates

Since the Bank is non-profit-making, the interest rates on its loans are similar to those on the markets where it procures its resources and as a rule are not subject to subsequent reviews; the loans are paid out on a par basis.

Generally the repayment of the loan takes the form of constant six-monthly capital and interest payments, which are deferred for the duration of the execution and running-in period of the project so financed. These payments must be made in the currency or currencies received by the borrower.

Article 19 of its Statute provides that the Bank may not grant any reduction in its interest rates. However, interest rebates may be granted by third parties and in many cases budgetary resources from the Member States or the Community have been used to reduce the real cost of EIB loans; they include the EMS, the Regional Fund, aid to the ACP countries and aid to the Mediterranean countries.

4. Projects financed by the EIB

From 1958 to the end of 1979 the Bank signed 1 164 loan and guarantee contracts for a total of 13 765 m u.a. Nearly four-fifths of this amount was approved since the enlargement of the Community in 1973. During the first stage, financing increased slowly, reaching about 500 m u.a. a year in 1971-72. Since then, the annual amounts have increased sharply to reach nearly 1 000 m u.a. in 1974 and 1975, more than 1 500 m EUA in 1977, nearly 2 200 m EUA in 1978 and nearly 3 100 m EUA in 1979.

The total amount of finance granted between 1973 and 1979 was 10 923 m u.a. of which 93.5% came from the Bank's own resources. Projects financed within the Community accounted for 9 476 m EUA, of which 9 199 m EUA derived from own resources and 277 m

EUA from NCI resources, i.e. 86.8% of the total. Outside the Community, about 70% of loans were effected from the Bank's own resources and some 30% from the special section.

A—Projects financed by the EIB within the Community

The rapid increase in the Bank's activities in the Member States in recent years is the result firstly, of the enlargement of the Community and secondly, of the guidelines adopted by the European Council in March 1977 and the more detailed provisions adopted subsequently, especially in July 1978, June 1979 and November 1979 (see Annex 3, pp. 353, 356, and 357). The European Council asked the Bank to take more active measures to ensure job creation, a higher level of investment and a reduction in the economic divergences between Member States, and the Bank therefore had to increase its financing of projects satisfying its criteria for intervention. The Bank's activities from own resources in the Member States increased from a little over 500 m u.a. in 1972 to 1 086 m u.a. in 1976, 1 401.3 m EUA in 1977, 1 966.5 m EUA in 1978 and 2 281.2 m EUA in 1979.

Moreover, following the Commission's decision on the eligibility of each project, the Bank may now, under the New Community Instrument for borrowing and lending, grant, on behalf of the Community, additional funds for projects complying with the Community's priority objectives in the sectors of energy, industry and infrastructure, taking account, *inter alia*, of the regional impact of the projects and the need to combat unemployment.

The relevant figures are given in the chapter on financing the Community's internal development policy (see p. 236).

B—Projects financed by the EIB outside the Community

Since 1963 the Bank has taken part in the implementation of the economic and financial cooperation policy of the Community which, on the basis of various agreements, financial protocols and decisions, links it with an increasing number of developing countries: Greece, Turkey, the African, Caribbean and Pacific States (ACP), overseas countries and territories dependent on Member States, Portugal, Yugoslavia, the Maghreb (Algeria, Morocco, Tunisia) and Mashreq countries (Egypt, Jordan, Lebanon, Syria) and Malta, Cyprus and Israel. Between 1963 and 1978 it helped finance 294 projects for a total of 1 833.5 m EUA, of which 1 165.8 m EUA came from loans from its own resources, generally carrying interest subsidies from budget resources, and 667.7 m EUA came from budget resources made available to it by Member States, either directly in the case of Turkey, or through the European Development Fund (EDF) in the case of the ACP States.

This financial activity will increase as a result of the entry into force in late 1978 and early 1979 of new financial protocols with the Mediterranean countries and the renewal of the ACP-EEC Lomé Convention.

Total financing by the Bank may be summarized as follows, on the basis of the table below. Loans from own resources between 1958 and 1979: 11 654.5 m u.a. within the Community and 1 165.8 m u.a. outside the Community, giving a total of 12 820.3 m u.a.; and from the special section: 944.7 m u.a., of which 277 m u.a. within the Community under the NCI and 667.7 m u.a. outside the Community.

EIB financing by origin of resources and location of investment projects

	1958-72			1973-79		
	Number	Amount (in m u.a.)	% of total	Number	Amount (in m u.a.)	% of total
Operations from own resources						
—Within the Community	310	2 455.5	86.4	551	9 199.0	84.3
• Belgium	6	67.2	2.4	7	165.4	1.5
• Denmark	—	—	—	37	207.8	1.9
• FR of Germany	44	353.6	12.4	34	533.2	4.9
• France	56	570.5	20	70	1 460.7	13.4
• Ireland	—	—	—	48	614.1	5.6
• Italy	196	1 412.3	49.7	207	3 377.5	30.9
• Luxembourg	3	9.0	0.3	—	—	—
• Netherlands	5	42.9	1.5	4	62.3	0.6
• United Kingdom	—	—	—	137	2 628.1	24.1
• Outside the Community (Article 18)	—	—	—	7	149.9	1.4
—Outside the Community	41	155.7	5.5	101	1 010.1	9.2
Total	351	2 611.2	91.9	652	10 209.1	93.5
Operations from the special section						
—Within the Community from NCI resources				9	277.0	2.5
—Outside the Community	57	230.8	8.1	75	436.9	4.0
Total	57	230.8	8.1	84	713.9	6.5
Grand total	408	2 842.0	100.0	736	10 923	100.0

C—Interest rebates on EIB loans

The notes in the 'remarks' column in the 1979 general budget show that 11 headings indicate the possibility of obtaining interest subsidies. These are the appropriations for financial cooperation with the Mediterranean countries (see p. 297). Moreover, the Regulation establishing the European Regional Development Fund (ERDF) provides, in Article 4(2)(b), that aid from the Fund for infrastructure projects may take the form in whole or in part of a rebate of three percentage points on loans granted by the EIB under Article 130(a) and (b) of the EEC Treaty in the eligible zones.

The EDF also grants interest rebates on Bank loans.

Moreover, the Council Regulation of 3 August 1979 makes provision, under the European Monetary System, for a 3% rebate on certain Bank loans from its own resources or NCI resources.

D—Guarantee provided by the general budget

As part of its emergency aid for Portugal, the Council decided on 7 October 1975 that the 100% guarantee granted to the EIB for its financing in Portugal would be entered in the Community budget. Later, by its decision of 8 March 1977, the Council included in the budget the guarantee to be granted for EIB loans from its own resources to the Mediterranean countries. The text it adopted reads as follows:
'The Council's assent for Community guarantees shall apply at the earliest to the budget of the Communities for the 1978 financial year and only to loans granted by the EIB to third countries under agreements concluded pursuant to Article 238 of the Treaty establishing the EEC and under the Financial Protocol with Portugal'. So there is now a token entry in the budget (Article 968). If the fifth EDF is included in the budget it would be logical for this budget heading to cover, in addition, the guarantee of EIB loans from its own resources to the ACPs and OCTs.

*
* *

The European Investment Bank makes a very effective contribution by collecting a substantial volume of resources and using them for priority investment projects aimed at promoting the Community's internal development. As a banking institution it is quite distinct from the other financing instruments available to the Commission.

The Bank's very uniqueness has thus far enabled it to escape the full rigour of Community scrutiny. Parliament is concerned about this. The more the Bank takes on tasks which could have been performed by the Commission (Euratom loans, NCI, various types of interest rebate), the stronger will become the demand that its activities should be brought under proper control.

Footnotes to Chapter X

[1] The Bank may guarantee loans granted by third parties for investment projects satisfying its usual intervention criteria.

[2] The Board of Directors of the Bank is constituted as follows: the Federal Republic of Germany, France, Italy and the United Kingdom nominate three directors and two alternates each; the five other countries nominate one director each, with one alternate for the Benelux countries. When Greece has joined the Community, on 1 January 1981, one Greek Minister will be nominated to the Board of Governors, one titular member of the Board of Directors will be nominated by Greece and one alternate member nominated by common accord by Denmark, Greece and Ireland.

[3] The definition of the EIB unit of account (u.a.) pursuant to Article 4 of the Statute, is identical to that of the European unit of account (EUA). The Board of Governors was made responsible for the definition of the unit of account by the Treaty of 10 July 1975, which entered into force on 1 October 1977—since a Treaty was required to amend the Protocol annexed to the Treaty of Rome—because the future development of the international monetary system cannot be foreseen and therefore—rather than the unit of account being redefined in the Bank Statute at this stage—the Bank should be enabled to adjust its definition and conversion methods to any changes, following a decision of the Board of Governors.

[4] In 1973 and 1974 the Bank raised two loans in European composite units made up of the sum of a fixed amount of all the currencies of the Member States.

[5] The specific provisions of the applicable agreements must of course be taken into account in the case of projects outside the Community.

Conclusion to Part Two

In the period 1952-79, the budget resources of the three European Communities covered more than 73 000 m u.a. of expenditure, to which should be added over 3 000 m u.a. under the EDF, i.e. more than 76 000 m u.a. of resources allocated to non-recoverable expenditure. Moreover, borrowed funds accounted for 19 000 m u.a. which means some 100 000 m u.a. of available resources (see Annexes 12, p. 398 and 13, p. 400).

In this case the unit of account was based on current prices and did not possess a fixed value throughout the 28-year period. The figures are therefore a computed total and not a measure of value in real terms; the position in this respect is the same as with national accounts, which are likewise based on the addition of current-price totals in national currencies.

In 1980, revenue derived from Community taxes and Member States' contributions amounted to about 16 600 m EUA and receipts from borrowed resources to about 4 000 m EUA, making a total of more than 20 000 m EUA. The scale of European finance is thus increasing at a fair pace, and the share taken by borrowed resources is becoming more and more significant. In the case of the EEC's and Euratom's own resources, the Member States of the Community were wise enough to introduce a system which is phased over a period of time but is also automatic, and which has worked perfectly and has guaranteed the sound development of the Communities at least until 1981 because of the dynamism of the EEC. Although the system was the same for the ECSC and was long applied satisfactorily, the situation deteriorated with the freezing of the levy rates at a fairly low level. Other ways had to be found of making up for this decline. These two trends give food for thought as regards the future of own resources to be made over to the Community.

So far, however, the budgetary history of the European Communities has followed the same lines of development as that of the federal systems which exist elsewhere. All federal constitutions allow the grant of customs duties to the federation; this has been put into effect in the European Communities, which receive the income from the Common Customs Tariff and agricultural levies treated as CCT income because they are levied on trade movements resulting from a common agricultural policy. Beyond this, a number of federal constitutions such as that of the United States provide for the federation to collect duties or taxes so long as they are uniformly applied throughout the federation's territory and distributed proportionally. This is true of the ECSC levies and the VAT percentage with its uniform assessment basis, which still leaves the question of the relationship between amounts paid to the Community and payments to the Member States. That is the problem called tax sharing.

It is clear that one cannot contemplate increasing the fiscal burden on the European taxpayer. If the VAT percentage assigned to the Community were increased, this could not be done by increasing the rate imposed by each Member State but only by a transfer of resources from the national to Community level without changing the national percentages.

This would be all the easier in that the amounts which make up Community VAT are made over to the Community by the Member States and not collected independently by them. This makes it even more clear that resources transferred to the Community must enable the Community to take measures which should no longer be taken nationally. The transfer of resources must go hand in hand with a transfer of responsibilities.

A further general comment must be made here, for in the final analysis, public finance activity, of whatever kind, simply reflects the aspirations which precede the formulation of specific needs. Similarly, the financing of Europe is a derivative phenomenon. Its evolution depends on the resolve to integrate Europe more closely, to create a 'European union'. That will be the achievement not only of the governments but also of the people, who now have their own voice thanks to the direct election of the European Parliament.

PART THREE

Financial intervention by the European Communities

It is now time to move on from the subject of the provision of the finances of the European Communities to turn our attention to the purposes for which those finances are used, i.e. the policies which they have served to promote for the past 28 years.

A point which should be made straight away is that the economies of the nine Member States are so developed and diversified, and the political and administrative systems of the Member States are so complex, of such long standing and so firmly rooted, that action by the Community as a whole is justified only if it is likely to prove considerably more advantageous than action taken separately by each country. As we shall see below, that aim has not always been achieved, but it is at the heart of many decisions on Community activities with financial implications. Where a different approach is taken, the reason lies in another major objective of the Community, namely solidarity between nations expressed by way of transfers from the richer ones to the less-favoured ones.

There are three ways of approaching the subject of financial intervention by the European Communities. All three approaches might provide the basis for arranging the material in Part Three of this book.

The first approach consists of classifying the financial operations of the European Communities according to their contribution towards the economic integration of the Member States. This is a *macroeconomic approach*. At the present stage of political progress towards economic integration, five categories of operation can be identified. The first category offers substantial economies of scale: e.g. research and development in the fields of energy (nuclear energy, hydrocarbons, solar energy, etc.), aerospace and certain advanced industrial equipment (such as computers). The second category whose value is just as self-evident as that of the first category, transcends frontiers: e.g. the battle against pollution, protection of the environment, building up transport infrastructures. The third category covers the solution of economic problems whose scale is beyond the scope of individual Member States and which therefore need to be dealt with in a spirit of Community solidarity: e.g. stabilization of agricultural markets and earnings, reduction of unemployment caused by economic or structural factors, elimination of balance-of-payments problems. The fourth category of measures arises from the very existence of the European Communities, i.e. from the need for a change of attitude towards self-sufficiency and independence, and for greater cooperation with non-member countries. The fifth and last class of operation involves aid to further structural change and modernization: e.g. the structure of industry and commerce, the structure of agriculture, and the structure of employment. This rather lengthy, though very compressed, summary of the macroeconomic approach to the financial policy of the European Communities shows that a very fine subdivision of Community operations would be achieved in this way. Although it has much to offer, the use of that approach would have the effect of dispersing the material, whereas this book should be seeking to concentrate on the financial aspect. This approach has therefore been ruled out.

A second possible approach to Community finances would be to *analyse both Community spending and any relevant expenditure by national exchequers*. Non-repayable Community outlays can be divided into four categories. The first category consists of expenditure completely replacing national expenditures: this is an exceptional situation and only concerns the agricultural 'guarantee' sphere, yet although a unique case, such expenditure amounts to 70% of the EEC budget funds. The second category involves expenditure which supplements that of the national governments, namely expenditure on regional development (although the 'supplementary' nature is in fact often theoretical) and some research expenditure in the energy field. The third category comprises expenditure partly replacing national expenditures: it covers expenditure under the Social Fund and the fund for agricultural structures (EAGGF guidance), expenditure on cooperation with the Third World and certain types of research expenditure. The fourth category comprises Community expenditure which would not be incurred but for the existence of the European Communities, namely administrative expenditure and the cost of research work carried out by the Community research establishment. Such an analysis would be incomplete if it did not also cover operations carried out with loans made possible by the financial resources of the Communities. Such operations come under the second category and to a lesser degree the third category mentioned above. Here it makes a difference whether Community finance is supplementary to or replaces finance from national budgets, since the operations may be carried out at national level, at regional level or even at local government level. Hence, in a federal or largely decentralized system of government, Community financial assistance may be given to authorities which have had no part in the burden of paying contributions to the Community budget. This can be an indirect cause of imbalance, as has happened in the Federal Republic of Germany. However, this approach is unsuitable for Part Three of this book, because it does not focus enough on Community finances as such.

An *approach by sectors of operations* would seem to be the most thorough and appropriate method. Part Three will therefore cover the four major areas of policy into which Community financial operations can be broadly divided, namely agricultural market guarantees, the internal development of the Community, energy and industry and cooperation with non-member countries. For each of these areas of policy I shall examine in turn the various objectives, the budgetary and legal framework, and the financial resources which are or have been available. These four chapters will be followed by a final chapter dealing with the administrative organization of the Community, since the financial resources could not be used if appropriate administrative machinery had not been set up.

Since this book is about the finances of Europe there will be no mention of those Community policies which, however vital they may be, do not have any financial implications. Cases in point are the policy concerning restrictive practices and the approximation of laws. However, the policies which do have financial implications are among the most important of the Communities' policies. Without them, and in particular without the agricultural policy, the European Communities would not be what they are today.

Chapter XI:
Financing the common agricultural policy
(agricultural market guarantees)

The agricultural sector in the Community is among the biggest in the world.[1] The problems which arise are commensurate with its size.

The EEC Treaty devoted a whole section containing ten articles (Articles 38 to 47) to agriculture. Article 38 provides that 'the common market shall extend to agriculture and trade in agricultural products' and that 'the operation and development of the common market for agricultural products must be accompanied by the establishment of a common agricultural policy among the Member States'. According to Article 39(1) of the Treaty, the objectives of the common agricultural policy shall be:

'(a) to increase agricultural productivity by promoting technical progress and by ensuring the rational development of agricultural production and the optimum utilization of the factors of production, in particular labour;

(b) thus to ensure a fair standard of living for the agricultural community, in particular by increasing the individual earnings of persons engaged in agriculture;

(c) to stabilize markets;

(d) to assure the availability of supplies;

(e) to ensure that supplies reach consumers at reasonable prices'.

The implementation of the common agricultural policy (CAP) was the subject of prolonged and heated argument in the early 1960s because of the difference in attitude between on the one hand France and the Netherlands, countries with a long tradition of producing and exporting agricultural products, and on the other hand the Federal Republic of Germany and Italy, whose interests were best served in their view, by obtaining supplies from the main exporting countries and which did not consider the creation of an agricultural policy for the Community a top priority. The CAP was set up at the end of 1961 under pressure from France which would not otherwise agree to carry on with setting up the common market. A great deal of integration has been achieved within the Community in this sphere. Of all the common policies this is the longest established, the most significant, the most successful and the most criticized. Accordingly, its financial aspects have frequently come under the scrutiny of the Heads of State or Government: at The Hague in December 1969 and November 1976, at Brussels in December 1977 and December 1978, and at Paris in March 1979 (see Annex 3, pp. 350 and 352 to 355).

The general term 'common agricultural policy' embraces market policy, structure policy and certain specific measures. These are three quite separate items and should therefore be analysed separately. This chapter is concerned solely with agricultural market guarantee policy, which differs from agricultural structures policy in that its decision-making and financial machinery are run entirely by the Community, which explains why it receives 70% of the Community's budget funds.

In this chapter I shall take a look at the following five topics: how the markets for agricultural products are organized, monetary difficulties and their consequences, the attempts to bring spending on agricultural policy under control and, as in each of the next three chapters, the legislative and budgetary framework and the financial resources deployed.

1. Policy concerning the organization of agricultural markets

The common organization of markets (COM) remains the most visible manifestation of the common agricultural policy. Over the years, the Council—acting on proposals from the Commission and after consulting the European Parliament—has enacted regulations subjecting 18 markets, covering 91% of agricultural production, to common organization arrangements. (The COM are listed in the table on guarantee expenditure by sector, on p. 191.)[2,25] It should be mentioned in passing that the COM for fishery products is administered separately. Since December 1962, the organization of markets has been based on the following three principles:

   (i) a single market, with free movement of goods, involving the abolition of customs duties and quantitative restrictions, backed up by progressive approximation of Member States' farm prices;

   (ii) Community preference, through the establishment of a system of levies at frontiers and a common customs tariff;

   (iii) financial solidarity, whereby the Member States, and ultimately the Community, are responsible for the financial consequences of the measures adopted.

As this book does not set out to cover all aspects of the common agricultural policy,[3] but only to those which affect the budget, I shall focus here on a description of the prices policy and intervention policy machinery, preceded by a description of the economic machinery involved.

A—The economic machinery

Merely deciding on a desired price level by setting a guide price offers no guarantee that the chosen price will actually be charged. In practice, two situations can occur:

(1) The actual price on the Community market may be lower than the guide price—as often happens—because production is too high, exports are too low, or there is too great a volume of low-priced imports. Suitable methods have been devised to deal with these three eventualities:

   (a) On the internal market, the Community can intervene to support prices, so that producers receive at least a 'support price' (also called 'intervention price', 'purchase price', 'withdrawal price' or 'minimum price') set by the Council at the same time as the abovementioned guide price. In order to maintain the 'intervention price', products may be stored, denatured or destroyed. These 'interventions' are financed by the Community budget;

(b) With regard to the volume of exports, the Community can intervene by paying exporters 'refunds' equivalent to the difference between the price within the Community and the world price. This enables exporters in the Community to bring their prices into line with those of their competitors outside the Community and they therefore enjoy a better trading position. The entire cost of 'refunds' is borne by the Community budget;

(c) With regard to the volume of imports, the Community can intervene by imposing on imports a 'levy' equal to or higher than the difference between the price on the world market and the price in the Community. This secures preference for Community products, especially if the levy is higher than the difference. The 'levies' go into Community funds, as 'own resources'.

(2) The actual price on the Community market may be higher than the guide price, because production is too low. To avoid this state of affairs, the Community may take the following action, which again has some effect on Community expenditure or revenue:

(a) On the internal market, the Community can intervene by raising the guide price in order to encourage production, but this must be done with caution, otherwise consumers will either grin and bear it or seek alternative products. If, on the other hand, stocks are available the Community may put them on the market at a low price;

(b) With regard to the volume of exports, the Community can intervene by making exporting more difficult, either by suspending any refunds still remaining or by imposing an export tax;

(c) With regard to the volume of imports, the Community can intervene by making importing easier, by reducing or removing levies and customs duties.

In the history of the CAP the frequency of occurrence of each of the two above scenarios has been markedly different. The first one has become increasingly predominant, in fact, since the Community is quite amply self-sufficient in almost all the sectors covered by the CAP. The main role of the Community budget is therefore to preside over the management of surpluses.

Four principles for the operation of the common organization of agricultural markets have gradually gained ascendancy:

(a) 'Price support', whereby export refunds are granted, and whereby intervention operations are carried out on the market. More than 70% of agricultural production is concerned, i.e. cereals, sugar, milk, beef and veal, pigmeat, some fruit and vegetables, table wine and fishery products. All these sectors are permanently or occasionally beset by over-production problems;

(b) 'External protection', which applies to 25% of agricultural production, i.e. flowers, other wines, rice and other fruit and vegetables;

(c) 'Additional aid', which is not unlike the system of deficiency payments the United Kingdom used to have.[4] This covers only 2.5% of agricultural products and makes it possible to keep consumer prices at a reasonable level, while maintaining producers' earnings. The products involved are principally durum wheat, olive oil and tobacco;

(d) 'Flat-rate aid per hectare' which covers 0.6% of products, and serves mainly to encourage productivity.

Thus, the agricultural markets are organized on the basis of a complex and flexible set of machinery which—in theory, at least—makes it possible to influence production, international trade and prices, in order to reconcile the conflicting interests of producers, who are concerned about their earnings, consumers, who are worried about rising prices, and the

Community as a unit, which needs balanced and secure supplies. The problem is that farmers are more or less at liberty to produce without having to worry about how much the market can absorb. A recurrent jibe is that farmers in the EEC countries produce with a view to benefiting from 'intervention', rather than in order to meet consumer demand.

Let us now turn to the prices policy pursued by the Community and then consider intervention which comes either as a direct result, or in most cases as an indirect result, of the ruling prices.

B—The prices policy pursued by the Community

The cornerstone of the common agricultural policy is the fixing by the Community of the prices to be applied throughout its territory. At the beginning of the year (in theory not later than 1 April) the Council, acting on a proposal from the Commission and after consulting the European Parliament, decides on the desirable price level (for the ensuing season) of each price subject to common marketing arrangements, with a view to satisfying the objectives specified in Article 39 of the EEC Treaty. Parliament is therefore merely asked to give its opinion and their conciliation procedure is not used in this case—a state of affairs to which it objects (see Annex 5, p. 368). Within the Council lengthy negotiations and hard bargaining about these prices take place (the infamous 'marathon sessions'). It is taking longer and longer to reach an agreement (the final decisions were not taken until February in 1975, March in 1974 and 1976, April in 1977, May in 1978 and 1980, June in 1979). This unfortunate development is partly due to the prevailing political circumstances in the Member States (political crises, forthcoming elections, etc.) or even the circumstances prevailing within the Community institutions, but the main cause is the growing tendency to reshape the marketing organizations when the prices are being fixed. Community problems of a more general nature may also delay matters (e.g. the British problem in 1980).

Although price fixing is the pivot around which the common market in agricultural products revolves, changes in the economic situation and in the economic structures on particular markets have prompted the Council to issue a growing number of regulations to alter the way in which the CAP is run. As a result, the annual negotiations have become concerned as much with the 'related measures' as with the prices themselves. The negotiations have in fact become much more involved in recent years, because the related measures have increasingly consisted in reshaping the arrangements regarding the common organization of markets, with the result that the decisions taken on prices are based on much wider considerations.

At first, the Community's prices policy was not altogether satisfactory. Having decided that the income of the agricultural community should come solely from the prices charged, the Community was inclined to set prices fairly high, in order to encourage the attainment of the levels of production judged to be desirable. For example, cereal prices were set at more or less the level in the Federal Republic of Germany, which was the highest in the Community of the Six. Other prices, in particular for sugar, were determined in much the same way. Thus, the policy was biased in favour of efficient farmers (50% of French cereals are produced by 7% of suppliers, who therefore pocket half the total Community aid given to French farmers). Moreover, this policy encouraged overproduction, which was very costly because of the guaranteed producer prices paid by the marketing organizations. The dairy products market was a good example of this. The bulk of the spending on that particular market, to which a growing proportion of EAGGF guarantee expenditure was directed, was on measures designed to dispose of products at an attractive guaranteed price when both the internal market and the external market were almost saturated.

Price relativity is just as important as price levels, but this has not been properly maintained, in that the prices of vegetable products have been increased by far more than the prices of animal products. In fact, the solution to the Community's agricultural problems does not lie in a policy of high prices but in a structural policy, which is a complex policy and a difficult one because of the social issues it raises. It would also be highly desirable for structural policy, which has not yet reached maturity, and markets policy to be complementary, instead of being independent of each other as they still are to a great extent at present.

Since 1977/78 the Community has deliberately been pursuing a policy of low prices. The increases in the prices of agricultural products decided on since then have been much smaller than before, as the table below shows.

(%)

	Commission's proposal in units of account[1]	Parliament's Opinion	Council's Decision
1976/77	+7.5	+9.5	+7.5
1977/78	+3	+3	+3.9
1978/79	+2	+2[2]	+2.1
1979/80	0	+3	+1.5[3]
1980/81	+2.4[4]	—[5]	+5.0[6]

[1] Common prices were calculated in u.a. until 1979/80; the ECU has been used since then.
[2] Excluding products in surplus.
[3] Excluding dairy products.
[4] Weighted average increase of 2.4% proposed on 6 February 1980, changed to 5% on 30 April 1980.
[5] Parliament rejected the Commission's proposal for a 2.5% increase, but made no alternative suggestion.
[6] Weighted average increase of 5%; i.e. increases of between 5.5% and 7%, but only 4% for milk.

However, because of the existence of the common market for agricultural products, the agricultural sector is less at risk in the present economic crisis than are other sectors of the economy. The system of guaranteed prices enables farmers to maintain their level of income by raising production, whereas in the present economic circumstances many other sectors of activity are not in such a fortunate position. It would therefore be logical that increases in the prices of agricultural products should be kept as low as possible, so that they do not contribute to the prices spiral.

An additional objective of the policy of holding down common market prices is to eliminate surpluses, on the assumption that price freezing will persuade producers not to produce more or even to produce less of the product in question. It is vital to the health of Europe's finances that surpluses should be eliminated.

Another important point is that the average level of prices in real terms, i.e. in national currencies, includes the effect of adjusting the 'green rates'; this adjustment is often made at the same time as the prices are decided. This adjustment chiefly affects the countries whose green rates (see p. 175) are too high in relation to the strength of their currency. (These are the countries with a comparatively weak currency: France, Italy and the United Kingdom.) For 1978/79, for example, the effect of the adjustment was an increase of 3% under the Commission's proposal and of 7% under the Council's decision. However, large cuts in the negative compensatory amounts in 1978, 1979 and 1980 have made it increasingly difficult for the countries with weak currencies to offset small rises in prices by devaluing their green rates (see Annex 6, p. 371, for the MCAs on 1 July 1980).

In the first half of 1980 there was a general lack of agreement within the Community and its institutions, and among the Member States and their governments, as to the future direction of the CAP. The Commission's prices proposal of 6 February 1980 advocated a price freeze for products in surplus (milk and sugar) and a small rise for the other products. On 26 March 1980, Parliament rejected the proposal made by its Committee on Agriculture for a price increase of 7.9%, and passed a Resolution which while not specifying any percentage referred to 'the need to guarantee farmers a fair income' and to 'the need to contain the increase in expenditure within limits compatible with a sound balanced budget'. The Council, for its part, is very divided when it comes to arriving at decisions, because of the delicate compromises that have to be made. As a result of the 'Community crisis' following the impasse at the European Council meeting in Luxembourg on 28 April 1980, the Council decision that same day to raise the prices by an average of 5% could not be confirmed. A decision was finally taken on 30 May 1980.

As a final word on this matter, I would mention that a 1% increase in prices in 1980 would increase the budget by about 150 million EUA over a full year. Therefore the financial implications involved are not all that great, even with an increase several times that percentage. A more important implication is that price increases could give rise to an increase in production in sectors which are already in surplus.

C—Means of intervention

Each of the 18 common organizations of markets has its own special features. In particular they vary in the amounts of price support. However, Community financing can be grouped in six main categories:

(1) *'Export refunds'* are intended to make up any difference between the market price in the Community and the price on the world market, so that Community products can be exported to non-member countries. The financial impact of the refunds is directly determined by world prices. In the present situation of declining prices for many agricultural products (milk, and until recently sugar and cereals) the total figure is quite high, amounting to 45% of total expenditure of the EAGGF Guarantee Section in 1979. In 1974, when world prices were often higher than prices in the Community, it comprised only 18% of the costs for agriculture.

(2) *'Storage'* is the device used to adjust supply and demand. When surpluses occur, either throughout the Community or in particular regions, the supply can be bought in and price levels in the Community maintained. The storage is usually carried out by official agencies (as 'public storage') if intervention is obligatory, i.e. where all available produce must be purchased by the official agency at the intervention price, as in the case of cereals, milk powder, butter, beef and veal. But since there are surpluses in the Community markets for most of its main agricultural products, the storage capacity of the official agencies is often fully taken up. 'Private storage' is then resorted to, because it is flexible and usually not much more costly than public storage. Long-established for pigmeat and wine, it has been extended to cereals and dairy products.
It is generally supposed that storage expenditure is confined to technical costs and financial costs (tied-up capital) arising from storage. In fact, the economic effects of

storage under the common agricultural policy do not stop at warehousing but extend to action which has to be taken to dispose of stocks, especially in the case of surpluses of butter and milk powder, which have been accumulating for several years. Clearance of stocks is a great deal more expensive and much more difficult than putting produce into storage.

The cost of price support through the storage intervention system can be estimated as 13% of the EAGGF guarantee appropriations in 1979, with a further 4% for private storage, making a total of 17%.

(3) '*Compensatory aid*' involves many kinds of measures and amounted to almost 29% of expenditure specifically on agriculture in 1979:

    (a) Compensatory aid to assist in the disposal of surplus produce not included in intervention in the form of storage but granted Community subsidy so that disposal can be achieved by lowering the price. Subsidy of this kind represented about 16% of the expenditure of the EAGGF Guarantee Section specifically on agriculture in 1979. It chiefly involves milk and wine.

    (b) Compensatory aid to support the processing industries is either for the purpose of obtaining the disposal of basic agricultural products, enabling processing industries to purchase them at competitive prices, or to allow these industries to be competitive in the world market, since the price of the products for processing is usually higher if they are bought within the Community than if they come from outside. Expenditure on these subsidies amounted to 5% of the EAGGF Guarantee Section appropriations in 1979 and is likely to rise substantially in the next few years. The items involved are predominantly starches and processed fruit and vegetables.

    (c) Regional compensatory aid whereby the Community can grant, directly to producers, a subsidy amounting to the difference between the producer price and the consumer price. These comprised more than 8% of expenditure specifically on agriculture in 1979. They apply to durum wheat, olive oil, tobacco and oilseeds and are similar to the British deficiency payments.

(4) '*Guidance premiums*' are intended for guidance of production or consumption. These include the calving premium, the premium for nurse cows, measures designed to expand the consumer market for dairy products and compensation for promoting Community citrus fruits. They amounted to only 2% of Guarantee Fund expenditure in 1979.

(5) *Expenditure on 'obligations' under other policies.* The above four kinds of expenditure include costs arising from decisions taken outside the CAP or costs directly engendered by such decisions. For example, the Lomé Convention contains a clause providing for the import of 1 300 000 tonnes of sugar produced in the ACP countries. Because of the present sugar over-production, the Community has to re-export the sugar, incurring the cost of refunds on export, which in 1979 amounted to 400 m EUA (see p. 280). The Community also imports at low rates of duty or duty-free certain products which compete with equivalent or alternative Community products. For example, it imports 100 000 tonnes of butter from New Zealand, which cost the Community 180 m EUA in 1980. As a result, compensatory aid has to be granted in order to maintain sales of the Community products. Altogether, these obligations under international agreements are quite a heavy burden on the budgetary funds for agriculture.

(6) Finally, a decreasing proportion of EAGGF Guarantee Section expenditure—13% in 1977, 9% in 1978 and 6.8% in 1979—goes to monetary compensatory amounts. These we shall now examine.

The monetary difficulties have had extremely troublesome effects on the guaranteed markets for agricultural products, disturbing both production and trading and giving rise to 'agri-monetary expenditure'.

A—Initial measures to deal with the monetary developments

The implementation of the common agricultural policy implies that common prices have to be set and that the intervention expenditure is to be met from Community financial resources; the policy therefore requires a common denominator for the currencies involved. The common denominator chosen, in 1962, under Regulation No 129, was the 'unit of account' used for the budget (see p. 24). Later, Council Regulation No 635/68 of 30 May 1968 established the arrangements for adjustment of the unit of account in the event of changes in the rates of exchange between the Member States. That Regulation had to be applied when the French franc was devalued on 8 August 1969, raising the rate for the unit of account from FF 4.93706 to FF 5.55419. However, the Council agreed that France need not bring its prices for agricultural products into line with Community prices immediately, i.e. that, to avoid aggravating the inflationary trends that had prompted devaluation and to avoid putting the group of producers concerned in an unduly favourable position, France could delay raising these prices by the devaluation proportion of 11.11%. In consequence, fixed 'compensatory amounts' had to be introduced to bridge the gap between the French prices and the Community prices; these amounts had the effect of a levy making French exports dearer and subsidizing French imports. When French prices had caught up with Community prices, in August 1971, these compensatory amounts were done away with.

A different method was adopted for the problems arising from the revaluation of the Deutschmark on 24 October 1969. Since, obviously—with the consumers in mind—the Federal Government did not wish to cut the prices of German agricultural products by 9.29%, it succeeded in obtaining for the German farmers for a four-year period an annual aid to offset their loss of income. The EAGGF was to make decreasing contributions towards this subsidy (90 m u.a. in 1971, 60 m u.a. in 1972 and 30 m u.a. in 1973, but in the event the last-mentioned payment was not necessary).

B—The monetary compensatory amounts (MCAs)

The balance of payments crisis of 1971 led the Community to make the application of the 'monetary compensatory amounts' (MCAs) system general (Regulation (EEC) No 974/71 of 11 May 1971), these amounts varying with the rates of exchange in the money market. This system envisages that:
(a) if the value of a Member State's currency is higher than its 'green rate' it may apply 'positive' MCAs, collecting amounts on imports and granting amounts on exports;
(b) if the value of a Member State's currency is lower than its 'green rate' it may apply 'negative' MCAs, collecting amounts on exports and granting amounts on imports.

There were also adjustments called 'accession compensatory amounts' (ACAs), applicable under Article 55 of the Act of Accession for the period from 1 January 1973 to 31 December 1977, to offset differences in price between the Six and the new Member States. However, these adjustments remained in effect for 1978.

Originally the main purpose of the MCAs was to preserve the traditional patterns of trade and protect consumers in the countries with weak currency from too sharp a rise in the prices of imported agricultural products. They were the price that had to be paid for failing to achieve economic and monetary union.

C—Green rates for the unit of account

From February 1973 onwards the unit of account applicable to the common agricultural policy was no longer the IMF parity unit of account but a unit of account picturesquely called 'green'. In practice, the indicators used for the common agricultural policy (seasonal prices and Community subsidies) expressed in units of account were converted into national currencies at 'representative rates' close to, but not identical with, the money market rates. The representative rates are not fixed for a period but are amended by Council decision according to the economic and monetary situation of each Member State. The prices in national currency of agricultural products, and all the Community aids, i.e. refunds, intervention payments of all kinds, and specific rates of duty under the Common Customs Tariff (for cheeses and wines only) are all fixed by Council decision under Article 43 of the EEC Treaty. Thus, a rise in the green rate means a rise in the prices of agricultural products in the Member State concerned, and vice versa.

The MCAs are based on the difference between the money market rate and the green rate. The percentage by which the green rate is higher or lower is multiplied by the price of each product sold within the EEC or exported, and this gives the financial adjustment to be made through the MCAs.

Broadly speaking, the bigger the gap between the green rate for the currency of a Member State and the true value of the currency, the larger the MCAs. If a Member State is a net importer and its currency has depreciated but, in order to limit the increase in the domestic prices of agricultural products, it refuses to devalue the green rate for its currency, then Community solidarity comes into play and the budget has to pay out increasing amounts in MCAs. Thus, in November 1976 the value of the pound sterling had fallen so much that the MCAs for a full year then totalled 1 000 m u.a.

D—Reducing the monetary compensatory amounts

The MCAs were intended as a temporary expedient but they have remained in force, making the general budget much bigger, sheltering the market for agricultural products from the influence of market forces and maintaining artificial distortions beyond the period of gradual adjustment in the price trend for the agricultural products to which the MCAs apply and the other products, both in respect of trade patterns and of internal Community expenditure. Moreover, within the agricultural sector MCAs make it difficult as regards the intended development of greater regional specialization in agriculture.

Several attempts to phase out the MCAs have failed, and risked causing a confrontation between Member States.

The initial attempts to reduce MCAs

Given the magnitude of MCAs at the time (see Annex 6, p. 370), on 21 October 1976 the Commission proposed to the Council a plan for almost automatic phasing-out of the MCAs, by means of gradual approximation of green rates and money market rates, until the MCAs had been eliminated completely. This proposal was not adopted by the Council, since the United Kingdom and the Federal Republic of Germany objected to the automatic nature of the scheme. In a new text submitted a year later, on 28 October 1977, the Commission proposed that existing MCAs should be cut by one-seventh a year and that the new MCAs introduced because of change in the money market rates should be completely removed one year after coming into operation. This second proposal was no more successful than the first, the Council of Ministers continuing to apply a pragmatic approach. Changes in the green rates are still being decided on an *ad hoc* basis, usually at the time of the annual fixing of agricultural prices. However, the European Council itself took up the problem of MCAs on 5 and 6 December 1977 (see Annex 3, p. 353); again on 4 and 5 December 1978 it debated the matter (see Annex 3, p. 355), emphasizing the seriousness of the problem, although there can hardly be any lack of awareness of this.

It must be pointed out that 'negative MCAs'—those applicable to countries with a depreciated currency—are much easier to eliminate than 'positive MCAs', because they can be removed if prices are raised and the 'green rate' is lowered. True, increasing the agricultural prices is an inflationary measure which a government may be reluctant to apply; on the other hand it is difficult for a government to cut the prices of home-produced agricultural products, especially by individual action not taken in the general context of Community decisions on prices and common measures.[5]

The EEC has suffered greatly as a result of its currency problems. The general instability of exchange rates has been highly damaging to the economic state of the Community and especially to the CAP. If this situation had continued it would have greatly weakened the former and destroyed the latter. The Community has therefore striven to find ways to combat the situation. In the agri-monetary sphere it has tried to organize the progressive elimination of the monetary compensatory amounts but has above all sought to create a zone of monetary stability.

The European Monetary System and the plan for aligning green rates with money market rates

Until the EMS was put into effect[6] and the ECU was introduced into the CAP, in March 1979, different kinds of exchange rates operated for the weak and the strong currencies. The former were 'floating', whereas the latter were linked together in the 'snake' and varied only within a margin of fluctuation. In consequence—unless the central rates for the 'snake' currencies were adjusted—the German, Dutch, Belgian and Luxembourg MCAs were stable, but the MCAs for the countries with a weak currency were recalculated weekly on the basis of the movements in these currencies in relation to the 'snake' currencies. However, so that changes should not be too frequent, two 'reducing' devices were applied: the application of an exempt proportion of 1.5%, and the requirement that the exchange rate must have moved by at least 1%.

176

Since the EMS came into operation and the ECU was introduced into the CAP, by Regula tion (EEC) 652/79 of 29 March 1979, applicable until 31 March 1980 but extended until 31 March 1981, there are only two currencies for which the MCAs still have to be adjusted weekly: the United Kingdom pound sterling and the Italian lira. The former does not par ticipate in the EMS and the MCAs are determined as before: weekly calculation of the deviation between the pound sterling and the EMS currencies linked together by fixed parities (central rates) and permitted margins of fluctuation; the lira does participate in the EMS but has a permitted margin of fluctuation of $\pm$ 6% which means that the MCAs for Italy can undergo considerable fluctuation.

As explained earlier (see p. 28), the value of the ECU is the same as that of the EUA but the method of conversion differs. In order to calculate the entitlements of recipients under the CAP, ECU conversion into national currencies is based on the latest representative rate adopted by the Council; for the purposes of entry in the accounts in implementation of the budget, however, agricultural expenditure is converted into EUA at the rate obtaining on the twentieth day of the second month preceding that in which it was entered in the accounts.

The adoption of the EMS and the introduction into the CAP of the ECU gave rise to a dis pute between France and the Federal Republic of Germany which must be mentioned. In return for agreeing to join the EMS, France wanted the Council to give an undertaking to phase out the MCAs, including positive MCAs. As we have already explained, although reduction of the negative MCAs does not present any great difficulties, because the prices in national currency rise as the green rates are lowered, the situation is entirely different for countries with a strong currency and positive MCAs. Any reduction in the positive MCAs made by raising the green rate and bringing it close to the money market rate means a cut in the payments to farmers, i.e. a net drop in their standard of living. The matter has not been settled and the German MCAs are still unchanged.

However, at the end of the first half of 1980, expenditure on MCAs dropped to a low level as a result of three developments:
(1) a spectacular rise in the UK pound, so that the MCA rate, which had been almost −45% in 1976, became positive by a small margin;
(2) a series of reductions in the green rates for the weak currencies: Ireland, France and Italy no longer have any MCAs; and
(3) the Benelux MCAs remained below 3%.

Only the German positive MCAs remain, at a rate below 10%, although they had not been increased for the revaluation of the Deutschmark on 23 September 1979. The bulk of the cost therefore comes from the countries which are net importers and have a weak currency; this expenditure is now only 2% of the budget. This improvement must be welcomed as one of the valuable achievements resulting from the smooth functioning of the EMS.

E—The position of MCAs in relation to the Community's finances

The MCAs are specially treated in the budget, in a manner contrary to the classical rules of budgetary practice, and especially to the rule of universality. The basic regulation es tablishing the MCAs—Council Regulation (EEC) 974/71 of 12 May 1971—was drawn up under Article 43 of the EEC Treaty and describes the cash flows involved in MCAs in intra-Community trade[7] as 'intervention measures under the common agricultural policy'. Consequently the MCAs collected are not regarded as 'own resources' in the sense of Article 201 of the EEC Treaty; the entries in the budget are shown in the 'expenditure' section of the general budget, whether they involve outgoings from Community funds or sums paid into Community resources. Accordingly, in the case of a country with a depreciated currency, the entry in the budget will be either a 'net expenditure', in the case of a net importer (for example the United Kingdom or Italy), or a 'net receipt', treated as 'negative expenditure', in the case of a net exporter (for example France or Ireland). This—unorthodox—presentation in the budget was devised at a time when it was impossible to foresee that the volume of MCAs would become so large. It does, however, offer the advantage of presenting in a simple form the net cost of the obligation to collect or pay MCAs in respect of the trade in agricultural products which results from instability.

One last point: a somewhat original procedure was adopted for inclusion in the budget of expenditure in MCAs payable to the United Kingdom and Italy. Article 2a of Regulation (EEC) 974/71 provided that Member States making exports to the United Kingdom or Italy could levy direct the MCAs on imports due to these two countries in intra-Community trade. This method was adopted so as to avoid the excessive costs resulting from the application of the dual rate of exchange at the time when the IMF unit of account was employed;[8] it was abandoned in 1980 since it is no longer necessary in a budgetary framework based on the EUA.

The table below is provided as a example showing the financial effects, calculated in millions of EUA, of the MCAs during the financial year 1978.[9] These effects were very substantial.

MCAs in 1978, in million EUA

	Belgium and Luxembourg	Denmark	FR of Germany	France	Ireland	Italy	Netherlands	United Kingdom	EEC
(1)	54.9	238.5	159.5	110.9	180.8	−42.3	226.6	−49	879.9
(2)	−43	−238.5	−172.9	−288.5	−210.9	+418.4	−179	+714.4	0
(3) = (1)+(2)	+11.9	0	−13.4	−177.6	−30.1	+376.1	+47.6	+665.4	879.9

(1) MCAs actually paid by the paying agencies of the Member States under Regulation 974/71 of 12 May 1971:
   (i) MCAs levied or granted for extra-Community trade;
   (ii) MCAs levied or granted for intra-Community trade, including compensatory amounts granted to Italy and the United Kingdom on imports and paid at the time of export from the other Member States (Belgium, Denmark, Federal Republic of Germany, France, Ireland and the Netherlands) by those countries, in application of Article 2a of Regulation 974/71 as from April 1976, after approval by the Council.
(2) MCAs granted on imports and paid by other Member States:
corrections to be made under Article 2a of Regulation 974/71. The sums comprise intra-Community MCAs paid by exporting Member States on behalf of importing Member States (minus sign = payment by the exporting States; plus sign = MCAs granted on imports and paid by the exporting Member State but to be re-entered in the account of the importing Member State). These sums are to correct cash movements between the own resources accounts opened in each Member State.
(3) MCAs paid by each Member State according to the true economy thereof and whatever the method of payment used:
   (a) Net expenditure (plus sign):
      (i) for countries with an appreciated currency and which were net exporters (Belgium, Luxembourg and the Netherlands);
      (ii) for countries with a depreciated currency and which were net importers (Italy and the United Kingdom);
   (b) Net 'negative expenditure' (minus sign):
      (i) for countries with a depreciated currency and which were net exporters (France and Ireland);
      (ii) for countries with an appreciated currency and which were net importers (the Federal Republic of Germany; but in 1977 it was a net exporter).

3. Containing the agricultural policy

The growth in expenditure on agriculture, at the rate of 23% a year from 1975 to 1979, and its 70% share in the EEC's budget expenditure, coupled with the fact that structural surpluses have occurred, has led the Commission to recommend that the policy of guaranteed markets for agricultural products should be contained.

A—General comments

It is widely accepted that the expenditure on agriculture is unavoidable, even 'open-ended'. This is not quite true, although from scrutiny of the budget at any given moment it may appear to be the case. Examination of the budget over a long period shows very clearly that the items which make up this expenditure can differ widely in nature.

The only truly unavoidable items of expenditure are those of unlimited duration, the magnitude of which is uncontrollable because it is governed by the fluctuations occurring in completely free markets. This expenditure results from the application of the major operating principles involved in the common organizations of markets, which are designed to ensure the equilibrium of the markets in agricultural products: refunds and public storage.

Other categories of expenditure on agriculture are also permanent, in terms of the regulations; they are for specific purposes and therefore easier to contain. They result from the attempt to achieve equilibrium and correspond to specific—but permanent—measures in particular sectors, e.g. aid for durum wheat, which is aimed at maintaining a certain level of income. Expenditure of this kind can be discontinued if the objective is judged to have been attained. Such items of expenditure can thus be contained, although it is always difficult to take away acquired rights.

A further category of expenditure on agriculture is that intended to overcome a temporary imbalance; this is therefore *ad hoc* expenditure to restore equilibrium. Clearly its value depends solely on its effectiveness. It could be brought under control if there is 'targeted' monitoring of the management thereof. Cases in point are the premiums for conversion and for non-marketing of milk, initially intended to cover 1 300 000 cows and to be for a limited period, the schemes being financed jointly by the Guarantee and Guidance Sections of the EAGGF. These schemes are still in operation. The same applies to the consumer subsidy for butter, intended to reduce the volume of surplus stocks, which has however been very costly and has had very modest results; yet the Council is continuing and expanding this scheme without heed to its effectiveness. Containing such expenditure would mean either stopping it or limiting it to worthwhile applications. Thus, whereas in the first case an explicit programme of action exists, in the second no such programme is formulated, so that there is no means of measuring the results, nor of bringing the expenditure under control. Clearly future efforts to contain agricultural expenditure should be directed along these lines, i.e. precise programmes should be drawn up, the results achieved should be assessed annually and the action should be suspended, increased or reduced according to the results observed.

To conclude, it seems clear that there exist different kinds of expenditure on agriculture:
  (i) the *ad hoc* expenditure to restore equilibrium can be contained, i.e. made as fruitful as possible;

(ii) the expenditure directed at achieving a permanent aim can be cut back over a long period;

(iii) only the items of expenditure governed by market forces are genuinely unavoidable.

B—The common organization in the milk products sector

The milk products sector is the most costly in the common agricultural policy. In the budget for the financial year 1979 it was assigned 38% of appropriations to the EAGGF Guarantee Section and 27% of the total of appropriations for payment; in the financial year 1978 it took up 46.5% of the appropriations. These figures alone call for some explanation concerning the undue place occupied by milk from the economic and political points of view. Milk and milk products make up some 19% of the value of final agricultural products in the Community and nearly one-third of the farmers in the EEC are milk producers (1.9 million milk producers out of a total of 5.6 million farmers). Moreover, there are great disparities in the dairy sector: about 1.5 million producers have fewer than 10 dairy cows (about 20% of the total) and the average herd size ranges from 5 cows in Italy to 23 cows in the Netherlands and 70 cows in Scotland. Thus a great many farmers in the EEC depend largely for their living on milk production; this is why the Community sets a 'political price' for milk.

In its 'Programme of action for 1977-80, for progressive establishment of equilibrium in the milk market', submitted to the Council on 9 July 1976,[10] the Commission found it necessary to emphasize the persistence of a structural imbalance in the milk and milk products sector:

(a) since 1960, to date, milk production in the Community has tended to resemble industrial production. The output has increased by about 1.7% per annum, and by as much as 2% in 1979, despite a gradual long-term decrease in the number of dairy cows, the average yield per dairy cow having risen (from 3 074 kg in 1960 to 4 036 kg in 1980); this is largely due to the growing use of animal feed compounds with a high nutritional content, based on soya imported from the United States, since the prices of these compounds are very competitive (and they are imported duty-free);

(b) the consumption of milk and milk products has been declining. As regards animal consumption, the changeover from farms' own skimmed milk to manufactured milk powder has speeded up in the last ten years, while the human use of the various milk products has markedly changed. Consumption of butter, liquid milk and fresh products has steadily decreased but consumption of cheese has increased. It is difficult to export these products other than at 'bargain' prices. Food aid has reached a maximum of 150 000 tonnes a year.

A similar situation of structural imbalance exists in most of the producing countries. Because of the worldwide surplus of dairy products, world prices are very low, making it a costly business to increase the quantities disposed of. Moreover, for reasons of trading policy the Community is often unwilling to compete too strongly with some of the traditional exporting countries (for example New Zealand and Australia, members of the Commonwealth) by setting refunds too high.

To sum up, expenditure of the EAGGF Guarantee Section on the milk products sector rose from about 600 m u.a. in 1968-69, in the original six Member States to about 1 500 m u.a.

in 1973 with the enlarged Community, rising to 4 527 m u.a. in 1979. Despite this considerable financial effort by the Community, by 1977 a skimmed-milk-powder mountain had formed. A total of 300 000 tonnes in storage would have been reasonable, but stocks increased from 465 000 tonnes at the beginning of 1974 to 580 000 tonnes at the beginning of 1975, 1 150 000 tonnes at the beginning of 1976 and 1 230 000 tonnes at the beginning of 1977. Special measures were therefore introduced, mainly in the form of aid for disposal for use in animal feed. As a result, the stocks were greatly reduced (to 200 000 tonnes at the end of 1979) but the cost of disposal was extremely high; there was too the fear that the surplus would immediately build up again if these measures were discontinued.

Evidence of the anxiety felt in the matter was provided by the motion of censure put down on 13 May 1976 by the Conservative Group in Parliament, criticizing the failure of the Commission's management. The debate on this, which took place in plenary session in June 1976, revealed that most of the members of Parliament blamed the Council rather than the Commission for the situation. On 16 June 1976 there were only 18 votes for the motion of censure, with 109 against.

Although the stocks of milk products are the highest—in view of the magnitude of the structural surplus—they are not the only stocks to be examined when speaking of the common agricultural policy. At the end of 1979 the Community was holding in stock about 215 000 tonnes of milk powder (equal to more than 10% of the year's output), 295 000 tonnes of butter (15% of output), 1 880 000 tonnes of cereals (less than 2% of output), 290 000 tonnes of beef and veal (about 5% of output) and 55 000 tonnes of olive oil (about 10% of output). Valued at the intervention price, the total public stocks were worth about 2 250 m u.a., a sum not shown in the budget of the Community of 31 December 1979.

C—The principle of co-responsibility

The Commission became worried enough to propose that a more direct link between the production and the disposal of milk should be formed by introducing a 'co-responsibility levy' on milk producers, in order to create a better economic and psychological climate for achieving equilibrium in the market for milk. The levy instituted by Council Regulation (EEC) 1079/77 of 17 May 1977 applies uniformly to all quantities of milk delivered to dairies and to direct sales of milk and products at the farm, except in hill farming areas (see p. 213). The proceeds of the levy are not an 'own resource' but are a part of the intervention arrangements incorporated in the common market organization for milk and milk products and are used to help finance measures to expand the market (advertising campaigns, the search for new products, and the financial contributions to the supply of school milk and to the disposal of surplus butterfats).[11]

This was not the first time that the principle of co-responsibility had been applied, since the Community invoked it when organizing the market for sugar in 1968. Sugar producers have to pay a 'production levy', to meet the cost of price support, on all production exceeding the individual basic quota; they may also pay a 'storage levy' to even out the charges imposed under a scheme of fair distribution of storage costs. In 1979 the receipts under these two heads were 465 m EUA, equivalent to 49.5% of the expenditure of the COM for sugar (see Annex 10, p. 384). Unlike the co-responsibility levy on milk, these levies are 'own resources'.[12]

The initial levy on milk was small (0.5% of the target price for milk); the Commission proposed on 31 January 1979 that it should be substantially increased for the 1979-80 season and become a progressive tax linked to the rise in output. Accordingly, the preliminary draft budget for 1980, submitted on 15 June 1979, showed a levy yield of 880 m EUA, to be directly offset against expenditure on milk and not used to finance special measures. However, on 22 June 1979, the Farm Ministers rejected this change from a fixed levy to a progressive tax which would more markedly discourage over-production. Since the Council had refused to approve the new co-responsibility tax on milk, the Commission had to bring in a letter of amendment to its preliminary draft budget on 6 July 1979, increasing EAGGF Guarantee Section expenditure. Thus, the old system continues to function, although it is incontestable that Community production of milk and milk products had to be reduced if the relevant expenditure were to be contained. The date of 22 June 1979 should be remembered as a sad day for the finances of the EEC; in actual fact, the levy yielded only 94.2 m EUA.

The Commission tried again a few months later, with proposals dated 29 November 1979 and 5 February 1980 for a co-responsibility tax on milk. The plan for this system was to charge a fixed tax of 1.5% of the target price on total production plus a surtax of 18 ECU per 100 kg of milk output above a reference quantity of 99% of the 1979 quantity. The Commission proposed that 80% of the price of milk should finance the bulk of the cost of marketing the extra output.

In connection with the 'Brussels compromise' of 30 May 1980, the Council had set a figure of 2% of the milk target price for the co-responsibility levy (and 1.5% for the first 60 000 kg of milk supplied by farmers in the less-favoured areas). In addition, it was agreed that if the total quantity of milk supplied in 1980 increased by more than 1.5% over 1979, a surcharge would be imposed for the 1981-82 season, on the principle that the cost of disposing of extra quantities of milk should be borne by the producers who increased their deliveries.

D—Containing the agricultural expenditure

Because the expenditure of the EAGGF Guarantee Section has risen steadily (by about 23% a year) and constitutes an almost constant proportion of EEC expenditure (about 70% of the budget), the Community institutions are demanding more and more insistently that expenditure on agriculture be brought under control. An old theme this, raised as long ago as the Summit meeting in The Hague in December 1969 (see Annex 3, p. 350). Since 1978 there has been growing concern, in view of the imminent exhaustion of the 'own resources' of the European Communities. So year after year, in the Communications which it sends to the Council and to the Parliament[13]—preparatory to establishing the priorities for the next year's budget—the Commission stresses the agricultural policy which needs to be pursued if the expenditure on agriculture is to be reduced:
(a) a sensible pricing policy;
(b) adjustments in some common market organizations with a view to reducing certain existing imbalances on certain markets (milk products, sugar and wine);
(c) progressive reduction of the monetary compensatory amounts.

Some people consider that these proposals are not enough to solve the problem of the cost of the common agricultural policy, even if they are on the right lines. The idea of putting a 'ceiling' on expenditure on agriculture or of setting an overall limit to the expenditure on markets is constantly present in the debates within the Community but not always explicitly stated.

The clearest expression of a wish for such control came from the Parliament shortly before the direct election of its members, in the budget debate for 1978. A motion tabled by Mr Spinelli and the Communist Group—carried on 26 October 1977—stated that:

'The Council undertakes to request from the Commission and subsequently to adopt during 1978 amendments to the regulations on agricultural prices as a result of which:

(a) a real and not an indicative ceiling will be placed on the commitments of the EAGGF Guarantee Section;

(b) the procedures and criteria for fixing prices will be changed so as to respect the aforesaid conditions;

(c) the share of the expenditure of the EAGGF Guarantee Section will be progressively reduced and that of the EAGGF Guidance Section increased'.

This motion was carried by 55 votes for, 52 against and three abstentions but was over-ruled by the Council and did not appear in the budget. However, such a heavy attack on expenditure on agriculture was significant. The same move was repeated the following year; the voting on 25 October 1978 was 56 for, 50 against and one abstention. As before, the Council omitted the text from the budget for 1979.[12]

But it was in the last quarter of 1979, during the procedure for approving the draft budget for 1980, that Parliament (now directly elected by universal suffrage) was more successful in asserting its views. On 7 November 1979 it adopted two modifications proposed by Mr Dankert (Socialist, Netherlands), General Rapporteur of the Committee on Budgets. The first and more striking amendment was on the lines of the Commission's initial budget proposal of 15 June 1979; it consisted of cutting the appropriations to the COM for milk (Chapter 62) by 280 m EUA and creating in Chapter 100 'Provisional appropriations', a reserve of the same sum to finance structural measures in agriculture. The second amendment aimed at reducing Chapter 62 by 280 m EUA and entering an additional 250 m EUA in Chapter 100, in order to put pressure on the Commission—and more especially on the Council—to spend less on the milk sector. On 23 November 1979, at the second reading of the budget for 1980, the Council set aside these two modifications, thus providing the Parliament with its main grounds for rejecting the budget on 13 December.

In the 'Agriculture' Council of 30 May 1980, important decisions (discussed above) were taken in respect of the co-responsibility levy in the milk market. The consequence thereof will be a better control of the expenditure in this sector. There is no certainty that it will lead to a genuine containment of agricultural production.

4. Budgetary and legal position of agricultural guarantee operations

A—EAGGF Guarantee Section

By Regulation No 25 of 4 April 1962 the Council established a European Agricultural Guidance and Guarantee Fund (EAGGF), in order to enable the common organization of agricultural markets to attain its objectives. The EAGGF is not a 'fund' in the sense of, e.g., French administrative law, because it has neither legal personality nor financial autonomy. Article 1 of the Regulation specifies that 'the Fund shall form part of the Community budget'. Moreover Article 2 establishes that the revenue of the Fund shall not be allocated to its expenditure, thus obeying the budgetary rule of universality, stipulating that: 'Revenue from levies on imports from third countries shall accrue to the Community so that the budget resources of the Community comprise those revenues together with all other revenues decided...'.

B—The budget estimates for the EAGGF Guarantee Section

We shall not again go into the difficulties inherent in making any kind of estimate in this sphere; it should however be recalled that, over and above the agricultural factors (levels of production and export-import possibilities) the currency situation has made estimation in the agricultural guarantee sector a very chancy matter. Moreover, because of the requirements of budgetary procedure and, since 1976, of the new budgetary timetable, the estimates have to be produced in May of the year before the budget is to be implemented, i.e. 20 months before the end of the financial year involved. True, the practice of issuing in September a letter of amendment to the preliminary draft budget does give an opportunity to adjust the estimates somewhat, because at that time crop yields are easier to estimate. But even so, it is usually necessary to bring in a supplementary budget during the financial year, to incorporate the financial effects of the decisions on prices for the season taken at the beginning of the year. To mention recent years only, a supplementary budget was needed in 1973 (864 m u.a.), in 1975 (260 m u.a.), in 1976 (717 m u.a.), in 1977 (934 m u.a.) and in 1979 (802 m EUA). The size of these sums in absolute terms and in relative value (29% in 1973) creates psychological and technical problems but also serious political problems.

C—Establishing the budget figures for the EAGGF Guarantee Section

Expenditure by the EAGGF Guarantee Section is regarded as compulsory expenditure; it is therefore the Council which has the last word as to the amounts entered in the budget. To tell the truth, the procedure for deciding what appropriations to enter in order to operate the agricultural markets policy occasions but little difficulty.[14] The Commission's preliminary draft budget for this section is almost always accepted as it stands. The expenditure on agriculture is in a sense self-fixing. It is very largely predetermined by the existing regulations (levels of prices and structure of common market organizations) and in the budget debates the Council usually simply ratifies estimates that are technical rather than political. Thus, this expenditure is not really decided by the Council meetings on the budget but by the Agriculture Council meetings, which set the prices and fix the rules.

It is however not beyond the bounds of possibility that changes are on the way. The first sign of this may well be the figures in the third supplementary budget for 1979, which were 10 m EUA less than the preliminary draft budget and was referred back and forth between the Council and the Parliament. Similarly, although Parliament rejected on 13 December 1979 the entire budget for 1980, this was primarily to underline its opposition to the budgetary provisions by the Council. The EAGGF Guarantee Section is on the way to becoming one of the central points of the budgetary procedure.

D—The structure of the budget for the EAGGF Guarantee Section

So that the Commission cannot freely use the money assigned to the Guarantee Section by making transfers from the appropriations entered for each product to other products, the Council has brought together in a single chapter the appropriations for each major product, so that if the Commission needs more money for these products it has to ask the Council to authorize a transfer from one chapter to another. As a result there are 18 chapters of the budget for the EAGGF Guarantee Section and since no title in the budget may contain more than 10 chapters, two titles have had to be allocated to the Guarantee Section; thus the latter uses headings in the general budget as profusely as it does Community finances.

Most of the chapters have two series of articles: one covering refund operations and the other intervention operations. Some articles for refunds contain two items: one for refunds in general and the other for refunds relating to food aid operations. The articles for the intervention operations can be distinguished by product (milk powder, butter, etc.) or by their economic nature (storage costs, premiums, etc.), each comprising a number of items dealing with specific budgetary measures.

Because of the volume of appropriations to the Guarantee Section, the Council, as legislator, has come to allow expenditure and revenue to be netted-off in some cases, contrary to the classical budgetary rule of universality. Thus, for public storage the provision in the budget covers net losses only. Similarly, there is offsetting of compensatory amounts levied on exports and the refunds made on exports, and also between compensatory amounts granted on imports and the levies. For 1976, for example, the cumulative sum of these various offsetting transactions has been estimated to be 1 850 m u.a., which lowered Guarantee Section expenditure figures by 26%—a sizeable proportion!

The temptation to net-off is therefore very strong. Thus, since 1977, when submitting the preliminary draft budget the Commission, for purposes of information, shows alongside the headings for the Guarantee Section what the total would be were the revenue from the agricultural levies or the sugar levies to be deducted. The Commission drew no conclusions as to the legal implications but that it had thought of this aspect was clearly apparent. Similarly, in the budgets for 1978 and 1979 the Council left in the 'remarks' column relative to the EAGGF Guarantee Section the figures for revenue from the agricultural and sugar levies, entered for information.

More recently, in order to try to obtain equilibrium in the milk and milk products sector, the Commission proposed in its programme of action for 1977-80 that the 'co-responsibility levy' should not be regarded as an 'own resource'. This proposal was based on Article 43 of the EEC Treaty to justify imposing the levy for the economic purpose of putting in order the market for milk and milk products; since this had no financial consequences, the Decision of 21 April 1970 on 'own resources' does not apply. This legal interpretation was employed to attain two points which the Commission considered indispensable:
  (i) that the introduction of the 'co-responsibility levy' should not require the application of Article 201 of the EEC Treaty, as this would have necessitated approval by the Member States in accordance with their respective constitutional procedures; and
  (ii) that the proceeds of the levy can be deducted from sums paid out by the Community under the head of some of the intervention operations in the market for milk.

Thus, offsetting would occur, but since certain items of expenditure were new in kind (publicity, research) the budgetary appropriations were increased accordingly. However, although in 1977 and 1978 the incomings from the co-responsibility levy covered entirely new measures, the thinking in 1980 is that the totality of expenditure on milk should be subjected to an offsetting operation.

Once incorporated in the expenditure, this revenue is called a 'negative expenditure'. When the sugar levies were introduced the thinking was quite different, because at that time the Commission was glad to be able to create an 'own resource' and was not worried about making the budget too big. However, it is clear that, since 1977, the tendency has been to bring the co-responsibility revenue and the sugar levies closer together, at least as far as their economic effect is concerned.

The legal status of the co-responsibility levy has caused some problems. A judgment handed down by the Court of Justice on 21 February 1979 nevertheless finds no legal objection to the principle of the levy, and confirms that levies of this kind could be introduced in the framework of the common organization of markets without the need to go through the procedure required for the creation of new own resources.

In its report on the 1978 financial year, the Court of Auditors, on the other hand, objected to the levy being entered into the budget as 'negative expenditure', as it is not covered by any of the rules contained in the Financial Regulation. Parliament meanwhile asked that revenue and expenditure in respect of this levy be entered in an annex to the budget and insisted that this kind of 'para-fiscal' levy should be applied solely in the agricultural field (report by a sub-group of the Committee on Budgets of 5 May 1980, p. 189).

E—The utilization of the EAGGF Guarantee Section budget appropriations

The Commission and its departments, in this case the Directorate-General for Agriculture and the Directorate-General for Fisheries,[2] are responsible for implementing the budget in accordance with the Regulations adopted by the Council. The Commission possesses considerable management powers, even though they are exercised after consultation with the Management Committees (see p. 78 and Annex 7, p. 373).

The Financial Regulation provides for a number of exemptions from the general rules for implementing the budget, because of the special nature of EAGGF Guarantee Section expenditure (the seven articles in Title VIII). For example, provisional global commitments are entered into, corresponding to advances to be made to Member States, because under Regulation (EEC) No 729/70 of 21 April 1970 the advances are made by the Community, not by the Member States. Commission decisions fixing the amounts of these advances, after consultation with the EAGGF Committee, have the force of provisional global commitments.

In practice, the expenditure is effected by the 44 national departments and agencies designated by the governments (12 in the Federal Republic of Germany, 10 in the Netherlands, 9 in France, 6 in Italy, 3 in Belgium and 1 each in the United Kingdom, Denmark, Ireland and Luxembourg). These are the true authorizing agencies for the expenditure. The expenditure is committed by chapter, article and item and booked as a payment, after examination of the statements sent in by the Member States; the expenditure is charged to a given financial year on the basis of payments made up to 31 December by the paying departments and agencies responsible for payments, provided that the formal authorizations for the payments have reached the Commission's Accounting Officer not later than 31 March of the following year. This special arrangement departs from the principle of annuality of the budget. As a result, the Community accounts cannot be closed before 31 March of the following year.

The Commission submitted a proposal on 23 April 1979 for amending the Financial Regulation to shorten this extra period.[15]

These few remarks show the exceptional character of the system, which combines centralization of the Community financing operations with decentralization of the individual payments. This has obviated the need to set up a vast Community administration which would have had to deal directly with farmers, exporters and others. The cost of running the 44 intervening departments and bodies is not charged to the EAGGF (Regulation (EEC) 729/70, Article 1(4)). But there is a danger in this highly satisfactory plan of organization, in that this decentralization could lead to disorder and slackness in the management of these activities.

Although the exceptional arrangements for implementation of the budget in respect of agriculture are the most significant feature, they are not the only peculiarity. Another is the scale of the disparities between the estimates and actual expenditure. We have already mentioned that supplementary budgets during the financial year have been necessary. Attention should also be drawn to the magnitude of transfers within chapters of the budget for the Guarantee Section and from one chapter to another,[16] to deal with the combined effects of fixing the prices for the marketing year and of the quantities produced, sold, exported or imported. Moreover 'second category' expenditure (for complicated intervention operations such as storage) is carried out only once a year, whereas the amounts involved in 'first category' expenditure are known at the time of commitment, because a precise rate of intervention has been fixed. A third peculiarity is the comparatively low figures for carry-overs from one financial year to the next, because the budget allocation for the EAGGF Guarantee Section is a 'cash budget' covered by an additional period after the end of the financial year for the booking of the payments.[17]

If—disregarding the transfers of budget appropriations made during or at the end of the financial year—we compare the actual expenditure with the initial budget estimates, we see how difficult it is to make reliable estimates when so much depends on chance. For example, implementation of the budgets for four financial years—1974, 1975, 1976 and 1977—produced an overall average difference of 8.8% between the initial estimates and actual expenditure.[18] The biggest differences were:

(i) for the MCAs (70% difference; average shortfall of appropriations 200 m u.a.): the full extent of fluctuations in rates of exchange is difficult to envisage when the budget is being drawn up;

(ii) for cereals (20% difference; average over-provision of appropriations 120 m u.a.) and for sugar (50% difference; average shortfall of appropriations 100 m u.a.): the difference was largely due to the difficulty of predicting fluctuations on the world markets;

(iii) for expenditure on milk and milk products (difference: less than 5% but a large amount in absolute terms; average over-estimation 80 m u.a.). Moreover, this difference is the result of balancing out the cost of the various support measures in the milk and milk products market. The average difference for export refunds in the milk and milk products sector, for example, was 22% (average shortfall of appropriations 80 m u.a.).

There is constant criticism of the use of the EAGGF Guarantee Section appropriations, and particularly in respect of the creation of structural surpluses, of certain export operations, e.g. the sales to the USSR in 1973 and 1977,[19] as well as great indignation at the major cases of fraud in 1979 and 1980.

F—Monitoring the implementation of the EAGGF Guarantee Section expenditure

The basic provisions governing the monitoring of EAGGF Guarantee Section expenditure derive from the Treaties and Council Regulation 729/70 cited above. The various kinds of audit can be summarized as follows:

(1) audits carried out by the governments of the Member States, for the most part as provided in Article 8 of Regulation 729/70;
(2) audit performed under the provisions made in pursuance of Article 209 of the EEC Treaty and now incorporated in the Financial Regulation;
(3) audit by the Audit Board as provided in Article 206a of the EEC Treaty;
(4) audit under the following provisions of Article 9 of the abovementioned Regulation:
    (a) officials appointed by the Commission to carry out inspections on the spot shall have access to the books and all other documents relating to expenditure financed by the Fund;
    (b) at the request of the Commission and with the agreement of the Member State, inspections or enquiries concerning the transactions referred to in this Regulation shall be carried out by the competent authorities of that Member State. Officials of the Commission may also participate'.[20]

Whereas Article 9(3) of the Regulation prescribes that 'the Council shall ... as far as is necessary, lay down general rules for the application of this Article' the Commission has not proposed any regulation for the purpose, considering that the provisions of Article 9 are sufficient as they stand and that no additional regulation on covering 'the officials appointed' is needed.

In practice, the monitoring operations are organized as follows during a budgetary period: the Directorate-General for Agriculture carries out a continuing series of operations in preparation for the decisions approving the Commission's accounts and to ensure that the requirements in respect of common policy on agricultural markets and prices are correctly observed by the Member States. For practical reasons, officials of the Member State concerned are usually present during such checks; sometimes officials of the national audit authorities attend. In addition, 'selective checks' are arranged by the Directorate-General for Financial Control. The distinguishing feature of these is that they concentrate on a particular type of expenditure, primarily to check on compliance with the principle of sound financial management and on correct practice.

The Member States usually show willingness to cooperate although sometimes concern is expressed about the 'superior position' of the various forms of investigation. To an outsider, the way in which the Community exercises financial control must seem cumbersome. Several different kinds of check can be made: examination by the authorizing agency (the Directorate-General for Agriculture), 'selective checks' (arranged by the Directorate-General for Financial Control), investigations by the Special Committee of Inquiry,[21] verifications which the Audit Board may decide to make and, lastly, checks on 'own resources' arranged by the Directorate-General for Budgets but not always involving the same administrative departments. Then there are the checks made by the various national audit authorities. Apart from these measures, cases of fraud or merely of 'irregularity' receive widespread publicity in the press and arouse public opinion. What is it all about? The answer is that under Community legislation (EEC Regulations 729/70, mentioned above, and 283/72) the Member States are required to take the requisite measures to prevent irregularities, to cover sums obtained by fraudulent activities and to supply to the Community all necessary information about their arrangements for preventing irregularities. The Commission has stated that on the whole the reporting system works satisfactorily. The number of cases reported has varied greatly: 8 in 1971, 20 in 1972, 51 in 1973, 89 in 1974, 130 in 1975, 226 in 1976, 150 in 1977, 113 in 1978 and 116 in 1979. From 1971 to 1979 inclusive, reported irregularities totalled 903, covering an amount of 40.8 m u.a. Twenty-two million u.a. were recovered in respect of 549 cases. It is also apparent that the irregularities are not proceeded against with the same vigour in all the countries.[22]

To sum up, it must be agreed that the Community makes every effort to organize the best possible system of monitoring to cover the largest block of expenditure in its budget, but the situation is definitely uncertain. While it may be true that not all the national authorities responsible for financial control are energetic enough, the Community organs are expected to perform the real monitoring; after a shaky start, which is understandable considering that major changes were taking place at the time, they seem to have become efficient enough to halve the number of cases of irregularity between 1976 and 1979. But we should not be too optimistic about this.

5. The resources applied to financing the agricultural guarantee operations

The basic legislation governing financing of the CAP is Regulation (EEC) No 729/70 of 21 April 1970, adopted at the same time as the 'own resources' arrangements. As we have already seen, the two measures were closely linked. The underlying principle of the Regulations is that since a single market for agricultural products has been set up, the prices have been approximated and a common agricultural policy has been achieved, the Community should bear the financial responsibility.

Let us now discuss the budgetary resources allocated to this policy from the outset, and then try to assess the results.

A—The budget resources allocated from 1965 to 1980

Over a 15-year period, from 1965 to 1979,[23] the European Economic Community has spent about 54 700 m u.a. on the CAP (see Annex 12, p. 399), and of this total 53 400 m went to guaranteeing agricultural markets. Allocations to the guarantee operations, which were 28.7 m u.a. in 1965, passed the thousand million mark in 1968, reached 4 336 m u.a. in 1975 (a year of enlargement), and then 10 418 m EUA in 1979.[24] The expenditure on guaranteeing the agricultural markets has thus rocketed, but it is, after all, the only truly common policy which has had financial effects. Even so, the 23% rate of increase per annum continues to cause concern.

The budget for 1980, approved on 9 July 1980, and based on the 'new budget proposal' as revised at 6 June 1980, is based on the agricultural price decisions for 1980-81 (see p. 172) and the associated measures, particularly in respect of co-responsibility (see p. 181). The appropriations allocated to guarantee operations total 11 486 m EUA, i.e. a 10.3% increase over the previous year's figures; this is a break in the four-year sequence of a 23% increase per year.

Using once more the classification given above (see p. 172), the expenditure can be broken down into four types of intervention:
(1) expenditure on refunds,
(2) expenditure on storage,
(3) subsidies,
(4) 'guidance premiums'.

Budget resources for the policy of guaranteed markets for agricultural products

(Million EUA)

COM	1979				1980			
Intervention measures	1	2	3	4	1	2	3	4
Milk and milk products	2 088	854	1 497[1]	89	2 669	226	1 820[1]	215
Cereals	1 185	89	290	–	1 122	207	287	–
Sugar	685	240	5	9	396	284	14	3
Beef and veal	270	417	–	61	460	514	8	196
Fats	1	23	582	–	8	16	763	–
Other COMs	503	151	693	–	572	189	1 180	60
Total in m EUA	4 732	1 774	3 067	159	5 227	1 436	4 072	474
%	48.6	18.2	31.6	1.6	46.6	12.8	36.3	4.3
MCAs in m EUA	708				276			
Grand total in m EUA	10 440[1]				11 485[1]			

[1] Including the receipts from the co-responsibility levy: 94 m EUA for 1979 and 223 m EUA for 1980.

The distribution of expenditure between the common organizations of markets (COMs)

A breakdown of the distribution of expenditure between COMs is given in the following table. The trends in the Guarantee Section expenditure by sectors from 1970 to 1979 are:
  (i) a relatively constant proportion for milk and milk products (although the percentage for 1975 was lower, there was considerable accumulation of stocks), for tobacco and for sugar (despite the shortage in 1975);
 (ii) a substantial increase in the proportion for beef and veal (from 1974 to 1976 inclusive) and for MCAs (introduced in 1973 but now being phased out);
(iii) a relative decrease for cereals.

Four COMs (cereals, milk, fats and beef and veal)—together representing slightly less than half the agricultural production in the Community in value terms—have been receiving at least three-quarters of the financial assistance given by the Guarantee Section.

The table also reveals that the share assigned to vegetable products has tended to decline in favour of animal products (milk and meat).

190

(%)[1]

Sector	1970	1971	1972	1973	1974	1975	1976	1977	1978	1979
Cereals	34.3	31.2	40.9	26.0	12.9	13.1	11	8.9	11.5	15.0
Rice	2.3	3.3	2.1	0.3	0	0.1	0.5	0	0.2	0.4
Milk and milk products	38.1	37.3	25.0	39.9	39.3	24.3	36.8	38.2	39.0	43.2
Fats	10.8	4.7	11.4	9.9	4.5	4.9	5.6	4.6	3.9	5.8
Sugar	7.4	7.4	6.8	3.5	3.5	6.6	4	8.1	8.9	9.0
Beef and veal	1.2	1.1	0.3	0.5	10.4	20.7	11.5	6.2	6.5	7.2
Pigmeat	1.7	3.4	2.3	2.5	2.2	1.1	0.5	0	0.5	1.0
Eggs and poultry	0.6	0.8	0.6	0.6	0.6	0.9	0.2	0	0.4	0.8
Fruit and vegetables	2.2	3.5	2.5	0.9	2.2	1.2	4.4	2.8	1.1	4.2
Wine		1.9	1.8	0.3	1.4	3.0	3.1	1.4	0.7	0.6
Tobacco	0.2	4.1	4.6	3.2	6.1	4.8	4.1	3.1	2.4	2.2
Fishery products			0.1	0	0	0.2	0.2)	1.7	0.2	0.2
Other 5 COMs	0.2	0.1	0.5	0.7	1.2	1.2	1.3)		0.9	1.2
Non-Annex II products	1.0	1.2	1.1	0.7	0.4	0.5	1.2	1.9	2.1	2.4
ACAs[2]				7.2	10.7	8.8	6.5	2.6	6.3	—
MCAs				3.8	4.6	8.6	9.1	12.9	2.3	6.8
Effect of the dual rate of exchange[3]								7.6	13.1	—
Total	100	100	100	100	100	100	100	100	100	100

[1] From the financial reports on the EAGGF, which do not correspond to a single financial year.
[2] Accession compensatory amounts (see p. 175).
[3] Not dealt with separately in budgetary implementation except in 1977 and 1978. Eliminated in 1979. (See p. 178 and footnote 8, p. 195).

B—Breakdown of the expenditure by Member State

Another breakdown of interest is the distribution of the expenditure among the Member States. The 'league table' for financial resources made available to the Member States in 1973 and in 1978 is as follows: Federal Republic of Germany (18.5%, 26.7%), France (29.9%, 16.7%), Netherlands (14.5%, 12.6%), Italy (17%, 13.4%), United Kingdom (4.2%, 13.3%), Denmark (8.1%, 6.5%), Belgium (5.3%, 6.4%), Ireland (2.4%, 3.9%), Luxembourg (0.1%, 0.1%).

These figures for the first six years of the enlarged Community show the increase in the share of the new Member States in guarantee for agricultural products, and also the marked expansion in German agriculture.

In September 1979, as part of the preparatory work requested of it for the meeting of the Council of Ministers in Dublin in November 1979 (see Annex 3, p. 357), the Commission worked out the figures for recipients of agricultural expenditure. These figures were updated for the Council meeting in Luxembourg in April 1980. They are worth quoting because they reveal an interesting aspect of the finances of the EEC (see also pp. 239, 269, 325 and 337). To understand the following table two pieces of information are needed. First, figures given for the percentages for the COMs (common organizations of markets) have been based on the purely agricultural expenditure on markets, but in working out the figures for the COMs+MCAs (monetary compensatory amounts) together (see p. 177) agri-monetary expenditure has been included. Secondly, in accordance with the Regulation governing the working of the financial mechanism (see p. 124), negative MCAs paid in the exporting country have been treated as expenditure in the importing country.[9]

191

Recipients of agricultural guarantee expenditure   (%)

	B	DK	D	F	IRL	I	L	NL	UK	Total
	Implementation in 1979									
COMs	7.1	5.3	22.0	22.5	3.7	17.0	0.1	12.4	9.9	100
COMs } MCAs	7.2	6.1	22.4	21.7	4.5	15.6	0.1	13.6	8.8	100
	Estimates for 1980									
COMs	6.3	6.6	24.5	23.0	4.6	16.5	0.2	13.3	5.0	100
COMs } MCAs	6.25	6.4	24.35	21.8	4.5	16.9	0.2	13.5	6.1	100

This table clearly shows that assignment of MCAs to the importing countries, namely Italy and above all the United Kingdom, markedly changes their share in agricultural expenditure. These two countries asked for different figures, claiming that the expenditure on green rates of exchange was not solely for their benefit. Recently this dispute has become more intense. However, since the middle of 1979 the volume of MCAs in trade between the United Kingdom and the rest of the Community has decreased considerably, as a result of devaluation of the green pound and the recovery of the pound on the foreign exchange markets. So long as this situation continues, the manner of assignment of MCA expenditure will be of little importance from the point of view of total agricultural guarantee expenditure.

If the figures for each Member State's proportion of the overall Community output of agricultural products are seen in conjunction with this table, some astonishing disparities appear. From 1975 to 1977 inclusive the share of the French agricultural sector averaged 26.8%, that of United Kingdom agriculture 11.1%, that of the Netherlands 7.7% and that of Belgium 4%. These percentages differ greatly from those shown in the table. The explanation lies in the structure of each country's agricultural industry, the level of domestic consumption of agricultural products and the eating habits of each nation, but also in the impact of European integration on the agricultural markets. It will soon be quite impossible to distinguish accurately the effect of the existence of a European common market on the nine economies involved. A qualitative threshold has been passed.

C—Rough balance of financial results

The agricultural guarantee policy is now costing more than 11 000 m u.a. a year. Yet this figure is not much more than 2% of consumer expenditure on food in the Community and is only 0.5% of the Community's GDP. But as a percentage of the GDP for agriculture of the Member States the expenditure of the EAGGF Guarantee Section is more than 10%—a very significant figure clearly indicative of the part played by the Community budget in this sector of the economy. But if one is content to leave these percentages out of account, one can claim—as did the Committee on Agriculture of the European Parliament in the debate on the draft budget for 1979 on 29 September 1978—that the cost of the CAP—or, to be precise, of the policy of equilibrium in markets, i.e. the operations of the EAGGF

Guarantee Section—is not unreasonable. It is sufficient to point out that in the budget for 1979:

(1) 620 million EUA were spent not on the CAP, but for reasons of international policy (purchases of sugar from the ACP countries and of New Zealand butter, see p. 173);
(2) 810 million EUA were spent on the MCAs, which 'reflect the inability of the Member States to coordinate their economies and establish an economic and monetary union';
(3) 350 million EUA were for refunds on food aid;
(4) 2 144.1 million EUA were to be collected from levies on agricultural products and sugar (a sum equivalent to 21% of the expenditure).

If these four sums are deducted, the guarantee operations amount to only 45% of the expenditure provided for in the budget. However that may be, the bulk of that expenditure, i.e. for the guarantee operations, is actually transfer expenditure, since in the absence of a common agricultural policy the Member States would have to bear at least as heavy a cost. So there is no extra burden on taxpayers in the Community; on the contrary, they pay less than they would otherwise do.

*
* *

Rivers of milk, butter mountains—these are the images often chosen to depict the common agricultural policy—to condemn it, of course. What is the truth of the matter? About 55 000 m u.a. have been spent (98% of this sum by the Guarantee Section) on guaranteeing markets for the agricultural products. This total comprised 77% of the expenditure entered in the EEC budget and 71% of non-returnable contributions (budgets + EDF). What has been achieved with this large outlay?

Have the five objectives laid down in Article 39(1) of the EEC Treaty been attained? A brief review reveals that the following results have been obtained:

(i) an increase in agricultural productivity, which has however been unevenly distributed, mainly because of the absence of a vigorous policy on structures, so that three-quarters of the producers supply only a quarter of the agricultural output;
(ii) an undeniable improvement in the standard of living of the agricultural community, although the gap between individual earnings in this industry and those of other occupational groups has not been closed. There has even been, on average, a slight drop in income in recent times;
(iii) a definite stabilization of markets, mainly in those with a price support scheme together with intervention arrangements (72%[25] of output). But it must be acknowledged that in some sectors there is increasing imbalance between supply and demand, creating, for example, structural surpluses of dairy products and of sugar;
(iv) a high degree of security of supplies, in that the Community is largely self-sufficient in food;
(v) the achievement of reasonable prices to consumers, which have helped to curb the inflationary trend of the last few years.

Thus, the overall result is not nearly as bad as some people claim or would like it to be. The aspirations involved are complex, namely achievement of a successful blend of an incomes and a prices policy with a development and a modernization policy. Some people argue that in any event the agricultural policy is too costly. The figures quoted above refute that allegation. But within the agricultural policy as a whole there is, indeed, a serious imbalance. Agricultural price support policy is decided and financed by the Community but a shortage of Community resources for the agricultural structures policy continues (3% of the appropriations made available for agricultural policy). Consequently the Community provides only 36% of the total amount spent on agriculture over the whole Community territory.

These percentages demonstrate that one can hardly speak of a Community policy on structures; instead there are nine national policies, largely disregarding common market considerations. This aggravates the disequilibrium between regions, causes economically detrimental competition, leads to non-specialization and results in the formation of structural surpluses. As an addition to the existing competition in agriculture between the nine Member States, there is the prospect of the enlargement of the Community to include three countries in southern Europe: Greece, Portugal and Spain. This presents a challenge, since the agricultural industries of those countries compete in varying degrees with French and Italian agriculture.[26] The common agricultural policy is based on organization of the markets for products coming largely from northern rather than southern Europe. In view of the possibility that a serious disequilibrium may arise, preventive measures should be taken while there are still nine countries in the market for agriculture. The Commission is therefore proposing the strengthening and modification of the existing structural guidelines to cater better for regional needs, for the specific market difficulties and for the changes in the economic environment; it believes that structural policy should work together with prices policy. The set of measures already adopted for the Mediterranean regions and for western Ireland are to be supplemented by additional specific regional measures. This will make a considerable call on the Community finances, and therefore forms the financial aspect of the CAP causing most concern to the Community's various organs at present. Since the Commission drew their attention to the situation, they have realized that agricultural guarantee expenditure was growing inexorably but that the ceiling for own resources assigned to the Community would soon be reached. The Community must find a way out of this dilemma (see footnote 15 on p. 135), since otherwise the common agricultural policy may collapse. In the general survey which the Community is to carry out in June 1981 (see footnote 30 on p. 245), two points are already firmly fixed: the common responsibility for financing, and the basic principles of the common agricultural policy.

But the political and electoral implications of a common agricultural policy that is complete, balanced and fully under control are such that the requisite expansion of the European Community's operations in this area will be a long-term task. It belongs in the sphere of the internal development policy, which is our next topic. The future of the people as 'citizens of the Community' is at stake.

Footnotes to Chapter XI

[1] Although the cultivable area is relatively very small (2% of the cultivable land in the world), Community agriculture ranks high in world production figures. The EEC is the world's leading producer of milk (25% of world production) and of wine (about one-half of world production), the second largest producer of beef and veal (16% of world production) and the third largest producer of cereals (10% of world production).

[2] The common organization of the market in fishery products almost completes the setting up of the common market for agriculture (only two sectors are still outside the Community system: potatoes and alcohol of agricultural origin).

Although fishing might be thought to have relatively special economic and social conditions the administrative system introduced by the Council in January 1976 is on exactly the same lines as for most of the major agricultural markets. Once a year the Council sets guide prices for the various kinds of fish, protecting production in the Community by means of reference prices which serve as import thresholds. If supply and demand do not match, aid for private storage may be granted, and if the producers' organizations recognized by the Council consider that withdrawal of fish from the market is necessary, compensation may be paid. The only difference for this market is that in addition to the normal administrative arrangements there are some special additional measures, partly arising from the law of the sea and the changes therein and partly because fishing extends into waters which are not exclusively Community territory (the North Sea, the Baltic, the Adriatic and off the coast of Africa).

[3] See A. Ries: 'The ABC of the agricultural common market', in the same series.

[4] So far the EEC has decided against the United Kingdom's method up to the time of its accession, namely, a policy of low prices for agricultural products, because of massive imports. The country's self-sufficiency in food was very low (50% of its needs), despite a high production capability. There was a system of deficiency payments for farmers, i.e. subsidies making up the difference between market prices, which were held down, and the desirable levels for farm prices decided each year by the authorities, so as to ensure a reasonable income for the farmers. This system meant that the cost of the subsidy was borne by the taxpayers instead of by the consumers.

[5] A good example is the 4% rise in exchange rates for the Deutschmark introduced on 16 October 1978, which produced a rise of 3.6 points (from 7.2 to 10.8) in the MCAs applied at the German frontier; this increased the subsidy for German exports by that amount, benefiting German exports, especially those to Italy. The alternative to raising the central rate for the Deutschmark would have been raising the rate for the green currency, thus lowering the prices of German agricultural products. The Federal Government rejected that possibility.

What is more, the export subsidy received by the German exporters was at the expense of Community finances. If prices had been lowered (by raising the green rate) expenditure on German agriculture would have been less and the smaller burden on the Community would have largely offset the increase in MCA 'revenue' produced by not changing the value of the green rate for the Deutschmark.

[6] Under the European Monetary System, the EMUA ('snake' unit of account) is replaced by the ECU, which is at par with the EUA and therefore about 21% below the value of the EMUA. The distribution of MCAs has been greatly affected by this drop in value. On the basis of the conversions carried out in November 1978 the German MCAs rose from +10.8% to +25.7%, Danish MCAs from 0% to +18.5%, Italian MCAs from −18.2% to +3.1% and French MCAs from −6.5% to +11.1%. Only the United Kingdom MCAs remained negative, with a rise from −30.8% to −6%. The Commission finds such an upheaval unacceptable. Whereas the figures for the common agricultural policy cannot be based on anything other than the ECU in future, this must not be allowed to lead automatically to altering the present price level, either expressed in national currencies or in Community units of account, nor alter the distribution of MCAs. The Commission therefore thought it necessary to convert into ECU all the prices and data in the common agricultural policy expressed in u.a., using a coefficient corresponding to the difference between the ECU and the EMUA (about 1.2). The green rates used in the common agricultural policy had to be converted at the same time using a similar coefficient (1:1.2, which gives about 0.833).

[7] The budgetary treatment of extra-Community trade is as follows:
MCAs *charged* are treated as *levies*. But Article 4a of Regulation No 974/71 provides that compensatory amounts charged on exports are to be deducted from refunds on exports; if the compensatory amount collected exceeds the refund, the balance is a gain for 'own resources';
MCAs *granted* are treated as *refunds*. But under Article 4a of Regulation No 974/71 compensatory amounts granted on imports are to be deducted from the levy; if the compensatory amount granted on importation exceeds the levy the balance counts as an expenditure for the EAGGF.

[8] When the system of the dual rate of exchange, now abandoned, was in operation the procedure was to enter in a separate chapter of the budget, under the titles for the EAGGF Guarantee Section, the expenditure resulting from differences between the amounts calculated in IMF units of account and those in green units of account. Until 1977 this expenditure was incorporated in each heading of the budget but then the gap became so large that it no longer seemed correct to disregard it, so it was decided to identify this cost in the budget. The effect of the differences was therefore shown separately in an *ad hoc* chapter of the budget. The expenditure was shown in this way mainly for political reasons, to demonstrate that the disorders affecting the monetary system were responsible for it. This attitude was not always entirely justified since—apart from the fact that the IMF had become outdated, this being a technical reason—the green rates themselves were often the fruit of political considerations and political negotiation. Since the EUA was introduced into the budget, i.e. from 1 January 1978, there have still been differences, because the source thereof remained, since the 'representative rates' are still being used, thus maintaining the separation of the unit of account used in respect of agricultural transactions from the unit of account used for all the other items in the budget. However, there no longer existed the particular distortions which were, up to the end of 1977, inherent in the fact that the IMF rates had not kept up with currency values. Beginning with the budget for 1979, it was no longer considered logical to set forth separately the effect of this dual rate. Henceforth, the ECU is the ap-

propriate means of measuring the impact on the budget of agricultural expenditure accurately. It remains true that the measures under the agricultural policy are still expressed in green units of account. The two standards do not match. But the effect of the dual rate of exchange thus appeared in the budget only in 1977 and 1978 (see p. 191).

⁹ Whenever the balances between Member States have been calculated, there has been a good deal of argument in the Community over the assignment of MCAs to countries which are net importers and have a depreciated currency (the United Kingdom and Italy). The British Government has always objected to receiving MCAs, since this reduced its balance of trade deficit and weakened its case for obtaining financial compensation.

¹⁰ See Supplement 10/76—Bull. EC. The conclusions to this programme were updated and reproduced in the 'New policy guidelines for the dairy products sector' submitted to the Council on 26 September 1978.

¹¹ The Commission gave the following reply to a written question in October 1978: 'The introduction for a limited period of the co-responsibility levy under Regulation No 1079/77 was proposed by the Commission on the basis of Article 43 and decided by the Council on that basis, because this measure involves a component of the common organization of the market for milk and milk products, even if it is not formally a component within the meaning of Regulation (EEC) No 804/68. The Commission emphasizes the close relationship between the levy as such and these specific measures, in the context of overall action designed to put the market in order. The revenue from this levy is entered in Chapter 62 of the budget and is deducted from intervention costs.' This is therefore 'negative expenditure'. A curious piece of legal/budgetary procedure occurs in Article 628, where the appropriations are preceded by a minus sign and are deducted from the remaining expenditure in the same chapter.

The co-responsibility levy on milk was 1.5% on quantities of milk and milk products delivered to a dairy undertaking or milk-processing undertaking, from 16 September 1977 to 30 April 1978. It was 0.5% until 1 June 1980 and was then increased to 2%. The revenue from the levy was 24 m EUA in 1977, 164 m EUA in 1978, and 96 m EUA in 1979. It should yield 223 m EUA in 1980. The appropriations for the market for milk and milk products entered in the budget have been as follows: 4 014 m EUA for 1978, 4 490 m EUA for 1979 and 4 930 m EUA for 1980.

¹² In the context of measures for stabilizing the agricultural markets there is other revenue which does not constitute 'own resources' within the meaning of Article 2 of the Decision of 21 April 1970; e.g. Regulation (EEC) No 352/78 of the Council of 20 February 1978 relating to the crediting of securities, deposits or guarantees furnished under the common agricultural policy and subsequently forfeited.

¹³ The Commission's anxiety is apparent in its communications to the joint meeting of the Council of Ministers for Foreign Affairs and Ministers for Finance and to the European Parliament, dated 27 February 1978 and 9 March 1979, and in the estimates for 1979, 1980 and 1981 and for 1980, 1981 and 1982.

¹⁴ See the author's comments on budgetary procedure (footnotes 9 and 13 to Chapter II).

¹⁵ On 23 April 1979 the Commission submitted a second amendment to the Financial Regulation (OJ C 116 of 9.5.1979), the first amendment having been made on 15 June 1978 (see footnote 3, p. 30). The main purpose was to eliminate the anomaly constituted by what is generally called 'additional period for the EAGGF' (see p. 75). The Commission proposed that this additional period—which was intended to enable accountancy data to be transferred from national accounts to Community accounts and processed, and which is at present three months (1 January to 31 March) following the end of implementation of the budget for each year—should be reduced by two months, by means of a system of provisional commitments and automatic carry-overs, so that the accounts could be closed by 31 January of financial year n+1. This proposal was later withdrawn, for technical reasons.

¹⁶ There have been numerous transfers between chapters in Titles 6 and 7 of the budget, which are for the EAGGF Guarantee Section, and the amounts have been large. For example, in 1975 the appropriations to 11 of the 17 chapters, pertaining to COMs in general were increased, in some cases to double (sugar, and beef and veal) or even treble (fisheries) the original amount and 6 (fats, rice, and eggs and poultrymeat) needed smaller totals of appropriations than had been entered. The sum of these transfers amounted to 1 090 m u.a., 25% of the total. In 1978 the amounts for 6 of the 17 chapters had to be increased, by a combined total of 1 115.3 m EUA (the biggest increase being for milk) and 11 had a surplus of appropriations (cereals and wine in particular).

In 1979, the appropriations for 10 out of 16 chapters were increased (the largest changes being for milk, fruit and vegetables, and beef and veal) and those for 6 were reduced (including in particular wine and sugar). The overall total of transfers was only 170.4 m EUA, because the third supplementary budget for 1979, adopted in December, itself made many rectifications.

¹⁷ Carry-overs of appropriations from one financial year to the next in Titles 6 and 7 of the budget, which are for the EAGGF Guarantee Section, are now small: 0.45% from 1978 into 1979. Carry-overs from 1975 into 1976, for example, amounted to 7.6%.

[18] This is a shortfall of appropriations, necessitating the introduction of supplementary budgets for 1975, 1976, 1977 and 1979. However, for 1976 and 1977 the appropriations in the supplementary budgets were too large (surpluses of appropriations of 4.8% for 1976 and of 7.8% for 1977), so that large amounts of appropriations were cancelled (265 m u.a. for 1976 and 530 m u.a. for 1977). By contrast, for 1979 the appropriations in the supplementary budgets were used in full.

[19] The scope of the powers in respect of the implementation of budgets and of the management of agricultural matters conferred upon the Commission sometimes gives rise to strong objection. Although entirely justified from the economic point of view, the export to the USSR in 1973 of 200 000 tonnes, at a cost of 300 m u.a., aroused bitter argument.

In 1977 a similar matter led to the tabling of a motion of censure of the Commission. The case is of some interest. At that time a salient feature of the Community market for milk and milk products, and especially for butter, was that there existed considerable over-production. (In 1976 the Commission had submitted to the Council proposals designed to apply fundamental remedies to this situation.) In an attempt to dispose of the structural surpluses that had already accumulated the Community used two devices: sales within the Community on special terms, under subsidies, and sales in the external market assisted by export refunds to exporters to make up the difference between the guaranteed price in the Community and the price on the world market. In using those two devices the Commission had to balance a complex set of political and commercial considerations and to observe the normal budgetary constraints.

On 5 February 1977 the Commission made a technical adjustment in the level of export refunds. Soon afterwards, a French exporter put in an application to benefit from the scheme of prior determination of refund, in order to sell 36 000 tonnes of butter to the USSR. (Both the quantity and the consignee involved were unusual, since the USSR was not a regular customer.) This contract received widespread publicity and rumours of other similar transactions circulated. In view of the risk that the repetition of these rumours might cause serious imbalance in the market and lead to the budgetary appropriations being exceeded, the Commission applied two safety measures provided for in the existing rules: on 25 February it suspended prior determination of refund, as an emergency measure, and on 2 March it introduced a control system for this system.

In the Parliament, agitation about these events was expressed first in committee and then in plenary session: on 9 March there was a lengthy debate on the subject. The following day two verbal questions were put to the Commission. The most important reaction was a motion of censure of the Commission tabled on 10 March by the Group of European Progressive Democrats; this motion censured the Commission for bad management and in particular for having acted precipitately without consulting Parliament, contrary to the formal undertaking given by the Commission to the Parliament on 14 December 1976. The Members of Parliament were divided in their views on other aspects of the matter but were unanimous on this point of procedure. However, the motion of censure was held to be uncalled for and inappropriate to the objectives in view; on 23 March 1977 it was rejected by 95 votes to 15, with 1 abstention.

The Parliament has held further debates on sales of butter to the USSR, for example on 25 September 1979, when there was a division of opinion between those who thought these sales should cease, notably the British Conservatives, and those who considered them to be perfectly acceptable.

[20] The provisions of Article 9 of Regulation No 729/70 form the basic text but they have been supplemented by subsequent provisions, namely:

(1) Regulation No 283/72 of 7 February 1972, containing a set of provisions concerning irregularities and arrangements for recovering sums paid which should not have been paid. It provides for close collaboration, on the one hand between the Member States and on the other hand between the Member States and the institutions of the Community, in this delicate matter of irregularities;

(2) the Council Resolution of 16 December 1975, adopted for the purpose of strengthening measures to prevent or prosecute irregularities;

(3) the Council Directive of 27 June 1977 on the monitoring by the Member States of operations partially financed by the EAGGF Guarantee Section. This Directive was issued in pursuance of the provisions of Article 8 of Regulation No 729/70 in particular, which requires Member States to take all necessary steps, in their internal administration, to exercise control. The features of this Directive are that it imposes on Member States an obligation to carry out systematic inspection of the operations of undertakings receiving payments from or liable for payments to the funds of the common agricultural policy: these inspections are required to cover not less than one-half of the undertakings whose receipts or liabilities under the EAGGF system in the year preceding the year of the inspection exceeded 100 000 u.a. Member States were required to take the steps necessary for the application of this Directive not later than 1 July 1979. On this basis much more widespread and systematic investigation will be carried out than was previously the case.

[21] A 'Special Committee of Inquiry' was set up by the Commission on 3 October 1973 in the context of the Commission's efforts to combat frauds against the EAGGF Guarantee Section. The existence of this Com-

mittee was extended on 5 March 1975. The Committee has submitted reports to the Commission—which has passed them on to the Council and to the Parliament—on milk and milk products, oilseeds and olive oil, beef and veal, wine, and cereals. Having investigated all the sectors of the EAGGF Guarantee Section for which it was set up, the Committee's duties were completed, as noted by the Commission on 28 November 1979.

[22] Frauds: the sums involved—expressed in units of account (with the amount recovered shown in brackets) were as follows: in 1971: 11 876 512 (11 747 072); 1972: 2 314 319 (1 045 751); 1973: 1 306 811 (654 091); 1974: 4 360 653 (976 809); 1975: 3 037 315 (1 283 629); 1976: 5 331 253 (2 277 229); 1977: 8 321 583 (2 041 688); 1978: 2 172 886 (988 454); 1979: 2 093 970 (1 210 055). By Member State and in descending order the figures are as follows: Federal Republic of Germany: 22 618 644 (17 175 780); France: 6 062 896 (637 493); United Kingdom: 4 968 023 (1 457 467); Netherlands: 1 787 264 (854 490); Denmark: 1 705 772 (1 182 271); Belgium: 1 577 928 (72 809); Ireland: 1 093 166 (839 407); Italy: 1 001 609 (5 061), giving a total of 40 815 302 (22 224 778).

[23] 1965 was the first financial year when payments by way of reimbursements were made to Member States. These were for the accounting periods 1962-63 and 1963-64. 'Reimbursements' have applied up to the end of 1970 and 'advances' from 1971 onwards.

[24] See Annex 12 (pp. 398 and 399) for the figures for expenditure from the budget, although these are for the whole of the common agricultural policy, not for the Guarantee Section alone. However, for the period from 1965 to 1978 inclusive, expenditure by the Guarantee Section comprised 98% of expenditure on the common agricultural policy. (In this connection see also the author's article in the *Common Market Review*, entitled 'Budgetary history of the EEC and Euratom', January 1977, p. 25.)

[25] The Council (Agriculture Ministers) decided to set up a common organization of the market in sheepmeat (and goatmeat) on 30 May 1980 as part of the Brussels compromise. The operating principles of this marketing organization are complex and give a fairly good indication of the many difficulties encountered in the lengthy negotiations between the Member States. As for the other sectors, a system of common prices, albeit on a regional basis, has been set up; this allows intervention to vary according to areas specified by regulation. However, provision is made for an alternative to intervention storage, in particular in the UK, entailing premiums paid directly to the producers. Import levies will be applied to the quantities traded but, although the principle of granting refunds is accepted, the details have not yet been laid down. In addition, this new COM will not enter into force until voluntary limitation agreements have been negotiated by the Commission with non-member countries. It is expected that matters will have been sorted out by 1 October 1980. The sum of 231 m EUA is already proposed in the 1981 budget.

[26] On 5 June 1980 President Giscard d'Estaing made the following pronouncement before the Assemblée des Chambres d'agriculture in Paris: 'Community preference and the single-market principle are sacrosanct. It cannot be gainsaid that certain items of expenditure are expanding too quickly and certain mechanisms are outdated. Leaving aside agricultural problems as such, the discussions of recent months have shown beyond any shadow of doubt that certain new members are not yet fully integrated, since they wish to be freed from some of the obligations inherent in being part of a Community. It hardly seems possible to cope with the problems and uncertainties connected with the first enlargement at the same time as those connected with the second one. The Community should therefore concentrate on completing the first enlargement operation before embarking on the second.'

198

Chapter XII:
Financing of a policy
to further the internal development
of the Community

This chapter seeks to analyse all the Community's financial instruments—apart from the EAGGF Guarantee Section (which was described in the previous chapter)—covered by the budget, i.e.:
(a) the Social Fund, the EAGGF Guidance Section and the Regional Fund,
(b) certain appropriations for specific aid, particularly for industrial conversion and restructuring and environmental protection, and
(c) EIB activities.

We have sought a common purpose behind all these financial instruments—'the internal development of the Community'. In speaking of a policy to further the internal development of the Community, however, we are employing a term which is broader than those generally used in Community parlance, such as 'financial instruments of a structural nature', 'coordination of the Community's financial instruments' and 'convergence of the Member States' economic performances'.

1. The Community's financial instruments and the convergence (or divergence) of the Member States' economic performances

The convergence (or divergence) of the economic performances of the Member States of the European Community, is a new term invented in the light of recent European Council meetings on the European Monetary System. It describes the development of independent economies in a compatible rather than a parallel fashion, towards comparable economic positions.[1]

A—The divergence of the nine Community economies

When establishing the European Economic Community in 1957, the parties to the Treaty of Rome declared they were 'anxious to strengthen the unity of their (countries') economies and to ensure their harmonious development by reducing the differences existing between the various regions and the backwardness of the less-favoured regions'. Their intentions were quite clear. Twenty years later they can only be reaffirmed.

What has happened since 1958? What do the most important macroeconomic indicators—the rate of price increases, *per capita* GDP and currency values—tell us?

There was definitely some convergence between the six founder Member States as far as inflation is concerned until 1972, but the 1973 crisis reversed this trend. In 1972 the spread between the highest and the lowest rates of inflation was 3.6%; it changed to 6.7% in 1973, 14% in 1974, 11.6% in 1975, 13.6% in 1976 and 14.3% in 1977. Since 1977 the spread has narrowed somewhat. In 1978 it was 10%, the lowest rate (in the Federal Republic of Germany) being 2.5% and the highest (in Italy) 12.7% with a Community average of 6.9%. However, this is still a very dangerous situation, since the highest rate is five times the lowest rate.

The second indicator—*per capita* GDP (at current prices and exchange rates)—points to a certain amount of convergence between 1960 and 1970, and divergence thereafter. In fact, the gaps in 1979 were even larger than in 1960. If *per capita* GDP is calculated at current prices and purchasing power parities, the spread becomes relatively smaller, although there is still divergence, as the following table shows. During the period the differences between the regions have stayed the same, the rich ones are still the most well off and the poor ones have not improved their relative position.

Finally, since 1958, the Deutschmark has risen by 20% against the guilder, by 35% against the Belgian franc, by 130% against the French franc and by 205% against the lira and the pound sterling (however, the latter has been a Community currency for only a third of this time).

We must therefore come to the conclusion that membership of the Community has not eliminated the factors causing divergence, the forces producing disparities or the centrifugal tendencies. This is serious and undoubtedly worrying, and something which we must always bear in mind. However, we must not forget that the Community has also made an active contribution to the improvement of living standards in all the Member States.

Per capita GDP in the European Community
EUR 9 = 100

Member State	At current prices and exchange rates					At current prices and purchasing power parities				
	1960	1965	1970	1975	1979	1960	1965	1970	1975	1979
Belgium	105.7	101.9	106.5	119.9	124.0	96.5	98.6	102.2	108.9	108
Denmark	112.3		130.9	141.6	137.9	112.6		120.5	118.7	115
FR of Germany	112.4	113.7	124.3	129.5	134.8	115.7	116.1	116.4	116.1	118
France	113.7	116.5	112.8	122.5	116.1	100.5	103.5	106.3	113.3	112
Ireland	54.0	54.2	53.6	49.5	49.3	57.8	57.6	60.8	61.2	60
Italy	59.6	65.2	70.2	60.2	62.0	68.8	71.1	76.4	72.9	76
Luxembourg	142.4	121.5	128	122.8	125.1	142.4	119.3	127.2	116.9	109
Netherlands	82.9	88.4	98.8	115.9	116.8	104.8	104.3	107.1	108.3	103
United Kingdom	117.4	106.1	89.3	77.5	76.1	112.8	106.5	97.3	93.6	93

B—The European Monetary System and the necessity for convergence of the economies

13 March 1979 is an important date in the history of the European Community for on that day the European Monetary System came into force as a result of a bold initiative by President Giscard d'Estaing and Chancellor Schmidt and the determination shown by the Community's members within the European Council. It was an event which proved to be a turning-point.

The European Monetary System—one stage on the road to economic and monetary union—reflects the determination to establish a zone of monetary stability in the Community by means of stable exchange rate relations between the Member States, and by introducing a common unit of account representing all the currencies involved according to the respective weights of the nine economies—a unit (the ECU) which is both an accounting and trade instrument and a symbol of unity.

Is the system likely to succeed? Have the obstacles which blocked the creation of such a system for nearly two decades been removed? Of course they haven't. There is a need for greater parallelism between monetary and economic developments. Progress on monetary solidarity must be accompanied by the less erratic development of the nine economies.

The convergence of economic performance, moreover, is a pre-condition for genuine stability in relations between European currencies and for the success of the European Monetary System, since the intention is that the economies should grow in such a way that parity changes within the system become increasingly rare and the Member States achieve levels of economic performance which are as identical as possible with regard to inflation rates, balance-of-payments equilibrium and a gradual return to full employment. In the longer term, moreover, and with a view to greater economic and monetary integration, the convergence of the economies should be achieved through the extensive harmonization of economic and social structures and production and trading conditions.

In short, the introduction of the European Monetary System will do much to pave the way for stable and lasting growth in the Community, but if the system is to succeed the economic performances of the Member States will have to converge more fully. Monetary and economic matters are closely linked.

C—Convergence of the economies and the use made of the Community's financial instruments

In 1980, the Community budget amounted to 15 683 m EUA (appropriations for payments) balanced by an equivalent amount constituting the Community's own resources. Loans granted will probably amount to some 3 800 m EUA. Although the sum of these two figures is considerable, it still represents only 1% of the GDP for the Community as a whole. It cannot be claimed, therefore, that these Community funds act as short-term regulators, nor has anyone in the Community ever claimed that they do. However, they include several instruments which have a structural purpose and, hence, an effect on convergence. There are eight such instruments and they provide for the granting of either non-repayable subsidies or repayable loans. In chronological order they are:

(i) since 1952, the funds of the European Coal and Steel Community (ECSC) for financing the modernization and conversion of the coal and steel industry and the resettlement of its workers;

(ii) nominally since 1952, but in fact since 1954, the financial activities of the ECSC designed to further the modernization and conversion of the coal and steel industry;

(iii) nominally since 1958, but in fact since 1960, the European Social Fund (ESF), the main purpose of which is to help finance vocational training aids. In recent years aids have been granted to the least-favoured regions at the rate of 85%, so they have a fairly considerable effect at regional level;

(iv) nominally since 1958, but in fact since 1961, the European Investment Bank (EIB) which is intended to contribute to the smooth and balanced development of the common market in the interests of the Community, and earmarks 70% of its loans to regional development;

(v) since 1970, the Guidance Section of the European Agricultural Guidance and Guarantee Fund whose task it is to help improve agricultural production and marketing structures;

(vi) since 1975, the European Regional Development Fund (ERDF), which is intended to further the development of the poorest regions in the Community, and is the most significant of the convergence measures;

(vii) nominally since 1978, but in fact since 1979, the New Community Instrument (NCI)—a borrowing and lending device for financing investment projects which contribute to the gradual convergence and integration of the Member States' economies, especially as regards energy and infrastructure developments;

(viii) since 1979, interest subsidies for NCI or EIB loans to the least prosperous Member States participating in the European Monetary System (Ireland and Italy).

The dates in the above list are not without significance, as they show that the first Community, the ECSC, set up some very modern mechanisms, which offered viable solutions to the problems of the late 1970s as well as those of the early 1950s. The list also shows that the second Community, i.e. the EEC, introduced, from the outset, as required by the Treaty, two instruments of a structural nature, but waited twelve years before introducing another one, and only since 1975 has it been allowed to exert a financial influence on the economic structure of the Member States of the Community.

It therefore took a long time for the awareness of such a need to crystallize, and new instruments only came into being after some fairly bitter arguments between Member States and by dint of a determined effort by the Community's institutions.

Since then, the Community institutions, and the European Council, have paid particular attention to convergence and the coordination of the Community's financial instruments. One only has to read the conclusions of the European Council meetings of November 1976, March 1977, March 1979, June 1979 and November 1979 (see Annex 3, pp. 352, 353 and 355 to 357) to see this.

Also, in January 1977 one of the Members of the Commission was given the specific task of coordinating all of the Community's financial instruments of a structural nature, and a small team was assigned to him. A special interdepartmental group has also been set up to coordinate the activities of the EIB and the Regional Fund. In a communication dated 17 May 1978, the Commission acknowledged the growing and fundamental importance of coordinating the EEC's financial instruments in the light of enlargement, economic and monetary union and the need to restructure sectors with excess capacity, while safeguarding access to markets and reviving the economy without encouraging inflation. The Commission observed that the economic crisis made it particularly necessary to coordinate the Community's financial instruments and that an overall structural policy was becoming increasingly essential; as were the concentration and rationalization of efforts at Community level, since financial resources, which were already limited, were running out. It emphasized, finally, the fact that the effectiveness of all the financial instruments should be improved and that their value to the citizens of Europe should be highlighted.

2. Community social policy

There are six million unemployed in Europe,[2] a Europe in which incidentally the standard of living has risen by 90% in 20 years. The parties to the Treaties wanted to raise the standard of living, but they did not foresee the possibility of such massive unemployment and, consequently, did not give the Community the means to remedy it.

The Treaties did, however, have much to say about social policy. They even declare in their preambles and in their detailed provisions that they have a social mission to perform.[3] The 'European constitution', however, unlike that of the United States, does not actually mention the word 'welfare'.

A—Financial foundations of social policy

The Community institutions have always attached great importance to the pursuit of an active social policy. However, they have found it difficult to state what the principles of such a policy should be, and even where this has been done, the money provided to finance the policy has always fallen far short of the original target. On at least three occasions—in Paris in October 1972, in December 1974 and in March 1979—the Heads of State or Government have stressed the need for sufficient funds to finance this policy (see Annex 3. pp. 350, 351 and 355). Despite their backing, the results have been disappointing.

That part of European social policy which has financial implications is primarily defined in the rules and aid procedures of the European Social Fund and the social action programme of 21 January 1974.

The European Social Fund

There have been two European Social Funds: the first was exhausted by the end of 1976, and the second was launched in 1971.

The old European Social Fund was created by the EEC Treaty itself in Articles 123 to 128, which laid down the Fund's task and its mode of operation. 'In order to improve employment opportunities for workers in the common market and to contribute thereby to raising the standard of living', this Fund, under the terms of Article 123, had 'the task of rendering the employment of workers easier and of increasing their geographical and occupational mobility within the Community'. The Fund's expenditure was non-discretionary in that under Article 125(1) the Fund was obliged, on application by a Member State, to meet 50% of the expenditure incurred by that State or by a body governed by public law for the purposes of ensuring productive re-employment of workers by means of vocational retraining or resettlement allowances, and granting aid to workers whose employment is reduced or temporarily suspended owing to the conversion of an undertaking to other production in order to maintain their pay pending full re-employment. The non-discretionary nature of the expenditure does not mean that it is open-ended. Aid under the Social Fund was and still is limited by the volume of appropriations included in the budget.

The new European Social Fund is as reformed by Council Decision 71/66/EEC of 1 February 1971. The reason for the reform was that it was thought that the provisions of the old Fund prevented it from effectively accomplishing the task assigned to it by Article 123 of the EEC Treaty. This Decision determined who should benefit from the Fund by stipulating that assistance may be granted to persons in active employment who will remain gainfully employed after receiving aid under one of the Fund's provisions, and, also, in special cases to be determined by the Council, to persons who will pursue some form of self-employment (Article 3).

Possible forms of aid under the new Fund are greater in number and more varied than with the old Fund. Two types of assistance are now provided for, some under Article 4 and the others under Article 5 of the Decision of 1 February 1971. The first type is essentially linked to Council decisions, and may arise when Community policies affect or are likely to affect employment or when the situation calls for joint action to improve the balance of manpower supply and demand within the Community. Under Article 4, whenever the Council sees fit, and the conditions are right, it may sanction a specific area for assistance from the Fund by a special decision on a proposal from the Commission. In nine years it has only made six decisions sanctioning assistance.

On 19 December 1972, the Council decided to grant assistance for operations designed to facilitate the employment and geographical and occupational mobility of persons ceasing to work, directly and as their main employment, in the *agricultural* sphere, in order to take up non-agricultural employment, whether as an employee or on a self-employed basis (Decision 72/428/EEC), and persons working in the *textile* industry who are to pursue activities either within that industry or outside it (Decision 72/429/EEC taken for a period of three years and extended by a decision of 9 February 1976 which also extended the application of these arrangements to the clothing sector).

In addition, on 27 June 1974, the Council decided that joint action could be taken under Article 4 to improve the working and living conditions of *migrant workers* (Decision 74/327/EEC). This action includes three types of operation which may qualify for assistance from the Fund: those forming part of 'integrated programmes' (measures covering all stages of migration, from the migrant's departure to his return to his country of origin), those covering 'integration' (measures to make it easier for migrant workers and members of their families to integrate into their social and working environment), and schemes promoting the training of welfare workers and teaching staff who run integration courses for migrant workers and their children.

On the other hand, again on 27 June 1974, the Council adopted a rather niggardly attitude with regard to the *physically handicapped* (of whom there are between 5 and 22 million in the Community, according to the method of counting), and agreed to sanction assistance under Article 4 only for the financing of pilot schemes for vocational training, whereas in its proposal the Commission had it in mind to carry rehabilitation arrangements much further and extend them to include all matters serving to improve the employment prospects and increase the geographical mobility of the handicapped (Decision 74/328/EEC). It was, however, accepted that the Social Fund could continue to provide help in this case within the framework of the much broader programmes directed against unemployment, namely, under Article 5 of the Decision of 1 February 1971, a proviso that created some confusion with regard to aid procedures, until, at the end of 1977, Decision 74/328/EEC lapsed and was not extended by the Council. The only aid for handicapped persons which still applies, therefore, is that granted under Article 5.

On 22 July 1975, the Council decided to make help available from the Fund for individual schemes aiming to improve the employment prospects and geographical and professional mobility of *young persons under 25* who are unemployed or seeking employment (Decision 75/459/EEC).[4] On the debit side, it should be recorded that two proposals put forward by the Commission failed to gain Council approval: the first related to persons employed in shipbuilding and the second to schemes intended to assist sectors and regions afflicted by the recession.

Most recently, Council Decision 77/804/EEC of 20 December 1977 extended the Fund to cover operations aiming to promote the employment of women over 25, a category particularly affected by employment difficulties.

Council Decision 78/1036/EEC of 18 December 1978, adopted at the instigation of the European Council of 6 and 7 July 1978 (see Annex 3, p. 354), provides for new aid schemes for young people under 25 to promote their recruitment either by means of new jobs or by means of projects for the creation of additional jobs which fulfil a public need which would otherwise not be met. This Decision does not, therefore, give access to the Fund, but instead amends Decision 75/459/EEC of 22 July 1975. On the same day, the Council adopted Regulation (EEC) No 3039/78 so that the two new types of aid for young people from the Social Fund could be created.

Apart from the one relating to farmers, which is not subject to a time-limit, all these decisions lapse at the end of 1980, in accordance with the basic decision.

The second class of assistance from the new Social Fund—that given under *Article 5 of the Decision of 1 February 1971*—is designed to remedy various difficult employment problems affecting underdeveloped or declining regions, sectors particularly affected by technical change, and the handicapped.

This type of assistance is much the same as that provided from the old Social Fund, except that it is given in advance, not retrospectively. The Decision of 1 February 1971 stipulates that at least 50% of the funds available must be allocated to assistance of this second kind during the first five years of the reformed Fund (Article 9(2) of the Decision). This figure then has to be reviewed by the Council, the understanding being that in the long run the greater part of the funds available should be earmarked for disbursement under Article 4 of the Decision. In addition, Article 2 of Council Regulation (EEC) No 2396/71 of 8 November 1971 provides that 60% of the amount appropriated for assistance under Article 5 of the Decision should be reserved in the first instance for operations aimed at eliminating long-term structural employment and underemployment.

Whether Article 4 or Article 5 is involved, assistance from the Fund generally matches that from the national budget, whether the recipients are governed by public law or private law (Article 8(1) and (2) of the Decision of 1 February 1971).

In accordance with Regulation (EEC) No 2396/71, the following types of aid may receive Fund assistance: aid for the organization of vocational training schemes or participation in such schemes, aid to promote geographical mobility in connection with employment and to promote integration into a new social and working environment, aid to remove obstacles to the employment of handicapped persons and workers over 50 and, finally, aid to enable firms in regions where employment has long been seriously affected to pay a temporary wage supplement to newly recruited workers (Article 3(2)). On a proposal from the Commission, the Council may also lay down the conditions for the granting of Fund assistance to aid to maintain the income of people who are on short-time working or wholly unemployed, to foster vocational information and guidance, and to promote employment in regions where employment has long been seriously affected (Article 3(3)). Finally under Article 7, the Commission may use the appropriations allotted for that purpose in the Community budget to promote, carry out or give financial assistance to preparatory studies and pilot schemes in order to give guidance to the Council and itself in the choice of areas in which the Fund should be able to intervene and to enable the Member States and those responsible for operations to choose the most effective aid and to organize the implementation thereof to the best effect.

The Social Fund's rules were revised on 20 December 1977. The basic Decision of 1 February 1971 had provided for a review by the Council of the operating rules of the new Social Fund not later than five years after their entry into force (1 May 1972). This review was carried out in 1977 on the basis of the Commission's proposals, which reflected the experience acquired over the five-year period. The review culminated in the adoption by the Council on 20 December 1977[5] of texts amending or supplementing the basic Decision and the Regulations implementing it.

The main amendments were as follows:
  (i) Fund aid to be made generally available to self-employed persons, rather than just to a few cases;
 (ii) greater emphasis on the regional aspect in the distribution of Fund aid; aid granted under Article 5 of the basic Decision for regions where employment has long been seriously affected (in practice the regions eligible for assistance from the European Regional Development Fund) to represent at least 50% of all the Fund's resources, even if, in the long run, aid under Article 4 continues to be more considerable. Assistance from the Fund was to be increased by 10%, moreover, for aid to Greenland, Ireland (both the Republic and Ulster), the Mezzogiorno and the French Overseas Departments;
(iii) aid payments to be speeded up. The new rules are not described here, but will be outlined later.

Like the 1971 Decision, the amended basic Decision contains a clause which provides for the Fund to be reviewed at the end of a five-year period, i.e. before the end of 1982.

In the context of the 1977 review, the Commission proposed extending the Social Fund's scope beyond vocational redeployment to help the young unemployed—whose number is increasing at present—by means of recruitment premiums and contributions from the Community to programmes for employing young people in activities of general interest. A decision was finally adopted by the Council on 18 December 1978, as already mentioned. This has created a precedent which may in future make it easier for the Fund to help other sectors or categories in difficulty in addition to supporting vocational redeployment schemes. This is a possibility which may open up a new area for the Social Fund whose measures have so far been very circumscribed.

Specific EEC social measures preceding the social action programme

Before the social action programme of 21 January 1974 was approved, the EEC had adopted certain specific measures falling into three groups. The first relates to migrant workers and their social security. The second relates to vocational training (Article 128 of the EEC Treaty and the Council Decision of 2 April 1963). The third relates to exchanges of young workers and the organization of training courses for national civil servants and social workers in the various fields of social welfare. Administrative appropriations are entered in Chapter 30 of the budget to finance these measures.

The EEC's social action programme of 21 January 1974

Following the recommendations of the Paris Summit of October 1972 (see Annex 3, p. 350), the Commission laid down its guidelines for a social action programme on 25 April 1973.[6] On 21 January 1974 the Council adopted a Resolution concerning a social action programme of which the three main objectives are as follows:
  (i) achievement of full employment of better quality in the Community;
 (ii) improvement of living and working conditions so as to enable them to be 'levelled up';
(iii) increased involvement of management and labour in the economic and social decisions of the Community and of workers in the life of their firms.

The sums placed at the Community's disposal are meagre, and so not a lot has been achieved in this area. The most important achievement was the setting up on 10 February 1975, under Regulation (EEC) No 337/75, of the European Centre for the Development of Vocational Training (see Annex 7, p. 375). It has legal personality and is supported by grants from the Commission. Its task is to provide encouragement at Community level for the promotion and expansion of vocational training and continuing education. It is based in West Berlin.

Mention should be made also of the provision of financial support for projects and pilot studies directed to the elimination of poverty, with a view to helping to solve the problems of what some call the 'Fourth World', and for pilot schemes aimed at improving housing conditions for handicapped workers and migrant workers. We should mention, finally, the Community grant to the European Trade Union Institute which was set up on 10 February 1978 by the European Confederation of Trade Unions (ECTU) as a result of the agreement signed on 7 June 1978. The Institute is to help trade-union organizations involved in the Community's work to train and inform their members to improve their knowledge of Community affairs and their linguistic abilities.

ECSC social policy

ECSC social policy includes two aspects with financial implications: resettlement aid for workers and aid towards the construction of subsidized housing.

Resettlement aid—The statutory basis for ECSC resettlement aid is Article 56(1) of the ECSC Treaty which provides that if the introduction, within the framework of the general objectives of the High Authority/Commission, of new technical processes or equipment should lead to an exceptionally large reduction in labour requirements in the coal or the steel industry, making it particularly difficult in one or more areas to re-employ redundant workers, the High Authority/Commission, on application by the governments concerned, may facilitate, either in the industries within its jurisdiction or, with the assent of the Council, in any other industry, the financing of such programmes as it may approve for the creating of new and economically sound activities capable of reabsorbing the redundant workers into productive employment. The scope of this Article was originally fairly narrow because it only applied in times of crisis, but it was later broadened by the addition of a second paragraph (OJ 33 of 16.5.1960) allowing resettlement assistance to be provided when there are 'fundamental changes in market conditions', as certainly occurred since 1958 with the crisis in the coal industry. In the minds of those who devised it, this extension was only meant to apply to the coal industry, but the Court of Justice took the view that the new provisions could not discriminate against the steel industry and extended their application to that sector as well. Intervention may take the form of loans (Article 56(1)(b) of the ECSC Treaty) or grants (Article 56(1)(c) and (2)(b) of the ECSC Treaty). No loans have been made since 1960. The detailed rules for the provision of Community grants are set out in general agreements concluded for an indefinite period with the various interested governments. The High Authority/Commission provides grants to cover 50% of the expenditure on the payment of tideover and resettlement allowances and the financing of vocational retraining for workers who have to change their employment.

In all, 73% of this type of aid has gone to the coal industry, 24% to the steel industry and 3% to the iron industry.

Aid for the construction of subsidized housing—Since 1954, under Article 54 of the ECSC Treaty, the High Authority/Commission has contributed towards the financing of eight housing programmes for workers in the coal and steel industries and three special experimental programmes. Under the ordinary programmes the Community does not itself get the houses built, but issues loans to banks or other financial institutions to help finance them. These long-term loans (15 to 30 years) represent a proportion of the total housing finance varying between 5% and 12% in the case of loans from the special reserve (72% of loans granted) and going up to 60% in the case of loans from a mixture of the Community's own funds and borrowed funds (28% of loans granted). The financial institutions borrowing from the Community in this way undertake to make loans in their turn to industrial firms or suitable specialized agencies financed partly from the sums they have received and partly from other borrowed resources. The amounts finally lent therefore carry a rate of interest better than that of the market owing to the low rate charged by the ECSC (1%).

By 31 December 1979, 165 500 dwellings had been financed by the ECSC.

Temporary social measures in connection with the restructuring of the steel industry—In its preliminary draft budget for 1980 the Commission proposed, under Article 235 of the EEC Treaty, that a one-off subsidy of 100 m EUA be paid from the general budget to the ECSC operational budget, to finance certain exceptional measures for 115 000 steelworkers. The very ambitious measures are as follows:
(1) early retirement to be extended;
(2) the work schedule to be adjusted, especially through the more widespread introduction of short-time working (reduced working week) and an extra shift;
(3) restrictions to be placed on overtime.
These measures would supplement, by virtue of a decision to be taken by the Commission after the Council has given its unanimous assent in accordance with Article 95 of the ECSC Treaty, those measures already authorized under Article 56 of the ECSC Treaty

concerning the resettlement of the workforce. Like the old measures, the new ones would be the subject of bilateral agreements between the Commission and the Member State concerned.

This package caused a great deal of controversy during the procedure for establishing the 1980 budget. The Council rejected the Commission's proposal, while Parliament supported it and even made it one of the reasons for throwing out the budget on 13 December 1979. A heading has been included in the 1980 budget (Chapter 54), but it contains only a token entry. In view of the threat of large-scale redundancies in the steel industry in the summer of 1980 this type of aid may be decided on, but the scope will no doubt be more limited.

B—Budgetary and legal framework of social policy

Because of the way it has evolved over the years and the difficulties experienced in putting it into practice, the social policy of the European Communities has a somewhat disjointed and peculiar basis. As already noted, appropriations for social policy are to be found in both the general budget and the ECSC operational budget.

Budgetary and legal framework provided by the general budget

The 'Social Fund'—The EEC Treaty pays the European Social Fund the excellent tribute of a whole chapter of six articles devoted to it. It does not, however, provide it with legal personality or financial autonomy. In consequence, the Social Fund is merely an offshoot of the Commission, and its resources are part and parcel of the general budget in accordance with the principle whereby all budgetary expenditure is bulked together (the unity principle).

Budget estimates for social policy—For a long time, the Commission took pains to draw up the best possible forecast of the Social Fund's financial requirements on the basis of annual estimates of the likely repayments to be claimed by Member States. In view, however, of the Council's persistent practice of merely setting an overall ceiling to expenditure, on the lines of an annual grant, it stopped making this detailed type of estimate in 1976 and instead put forward a proposal for a grant determined on political grounds. This development largely eliminated the need for supplementary budgets in this field, since the task was no longer one of meeting specific needs but of redistributing certain specified sums between Member States of the EEC.

Since the commitment appropriations are granted on a political basis, the only problem is to decide what level of payment appropriations to provide for. The theoretical schedule is as follows: Financial year $n = 40\%$; $n+1 = 25\%$; $n+2 = 20\%$; $n+3$ and following years $= 15\%$.

Establishing the budget for social policy—Expenditure on social policy is considered to be non-compulsory expenditure: it is the European Parliament, therefore, which has the final say. Every year, the latter has resolutely exercised its powers by using its margin for manoeuvre. The Commission has thus been able to obtain virtually all the appropriations it has asked for. Without Parliament's intervention, the appropriations for social policy would certainly not be as high as they are.

The structure of the budget for social policy—In the general budget, the appropriations for social policy are grouped together fairly closely, there being four budget chapters set aside for the EEC's social policy, three for the Social Fund in Title 5 and one for specific tasks (social action policy and miscellaneous) in Title 3.

Since 1976, the chapters of the budget dealing with the Social Fund have been divided into separate articles dealing with the various different types of intervention.

Implementation of the budget for social policy—The appropriations for social policy are administered by the Commission and more specifically by the Directorate-General for Employment and Social Affairs.

Requests for aid put in by Member States under Articles 4 and 5 are submitted to the Social Fund Committee for its opinion (see Annex 7, p. 373) before endorsement by the Commission. As stated in Article 7 of the Decision of 1 February 1971, such endorsement is conditional on availability of funds. So there is no binding commitment to meet these claims, as was the case with the old Fund. The grant of assistance, corresponding to 50% of the total outlay, is discretionary and depends on criteria to be determined and on the availability of funds.

Implementation of the Social Fund budget has long been fraught with difficulty and much criticized. The disorderly submission of requests for grants of aid and the delays in requesting actual payment have given rise to automatic and non-automatic carrying over of appropriations, at times on such a scale as to call into question the validity of the whole system.[7] Subsequent cancellations have given rise to severe censure and the adoption of such short-term legal palliatives as Regulation 75/717/Euratom, ECSC, EEC of 24 November 1975 making it possible to carry forward committed appropriations for two years instead of one. The bringing in of two-part appropriations as of the financial year 1977 should have allowed the Social Fund's resources to be more smoothly administered, but unfortunately this has not been the case.

The administrative and financial arrangements provided for in 1972 have not really enabled the Social Fund to provide a back-up for the operations which it assists. It has functioned simply as an instrument for making repayments, often very late repayments. The new provisions which have applied since 1 January 1978 are intended:
(a) to ensure that Commission decisions on the granting of assistance take effect before, or at least while, the operations in question are being carried out, and
(b) to speed up payments by means of a system of two advances, each of 30%, the first of which is paid as soon as the Member State certifies that the operation in question has begun, and the second when it is half finished.

Since 1978, the Commission has set certain rules for the management of the Social Fund. On 23 April 1980 it adopted the guidelines for the period 1981-83, of which the following are noteworthy: '... In view of the extent to which the volume of applications exceeds available appropriations the Commission is obliged to select applications for assistance according to priorities fixed for types of operations in each intervention field. First priority will be accorded in the various intervention fields to operations for which joint financing from several Community Funds is envisaged as well as operations carried out jointly by several Member States ...

In fields of intervention where total applications exceed the appropriations available, a reduction will be applied. This will be calculated on applications at the lowest level of priority for which appropriations remain available. For each Member State, a weighted reduction coefficient will be calculated on the basis of the average unemployment rate and the gross domestic product *per capita* for each Member State at current exchange rates. The total amount to be deducted is obtained by applying this coefficient to the applications for that Member State classified at the priority level subject to the weighted reduction. The amount thus arrived at will be apportioned between the individual applications after consultation with the national authorities.'

Checks concerning the implementation of the budget for social policy—Council Regulation (EEC) No 858/72 of 24 April 1972 allows the Commission to carry out on-the-spot checks very similar to those made under the EAGGF inspection arrangements. Officials authorized by the Commission have access to the books and any other relevant documents which make it possible to check that national administrative practices comply with Community rules, that the requisite supporting documents exist and tally and the manner in which the operations are carried out. The Member State's own officials may take part in the inspections carried out by the officials from the Directorate-General for Employment and Social Affairs, who are regularly accompanied by officials from the Directorate-General for Financial Control. The Commission may also require inquiries to be made by the national authorities, subject to the approval of the Member State concerned. Officials from the Commission may take part in such inquiries.

In 1978, Social Fund staff made 52 on-the-spot visits (38 in Italy, 8 in the United Kingdom, 4 in Ireland, 1 in France and 1 in Luxembourg), compared with 82 in 1975. This lower figure is explained by a shortage of staff. It should also be mentioned, however, that the wide range of measures supported, the large number of categories of eligible aid and the many and varied supporting documents which have to be submitted generate a considerable volume of internal and external control work. The complexity and cost of these checks seem out of all proportion to the benefits they bring, since the Social Fund operates essentially as a redistributive mechanism. The actual effectiveness of the measures supported is never properly analysed.

Budgetary and legal framework provided by the ECSC operational budget

Appropriations for social policy are to be found under two different headings in the ECSC operational budget. One of these, aid to resettlement, is covered by levy revenue. Resources used for the construction of subsidized housing, however, are shown 'below the line' because these funds do not accrue directly from levies. Implementation of the ECSC operational budget is an extremely simple matter compared with implementation of the general budget, because expenditure under the first two headings is not subject to the traditional rule whereby expenditure and receipts have to balance. This relaxation is helpful since resettlement expenditure, being non-discretionary in character, must be financed even if this involves overspending. This happened, for example, in 1973 when expenditure amounted to 42.9 m u.a. against estimates of 40 m u.a. and gave rise to an overall deficit in the ECSC operational budget of 1.14 m u.a. By contrast aid towards the building of subsidized housing is kept within the limits of repayments income plus resources available in the special reserve and pension fund. A special contribution from the general budget to the ECSC operational budget appears in Chapter 54 of the 1980 budget as a mere token entry.

3. Community policy on agricultural structures

The focal point of policy on agricultural structures is the EAGGF Guidance Section, which is a component part of the common agricultural policy, but also a structural policy instrument, and a means of attaining greater economic convergence. The Community's agricultural structures policy complements prices policy in significant fashion by helping to raise farmers' incomes (mainly by increasing productivity), and by means of direct income subsidies and special measures to assist farming in mountain and hill areas, less favoured areas and regions where farming structures are lagging behind. Some operations in this field are intended to help reduce structural imbalances in the markets for certain products. In this connection, the Community's investment aid is channelled to those sectors offering outlets on internal and external markets and not to sectors where there are surpluses (e.g. the dairy sector).

At the same time, however, the Community's structural policy has to take social structure and regional agricultural differences into account and improve the economics of farming. As a result, it encourages the maintenance of agricultural prices in the Community within limits which are more advantageous to the consumer, while ensuring that the other aims set out in Article 39 of the EEC Treaty for the common agricultural policy are achieved, especially the objective of ensuring a fair standard of living for the agricultural community. In order to achieve the goals of Community structural policy, financial contributions from the EAGGF Guidance Section cover about 25% of the cost of the operations. The rate may be varied and advances may be granted in the light of particular regional or sectoral situations.

A—Financial foundations of agricultural structures policy

The various components of the agricultural structures policy are set out in the new budget nomenclature (four chapters in Title 8) proposed by the Commission in the preliminary draft budget for 1980. In addition, appropriations earmarked for specific tasks in the agricultural sphere are grouped together in one of the chapters of Title 3.[8]

Projects for the improvement of agricultural structures

The Community finances projects designed to improve the infrastructure of agriculture and the conditions under which agricultural produce is processed and marketed which are still very inadequate in certain regions and sectors. Particularly favourable conditions are offered, e.g. through large financial contributions from the Community: Mezzogiorno (50%), Languedoc-Roussillon (35%) and the West of Ireland (50%). Aid is also provided for certain sectors with structural shortcomings, such as pigmeat processing in France and the United Kingdom. These measures are in the form of projects carried out under specific programmes for a given sector or geographical area. Such projects take a great deal of time to carry out and ceilings are set to the amount of financial support provided.

General socio-structural measures

Three Directives with a broad scope (the 'socio-structural' Directives) were adopted on 17 April 1972.[9]

They cover:
(a) the modernization of farms,
(b) the cessation of farming and the reallocation of land for structural improvement, and
(c) socio-economic guidance and the training of persons engaged in agriculture.

Their main aim is to direct national structural policies towards objectives defined at Community level, whilst ensuring a measure of financial solidarity as a result of aid from the EAGGF Guidance Section. Expenditure incurred by the Member States is generally refunded at the rate of 25% (65% in the case of Ireland and the less-favoured regions in Italy as regards the cessation of farming), and no advances are permitted. The Commission presented the Council with a batch of proposals on 19 March 1979 containing various amendments to the Directives seeking to make them more attractive and effective. The Commission also proposed that the Council ought to prohibit the granting of production aid in certain sectors of the market experiencing considerable difficulties in marketing products, i.e. the dairy sector, pigmeat and glasshouse production.

Measures to assist less-favoured areas

A new approach to structural policy emerged in 1978, the intention being to combat regional inequalities by introducing a number of measures designed to solve specific and regional problems, e.g. in the Mediterranean regions. Whereas the socio-structural Directives are general, it can be said that these measures are specific. It is essential to help the Mediterranean regions and the West of Ireland to make up their considerable leeway in terms of economic development, in particular through high rates of contribution and by allowing advances. A high percentage of the population in these regions is employed in agriculture, the infrastructure is inadequate and there is a high rate of unemployment or underemployment.

These regional measures can be subdivided into four groups: the measures to assist mountain and hill farming adopted in 1975, the measures decided by the Council in 1978 and at the beginning of 1979, those decided in 1980 and measures on which a decision has not yet been taken.

Measures to assist mountain and hill farming

In most of the Member States concerned implementation of Council Directive 75/268/EEC of 28 April 1975 is now in full swing. However, in some of the regions which are particularly at a disadvantage, the aid opportunities afforded by the Directive cannot be exploited adequately, either because Member States (in the case of Ireland and Italy) have insufficient resources or because farms are too small to meet the aid conditions (in the case of the Mezzogiorno). On 24 June 1980, the Council therefore adopted certain amendments to ensure that the Directive is applied more extensively in the least-favoured agricultural areas of the Mezzogiorno and the West of Ireland and to raise the Community's financial contribution from 25% or 35% to 50%.

213

Measures decided by the Council in 1978 and 1979

Implementation of these measures is now going along smoothly: drainage in Ireland (the first EAGGF funds for this were spent in 1979); forestry measures in certain dry Mediterranean areas, an agricultural advisory service in Italy, irrigation in the Mezzogiorno and Corsica, winegrowing in Languedoc-Roussillon, conversion of areas under vines in Charentes, collective restructuring of vineyards and infrastructure improvements in certain less-favoured areas. The outline programmes were all adopted in 1979 or early 1980, and, in some cases, the first projects have already been received. The only delay that has occurred concerns the preparation of the outline programme for drainage in catchment areas on both sides of the border between Ireland and Northern Ireland. As a general rule, the Community covers 50% of the costs incurred by the Member States, and they can ask for an advance of up to 80% of the Community's contribution.

Measures decided in 1980

On 24 June 1980, the Council decided on two new specific measures: one concerning Greenland (development of sheep farming) and one concerning the West of Ireland (stimulation of agricultural development).

Measures on which a decision
has not yet been taken

The Commission put forward new proposals in March 1979 concerning specific measures in Italy (development of beef cattle and sheep farming), and three integrated development programmes covering farming and other activities. The three pilot regions are: the Western Isles of Scotland, Lozère and south-eastern Belgium. The Council has not yet taken any decision concerning these measures.

Structural measures relating to the
common market organizations

These measures are designed to bring about improvements in certain problem sectors, i.e. the dairy, meat, wine and fruit sectors. The measures complement or back up similar ones under the common organization of markets. There is a particularly close link in this case between the Guarantee Section and the Guidance Section of the EAGGF.

B—Budgetary and legal framework of agricultural structures policy

EAGGF Guidance Section

Guidance Section expenditure is financed from the same Fund as Guarantee Section expenditure, so the distinction between the two sections is purely formal (see p. 183).

Budget estimates for the EAGGF Guidance Section

When the EAGGF was first established, it was thought that the expenditure of the Guidance Section ought to be one-third of the expenditure of the Guarantee Section in order to ensure that a major effort was made to improve the structure of farming. However, the increase in Guarantee Section expenditure over the years led to a decision to restrict Guidance Section expenditure to 285 m u.a. per annum. This was done by Regulation No 729/70 of 21 April 1970. The ceiling was subsequently raised to 325 m u.a. by Regulation (EEC) No 2788/72 of 28 December 1972, to take account of the enlargement of the Community. In consequence, the task of forecasting expenditure is not one of fixing an overall limit but of allocating resources, up to the limit already fixed, between the different types of activity specified above. This task is made simpler still by Article 6(4) of Regulation (EEC) No 729/70, which requires the financing of individual projects under Regulation No 17/64/EEC to be continued so long as the appropriations to fund common measures do not reach the ceiling of 325 m u.a. Until 1977, it was merely a matter of forecasting reimbursement requests from Member States and determining, by subtraction, the provision to be made for individual projects.

From 1978, however, the estimates of expenditure for all existing and proposed common measures described above have exceeded the allocation of 325 m u.a. On 22 September 1978 the Commission therefore introduced (at the Council's request) a proposal for a Regulation amending Regulation (EEC) No 729/70 as regards this allocation. The Commission's proposal provided for an average annual target figure of 840 m EUA to be fixed every year through the budgetary procedure and a five-year ceiling of 4 200 m EUA.

Council Regulation (EEC) No 929/79 of 8 May 1979[12] cleared up the situation, as far as the past was concerned, by laying down that EAGGF Guidance Section appropriations were to remain at 325 m EUA until 31 December 1979. It then went on to state that for the five-year period 1980-84 the total amount of financial assistance which may be charged to the Fund shall be 3 600 m EUA, the exact annual figure being determined through the budgetary procedure in the light of the volume of expenditure to be financed for each particular year.

The overall budget estimates for the EAGGF Guidance Section are therefore largely predetermined by the Regulation. The Commission bases its detailed estimates on the figures provided by the nine governments.

Establishing the budget for the EAGGF Guidance Section

As the ceiling for EAGGF Guidance Section expenditure is laid down in Regulation (EEC) No 729/70, the European Parliament has accepted that this expenditure should be regarded as compulsory. The Council is therefore the sole budgetary authority for this expenditure. When the 1979 budget was being drawn up, Parliament tried to change this classification. No solution to this dispute emerged from the budget crisis of 1978-79 (see p. 45). In its preliminary draft budget for 1980 the Commission, realizing that the Council Regulation of 8 May 1979 had created a new situation,[10] proposed that where this Regulation does not give rise to entitlements for third parties and expenditure depends on the availability of funds, the expenditure in question should be regarded as non-compulsory. In practice this concerns the projects for the improvement of agricultural structures. No agreement was

215

reached between the institutions on the question of changing the classification of this expenditure when the 1980 budget was drawn up.

The structure of the budget for the EAGGF Guidance Section

Part of Title 8 of the Commission's budget is devoted to the EAGGF Guidance Section.[11] Its nomenclature has gradually been improved to put into a more orderly form a classification that for a long time has grown somewhat haphazardly. There are four relevant chapters in the 1980 budget, one for each of the four financial foundations of the agricultural structures policy we have just described (p. 212). They contain many budget headings, although some have only received token entries, especially if they are to finance measures which the Council has not yet authorized.

Implementation of the appropriations for the EAGGF Guidance Section

Because of the very great difficulties attending the adoption of decisions on structural policy in the field of agriculture, along with the slowness of national legislative procedures in implementing directives, Guidance Section appropriations have in practice hardly ever been committed during the year in which they are allotted. But it must be admitted that, in addition to the multiplicity and complexity of the individual cases, the consultation procedures are very lengthy, since the files must go first to the Standing Committee on Agricultural Structures and then to the EAGGF Committee (see Annex 7, p. 374) for an opinion before the Commission, which is the authorizing authority for this expenditure, can make its decision. The Directorate-General for Agriculture is the Commission's administering department for this expenditure.

Several years ago, to avoid having to cancel these precious appropriations, the Council accepted that they could be carried forward. However, from 1969 to 1975 it preferred to cancel them and enter them in the remarks column of the budget (the procedure known as the Mansholt Reserve system). These appropriations may then serve as commitment authorizations for common measures if the total allocation of 325 m u.a. proves inadequate. If they are to be used in this way, the appropriations must be 're-entered' in the budget which treats them as appropriations for the financial year as far as their financing from revenue is concerned. Drawings on this 'reserve' through the budget began in 1978.[12]

With regard to the unit of account, the Guidance Section also uses the green rates, but in a modified form.[13]

Since 1977, Guidance Section appropriations have been 'differentiated', meaning that a distinction is made between commitment appropriations and payment appropriations in order to make implementation easier. Very considerable difficulties remain, however, to do with the nature of the expenditure, i.e. whether it is 'open-ended' or not. Expenditure which is not open-ended almost always consists of subsidies to individual projects or investment programmes for which the Council has set an annual ceiling that the Commission may not exceed. If there are enough worthwhile projects, there is generally no difficulty about committing expenditure; problems arise with payments, however, since they depend on how quickly the work is completed and on the Member States submitting accurate payment claims in good time. In 1978, for instance, operations begun in 1968 had still not been finalized. The other common measures, where expenditure incurred by Member States is reimbursed, are almost always open-ended, which means that for every eligible item of expenditure which complies with Community legislation, the Member State has the right to be reimbursed by the Community the following year. This explains why, in the majority of cases, the commitment appropriation matches the payment appropriation.

Be that as it may, the differentiation of appropriations does simplify the implementation of the budget. In the past, the Commission had some difficulty in committing appropriations in the year in which they were allocated and, with some individual projects, needed special regulations in order to carry over appropriations which had not been committed. Similarly, the 1973 Financial Regulation provided for special exemption arrangements for the Guidance Section by specifying that commitment appropriations could be carried over automatically for a five-year period;[14] these arrangements are no longer necessary now that the principle has been accepted that appropriations which have not been committed remain available the following year and that appropriations which have been committed remain committed until they are used up. To avoid having appropriations committed under the Guidance Section remaining unused for too long, they may be released and re-used—breaking the rule of annuality—in accordance with Council Regulation (EEC) No 3171/75 of 3 December 1975.

Checks concerning the implementation of EAGGF Guidance Section appropriations

Auditing the implementation of Guidance Section expenditure is primarily the responsibility of the Member States. Under Article 8 of Council Regulation No 729/70, Member States must satisfy themselves that the operations financed by the Fund are actually carried out and are executed correctly, prevent and deal with irregularities and recover sums lost as a result of irregularities or negligence.

Under Commission Regulation No 99/64, the Commission may carry out inspections on the spot, provided it gives prior notice to the Member State concerned. Article 9(2) of Regulation No 729/70 specifies the objectives of on-the-spot inspections and stipulates how they are to be carried out. The Commission initiates these inspections. Officials of the Member State concerned may take part in them. The Commission may also request the Member State to carry out certain specific checks itself, with or without Commission officials being present.

The Directorate-General for Agriculture and the Directorate-General for Financial Control are involved in the carrying out of Commission inspections; these may involve audits of adjustments to accounts, one-off inquiries for special reasons or investigations of one particular aspect. The latter deal with problems arising in a given sector and generally concern all the Member States.

The Court of Auditors is also entitled to carry out on-the-spot checks under Article 206a(3) of the EEC Treaty and Article 80 of the Financial Regulation.

In 1977, the Commission organized on-the-spot checks in the case of 9 individual projects and 6 common measures and special measures; the Court of Auditors (or Audit Board as the case may be) has taken part in the audit of 2 individual programmes and 5 common measures or special measures. It has to be said that, although the amount of checking is increasing year by year, it is still far short of what is actually required.

4. Community regional policy

Despite the persistent advocacy of the Commission over many years, it remained impossible for a long time to get a Community regional policy accepted. Not until the Paris Summit, in the Communiqué of 21 October 1972, did the Heads of State or Government give regional policy top priority and ask the Community institutions to set up a Regional Development Fund by 1 January 1974. The year 1973 was spent first in preparing the Commission's proposal of 31 July, then in an inconclusive discussion in the Council on the amount (proposed as 2 250 m u.a. for 1974-76) and allocation of the aid to be granted and the criteria that should govern operations. The Copenhagen Summit, on 15 December 1973, could do no more than reaffirm the desire to see the Fund created. Another whole year passed without result. But at the next Paris Summit, on 10 December 1974, the Heads of State or Government decided that the Fund would be put into operation with effect from 1 January 1975. For various reasons, this did not actually happen until several months later.

In fact, three meetings of Heads of State or Government were required before sufficient impetus could be achieved for a Regional Fund to be set up. A meeting of the European Council in Brussels (on 6 December 1977) was also required so that the Fund's activities could be continued after the first phase of its operations (see Annex 3, pp. 350, 351 and 353). The Regional Fund has therefore been and still is one of the most controversial areas of Community action as far as the Member States and the Community institutions are concerned, whereas is should be a cornerstone of Community activities and, therefore, of Community finances.

A—Financial foundations of regional policy

The regional policy of the European Communities has been pursued on three separate fronts: the EEC, the ECSC and the EIB. EEC activities can be divided into two parts.

The EEC Regional Fund

As the reader will have already gathered, the present Regional Fund is not the first of its kind; there is very little, however, to distinguish it from its predecessor.

The Regional Fund (1975)—On 18 March 1975—after discussions lasting 20 months—the Council adopted a package[15] concerning the European Regional Development Fund (ERDF) which was set up on an experimental basis for three years and allocated 1 300 m u.a. in appropriations (split into national quotas) to support the development of Community regions in difficulty as a result of the predominance of agriculture, industrial changes or structural underemployment.[16] The objective of the ERDF is to correct the main regional imbalances in the Community. Fund operations are Community measures in support of Member States' regional policy measures and they fit into regional development programmes. The map shows which these regions are.

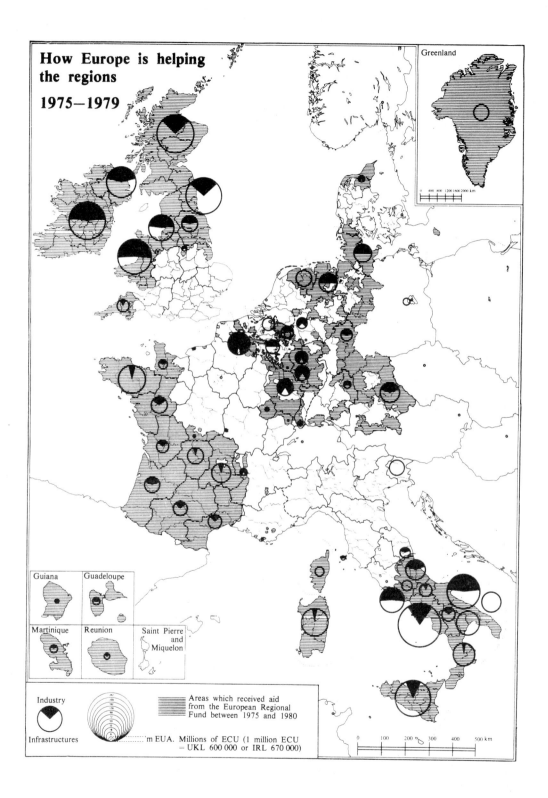

How Europe is helping the regions
1975—1979

Greenland

0 400 800 1200 1600 2000 km

Guiana
Guadeloupe
Martinique
Reunion
Saint Pierre and Miquelon

Industry

Infrastructures

'm EUA. Millions of ECU (1 million ECU = UKL 600 000 or IRL 670 000)

Areas which received aid from the European Regional Fund between 1975 and 1980

0 100 200 300 400 500 km

The Community measures involved cover investment projects costing more than 50 000 u.a. in one of the following categories:

(i) *Investment in industry, crafts or services.* These activities must be economically sound and be in receipt of State regional aid and create or preserve at least ten jobs. In the craft and tourist sectors a group of interrelated investment projects may be regarded as a single investment. The Fund's contribution is 20% of the investment cost. It may not, however, exceed 50% of the national aid granted to each investment under regional assistance arrangements. It is also restricted to that part of the investment not exceeding 100 000 u.a. per job created and 50 000 u.a. per job preserved. Where services are concerned, the Fund's contribution may be more than 20% of the investment cost but may not exceed 50% of the national aid or 10 000 u.a. per job created or preserved.

(ii) *Infrastructure investment.* Such investment must contribute to the development of the region or zone concerned, and must be warranted under one of the regional development programmes. This category includes the infrastructure investments referred to in the Council Directive on mountain and hill farming and farming in certain less-favoured areas (see p. 213). The Fund's contribution is 30% of the amount spent by the public authorities if the investment costs less than 10 m EUA,[17] and between 10 and 30% if it costs 10 m EUA or more. The new Regional Fund Regulation states that this rate may be as much as 40% in cases where projects are specially important for the development of the region in question. It also states that Fund operations for the financing of infrastructure investment may not exceed 70% of total Fund aid.

All assistance from the Fund is supposed to be additional to national aid to the regions to create new jobs or save those under threat. All the main forms of national aid to regional investment at present operated by Member States are eligible for assistance from the Fund. Applications for aid must be submitted to the Commission by the authorities of the Member States and not by those investing in projects. It is fair to ask however, whether the appropriations from the Regional Fund really provide assistance additional to that of the Member States or whether they use it to reduce their own national expenditure. This was emphasized by Parliament in its Resolution of 15 April 1980, paragraph 22 of which pointed out 'that the effectiveness of the available funds—which are small by comparison with requirements—depends on the principle that they are additional to national expenditure and must have a multiplying effect', while paragraph 23 pointed out and deplored 'that the Member States have used aid granted from the Fund for industrial projects as partial repayment of national aid, whereas Community aid is intended to supplement aid and thus facilitate control and publicity'.

Be that as it may, the establishment of a Fund by the Community does not interfere with the regional policies of the Member States. They are still free to choose the instruments of regional policy best suited to the particular need of their regions. In a Community with such widely different regions as Sicily, Clydeside and Greenland, a uniform approach would not work. But one of the aims of Community regional policy is to place more emphasis on coherent overall planning for the less-favoured regions. It is therefore necessary that the projects submitted by Member States for aid from the Fund should fit in with overall development plans drawn up at the local or national level for each region.

The Regional Fund since 1978—On 3 June 1977, the Commission proposed various amendments to the Fund Regulation in its guidelines for the Community's regional policy. On 6 February 1979—after 20 months had elapsed, as in the case of the basic Regulation—the Council adopted legislation[18] which differed from the previous rules on the following three points only:

(i) a non-quota section, for which 5% of the Fund's total resources would be reserved was introduced,

(ii) national quotas were adjusted, enabling a 2% increase in France's share, for the benefit of the Overseas Departments, and

(iii) the infrastructure projects eligible for Fund aid were defined more flexibly.

The non-quota section of the Fund—The provision of a non-quota section is definitely the most significant amendment made in the Regulation of 6 February 1979. Under it, the Fund may help to finance specific Community measures in the field of regional development which are either wholly or partly different from Community action in support of the Member States' own regional policy measures. A further advantage is that this section may operate, where necessary, outside the assisted areas defined for Community action in support of Member States' own regional policy measures. The nature of the operations which the Fund may support, its contribution and the financial procedures are all to be laid down in the special programmes adopted by the Council on a proposal from the Commission for each of the specific Community measures to be introduced. Budget implementation therefore involves tertiary legislation to be adopted by the Council as well, with all the attendant problems that this entails.

In fact, it was not until 16 October 1979 that the Commission put forward programmes involving 220 m EUA of aid to be granted up to the end of 1984 under the non-quota 5% of the Fund (probably 350 m EUA). The intended recipient countries are Belgium (6 m EUA), France (65 m EUA), Ireland (16 m EUA) and the United Kingdom (58 m EUA). The five sets of measures proposed are as follows:

(i) Measures contributing to the development of certain regions affected by the enlargement of the Community (120 m EUA to help develop rural tourist facilities and small and medium-sized businesses in the Mezzogiorno, Aquitaine, Midi-Pyrénées and Languedoc-Roussillon—the regions which will be most directly affected by the accession of Greece, Portugal and Spain to the Community);

(ii) Measures contributing to the development of certain areas severely affected by the difficulties in the steel industry (43 m EUA to improve the environment, promote small and medium-sized businesses and encourage industrial innovation in the counties of Strathclyde, Cleveland, Clwyd, South and West Glamorgan and Gwent and the district of Corby in the United Kingdom, the province of Naples in Italy and certain areas in the provinces of Liège, Hainaut and Luxembourg in Belgium);

(iii) Measures benefiting certain areas severely affected by the difficulties in the shipbuilding industry (17 m EUA to improve the environment, promote small and medium-sized businesses and encourage industrial innovation in the following counties in the United Kingdom: Strathclyde, Cleveland, Tyne and Wear, Merseyside and Belfast);

(iv) Measures helping to diversify energy sources in the Mezzogiorno (16 m EUA for the installation and promotion of new techniques for hydroelectricity and alternative energy sources especially those using mini-turbines at small waterfalls in the mountainous areas of the Mezzogiorno);

(v) Measures to help the development of tourism in Ireland and Northern Ireland (24 m EUA to promote tourism and craft activities in the frontier areas of Ireland and Northern Ireland).

This first group of proposals is a good illustration of the intended aim of the new non-quota section. It demonstrates the Commission's right of initiative and clearly reveals the link between the various Community policies and the situation in certain regions. The fact that the method employed is based not on projects but on programmes should make it possible to monitor the success of the operations more effectively, since the Member States con-

221

cerned are required to present an annual report on the programmes. The type of measure envisaged is also new. It concerns not simply investment aid, but rather forms of aid which are designed to enable specific sectors in specific regions to adapt properly to new conditions (market studies for small and medium-sized businesses which are the industrial fabric of certain regions in France and Italy, information on new technology, and feasibility studies). Under the Commission's proposal, the Community contribution could be as much as 70%.

The Council finally agreed to the Commission's proposals of 10 October 1978[18] in July 1980.

Measures to assist the less-prosperous Member States in the context of the European Monetary System

To facilitate the entry into force of the European Monetary System, the European Council agreed on 4 and 5 December 1978 to take measures 'to assist the less-prosperous Member States which are participating effectively and fully in the exchange and intervention mechanism' (see Annex 3, p. 354). Two measures are involved:
(a) loans for a period of five years, to the extent of 1 000 m EUA a year to be granted by the Community (NCI) and the EIB, and
(b) interest subsidies for those loans amounting to 3% during the same period, costing 200 m EUA each year.

It was decided, with regard to the implementation of these measures, that two-thirds would concern Italy and one-third Ireland (the United Kingdom is not in the EMS).

All these measures, then, are part of regional policy in its widest sense, since they are aid for the development of two of the least-prosperous States, one of which (Ireland) constitutes, on its own, a priority ERDF region. For the budget preparations, and in order, in particular, to find a solution to the budget crisis of December 1978 (see p. 45), it was decided that these measures should be regarded as regional policy measures. However, the refund paid to the United Kingdom because it is not in the EMS (see p. 127), does not come under the heading of regional policy. Instead, the appropriations in question have been entered alongside interest subsidies.

Supplementary measures for the benefit of the United Kingdom

The European Council meeting in Dublin in November 1979 asked the Commission to act as arbitrator in order to help find a solution to the 'British problem', i.e. the fact that the United Kingdom is now a net contributor to the Community budget. The Commission proposed two possible courses:
(a) to amend the 1976 financial mechanism so that larger repayments can be made to the United Kingdom (see p. 126), and
(b) to devise specific measures concerning expenditure.

The Commission suggested that Article 235 of the EEC Treaty could be the legal basis for these measures, as was the case when the financial mechanism was introduced in 1976. Invoking this article means in particular that the measures to be taken should contribute to the attainment of the Community's objectives, and the very fact of invoking it shows that the solution is to be found in the context of normal Community procedures.

On May 30 1980 (on the occasion of the Brussels compromise), the Council accepted the principle of specific or, as they were called, 'supplementary', measures to assist the United Kingdom. The sums granted for 1980, 1981 and probably 1982 (see footnote 7 on p. 340) will be considerable, far greater in fact than the UK's quota under the Regional Fund. At the request of Her Majesty's Government, it was agreed that the Council, on a proposal from the Commission, could decide each year to grant advances which would enable these measures to be implemented more quickly, and that the appropriations in question would be in the following year's budget.

In the explanatory memorandum to its proposal for a Regulation put forward on 12 June 1980, the Commission placed these supplementary measures within the context of the solution to the United Kingdom's main structural problems, a solution which ought to be consistent with the gradual achievement of convergence of the Member States' economies. The supplementary measures should help improve the economic performance of the United Kingdom by developing the economic and social infrastructure, especially in the assisted areas, and by investment in the exploitation of coal resources.

The Commission proposes that these measures should involve investment expenditure to be implemented in special multiannual programmes such as those for the non-quota section of the Regional Fund just described. It also asks that it, the Commission, should decide, after consulting the Regional Policy Committee and the Energy Committee (see Annex 7, p. 374), how this Community finance should be distributed.

The measures in question are therefore of a political, exceptional and temporary nature. The measures have two special features worth mentioning:
(a) the maximum Community contribution is 70%, compared with 55% for the Social Fund, 40% for the Regional Fund and 65% for the EAGGF Guidance Section, and
(b) provision is made for 90% of this contribution to be paid immediately, the remaining 10% being made over, once the first 90% has been used up (and the UK Government has notified the Commission to that effect), at the latest before the end of the year following that of commitment, on condition that the programme is being accomplished according to plan. This rate (90%) is also the highest ever reached compared with 30% in the case of the Social Fund, 75% in the case of the Regional Fund and 80% in the case of the EAGGF Guidance Section).

ECSC structural policy

The Regional Fund may be the main instrument of Community regional policy, but it is neither the only one nor the oldest. The ECSC has been pursuing its regional policy, under Articles 54 and 56 of the ECSC Treaty, much longer. We will not reproduce these articles here since we quoted from them when discussing the financial aspects of the ECSC (see p. 137). Suffice it to say that Article 54 authorizes loans for investment purposes and Article 56 promotes conversion. The policy of the High Authority/Commission since 1968 has been to grant interest subsidies on some of the loans it grants.

The loans which do carry interest subsidies represent an important financial instrument for promoting priority investment, in particular that connected with Community restructuring and conversion policies. To qualify for interest subsidies, the loans must fulfil certain criteria published in the *Official Journal*.

As far as *investment* is concerned, the main objective of the reduced interest rate loans at present is to further the structural improvement and reorganization of the coal and steel industries. The criteria for granting interest subsidies relate principally to:

 (i) The environment: interest subsidies are confined to exceptionally large capital expenditure on existing plant and investment in pilot plants (OJ C 146 of 25.11.1974);

 (ii) Research and training centres and the removal of bottlenecks: interest-subsidies are reserved for investment to increase coking capacity (OJ C 73 of 18.6.1970);

(iii) The stabilization of coal production: interest subsidies are confined to investment in pits, work underground and haulage and mining equipment. To assess the merits of investment of this kind, the Commission takes into account its size (completion time), location (significance of the coalfield), purpose and employment content. This is a new category of aid proposed by the Commission on 10 October 1979 (OJ C 49 of 29.3.1980);

(iv) Restructuring: interest subsidies may be granted for investment which is very attractive with a view to restructuring and a return in the long run to a competitive Community steel industry (OJ C 174 of 22.7.1977). The Commission considers this category of aid a particularly important part of its steel policy.

Where *conversion* is concerned, loans are granted to firms or public bodies promoting investment which will generate new jobs in the areas hit by declining employment in the coal and steel industries (OJ C 178 of 27.7.1977 and OJ C 82 of 29.3.1979). The maximum loan which qualifies for an interest subsidy is currently 20 000 EUA per job created. Recipients must give precedence to former ECSC workers when it comes to recruitment.

Jobs are still being lost in the Community steel industry at an alarming rate, and it looks as though this trend will continue for some years to come. As a result, without exaggerating the short-term effectiveness of conversion measures, it is possible, as far as job-creation is concerned, to arrive at a few orders of magnitude in relation to the scale of the problem. If, in 1980, the ECSC, through its conversion policy, was to encourage the replacement of all 25 000 jobs which are likely to disappear in the steel industry alone, reduced interest rate loans would have to be granted to the tune of 500 m EUA, with non-repayable interest subsidies amounting to 75 m EUA (3% interest subsidies per year for five years).

It is worth noting, finally, that interest subsidies on ECSC loans cannot be financed by levy revenue, as Article 50 of the ECSC Treaty does not provide for this; instead it is possible to use revenue from own funds.

EIB activity

Financing regional development projects is one of the tasks assigned to the Bank by Article 130 of the EEC Treaty. The general directives for credit policy adopted by the Board of Governors in December 1958 state that a large part of the Bank's resources must be devoted to financing projects which are likely to help improve the situation in the less-developed regions. In fact, more than two-thirds of the Bank's financing operations in the nine Member States are investments with regional significance.

The second major task assigned to the Bank concerns investments of importance to several Member States or indeed to the Community as a whole. Financing operations in this field initially focused on economic infrastructure projects designed to further intra-Community trade and improve communications, e.g. projects concerning road, rail and maritime links. Since 1973, the focal point has been the security of the Community's energy supplies (development of indigenous resources, diversification of imports and energy conservation). Because of their European significance, the Bank has also supported projects carried out in the context of close cooperation between firms in two or more Member States, projects which make use of new technologies, and more recently, projects relating to the protection of the environment.

The Bank may also finance (under indent (b) of Article 130 of the EEC Treaty) projects for the modernization, or conversion of firms and the creation of new activities. These projects are aimed at problem sectors, and are generally part of the policy laid down by the Community and the Member States for the sectors concerned.

B—Budgetary and legal framework of regional policy

The very history of regional policy explains why the budgetary and legal framework is so diverse.

Budgetary and legal framework provided by the general budget

The Regional Fund—The ERDF is not a proper fund, any more than the Agricultural or Social Funds are. It has neither legal personality nor financial independence. Its appropriations are set out in the budget and are covered by the Community's own resources under the comprehensiveness rule.

Budget estimates for the Regional Fund—Prior to 1979, there was no proper budget estimate for regional policy, since the Fund allocation was agreed for the period 1975-77 at the Paris Summit of 10 December 1974, and later confirmed in the Regulation of 18 March 1975: 1 300 m u.a. (300 m u.a. + 500 m u.a. + 500 m u.a.). Similarly, the allocation for 1978-80 was agreed by the European Council meeting in Brussels on 6 December 1977: 1 850 m u.a. (580 m u.a. + 620 m u.a. + 650 m u.a.).[19] The only difficult problem was to decide what payment appropriations should be provided for these appropriations which were themselves considered to be commitment appropriations. A theoretical schedule was drawn up and gradually revised in the light of experience. The present schedule for payments is: financial year n = 25%; n+1 = 45%; n+2 = 10%; n+3 = 10% and n+4 = 10%.

Establishing the budget for the Regional Fund—the ERDF budget was one of the main bones of contention as regards the classification of Community expenditure as compulsory expenditure (CE) or non-compulsory expenditure (NCE). Since the 1975 budget, Parliament, supported by the Commission, has considered ERDF expenditure as NCE. The Council, on the other hand, has taken the view that, under Article 2(1) of the Regulation of 18 March 1975, the expenditure involved for the period 1975-77 should be regarded as necessarily resulting from an act adopted in accordance with the Treaty. In its desire to meet Parliament half-way, and in view of the fact that the Commission was to put forward proposals for the period after 1977, the Council declared on 22 April 1975 that it was ready to decide that, after the period 1975-77, expenditure under the Fund would no longer be regarded as necessarily resulting from the Treaty or an act adopted in accordance with the Treaty. Rather reluctantly, Parliament accepted this. However, when the 1978 budget was being negotiated, the Council exerted considerable pressure on Parliament to get it to accept the figures which the European Council, not without difficulty, had managed to arrive at on 6 December 1977. Parliament finally accepted, after some initial misgivings.[20] When the 1979 budget came up for discussion, the same dispute recurred, as has already been explained. The Commission, in accordance with the decisions of the European Council of 6 December 1977, proposed the inclusion of 620 m EUA in the budget. The Council accepted this figure, but Parliament proposed raising it to 1 100 m EUA—the figure which in fact appears in the budget finally adopted. To find a way out of the December 1978 budget crisis, the three institutions concerned finally agreed on a supplementary and amending budget of 945 m EUA (900 m EUA for the quota section and 45 m EUA for the non-quota section) plus 200 m EUA in the form of interest subsidies. The Council (Budget) therefore agreed that the figure which the European Council laid down in December 1977 and confirmed in December 1978 could be exceeded; this was quite an event.

For the 1980 budget, the Commission proposed 1 200 m EUA (1 140 m EUA for the quota section and 60 m EUA for the non-quota section). This was cut by the Council to 945 m EUA, one of the reasons why the European Parliament rejected the budget on 13 December 1979. In the Commission's new budget proposal of 29 February 1980, the sum of 1 200 m EUA is maintained however. The Council reduced this to 1 165 m EUA, a figure which Parliament finally reluctantly agreed to. Consequently, the ERDF is still a subject of controversy among the Community institutions.

As the Regulation of 6 February 1979 sets the resources of the non-quota section at 5% of those for the quota section, there is no need to make a separate estimate for the non-quota section.

Structure of the budget for regional policy—Regional Fund appropriations are given in Title 5 of the Commission's statement of expenditure. Chapter 55, for instance, was included as from the 1974 budget as the first practical application of the Resolution of the Paris Summit of October 1972. At first, it had only a token entry, but appropriations were included from 1975. In the 1979 budget there is also a Chapter 56 for non-quota appropriations. The Fund's appropriations, unlike those of the Social Fund, are not subdivided into articles, so this heading is consequently one of the most richly endowed in the general budget.

The appropriations for interest subsidies and financial compensation to the United Kingdom are in Chapter 57, although the latter might be more at home in Title 4 under the heading of repayments to Member States.

Implementing the budget for the Regional Fund—The Commission and its departments, primarily the Directorate-General for Regional Policy, are responsible for implementing the Regional Fund budget. They are advised by the Regional Policy Committee and the Regional Fund Committee (see Annex 7, p. 374). The most striking, and at the same time the most exceptional, feature is that the implementation of the Fund is settled in advance in that the appropriations are allocated on a geographical basis, as laid down in Article 2 of the two Fund Regulations. The European Parliament has criticized the quota arrangements, the most recent example of its criticism being in its Resolution of 15 April 1980 on the Fourth Annual ERDF Report (1978). The quotas are as follows (the first figure is for 1975-77, and the second for 1978-80[21]): Italy 40% and 39.39%; United Kingdom 28% and 27.03%; France 15% and 16.86%; Federal Republic of Germany 6.4% and 6%; Ireland 6% and 6.46%;[22] Netherlands 1.7% and 1.58%; Belgium 1.5% and 1.39%; Denmark 1.3% and 1.2% and Luxembourg 0.1% and 0.09%. These quotas will have to be amended when the Community is enlarged (see p. 411).

When the ERDF was set up, the need for differentiated appropriations was realized.[23] The Fund has had the benefit of differentiation from the start, although admittedly the quota system does have certain snags as well as advantages. This has had various consequences: commitment appropriations have been implemented with scarcely a hitch, but some delay has been experienced in implementing payment appropriations. In 1978, commitments not followed by payments amounted to 705.8 m EUA, rising in 1979 to 1 132.9 m EUA.

Under the Regulation of 6 February 1979, accelerated payments may be agreed to by the Commission at the request of a Member State. These may not exceed 75% of the total amount of Fund aid and are conditional on at least 30% of the payments forming the basis of the aid having been made.

The non-quota section of the Regional Fund has not yet come into operation. For it to do so, the Council must adopt various Regulations unanimously. There is, therefore, a third set of rules which govern Community intervention, and this constitutes a restriction of the Commission's budget implementation powers.

Checks concerning the implementation of the budget for the Regional Fund—Under Article 9(2) of the Council Regulation of 18 March 1975, the Member States provide the Commission with all the information required for the Fund to operate effectively, and are required to take all steps to facilitate supervision by the Commission, including on-the-spot checks. Under Article 9(3) of the same Regulation, on-the-spot checks are carried out, at the Commission's request and with the agreement of the Member State concerned, by the competent authorities of that State. Commission officials may take part in these checks. In this case it is staff from the Directorate-General for Regional Policy who take part in the checks, in 9 cases out of 10 accompanied by officials from the Directorate-General for Financial Control. The purpose of on-the-spot checks is to ascertain:
(a) whether administrative practices are consistent with Community rules,
(b) whether supporting documents exist and tally with the operations concerned,
(c) the conditions under which operations are implemented and investigated, and
(d) whether the projects implemented are in line with the original intention.

The main purpose of the checking arrangements is to ensure, in cooperation with the competent authorities in the Member States and in accordance with the Fund Regulation, that the projects which receive Fund backing are properly administered and correctly implemented. The programme of on-the-spot checks is designed to cover a reasonable sample of the different types of project supported by the Fund. Checks have been carried out particularly in those regions which are the main recipients of Fund aid—148 in the United Kingdom, 95 in Italy, 68 in the Federal Republic of Germany, 66 in France, 35 in Ireland, 27 in Denmark, 13 in Belgium, 4 in the Netherlands and 2 in Luxembourg, giving a grand total of 458 between 1975 and 1978. In all, about 9.6% of the projects have been investigated on the spot; this is slightly below the 10% considered by the Commission to be the minimum which can be accepted.

Financial and legal framework provided by the ECSC and the EIB

The ECSC borrows money for on-lending. The High Authority/Commission is the sole arbiter of the amounts of the loans involved which are administered by the Directorate-General for Credit and Investments. The loans may receive interest subsidies which constitute non-repayable expenditure charged to the ECSC operational budget. The subsidies are covered not by the levy but from income from own funds. The administering department is the Directorate-General for Regional Policy in the case of industrial conversion pursuant to Article 56 of the ECSC Treaty, and the Directorate-General for Credit and Investments in the case of investments under Article 54. These activities, and EIB loans, have no special features and follow the normal rules.

5. The Community's industrial restructuring and conversion policy

There is at present in the Community surplus production capacity in industries such as steel, shipbuilding, man-made fibres and paper. To enable the problem industries to restructure so that they can become competitive enough to face up to international competition, support is required at Community level for the essential restructuring and diversification measures. The efforts to adapt capacity in terms of quantity and quality are primarily the industries' responsibility, but it is the job of the public authorities in the Community to guide and stimulate them in this task. In this context, it is essential for the Community to provide financial support to enable adjustments to take place with as little social disruption as possible and as fairly as possible.

A—Foundations of the Community's restructuring and conversion policy

Under Article 235 of the EEC Treaty, the Commission put to the Council a proposal for a Regulation on 26 October 1978 relating to Community aid, the intention being to acquire on behalf of the European Economic Community similar powers to those which it holds under Articles 54 and 56 of the ECSC Treaty. On 11 January 1979 it proposed shipbuilding and textiles (especially man-made fibres) as the first suitable areas for receiving such aid.

The proposed operations are intended:
(a) to support rationalization measures covering all the firms in a particular industry, and
(b) to provide a particular category of firm, such as small and medium-sized businesses, with resources which they have difficulty in obtaining at present.

Community financial assistance has a two-fold purpose. It is not aimed just at programmes for restructuring through investment in rationalizing and updating equipment, production techniques, and management and sales strategies, but, if the employment situation in the region where the firm in question is situated so warrants, it also covers conversion investment programmes designed to ensure that employment is maintained, either in the same industry or in other activities. In both cases, Community aid must be consistent with the attainment of common objectives defined at Community level.

Community aid can take the form of direct assistance (investment premiums) or interest subsidies.

The substance of the Commission's proposal was endorsed by Parliament on 26 April 1979, except as regards the decision-making process (further details will be given later). The Council, however, has not yet reacted to the proposal.

B—Budgetary and legal framework for industrial restructuring and conversion policy

We can be very brief here, since the legal basis is in fact non-existent.

Establishing the appropriations for industrial restructuring and conversion policy

The inclusion in the budget of an Article 375 for Community aid for industrial restructuring and conversion operations constitutes an exceptional event and yet has been a source of disappointment.

This heading was proposed by the Commission in September 1977 in a letter of amendment to its preliminary draft budget for 1978 and was included in the 1978 budget. In allocating funds for this purpose, the Council departed considerably from the principle of allocating appropriations only if there is a legislative basis for their use (see p. 57). Despite the fact that funds were available—and under a specific heading at that—the Commission waited 13 months before putting forward its proposal for a Regulation. Although Parliament had been basically very much in favour of the scheme, on 26 April 1979 it gave an opinion which was only partly favourable. In acknowledging the need for a legislative basis, it departed from its previous standpoint.

The practical outcome of this legal and political muddle, resulting from the growing uncertainty as to the relevance of such a Community scheme, was that in the 1978 budget the heading received 20 m EUA in the form of commitment appropriations and 17 m EUA in payment appropriations; 20 m EUA in commitment appropriations and 10 m EUA in payment appropriations were entered in the 1979 budget, but in Chapter 100 and were to be shared with the Social Fund for an unspecified measure under the heading of industrial conversion. In the 1980 budget the heading in question has received only a token entry.

Implementing the appropriations for industrial restructuring and conversion policy

There is a problem of principle here. On 26 October 1978, the Commission proposed a decision-making process whereby requests for aid would be referred to an Advisory Committee, whereas in the case of measures to implement the Regulation, the Council would be able to reach a different decision from what the Commission itself had in mind, although admittedly it would have to do so within two months. In its Opinion of 26 April 1979, Parliament did not agree with this proposal as it thought that it was contrary to Article 205 of the EEC Treaty.

In view of the need to use up the 1978 appropriations carried over to 1979 and due to lapse on 31 December, the Commission put forward a Regulation which the Council adopted on 20 December 1979. As a result, it has been possible to grant Community assistance worth 13.9 m EUA to a number of projects in the man-made fibre industry in Italy.

6. Community environment policy

Community environment policy is mentioned in a short paragraph in the final communiqué of the Summit Conference held in Paris in October 1972. The Heads of State or Government stressed the value of such a policy and requested the Commission to draw up an action programme with a detailed timetable before 31 July 1973.

A—Financial foundations of environment policy

Community environment policy is pursued under the aegis of all three European Communities and the EIB.

Policy pursued by the European Economic Community

On 17 April 1973, the Commission put forward an action programme the broad lines of which were adopted by the Council on 19 July 1973. Formal approval was given in a declaration made on 22 November 1973,[24] which states that the aim of the Community environment programme is to improve the setting and quality of life and the surroundings and living conditions of the peoples of the Community. It goes on to state that this policy must help to place economic growth at the service of man by providing him with an environment offering the best possible living conditions, and to reconcile this growth with the increasingly imperative need to preserve the natural environment. The programme of 22 November 1973 specifies three main types of action: action to reduce pollution and nuisance, action to improve the environment, and pursuit of Community action or joint action by the Member States within the framework of international organizations. On the basis of this programme the Commission submitted to the Council, on 5 March 1974, a draft Recommendation to Member States to apply the rule that 'the polluter pays'; this was accepted by the Council on 7 November 1974. A division of responsibilities was thus arrived at whereby the Community studies the problems and determines methods for dealing with them, and the Member States choose and carry through actual measures for the protection of the environment.

In May 1975, a European Foundation for the Improvement of Living and Working Conditions was set up; its task is to contribute to the definition and achievement of improvements in living and working conditions by expanding and spreading the knowledge needed to make progress in this direction. The Foundation has legal personality and is maintained by a grant from the Commission. It is located in Dublin.

On 17 May 1977, the Council adopted a Resolution approving a second action programme which is the continuation of the first and will run until 1981. Apart from continuing with the action taken under the first programme, it emphasizes the management of natural resources and, in particular, anti-wastage measures.

It has to be admitted, however, that if progress is being made in this area, it is because of the repercussions of disasters like Seveso in 1977, the Amoco Cadiz in 1978 and Three Mile Island in 1979. When all concerned ultimately agree on the need to act, the Community is often the obvious forum.

Policy pursued by the European Atomic Energy Community

The Euratom Treaty is concerned with the environment from the health angle. Chapter 3 of the Euratom Treaty devotes 10 articles to health and safety. The basic standards to be laid down for protection against the dangers arising from ionizing radiation include maximum permissible dosages compatible with proper safety levels, maximum permissible levels of exposure and contamination, and the fundamental principles governing the health surveillance of workers. It should be noted that Euratom is also involved in environmental research. The current four-year research programme has considerable funds for this.

Policy pursued by the European Coal and Steel Community

Under Article 54 of the ECSC Treaty, the High Authority/Commission has for several years been pursuing a policy of encouraging the protection of the environment. It helps firms bear the substantial costs they have to pay to combat pollution, in particular by granting interest subsidies on loans.

Policy pursued by the European Investment Bank

The EIB has granted a number of loans to industrial firms or public authorities for projects of a pioneering character or ones that reduce pollution to the benefit of more than one Member State. More generally, it is the practice of the Bank to pay special attention to the impact of proposed projects on the environment when it scrutinizes individual applications for assistance.

B—Budgetary and legal framework of environment policy

There is not a lot to say on this subject. Funds for the environment policies pursued by the EEC and Euratom have been grouped together in a single chapter of the budget (Chapter 35 of Title 3) as a sign of their common purpose. The appropriations are classed as being for NCE so the final decision rests with the European Parliament. The EEC appropriations are for studies, while the Euratom appropriations are to cover administrative costs (meetings, experts' fees, training, missions and inspections, purchase of equipment, publications). The only item worth mentioning in particular is the subsidy granted to cover the running costs of the European Foundation for the Improvement of Living and Working Conditions. In 1973, the Commission set up the Environment and Consumer Protection Service which has responsibility for environmental matters and therefore administers the relevant appropriations. The health and safety appropriations are administered by the Directorate-General for Employment and Social Affairs.

7. Resources used to finance internal development policy

Let us now turn to the financial resources allocated for internal development policy from 1952 to 1980 and try to assess the regional impact of the different resources made available. We shall then examine the purposes for which Community funds are allocated.

A—Resources used, 1952-80

As the Community has been particularly active in the internal development field in the last few years, let us start by giving the figures for 1979 and 1980. As these figures are rather complicated they are presented in a table, and a few preliminary remarks are called for. First of all, the table does not follow the standard pattern as it lumps together general budget appropriations and ECSC operational budget appropriations. Secondly, it brings together all the subject matter covered by this chapter on how the internal development of the Community is being financed. This concept of internal development is not covered by the budget nomenclature or the Commission's presentation in its general introduction to the preliminary draft budget. Consequently, the table does not include some of the appropriations of Title 5 (Social and Regional Funds), e.g. the amounts repaid to the United Kingdom by way of financial compensation since she is not in the EMS. Similarly, appropriations for Community industrial restructuring and conversion operations (Article 375) have been taken from the appropriations for energy and industrial policy so that they can be included here. Consequently, the table differs from the one in Annex 12 (pp. 396 to 399).

The very high figures quoted must, however, be seen in perspective. To take an example, the money designed to help unemployed young people in 1980 is likely to benefit only 80 000, when there are in fact two-and-a-half million of them. Although this example is not necessarily typical of all cases it has to be said that the effect of Community aid is limited. It is more of a partial substitute than a form of supplementary assistance. Nevertheless, before looking back to the past, we should note the extremely rapid increase in these resources. However, although they doubled in the three years from 1977 to 1979, they still represent only 15.8% of the appropriations for commitments and 8.3% of the appropriations for payments in the 1980 budget.

A distinction should be made between non-repayable grants and repayable loans.

Budget resources disbursed as grants from 1952 to 1979

As the Social Fund was reformed in 1971, we shall examine the old Social Fund and the new Social Fund in turn. Six financial instruments are involved and we shall examine them in order of appearance, along with various specific measures.

ECSC aid (1953-79)—The earliest grants were allocated by the ECSC. They amounted to 446.7 m u.a. in resettlement aid and 158.3 m u.a. in interest subsidies on industrial conversion loans (96.3 m u.a.) and aid for industrial modernization (62 m u.a.). The total cost of ECSC aid from its operational budget amounts to 605 m u.a.

Budget resources for internal development policy

(m EUA)

Policies and measures				1979		1980	
				For commitment	For payment	For commitment	For payment
Social policy	Social Fund		1	767.5	527.5	909.5	374.3
	Social programme		2	13.7	11.6	9.6	14.5
	Disasters		3	5.0	5.0	5.0	5.0
	Contribution to the ECSC		4	—	—	token entry	token entry
	EEC—Total		5=1+2+3 +4	786.2	544.1	924.1	393.8
	ECSC resettlement		6	67.0	67.0	67.0	67.0
		Total	7=5+6	853.2	611.1	991.1	460.8
Agricultural structures policy	EEC		8	529.8	372.8	462.8	322.3
Regional policy	Regional Fund		9	945.0	499.0	1 165.0	1 403.0
	Interest subsidies		10	200.0	200.0	200.0	200.0
	EEC—Total		11=9+10	1 145.0	699.0	1 365.0	603.0
	ECSC		12	25.5	25.5	23.0	23.0
		Total	13=11+12	1 170.5	724.5	1 388.0	626.0
Industrial restructuring and conversion	EEC		14	20.0	10.0	token entry	token entry
	ECSC		15	21.7	21.7	43.0	43.0
		Total	16=14+15	41.7	31.7	43.0	43.0
Environment	EEC		17	7.8	7.8	8.6	8.6
		Grand total	18=7+8+ 13+16+17	2 603.0	1 747.9	2 893.5	1 460.7

The old Social Fund (1960-76)—In just over 16 years (from 20 September 1960 to 31 December 1976), the old Social Fund paid out 394.3 m u.a.—382.6 m u.a. in aid for retraining and 11.7 in resettlement aid. In all, 1 900 000 workers benefited from this expenditure (1 130 000 retrained and 770 000 resettled). The cost of retraining is high (339 u.a. per worker) compared with the cost of resettlement (15 u.a. per worker).

Although the Social Fund was set up chiefly to help Italy (which received 37% of total payments), a greater proportion of its aid was granted to the Federal Republic of Germany (43.5%). The other countries shared the remaining 19.5% as follows: France 12%, the Netherlands 3.8%, Belgium 3.2% and Luxembourg 0.5%. The Federal Republic benefited more because the authorities there were sufficiently well-organized to put in claims that were likely to be met and were in a position to contribute their half of the aid in question. But to give the whole picture, it should be added that Member States deliberately refrained from submitting all the claims they could have made, exercising voluntary restraint in order to maintain some degree of balance amongst themselves in view of the limited amount of Community budget resources available.

The new Social Fund (1972-79)—Aid from the new Social Fund dates from 1 May 1972. In the eight years from 1972 to 1979, this aid amounted to 3 500 m EUA in commitments and 1 877 m EUA in payments. Strangely enough, the Social Fund suffers from too few commitment appropriations and too many payment appropriations.

The Commission is finding that the total amount of assistance requested from the Social Fund is increasingly exceeding the resources available. The number of applications in 1977 exceeded budget resources by 52.3%, in 1978 by 93.3% and in 1979 by 70.4%. However, the shortage of funds does not affect all the fields of intervention in the same way. It is particularly acute in the case of migrant workers, young people and handicapped persons; applications for these categories exceeded the amounts allocated by 340%, 66.4% and 71.5% respectively in 1978. In absolute terms, the most seriously affected by the shortage were young people (302 m EUA available compared with 502.5 m EUA requested) and the regions (326 m EUA available compared with 542.7 m EUA requested). The Commission has therefore had to apply very stringent selection criteria. A total of 772.5 m EUA in commitment appropriations was available in 1979, a 35.5% increase compared with the previous year. The total number of people who directly benefited from programmes approved in 1979 has been estimated at 1 200 000 (of which 460 000 received money by way of regional aid, 450 000 benefited as young people and 285 000 as migrant workers). In 1979 more than 85% of the Social Fund's resources were allocated to regions with priority status, compared with 80% in 1978.

Moreover, for some time now the Commission has been concerned at the continuing delays in paying over funds in spite of its attempts to facilitate and improve payment procedures. A number of improvements were made to the payment procedure when the Council reviewed the Fund in 1977. These included the possibility of an advance of 85% of the total amount of assistance for all operations carried out before 31 December 1977, and—for new operations to be carried out from 1 January 1978 onwards—the possibility of an advance of 30% of the amount of assistance once the Member State certifies that the operation has commenced and a second advance of 30% when it certifies that the operation has been half completed. Since these new rules have been in force, the first indications are that to a large extent the Member States have been slow to take advantage of them. At the end of 1978, the commitments entered into against which no payments had been made amounted to 1 222 m EUA. In 1979, however, there was considerable progress as payments amounted to almost 600 m EUA, more than double the amount paid in 1978 (285 m EUA). To the Commission's way of thinking, the major obstacle is that some Member States take too long to send in payment claims, the worst offenders being Luxembourg (only 12% of commitments settled), Italy (36.7% settled) and France (39.5% settled). The overall average settlement rate was 50.8%. As this problem is not peculiar to the Social Fund, but is common to all the structural funds, we shall be discussing it later.

EAGGF Guidance Section (1965-79)—A total of 4 081 m u.a. in appropriations were made available for the EAGGF Guidance Section from 1965 to 1979. Because of difficulties in making actual disbursements, commitments began to pile up, reaching a total of 3 155 m u.a., or 77% of all the appropriations in question. In order to prevent these appropriations being cancelled, the Mansholt Reserve[12] was set up in 1969. In addition, a sum of 150 m u.a., which had been placed in reserve, was entered in the budget against the Regional Fund.[15, 16] In the end, only 93 m u.a. lapsed (2.3%). By the end of 1979, only 2 038 m u.a. out of the 3 155 m u.a. committed had been paid,[25] with 905 m EUA still to be paid at the end of 1979.

It should not be forgotten that whereas policy for supporting agricultural markets is decided upon and financed almost entirely by the Community, this is not the case for structures policy, where only a proportion of certain eligible expenditure incurred by the Member States in the framework of Community legislation, which itself only covers part of the overall structures policy, is reimbursed by the EAGGF Guidance Section.

Regional Fund (1975-79)—The following amounts were allocated: 1 300 m u.a. for the period 1975-77 (see p. 225), 581 m u.a. for 1978[20] and 945 m u.a. for 1979, a total of 2 826 m u.a. over five years. Total payments over the same period amounted to 2 074 m u.a.

Interest subsidies in the context of the EMS (1979)—In 1979 (the first year of operation of this scheme), 34 subsidies, totalling 200 m EUA, were paid to Italy and Ireland.

Industrial measures (1979)—Non-repayable grants in 1979 (the first year of operation of this scheme) totalled 13.9 m EUA.

Specific or exceptional measures (1959-79)—Expenditure on specific measures of a *social* nature amounted to 50.8 m u.a. (expenses incurred by the Administrative Commission on Social Security for Migrant Workers, vocational training aid, *environmental* measures, training periods, conferences and congresses and, since 1976, Community contributions towards schemes to combat poverty and measures to improve the housing conditions of migrant workers and handicapped people). Expenditure on specific *agricultural* measures, the first of which were launched in 1966, amounted to 6.5 m EUA in 1978. After being less than 600 000 u.a. a year up to 1971 (with the exception of 1968), the figure has been in excess of 1 m EUA ever since, because of expenditure on agricultural research[26] and on the Farm Accountancy Data Network. Between 1966 and 1978, this expenditure accounted for a total of 37.9 m u.a., i.e. 0.07% of agricultural expenditure.

We should not forget either the large amounts of aid granted by the European Communities to the region of Friuli-Venezia Giulia following the earthquake there in 1976,[27] and to Martinique and Guadeloupe after hurricanes devastated the islands in 1979.[28]

Exceptional aid—involving smaller amounts than in the two cases mentioned above—was also granted to victims of other disasters: in 1976, the earthquake in Sicily, the floods in Tuscany and the mining disaster in Flixborough; in 1977, the floods in south-west France in July, the hurricane in Tuscany in August and the floods in northern Italy in October; in 1978, the storms and floods in Great Britain and France in January, the Amoco Cadiz disaster in Brittany, the floods in Germany in May, the earthquake in Germany in September, the floods in the Val d'Ossola in Lombardy in August; and, in 1979, the earthquakes in Umbria, Latium and Marches in October, and the floods in the islands off the coast of Scotland in December.

Loans granted (1954-79)

During this period, loans were granted by the ECSC, the EIB and the NCI. The NCI became operational in 1979.

Loans granted by the ECSC (1954-79)—In 25 years, the ECSC has granted loans totalling 6 058.7 m u.a. from borrowed funds (5 844.5 m u.a.) and from its own funds (214.2 m u.a.).

The loans from borrowed funds were to the iron and steel industry (3 524.9 m u.a.) the coal industry (1 529.4 m u.a.) and the iron-ore sector (97.3 m u.a.), giving a total of 5 151.6 m u.a. under Article 54 of the ECSC Treaty. Almost unnoticed, therefore, the High Authority/Commission has become the leading investment bank for the coal and steel industries in the Community. In 1978, for example, it financed 20% of all the capital expenditure in the steel industry (no more than 30% of the amount invested by the industry in any particular case) and 26% of all the capital expenditure in the coal industry (no more than 50% of the amount invested by the industry in any particular case).

In addition, again from borrowed funds, the ECSC granted 623.4 m u.a. under Article 56 of the ECSC Treaty to encourage redeployment. It also granted 69.5 m u.a. for the building or renovation of subsidized housing.

From its own funds, the ECSC made grants of 206 m u.a. for subsidized housing, 3.8 m u.a. for industrial conversion, 3.9 m u.a. for the steel industry and 0.5 m u.a. for resettlement.

Loans granted by the EIB (1958-79) and the NCI (1979)—in 22 years, the EIB granted loans totalling 11 654.5 m u.a. from its own resources, 8 551.1 for regional development, 243.3 for modernizing and converting firms and 4 457.7 for projects of common European interest.

Apart from these overall amounts, it is worth mentioning some of the more important figures for the period after enlargement. Since 1973, more than two-thirds of the Bank's financing in the Community has been channelled into investment of regional benefit (6 600.8 m u.a., 152.2 of which under the NCI, out of a total amount of 9 476.0), chiefly in the Italian Mezzogiorno and in the UK development areas and Ireland. The annual amount of this aid has been increasing: 424.5 m u.a. in 1973, 964.4 m u.a. in 1977, 1 457.6 m u.a. in 1978 and 1 570.6 m u.a. in 1979 from the Bank's own resources, with another 152.2 m u.a. in NCI loans.

Since 1973, there has been a marked increase in the financing of projects of benefit to several Member States or the Community as a whole (3 796.3 m u.a. from 1973 to 1979, including 124.8 m u.a. in NCI loans, particularly as a result of the growth of finance for investment to help improve the Community's energy supplies (3 079.1 m u.a. from 1973 to 1979, including 124.8 m u.a. under the NCI). The annual amount of finance for this purpose increased from 219.2 m u.a. in 1973 to 545.4 m u.a. in 1978, and totalled 910.7 m u.a. in 1979. Still in the field of projects of common European interest, the Bank granted some 470 m u.a. in loans between 1973 and 1979 to improve transport and telecommunications between Member States and to protect the environment. Incidentally, some investment of common European interest is also of regional importance, so the amounts quoted cannot be lumped together.

The Bank's activities cover all sectors of the economy. More than a fifth of its loans have been granted to industry (some 2 100 m u.a. between 1973 and 1979), both in the form of individual loans for fairly sizeable projects (171 loans from 1973 to 1979) and in the form of global loans to financing bodies which then allocate the amounts in question to smaller investment projects, according to the criteria laid down by the Bank and subject to its approval. Between 1973 and 1979, the Bank granted 55 global loans, totalling more than 640 m u.a., which enabled 1 129 smaller loans to be granted for investment in a wide variety of labour-intensive industries.

More than one-third of the assistance granted from the Bank's resources and from the NCI was for energy plant (3 586.2 m u.a. between 1973 and 1979), mainly for electricity generation (2 225.7 m u.a.), e.g. the construction of nuclear power stations (1 299.6 m u.a.), and for the exploitation and transport of oil and natural gas (967 m u.a.). Next come the big infrastructure projects: transport (972.1 m u.a. between 1973 and 1979), telecommunications (1 390.6 m u.a.), water catchment and abstraction schemes, effluent disposal and purification plants (1 107 m u.a.) and irrigation facilities (326 m u.a.).

More than two-thirds of the projects financed in the Community are in the countries with the most serious regional problems: Italy, the United Kingdom and Ireland. Loans for projects in Italy (3 462.5 m u.a. between 1973 and 1979—see (a) below) accounted for 36.5% of the total amount of financing provided in the Community, and were basically for projects in the south of Italy. In the United Kingdom, 2 733.4 m u.a. (see (b) below) (28.9%), were spent chiefly on developing North Sea oil and gas resources, restructuring the iron and steel industry and on major water schemes. In France, 1 460.7 m u.a. (15.4%) were granted, chiefly for large-scale energy and communications projects. Next come Ireland (700.8 m u.a.—see (c) below), Federal Republic of Germany (533.2 m u.a.), Denmark (207.8 m u.a.), Belgium (165.4 m u.a.) and the Netherlands (62.3 m u.a.). Another 149.9 m u.a. were for projects which, although outside the Community, offer the prospect of considerable benefits for Community energy supply.

The New Community Instrument (NCI) comes within the range of this banking activity. Thus the figures quoted in the previous paragraph include 277 m EUA lent under the NCI (see Annex 13, p. 401), namely:
(a) 85 m EUA in Italy,
(b) 105.3 m EUA in the United Kingdom, and
(c) 86.7 m EUA in Ireland.

Total Community aid

A total of 7 197 m u.a. was disbursed in non-repayable grants between 1953 and 1979, and a total of 17 713.2 m u.a. was distributed in the form of loans between 1954 and 1979. This area thus ranks third of all the Community's intervention policies from the point of view of the resources deployed.

B—Regional impact of the resources used to finance internal development policy

A common feature of all the financial instruments described in this chapter is their regional aspect. The prime example is, of course, the Regional Fund, which I shall not go into here. A few words should be said about three of the other instruments, however.

In 1979, the *Social Fund* continued to be used to offset structural inadequacies, particularly in the less-developed regions of the Community, by expanding the regional side of the operations financed under Article 4, while at the same time continuing with the regional measures under Article 5. In 1979, therefore, an estimated 85% of its impact was of a regional nature, compared with 80% the year before. Some 37.8% of the Fund's resources were used to help the five regions accorded top priority under Council Regulation (EEC) No 2895/77—Greenland, the French Overseas Departments, Ireland, Northern Ireland and the Mezzogiorno—compared with 25% in 1977 and 37.6% in 1978.

The increase in the amounts committed to helping the five top-priority regions is the result of the decision to increase the rate of contribution in these regions by 10% as of 1 January 1978 (the rate was increased from 50 to 55% for each operation). This higher rate brought the commitment appropriations up to 293.3 m EUA. The increase in the proportion of the Fund's resources allocated to these five regions is also a reflection of the desire to concentrate the Fund's operations in these regions because of the seriousness of their unemployment problems. Commitments in the other ERDF regions in 1979 totalled 366.9 m EUA (47.3%), while only 115.6 m EUA (14.9%) were committed elsewhere.

The EAGGF Guidance Section has been concentrating more and more on regional projects. In 1975, the directive on mountain and hill farming and farming in certain less-favoured areas was adopted and, in 1978 and 1979, regulations and directives concerning Mediterranean regions were adopted, although these measures have not yet been fully translated into financial terms. A look at the accounts of the EAGGF Guidance Section in a few years' time should certainly confirm that it has a definite regional function.

Since 1958, *the EIB* has allocated three-quarters of its financial aid in Member States for investment of regional benefit; in 1979 alone, this amounted to 1 722.8 m EUA, of which 1 570.6 came from the Bank's own resources and 152.2 from those of the NCI. Some of its financial operations also help to achieve other objectives at the same time. For example, most of the projects for industrial modernization and conversion and job creation concern ailing industries which are heavily concentrated in certain areas and thus eligible for regional aid. Similarly, a number of energy and communications projects of general benefit to Europe also help further the development of less-favoured regions.

The Bank's operations to assist regional development are governed by a number of criteria. The EIB pays great attention to the Community's regional policy objectives and the priorities established by the Member States. Thus, regions which already receive considerable assistance under the regional aid schemes coordinated by the Commission are automatically considered eligible for EIB support. Investment in other areas may also be considered on an individual basis if there are particular structural difficulties which would seem to justify intervention. The Bank also tries to channel its assistance into regions whose problems are particularly acute. Thus, between 1973 and 1979, more than 70% of the amount of financing provided for projects of regional benefit was allocated to projects in the assisted regions of Italy, the United Kingdom and Ireland. Lastly, in 1969, in order to extend its operations to assist small and medium-sized businesses which, because of their diversity and the fact that they are very labour-intensive, have a particularly effective contribution to make in developing a region's economy, the Bank adopted the global loans system. Thus, between 1973 and 1979, more than 1 130 subloans were granted for small or medium-sized projects, totalling nearly 470 million u.a.

On 21 March 1979, the Commission introduced a system of integrated operations to coordinate its financial instruments for structural purposes. An integrated operation is a consistent set of public and private schemes and investments covering a limited geographical area, the financing of which is supplemented by the national and local authorities of the Member States and the Community by means of its financial instruments for structural purposes. An integrated operation must include at least:
(a) a definition of the area covered by the planned investment and schemes;

(b) the deadline for the completion of the investment, which may be spread over several years;

(c) a description of the schemes or investment planned (infrastructure, public services, industry, services, tourism, farming schemes, etc.); this should not be too inflexible, but should be designed to meet the real needs of the area;

(d) the financial resources required, their source (local, regional, national, Community) and type (loans, grants, interest subsidies).

The first integrated operations will constitute something of a trial run, and will have to be implemented pragmatically. The plan is that a gradualist approach will be followed, beginning with only a few integrated operations in a small number of countries (Italy, United Kingdom, Ireland and France). Then, in the light of the experience gained, it will be decided whether or not to carry on. It is extremely unlikely, in fact, that their use will become very widespread, one reason being that they require the combined use of a number of Community instruments, and this will not always be possible. It is more likely that they will be used to a much smaller extent than the conventional operations of the various Funds, but they may well prove a useful and worthwhile instrument in cases where they can be used, as they provide a facility which is not at present available.

C—Financial results of internal development policy and the convergence of the Member States' economies

Given below are figures which were worked out for the European Council meeting in Dublin in November 1979 and revised in March 1980. They show where the appropriations for commitments of the four financial instruments covered by the general budget were spent in 1979 and where they are expected to be spent in 1980.

Disbursements under the four structural Funds
covered by the general budget

(%)

Member State	B	DK	D	F	IRL	I	L	NL	UK	Total
	Actual amounts in 1979									
Social Fund	0.9	2.8	10.1	16.0	6.0	28.3	0.01	1.9	33.9	100
EAGGF guidance	4.2	3.6	31.5	22.3	6.9	9.4	0.1	6.1	15.9	100
ERDF	0.6	1.8	9.0	20.2	6.4	28.0	0.0	1.7	32.3	100
EMS subsidies	0.0	0.0	0.0	0.0	42.0	58.0	0.0	0.0	0.0	100
% in 1979	1.5	2.4	14.0	17.3	9.8	26.4	0.1	2.7	25.8	100
	Estimates for 1980									
Social Fund	3.0	4.0	13.0	16.0	8.0	25.0	0.0	3.0	28.0	100
EAGGF guidance	2.5	2.9	24.3	25.0	8.1	15.1	0.4	4.2	17.5	100
ERDF	1.39	1.20	8.0	16.86	6.46	36.85	0.09	1.58	27.57	100
EMS subsidies	0.0	0.0	0.0	0.0	33	67	0.0	0.0	0.0	100
% in 1980	1.9	2.3	12.3	16.0	11.4	·32.6	0.1	2.4	21.0	100

What does this table show? The funds seem to be deployed very sensibly. In fact, of the non-repayable grants, 62% in 1979 and 65% in 1980 are shown to be allocated to the three least-wealthy Member States of the Community—the United Kingdom, Italy and Ireland—whose combined GDPs represent a little less than 32% of the Community's overall GDP. Moreover, 65% of the repayable loans are also granted to these three Member States. The other six Member States are thus displaying deliberate solidarity with these countries.

The actual amounts of these loans are also important. In 1979, non-repayable grants amounted to 1 632 m EUA in payment appropriations and 2 596 m EUA in commitment appropriations, in other words, in authorizations given to the Commission to enter into commitments on the Community's behalf during that or the following financial year, and repayable loans amounted to 3 600 m EUA. This means, therefore, that 17.5% of budget resources and 85% of borrowed funds are spent on measures which help promote the convergence of the economies, in that they will be concentrated chiefly in the less-favoured areas. A comparison of these figures with the Community's GDP shows that efforts by the Community to encourage regional development and the convergence of the national economies account for 0.25% of its GDP. If on the other hand, instead of this average percentage, we work out what each Member State receives as a percentage of its GDP, the results are rather different: over 1% for Ireland, over 0.5% for Italy and much more than average for the United Kingdom.

Moreover, it should not be forgotten that in a unit such as the European Community which is still in the process of integration, what is beneficial to each individual region is of benefit to the Community as a whole. Anything than can be done to promote convergence and harmonization is basically for the good of all. We should not therefore only consider the net benefits accruing to each constituent part of that unit.

*
* *

Economic convergence between the Member States of the Community will be achieved in the first place through national economic, monetary and social policies, but these policies also require coordination at Community level. The machinery for achieving this goal should therefore be strengthened and resolutely given a leading role to play. Where Europe's finances are concerned, efforts should focus not on setting up new instruments but on allocating more resources to existing instruments and coordinating them, particularly by encouraging integrated operations. To be sure, the amounts of budget resources and funds lent doubled in the three years from 1977 to 1979. This is a tremendous increase, but the trend is only recent. There is an urgent need for a dynamic adjustment of expenditure as far as this is possible within the limits of the own resources allocated to the Community. As the Commission wrote in its Communication to the Council of 5 February 1980 on convergence and budgetary questions: 'Real progress will anyway need to be made towards a better balance within Community policies in terms of stabilizing expenditure on surpluses under the agricultural policy, strengthening the existing structural policies, and establishing policies whose need is not questioned but on which the Council have not yet succeeded in reaching agreement'.[29] Judging by the steps taken to resolve the 'British problem', on 30 May 1980, the Council would appear to have committed itself to this policy in its future deliberations and action.[30]

However, it goes without saying that it is only by allocating the Community new own resources that this dynamic adjustment of expenditure can take place. On 15 October 1979, when preparing the November European Council meeting in Dublin, the Italian Govern-

240

ment proposed that appropriations for structural purposes should constitute at least 25% of the budget by 1982. This proposal has not yet been agreed to although it obviously goes right to the heart of the matter and would bring the deadline closer. The solution of the British problem and the enlargement of the Community should also help to speed things up.

It has to be admitted, however, that increasing the financial resources with which the Community instruments are endowed will encourage the convergence of economies only if the increase in own resources this implies does not have a regressive effect, in other words only if the poorer Member States do not have to contribute an unreasonable proportion of the increase. In any event—and this is the simplest approach—expenditure should be channelled in such a way as to benefit the least healthy economies. The poorer countries should not be net contributors. To allow such a situation to come about and, what is more, persist would negate the very idea of the Community. This word 'Community' is both the name and the slogan of the Europe we have been building over the last 28 years. However, although the development of a Community implies respect for one's neighbour, solidarity and the pooling of resources, this is only possible by means of open discussion, self-discipline and endeavour on all sides. In less abstract terms this means, as far as Europe's finances are concerned, that those Member States for whose benefit the Community's instruments should be developed must act in such a way that their national macroeconomic and structural policies are consistent with jointly-agreed overall objectives. The European public must have a guarantee that the financial sacrifices made to help the less-prosperous countries genuinely promote convergence.

Footnotes to Chapter XII

[1] The points made concerning the convergence or divergence of the economic performance of the Member States of the Community are taken from a paper read by the author when he was awarded an honorary Doctorate by the University of Oviedo, Spain, on 18 June 1979.

[2] The average unemployment level in 1978 was 5 969 000, or 5.6% of the working population. The corresponding figures were 1 166 900 (5.3%) for France, 333 400 (8.4%) for Belgium and 1 200 (0.8%) for Luxembourg.

[3] Those who drafted the Treaties certainly paid particular attention to the social aspects of European integration. Thus, the ECSC Treaty states in its preamble that the signatories are 'anxious to help, by expanding their basic production, to raise the standard of living' and goes on to provide, in Article 3(e), that the institutions of the ECSC shall 'promote improved working conditions and an improved standard of living for the workers in each of the industries for which it is responsible'. For its part, the EEC Treaty states, in its preamble, that the signatories 'affirm as the essential objective of their efforts the constant improvement of the living and working conditions of their peoples' and then goes on to develop this theme in two articles. Article 2 provides that one of the Community's aims is 'to promote throughout the Community a harmonious development of economic activities and a continuous and balanced expansion', a task that cannot conceivably be pursued without an active social policy, a coherent regional policy, and effective pursuit of measures to improve the quality of life and the protection of the environment. Article 3(i) of the EEC Treaty provides that the Community's activities shall include 'the creation of a European Social Fund in order to improve employment opportunities for workers and to contribute to the raising of their standard of living'. In the course of the preamble to the EEC Treaty, the signatories also declare themselves 'anxious to strengthen the unity of their economies and to ensure their harmonious development by reducing the differences existing between the various regions and the backwardness of the less-favoured regions'. Finally, the Euratom Treaty indicates, in its preamble, that its signatories are 'anxious to create the conditions of safety necessary to eliminate hazards to the life and health of the public', and stipulates in Article 2(b) that the Community must 'establish uniform safety standards to protect the health of workers and of the general public and ensure that they are applied'. At the Paris Summit, on 21 October 1972, the Heads of State or Government declared very firmly that the European Community is not intended to be a community of traders but a social community.

[4] In 1978, 2 263 000 young people below the age of 25 were unemployed in the Community, representing 38.2% of all the unemployed. The average rate of unemployment among young people in the Community was 12.4%.

[5] Social Fund legislation of 20 December 1977:
(a) Council Decision 77/801/EEC amending Decision 71/66/EEC of 1 February 1971;
(b) Council Regulation (EEC) No 2893/77 amending Regulation (EEC) No 2396/71 of 8 November 1971 implementing the Council Decision of 1 February 1971 on the reform of the European Social Fund;
(c) Council Regulation (EEC) No 2894/77 amending Regulation (EEC) No 858/72 on certain administrative and financial procedures for the operation of the European Social Fund;
(d) Council Regulation (EEC) No 2895/77.
All this legislation was published in OJ L 337 of 27.12.1977. The European Parliament waived the conciliation procedure (see Annex 5, p. 367) even though the legislation was not in accordance with the opinion it had published on 12 May 1977.

[6] Guidelines for the social action programme were published in Supplement 4/73—Bull. EC and the Resolution concerning a social action programme in OJ C 13 of 12.2.1974.

[7] The percentages of appropriations cancelled were 43% in 1969, 42% in 1970, 0.4% in 1971, 14.3% in 1972, 12.4% in 1973, 18.2% in 1974, 58.5% in 1975, 45.7% in 1976, 1.5% in 1977, 0.6% in 1978 and 0.2% in 1979.

[8] The EEC has gradually built up a whole arsenal of specific measures in the agricultural field, the major ones being, in descending order: since 1966, action in campaigns against epidemics to which livestock may be exposed; since 1967, financing the application of directives on veterinary matters and the marketing of seedlings and seeds; since 1968, the Farm Accountancy Data Network (in 1979 this covered 30 800 farms); and, since 1974, a programme for coordinating agricultural research. Budget appropriations for these various operations are administered in accordance with the general rules for implementing the budget and appear together in Chapter 30 of Title 3.

[9] See OJ L 96 of 23.4.1972.

[10] In the general introduction to the preliminary draft budget for 1980, the Commission states (on p. 99): 'The position is different with regard to the financial year 1980, since the Council recently took a decision (on 8 May 1979) whereby the annual allocation has been replaced by a new concept—total amounts fixed for five-year periods—with the result that annual appropriations will now have to be determined in the context of the normal budgetary procedure . . .
As a result of this new legal context, Guidance Section expenditure is no longer automatically compulsory expenditure. The Commission has therefore analysed the various budget headings in the Guidance Section to determine which should remain classed as compulsory expenditure and which, in its opinion, should now be classed as non-compulsory expenditure.'

[11] In the budgets for 1979 and 1980, the appropriations for the fisheries sector were grouped together in four chapters of Title 8. They have already been dealt with in the previous chapter of this book.

[12] The 'Mansholt Reserve' was set up by Regulation (EEC) No 2010/68 of 9 December 1968 (OJ L 299 of 13.12.1968). Between 1969 and 1975, it was credited with appropriations totalling 531 089 932 EUA. These appropriations were intended to finance special measures and common measures adopted following decisions on agricultural structures taken after examination of the Commission's memorandum to the Council on the reform of agriculture in the EEC. The amount is substantial because the structural reform was slow to be implemented. The consequent immobilization of huge sums of money was a problem which has been raised on several occasions by certain Council delegations and by the European Parliament's Committee on Agriculture.
The reserve is made up as follows:
(a) 59 799 418 EUA reserved in respect of 1969 in accordance with Regulation (EEC) No 2010/68 (25 m u.a. were assigned to the ERDF under Regulation (EEC) No 725/75 in supplementary budget No 1/1975),
(b) 83 562 310 EUA reserved in respect of 1970,
(c) 185 117 684 EUA reserved in respect of 1971,
(d) 92 846 288 EUA reserved in respect of 1972,
(e) 93 211 316 EUA reserved in respect of 1973,
(f) 15 035 130 EUA reserved in respect of 1974,
(g) 1 517 786 EUA reserved in respect of 1975.
However, the mere fact of putting the reserve into the budget was no guarantee that it would actually be used. The appropriations in question were entered in the budget by the budgetary procedure as soon as commitment appropriations for common measures exceeded the annual allocation of 325 m EUA. Thus, the financial requirements for special and common measures led to the entry of 153.5 m EUA in the 1978 budget

and 239.230 m EUA in the 1979 budget, i.e. 392.730 m EUA of the reserve, leaving 138 359 932 EUA not entered in the budget. However, the budget implementation in respect of the EAGGF Guidance Section as at 31 December 1979 shows an unused amount of 202 323 000 EUA, 182 404 000 EUA of which was still available in 1980, the remainder having lapsed.

It was decided in 1978 and 1979 to allocate to other measures an amount of 195.36 m EUA originally reserved for the financing of common and special measures. Accordingly, Regulation (EEC) No 2992/78 of 19 December 1978 earmarked 70 m EUA for the financing of individual projects and supplementary and amending budget No 3/1979 cut the commitment appropriations for the Guidance Section by 105 m EUA and the payment appropriations by 100 m EUA, allocating 100 m EUA to the Guarantee Section. Furthermore, 20.36 m EUA have been transferred from the Guidance Section, including 9 m EUA for emergency assistance to disaster victims in Kampuchea. So far only the ridiculously small amount of 47 000 EUA has been used to finance agricultural reform measures.

On 8 May 1979, when making new provisions on the financing of measures eligible under the EAGGF Guidance Section, the Council decided to discontinue the reserve. On the assumption that the reserve will have been used up in 1980 and that progress will have been made with the structures policy, Regulation (EEC) No 929/79 of 8 May 1979 (OJ L 17 of 12.5.1979) provides for an amount of 3 600 m EUA (including the 1979 appropriation still available for 1980) for the period 1980-84 (the annual appropriations to be determined in the course of the budgetary procedure). Paragraph 1 of Article 6(b) of that Regulation abolishes the reserve by providing that if appropriations are not entered in the budget before 1 January 1980 they can no longer be entered in it. The inevitable conclusion, therefore, is that all the misgivings and criticisms voiced when the reserve was set up were justified and that the fact that it has not been used and has now been discontinued merely underlines the failure of certain Community efforts to reform agricultural structures.

[13] Council Regulation (EEC) No 129/78 of 24 January 1978 provides for different arrangements for the exchange rates to be applied for the purposes of the common agricultural structures policy (guidance) and for guarantee purposes. Since the amounts expressed in units of account in the instruments relating to the agricultural sector (the green rates) are converted at the representative rates obtaining when the operative event giving rise to a claim occurs and as the main purpose of adjusting these representative rates is to preserve the unity of markets and reduce compensatory amounts, it was felt that the dates of entry into force of the new rates scarcely suited the requirements of the structures policy, particularly where repeated adjustments were made during a single calendar year and that the system should be changed. As a result, the Regulation stipulates that the rates to be applied to guidance expenditure shall be those obtaining on 1 January of the year during which the instalment of aid becomes payable.

[14] Article 6(5) of the Financial Regulation of 1973 provided a special arrangement for the Guidance Section whereby committed appropriations could be carried forward automatically for a period of five years as an exception to the general rule. This measure was decided upon in order to avoid administrative complications, since the actual completion of projects to improve structures generally takes many years. After each particular five-year period, approval for carry-overs could still be obtained from the Council on a yearly basis. This arrangement still applies to appropriations committed before 1977.

[15] The legislation of 18 March 1975 on the Regional Fund consists of:
(a) Council Regulation (EEC) No 724/75;
(b) a Regulation on the transfer to the ERDF of 150 m u.a. from the appropriations held in reserve for the EAGGF Guidance Section;
(c) Decision 75/185/EEC setting up a Regional Policy Committee (see p. 374).
All this legislation appeared in OJ L 73 of 21.3.1975. It was adopted after a nebulous and unproductive conciliation meeting with the European Parliament (see Annex 5, p. 363).

[16] On this occasion, the Commission withdrew its proposal of 2 June 1972 on development in the priority farming areas, for which it was intended that 250 m u.a. would be granted for five years under the EAGGF Guidance Section by virtue of a Council Decision. The appropriations in the budget from 1972 to 1974 (125 m u.a.), which went into the Mansholt Reserve, were included in a supplementary budget in 1975 and are part of the 1 300 m u.a. allocated to the Regional Fund. This switch of appropriations was justified by the fact that the Regional Fund was to aid these very same areas (less-favoured farming areas).

[17] Regional Fund assistance may be entirely or partly in the form of a three point interest subsidy on EIB loans granted under subparagraphs (a) and (b) of Article 130 of the EEC Treaty. However, none of the Member States has yet used this facility in the three years it has been available.

[18] The main legislation of 6 February 1979 on the Regional Fund consists of:
(a) Council Regulation (EEC) No 214/79 amending Regulation (EEC) No 724/75 establishing the ERDF;
(b) Council Decision 79/137/EEC amending Decision 75/185/EEC setting up a Regional Policy Committee.
This legislation was adopted after lengthy consultation with Parliament which was not very productive (see Annex 5, p. 323). It appeared in OJ L 35 of 9.2.1979.

This legislation was adopted after lengthy consultation with Parliament which was not very productive (see Annex 5, p. 364). It appeared in OJ L 35 of 9.2.1979.

(a) On a request from the German Delegation, the Council and the Commission made a statement agreeing that in future 'the zones and regions for each measure will be defined on the basis of comparable indicators and that standard thresholds will be applied'.

(b) On the subject of the financial allocation, the Council's statement stresses that 'this is an initial set of projects undertaken on an experimental basis directly linked to certain Community policies and that this agreement is without prejudice to the contribution which the ERDF might take eventually towards resolving the problems of convergence of economies and certain problems concerning industrial conversion'. The United Kingdom's statement emphasizes 'an important function of the quota-free section is the promotion of convergence within the Community'. The UK Delegation therefore 'regrets that the proposals for the first tranche emphasize the imbalance in favour of agriculture in the Community budget, and in particular that it takes less account of the needs of the less-prosperous Member States than does the quota section'. The Belgian declaration states that 'Belgium has drawn up a substantial programme of conversion measures in the steel-producing regions' and that 'it is preparing to do the same in the textile-producing regions'.

The decision also adds fresh fuel to the arguments about the budget implementation powers of the Commission.

[19] In its proposal for a Regulation of 3 June 1977, the Commission proposed that from 1978 the amount allocated to the ERDF should be fixed each year via the budget, in other words in the course of the budgetary procedure. For 1978, it proposed commitment appropriations of 750 m EUA. The allocation ultimately decided upon by the Council (1 850 m EUA) is not mentioned in the Regulation of 6 February 1979, however—unlike what happened for the initial period—but only in the minutes of the Council meeting of 6 February 1979.

[20] This story is worth telling. On 7 December 1977, a 'Budget' Council meeting entered 580 m EUA in commitment appropriations and 460 m EUA in payment appropriations in the revised draft budget. Finally, after arguments between the hard-liners and the moderates, an amendment restoring the allocation of the ERDF to the level proposed by the Commission (750 m EUA in commitment appropriations) did not obtain the required parliamentary majority of 100 votes (there were 82 votes in favour, i.e. the socialists, communists, and a few from other groups—28 votes against and 12 abstentions). However, Parliament was united in its anger at the European Council. First, it voted by 126 votes to 10 (the communists) with no abstentions, in favour of an amendment making a symbolic increase of 1 m EUA in commitment appropriations (to 581 m EUA) and, somewhat irrationally, an increase of 65 m EUA in payment appropriations (to 525 m EUA, in other words, the amount the Fund would have had if it had been allocated 750 m EUA in commitment appropriations). Then, with all the groups, except the communists, in favour it passed a Resolution castigating the Council in the following terms: 'Parliament considers that the fixing by the European Council of the appropriations allocated to the Regional Fund is a deliberate challenge to the right of Parliament in an area of expenditure which has finally been recognized by all the institutions as being non-compulsory expenditure on which Parliament therefore has the last word'.

[21] The change in percentages is due to the fact that France's share has been increased by 2% for the French Overseas Departments (Guadeloupe, Guiana, Martinique and Reunion).

[22] Article 2 of the Regulation of 18 March 1975 also allocated an additional 6 m u.a. to Ireland. This clause was deleted after 1978.

[23] Regulation (EEC) No 724/75 of 18 March 1975 amended the Financial Regulation of 25 April 1973 applicable to the general budget and authorized the allocation of commitment and payment appropriations for the ERDF. Moreover, as an exception to the general rule, the commitment appropriations could be carried over for one year; this became the rule when the Regulation of 21 December 1977 came into force.

[24] See OJ C 112 of 20.12.1973.

[25] According to the general rule, payments against expenditure commitments must be made in the year of commitment or the following year (to which the appropriations can be carried over automatically). This being the case, the EAGGF Guidance Section has made payments totalling only 1 314 m u.a. (which is the figure given in the table in Annex 12, p. 396, compared with the total of 54 740 m u.a. for the whole of the agricultural policy). In fact, because of the special arrangement for the EAGGF Guidance Section (see p. 217), appropriations may be carried over for a number of years (thus in 1979 there were appropriations which had been carried over since 1967) and payments made against them (724 m u.a.).

[26] As the book is arranged, it would have been more logical to examine expenditure on agricultural research, for example, in the next chapter, but I did not wish to stray too far from the official nomenclature.

[27] The aid granted to Friuli was in the form of subsidies of 60 m u.a. not unlike those from the EAGGF Guidance Section (Council Regulation (EEC) No 1505/76 of 21 June 1976) and the Regional Fund (Council

Regulation (EEC) No 1506/76 of 21 June 1976). The ECSC has also granted loans for rebuilding workers' housing (6 m u.a.) and for rebuilding steel mills (5 m u.a.). Lastly, the EEC has granted 0.5 m u.a. from its fund for aiding disaster victims in the Community.

[28] The aid granted to Martinique and Guadeloupe was in the form of a subsidy of 12 m u.a. not unlike those from the EAGGF Guidance Section. This grant was in addition to a sum of 1 m u.a. paid from the disaster aid appropriations.

[29] To the Commission's way of thinking the proposals of March 1979 on agricultural structures (see p. 214) and its proposal for a second NCI tranche (see p. 145) come under the heading of 'policies whose need is not questioned'.

[30] The Council's conclusions of 30 May 1980 state: 'For 1982, the Community is pledged to resolve the problem by means of structural changes (Commission mandate, to be fulfilled by the end of June 1981: the examination will concern the development of Community policies, without calling into question the common financial responsibility for these policies which are financed from the Community's own resources, or the basic principles of the common agricultural policy. Taking account of the situations and interests of all Member States, this examination will aim to prevent the recurrence of unacceptable situations for any of them).' (See OJ C 158 of 27.6.1980.)

Chapter XIII:
Financing intervention in the sphere of energy, industry and research and development

Europe's strong points are now becoming its weaknesses. Following in the wake of the coal industry, textiles, shipbuilding and steel have ceased to be assets and turned into liabilities.

Since their inception, the European Communities have gradually laid the foundations for a Community policy in the sphere of research, technology, energy and industry, based on provisions contained in the three Treaties but also on genuine new policy initiatives under Articles 235, 203 and 95 of the EEC, Euratom and ECSC Treaties respectively. The storm which has been brewing since 1974 has often demanded solutions at Community level and this has given Community Europe a real boost in these fields, although there have not been any really impressive practical achievements as far as Europe's finances are concerned.

European Community action in these areas involving financial intervention is described in five sections. The first covers energy policy, the second various branches of industry, the third research and development policy, the fourth information and scientific and technical documentation and the fifth the financial resources deployed in these fields.

1. European Community energy policy

An energy policy—although this term is something of an overstatement—was arrived at gradually. The coordinated efforts of the three Communities have produced a reasonably coherent whole, but there are still significant gaps. However, thanks to the efforts of the Commission and encouragement from the European Parliament, and in spite of the hesitations of the Council, a certain willingness to work towards a European energy policy is now emerging in the Community.

A—Financial foundations of Community energy policy

Looking at the Treaties, the first European Community, the ECSC, was a manifestation of the desire of six countries to act together in the coal and steel sectors, in particular the

Community coal industry. Euratom represented a similar attempt at joint action at the technological level in the nuclear field. The third Community, the EEC, had no particular designs in the energy field any more than it had in the industrial field, come to that, but nevertheless found itself increasingly obliged to define certain Community approaches.

Objectives of the ECSC's energy policy

Obviously no discussion of energy policy would be complete without a mention of ECSC policy. However, as this policy has already been covered in the chapter on the Community's internal development policy, there is no need to go over the same ground again (see p. 223). Suffice it to say that when the ECSC Treaty was being negotiated, and when it came into force, coal was king. Several years later a crisis hit the coal industry, forcing the ECSC to change its policy. Even today, coal is still the main source of energy in the Community and provides 20% of the Community's total energy supplies.

The medium-term guidelines for coal 1975-85 published by the Commission in 1975 include a target for Community coal production of 250 m tce in 1985. In 1979, output totalled 238 m tce. The Community now realizes that it has become difficult to maintain coal production and that we are heading towards a coal shortage.

Sales aid for coking coal—After helping to close down the least viable mines, the ECSC has endeavoured, since 1967, to support the production of coking coal and coke in the interests of security of supply. These measures come within the scope of this chapter.

Two types of coal are of major importance for the Community's energy balance: coking coal for making steel (67.5 million tonnes in 1977) and steam coal for generating electricity (120.8 million tonnes in 1977 or 40% of the fuel used in conventional power stations). ECSC intervention was not originally financial, but this changed in 1970: Decision No 70/1/ECSC of 19 December 1969 (under Article 95 of the ECSC Treaty) instituted the first ever marketing aid to subsidize intra-Community deliveries to areas remote from the point of production. Intra-Community trade totalling 17 million tonnes was subsidized each year at a cost of 7.65 m u.a. to the ECSC and 20.40 m u.a. to the Member States, spread over three years.

In 1973, Decision No 73/287/ECSC of 25 July 1973 amended by Decision No 1613/77/ECSC of 15 July 1977 set up a new system of Community aid for the sale of coking coal to run from 1973 to 1981. This new Community aid applies to a maximum of 15 million tonnes of coking coal a year. Between 1973 and 1979 the maximum amount payable was limited to 216.628 m u.a. The timetable is as shown in the following table.

(in m u.a. and m EUA)

Year	ECSC	Member States	Steel industry	Total
1973	4.00	9.400	16.60	30.000
1974	5.00	8.400	16.60	30.000
1975	6.00	7.400	16.60	30.000
1976	6.33	7.807	17.52	31.657
1977	6.33	7.807	17.52	31.657
1978	6.33	7.807	17.52	31.657
1979	6.33	7.807	17.52	31.657
Total	40.32	56.428	119.88	216.628

Decision No 3058/79/ECSC of 18 December 1979 amending Decisions Nos 73/287/ECSC and 1613/77/ECSC settled the financing of Community aid for 1980 and 1981 as follows: 6 m u.a. to be paid by the ECSC, 24 m u.a. by the Member States and 17 m u.a. by the steel industry each year. Between 1970 and 1981 a total of 338.678 m u.a. is to be paid in aid for the sale of coking coal, 59.97 m u.a. by the ECSC, 124.828 m u.a. by the Member States and 153.88 m u.a. by the steel industry.

Aid for investment in the coal industry—As already mentioned (see p. 224), the Commission decided, on 10 October 1979, to assist certain types of mining investment by granting interest subsidies to allow the creation of modern production capacity and to help stabilize Community coal production.

Objectives of Euratom's energy policy

Like the ECSC, Euratom is concerned with a specific sector—atomic energy in Euratom's case—but the resources originally placed at its disposal were more ambitious. The Euratom Treaty was drafted with a view to achieving cooperation and integration which would enable the Europe of the Six to rapidly acquire a nuclear energy capacity for peaceful purposes. That is why the Community was richly endowed with resources for coordinating and integrating the efforts of the six Member States. However, for a number of different reasons, these resources have not always been deployed. The Euratom Treaty, like the ECSC Treaty, for that matter, provides, in Article 40, that the Commission shall publish illustrative programmes indicating in particular nuclear energy production targets and all the types of investment required for their attainment. In fact, the Commission has drawn up only two such programmes, the first in 1966 and the second in 1972. Again, Article 5, which provides for the coordination of national research, has scarcely been applied. This constitutes a basic setback as far as this Community is concerned. In fact, the most successful of Euratom's ventures has been research and development, on which subject I shall have more to say further on.

Uranium prospecting—Since 1976, at the Commission's request, the budget has contained appropriations for uranium prospecting allocated by Parliament in accordance with its right to have the final word on non-compulsory expenditure. Although the sums involved are fairly small, they have made it possible to promote uranium prospecting programmes aimed at reducing the Community's dependence on outside suppliers under Article 70 of the Euratom Treaty. Annual Community requirements at the end of the next decade can be estimated at some 40 000 tonnes so it would seem a reasonable aim to provide a quarter of this from Community production. Such a scheme would cost 100 m EUA.

Nuclear industry loans policy—Since 29 March 1977, the Commission may borrow and on-lend to help finance nuclear power stations. The Council took the view that 'the use of nuclear energy can reduce the Community's excessive dependence on external sources of energy and thus improve the terms on which energy is imported'. Since, in the present technological and economic climate, the use of nuclear energy to generate electricity is economically viable and more advantageous than the use of petroleum products, it was thought that the Community could provide substantial aid to increase the financing potential of the nine Member States. The Commission is to borrow no more than the amounts of the loans for which it has received applications, and loans should not normally exceed 20% of the investment cost (see p. 143).

The Supply Agency—Mention should also be made of the Supply Agency, set up under Article 52 of the Euratom Treaty, which provides that the supply of ores, source materials, and special fissile materials must be 'ensured by means of a common supply policy on the principle of equal access to sources of supply'. The Supply Agency, which has capital resources subscribed by the Member States, has legal personality and financial autonomy under the supervision of the Commission, which issues directives to it and has a right of veto over its decisions. In fact there has never been a common policy on uranium supply, and the Agency has had to content itself with importing ores and fissile materials, chiefly enriched uranium from the United States, on behalf of the Member States.

The Supply Agency's expenses are met from a subsidy paid by the Commission to balance its general revenue and expenditure account.

Safeguards—Chapter VII of the Euratom Treaty deals with safeguards. Under the provisions of Article 77, the Commission must satisfy itself that, in the territories of Member States, ores, source materials, and special fissile materials are not diverted from their intended uses as declared by the users, and that the provisions relating to supply and any particular safeguarding obligations assumed by the Community under an agreement concluded with a third State or an international organization are complied with. Under Article 81 of the Euratom Treaty, the Commission may send inspectors from time to time or sometimes even on a permanent basis to examine the 350 nuclear installations situated on the territory of the Community: production or reprocessing plants and small units belonging to research centres or universities (35% of these are in France, 25% in the United Kingdom, 25% in the Federal Republic of Germany and 15% in the rest of the Community).

On 5 April 1973, an Agreement was signed between the International Atomic Energy Agency (IAEA) in Vienna, the Commission of the European Communities and those Community countries which do not have military installations—that is, all Member States except France[1] and the United Kingdom[2]—providing for the safeguards service of the Commission of the European Communities to carry out the inspection duties for which the International Atomic Energy Agency is responsible. It is worth observing that this means that almost all the inspection work of the International Atomic Energy Agency is done by the Commission of the European Communities, since outside Community territory only 35 major nuclear installations fall within the jurisdiction of the Agency.

This safeguarding activity is particularly noteworthy because it gives the Commission direct power as a public authority over all nuclear installations except those with military objectives.

Objectives of EEC energy policy

The EEC Treaty, while providing for the implementation of common policies, is silent on the subject of energy. The only relevant instrument it has created is the European Investment Bank, which does in fact have an important part to play in this field.

However, the Community is dependent on imports for 56% of its supplies, so when these supplies began to become a highly sensitive political issue it had to work out a policy[3]— which it did. The most recent definition of this was given at the European Council meetings of 12 and 13 March 1979 and 21 and 22 June 1979 (see Annex 3, pp. 355 and 356).

On 14 June 1979, the Commission proposed to the Council energy objectives which it later confirmed on 4 October 1979 in its energy programme. The objectives adopted a year later, on 9 June 1980, are as follows for 1990:
(a) the gradual reduction to below 0.7 of the ratio between the growth of energy consumption and economic growth;

(b) to limit the Community's dependence on energy imports to 50%, and, particularly, net oil imports to 472 million tonnes (the level reached in 1978).

In order to do this—and this is not straying from the subject of Community public finances—the Commission emphasizes the need for convergence in Member States' and Community policy in the following areas:

(a) stepping up energy saving measures;

(b) increasing the use of solid fuels and nuclear energy, so that together they can generate at least 70 to 75% of our electricity, by trying to achieve the coal production figures of 1973 (175 million tonnes oil equivalent—m toe) under satisfactory economic conditions, by considerably increasing imports of coal from non-member countries compared with 1978, by creating additional solid fuel capacity in electric power stations and certain industries and by relaunching nuclear programmes where this is possible under perfectly safe conditions;

(c) adapting refinery capacity to changes in the structure of the world oil market;

(d) increasing the production of oil and gas towards the upper end of the range of present forecasts (oil 147 m toe, natural gas 130 m toe) and encouraging exploration to this end;

(e) promoting research into and the use of new energy sources.

Under the EEC Treaty and in particular its all-purpose Article 235, the Commission of the European Communities has planned a vast edifice in the last five years, but only a few parts of it have so far been erected.

Measures in the hydrocarbons sector—The first operation was launched via Council Regulation (EEC) No 3056/73 of 9 November 1973 on the support of Community projects in the hydrocarbons sector. The object is to promote technological development of direct relevance to prospecting for, extracting, storing, or transporting hydrocarbons in cases where the work seems likely to improve the security of the Community's energy supplies. The Commission considers that the most suitable instrument will as a rule be a grant, refundable in the event of commercial success, because the bulk of these projects necessarily entail such technical risks and financial burdens that in the absence of external support they could not be undertaken—at present.

On 29 November 1974, the Commission made another proposal envisaging financial assistance not for technological research but for exploration work (north of the 60th parallel and in deep water) which could help reduce the Community's dependence on external supplies of oil. Here again and for the same reasons, the Commission proposed that aid should be granted in the form of a subsidy repayable if results prove successful, with the Community bearing up to 75% of the costs of geophysical work and 50% of the cost of hiring an offshore drilling ship. The amount of appropriations envisaged should permit an average of two test borings a year. The costs involved vary between 5 and 15 m EUA per boring according to its position, the depth of the water and the depth of the boring. The Commission's proposal has not yet been accepted by the Council although on 8 May 1979 it did agree to support a joint hydrocarbon exploration project in Greenland. However, Parliament has been entering appropriations against a specific heading for these activities since the 1977 budget.

Measures in the coal sector—The Commission has proposed several aid measures to improve the position of the coal industry based on the energy policy guidelines given by the European Council at its meeting in Rome on 1 and 2 December 1975 (see Annex 3, p. 352) and in order to overcome the recent difficulties facing the coal industry as a consequence of the steel crisis.

251

On 31 December 1976, the Commission submitted a proposal to the Council aimed at encouraging the use of coal instead of liquid fuels in power stations by granting non-repayable financial subsidies to offset a proportion of the additional costs incurred by operations when building, modifying or modernizing power plant for the purpose of burning coal. Between 25 and 40 million tonnes of oil could be saved each year in this way.

On 18 March 1977, the Commission proposed a system of Community financial aid for the stockpiling of 20 million tonnes of coal. The aim of this is to maintain the coal production levels agreed upon by the Community and thus to prevent cyclic fluctuations from adversely affecting coal undertakings. In order to do this, it wants the Community to shoulder some of the vast amount of expenditure involved in stockpiling as a result of the slump on the coal market.

On 28 September 1978, the Commission sent the Council a proposal for a Community aid system for intra-Community trade in power-station coal whereby an annual amount of 100 m EUA in Community aid would be granted for a period of three years for intra-Community trade in steam coal. This scheme is designed to increase trade from around 3 million to 10 million tonnes a year.

Since, in spite of its efforts, these three proposals have still not been approved by the Council, the Commission was intending, in mid-1980, to make alternative proposals.

Demonstration projects relating to energy saving and new sources of energy—On 12 June 1978, on a proposal from the Commission dated 31 May 1977, the Council adopted two programmes involving aid for demonstration projects. The first programme covers the financing of demonstration projects relating to methods, processes, materials or new products whose use would help save energy. The second provides for financial contributions from the Community for the carrying out of demonstration projects or pilot plants using new methods or technologies to harness alternative sources of energy. An unproductive attempt at conciliation was made when adopting these two Regulations (see Annex 5, p. 365).

It had been agreed that implementing regulations would be enacted and these were adopted on 9 April 1979. An amount of 55 m EUA has been allocated for demonstration projects (the programme runs for four years) and 95 m EUA as financial support for projects to exploit alternative energy sources (a five-year programme). Three kinds of new energy source were specified: geothermal energy, liquefaction and gasification of solid fuels and solar energy.

The proportions contributed by the Community may, and in fact do, range from 29 to 45% for energy-saving projects. They must be less than 50% for alternative energy projects. In practice the Community contributes between 30 and 40%.

Reduction in refining capacity—A new heading (Item 3751), with a token entry, was included in the 1979 budget in order to make it possible to grant direct subsidies or interest subsidies to speed up reductions in refining capacity (60 million tonnes of capacity have to be eliminated). The legal basis would be the same as for industrial restructuring and conversion (see p. 228).

EIB activities in the energy sector

The European Investment Bank's financial operations fit into the Community's policy (which was restated at the European Council meetings of 1979) of seeking to reduce the Community's dependence on imported energy, to reduce its net oil imports, to work at energy saving and to make better use of its indigenous resources. From 1967, and especially from 1973 onwards, it has granted aid for:

(i) the exploitation of the Community's primary energy resources: hydroelectric power plants and pumped storage stations, coal-fired power stations, exploitation of oil and gas fields, particularly in the North Sea, geothermal plants, uranium deposits;

(ii) diversifying and securing Community energy supplies: light-water and breeder reactors, uranium enrichment plants, gas pipelines linking the Community with external sources of natural gas and the establishment of a trans-European gas pipeline network, and gas storage facilities;

(iii) energy saving.

With the specific approval of the Council and the Governors of the Bank, some financing operations have involved projects located outside the territory of Member States because of their considerable benefits in terms of the Community's energy supplies. Examples are the exploitation of the Ekofisk field in the Norwegian sector of the North Sea and the pipeline bringing gas from the Soviet Union through Austria.

Lastly, in 1977, 1978 and 1979 the Bank, acting as an agent for Euratom, signed loan contracts for nuclear plants jointly with the European Commission after scrutinizing all the applications.

B—Budgetary and legal framework of energy policy

At this point it is worth having another look at the above policies to see the differences resulting from the application of the three Treaties.

Budgetary and legal framework provided by the general budget as regards energy policy

The only appropriations in the 1979 and 1980 budgets are for hydrocarbons (technological development and exploration), uranium (prospecting), energy saving, new sources of energy and studies. There is no need to dwell on these. There are also appropriations for safeguards[4] and the Supply Agency.[5] We will however, follow the usual pattern, keeping it as short as possible.

The budget for energy policy—Although the idea of an Energy Fund is raised from time to time, there have been no serious proposals on the subject, which is not a bad thing because the time is not yet ripe to abandon the rule of non-assignment of revenue.

Estimating the appropriations for energy policy—These appropriations are estimated as carefully as possible, but the estimate is converted into an allocation, which is always much smaller, to make it more politically acceptable.

Establishing the appropriations for energy policy—These appropriations are regarded as being for non-compulsory expenditure so Parliament has the final say. It is fair to say that if this had not been the case, there would be hardly any energy appropriations in the budget. Year after year, Parliament tries to initiate (e.g. prospecting for uranium and hydrocarbons, encouraging the use of coal in power stations) or develop (technological development of hydrocarbons) measures by using its margin for manoeuvre. This has given rise to disagreement between the institutions, with the Parliament and the Commission somewhat resenting the way the Council always manages to evade the issue.

Structure of appropriations for energy policy—These appropriations are all in Chapter 32 of Title 3, guarantees for Euratom loans are also covered in that Chapter.

Implementation of appropriations for energy policy—The Commission is responsible for implementing these measures. It has extensive powers vested in it by Article 70 of the Euratom Treaty as regards uranium prospecting. This is not the case with hydrocarbons where it can only act with the full agreement of the Council, which in practice means that it is the Council which authorizes the appropriation, while the Commission can merely examine the projects submitted to it, make its own choice and put forward technical and financial arguments. This therefore infringes Article 205 of the EEC Treaty, which specifies the powers of the Commission. Its powers in respect of demonstration projects relating to energy saving and alternative energy sources may also be blocked by the Council.[6]

The management of these appropriations, which had been very difficult because the projects concerned cover several years, was made much easier by the allocation of differentiated appropriations. There are two peculiarities about the management of these appropriations: they are the subject of public invitations to submit applications published in the *Official Journal of the European Communities*; also, if a project subsidized by the Commission proves successful, the aid has to be repaid, as now happens in the case of technological development in the hydrocarbons sector. The Commission's administering department is the Directorate-General for Energy.

Commitment appropriations (10 m EUA) made available by Parliament in the 1978 budget have been cancelled because there was no legal basis for implementation, which is another example of inconsistency as far as Community matters are concerned.

Checks concerning the implementation of appropriations for energy policy—The only area involved is that of hydrocarbons: Article 8 of Council Regulation (EEC) No 3056/73 states that 'those responsible for implementing a project in receipt of Community support shall each year submit to the Commission, which shall inform the Council thereof, a report on the progress of work on the scheme and on the expenditure involved in its implementation. The Commission shall at all times have access to the accounts of the project'. The Member States are not therefore directly involved in inspection procedures as they are with the various Funds.

Apart from checking supporting documents, there are also on-the-spot checks carried out jointly by the Directorates-General for Energy and Financial Control. These checks may be made at the beginning of the contract, while it is being carried out or once the contract has been completed. The most difficult thing to check is whether a project can yield sufficient commercial benefits to warrant repayment of the aid granted. There are currently 180 projects in progress.

Financial and legal framework provided by the ECSC and the EIB

The same remarks apply here as were made in the previous chapter (see p. 227).

Two Commission departments manage these areas: the Directorate-General for Energy is responsible for budget appropriations and the Directorate-General for Credit and Investments for loans.

2. European Community action relating to various branches of industry

This section is much shorter than that on energy policy, as Community industrial policy has not yet been fully worked out and, as far as the finances of Europe are concerned, is still in its infancy. In fact, it is more a case of action in specific sectors than of a coherent policy. We have already covered industrial restructuring and conversion in the previous chapter.

A—Financial foundations of action relating to various branches of industry

Two of the Communities have tried to set up an industrial policy. Whereas the ECSC was successful, the EEC has been only moderately so.

Objectives of ECSC industrial policy

In this field the emphasis has been on specific technical objectives (for example, the introduction of the oxygen process for steelmaking, which now accounts for 70% of the Community's output as against only 10% in 1960) or specific economic objectives (for example, siting of steelworks on the coasts). The Commission has drawn up general objectives for the period 1980-85. These pay particular attention to the problem of energy supply and finance.

The steel crisis prompted the Commission to amend these objectives. Its initial findings show that crude steel production capacity in 1978 exceeded the capacity required to meet demand in 1983 by more than 25 million tonnes. The aim must therefore be to restructure, in other words, to maintain a modernized production capacity based on tools and products which are economic, and therefore competitive. The Commission is using all the scope for financial intervention provided by Article 54 of the ECSC Treaty—loans and interest subsidies—to encourage investment to bring about this restructuring.

One of the main aims of the restructuring programme, which has already been alluded to, is to make the Community steel industry more competitive in order to consolidate its position on domestic markets and its position as a major steel exporter. Action must be taken therefore in respect of foreign competition on Community markets in all steel products and, as far as exports are concerned, we must concentrate on all types and qualities of specialized and finished products. In order to do this, ECSC steel research must continue to figure prominently in achieving these objectives, which are important for all in the Community (see p. 260).

Objectives of the EEC

As already noted, the EEC Treaty does not specifically provide for an industrial policy. At the Summit meeting at The Hague on 2 December 1969 the Heads of State or Government reaffirmed their readiness 'to coordinate and promote industrial research and development in the principal pacemaking sectors, in particular by means of common programmes, and to supply the financial means for these purposes' (see Annex 3, p. 350).

Since that time, a number of plans have been formulated, on the basis of the Council's Resolution of 15 July 1974 on data processing and the Council's Declaration of 14 March 1977, which—in the light of the proposal for an action programme for the European aeronautical sector made by the Commission of 3 October 1975—fixed certain objectives for industrial policy in that sector. In the field of data processing, the Commission has adopted an initial Community-financed programme (Council Decision 76/632/EEC of 22 July 1976) involving such joint projects as the creation of a data bank for blood and organ-matching and a study of requirements for legal information retrieval systems. A second programme was adopted under Council Decision 77/615/EEC of 27 September 1977 which includes joint projects on software portability, high-speed data transmission techniques and a group of studies on support for the use of data processing.

On 9 November 1976, the Commission proposed a third four-year programme based, like its two predecessors, on Article 235 of the EEC Treaty. The programme (which runs from 1979 to 1983) was adopted by the Council on 11 September 1979 and aims to develop the data-processing industry in the Community and make it more competitive. The programme is in two parts:

(i) general measures, which have been allocated 10 m EUA for four years and include standardization, public contracts, research cooperation and general studies; and

(ii) financial support measures to promote data processing applications within the Community, which have been allocated 15 m EUA for between two and four years.

On 17 July 1980, the Commission proposed Community measures in the field of microelectronics in order to provide the Community with a modern microelectronics capacity by 1985. It does not propose to finance this from the budget except where at least three Member States are working together on the same project, in which case 50% of the expenditure incurred by those Member States could be reimbursed.

The projects put forward by the Commission concerning the aircraft industry are particularly ambitious. The first, dating back to 3 October 1975, is an action programme for the European aeronautical sector.[7]

The Commission advocates the establishment of a joint programme to develop, build and market large civil transport aircraft and establish a Community programme for basic research. It calls for Community financing to replace national aids, both for research and development and production tooling. Finally, it proposes Community financial support for marketing. On this basis, and in accordance with Article 235 of the EEC Treaty, the Commission submitted to the Council on 2 August 1977 a first series of aeronautical research measures dealing mainly with increasing the life of airframes and improving helicopter performance. The Council has failed to adopt them so far even though Parliament earmarked appropriations for this purpose in the budget back in 1977.

Industry and transport are two sectors which tend to be linked together. In the budget nomenclature, for example, they are both in Chapter 37. I have no desire to go against the trend, so an ambitious plan relating to transport policy is examined here. If it had lived up to expectations it would have been included with the internal development policy described in the previous chapter. This plan dates back to 30 June 1976 and contains proposals for action in the sphere of transport infrastructure. Noting the likelihood that a number of schemes in this field would not be carried through, despite the interest they arouse from a national viewpoint, by a given Member State in isolation, the Commission advocates providing financial assistance if they are also of interest to one or more other Member States. It therefore asks to be given resources to be used to enable schemes of European importance to go ahead. On 5 July 1976 the Commission drew up a draft Regulation on support for projects of Community interest. Later, on 18 February 1980, it proposed that it should be possible for Community assistance to be given to investment projects outside the Community. A token entry has been included since the 1979 budget, but the Regulation has not yet been adopted.

It should also be noted that a Community Business Cooperation Centre was set up on 21 June 1973 with responsibilities for promoting cooperation between firms in the Community by disseminating information and bringing firms into contact. Up to 31 December 1979 this 'marriage bureau' had received 4 374 requests for information and had circulated 696 enquiries for partners, to which 7 101 firms had replied, giving rise to 509 contacts between firms and many actual agreements. The Centre is formally independent, but the Commission staffs it and bears its operating costs.

The objectives of the EIB

Between 1958 and 1978 the EIB granted a large number of loans for the financing of major intra-Community transport infrastructure projects, particularly those involving road and rail links between national networks in the Community. Mention has already been made of these.

B—Budgetary and legal framework for measures concerning various branches of industry

The budgetary and legal framework is rather limited.

Budgetary and legal framework provided by the general budget

Title 3 contains a Chapter 37 for expenditure in the industrial and transport sectors. This is non-compulsory expenditure on which the final word rests with Parliament which has often allocated further funds, using its margin for manoeuvre.

The use made of the appropriations available for data processing has followed the normal pattern, but the appropriations voted for the aeronautical sector in 1977 and 1978 have not given rise to commitments. They are one of the main bones of contention between the European Parliament and the Council of Ministers as regards the budget and whether or not there is an adequate legal basis for the pursuit of new policies.

Financial and legal framework provided by the ECSC and the EIB

The points already made concerning financial operations in the energy sector (see p. 254) also apply to financial operations in the industrial sector. The Directorates-General for the Internal Market and Industrial Affairs, Energy and Credit and Investments are the Commission's administering departments for this sector.

3. The European Community's research and development policy

Since their inception, the three Communities have been involved in research programmes in the coal and steel, nuclear and agricultural sectors, as is allowed under the Treaties. However, it was not until 1974 that the Council adopted its first Resolution on a genuine common policy in the field of science and technology. By definition multidisciplinary, this scientific policy focuses on the Community's sectoral policies and has four general objectives:

 (i) long-term security of supply and measures to conserve resources (raw materials, energy, agriculture);
 (ii) promotion of economic development in the Community to cope with international competition;
 (iii) improvement of living and working conditions in the Community;
 (iv) protection of the environment and nature.

The Member States give priority to the same objectives and adhere to them when drawing up their own domestic programmes. As a result, the common policy not only gives an extra dimension to efforts undertaken by the Community countries but also makes it possible to coordinate national activities under programmes which have priority at Community level.

Action by the Community under the common R & D policy is carried out using the funds made available to the Community and the instruments set up by the Treaties, in particular:

(a) intramural research or direct action conducted by the Joint Research Centre set up by the Euratom Treaty. Most of its activities relate to energy (nuclear and non-nuclear) and the environment;

(b) extramural research on a shared-cost basis, also called indirect action, conducted in the specialized laboratories of national, university or industrial research centres. The Commission administers and coordinates this research work. Such research is also conducted within the following frameworks:

  (i) ECSC Treaty for research into coal, steel and safety in the coal and steel industries;
  (ii) Euratom Treaty for research into controlled thermonuclear fusion, radiation protection and fission nuclear energy (reactor safety, nuclear fuel cycle, radioactive waste, decommissioning of nuclear power stations);
  (iii) EEC Treaty for research currently being conducted into the following fields: agriculture, new energy sources (solar energy and geothermal energy), hydrogen, energy conservation and energy systems analysis, environment, raw materials (primary raw materials, paper and board recycling, uranium), the aircraft industry, data processing, textiles, footwear, the Community Bureau of References, forecasting and assessment in the field of science and technology;

(c) concerted action at national level without financial assistance from the Community, but coordinated and programmed by the Community. Research of this type is currently being carried out into medicine and public health, town planning, foodstuffs, sewage sludge, atmospheric pollutants, and micropollutants in water;

(d) cooperation with ten European countries (COST) with the participation of the Community or the Member States, as the case may be.

The following criteria have proved reliable for selecting Community R & D activities:

 (i) no one Member State can carry out the project because of the large amount of money and staff required (e.g. thermonuclear fusion);

(ii) implementation of programmes or projects at Community level is more efficient and will rationalize activities as small research teams are scattered throughout the Member States (e.g. in the case of some sectors of research into new energy sources, raw materials, medicine, town planning, social research);

(iii) some common needs at Community level require collective action (e.g. action concerning the environment, nuclear safety, reference materials and radiation protection);

(iv) activities in which the Community has an important role to play by coordinating or encouraging (e.g. encouraging the exploitation of new energy sources, conservation of energy and raw materials);

(v) research and technology projects which require action within a transnational framework (e.g. the aircraft industry, data processing).

A—Foundations of the European Community's research and development policy

The ECSC and Euratom have active and successful research and development policies which are a credit to the European Community.

The ECSC's objectives

Article 55 of the ECSC Treaty clearly requires the High Authority to promote technical and economic research relating to the production and increased use of coal and steel and to occupational safety in the coal and steel industries. After consulting the Consultative Committee, the High Authority/Commission may initiate and facilitate this research by inducing joint financing by the companies concerned, or by allotting for that purpose any funds received as gifts or, with the assent of the Council, funds derived from levies. The third method is the one which is used.

Coal research—In 1961, the High Authority published the general outlines of its research policy: i.e. to concentrate effort on projects which, by virtue of their size, their cost, the risks involved, and uncertainty as to whether the results would be commercially exploitable, were unattractive to firms and research institutes. Financial aid from the High Authority, normally in the form of non-repayable grants, was limited to a contribution representing only a part of the total expenditure. The research work had to be compatible with the Community's general objectives and was usually basic research or applied research rather than development work aimed at enabling new production methods to be introduced on an industrial scale. In 1963 the High Authority formulated a policy for technical research. This was followed by a medium-term programme (1970-74, revised in 1972). Recently, a new programme has been drawn up for 1975-80. This sets three objectives for the coal industry and for coal research in particular: to reduce costs, mainly by increasing productivity; to promote product beneficiation and product utilization; and to further improvements in conditions of work, occupational safety, and care of the environment. The coal crisis did not reduce the value of such research and the present energy crisis has made it all the more necessary. Substantial and decisive Community action is required to take advantage of coal, a resource which has long been looked down on in Europe.

The ECSC covers 60% of total costs. It should be noted, however, that Community aid represents no more than some 35 to 40% of total Community research expenditure in this field.

Steel research—The High Authority published an account of its activities in 1963 and 1966, but the first medium-term research programme to be presented was for the period 1967-70. This was followed by a second one for 1971-75. In fact, from 1955 to 1962 research focused almost exclusively on production processes, one of the determining factors being the desire to use raw materials—coal and iron ore—mined in the Community, in order to improve the economics of production. By contrast, from 1962 to 1966, a period in which competition became sharper, emphasis was placed on process automation in blast furnaces, steelworks and rolling mills. In the period 1966 to 1976, research effort was still directed toward the same objectives as before, but with the additional aim of promoting a number of fundamental research projects, particularly in the field of physical metallurgy. A further aim has now been added involving research into the application of computers to the steel industry's administration problems.

As of 1976, as stated in the industry's new general objectives for the period 1980-85, steel research will be directed toward increasing capacity, reducing production costs, and improving quality. From the competitive point of view, emphasis will be placed on security of supply of raw materials on the most favourable possible terms and on measures to rationalize the industry.

The ECSC covers 60% of total costs. It should be noted however, that Community aid represents no more than some 20 to 30% of total Community research expenditure in this field.

Social research—The multiannual research programmes pursued since 1955 have been designed to promote both basic laboratory research, and more especially, applied research in the field of hygiene, medicine, occupational safety, and ergonomics (physiology and psychology of work) with the general aim of preventing and treating occupational diseases and accidents at work. Aid is granted by the High Authority/Commission on the basis of applications from industrial firms or scientific and technical research institutes. It is discretionary in character. Selection of projects is both possible and necessary. Community aid is normally limited to 60% of their direct cost (expenditure on staff, consumable supplies, and equipment).

Euratom's objectives

A distinction should be made from the outset between direct action and indirect action in the Euratom context.

Direct action—Direct action projects are those carried out by the Joint Research Centre (JRC) set up under Article 8 of the Euratom Treaty. They are intramural research projects and more funds and staff are required.

The JRC is a Commission department, consisting, apart from its Directorate-General in Brussels, of four establishments in Ispra (Italy), by far the biggest, Geel (Belgium), Karlsruhe (Federal Republic of Germany), and Petten (Netherlands). Since its foundation it has concentrated on the technological development of reactors (improvement of nuclear materials and fuels and development of heavy-water reactors (the Orgel project)) and on research topics of public interest (nuclear measurements, dissemination of information, data processing). It must be recorded that the Orgel project, Euratom's main venture, was a failure, not because of technological shortcomings but for economic and industrial reasons.

Although a first programme was adopted at the same time as the Euratom Treaty itself, to cover the period 1958-62, followed by a second programme covering the period 1963-67 (extended to 1968), only annual programmes were adopted for the years 1969 to 1972, owing to the impossibility of reaching agreement within the Council. It was not until 5 February 1973 that the Community, by this time enlarged, approved a series of new multiannual programmes of direct and indirect action projects (some of them based not only on the Euratom Treaty, but also on Article 235 of the EEC Treaty). The programme for 1973-76 was followed by the programme for 1977-80.

The JRC is an ideal instrument for the common policy for science and technology because of the size of its staff complement and the fundamental importance of its functions:
 (i) catalyst for projects of Community interest;
 (ii) scientific and technological support for the Member States and the Commission;
(iii) tests in large centralized installations of materials developed in the Member States;
 (iv) Community public service activities; and
 (v) contribution to scientific and technological cooperation between the Community and the developing countries.

Whereas the JRC programme for 1973-76 could be described as a programme of transition and change, the programme for 1977-80 adopted on 18 July 1977[8] already takes full account of the change of direction of Community research. This programme, allocated an overall budget of 346 m EUA (60% for staff costs and 40% for operating expenditure) centres on two main concerns: energy research and environmental research, accounting for 55% and 10% respectively of the JRC's financial resources. Public service activities and support for other JRC activities account for 15% and 20% respectively of these resources. The effort, moreover, is more concentrated than in the previous programme, since the number of research objectives is limited to 10 compared with 22.

This tendency to narrow down the JRC's programme objectives is even more accentuated in the four-year programme for 1980-83 adopted by the Council on 13 March 1980.[9] The sum of 510 m EUA is allocated as follows among the six main programme topics: nuclear safety and the fuel cycle (48%), new energy sources (16%), environmental studies and protection (10%), nuclear measurements (9%), specific support for the Commission's sectoral activities (7%) and operation of major installations (10%).

Of these projects, mention should be made of the operation of the HFR reactor at Petten (accounting for 52.22 m EUA) which is a complementary programme financed equally by two Member States (the Federal Republic of Germany and the Netherlands). This is a breach of the Community's basic principles. It is a case of 'Europe à la carte', a Europe, that is, whose activities are financed by common resources only in so far as all Member States consider the project concerned to be directly beneficial to themselves. If this is not so, contributions are made only by Member States who do find it to their advantage. However, this regrettable state of affairs is no longer quite so common and is in fact now restricted to the case in point.

Indirect action—These projects fit in with the four general objectives of the common policy in the field of science and technology: resources (energy, raw materials, agriculture), industrial development, living and working conditions and the environment.

Energy, the most important sector in terms of the resources allocated for indirect action projects, includes non-nuclear energy as well as research into thermonuclear fusion and fission (reactor safety, plutonium recycling, radioactive waste, decommissioning of nuclear power stations).

The most important energy project, as regards both its ultimate aim and the financial outlay[10] by the Community and the Member States, involves controlled thermonuclear fusion. The ultimate aim of the programme for 1976-80 is to demonstrate the feasibility of obtaining energy at commercial prices from nuclear fusion reactions between light nuclei, and, if this can be done, to construct joint prototypes with a view to industrial and commercial development.

This programme has been pursued without a break since the Euratom Treaty came into force in 1958 and is a forum for long-term cooperation covering all national activities in this sector. It includes:
(a) the general research programme carried out in specialized laboratories in the Member States[11] by means of association between the Commission and the appropriate national bodies and, since 1977, by the JRC, and
(b) since 1978, the programme covering an ambitious experimental project known as JET (Joint European Torus) which is intended to demonstrate the scientific feasibility of controlled fusion using a magnetic confinement.

Activities under the general programme have led to the establishment of an impressive range of experimental facilities and the achievement of scientific and technical advances allowing the Community to keep up with the front runners, the United States and the USSR. The Community's financial contribution to these activities varies from 15% to 80%, and averages 50%.

Activities under the five-year programme for 1976-80 will be continued as part of the new 'rolling' programme for 1979-83 adopted by the Council on 13 March 1980,[12] the main aims of which are:
(a) to complete the construction of JET and put it into operation, and
(b) to obtain sufficient information concerning physics and technology to be able to define the subsequent stages towards obtaining a new source of energy from thermonuclear fusion.

Apart from the JET project, this programme covers the construction and operation of a number of medium-sized facilities and the carrying out of a large-scale technological programme (materials, superconductivity, tritium, remote handling, systems analysis, environmental impact, etc.).

A Joint Undertaking, as defined in Articles 45 to 50 of the Euratom Treaty, was set up for the JET project in 1978. Although use has already been made of these Articles six times in the past for the building of demonstration nuclear reactors, the JET project is the first example of a genuine Joint Undertaking in which the Community is participating directly. Apart from the Community itself, the JET Joint Undertaking, which is based in Culham, UK, where the device will be built and operated, has 11 members representing nuclear research bodies in the Member States and, as a result of the cooperation agreements concluded between the Community and Sweden and Switzerland, the competent bodies of these two countries. This Joint Undertaking operates according to rules specially drawn up and approved by the Council in the JET Statutes. These Statutes and the Financial Regulation drawn up on the basis of them give the JET Joint Undertaking a good deal of managerial flexibility. The drawback is that the Commission does not have overriding control of JET, despite the fact that 80% of the cost is paid from the Community budget. The Member States, however, preferred this approach, which reveals their desire to restrict the Commission's executive powers.[13]

As regards non-nuclear energy, special mention should be made of the four-year energy research programme adopted by the Council on 11 September 1979. It has been allocated 105 m EUA as follows: 46 m EUA for solar energy, 27 m EUA for energy conservation, 18 m EUA for geothermal energy, 8 m EUA for the production and utilization of hydrogen and 6 m EUA for energy systems analysis.

B—Budgetary and legal framework for research and investment appropriations

As there is nothing of note to be said about the ECSC operational budget, we shall focus our attention on the research and investment appropriations in the general budget which do have some noteworthy features.

The research budget

The research and investment appropriations have been part and parcel of the general budget since 1971. They have thus lost their independence and a good deal of their individuality. However, they deserve to be examined separately because of what remains of their special nature.

Estimating research and investment appropriations

The budget issued from the research programmes proposed by the Commission which consults the Scientific and Technical Committee set up under Article 134 of the Euratom Treaty (see Annex 7, p. 373) on the programmes based on Article 7 of the Euratom Treaty and the General Advisory Committee of the JRC, set up under Article 4 of the Commission Decision of 13 January 1971 on the reorganization of the JRC, for the JRC's programmes (see Annex 7, p. 374). The Commission also has to consult a number of other committees, in particular the Scientific and Technical Research Committee (CREST) set up by the Council Resolution of 14 January 1974 (see Annex 7, p. 374) mainly to coordinate national and Community policies and define and implement projects of Community interest. The Commission asks for the European Parliament's opinion on Euratom research and training programmes even though the procedure laid down in Article 7 of the Euratom Treaty does not actually stipulate that it has to. The European Parliament must, however, be consulted on proposals for research programmes based on Article 235 of the EEC Treaty as regards non-nuclear projects. The programmes finally adopted by the Council specify the funds required for their implementation and their budget specifies the amounts and staff actually authorized each year. As a result, the budget estimates are inevitably no more than an annual remoulding; this has prompted the argument, as yet unresolved, about the illustrative character of the programmes and the question of ceilings.

Establishing the research and investment appropriations

These appropriations have been regarded from the outset as non-compulsory expenditure on which the European Parliament has the final word, even though this is not self-evident as they derive from programmes laid down by the Council. This ambiguity has not sparked off any major arguments. However, it did necessitate an interpretation of Article 203 of the EEC Treaty in 1976 and 1977 (see p. 45). However, if the situation is analysed in detail, it will be found that the Council actually has the final say as more often than not the Commission cannot act without a programme.

The structure of the research and investment appropriations

Under Title VII of the Financial Regulation, as amended on 25 June 1979, research and investment appropriations are classified in Chapter 33 of the budget according to the purpose of the expenditure arising from the programme decisions. Each item basically corresponds to a research objective, possibly consisting of several projects grouping together under one budget heading all the funds needed to carry out this objective, i.e. appropriations for staff expenditure,[14] administrative and technical operating expenditure, expenditure on investment and contracts, etc.

A table of equivalence attached to the budget breaks down the appropriations for Chapter 33 by project, i.e. according to the purpose of the expenditure, and by type of expenditure using the old subheadings of Chapter 33 from the 1978 budget. This table thus summarizes for the Budgetary Authority the breakdown of appropriations for each project contained in a particular programme and makes it easier to compare the amounts budgeted for with actual expenditure at the end of the financial year.

This annex to the budget also contains a rough timetable for each research project recording the overall financial allocation, the tranches of appropriations made available and the expected rate of utilization of commitment and payment appropriations over the life of the programme. These timetables, first drawn up to assess the financial ceilings for the programmes, are adjusted every year as the research work in question progresses.

Finally, to administer the research and investment appropriations, the Financial Regulation calls for extra-budgetary financial plans for the JRC and indirect action. Part I of these financial plans contains the appropriations for implementing the various programme projects as they feature in the items of Chapter 33, first of all itemizing them into subheadings and then, in greater detail, into categories of expenditure, each of these categories corresponding roughly to the chapters of Titles 1 and 2 of the general budget. Part II of the financial plans consists of appropriation accounts recording the appropriations for the means of attaining the research objectives, e.g. in the JRC's case the scientific divisions, general services and scientific and technical support services. Part III of the financial plans contains the expenditure on the staff assigned to the objectives in Part I or to the appropriation accounts in Part II.

The research budget now consists of no more than a few pages which are easier to follow and therefore easier to audit.[15]

Implementing the research and investment appropriations

Responsibility for implementation falls to the Commission, and in particular to the Directorate-General for the JRC. It was decided on 13 January 1971 that independent powers should be given to the Director-General concerned. He is empowered to take decisions on the Commission's behalf in implementing the research programme, implementing the JRC budget, and appointing most of the established and other staff employed on direct-action projects. Indirect-action projects are administered by a different Commission department: the Directorate-General for Research, Science and Education.

As already mentioned, the appropriations in Chapter 33 are administered on the basis of financial plans produced first of all to support the preliminary draft budget and then adjusted in line with the budget finally adopted. Implementation of the budget on the basis of these financial plans is a very complicated business because of the cascading charging system which operates as follows each month:

(a) The amounts charged to the staff expenditure accounts are divided between the research objectives (Part I) and the appropriation accounts (Part II) on the basis of the staff assigned.

(b) The operations charged to the appropriation accounts are divided between the research objectives in Part I according to the extent to which they have made use of the resources (or means of attaining objectives).

(c) The operations relating to the objectives in Part I are charged against the relevant headings in Chapter 33 of the budget.

Where there are no excess resources these accounts balance in the sense that all such resources can be charged to the relevant objectives. If resources and requirements do not exactly match, which seems almost bound to happen, then the figures will no longer balance. But the Council, in its capacity as Budgetary Authority, will not accept that this is so. This attitude has merely resulted in the artificial booking of resources which glosses over any possible underutilization. For all its complexity, the functional budget for research appropriations is thus rather ineffective since it does not enable a proper cost-benefit analysis to be made of the research programme and the Council's instruction that the appropriation accounts must be balanced come what may falsifies any assessment that may be attempted.

The functional research budget nevertheless enjoys some significant exemptions from normal budget rules. The Commission has, for example, delegated to the Director-General for the JRC the authority to make transfers between chapters, that is, between programme objectives, up to a limit of 7% which gives great flexibility to the administration of the JRC, making it less bureaucratic and more commercial in character. Similarly, commitment appropriations do not lapse after being carried forward for one year but remain valid until such time as cancellation is carried out through the budgetary procedure. Payment appropriations, on the other hand, do follow the normal rules.

Checks concerning the implementation of research and investment expenditure—Direct action is subject to the usual checks stipulated in the Financial Regulation. They are conducted by the Commission's Directorate-General for Financial Control. The dual accounting system just discussed makes the task of checking complicated. The Audit Board has, however, paid particular attention to auditing the JRC's financial management.

The auditing of indirect action projects is based on the Euratom Treaty and the Financial Regulation; auditing provisions are usually included in the contracts of association. The audits are conducted by the Directorate-General for Financial Control and the Directorate-General for Research, Science and Education during and at the end of the contract.

4. Scientific and technical information and documentation policy of the European Communities

The Treaties establishing the European Communities recognize that access should be provided to the results of research financed by the Communities and that there should be an exchange of scientific and technical information (Article 55(2) of the ECSC Treaty, Articles

13, 14 and 15 of the Euratom Treaty and Article 41 of the EEC Treaty). As an outcome of the Summit meeting in The Hague in December 1969 (see Annex 3, p. 350), the Council adopted a Resolution on 24 June 1971 with a view to coordinating the action of the Member States regarding scientific and technical information and documentation (STID). This Resolution was followed by a Council Decision of 18 March 1975 adopting a three-year plan of action (1975-77). A second three-year plan of action (for 1978-80) was adopted by the Council on 28 October 1978 to permit the completion of a new series of projects launched during the first plan of action. These plans of action cover three inter-related fields.

The first project is the establishment of the Euronet-Diane computer network which, on the basis of the telecommunications network set up by a consortium of the nine PTT authorities, links 30 or so host computers scattered throughout the Community which manage more than 100 information systems (data banks and bases). It will be possible to connect more than 700 users to this network which will also be accessible to many non-Community countries both inside and outside Europe. This network was inaugurated in Strasbourg on 13 February 1980 by the Presidents of the European Parliament, the Council of Ministers and the Commission. It will be used for applications other than STID. The Euronet telecommunications network is in fact intended to develop into a public European data transmission network. The size and scope of this project will help the Community to catch up with the other leaders in the field of scientific and technical information.

The second project is the establishment of a number of new information systems. On this subject, it should be recalled that information systems already exist in some sectors, such as the European Nuclear Documentation System (ENDS), which has built up a library of some 1.5 million documents, the Metallurgical Documentation and Information System (MDIS) and the International Scientific and Technological Information System for the Agricultural Sector, established under the auspices of the FAO (Agris 1). Other systems are being launched, in particular in connection with environmental matters, veterinary science, tropical and subtropical agriculture, and biomedicine. Most of the revenue will in future be used to back the development of information systems which have already been set up or are to be set up by European organizations and which are likely to be used by the Community as a whole because of the Euronet-Diane system. This venture entails exporting to non-Community countries and will create new jobs and revenue.

The third project is the development of new advanced information technologies to expand and facilitate the use of Euronet and overcome the language barriers which still impede the transfer of information between the six official languages of the Community. Work has, for example, been done on machine translation and machine-assisted translation and in new fields such as videotext and other data or image transmission systems.

Apart from these specific STID activities, the Commission has undertaken and intends to actively develop a wide range of projects concerning the dissemination, assessment and utilization of the findings of private and public research in the Community, to stimulate industrial innovation which is becoming increasingly necessary at Community level.

The measures implemented in this sector have much in common with Euratom's extramural indirect action projects (see p. 261). The Commission often does not have actual decision-making powers in this sector.

The appropriations for these purposes appear in a special chapter in Title 3. They are subject to normal budget implementation rules and are administered by the Directorate-General for the Information Market and Innovation.

5. Resources used to finance energy and industrial policy measures

We shall analyse first of all the resources which have been allocated since 1952 and then the use to which the money in question has been put.

A—Resources used in the period 1952-80

As in the two preceding chapters, the intention is to analyse the resources available in 1979 and 1980.

The following table is based on the same principles as the one appearing in the preceding chapter (see p. 233). It adds the funds from the ECSC operational budget to those from the general budget. It includes the appropriations in Chapter 37, with the exception of those for Community aid for industrial restructuring and conversion operations (Article 375) which were included in the table in the preceding chapter. However, it does include the appropriations for Chapter 39 which is rather a motley assortment.[16]

The money provided for these policies and measures is in the form of grants and loans, as already mentioned.

Funds for energy policy, industrial policy and research and development

(m EUA)

Policies and measures				1979 For commitment	1979 For payment	1980 For commitment	1980 For payment
Energy	EEC		1	57.0	50.5	100.0	77.1
	Safeguards		2	1.5	1.5	1.5	1.5
		EEC—Total	3=1+2	58.5	52.0	101.5	78.6
	ECSC		4	6.0	6.0	6.0	6.0
		Total	5=3+4	64.5	58.0	107.5	84.6
Industrial	EEC		6	4.2	3.9	12.1	7.0
Research and development	Euratom		7	181.4	216.7	312.9	276.7
	ECSC		8	46.6	46.6	44.0	44.0
		Total	9=7+8	228.0	263.3	356.9	320.7
Dissemination	Euratom		10	6.2	6.5	5.9	6.1
Miscellaneous	EEC		11	9.0	9.0	16.9	17.2
		Total	12=5+6+9 +10+11	311.9	340.7	499.3	435.6

Non-repayable aid (1953-79)

We shall analyse in turn the assistance granted by the ECSC, Euratom and the EEC.

ECSC aid (1953-79)

ECSC aid is directed mainly towards research: steel research (150.7 m u.a.), coal research (139.4 m u.a.) and social research (81.5 m u.a.), giving a total of 371.6 m u.a. There are also various aids for coal stockpiling amounting to 51.3 m u.a. Altogether, ECSC aid has totalled 422.9 m u.a. over 27 years.

Euratom aid (1958-79)

The budget resources expended under the Euratom Treaty amount to 1 848.3 m u.a. (see Annex 12, p. 393 and the table on pp. 398 and 399), a considerably larger sum, but quite different in its impact since the main thrust of the Community's activities, in financial terms, was towards direct action projects (JRC) rather than indirect action projects, it being the latter that bear direct comparison with the ECSC operations. Indeed, the bulk of the JRC's expenditure has been in staff costs.

EEC aid (1974-79)

Aid under the EEC Treaty is very recent. Between 1974 and 1979 aid totalling 235.5 m u.a. was granted to oil and gas technology projects and to uranium prospecting in the Community, and to measures relating to industry.

Total non-repayable aid

Adding up the abovementioned figures, we obtain a total of 2 506.5 m u.a. granted since the European Communities were set up. Of all the policies involving financial aid, this policy thus brings up the rear.

Loans granted

Loans are granted by the ECSC, the EIB and Euratom. ECSC loans have already been discussed in the previous chapter as it was preferred to include them with the funds to further the Community's internal development (see p. 236).

Since 1973, the most significant development in EIB loans has been in the energy sector; in seven years, they have totalled almost 3 080 m u.a., i.e. 81% of the assistance for projects of common interest (see p. 236).

Euratom loans granted between 1963 and 1979 amounted to 352 m u.a.

B—Breakdown of expenditure by Member State

As part of the preparatory work for the European Council in Dublin, the Commission drew up tables showing the breakdown of expenditure by Member State. These figures, updated in March 1980, show the following:

Expenditure on energy, industrial policy and research and development

(%)

Member State	B	DK	D	F	IRL	I	L	NL	UK	Sub-total	Other	Total
	1979 Expenditure											
1. Research and investment	10.4	0.7	18.8	10.0	0.3	29.8	0.1	8.1	21.8	100		100
2. Energy	0.8	0.8	16.7	39.1	2.6	18.9	0.0	5.2	15.9	100		100
3. Industry	7.5	0.6	4.6	14.9	0.0	68.4	0.0	1.1	2.9	100		100
4. Other												
5. Total (1 to 4)	9.1	0.7	17.1	12.8	0.5	33.0	0.1	7.2	19.5	100		100
	1980 Estimates											
1. Research and investment	10.0	0.6	19.1	7.6	0.2	31.4	0.0	9.6	21.5	100		100
2. Energy	3.3	0.7	16.0	36.6	1.4	12.5	0.0	4.7	16.8	92.0	8.0	100
3. Industry	13.5	1.3	13.5	27.0	0.0	31.1	0.0	4.1	8.1	98.6	1.4	100
4. Other												
5. Total (1 to 4)	8.5	0.6	18.3	14.8	0.4	27.0	0.0	8.3	20.2	98.1	1.9	100

This aggregate—Aggregate III (see p. 333)—does not provide a particularly meaningful breakdown. The large amount of money spent in Italy is due to the presence on its territory of the JRC's Ispra Establishment (see p. 260), and the United Kingdom is second in line due to the JET project being based on its territory (see p. 262).

In a way, the Community issued from the energy sector, as the ECSC and Euratom testify. Nevertheless, energy policy is still in its infancy in 1980. The Commission has admittedly proposed a whole panoply of measures to give the Community the role of catalyst, but the interests of the Member States vary considerably, as do their dependence on foreign supplies and their political philosophies for tackling these problems. However, energy is the basic problem facing us today, though it must be recognized that, if Community public finance was to make an active contribution towards energy investment, the resulting burden would be overwhelming since it is expected that the Member States will spend 400 000 m EUA—or 2% of Community GDP—between 1980 and 1990. The question of resources allocated at Community level would take on even greater significance.[17] Nevertheless, the European Council meeting in Luxembourg in April 1980 considered that 'structural changes could be speeded up by support at Community level, for a set period and subject to the financial constraints which the Community sets itself' (see Annex 3, p. 357).

The term 'industrial policy' is a euphemism. Community achievements to date in this field are so limited that they would scarcely deserve a mention were it not for the ECSC's role in the steel industry. Within this particular Community, however, the achievements have been quite remarkable. To be sure, in 1975 the steel industry faced the most serious crisis in its postwar history, but the blame for this did not lie at the door of the Community. As far as finance is concerned, the Community offers major assistance for investment and research programmes aimed at making the industry more modern and more competitive. Community action in other industrial sectors is either diffident and limited (data processing and textiles) or no more than conjectural (aerospace and shipbuilding). Despite the creation of the free-trade zone in industrial products, and the signing of large numbers of agreements, often, it must be said, restricted by national frontiers, rather than transcending them, and the economic progress made in the last 25 years and the ensuing recession, no desire to act in concert at the level of the Community has emerged. To be sure, financing on a European scale could never have been more than a catalyst. In practice, it was not sought.

Instead, the major agreements have been reached outside the Community framework: e.g. Concorde, the Airbus, Ariane, the communications satellites and data processing. This is not necessarily something to lament. However, it has to be admitted that industry has bypassed Brussels (where the Community has its headquarters) in these cases.

However, Community financing can play a role in the research and development sector, since the Community is an eminently suitable framework for coordination, the exchange of information, harmonization and economies of scale. The efforts made here have been considerable and usually successful.

Footnotes to Chapter XIII

[1] On 19 July 1978 France signed a similar agreement for a number of civil nuclear plants; this agreement has not yet taken effect.

[2] The United Kingdom signed a similar agreement for non-military nuclear plants which took effect on 14 August 1978.

[3] In its Communication to the Council of 27 April 1973 on guidelines and priorities for a Community energy policy, the Commission emphasized the risks involved in the Community being so dependent on external oil supplies. The Copenhagen Summit of 14 and 15 December 1973, in the midst of the oil crisis, asked the Commission to propose measures for tackling the problems raised by the energy crisis (see Annex 3, p. 351). On 5 June 1974 the Commission put forward a number of detailed proposals for a new energy policy strategy for the years ahead. On 17 December 1974 the Council adopted targets for 1985 and decided what should be done to use energy more rationally, increase indigenous energy production and, as a result, reduce the Community's dependence on imported energy from 63% in 1973 to 50% or preferably 40% in 1985.

[4] Title 3 contains a chapter including all the funds earmarked for the Commission to carry out its duties as regards *safeguards*. These appropriations are classified according to purpose and are intended to finance inspection visits, sampling and analysis and the procurement of equipment. The funds are administered in accordance with the normal administrative rules.

[5] The operating subsidy for the *Supply Agency* appears in Title 2 (Buildings, equipment and miscellaneous administrative expenditure). This is administrative expenditure and does not call for special comment.

[6] Article 6(2) of Council Regulation (EEC) No 1302/78 of 12 June 1978 on the granting of financial support for projects to exploit alternative energy sources and Article 5(2) of Council Regulation (EEC) No 1303/78 of 12 June 1978 on the granting of financial support for demonstration projects in the field of energy saving state: 'The Commission shall decide whether to grant or refuse support for projects after consulting the Advisory Committee on the management of the projects concerned composed of representatives of the Member States. The Commission's decision shall be communicated to the Council and to the Member States forthwith and shall apply upon expiry of a period of 20 working days if during that period no Member State has referred the matter to the Council. At the request of a Member State, the Council shall rule on the Commission decision, acting unanimously in the case of the first set of projects and by a qualified majority in the case of subsequent projects.' This provision caused difficulty with the European Parliament (see Annex 5, p. 365).

[7] See Supplement 11/75—Bull. EC.

[8] See Decision 77/488/EEC, Euratom of 18 July 1977 adopting a research programme (1977-80) for the JRC which provides for funds of 346 m u.a. and a staff of 2 038 as a guide (OJ L 200 of 8.8.1977).

[9] See Decision 80/317/EEC, Euratom of 13 March 1980 adopting a research programme (1980-83) for the JRC which provides for funds of 510 m EUA and a staff of 2 260 (OJ L 72 of 18.3.1980).

[10] The five-year programme (1976-80) was allocated 124 m EUA, approximately one-quarter of the total financial outlay in the Community.

11 Sweden and Switzerland joined the Community in this field in 1976 and 1979 respectively.

[11] Sweden and Switzerland joined the Community in this field in 1976 and 1979 respectively.

[12] See Decision 80/318/Euratom of 13 March 1980 adopting a research and training programme in this field of controlled thermonuclear fusion (1979-83). Excluding the JET project, the funds involved total 190.5 m EUA and the staff 113, i.e. about 30% of the resources involved in the 'general programme' in the Community. Another 145 m EUA and 150 temporary staff are provided, representing 80% of the cost of the JET Joint Undertaking.

[13] The JET story is worth telling:
   (1) On 31 July 1975, the Commission made a proposal to the Council concerning the fourth five-year programme (1976-80) in the field of controlled thermonuclear fusion, including the JET project;
   (2) On 18 December 1975, the European Parliament approved this proposal;
   (3) On 15 December 1975, the first meeting of the Council of Research Ministers took place. No decision was reached on the rest of the fusion programme (i.e. excluding JET) or on the JET project itself because of disagreement on the siting of JET;
   (4) On 28 January 1976, the Commission sent a Communication to the Council on the site for JET (the candidates being: Cadarache, France; Culham, United Kingdom; Garching, Federal Republic of Germany; Ispra, Italy; Jülich, Federal Republic of Germany and Mol, Belgium) and on the structure of the fusion programme;
   (5) On 11 June 1976, another Commission Communication was sent to the Council, this time proposing solutions for each of the scientific, technical, financial and administrative problems with the project and urging the Council to take a speedy and final decision on the matter;
   (6) On 22 December 1976, a Commission Communication was sent to the Council indicating the extreme gravity of the situation concerning the project, after nothing had been achieved in six ministerial meetings;
   (7) On 10 January 1977, a third European Parliament Resolution was adopted on the need to decide on the site for JET;
   (8) On 1 February 1977, the European Parliament asked the Council to institute joint consultations on the site for JET;
   (9) On 29 and 30 March 1977, at the Council of Research Ministers, Belgium withdrew its application to have the site at Mol, France was prepared to accept a site other than Cadarache, and Italy was ready to withdraw Ispra as a candidate in the light of decisions to be taken concerning the JRC. The remaining candidates were Culham and Garching. However, the proposed majority vote did not take place. The meeting was finally adjourned;
   (10) On 19 April 1977, a meeting was held between the President of the Council and the President of the European Parliament;
   (11) On 29 and 30 June 1977, the European Council meeting in London asked the Council to continue its efforts so that a decision could be reached on the site of the JET installation at the next Council meeting;
   (12) On 25 October 1977, the Council of Research Ministers selected Culham as the site for JET and approved the arrangements for implementing this decision;
   (13) On 7 April 1978, another Commission proposal was submitted to the Council, this time to include the JET project in the fusion programme and to set up a JET Joint Undertaking;
   (14) On 30 May 1978, the Council Decision was published in OJ L 151 of 7.6.1978.
   At least two years were wasted. In August 1978, the University of Princetown announced that, for the first time, conditions approaching those required for thermonuclear fusion had been achieved in an experimental device. Has the Community fallen behind in fusion research?

[14] The research and investment appropriations include staff appropriations; as a result, JRC staff and the staff for indirect action projects appear in two different establishment plans separate from the Commission's establishment plans (see pp. 304 and 310).

[15] It is worth noting the remarkable fact that in the 1976 budget Annex 1 (where the research and investment appropriations are entered) contains 166 of the 369 pages devoted to the Commission (45% of the document devoted to only 1.81% of the budget). The sole purpose of this crude comparison is to show how complicated the budgetary presentation of these appropriations is.

[16] Chapter 39 is for other expenditure on specific projects undertaken by the Commission. It contains six Articles which were allocated the following amounts for 1979 and 1980: Article 390 'Research projects in the field of technology and industry' (token entry for each year); Article 391 'Preparation of new research programmes' (1 150 000 EUA for each year); Article 392 'Educational measures' (5 490 000 EUA and 6 700 000 EUA); Article 393 'Cultural measures and events' (315 000 EUA and 570 000 EUA); Article 395 'Specific measures to improve knowledge of the Japanese market' (1 500 000 EUA and 1 500 000 EUA) and Article 396 'European Foundation' (500 000 EUA for each year), a total of 8 955 000 EUA and 10 420 000 EUA respectively.

[17] In its Communication of 21 March 1980 to the European Council entitled 'Energy—Community initiative', the Commission raises the question of financing Community energy policy: 'Until we have a clearer idea of the amount required, it would be premature to draw any conclusions about methods of financing. There are a number of possibilities, from raising Community loans for the purpose to increasing revenue under the Community's existing system of own resources, to introducing a specific Community energy tax designed to contribute to the objectives of energy policy as a whole. If the choice were to be some form of Community energy tax, it would be desirable:

  (i) to adopt a system which is administratively simple and easy to operate, raises least political and constitutional difficulties, and can be rapidly introduced;

 (ii) to minimize complications with third countries, in particular oil suppliers and those with whom we have preferential agreements;

(iii) to ensure that the tax was an own resource of the Community with its yield going directly into the Community budget.

The main possibilities—not mutually exclusive—for taxation would be to impose a tax on the consumption of energy, either in all its forms or on oil or specific oil products; a tax on production of energy in general or oil in particular; a duty or levy on imports either of energy in general or of oil or specific oil products. The Commission is sending the Council a detailed examination of possible fiscal instruments for raising Community revenue from energy. Each form of taxation has its advantages and disadvantages. Various combinations of taxes might also be considered.'

On 13 February 1980, the European Parliament came out against a common energy tax without a coherent energy policy. A tax of 2 EUA on each tonne of imported oil would raise 1 000 m EUA and would only increase the cost to the consumer by just under 0.5%.

Chapter XIV:
Financing of policy concerning cooperation with non-member countries

The contemporary world has become divided into two groups of countries: on the one hand, the industrial countries and those countries that have succeeded in 'taking off' economically, with a combined population of a little over 1 000 million, and on the other hand, the developing countries with a population of 2 500 million. The first group provides 87.5% of the world's production. This unbalanced structure, which contains the seeds of possible conflict between rich and poor, is likely to get worse unless some drastic remedy is found. For it has been found that production is rising much faster in the industrialized countries than in the others—where the trend of production is barely keeping pace with the increase in population.

From the outset, the European Community of the Six was faced with the choice between a regional and a world approach in working out a policy for development aid to the Third World. Quite naturally, the Member States with recent responsibilities as colonial powers wanted their former colonies, generally in Africa, to receive Community aid. On the other hand, the Member States that had not had such responsibilities supported the principle of granting aid that made no distinction on geographical or historical grounds but was based solely on the needs inherent in underdevelopment. The first principle was dominant at the beginning, then the second gradually gained ground, though without really affecting the entrenched position of the other. Thus at the Paris Summit on 21 October 1972 the Heads of State or Government invited Member States 'progressively to adopt an overall policy of development cooperation on a world-wide scale'. With the enlargement of the Community, these differences were given a fresh airing and finally narrowed to the point where the Communities' activities are now gradually assuming a reasonably balanced form in political terms, although it must be acknowledged that it is taking longer to follow this up financially.

The Community has extended its financial cooperation arrangements, particularly since 1976, to some countries not in the category of developing countries as defined by the Development Aid Committee (DAC) of the Organization for Economic Cooperation and Development (OECD), notably certain Mediterranean countries. This chapter will consider in turn cooperation with associated countries, that is, the ACP (African, Caribbean and Pacific) countries, cooperation with developing countries in general, cooperation with countries in the Mediterranean area, and finally, the resources applied to finance these various forms of cooperation.

1. Policy concerning cooperation with countries associated with the European Community

Article 3(k) of the EEC Treaty states that the activities of the Community shall include 'the association of the overseas countries and territories in order to increase trade and to promote jointly economic and social development'. Part 4 of the Treaty relates to the 'Association of the Overseas Countries and Territories' (Articles 131 to 136) and an Implementing Convention of 17 articles is annexed to the Treaty. It was thus the EEC Treaty itself that laid down the legal framework and the means of action of the first European Development Fund (EDF). There is also provision in the EIB's Statute for the possibility of financing projects outside the Community.

A—Foundations of policy on cooperation with countries associated with the European Community

Article 131 of the EEC Treaty (as amended by Article 24(1) of the Act concerning the Conditions of Accession and the Adjustments to the Treaties, annexed to the Treaty of Accession of 22 January 1972) states that the purpose of association shall be to promote the economic and social development of the non-European countries and territories that have special relations with Belgium, France, Italy, the Netherlands, and the United Kingdom. It stipulates that association shall serve primarily to further the interests and prosperity of the inhabitants of these countries and territories in order to lead them to the economic, social and cultural development to which they aspire.

Association thus has two facets. On the one hand, its aim is to create a vast economic area enjoying maximum freedom. This goal is limited, however, by the need to take account of both the historical situation of the associated countries and certain essential requirements of the EEC such as the common agricultural policy. On the other hand, association constitutes an organization for the multilateral distribution of public financial aid, the expense of which is borne according to variable scales. The agency created to carry out this distribution is the European Development Fund.

As association originally covered many countries that at the time—1957—were on the point of becoming independent, it was designed to run for five years in order to allow those countries to decide for themselves as sovereign States whether to renew, modify, or abandon the relationship. There have since been four subsequent association conventions.

Treaty of Rome: The First EDF (1959-64)

The Implementing Convention signed on 25 March 1957 at the same time as the Treaties of Rome was, as we have said, concluded for a period of five years (1959-64). According to Annex IV to the EEC Treaty in the version of 1957, the associated overseas countries and territories (OCTs) to receive aid comprised the eight countries of French West Africa, the four countries of French Equatorial Africa, the seven French overseas territories, Togoland and the Trust Territory of the Cameroons under French administration, the Belgian Congo and Rwanda-Burundi, the Trust Territory of Somaliland under Italian administration, and Dutch New Guinea.

274

The Fund was allocated 581.25 m u.a. Of this sum, 568.8 m u.a. were committed. In 1979, its operations had not yet been wound up (total payments amounted to 568.6 m u.a.). The Fund's main emphasis has been on transport and communications (this heading accounts for 44% of the assistance granted), education and training (19%), health and water engineering (17%) and rural production (16%).

First Yaoundé Convention: The Second EDF (1964-70)

After they had become independent, most of the States associated with the Community under the Treaty of Rome decided to continue their association. This led to the formation of the group of 18 Associated African States and Madagascar (AASM); it consisted of all the original countries except New Guinea, which decided to join Indonesia, and Guinea, plus two territories under British administration, West Cameroon (since integrated into the Federal Republic of Cameroon) and Somaliland (since integrated into the Somali Republic). On 20 July 1963, at Yaoundé, these countries signed the Convention known as the First Yaoundé Convention. It should be noted that in addition to the AASM countries there were two groups of countries to which special arrangements applied: first, certain OCT countries with special relations with Member States of the Community and second, the four French Overseas Departments (Guadeloupe, Guiana, Martinique, and Reunion).

The First Yaoundé Convention demonstrated the continuity of the activities initiated by the Treaty of Rome, since its preamble declared that the signatories were determined to pursue their efforts together with a view to the economic, social and cultural progress of their countries. This joint desire to work together on the basis of complete equality and friendly relations, observing the principles of the Charter of the United Nations was reflected in the creation of institutions with strict parity of composition. This EDF was given more funds than its predecessor: it received appropriations of 730 m u.a., supplemented by loans of 70 m u.a. from the capital resources of the European Investment Bank. The Convention entered into force on 1 June 1964 and came to an end, after an extension, on 31 December 1970.

The capital expenditure related to the following sectors, in decreasing order: rural production (37%), transport and communications (34%), health and water engineering (11%), and education and training (9%). By 1979, a total 726.5 m u.a. had been paid.

The EIB's operations, on the other hand, were mainly in the industrial sector, which accounted for over 95% of the loans granted.

Second Yaoundé Convention: The Third EDF (1970-75)

Negotiations starting toward the end of 1968 resulted in the signature of a new Convention at Yaoundé on 29 July 1969, known as the Second Yaoundé Convention. The signatories set themselves the same main objectives and retained the institutions and procedures of association unchanged. As far as finance was concerned, the EDF was allocated 900 m u.a., supplemented by loans of 100 m u.a. from the EIB. This Convention expired on 31 January 1975. The Third EDF, like the Second EDF, focused on basic economic investment: transport and communications (38%), rural production (26%), education and training (11%). By 1979 some 801.4 m u.a. had been paid.

As regards the EIB, some 66% of its loans were for projects in the industrial sector.

In a declaration dated 1 and 2 April 1963 and confirmed in 1969, the Six had offered countries with an economic structure and production similar to those of the AASM the opportunity either to join the association convention or to conclude individual association agreements. Apart from the accession of Mauritius to the Second Yaoundé Convention on 12 May 1972, the most tangible result of these overtures was the Convention signed at Arusha on 24 September 1969 with Kenya, Uganda and Tanzania. Under that Convention, the three States in question obtained the benefit, like the AASM, of exemption from customs duties and equivalent charges. But they were not granted financial aid. This Convention, like the Second Yaoundé Convention, expired on 31 January 1975.

First Lomé Convention: The Fourth EDF (1976-80)

As expressly requested by the countries involved, the Second Yaoundé Convention and the Arusha Convention provided that 18 months before the Convention expired the Contracting Parties would examine the arrangements to be made for a new period in order to avoid a hiatus between two Conventions. This led to the opening of negotiations in Brussels, on 25 July 1973. It was not until 28 February 1975, at Lomé, that the resulting new Convention was signed, but the agreement then made involved all 46 of the countries who had entered into the negotiations. This Convention was scheduled to run from 1 April 1976 to 29 February 1980.

At the time of signature, this Convention accordingly applied to the 9 EEC Member States and 46 ACP countries, comprising the 19 States (African States and Madagascar and Mauritius) who had signed the Yaoundé Convention (Benin*, Burundi*, Cameroon, the Central African Republic*, the Congo, the Ivory Coast, Gabon, the Upper Volta*, Madagascar, Mali*, Mauritania, Mauritius, Niger*, Rwanda*, Senegal, Somalia*, Chad*, Togo*, and Zaire); 21 Commonwealth countries (in Africa the three signatories of the Arusha Convention (Kenya, Uganda*, and Tanzania*), along with Botswana*, Gambia*, Ghana, Lesotho*, Malawi*, Nigeria, Sierre Leone, Swaziland*, and Zambia, six Caribbean States (Barbados, Guyana, Jamaica, the Bahamas, Grenada, Trinidad and Tobago), and three Pacific States (Fiji, Western Samoa*, and Tonga*)); and lastly, a further six African States (Ethiopia*, Guinea*, Equatorial Guinea, Guinea-Bissau*, Liberia, and the Sudan*).

The French Overseas Departments already mentioned on p. 275, plus St Pierre and Miquelon whose status changed from that of Overseas Territory to Overseas Department on 19 July 1976, no longer receive EDF aid, but receive ERDF aid instead (see p. 220).

Any former OCT State may join the Convention and so may any State whose economic structure and production are similar to those of the ACP States. Since the Convention was signed, the following former OCTs have acceded on the basis of the first criterion: Surinam on 16 July 1976, the Seychelles* on 27 August 1976, the Comoros* on 13 September 1976, Jibuti* on 2 February 1978 and the Kiribati Islands on 30 October 1979. The following have acceded on the basis of the second criterion: the Solomon Islands* on 27 September 1978, Sao Tome and Principe* and Cape Verde* on 1 November 1978, Papua New Guinea on 1 November 1978, Tuvalu* on 17 January 1979, Dominica* on 26 February 1979 and St Lucia on 28 June 1979. Three other former OCTs have applied—St Vincent, the New Hebrides and St Kitts-Nevis. Zimbabwe and the Cook Islands have also been informed of the possibilities of acceding to the Convention in early 1980.

The map on p. 277 shows that there are at present 58 ACP countries. These countries have a total population of around 270 million. Special aid measures are available for the least-

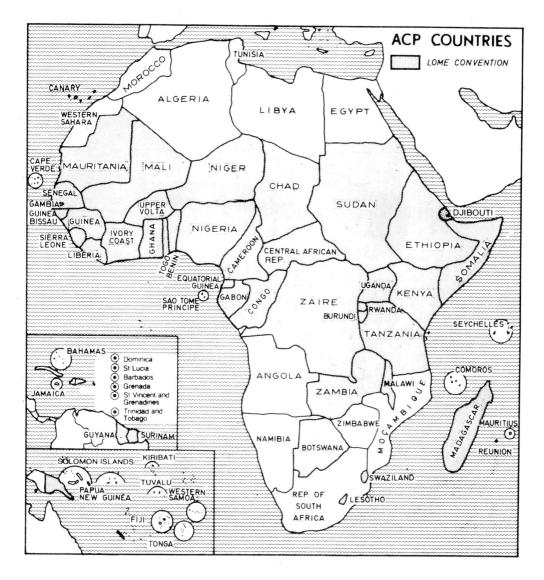

ACP COUNTRIES

LOME CONVENTION

developed ACP States under Article 48 of the Convention. Originally 24, these countries now number 32 following accessions since the Convention was signed. These countries are marked with an asterisk.

The Lomé Convention is an agreement of considerable scope both because of the large number of signatories—in particular, all the independent black African countries—and also because it establishes a new type of relation between the industrialized world and the developing countries based essentially on equality and cooperation. Its new features are adjustments in trade relationships (customs-free access to the European market for 99.3% of ACP exports), the setting up of a stabilization scheme for export earnings, and the inauguration of industrial cooperation. Only the second of these provisions has financial effects that need to be mentioned here.

The stabilization scheme for export earnings (Stabex) works like this. When the export earnings of an ACP State for a given product (groundnut products, cocoa products, coffee products, cotton products, coconut products, palm products, hides and skins, wood products, fresh bananas, tea, raw sisal, and, exceptionally, iron ore) represent at least 7.5% (or in the case of sisal, 5%) of its total earnings, that State has the right to request a cash transfer if its earnings from exporting one of these products to the Community are at least 7.5% below the reference level, which is the average of the previous four years. These two thresholds—the dependence threshold and the activating threshold—are reduced to 2.5% for the 34 least-developed, landlocked, or island ACP States. For some of these countries (Burundi, Ethiopia, Guinea-Bissau, Rwanda, and Swaziland) in view of their economic situation, the system applies to exports irrespective of destination. The Convention further stipulates that ACP States which have received cash transfers must—provided certain conditions are fulfilled in the five years following the grant of the transfers—contribute to the replenishment of the system's resources. The 29 least-developed countries àre exempt from the obligation to contribute in this way toward the replenishment of funds. This arrangement is a remarkable innovation without precedent in history in that it is an insurance against bad years. It constitutes a most welcome improvement on the traditional type of financial aid.

The Lomé Convention of 28 February 1975 allocates 3 390 m EUA for the five years it covers. Of this 3 000 m EUA is for the Fourth EDF and 390 m EUA for loans financed by the EIB from its own resources. The aid of 3 000 m EUA can be broken down as follows: 2 100 m EUA in grants (100 m EUA as interest relief on EIB loans, generally 3%), 375 m EUA for the stabilization of export earnings, 430 m EUA in special loans and 95 m EUA in risk capital. The Lomé Convention, after being duly ratified by all signatories, took effect on 1 April 1976. Indicative financial and technical cooperation programmes were drawn up in line with the *objectives* defined by each of the ACP States during the programming missions; this resulted in 37% of Community aid going to rural development, 12% to industrial projects, 28% to economic infrastructure and 15% to social development. An amount of 150 m EUA is available for emergency aid (see p. 289).

Investment has been directed towards rural production, transport and communications and industrialization. Some 992.2 EUA had been paid by the end of 1979.

Second Lomé Convention: The Fifth EDF (1980-85)

The First Lomé Convention was due to expire on 1 March 1980, and final provisions required the Community and the ACP States to begin negotiations 18 months before then to work out the framework for their future relations. Negotiations opened officially at ministerial level on 24 July 1978 in Brussels but the real work of negotiation got underway on 18 September in Brussels. The Convention was signed on 31 October 1979.

The underlying principles which gave the previous Convention its distinctive features have been retained. In terms of Community financing, the new Convention introduces three improvements. The first is an extension of the Stabex system to cover 44 products, thus ensuring much wider and more balanced protection in the light of the diversity of products exported. Chief among the new products are rubber, cashew nuts, pepper, shrimps, prawns and squid, cotton seeds, peas, beans and lentils and oil cake. The dependence thresholds have been lowered from 7.5% to 6.5% (and from 2.5% to 2% for the least-developed States).

The second improvement is a special arrangement for minerals to complement the Stabex system which covers only agricultural raw materials and iron ore. This special financing facility for minerals (minerals facility for short) covers the main minerals exported by the ACP countries, namely: copper and cobalt (Zambia, Zaire, Papua New Guinea); phosphates (Togo, Senegal); bauxite and alumina (Guinea, Jamaica, Surinam, Guyana); manganese (Gabon); tin (Rwanda); iron ore (Mauritania, Liberia) and iron pyrites.[1] The system comes into play in respect of a given State only if:

(a) as a general rule, one of these minerals has, in the preceding four years, represented at least 15%, on average, of the State's total exports to all destinations (10% for the least-developed, landlocked or island States), or

(b) the State's production capacity or its capacity to export to the Community is likely to be substantially reduced (by at least 10%) either owing to a drop in export earnings such as would threaten the profitability and maintenance of an otherwise viable line of production or to fortuitous events of any kind.

In these cases, the country in question may obtain Community assistance for financing projects or programmes designed to maintain or restore its production or export capacity; this aid is in the form of special loans (bearing interest at the rate of 1% per annum, repayable over 40 years and with a grace period of 10 years). Advances may be made as a means of prefinancing projects or programmes.

This system to protect the mining industry of ACP States is backed up by a set of provisions, the combined aim of which is to ensure the development of their mining and energy potential by means of:

(a) technical and financial assistance for exploration and mining programmes through the establishment of national or regional exploration funds;

(b) assistance in the form of risk capital for research and investment prior to the launching of mining and energy projects;

(c) aid from the European Investment Bank (whose resources have been substantially increased) for projects of mutual interest, and

(d) encouragement of private investment backed up by the conclusion of specific investment protection agreements with interested ACP States.

The third improvement concerns the overall amount of the Community's financial assistance which, in EUA terms, has been increased by 62% (72.3% in terms of dollars and 69.7% in terms of CFAF). The overall amount for the ACP countries breaks down as follows: EDF—3 712 m EUA in project aid (2 928 m EUA for subsidies, 500 m EUA for special loans and 280 m EUA for risk capital); Stabex—550 m EUA; minerals facility—280 m EUA; total—4 542 m EUA; EIB—685 m EUA in loans. Apart from the financial provisions of the Convention, a sum of 180 m EUA has been earmarked in the general budget to cover the administrative expenditure of Commission Delegations in ACP States (expenditure hitherto charged to EDF appropriations), plus 200 m EUA in EIB loans for mining and energy projects. The total amount for the ACP countries is therefore 5 607 m EUA to which should be added 109 m EUA for the OCTs: 85 m EUA under the EDF (51 m EUA for subsidies, 27 m EUA for special loans and 7 m EUA for risk capital), 9 m EUA under Stabex and 15 m EUA under the EIB, giving a grand total of 5 716 m EUA.

Leaving aside the financial aid available from the EIB outside the terms of the Convention, the ratio between grants and repayable aid has been maintained (80% and 20%). Furthermore, as far as repayable aid is concerned there has been a substantial increase in the amount of aid granted in the form of risk capital as compared with normal loans. As a result of this adjustment, the European Investment Bank should be able to provide more aid, particularly for the least-developed countries where the financing of industrial products is often possible only if these two types of financing are combined. Under the new Convention, the least-developed States already enjoying more privileged treatment under the First Lomé Convention will obtain even further advantages thanks to a special chapter covering the special measures for these States. These special provisions concern both financial cooperation (determination of the volume of aid and the conditions under which it is granted, reduction in the interest rate on special loans from 1% to 0.75%) and Stabex. A total of 200 million EUA has been earmarked for emergency aid purposes (see p. 289).

To these figures must be added the amounts allocated to food aid and cofinancing arrangements with non-governmental organizations (NGOs) undertaken outside the Convention. In this connection, the Community has notified its partners of the estimated amount of aid to which they are eligible for the duration of the Convention, i.e. at least 300 m EUA in food aid and 25 m EUA in aid to NGOs.

Sugar Protocol concluded
with the ACP States (and India)

Reference should again be made in this context to the Sugar Protocol already mentioned in the chapter on guaranteed agricultural markets (see p. 173). Under Protocol No 3 to the Lomé Convention and Annex IV of the Council Decision on Overseas Countries and Territories (OCTs) and the agreement with India, the Community guarantees imports of specific quantities of raw or white cane sugar at annually negotiated guaranteed prices on condition that the States concerned undertake to supply these quantities. The total quantity, expressed in terms of white cane sugar, is 1 300 000 tonnes. However, because of the Community's own sugar surplus, it has to export a corresponding volume of Community sugar to non-member countries. As a result, the Sugar Protocol entails expenditure which has to be met from the Community budget. In 1978, this expenditure totalled 350 m EUA. In 1979, it totalled 400 m EUA and it may well amount to 210 m EUA in 1980. In its preliminary draft budget for 1980, the Commission proposed that this amount for refunds on sugar (Item 6400, EAGGF Guarantee Section) should be transferred to a newly created Article 972 to be included under the heading of cooperation with these non-member countries, but the Budgetary Authority rejected this proposal.

B—Financial and legal framework for policy
concerning cooperation with
countries associated with the European
Community

A distinction must be made between EDF financing and EIB financing.

Framework provided
by the European Development Funds

EDF resources

The Member States of the European Economic Community contribute certain sums which are quite separate from those paid up to and including 1974 in order to balance the general budget (see p. 377). They are for the specific purpose of aid to associated developing countries. The money is duly spent, but it does not pass through the budget. It has been or is being used to finance the European Development Fund (EDF) which has already financed four Community aid programmes for associated States.

Consequently, the EDF's resources are funds contributed by the Member States outside the budget, according to a scale of contributions determined for each Fund after long negotiations. However, the Commission wanted the Fourth EDF to be included in the budget.

On 12 June 1973, the Commission put this proposal to the Council, arguing that since the Council had decided, through its Decision of 21 April 1970, to replace the Member States financial contributions to the general budget by the Community's own resources, it was logical, if not inevitable, when next the association agreement was renewed, that Community expenditure on financial cooperation should be included in the budget. The Commission gave six reasons for including the expenditure in question in the budget. These can be summarized in the three following arguments:

(i) Including the EDF in the budget would give Community aid a genuine Community stamp and make it part of the financing of the overall Community aid policy advocated by the Paris Summit. At the same time this would, pursuant to Article 199 of the EEC Treaty which lays down the principle of comprehensiveness as regards the budget, make for greater clarity by grouping together in the budget all the resources deployed by the Community.

(ii) Including the EDF in the budget would guarantee parliamentary control by the European Parliament whereas, under the present system, these appropriations are outside the scope of Parliament's budgetary powers. Ever since its sitting of 21 June 1971, the European Parliament has been a strong supporter of this view. At the same time, Community expenditure would be diversified, in line with the wishes of Parliament and the Commission in particular, by reducing the proportion of agricultural expenditure.

(iii) Including the EDF in the budget would end any argument about how much individual Member States would contribute, since the application of the Community own resources system would resolve this question from the outset. It could also be a way of avoiding a break in continuity between successive agreements since this type of hiatus has created difficult problems in the past which have never been settled. All that would be necessary would be to include a provision in future agreements specifying the amount of appropriations to be provided for any interim period.

In fact, the question of the scale of contributions and the question of the unit of account to be used were the main stumbling-blocks which prevented the Fourth EDF from being brought into the budget. It therefore continued to operate outside the budget. The scale of contributions (see Annex 10, p. 380) was determined in an internal agreement on the financing and administration of Community aid approved by the nine Member States in accordance with their constitutional requirements on 11 July 1975.

On 10 January 1979, the Commission proposed the inclusion of the Fifth EDF in the budget, again setting forth its reasons. The Council rejected this proposal, however, and retained the system of contributions based on a political scale (see Annex 10, p. 380) in another internal agreement signed on 20 November 1979. This refusal to include the EDF in the budget was one of the main reasons why the European Parliament rejected the 1980 budget on 13 December 1979. In an attempt to find some common ground, the Commission annexed to its new budget proposal for 1980 of 29 February 1980 a discussion paper entitled 'The European Development Fund. Estimate of appropriations for 1980. Three-year financial estimate. Financial information'. On 12 March 1980, Parliament called for joint consultations (conciliation) (see Annex 5, p. 368). Such consultations had not taken place at the time of writing (summer 1980). The funds for the EDF are not included in the 1980 budget any more than they were included in the 1979, 1978 or 1977 budgets. All that has been done is to reserve two chapters for it.

Structure and functioning
of the Lomé Convention
and the European Development Fund (EDF)

Contributions are administered in a unique fashion reflecting the nature of the aid given to the States linked to the Community. We should therefore examine in turn the structure and functioning of the Lomé Convention and then the structure and functioning of the EDF itself.

Structure and functioning of the Lomé Convention

Under the Lomé Convention, the Community and the ACP (African, Caribbean and Pacific) States have two unprecedented joint institutions, namely:
(i) a Council of Ministers, comprising the members of the Council of the European Communities, a member of the government of each of the ACP States, and members of the Commission of the European Communities. It takes decisions and is assisted by a Committee of Ambassadors whose composition is similar to its own. A Joint Secretariat is provided;
(ii) a Consultative Assembly, comprising equal numbers of members of the European Parliament and representatives nominated by the ACP States, which may pass resolutions.

There is also an agreed arbitration procedure for settling disputes over the interpretation or application of the Convention which the Council of Ministers has been unable to settle amicably.

These two joint institutions are responsible for managing the political affairs of the association. The EDF is involved where implementation is concerned.

Structure and functioning of the EDF

The EDF is a different kettle of fish altogether from the European Agricultural Guidance and Guarantee Fund (EAGGF), the European Social Fund (ESF) and the European Regional Development Fund (ERDF), because it has resources of its own which it can use to enter into and meet expenditure commitments.

Structure of the EDF—The EDF is administered by one of the Commission's departments (the Directorate-General for Development) and not by an independent body. A non-profit-making international organization, the European Association for Cooperation (EAC), has also been set up to look after the recruitment, installation and management of staff required to carry out scientific and technical cooperation and supervision duties, generally on the spot. The EAC draws up an estimate of its expenditure, which is covered by a subsidy from the EDF for supervision and technical cooperation costs (95% of the total) and a subsidy from the Commission for headquarters costs (5% of the total).

With the Lomé Convention, the role of the 42 Commission delegates in the ACP States has increased significantly. Their tasks and duties are now those of public administrators and Commission representatives.

Performance of these duties and responsibilities is therefore no longer compatible with a situation in which the delegate is linked only indirectly to the Commission by means of a mere service mandate and an employment contract with a private association, the EAC. On the contrary, it is important that a direct hierarchical link be established—under public law—between the Commission and its delegates, a link which the Commission will then formalize by assigning delegates to temporary posts.

Functioning of the EDF—The operation of the EDF, like that of the general budget, is governed by a Financial Regulation (Regulation 76/647/EEC of 27 July 1976 in the case of the Fourth EDF). The following summary of the main points analysed is intended to show how the appropriations administered by the EDF differ from those of the general budget.

Framework and principles—The conventional rules applying to budget appropriations do not apply to the EDF, since its appropriations are allocated for certain specific operations and are multiannual, i.e. extending over five years, with ceilings determined in detail at the time of signature of each Convention. In common with budget appropriations, however, up to the stage of the Third EDF, they were expressed in a unit of account whose value was the same as the unit of account used in the general budget, the conversion rate being that of the IMF parities. As with the general budget, this produced unfortunate effects, with the result that, pursuant to a Decision of 21 April 1975, the unit of account chosen for the Fourth EDF was the EUA.[2]

Moreover, EDF appropriations are not presented in the form of a budget but are simply set out, after the event, in a balance sheet which constitutes a statement of expenditure (commitments and payments) and revenue.

Estimating and preparation—Here again the procedures are quite different, because the total amount of each successive EDF is the outcome of international negotiations. It is therefore a 'political' figure which, once agreed, can no longer be called into question unless non-OCT States subsequently accede to the Convention. Approval of this figure, however, is a much more complicated matter since, given the need for an internal agreement among the nine Member States, it must first undergo national ratification procedures.

Financial implementation—Although the financial administration of the Fund complies with the general rule requiring separation of the functions of Authorizing Officer, Accounting Officer and Financial Controller, it does have a number of peculiarities. The functions of the Authorizing Officer are exercised at two levels, (a) at the level of the Commission by the Chief Authorizing Officer who has overall responsibility and (b) at the level of each ACP State by the National Authorizing Officer who has limited powers as laid down in Article 30 of Protocol No 2. All financing proposals submitted to the Commission by ACP States must be examined either by the EDF Committee (see Annex 7, p. 375), or by the Article 22 Committee where financing is to be provided from resources administered by the EIB.

In addition to the checks carried out on the basis of records and on the spot by the Financial Controller and the Court of Auditors, the Commission Delegates in the ACP countries are also responsible for supervising the proper financial and technical implementation of the projects and action programmes financed from Fund resources.

In an attempt to promote more efficient management and more effective participation by the ACP States in this management, the new Lomé Convention has introduced a whole range of new provisions. The division of responsibilities between the Community authorities and the ACP States has now been clearly defined. An EEC-ACP Ministerial Committee is responsible for monitoring financial and technical cooperation measures. Most important of all, however, operations will be carried out according to advance timetables laid down for the implementation of the various stages of project programming, appraisal and implementation.

Audit—From its inception, the financial affairs of the EDF were audited by the Audit Board pursuant to Article 15 of Regulation No 5 which lays down the procedures for the collection and transfer of financial contributions, the rules for budgeting and the management of resources held by the Development Fund for the Overseas Countries and Territories. At the close of each financial year the Commission adopted the revenue and expenditure account for the financial year ended and the balance sheet of the Development Fund. It then submitted these documents together with supporting evidence by 31 March of the following financial year for scrutiny by the Audit Board provided for in Article 206 of the EEC Treaty. In carrying out this task the Audit Board had the same powers as those bestowed on it by Article 206 of the Treaty with regard to the Community budget. The Court of Auditors has now taken over this task from the Audit Board. The European Parliament, in particular its Committee on Budgetary Control, has a keen interest in the activities of the EDF.

Framework provided by the EIB

The exception provided for under Article 18 of the Statute of the EIB empowers the Board of Governors to authorize the Bank to grant loans for investment projects to be carried out outside the European territories of the Member States. Since 1963, therefore, the Bank has helped to implement the Community's financial cooperation policy under various agreements, financial protocols and decisions, mainly relating to ACP States.

The two Yaoundé Conventions set a ceiling of 170 m u.a. on the amount of assistance the Bank could provide from its own resources, and a ceiling of 140.5 m u.a. on the total amount of special loans or contributions from EDF resources towards the formation of risk capital. Virtually all of these amounts have been committed.

Under the First Lomé Convention, the Bank grants loans from its own resources[3] up to a maximum amount of 390 m EUA (400 m EUA if account is also taken of the Decision concerning OCTs). As with the Yaoundé Conventions, Community aid basically takes the form of grants or very favourable loans used mainly to finance agricultural projects, infrastructure projects or social projects. However, in contrast to the procedures adopted under the Yaoundé Conventions, the Commission alone is responsible for the appraisal and approval of applications for special loans. On the other hand, industrial projects are submitted to the EIB, which may decide to grant a loan from its own resources if, on examination of the project dossier, favourable conclusions are reached, particularly with regard to the technical, economic and financial viability of the project. The EIB may also finance economic infrastructures provided they help increase productivity. The Bank is also responsible for the utilization of 97 m EUA (101 m EUA if account is also taken of the Decision concerning OCTs), earmarked from budget funds for risk capital assistance. This assistance is granted by the Bank on the instructions and on behalf of the Community and is intended to finance either the acquisition of holdings or loans to an ACP State or a national development institution in order to increase firms' own funds, or to finance quasi-capital aid. This type of aid takes the form of subordinated loans repayable only after settlement of first-rank loans, or conditional loans the repayment and term of which depend on the fulfilment of specific conditions laid down when the loan was granted.

Out of a total volume of Community aid of 5 607 m EUA under the Fifth EDF, the ceiling on loans which may be granted by the EIB from its own resources has been set at 700 m

EUA; the ceiling on risk capital assistance is 287 m EUA. The EIB may, in accordance with its Statute, commit its own resources on a case-by-case basis beyond this amount in mining investment projects and energy investment projects recognized by the ACP State concerned and by the Community as being of mutual interest. Any such additional aid must be authorized by the Board of Governors of the Bank in accordance with the second subparagraph of Article 18(1) of its Statute. The maximum amount of additional aid which may be granted during the term of the Convention is 200 m EUA. Provision is also made in the new Convention for interest rate subsidies on EIB loans; a maximum of 175 m EUA must be earmarked for this purpose from the appropriations provided for grants.

2. Policy concerning cooperation with developing countries

Having settled the argument between the partisans of regional aid and world aid. the EEC has developed a cooperation policy addressed to all developing countries.

A—Foundations of policy concerning cooperation with developing countries

The most striking manifestation of this policy is still food aid, but this has been supplemented for some years by various *ad hoc* operations, and since 1976 an overall policy for technical and financial cooperation with non-associated developing countries has begun to take shape.

Food aid policy

Under the Kennedy Round of multilateral trade negotiations conducted within the framework of the General Agreement on Tariffs and Trade (GATT)—which failed, in particular, to produce comprehensive arrangements to regulate the world cereal market—the Community agreed to take part in a defined programme of food aid amounting to 4 500 000 tonnes of cereals a year for three years, of which 42% was to be supplied by the United States and 23% by the Community (namely 1 035 000 tonnes of which 300 000 to 350 000 tonnes was to come from Community sources). The aim of this operation was to create fresh demand for cereals in the wealthy countries, thus opening up their markets, and simultaneously provide direct benefit to cereal exporters and aid to people suffering from malnutrition.

On 3 May 1971, the Community signed a new Convention—which entered into force on 1 July 1971—under which a fresh undertaking was given to supply 1 035 000 tonnes a year over a three-year period (raised to 1 287 000 tonnes following enlargement of the Community, 643 500 tonnes being provided from Community sources). In addition, in April 1969, on its own initiative, the Commission devised a food aid scheme based on dairy products (skimmed milk and butteroil) as part of its policy for the absorption of certain agricultural surpluses.

As the 1971 Convention expired on 30 June 1974, the Commission was prompted to make fresh proposals and this led it to examine the matter in some detail. In a Memorandum on the EEC's food aid policy dated 6 March 1974 the Commission stated that the developing countries were faced with an unprecented food crisis and that the deterioration in the world food situation was the result not only of certain unforeseen events such as the drought in the Sahel but also of a general trend much more prejudicial than expected, because the 'green revolution' in the developing countries was not taking place at the expected rate, and also because population growth had been greater than expected. The Commission therefore considered that if the Community was to shoulder its responsibilities it would have to be in a position to pursue a valid food aid policy for at least the next five to ten years, and proposed that the six fundamental principles of Community policy should be as follows:

(i) The Community should give firm undertakings for a specified period.
(ii) The Community's aid effort should bear no relation to Community surpluses. This is an important innovation.
(iii) The aid effort should involve not only cereals but also dairy products, sugar, and perhaps corned beef.
(iv) Aid should be supplied, free of charge, to the governments concerned, leaving them to sell the commodities concerned at normal prices so as not to discourage efforts within their own countries to increase production of the foods in question. The proceeds of the sales should be used to finance development projects, particularly in agriculture.
(v) Procedures should be simplified, preferably by sending consignments directly from the Community to the recipient States.
(vi) It should not be insisted that all aid be immediately channelled through the Community. Member States would thus be able to continue with certain 'national' aid for a time.

The Commission's Memorandum, with its six fundamental principles, thus lays down a coherent and reasoned overall policy for food aid. The upper and lower limits for the annual aid targets are as follows:

(a) 1 700 000 to 2 500 000 tonnes for cereals. The Commission proposes that all deliveries should be made by the Community itself or that, if Member States wish to continue their bilateral aid, it should at all events be limited to 700 000 tonnes. It may be noted that the worldwide aid amounts to between 6 and 7 million tonnes and that in November 1974 the World Food Conference asked that this figure be increased to 10 million tonnes;
(b) 80 000 to 120 000 tonnes for skimmed-milk powder and 45 000 to 65 000 tonnes for butteroil;
(c) 10 000 to 40 000 tonnes for sugar.

Since that time, the Commission's Memorandum of 6 March 1974 has been used as the basis for discussion in drawing up successive budgets, but no real decision has in fact been made on it. Although the Food Aid Convention, itself part of the International Wheat Agreement, has been renewed, the quantities to be provided are below those proposed by the Commission. Given the increasing urgency for longer-term programming of food aid and the misgivings of certain Member States about channelling all such aid through the Community, the Commission submitted a new three-year indicative programme for 1977-79 to the Council on 14 September 1976. The differences between this programme and that outlined in the Memorandum of 6 March 1974 were:

(a) Programming to be limited to three basic products: cereals, skimmed-milk powder, and butteroil. Deliveries of other products would be decided year by year.
(b) A smaller share of cereal aid to be provided on a Community basis. Thus Member States would be free to decide to what extent they would be offset by an increase in Community aid.

(c) Certain quantities to be adjusted: the minimum target for cereals to be changed from 1 700 000 tonnes to 1 650 000 tonnes; the range for skimmed-milk powder from 80 000 to 120 000 tonnes to 150 000 to 175 000 tonnes; no change was proposed for butteroil quantities.

The Commission's proposal of September 1976 was only partly accepted by the Budgetary Authority (essentially, the Council). It was not until March 1980 that the Council agreed to increase EEC food aid in cereals from 1 287 000 tonnes to 1 650 000 tonnes, the total being made up of direct Community aid (i.e. 720 000 tonnes up to and including the 1980 budget) and aid from the nine Member States. On the other hand, because of the situation on the milk market (see p. 180), skimmed-milk powder aid was set at 150 000 tonnes for 1976, 105 000 tonnes for 1977 and 150 000 tonnes for each of the years 1978, 1979 and 1980. But it must be acknowledged that the Community has long experienced great difficulty in implementing its programmes of skimmed-milk powder aid because the recipient countries have reception and processing problems. For butteroil, the quantity assigned has been 45 000 tonnes each year since 1976 and for sugar, 6 100 tonnes in 1976 and 1977 and 6 153 tonnes in 1978 and in 1979.

While only part (56%) of cereal food aid to developing countries is channelled via the Community, all aid in the form of milk powder and butteroil goes through Community channels.

The poorest countries have precedence as regards the granting of aid. Lately, they have received 95% of the Community's cereal food aid programme. The Commission has proposed that 93% of the butteroil programme be earmarked for them, and 88% of the skimmed-milk powder programme (first instalment). Roughly half the aid is distributed directly to the sections of the population with the most urgent needs, on a regular or emergency basis (see p. 290): 51% in the case of cereals, 46% in the case of butteroil and 42% in the case of milk powder. The remainder of the aid is intended for sale on the local markets, the income therefrom benefiting the population as a whole as it is assigned to 'counterpart funds' devoted to financing development projects.

Specific operations in the context of financial cooperation with developing countries

Over the years the Community has organized a number of specific operations for the benefit of the developing countries. In chronological order, these operations are as follows.

Assistance to Palestine Refugees—On 19 December 1972, the Council, on a proposal from the Commission, signed an agreement with the United Nations Relief and Works Agency for Palestine Refugees (UNRWA) undertaking to make contributions in cash and in kind to this organization, phased over three years, to enable it to maintain and extend its food-aid operations for the benefit of Palestine refugees living in the Middle East. A second agreement was concluded on 20 July 1976 covering the period from 1 July 1975 to 30 June 1978. It has been extended by a third agreement which runs until 31 December 1980.

Assistance to the Sahel countries—For several years a drought of a severity not experienced since 1913 gripped the Sahel, involving the following seven States: Chad, Ethiopia, Mali, Mauritania, Niger, Senegal and Upper Volta, bringing disaster upon the 7 or 8 million inhabitants of that region. Harvests dwindled to almost nothing and between 30% and 100% of the livestock, whose milk forms the staple diet of the pastoral population, has perished. The Council accordingly, on a proposal from Parliament, and in addition to a food-aid grant to the value of 48 m u.a. included in the programmes already mentioned, provided in the 1974 budget for exceptional aid amounting to 35 m u.a. plus 5 m u.a. to cover exceptional transport costs. This aid served in particular to restore the region's productive capacity. The Council's decision, taken on 10 December 1973, is of particular interest in that it supplemented EDF assistance and benefited a non-associated State, Ethiopia.

Community contribution to the United Nations International Emergency Scheme to assist the developing countries most affected by recent movements in world prices (the Cheysson Fund)—In a Communication to the Council, dated 20 March 1974, the Commission proposed that the Community should take the initiative in appealing to the rich countries to make a special effort to assist the poor countries most affected by the rises in the prices of energy products, cereals, and essential industrial products. At a special session, held from 9 April to 2 May 1974, the UN General Assembly agreed in principle that emergency assistance should be given to the most seriously affected countries, thus establishing a category of countries different both from the list drawn up by the EDF (see p. 276) and from that of the Development Aid Committee (countries with a GDP of less than USD 200 *per capita*). It was considered that USD 3 thousand million would be needed to enable these countries to obtain essential imports between April 1974 and May 1975. On 25 June 1974, the Council decided that the Community's contribution should be one-sixth of total funds or not less than USD 500 million. USD 150 million were paid from the Community budget in 1974 (124.5 m u.a.) and USD 100 million in 1975 (89 m u.a.). Bilateral contributions from the Member States came to more than USD 400 million.

The adoption of emergency procedures made it possible to distribute the aid very quickly, and its impact was considerable, both economically (for imports of absolutely essential products) and psychologically. Help was given to 42 countries, including 25 associated (or potentially associated) countries under the Lomé Convention.

Special measures—In addition, in two resolutions adopted on 30 April 1974, the Council agreed in principle to measures to assist the promotion of exports from non-associated countries on Community markets and measures to assist efforts to achieve regional or sub-regional integration between developing countries.

Aid for work done by non-governmental organizations—In 1975, the Commission recommended the co-financing in partnership with non-governmental organizations (NGOs) of microprojects for the benefit of the most underprivileged sections of the population in developing countries, whether associated or non-associated. The Council did not give this plan a favourable reception, but Parliament none the less created a budget heading for this purpose and granted funds as from 1976. This means that specific operations, limited in scope but very useful in their effect, can be implemented.

Cooperation on energy—On 31 July 1978, the Commission approved a Communication to the Council on cooperation with the non-oil-producing developing countries with a view to helping them take stock of and develop indigenous sources of energy. The Commission thought that 10 m EUA would be enough to get such cooperation off the ground, i.e. to make an initial inventory of the requirements and potential resources of certain developing countries, and for suitable pilot schemes. The Commission is also of the opinion that this avenue could be explored within the framework of the North-South Dialogue, various UN bodies and the Euro-Arab Dialogue. This project is the logical extension of efforts by the Community, and other industrialized nations, as evidenced by the Bremen and Bonn agreements, to reduce dependence on external sources of energy and cut down the use of oil as much as possible. The Commission hopes that this project will help the developing countries to avoid making the mistakes the industrialized countries made before the 1973 oil crisis, mistakes which caused them to become overdependent on imported oil. A token entry has been included in the 1980 budget.

Financial cooperation with non-associated developing countries

Following the enlargement of the European Communities, increased emphasis was placed on the aim of balancing the Community policy for cooperation with associated countries by a parallel policy relating to non-associated countries. On 16 July 1974, the Council agreed in principle to grant financial and technical aid to non-associated developing countries and on 5 November 1974 the Commission presented a 'fresco' on development aid[4] based on the formula 'to each according to his needs by bringing all our means to bear'. In it the Commission put forward a selective cooperation policy which may be summarized as follows:

(a) for 42 very poor countries (*per capita* GNP lower than USD 220; this category covers 64% of the population considered): financial and food aid and technical assistance;

(b) for 36 medium-income countries (*per capita* GNP between USD 220 and USD 530; this category covers 26% of the population considered): guarantee of export earnings, access to markets, sales promotion, and, to a much lesser extent, financial cooperation;

(c) for 21 relatively high-income countries (this category covers 10% of the population considered): industrial cooperation.

In the discussions in the Council on 22 January 1975 a fairly wide consensus was reached on this 'fresco', so the Commission, on 5 March 1975, put forward a proposal for financial and technical aid from the Community to the non-associated developing countries for the period 1976-80.[5] It asked for appropriations to be provided in the general budget to cover the food needs of the developing countries (measures designed to secure a direct increase in the quantity and quality of production; operations connected with marketing and storage; aid for applied research, vocational training, the food industry, and so on) amounting to 730 m u.a. over five years. This money was to be additional to food aid proper, but could also be used to encourage regional cooperation and integration between developing countries and to cover the cost of emergency operations in times of disaster. In addition, however, to this sum, 36 m u.a. would be provided for technical assistance in connection with the promotion of exports from non-associated developing countries.

The Council has taken no decision as to the principle on this matter, but Parliament's action in entering appropriations in the budget for this purpose has made it possible to start *ad hoc* operations.

On 18 February 1977, the Commission submitted a proposal for a Regulation concerning which Parliament gave its opinion on 16 May 1977 and the Council arrived at a common approach on 25 April 1978. An attempt is now under way to achieve conciliation between Council and Parliament on this matter (see Annex 5, p. 365).

Emergency and exceptional aid to developing countries

The European Community has made a habit of contributing towards international action to assist developing countries hit by natural disasters or serious political upheavals. There is a chapter in the Community budget for this purpose similar to that provided to deal with disasters within the Community (see p. 235). Since 1977 this chapter has been in Title 9.

Significant as these Community contributions were, they remained on the small side until 1978.[8] Since 1979, they have grown considerably, mainly because of the political situation in certain countries. In 1979, for example, one of the main causes for concern was the problem of refugees, particularly South-East Asian refugees. Several operations were mounted to help them, costing a total of 55 m EUA, 16 m EUA by way of food aid and 39 m EUA by way of emergency aid consisting of supplies of essential goods such as food, medicines, clothing, lorries, medical attention and the like. The Community has also had to come to the aid of refugees in other parts of the world: refugees from Zimbabwe in Angola and Mozambique, refugees from Ethiopia in Somalia, Ugandan refugees in the Sudan, refugees from Nicaragua in Costa Rica and Honduras and Afghan refugees in Pakistan. In all, Community emergency aid for refugees in the Third World has amounted to 65 m EUA, i.e. 52% of total aid.

In all, the Community undertook to provide 122.5 m EUA in emergency aid in 1979. There are three instruments it can use to provide rapid assistance to developing countries—whether they are associated or not—which find themselves faced with exceptional problems.

Emergency aid to disaster victims (Chapter 95 of the budget)

Twenty-three operations totalling 41.5 m EUA were carried out in 1979 for:
 (i) refugees, as mentioned above;
 (ii) victims of hurricanes in Mozambique, India, the Dominican Republic, Haiti, Saba and St Kitts;
 (iii) victims of political conflicts (Yemen), floods (Thailand and Paraguay) and volcanic eruptions (St Vincent).

As Chapter 95 was allocated only 3 m EUA in 1979, 39 m EUA had to be transferred from elsewhere (including 0.5 m EUA for floods in Portugal and an earthquake in Yugoslavia). Some of the funds needed were transferred from the EAGGF Guidance Section—which shows that a degree of flexibility has been achieved in the administration of Community finances (see footnote 12 on p. 242).

Emergency food aid

Under the food aid programme (see p. 287), the purpose of emergency aid is to respond to exceptional situations caused by events which cannot be foreseen when the annual aid programmes are drawn up. In 1979, such operations involved 186 000 tonnes of cereals, 6 800 tonnes of milk powder and 850 tonnes of butteroil, as well as an *ad hoc* supply of kidney beans to Nicaragua. Twenty-one countries received food aid, the largest proportion of which went to Cambodia and South-East Asian refugees, i.e. 107 500 tonnes of cereals (58% of the total) and 3 000 tonnes of milk powder (44% of the total). The total cost of these operations to the Community was 55 m EUA. Their corresponding value at world prices was 36 m EUA.

Exceptional aid under Article 59 of the Lomé Convention

The Lomé Convention also provides that exceptional aid may be accorded to ACP countries faced with serious difficulties resulting from natural disasters or comparable extraordinary circumstances. Thirty-one operations were launched by the Community in 1979 at a total cost of 26 m EUA. Apart from climatic hazards such as drought, floods and hurricanes, the biggest requests for aid were occasioned by political conflicts.

Apart from refugee problems in several regions of Africa, some countries have suffered, as a result of their geographical position, because conflicts cut their traditional supply lines. This is the case with landlocked countries such as Rwanda and Burundi, which received aid because of the problems caused for them by the conflict between Uganda and Tanzania. It is also the case with Zambia and Malawi, which have suffered from events in Southern Africa.

Conflicts also produce emergency situations in the countries themselves—a fact which led the Community to grant aid to Uganda, Tanzania and Chad.

Emergency and exceptional aid in 1979

In 1979, 71 m EUA of such aid went to Asia (69 m EUA to South-East Asia, mainly Cambodia), 31.5 m EUA to Africa, 19 m EUA to Latin America and 1 m EUA to the Middle East. This aid has thus acquired proportions such that it can no longer be regarded as the sum of a series of *ad hoc* measures but as the beginning of a fully-fledged policy of helping to combat misery in the Third World.

B—Budgetary and legal framework of policy concerning cooperation with developing countries

This subject warrants a certain amount of discussion, since the policy involved is an evolving one and the methods of implementing it in the context of the budget are still being hammered out.

The budget for cooperation with developing countries

It should be stressed at the outset, however, that the principle of including the funds in question in the budget has never been contested and there is no question of resorting to a solution such as that for the EDF.

Estimating appropriations for the policy concerning cooperation with developing countries

The Commission takes considerable pains to quantify the cost of each of its proposals by defining an overall amount covering a period of years (Memorandum of 6 March 1974 on food aid policy, proposal of 20 March 1974 on the Cheysson Fund, and Communication of 5 March 1975 on financial aid for non-associated countries).[5] Although these estimates go into the greatest possible detail, the figures involved nevertheless amount, in the final analysis, to allocations of a political nature.

Establishing appropriations for the policy concerning cooperation with developing countries

Apart from the food aid appropriations which are regarded as being akin to those for the EAGGF Guarantee Section, i.e. for compulsory expenditure, these appropriations are regarded as being for non-compulsory expenditure on which the European Parliament has the final word. It is in fact the leeway, or margin for manoeuvre, which Parliament has in this field which has allowed these funds to increase so significantly in recent years. However, the Council has kept the appropriations for food aid as low as it could, at levels far below those the Commission proposed.

However, what distinguishes these appropriations from those in other parts of the budget is the fact that often they have been voted even though no formal legislative basis existed. Financial aid to non-associated developing countries and aid for sales promotion and regional integration have their foundation in Council Resolutions, while the aid for the Sahel countries and for NGOs was authorized solely through the budget process. This is thus an important departure from normal Community practice, a departure which need not be regretted, since it imparts a welcome flexibility to the Community's aid mechanisms. At the same time, however, this procedure causes serious difficulties as regards budget implementation.

Structure of budgets for the policy concerning cooperation with developing countries

The Commission has made a series of adjustments to rationalize the budget nomenclature. As from 1977, Title 9 of the budget is given over entirely to cooperation with developing countries and other non-member countries. Four chapters are devoted to cooperation with the developing countries, while two are reserved for EDF appropriations. It should, however, be noted that food aid appropriations are entered both in Title 9 (Chapter 92) and in Title 6. In Title 9 they are grouped together in a chapter with separate articles for cereals, dairy produce, sugar, other products and other expenditure, and cover the value of the products donated at world prices. In Title 6 they cover refunds granted where world prices are below Community prices.[6] The Commission has proposed, without success, that these refunds be included in Chapter 92.

Implementation of appropriations for the policy concerning cooperation with developing countries

Implementation of food aid undoubtedly deserves particular mention. At the present time, most decisions in this field are taken by the Council, acting by a qualified majority (budget procedure for quantities; procedure under Article 43 of the EEC Treaty for aid in the form of dairy produce and that under Article 113 of the EEC Treaty for aid in the form of cereals). The Council, therefore, decides which countries are to receive food aid and such details as arrangements for transporting the products. The Commission is responsible for day-to-day management, including the granting of emergency aid to disaster areas, provided the Council agrees. The Commission also negotiates and concludes agreements with recipient countries. On 19 June 1978, the Commission made proposals aimed at improving and speeding up the procedures for managing food aid, in particular by acknowledging the

Commission's role under Article 205 of the EEC Treaty.[7] These proposals are still under discussion.

Turning to more general considerations going beyond the subject of food aid, it should be noted that, although implementation of these appropriations usually extends over several years, they have been differentiated only since 1978—a fact which for a long time hampered the Commission in exercising its responsibilities, through its Directorate-General for Development which is the administering department in this case. The Commission is unable to carry out to the full its task of implementing the budget, for the Council either tries to reserve authorizing powers for itself—as we saw in connection with food aid—or implementation depends on international arrangements such as those for the Cheysson Fund or aid for UNRWA. At the very least, the Council insists that the Commission submits its aid programme to it in advance (aid for the Sahel, emergency aid, etc.).

The Community's aid activities are carried out indirectly as much as directly. Food aid, for example, is often channelled through international organizations (World Food Programme, UNRWA, International Red Cross Committee, Caritas, Ecumenical Council and Unicef), the Cheysson Fund is handled by the UN and some *ad hoc* operations by NGOs. It is also worth mentioning that the dispute between the institutions over the legal basis for entries in the budget has been transferred by the Council to the question of implementation. The Council takes the view that the Commission may not commit expenditure simply because it is authorized to do so for the budget. Thus, not content with examining the aid programmes for non-associated developing countries which the Commission intends to adopt, the Council insists on approving them itself to show that it is not the Commission which has the final word. This situation provoked a hostile reaction from Parliament, and so the draft Regulation is at present blocked because of the decision-making machinery proposed by the Commission, even though the procedure (akin to the ERDF procedure) is more favourable than the present practice (see p. 78 and Annex 5, p. 368).

Checks concerning the implementation of appropriations for the policy concerning cooperation with developing countries

Checking relates to the choice of recipient countries or bodies (in the context of the annual distribution programmes) and the use to which the aid is put by the recipients. Programme preparation is based on information from various authorized sources: Commission delegates, the FAO, other donors and, above all, on the requests from the developing countries and specialist bodies. To obtain from aid applicants all relevant information regarding the purpose of the aid requested, the Commission has drawn up a questionnaire for each product concerned, which must be duly answered and sent to the Commission in support of the aid request. With the help of the answers to these questionnaires the Commission endeavours to determine in a highly precise manner not only the needs of the applicant countries (including the standard of living and the state of external finances) but also the various types of recipients envisaged. In making its proposals, the Commission gives priority to free distribution to the most underprivileged population groups and takes into account the capacity of each country's distribution infrastructure.

The arrangements for checking the use made of aid include reports submitted by the recipient countries, the Commission delegates, the recipient bodies and inspection reports made by Commission officials. As with the EAGGF, on-the-spot inspections are primarily the responsibility of the Member State whose departments are responsible for the payment of the expenditure in question under Article 8 of Regulation (EEC) No 729/70 to which Article 4 of Council Regulation (EEC) No 2681/74 of 21 October 1974 refers.

The on-the-spot inspections which the Commission is authorized to make are also similar to those provided for as regards the EAGGF since, pursuant to Article 4 of the basic Regulation No 2681/74, the provisions applicable to this Fund, i.e. Article 9 of Regulation No 729/70, also apply to the monitoring of food aid expenditure.

3. Policy concerning financial cooperation with countries in the Mediterranean area

Since 1961 the Community has signed agreements incorporating provisions for financial aid with a number of countries in the Mediterranean area.

A—Foundations of policy concerning financial cooperation with countries in the Mediterranean area

The Community signed an Association Agreement with Greece in 1961 and with Turkey in 1964. Attached to the two Agreements were Financial Protocols entitling these countries to financial aid, the purpose of which was to help them to catch up economically. Many other agreements have since been signed. The fact of the matter is that the Community is developing, with regard to the Mediterranean countries—with which it has historical, cultural and economic links—a large-scale policy comparable to that concerning the ACP countries. It is an ambitious and promising policy.

Agreements with Greece

The Association Agreement with Greece provided, in the *First Financial Protocol*, for the Community to provide financial assistance of USD 125 million in the form of loans to finance investment projects. On instructions given by the Member States, the EIB issued these loans from its own resources. To reduce the burden of debt on projects offering a limited or considerably deferred return on investment, interest relief of 3% a year, paid for by the Member States, was applied, under the terms of the Protocol, to approximately two-thirds of the total lent. Although planned to extend over a period of five years, the aid was paid out between 1963 and 1975, having been suspended in May 1967 after the Greek *coup d'état* and resumed in August 1974. Of the loans granted under the Protocol, 58% were used to finance infrastructure projects, mainly for agriculture, and the remainder were used to finance industrial projects—mostly on a small scale.

The *Second Financial Protocol*, signed in February 1977, came into force in August 1978. In 1979, the EIB granted loans totalling 114 m under this Protocol, including 104 m from its own resources. This Protocol, which is scheduled to expire at the end of October 1980, provides for aid not exceeding 280 m, including 225 m from the EIB's own resources, in some cases with interest subsidies amounting to three points from budget resources. These new loans are connected with Greece's forthcoming accession to the Community on 1 January 1981 under the Accession Treaty concluded on 28 May 1979.

Agreements with Turkey

The Association Agreement with Turkey also made provision for financial aid. Since 1964, two successive Protocols have been in force. The *First Protocol*, running from 1965 to 1969, provided for 175 m u.a. of loans at a favourable rate (between 3% and 4.5% yearly interest with a 30-year repayment period and an 8-year grace period). These loans were financed from the Member States' budgets and issued and managed by the EIB under its Special Section. The *Second Protocol* came into force in January 1973 and provides for further loans under the Special Section amounting to a total of 195 m u.a. with a further 25 m u.a. financed from the EIB's own resources. The EIB committed the whole of these sums between 1965 and 1978, mainly for industry (39%), energy (35%), transport infrastructure and agricultural improvements. In 1979, the EIB granted the first loans under the *Third Financial Protocol* totalling 82 m EUA, including 36 m EUA from its own resources.

Agreements with Portugal

Since the establishment of a new regime in Portugal in April 1974, the Community has been favourably disposed towards establishing closer relations. To help Portugal cope with its economic difficulties, the Council decided on 7 October 1975 to grant *emergency aid* in the form of EIB loans up to a ceiling of 150 m u.a. from the Bank's own resources carrying a three-point interest subsidy financed from the Community budget. In September 1976, an *Association Agreement* was signed by Portugal and the Community which provides for 200 m u.a. in the form of ordinary EIB loans, which, up to a maximum of 150 m u.a., attract a three-point interest subsidy financed from the Community budget to the value of 30 m u.a. By the end of 1977, the 150 m u.a. of emergency aid had been lent. In 1978 and 1979, 81 m u.a. of loans were granted under the Financial Protocol, (41% for industry, 32% for energy, and the rest for communications, water engineering infrastructure and agricultural improvements. Special consideration is given to investment projects helping to further Portugal's economic integration into the Community. To pave the way for accession, the Council decided in principle on 22 July 1980 to provide additional aid (see Annex 16, p. 412).

Agreements with Yugoslavia

In January 1976, the Council agreed that Yugoslavia should have access to ordinary EIB loans up to a ceiling of 50 m u.a. for investment projects of common interest. This sum was exhausted with the granting of two loans for the extension of the high-voltage electricity grid and the building of the trans-Yugoslavia motorway.

On 2 April 1980, an Agreement, with a Financial Protocol providing for the granting of 200 m u.a. of EIB loans from its own resources, was initialled by Yugoslavia and the Community. It may be implemented as from 1 July.

Agreements with the Maghreb and Mashreq countries, Malta, Israel and Cyprus

In 1976 and 1977, as part of its new Mediterranean policy, the Community concluded a series of cooperation agreements firstly with Morocco, Algeria, Tunisia and Malta and subsequently with Egypt, Jordan, Syria, Lebanon, as well as with Israel and Cyprus.

Three loans totalling 20 m EUA were granted to *Lebanon* by the EIB from its own resources as exceptional aid for the reconstruction of the country, thereby committing the whole amount authorized in November 1977 by its Board of Governors. The Agreements with the Maghreb and Mashreq countries, Malta, Cyprus and Israel came into force between August 1978 and February 1979. The first loans to these countries, totalling 184.5 m EUA, including 22.8 m EUA on special conditions, were granted in 1979. These loans generally attract an interest subsidy of two or three points financed from the Community budget, which also provides an overall guarantee covering any risks up to a limit equivalent to 75% of the total loans granted by the EIB to these countries.

B—Financial framework of policy concerning financial cooperation with countries in the Mediterranean area

The financial framework of this policy has two aspects, the first being the general budget and the second the EIB.

Framework provided by the general budget

The budget for financial cooperation with countries in the Mediterranean area—The inclusion in the budget of the aid provided for in the Financial Protocols annexed to the Agreements with the countries in the Mediterranean area sparked off a long and impassioned discussion within the Council because the parity unit of account was obsolete. In fact, its inclusion in the budget was accepted only after it had been agreed that the EUA would be applied to the general budget.

Estimating the appropriations for financial cooperation with countries in the Mediterranean area—The appropriations to be written into the budget are predetermined by the Agreements concluded by the Community with the associated countries. The problem is how to establish within the budget the pattern of commitments and payments throughout each Agreements' period of validity. The table on the following page attempts to define this process more precisely.

Establishing the appropriations for financial cooperation with countries in the Mediterranean area—These appropriations relate to compulsory expenditure decided by the Council alone. Classifying these appropriations in this category has not so far caused any real problems, although the classification is disputed by Parliament. The 1976 budget was the first to contain money for this policy, although the amounts involved were still only modest sums to cover interest subsidies on loans granted by the EIB to Portugal.

The discussions on the 1977 budget produced a major dispute over the inclusion in the budget of aid for the Maghreb countries and Malta. In fact, Parliament pushed this through, even though it lacked decision-making powers.

Structure of the appropriations for financial cooperation with countries in the Mediterranean area—One chapter was reserved in Title 9 of the 1978 budget to accommodate these appropriations. There are seven articles for this purpose. An eighth article is for a guarantee

The Community's Mediterranean commitments

(m EUA)

Recipient countries		Sums granted		Total
		EEC budget	EIB	
Portugal				
Emergency aid (*)		30	150	180
Financial Protocol (**)		30	200	230
	Total	60	350	410
Greece		55	225	280
Turkey		220	90	310
Malta (**)		10	16	26
Cyprus (**)		10	20	30
Maghreb				
Algeria		44	70	114
Morocco		74	56	130
Tunisia		54	41	95
	Total	172	167	339
Mashreq				
Egypt		77	93	170
Syria		26	34	60
Jordan		22	18	40
Lebanon				
— Financial Protocol		10	20	30
— Emergency aid			20	20
	Total	135	185	320
Israel			30	30
Yugoslavia (*)			50	50
	Grand total	662	1 133	1 795

These agreements expire on 31 October 1981, apart from those whose funds are exhausted (*) and those scheduled to run until 31 October 1983 (**).

for the EIB in respect of the repayment of the loans it grants at the Community's request. To this end, a budget heading has to be created with a token entry, so that—should the debtor default—funds can be transferred to cover the repayments to the EIB. The Community guarantee covers 75% of the total outstanding debts of the countries of the Mediterranean area and 100% in the case of the emergency aid for Portugal. A ninth article is for appropriations for cooperation with the Arab countries at regional level.

Implementing the appropriations for financial cooperation with countries in the Mediterranean area—Formal implementation has been delayed because of the time needed to ratify the Agreements. This subject has in the meantime led to a discussion of the Commission's right to set up delegations in these countries in order to see to it that these Cooperation Agreements are properly applied. The Council ultimately denied the Commission such powers—although, legally speaking, this would seem to be covered by the Commission's organization powers—and itself authorized the setting up of delegations in the Maghreb and

Mashreq countries and in Israel. The delays in the ratification procedures shortened the implementation period, since the cut-off date was generally fixed in advance at 31 October 1981. However, implementation was not held up, since the Commission (the Directorate-General for Development and the Directorate-General for External Relations) and the EIB did not wait for the agreements to come into force formally before compiling their dossiers. As with the non-associated developing countries (see p. 293), the Council takes over from the Commission when it is a matter of deciding on the financing of projects, and the Commission can merely express a reservation regarding the manner of depriving it of its budget implementation powers.

The type of expenditure varies, though it usually covers interest subsidies on loans granted by the EIB,[3] grant aid or loans on special conditions, i.e. a long term (30 to 40 years, for example), a grace period for repayment (8 to 10 years, for example) and a very low interest rate (1 to 2.5%).

Framework provided by the EIB

The exception provided for in Article 18 of the Statute of the EIB has been used in a more general manner since 1962 to authorize the EIB to help the Community to cooperate financially with an increasing number of developing countries. The financing provided by the EIB under various cooperation agreements, conventions and decisions is for investment projects designed to further the economic development of the countries concerned.

In this way the EIB's activities have been gradually extended to include Greece, Turkey and Portugal, as well as the associated countries. In 1977, the EIB began helping Yugoslavia at the Community's request and, in 1978, began providing funds, authorized by its Board of Governors, for the reconstruction of Lebanon. Finally, in 1979, it provided assistance for the first time for various countries in the Mediterranean area under agreements signed by the Community and the Maghreb countries (Algeria, Morocco and Tunisia), the Mashreq countries (Egypt, Jordan, Lebanon and Syria), Malta, Cyprus and Israel.

The loans are from the EIB's own resources[3] or from budget funds.

4. Resources used to finance cooperation with non-member countries

After analysing these resources since 1958, we shall endeavour to place this political aid in its proper context.

A—Resources used from 1958 to 1980

As in the three preceding chapters, we shall first point out the resources available in 1979 and in 1980. A few words are needed to introduce the table concerning these resources. It shows both budget funds and EDF resources.

Budget and non-budget funds for policy concerning cooperation
with non-member countries

(m EUA)

Instrument	1979		1980	
	For commitment	For payment	For commitment	For payment
1st, 2nd and 3rd EDFs	–	42.0	–	35.0
4th EDF	600.0	420.3	–	522.5
5th EDF			300.0	106.0
Food aid	289.9	289.9	395.4	395.4
	(351.8)[1]	(351.8)[1]	(294.5)[1]	(294.5)[1]
Non-associated developing countries	139.6	60.6	145.3	26.8
Specific and exceptional measures	17.5	13.0	18.5	55.2
Cooperation with countries in the Mediterranean area	195.1	128.7	178.2	137.6
Cooperation concerning commodities	(379.8)[2]	(379.8)[2]	(210.0)[2]	(210.0)[2]
Operation of the Commission delegations in the developing countries	5.3	5.3	26.5	26.5
Total	1 247.4	959.8	1 103.9	1 305.0
	(1 979.0)[3]	(1 691.4)[3]	(1 608.4)[3]	(1 809.5)[3]

[1] The appropriations for food aid refunds (see p. 185) are in Titles 6 and 7 (EAGGF Guarantee Section). They are shown here in brackets for information purposes.
[2] The appropriations for ACP/India sugar (see p. 280) are in Titles 6 and 7 (EAGGF Guarantee Section). They are shown here in brackets for information purposes.
[3] Total, including the appropriations in brackets.

The resources used from 1958 to 1979 took the form of non-repayable expenditure (see Annex 12, pp. 393 to 399) or EIB loans.

Non-repayable expenditure

Expenditure under the First EDF covered by contributions from the Member States amounted to 568.6 m u.a., under the Second EDF 726.5 m u.a., under the Third EDF 801.4 m u.a. and under the Fourth EDF 992.2 m u.a., giving a total of 3 088.7 m u.a. The expenditure included in the budget amounted to 1 995.1 m u.a., as follows: 1 353.3 m u.a. for food aid (not including refunds, which are included in the expenditure of the EAGGF Guarantee Section), 144.3 m u.a. for cooperation with non-associated developing countries, 213.5 m u.a. for the Cheysson Fund, 35 m u.a. for aid to the Sahel countries and 249 m u.a. for interest subsidies on loans granted to Portugal, payments to UNRWA and various other schemes.[8]

The breakdown of EDF operations is as follows: 42% relate to infrastructure, 37% to rural modernization and 21% to social development. The allocation of contracts among the Member States of the Community is by no means proportionate to their respective financial contributions. Some Member States—France, Italy and Belgium for example—are very active in this field, while others are less so.

Expenditure on emergency aid is growing: 2.4 m u.a. in 1976, 1.7 m u.a. in 1977, 2.2 m EUA in 1978 and 42 m EUA in 1979 (see p. 289).

EIB loans

Between 1963 and 1978, EIB *operations using its own resources* in the field of financial cooperation with non-member countries amounted to 1 165.8 m u.a., as follows: 146.1 m u.a. under the First and Second Yaoundé Conventions, 272.6 m u.a. under the First Lomé Convention, 240.4 m u.a. as aid to Greece, 61 m u.a. as aid to Turkey (First and Second Protocols), 231 m u.a. for Portugal, 50 m u.a. for Yugoslavia, 50 m u.a. for the Maghreb countries, 111.7 m u.a. for the Mashreq countries and 3 m u.a. for Malta. *Operations involving the resources of the Special Section* amounted to 667.7 m u.a. The Member States make financial contributions according to a scale similar to that for the EDF. The breakdown is as follows: 10 m u.a. for Greece, 416 m u.a. for Turkey, 14 m u.a. for Morocco, 3.8 m u.a. for the Maghreb countries and 5 m u.a. for Malta, and 142 m u.a. under the First and Second Yaoundé Conventions and 76.9 m u.a. under the First Lomé Convention.

In all, the EIB carried out operations amounting to 1 833.5 m u.a. as follows: 1 195.9 m u.a. in countries in the Mediterranean area and 637.6 m u.a. in ACP and OCT countries.

B—The role of EEC public aid

Substantial as it is, Community aid represents barely 5% of the public development aid granted by the nine Member States. For years the Community has been trying to achieve the target, set by a UN recommendation, of devoting 0.7% of GNP to public development aid. In 1979, the average 'score' for countries on the OECD's Development Aid Committee was 0.34% (better than that of the United States (0.19%) and Japan (0.32%), but in general worse than that of the Member States of the Community, the Netherlands achieving 0.93%,[9] Denmark 0.75%, France 0.59%, Belgium 0.56%, the United Kingdom 0.52%. However, the Federal Republic of Germany and Italy are only 0.44% and 0.10% respectively.

Cooperation policy is undoubtedly one of the most successful of the Community's policies which have financial implications. Though it is by no means fully on a Community footing, it still covers a very wide range of activities. However, it is undoubtedly the spirit underlying the whole endeavour, and in particular the Lomé Conventions, which is the most notable feature, for the Community and the ACP countries have embarked on an unprecedented undertaking based on human solidarity and mutual respect within the general context of North-South relations. As Mr Claude Cheysson said at the signing of the Second Lomé Convention on 31 October 1979: 'What is fundamental, I think, is the contract between the two groups of countries—the European Community and Africa with its Caribbean and Pacific brothers. Both groups have a single voice, so that neither can the one side interfere in the issues uniting or opposing Europeans, nor the other in those linking or dividing the ACP. Thus all of us are bound to respect each other's individuality, the right to differ, to choose alliances, economic systems and cultural patterns freely.'

In terms of resources, cooperation policy is the second largest Community policy, albeit a long way behind agricultural policy. There is now a major discussion going on within the Community and its institutions about hunger in the world. What will be Europe's response to this problem? Our future depends on it.

[1] Exports of iron ore from deposits now being worked will continue to be covered by Stabex for five years (1979-84).

[2] The Fourth EDF is implemented in European units of account (EUA), and the Member States' contributions are called in twice a year by the Commission in EUA. They are paid over by the Member States in their respective currencies at the exchange rates on the due date. The Community's commitments to the ACP countries are then expressed in EUA. These commitments are formalized for each project in a financing agreement which specifies the maximum amount in EUA.

On the basis of these appropriations in EUA, the ACP States conclude project contracts with construction firms, equipment suppliers, consultants, etc.

Under the EDF Financial Regulation, contractors may express their claims (in part at least) in EUA. Where this option is exercised by the contractor, payment of the claim expressed in EUA is made in the currency of a Community Member State or an ACP State on the basis of the parity on the day preceding payment (Article 45(4) of the EDF Financial Regulation).

Payment orders issued by the national authorities of the ACP countries are presented to the EDF paying agents with which the Commission has accounts expressed in the currency of a Member State. The Commission's account with the paying agency is debited by the requested amount in the currency or its equivalent value in the currency of the ACP State (at the rate on the day of conversion). The central accounts department of the European Development Fund records in EUA the amounts debited from the accounts of these paying agents on the basis of the rate for converting between the EUA and the European currency in question on the day when the debit entry is made.

The EUA is therefore used extensively, though not fully, for EDF purposes; and this fact can be regarded as a step in the right direction.

[3] Outside the Community, in the African, Caribbean and Pacific countries, in Greece and Portugal and in the other Mediterranean countries (except Israel, Turkey and Yugoslavia), loans from the EIB's own resources qualify, as a general rule, for interest rate subsidies from Community resources. The interest subsidy is three points in the case of the ACP States, Greece and Portugal and two points for other countries in the Mediterranean area.

[4] See Supplement 8/74—Bull. EC.

[5] In its Communication to the Council of 5 March 1975, the Commission proposed a five-year timetable for non-associated developing countries starting in 1976: 100 m u.a. in 1976, 120 m u.a. in 1977, 140 m u.a. in 1978, 170 m u.a. in 1979 and 200 m u.a. in 1980. The Budgetary Authority, however, only authorized a 20 m u.a. payment appropriation in the 1976 budget, 45 m u.a. in the 1977 budget, 70 m u.a. in the 1978 budget, 110 m u.a. in the 1979 budget and 138.5 m EUA in the 1980 budget. Accordingly, and as no mechanism for implementing the aid in question has yet been defined, the Commission proposed regarding 1976 and 1977 as the preparatory phase and 1978 as the first full year of the scheme and reviewing the original timetable. The Commission would like it extended by two years so that the 200 m u.a. target is reached in 1981.

[6] Mention should be made of the judgment of the Court of Justice of the European Communities of 11 January 1973 (*Government of the Kingdom of the Netherlands v Commission of the European Communities*). In it the Court finds that, if refunds are payable, the Community must pay them to the exporting State regardless of whether commercial operations or food aid operations are involved. In upholding that refunds can also be made in the latter case if they contribute towards fulfilling the aims of the common agricultural policy, the Court allowed that Article 39 of the EEC Treaty was a valid legal basis for food aid. The Community is now seeking to establish a legal basis specifically for food aid; this entails going beyond the Court's interpretation.

[7] See OJ C 168 of 13.7.1978. The Commission's proposal on food aid is that:

(a) The Council, acting on proposals from the Commission, should specify the commodities to be supplied as aid; decide on the total quantities of each product on an annual or multiannual basis (in particular apportioning cereal aid between Community and national operations); decide as to the principle of renewing and concluding food aid agreements (the Commission conducting the negotiations with the help of the Article 113 Committee); determine in good time (before the end of October each year) the general guidelines for aid in the following year and the criteria for examining applications for aid.

(b) The Commission should have general powers over food aid, and in particular that it should decide the annual or multiannual apportionment of the quantities in question among countries and organizations, and the volume of the reserve; decide on the derived products to be supplied as food aid; decide on matters relating to the transport of products. The Commission also proposed the setting up of Food Aid Committees (along the lines of the ERDF Committee) to assist it, consisting of representatives of the Member States and chaired by the Commission. This Committee would have to be consulted on matters within the Commission's jurisdiction and would express opinions by a qualified majority. In the event of disagree-

ment with the Commission, the Council would be able to take a decision differing from that of the Commission within two months.

Some progress has undoubtedly been made with reducing the time it takes to deliver food aid, and the Council has adopted measures to streamline the procedures for emergency and normal food aid, but the Commission still feels that new measures are needed to end the anomalous way responsibilities are divided at present between it and the Council.

[8] Urgent or exceptional aid was granted in 1975 to Vietnam (refugees), Angola (refugees), Turkey (earthquake); in 1976 to Guatemala (earthquake), Lebanon (political troubles), Mozambique (refugees), Turkey (earthquake) and Ethiopia (political troubles); in 1977 to Romania (floods), Cape Verde (drought), India (typhoon); and in 1978 to Laos and Thailand (floods), Sri Lanka (hurricane), Burma (refugees from Bangladesh) and Nicaragua (refugees from Costa Rica).

[9] The two countries which devoted the highest percentage of their GDP to public development aid in 1979 were Sweden with 0.94% and Norway with 0.93%. The Netherlands was third, followed by Denmark in fourth place, and France fifth.

Chapter XV:
Financing the administrative organization of the European Community

One part—even if a relatively small one—of the Communities' resources is used to cover the administrative operating costs. It is nevertheless interesting to consider the policy which the Community authorities wanted or have been able to apply with the funds earmarked for organization. We shall first look at the expenditure assigned to this policy and then examine two major elements thereof: staff and organization policy, and the recruitment of extra staff, or the addition of technical and material resources, looking lastly at the developments in the budget sector and the budget resources allocated to this organization.

1. The management costs of the Community's administrative organization

The budget framework considered will be that of the financial year 1980. It is not possible within this book to analyse the development of this framework over a period of 27 years, but in fact there has been little change in the overall structure since 1968, when the Executives were merged. On the other hand, the total resources allocated to running the Community's administrative organization have increased considerably over the years, although at the same time their relative share in the budget has decreased.

From 1968 to 1976, the administrative operating appropriations of the European Communities appeared in Titles 1 and 2 of the sections of the budget devoted to the Community institutions (Council, Parliament, Commission and Court of Justice) and in the three annexes reserved for certain bodies (Economic and Social Committee, Audit Board and ECSC Auditor). From the 1977 financial year onwards a fifth section was added for the Court of Auditors, and the annexes for the Audit Board and the ECSC Auditor were discontinued.

In the appropriations for the first two titles of the budget, a fundamental distinction has to be made between those earmarked for the operation of the administrative machinery of the Community and the other appropriations.

A—The costs of the administrative machinery of the European Community

The costs of the administrative machinery of the European Community comprise staff costs and operating costs.

Staff costs

The appropriations expenditure on staff appear in Title 1 of each section of the budget under 'Expenditure relating to persons working with the institution'. This title generally contains the same six chapters for each institution or organ; Chapters 10 (Members of the institution), 11 (Staff), 12 (Allowances and expenses on entering and on leaving the service and on transfer), 13 (Missions and duty travel), 14 (Social welfare) and 15 (In-service training and further training of staff). The only differences arise from the differences between the institutions. For instance, only in Chapter 10 of the sections relating to the Commission, Court of Justice and Court of Auditors are appropriations entered to cover the salaries and other entitlements of the Members of these institutions. Chapter 10 of the section relating to Parliament, on the other hand, includes only appropriations for 'Travel and subsistence allowances. Notice of meetings and connected expenditure', to reimburse the Members of the European Parliament for their travel and subsistence expenses; it does not include any appropriation for salaries since these are paid at national level in accordance with national rules; this chapter also includes the secretarial allowances for Members of Parliament.[1] The Council section does not include this chapter at all, as the members of the national governments who attend meetings of the Council are not paid salaries or allowances by the Communities. There are other distinctive features, involving only very small sums, in the appropriations for the various institutions. The section relating to the Council, for instance, does not include appropriations for in-service training (Chapter 15).

Each section of the budget is accompanied by an establishment plan which forms an integral part of the budget and which has binding effect, as do the appropriations entered under the various budget headings. There are eight establishment plans, of which the Commission has four: one for staff paid out of the operating appropriations (Title 1), two for staff paid out of the research and investment appropriations and one for the Office for Official Publications, the other four institutions having one each. The budget of the Economic and Social Committee is an annex to the Council budget. The Committee does not have its own establishment plan either, as the staff it may recruit are listed in a column of the Council's establishment plan.

The eight plans give a very detailed breakdown of the posts which may be filled, showing category, service and grade (28 headings).

Operating expenditure

The appropriations for the operating expenditure are contained in Title 2 of each section of the budget. This title covers 'Buildings, equipment and miscellaneous operating expenditure'. It includes ten chapters which usually occur in the section devoted to each institution; each chapter covers a different category. Only the first seven form part of the administrative machinery of the Community. In the budget nomenclature for 1980 this includes expenditure on immovable property (Chapter 20), data processing (Chapter 21), movable property (Chapter 22), current administrative expenditure (Chapter 23), entertainment expenses (Chapter 24), meetings and experts (Chapter 25) and studies (Chapter 26). Within this expenditure there are sometimes differences between the institutions because of the functions assigned to them by the Treaties and the facilities which the Budgetary Authority wishes to grant them. For instance, only the Commission has substantial appropriations for data processing.

B—Expenditure on publishing and information

In Chapter 27 of Title 2, each institution has appropriations for publishing, to cover the publication in the *Official Journal* of texts relating to the institution and its own publications. On the other hand, only the Commission and Parliament have appropriations for information which, for the first time, are fairly substantial because of the duties of these institutions. It has been pointed out, however, that these appropriations are not as high as the advertising expenditure of a large company.

C—Subsidies

The Commission can grant subsidies of two kinds:

Subsidies for balancing budgets
(Chapter 28 of Title 2)

Certain agencies are, as it were, satellites of the Community. The administrative operating costs they incur are generally covered in full by a Community subsidy, which is entered in the Commission section of the budget. There are four balancing subsidies in this chapter: the Supply Agency, the Business Cooperation Centre, the European Schools and the Office for Official Publications.

On the other hand, three other subsidies occur among the appropriations entered for specific purposes: in Title 3, the subsidies to the European Centre for the Development of Vocational Training and the Foundation for the Improvement of Living and Working Conditions, and in Title 9, the subsidy to the European Association for Cooperation.

Subsidies and financial contributions
(Chapter 29 of Title 2)

This chapter comprises a number of rather disparate appropriations, but their common feature is that they are used by the Commission on behalf of the Community to assist certain organizations dedicated to the cause of European integration and to finance certain European activities.

Parliament also has appropriations of this type.

D—Lump-sum repayment to the Member States of the costs incurred in collecting own resources

Another category of expenditure can be likened to that involved in the management of the administrative organization of the Community and appears in Chapter 40 of Title 4: 'Repayments and aid to Member States—miscellaneous'. The last paragraph of Article 3(1) of the Decision of 21 April 1970 lays down that the Communities shall refund to each Member State 10% of the amounts paid as own resources to cover the expenses incurred in the collection of these resources; this is because there is no Community service for the fiscal collection thereof (see p. 83), the administration of the collection system being delegated but paid for out of the Community budget under the section relating to the Commission.

The disadvantage of this system of repayment is that it inflates the Community budget. Some people therefore recommend streamlining the procedure and only paying to the European Communities the net proceeds of own resources. If this arrangement were adopted, it would compromise the gross budget principle.

In the Commission, the appropriations earmarked for the administrative machinery are generally administered by the Directorate-General for Personnel and Administration. Repayments to the Member States are the responsibility of the Directorate-General for Budgets.

2. Staff and organization policy of the European Community

The European Communities have the largest payroll of any international organization at the present time, numbering almost 18 000 persons in 1980 (17 941 to be exact).

We shall consider in succession some fundamental aspects of the European Communities' staff policy, i.e. the status and remuneration of the staff, the numbers, the organization and operation of the various services and the European Schools.

A—The legal status and remuneration of European Community staff

The decisions taken as regards the status and remuneration of the staff of the European Communities have had implications for the budget.

The legal status of European Community staff

The European Communities possess a very elaborate and diversified legal system for the benefit of their staff, defined by the 'Staff Regulations of Officials' and 'Conditions of Employment of Other Servants'.

Evolution of the legal status of
European Community staff

This was not the case at the very beginning, when the ECSC institutions only awarded contracts for specific periods, which basically stated the remuneration (in fact a percentage of that of the members of the High Authority) and described the duties to be performed. Soon, however, in fact in 1956, Staff Regulations were introduced, giving the employees job security, a career system, an up-to-date system of pay and its modern adjuncts (various allowances, social security system and pension scheme). With the creation of the EAEC (Euratom) the question was raised as to whether this civil service system was appropriate for the recruitment of scientists and technical staff working on multiannual nuclear research programmes. This question was answered in the affirmative at the time, in 1962, although the decision was subsequently held to be somewhat over-rigid.

Later, the Commission of the European Communities proposed a system of contracts for all staff whose work was directly connected with a research programme. This change took place on 29 October 1976, giving all staff paid from the research appropriations the status of staff on contract ('temporary staff'), so that only established officials with 'acquired rights' were covered by the Staff Regulations.

There have been two other relatively important changes to the legal provisions of the Regulations: one on 30 June 1972, the other on 4 May 1978.

Under the Staff Regulations, no appointment (or promotion) of an official may be made for any purpose other than that of filling a vacant post in the list of posts appended to the section or annex to the section of the budget relating to an institution or organ of the Communities. The posts are classified into four categories A, B, C and D in descending order of seniority depending on the nature and importance of the official's duties.

There is also a Language Service comprising six grades equivalent to the lower six grades of Category A. 93.4% of the staff of the European Communities are officials, and 6.6% are 'other servants', i.e. staff on contract not covered by the Staff Regulations. The latter comprise the following four groups: temporary staff occupying a post in the 'list of posts', and the staff paid from the overall appropriations: auxiliary staff, local staff and special advisers.

The Staff Regulations of the European Communities soon became a model and a target to be achieved for the staff of international organizations, although some governments find it too rigid a system and too favourable. One might in fact consider it only natural for the European Communities to give the status of official to the forerunners of those who will one day be the civil servants of a European Confederation. The system is admittedly more expensive and binding than a system of contracts, but it is a modest price to pay for the construction of one of the pillars of Europe.

The 'termination of service' operations

One should not conclude, however, that the European public service is a privileged body, protected from every kind of difficulty. Three times, in fact, in little more than a decade, it has been shaken up by special termination of service operations, although the 'volunteers' concerned did admittedly receive generous severance payments.

The first of these occasions was in 1968, when the single Commission had the difficult task of simultaneously merging the services of the three former Executives and reducing the staff establishment by 254 posts. Council Regulation (EEC, Euratom, ECSC) No 259/68 of 29

February 1968—the so-called 'termination of service regulation'—waived the Staff Regulations, made it possible to appeal for voluntary redundancies and encouraged certain departures among the highest administrative grades (A/1, A/2 and A/3). The breakdown by category was as follows: 114 A grades (8 A/1, 12 A/2, 44 A/3—i.e. 64 top administrative officials—and 50 A/4 to A/7), 13 LA, 62 B, 54 C and 11 D.

The second of these operations was carried out in 1973 at the time of the first enlargement. To complete it successfully, the Commission was authorized in the 1973 budget to recruit a further 1 008 staff. At the same time, a new 'termination of service regulation' waiving the Staff Regulations—Council Regulation (ECSC, EEC Euratom) No 2530/72 of 4 December 1972—was adopted in order to free certain posts filled by nationals of the Six for occupation by nationals of the three new Member States. Only the five highest administrative grades were involved this time, not posts from all categories as in 1968. The aim which the Commission had courageously adopted was to welcome the nationals from the new Member States without at the same time expanding the upper strata of the pyramid by creating additional administrative posts. The aim was achieved. In all, 247 posts were made vacant, taking to 1 255 the number of posts to be provided at the time of the enlargement for administrative needs. The breakdown by grade was as follows: 14 A/1, 42 A/2, 83 A/3 (i.e. 139 top administrative officials), 72 A/4 and 36 A/5.

Research staff were not included on this occasion, although a 'termination of service regulation' was also adopted—Council Regulation (ECSC, EEC, Euratom) No 1543/73 of 4 June 1973—enabling 110 posts to be freed, as it happened, from among all categories. The breakdown in this instance was: 65 A (1 A/1, 6 A/2 and 16 A/3—i.e. 23 top management officials—12 A/4, 20 A/5, 9 A/6 and 1 A/7), 38 B and 1 C.

The third of these special operations is in the process of being decided. In view of the forthcoming accession of Greece and the consequent need to recruit a number of officials from that country to the Community's institutions—but also in order to offset the unusual, temporary, impasse to careers and re-establish a sounder career pattern—the Commission presented the Council on 13 June 1979 with an amendment to the Staff Regulations designed to facilitate retirement at 60 by introducing pension bonuses and the possibility of buying supplementary pension rights. The Commission also decided on 31 July 1980 to put a further, supplementary, measure (lasting till 1986 only) to the Council, which would mean that the existing organization of departments—after restructuring—would be unaffected by successive enlargements. This new temporary measure concerning staff management should enable the Community's institutions to offer A/3 and A/4 officials, who have been in the last step of their grade for at least two years and are aged 55 or over, the possibility of early retirement with an allowance equal to 70% of their basic salary up to the age of 65, when they would receive a pension taking into account the period of allowance.

The remuneration of European Community staff

In 1952 the High Authority of the ECSC, which had to recruit high-grade staff quickly, laid down a system of remuneration to enable it to attract suitable staff from the coal and steel industries, i.e. by giving them higher salaries than those offered by these two industries. This—initially—extremely favourable system gradually deteriorated because the salaries were not updated. In 1962, following the adoption of Staff Regulations to cover the staff of the three European Communities, a new system was instituted (Article 65 of the Staff Regulations) which provides: first, for a review of remunerations in line with increases in the cost of living, using a joint index prepared by the Statistical Office of the European Communities; and, secondly, an adjustment to take into account increases in salaries in the public service and the needs of recruitment. As the staff did not consider this system was properly applied, over several years they launched a series of strikes, led by the trade unions, which paralysed the Communities. On 21 March 1972 the Council, in agreement with the Commission and the Liaison Committee of the Trade Unions and Staff Associations, adopted a method to apply for three years which based the variation in purchasing power on two indicators, i.e. the specific index of salaries in the national public services and the *per capita* emoluments indicator in the public services; the method made no change in the system for offsetting rises in the cost of living. Since then a semi-automatic system has operated, enabling European officials to enjoy adjustments to their salaries to take account of rises in the cost of living and updating their remuneration in line with the weighted average increase in purchasing power in the Community. On 29 June 1976 a new agreement was reached, in which the adjustment of the salaries of European officials would be covered by a policy designed to ensure, in the medium term, that these salaries progressed in line with the average remuneration of the national civil servants of the Member States. The automatic arrangement set up by the agreement of 21 March 1972 thenceforth disappeared. From a base of 100 in 1962, remuneration had reached a figure of 435.4 in nominal value on 1 January 1980 and 156.6 in real terms. The difference between the salaries of European officials and national officials has remained fairly constant, the former still being higher than the latter in spite of the erosion which has taken place. It is sometimes asked if this difference is justified. In our view it is so, for two reasons: work in an international organization is demanding and calls for special qualities; secondly, the European officials live for the most part in a country which is not their own, which involves them in undeniable financial burdens.

B—The staff complement of the European Community

In a praiseworthy but at the same time unrealistic spirit, the drafters of the Treaty of Paris included the following clause: 'The institutions of the Community shall carry out these activities with a minimum of administrative machinery and in close cooperation with the parties concerned' (last paragraph of Article 5). On the merging of the Executives in 1967, however, the High Authority had 949 officials on its establishment, including 257 officials in Category A. This comment is not intended as a criticism of the policy conducted by the High Authority of the ECSC between 1952 and 1967, but is simply a general comment. It has to be made at the beginning of this section, since there is no doubt that the staff of the Community institutions is numerous and sometimes inadequate, because of the difficulties facing European integration.

In considering the staff complement of the European Communities, a distinction has first to be made between those of the Commission and those of the other Community institutions or organs, because of the duties entrusted by the Treaties to the different institutions. While the staff of the Council, Parliament or the Court of Justice or the Court of Auditors constitute a secretariat, a court record office or an audit office, the Commission staff form an executive responsible for initiating policies, drafting legislation and performing administrative functions, i.e. duties requiring a large staff. We shall first consider the staff of the Commission and then the other Community institutions or agencies.

Staff complement of the Commission of the European Communities

In 1980 the Commission had a staff of 12 723. According to the staff tables annexed to the budget, it is authorized to fill 11 874 posts shown in its 4 lists of staff. This figure is made up of 11 254 permanent posts, i.e. 8 435 operational staff, 2 574 paid from the research appropriations (of the 2 724 in the list, 150 are temporary posts) and 245 for the Office for Official Publications, plus 620 temporary posts: 450 under the operating budget and 150 on research activities, and 20 temporary posts authorized for the Office for Official Publications. The Commission also has about 849 staff paid out of the total appropriations.

This staff is divided into two groups: the 'administrative' staff, generally working in Brussels and Luxembourg, although sometimes elsewhere in the world (see p. 317), and the 'research' staff, assigned to the four establishments of the JRC, or to 'indirect action', i.e. in public or private organizations associated with the Community; the latter staff work all over the territory of the Community.

Mention should be made here of the staff of the European Association for Cooperation (EAC) (see p. 282), since they are in the service of the Commission. There are 1 303 staff, broken down as follows: the staff posted to the headquarters of the EAC in Brussels (53), the delegates, advisers and attachés to the delegations, the technical assistants and staff on special contracts (342), and the local staff assigned to the delegations and to technical assistance (908). At present the expenditure to cover the remuneration of this staff and the other operating costs are borne by the general budget (Commission section) in respect of the headquarters staff and by the European Development Fund (EDF) as regards the rest. On top of this figure of 1 303 staff, we must mention a further 97 persons in the eight

Total staff complement of the Commission in 1980

Posts	Operating budget		Research appropriations		Office for Official Publications	Total
	Permanent	Temporary	Scientific	Administrative		
Category A	2 163	160	771	47	14	3 155
Category B	1 740	91	801	125	128	2 885
Category C	2 865	115	589	337	106	4 012
Category D	443	10	31	23	17	524
LA	1 224	74	0	0	0	1 298
	8 435	450	2 192	532	265	11 874
Total of 4 lists of staff (1)	8 885		2 724		265	11 874
Local staff	606		0		51	657
Auxiliary interpreters	3		0		0	3
Other auxiliaries	95		60		5	160
Special advisers	29		0		0	29
Total other staff (2)	733		60		56	849
Grand total (1)+(2)	9 618		2 784		321	12 723

delegations to the southern Mediterranean countries, whose salaries and operating costs are borne by the general budget (Commission section).

The staff at the disposal of the Commission is thus in excess of 14 100 (14 116 to be precise).

Staff complement of the other European Community institutions and organs

The numbers of such staff in 1980 were as follows:

Total staff complements of the other institutions and organs in 1980

Staff	Parliament	Council	Court of Justice	Court of Auditors	Economic and Social Committee	Total
Officials: A	253	184	57	74	41	609
B	334	142	71	54	54	655
C	941	758	113	60	146	2 018
D	265	209	31	21	26	552
LA	376	300	89	22	67	854
Temporary staff: A	72	3	0	22	0	97
B	25	3	0	0	0	28
C	61	0	2	6	2	71
D	2	0	0	0	0	2
LA	0	0	0	0	3	3
Total in lists of staff (1)	2 329	1 599	363	259	339	4 889
Other staff						
Local staff	30	36	9	4	11	90
Auxiliaries	177	13	25	4	18	237
Special advisers	1	0	1	0	0	2
Total other staff (2)	208	49	35	8	29	329
Grand total (1)+(2)	2 537	1 648	398	267	368	5 218

The staff of these other institutions and organs are posted either to Brussels (Council and Economic and Social Committee), or Luxembourg (Parliament, Court of Justice and Court of Auditors).

Staff trends in Community institutions since 1968

Having thus sketched the situation in 1980, it is interesting to analyse the trends in the number of posts authorized since the merging of the 3 Executives in 1967, the 1968 budget having been the first 'merged' budget. The authorizations given for that year therefore provide the basis for comparisons (except for the Office for Official Publications which was not set up until 1970). The following three tables show how the numbers of posts (permanent and temporary) have changed, first for Categories A, B, C and D, then for LA, and finally the totals for all posts.

Increase in Category A, B, C and D posts from 1968 to 1980

New posts		Percentage increase	
Commission (operating budget)	+3 101	Court of Auditors	+1 147.4
Parliament	+1 537	Parliament	+ 369.4
Council	+ 831	Economic and Social Committee	+ 183.2
Office for Official Publications	+ 265	Council	+ 177.6
Court of Auditors	+ 218	Court of Justice	+ 188.4
Economic and Social Committee	+ 174	Office for Official Publications	+ 167.7
Court of Justice	+ 179	Commission (operating budget)	+ 69.1
Commission (research)	− 26	Commission (research)	− 0.9
Total	+6 279	Average	+ 75.4

This table shows that the increase in the number of posts authorized for each institution has varied considerably. A substantial increase was authorized for all the institutions in 1973 because of the enlargement of the Communities as a result of the accession of three new Member States (plus 15.8% on average). The increases for the Court of Auditors are explained by the change in the nature of that institution; the same applies to Parliament.

Increase in posts in the Language Service (LA posts) from 1968 to 1980

New posts		Percentage increase	
Commission (operating budget)	+ 831	Court of Justice	+493.3
Parliament	+ 278	Parliament	+283.7
Council	+ 205	Economic and Social Committee	+218.2
Court of Justice	+ 74	Council	+215.8
Economic and Social Committee	+ 48	Commission (operating budget)	+177.9
Court of Auditors	+ 22	Court of Auditors	+ 15.8
Total	+1 458	Average	+209.2

The increase in the number of linguists is therefore considerable and is the result of the Community's inevitable communication problem. We shall refer to this again.

Total increase in numbers of officials from 1968 to 1980

New posts		Percentage increase	
Commission (operating budget)	+3 932	Court of Auditors	+1 263.2
Parliament	+1 815	Parliament	+ 353.1
Council	+1 036	Court of Justice	+ 230.0
Office for Official Publications	+ 265	Economic and Social Committee	+ 189.7
Economic and Social Committee	+ 222	Council	+ 184.0
Court of Justice	+ 253	Office for Official Publications	+ 167.7
Court of Auditors	+ 240	Commission (operating budget)	+ 79.4
Commission (research)	− 26	Commission (research)	− 0.9
Total	+7 737	Average	+ 85.7

The increase in staff was authorized as a number in the Commission and as a percentage in the other institutions. The Budgetary Authority has thus been particularly restrictive as regards increases in Commission staff, wishing to encourage it to achieve greater mobility among its staff, which the Commission has endeavoured to do.[2] Thus the increases in staff, other than language staff, lay between 1.4% and 3.3% for the Commission in the last 3 years, and between 11.9% and 23.4% for Parliament. The Council has been fairly strict as regards its own staff, the percentages being between 0.7% and 4.2%.

Sociological analysis of the staff of the European Community

On examining the various lists of staff, certain comments can be made, bearing in mind that the figures given are those for posts authorized, and so are slightly higher than the numbers in post, and also bearing in mind that the national officials working for the European Communities are not counted (staff of the Permanent Representations of the nine Member States assigned to the Community in Brussels, and staff working in the nine capitals on Community problems, in the specialist departments on European matters within the ministries, or the paying agencies of the EAGGF, Social Fund, etc.). There are four such comments:
 (i) the Budgetary Authority (Council and Parliament) has included 93.4% of the staff of the Communities (16 763 out of 17 941) in the lists of posts, leaving only 6.6% of this staff to be paid from total appropriations. It thus has a complete check on the number of staff available to the Community institutions;
 (ii) the European Communities have clearly opted for the status of official, since 88.9% of their staff enjoy this status (15 942 out of 17 941);
 (iii) the European Communities have a high proportion of graduate (or equivalent) staff (Category A and Language Service staff together: 33.7% (6 051 out of 17 941)). Of this staff there is a large proportion entrusted with administrative and advisory duties (Category A): 21.5% (3 862 out of 17 941);
 (iv) the staff of the Commission form the major part of the staff of the Community institutions: 70.9% (12 723 out of 17 941). Of these, the number of graduates and equivalent is the same as in the other institutions: 35.3% (4 486 out of 12 723), but the proportion of Category A officials is much higher: 24.8% (3 155 out of 12 723) than in the other institutions: 13.6% (706 out of 5 205); this is explained by the role of the Commission in the interplay of the Community institutions, which is to examine, propose and conciliate.

C—The organization and operation of the departments of the institutions of the European Community

In view of the scope of this book, only the Commission departments will be considered. Their structure and operation are particularly interesting because of the role the Commission plays in the Community machinery and of the size of its staff. The administration of each of the other institutions, except the Court of Auditors, is like that of a general secretariat or a court record office, the function of which is essentially to assist the Members of the institution in their duties and record the minutes of meetings (see Annex 14, p. 402, for some details of the organization of the General Secretariat of the Council and the Secretariat of Parliament).

Organization of the Commission departments

The Commission departments consist of 23 main administrative units headed by a Grade A/1 official (Director-General) and under the authority of a Member of the Commission. There are also five lesser administrative units headed by a Grade A/2 official (Director) but also directly under the authority of a Member of the Commission. Nineteen of the major administrative units are called Directorates-General, while the other four are of the same level but have a different name. They are generally divided into from one to eleven directorates, these in turn being broken down into divisions and specialized departments, varying in number from two to eight. The Commission is at present endeavouring to reduce them in number.

The major administrative units are either vertical (specific) or horizontal (general) in function. The former category cover matters relating to a specific field under the Treaties or secondary legislation; the latter category covers general matters affecting all sectors, or has a coordinating function, sometimes in the sphere of administration (see Annex 14, p. 402).

Operation of the Commission departments

The coordination problem—The Commission is a collegial political body, which means that its departments form a single administration. Matters are referred to it by each of its Members according to the responsibilities assigned to them on their appointment, and not by the Directors-General, whose responsibility in essentially technical in character.

The problem which arises is therefore one of coordination of the activities of the Directorates-General and departments, to ensure the effective execution of the preparatory work for the decisions and initiatives which the Commission has to take by virtue of the Treaties and the secondary legislation. The single Commission and the three former. Executives before they merged often had to ponder this problem. The former High Authority of the ECSC and the former Commission of the EEC tried to solve it by setting up working parties consisting of members specializing in some major area of activity of the Community concerned. This arrangement was fairly successful in the former High Authority, because the Treaty of Paris only covered two sectors of the economy; on the other hand, it was hardly ever used by the former Commission of the EEC because it was under such great pressure and because its responsibilities were so multifarious, which prevented Members concerning themselves with any sectors other than those which were their particular responsibility. It should also be added that the Members of the former Commission of the EEC were not averse to this state of affairs, since it helped to put a personal stamp on certain policies or projects, each Member being pleased to attach his name to a major sector of European integration. The single Commission since 1967, and the enlarged Commission since the entry of the three new Member States into the Community have not attempted to achieve such coordination at the level of the Members of the Commission, preferring to adopt other systems.

Practice has thus endorsed the meeting of 'Chefs de cabinet' (Grade A/2) or their staff (other A Grades) every week—and, increasingly, several times a week—to prepare for the deliberations of the Commission. This arrangement has proved to be effective in the preparation of subject matter, but psychologically it raises a problem, since it tends to exclude the Directors-General and Heads of Department from the exercise of responsibilities which are partly theirs, despite the fact that they or their staff are invited to attend the meetings of the 'Chefs de cabinet'.

Apart from this operating practice of the institution, the Commission has tried to strengthen the coordinating powers of some of its departments which are horizontal in function. Thus the Secretariat-General and the Legal Service play a valuable part. Similarly, the Directorate-General for Budgets is playing an increasingly active part. The Commission has endeavoured to maintain the traditional powers of the Directorate-General for Personnel and Administration by refusing to take action on the demands of the major operational Directorates-General, which have always sought to obtain administrative departments of their own by decentralization.

It is none the less true that the problem of coordination, discussion and action by the Commission departments is a permanent problem and completely typical of our era, which has brought forth vast technocratic organizations which are difficult to administer. The Commission of the European Communities is not alone in this, it is simply another symbol of Europe.

Departmental flexibility—There is another fairly serious problem, that of the adaptability of the structures to the Commission's tasks. The Commission has always had great difficulty in moving staff from one department to another because those in charge and even the persons concerned put up considerable resistance. It is only by means of new posts authorized each year in the budget that it has been able to strengthen the departments which needed it. The result is that the Commission is able to tackle immediately any new work in a sector where activity has been at a low level. In the sectors which are always busy, new work can be taken on but only by making a great effort and sometimes by the creation of a temporary task force.

The best illustration of this ability to consider, devise and formulate major proposals was given in 1973 when the Commission and its departments were able, within a few months, to prepare the many proposals called for by the Paris Summit in October 1972; in actual fact, little action was taken on these proposals. The Commission has given less attention to the management side than to the advisory and negotiating departments. Thus the Directorates-General responsible for general administration, budgets, financial control and the management of certain funds (EAGGF, Social Fund, Regional Fund, energy policy) are understaffed.

Internal integration—Another hallmark of the European spirit is the excellent degree of integration achieved by the staff of the European Communities. In the beginning it did not seem that this would be easy. It seemed a chancy business to assemble, on a permanent basis, the citizens of six countries, speaking four different languages, the products of different educational systems and having different traditions and customs, and to get them to work together. Nevertheless, success was immediate, doubtless as a result of the team spirit developed by Jean Monnet, the first President of the High Authority, but also because of the very high European ideals which animated the pioneers of the ECSC. These same ideals were present at the cradle of the Communities in Brussels, and, although the administrative machinery created—particularly that of the Commission of the EEC—was strongly hierarchical, this did not prevent the immediate formation of an extremely homogeneous corps of European officials. True, it would be foolish to claim that national differences do not exist, but they do not put at risk the efforts to reconcile national interests with the Community interest.

Geographical balance—Article 27 of the Staff Regulations provides that staff shall be 'recruited on the broadest possible geographical basis from among nationals of Member States' and that 'no post shall be reserved for nationals of any specific Member State'. On the basis of this rule, practice has produced the law of 'geographical balance'. In the Europe

315

of the Six there was to have been a division into four equal parts, i.e.: 25% French, 25% German, 25% Italian and 25% Benelux nationals in the Communities in Brussels; this was because the percentage of Italian nationals in the staff of the High Authority was smaller because of the small contribution made at that time by Italy to the Community's coal and steel output. In fact, this four-part balance was never achieved, except roughly in Category A, which is obviously the most important politically, and very punctiliously in Grades A/1, A/2 and A/3, which form the three higher management grades. On 31 December 1972, the last year of the Community of Six, the geographical breakdown as a percentage of the total and of the A Grade officials was as follows: German: 20% (A—25%); French: 17% (A—23%); Italian: 18% (A—21%); Benelux: 41% (A—30%); other nationalities: 4% (A—1%). With the enlargement of the Community, the geographical breakdown was made on the following theoretical basis: the four groups of the Community of the Six and the United Kingdom: 18.4% each; Ireland and Denmark: 4% each.

In fact, the breakdown was as follows on 31 December 1979: German: 14.7% (A—19%); French: 14.2% (A—20.2%); Italian: 17% (A—17.4%); Benelux: 38% (A—22.4%, of which Belgians made up more than half); British: 9.5% (A—14.5%); Danish: 3.8% (A—3%); Irish: 1.9% (A—2.9%); other nationalities: 0.9% (A—0.53%).

This system of geographical breakdown has not had the inevitable consequence it has generally had in federal States, because the Community institutions have not tried to recruit two or three officials for the same duties in order to avoid discrimination between nationalities; they have rather created a mixed pyramidal administration based on a system of allocation by nationalities for the senior grades. This allocation on the basis of nationality is fortunately not sacrosanct, but can be modified by exchanges, always provided that the balance of the geographical breakdown is preserved, at least at the upper level, i.e. in respect of the Directors-General. Thus, the five groups referred to above have finished up with four Directors-General each—a total of 20 posts—plus three Directors-General of either Danish or Irish nationality.

After sharing out the portfolios, i.e. the Directorates-General, among its Members, the Commission assigned a nationality for each post of Director-General (A/1), Director (A/2) and sometimes even Head of Division (A/3) or Specialized Department (A/5-4), making sure as far as possible that none of these officials answers to a compatriot or has too many compatriots as colleagues. This intermingling of nationalities has contributed greatly towards the creation of a sense of unity and *esprit de corps* among the European officials. Finally, it should be noted that duties are assigned with regard to the interest which the governments have in the subject in question. Thus, for instance, a Frenchman is Director-General for Agriculture. The opposite principle might, of course, have applied, but the institutions preferred to have this kind of guarantee.

Inflation in the number of management posts has also been avoided, sometimes even by being very strict. On the enlargement of the Communities, for instance, the Commission did not increase the number of its Directorates-General and by means of a 'termination of service' operation it freed a number of posts for nationals of the three new Member States. On the other hand, there is some inflation of duties because of the link between grades and duties. For example, of the 145 permanent A/2 Grade officials in the central services of the Commission (including 20 who have the Grade of A/1 on a personal basis), about 70% carry out management duties, the other 30% having advisory functions or holding this grade on a personal basis. In any case, the senior posts (A/1, A/2, A/3 and the A/5-4 officials acting as heads of specialist services) represent about 5% of the total staff.[3]

The language problem—The European Communities could quite easily have become a real Tower of Babel. In fact, nothing of the sort happened. As practically all the officials whose mother tongue is not French know French well, it became the working language of the Six, both written and spoken. The enlargement of the Community did not radically change this state of affairs, but English came to be a second working language. In practice this means a considerable saving of budget funds, since it is not necessary to have all working documents translated or to provide interpretation services at all internal meetings. On the other hand, when the institutions hold their official meetings, the six languages are spoken and interpreted into the other languages, except at the Commission which only uses French, English, German and Italian, and at the Court of Justice which only uses French. All the documents officially submitted to the institutions are produced in the six languages. Similarly, all the documents published in the *Official Journal of the European Communities,* and a large number of other publications, are published in the six languages. As a result, the language services of the Communities have large staffs, comprising 2 155 linguists, all with university education or equivalent. Of the total, 77.8% are translators or revisers and 22.2% interpreters, the former having at their disposal the services of some 840 secretaries. The language burden is still therefore very considerable, even though the Communities have been able to arrange a very reasonable system pragmatically. It should be pointed out, however, that the desire to set up a 'comprehensive language service', i.e. with all documents being translated and all meetings interpreted into six languages, is becoming more and more evident.

At the same time, the European Communities are making great efforts to produce an operational automatic translation system. Studies currently being undertaken show that such a system may cost between one-half and one-third as much as having the work done by human translators, though the degree of error before correction by a reviser is 15% for machine translation and only 3% for human translators. Technical progress can still be made however.

Nevertheless, the future of the Language Service still remains a crucial problem for the operation of the European Communities. Further enlargement must bring a complete reappraisal, since, however essential it is for all the legislation to appear in all the Community languages, it would seem equally indefensible to use nine languages at all times for all the written or spoken work of the European institutions.

The siting of the places of work—Because of the multiplicity of cities willing to house the Community offices and the not very serious character of some of the proposals, in 1952 the Luxembourg Government succeeded in having the ECSC institutions located in Luxembourg, although Parliament had to meet in plenary session in Strasbourg. In 1958, the Belgian Government was likewise able to arrange for the provisional location of the two new Communities (the Commissions and Councils thereof) to be established in Brussels. The question of location arose again at the time of the Merger Treaty, but the acquired rights of the three cities were maintained: they remained the provisional places of work of the Community institutions (Decision of the Representatives of the Governments of the Member States on the provisional location of certain institutions and departments of the Communities of 8 April 1965). To be precise, the present arrangements are as follows: the Commission in Brussels and Luxembourg (three Directorates-General, Computer Centre and Office for Official Publications in the latter city); the Council in Brussels (but in three separate months of the year all its meetings are held in Luxembourg); Parliament in Luxembourg (the Secretariat is housed there; Parliament holds three part-sessions there in each year), in Strasbourg (where the other part-sessions are held) and in Brussels (most committee meetings being held there); the Court of Justice in Luxembourg; the Court of Auditors in Luxembourg; the Economic and Social Committee in Brussels; the ECSC Consultative Committee in Luxembourg and the European Investment Bank in Luxembourg.

Thus, the European Communities are still without fixed abode, they only have provisional places of work. The minor consequence of this is that they cannot build and are forced to rent offices at great expense, but the major disadvantage is that the operation of the institutions is made difficult, and expensive, because of their geographical dispersal. Some people, especially Members of Parliament—and the Court of Auditors—are questioning the arrangement and asking for a more realistic solution.

It may be pointed out at this juncture that the Commission has:
(a) *Two places of work,* Brussels and Luxembourg, where its central services are based.
(b) *Press Offices* in all the capitals of the Community (sometimes with branch offices: Berlin, Belfast, Cardiff, Edinburgh, Milan) and in Athens, Ankara, Madrid and Lisbon.
(c) *Delegations,* often with press offices, to governments or international organizations (Australia, Austria, Canada, United States, Japan, Yugoslavia, Latin America (Caracas and Santiago, Chile); GATT, OECD, UN (New York and Geneva)).
(d) *Forty-two delegations in the ACP countries.*
(e) *Eight delegations in the southern Mediterranean countries.*

This gives a total of 79 cities. Eighteen hundred people work in these out-stations.[4]

D—European education

The European Schools are amongst the most original and most fruitful creations of the European Communities. The agreements governing the European Schools reflect an experiment in the education of children of different mother tongues and nationalities, which was begun in October 1953 on the initiative of a group of ECSC officials with the support of the Community institutions and the Luxembourg Government. The collaboration between the Ministries of Education and the Directorates-General for Cultural Relations of the six countries and the Parents' Association, which began in June 1954, became more and more intense and finally the governments accepted responsibility for the European School. By signing the Protocol of 12 April 1957 they set up the first official inter-governmental school in Luxembourg, soon to be followed by a European School in Brussels in 1958 and a second in 1976, in the establishments of the JRC at Mol/Geel and Varese (Ispra) in 1960, at Karlsruhe in 1962, at Bergen (Petten) in 1963, and at Culham in 1978.

At the beginning of the 1979-80 school year the eight European Schools had 10 711 pupils (855 in the kindergarten, 4 110 in the primary and 5 746 in the secondary sections); true, these are not all children of members of the Community's staff. The latter are sometimes even in a minority in their school, except in Brussels and Luxembourg where they are well in the majority; in all 782 teachers are employed in these establishments.

There are between four and six language sections in each of the schools (German, English, French, Italian, Dutch and Danish, but certain classes are given in a language other than the language of the section. Since 1959, 3 342 pupils have passed out from the European Schools with a *baccalauréat* (school-leaving examination) and gone in the normal way to the higher education establishments of the nine countries of the Community, as well as those of Austria, Switzerland and the United States.

The expenditure on the European Schools can be divided into two categories: expenditure borne by the Member States, i.e. the national salaries of the teachers, and the expenditure borne by the European Communities in the form of a balancing subsidy entered in the Commission section of the budget (34.3 m EUA in 1980). Actually the real budgetary authority for determining the level of this expenditure is the Board of Governors of the European Schools.

In addition to these eight European Schools, a ninth was set up in 1977 in Munich where the European Patents Office is located. Since this school is financed directly by the 16 States forming this new authority, there is no appropriation for it in the general budget of the European Communities.

Another important European educational institution is the European University Institute in Florence. This institution of higher education, created by the Convention signed on 19 April 1972, has as its aim 'to contribute, by its activities in the fields of higher education and research, to the development of the cultural and scientific heritage of Europe, as a whole and in its constituent parts'. The controlling body is a High Council made up of representatives of the Member States. On the financial side it approves the budget of the Institute on the basis of a proposal from the Principal of the Institute. The revenue side of its budget is covered by financial contributions calculated on the basis of a political scale (21.16% paid by the 'big four'). From 1 January 1978 there has been the alternative possibility of finance from the general budget. So far this has not been adopted.

3. Supplementary staff resources and the technical and material resources of the European Communities

In addition to the staff we have been discussing, the Community has appropriations enabling it to have work done by outside staff. It also has often substantial technical and material facilities at its disposal. We shall briefly consider these two aspects.

A—Supplementary staff resources

These resources comprise mainly the research and studies appropriations, the appropriations for support staff and the appropriations for services.

Studies and research appropriations

Scattered throughout the various titles of the section of the budget devoted to the Commission there are thirty-four budget headings (articles or items) against which a total of 26.39 million EUA were entered in 1980 for studies and research. These appropriations are mainly earmarked for statistical studies and surveys, studies and surveys of market conditions, actions under the scientific and technological policy, environmental studies and funds to allow the Commission to further its examination of areas in which it has a particular interest. The term 'studies' is to be understood in the widest meaning of the word. The other institutions of the Communities have little in the way of study and research appropriations, or none at all.

These appropriations have always been considered very useful by the Commission, since they have enabled it to carry out surveys of a highly technical nature, or work which its own departments could not do. The Budgetary Authority has always been restrictive in granting these appropriations, believing that very often the work could have been done by the Commission's permanent staff. The Commission's insistence has—despite the reluctance of the Council—none the less enabled the European Community to be provided with substantial appropriations.

Appropriations for supplementary staff

These are overall appropriations to enable certain work to be carried out which cannot be done by the permanent staff because of the work load. In the case of the Commission the work involves interpretation at meetings, the translation of highly technical or very long documents which are not urgent, the typing of documents and proof-reading of texts for printing. On some days such work may require several hundred people actually working on the Commission's premises. In addition there are some 70 experts seconded by the national authorities to the services of the Commission on a full-time basis for a specific period.

All these appropriations for the Commission entered in Title I (Staff appropriations), while being substantial (6.6 m EUA) nevertheless represent only 1.6% of the appropriations under this title. The same appropriations exist for the other institutions, but the proportions vary (1.6% for Parliament, 0.74% for the Economic and Social Committee, 0.57% for the Council, 0.21% for the Court of Justice and 0.13% for the Court of Auditors).

Appropriations for services

There are appropriations for services, i.e. for the payment of firms on contract employed to carry out practical work needed for the smooth running of the institutions, but which need not be carried out by the latter's staff, for instance work on buildings (maintenance and cleaning), equipment and furniture (maintenance, repair, removals) and data processing. It may involve several hundred people working on the institutions' premises, usually on a part-time basis. The Commission, like the other institutions, is therefore provided with the appropriate resources. It is interesting to note, however, that there is one legal/budget problem, that of the 'appaltati', which is specific to the Joint Research Centre at Ispra but could one day have general implications. According to Italian legislation, 'contratti d'appalto' (service contracts) cannot be awarded for work carried out on the site of the undertaking, or for the ordinary and continuing maintenance work, with the exception of work that can be done only outside normal working hours. As a result, the 'appaltati'—i.e. the staff of the companies providing services—have to be engaged by the firm for whom they do the work, in this case the Commission of the European Communities. Only those actually doing cleaning work on the premises outside normal working hours can remain 'appaltati'. In 1974, therefore, 105 'appaltati' at Ispra received contracts as local staff. This is a problem of the modern era, reflecting the desire to tighten the links between the real employer and the worker and give the latter the maximum job security.

B—The technical resources of the Community

The real technical resources of the Community are the computer centres, the various documentation facilities and the Office for Official Publications.

Computer Centres—The Community has two major computer centres in the Commission: at Luxembourg and Ispra. The Commission has at its disposal 16.63 m EUA and 239 officials and other staff to run the former, and 3.5 m EUA and some 40 officials and other staff for the latter.

Documentation facilities: CIRCE system—In 1973 the Commission set up an internal automatic documentation system to update the information available in the institution—and even in the Community—to broaden its coverage, and to speed up access thereto. The system at present contains 130 000 documents (25% dealing with budgetary, monetary, financial control and tax matters) growing at the rate of 2 500 documents a month. The system cost 4.1 m u.a. to set up and develop from 1974 to 1979, and it has rationalized the work and ensured more complete and more exact information. In the meantime, other data bases have been created:

(a) a data base covering the decisions of the Commission; this base—comprising 29 000 documents—is continuously updated;
(b) a data base for administering the matters pending between the Commission and the Council (5 300 documents);
(c) another base—of 7 000 documents—for administering the application of the Directives is at the experimental stage. These bases thus comprise in all 41 300 documents.

The Commission has also brought into operation an automatic legal documentation system enabling any Community legal reference to be found easily from a collection of 48 000 documents. By a Commission decision of December 1976 these two systems were merged to form the 'European Communities Information and Documentary Research Centre' (CIRCE). This base is growing at the rate of 200 documents a month in the six official languages.

Finally, the Commission has a large documentation centre and a library (483 000 works), the administration of and access to which is itself being automated (computer-prepared catalogues by subject, author, country).

Office for Official Publications—In 1969 the four institutions of the Community and the Economic and Social Committee set up the Office for Official Publications of the European Communities which has considerable resources: 265 officials, 51 local staff and 13.3 m EUA in operating appropriations.

It works for the institutions, which place orders with it for printing, and carries out certain work itself with its own resources. It is also responsible for the *Official Journal of the European Communities* which it has printed by an external printer (171 900 pages in 1979).

The Financial Regulation of 21 December 1977 lays down that all the appropriations of the Office for Official Publications shall be charged to an annex to the section of the budget applicable to the Office, and that the other institutions will only have pro-forma appropriations in order not to inflate the general budget of the Communities, the expenditure of the other institutions having previously been Commission revenue.

4. Budgetary and legal framework of the Community's administrative organization

The expenditure on the Community's administrative machinery also calls for some comments.

A—The administrative budget

Administrative expenditure occupies only a modest place in the budget of the European Communities for 1980. It may be recalled that originally the administrative expenditure of the ECSC formed, by virtue of Article 78(3), third subparagraph of the ECSC Treaty, the subject of a 'general estimate' which was in fact a budget. Similarly, the administrative expenditure of Euratom was the subject of a special budget pursuant to Article 174 of the Euratom Treaty. The administrative expenditure of the EEC for a long time formed the bulk of the budget referred to in Article 199 of the EEC Treaty. The administrative budget now appears in Titles 1 and 2 of each of the sections relating to the five institutions of the Community.

B—Budget estimates for administrative appropriations

The Commission and the other institutions prepare very detailed estimates of their requests for appropriations. In the highly sensitive area of requests for more staff, in particular, they have to provide a very precise justification by virtue of Article 12(4)a of the Financial Regulation.

C—Establishing the administrative appropriations

The appropriations intended for the administrative machinery of the Community are non-compulsory expenditure which, therefore, are ultimately fixed by Parliament; nevertheless, the Council plays a considerable part in this matter. Its Budget Committee devotes particular attention to the subject and its Permanent Representatives Committee does not neglect it either. Because of their institutional autonomy, the Council and Parliament are each free to adopt their own administrative budget. On the other hand, the Council considers very strictly the requests by the Commission, the Court of Justice, the Court of Auditors and the Economic and Social Committee and rejects them to a great extent. Parliament is more sympathetic, but it is not true to say that it systematically accepts the Commission's requests for staff.[5] The operating appropriations are in practice fixed by the Council alone, Parliament giving its attention rather to the intervention appropriations, although it does not ignore the appropriations for information activities.

D—Implementation of the administrative appropriations

The appropriations for Titles 1 and 2 of each section of the budget are to cover the expenditure of the administrative machinery of the Community and not to carry out financial operations. The consequences of this are as follows: these appropriations are non-differentiated appropriations, since the commitments can easily be followed by payments during the financial year and the following financial year, to which appropriations can be carried over (see p. 74). Staff appropriations cannot be carried over. The payments in fact coincide with the commitments.

Particularly in those institutions whose staff is limited, a great many transfers have to be made to adapt the budget to the needs of implementation.

While not wishing to analyse in detail the conditions of such implementation, we may point out two things. The first is that because of the provisional nature of the locations of the Community, which are only provisional places of work (Article 1 of the Decision of 8 April 1965 of the Representatives of the Governments), the institutions have only been able to rent the buildings needed to accommodate their departments and not to buy or build. On the other hand, the Commission has been able to buy premises for its delegations or offices outside Brussels and Luxembourg. The second point is that the Commission covers itself by numerous safeguards in the implementation of its operating appropriations by obtaining the opinions of advisory committees: advisory committees on procurements and contracts (one for all the transactions except those of the JRC, the other for the JRC), set up pursuant to Article 54 of the Financial Regulation, the Advisory Committee on Commissioned Studies, the Consultants Committee and the Advisory Committee on Publications, all three set up by decision of the Commission. All these committees are made up of senior officials, the first three being headed by the Directorate-General for Budgets and the fourth by the Directorate of the Office for Official Publications.

E—The auditing of the implementation of administrative appropriations

The administrative expenditure is one of the categories of Commission expenditure subject to the closest control. Both the internal Financial Controller and the external audit body, and even Parliament of more recent times, examine it closely. In the past the Audit Board devoted as much as one-third of its report to it; nowadays the Court of Auditors devotes its attention to a wider field.

5. The budget resources assigned to the administrative organization of the European Community from 1952 to 1980

One of the fundamental budget rules is that the Community cannot finance its administrative expenditure by borrowing. The ECSC even incorporated this rule in the Treaty which established it. Article 51(1) thereof reads: 'The High Authority may not use the funds obtained by borrowing except to grant loans'. The resources allocated by the Community to the operation of its own administrative machinery therefore originate from the budget.

A—The budget resources used from 1952 to 1980

In the following table we show—in decreasing order of size—the appropriations granted to each institution in 1979 and 1980. We have used the breakdown described earlier (see p. 304) between resources spent on the administrative machinery and other expenditure. Then we added the expenditure for the delegated administration of own resources (customs duties and agricultural levies).

Since these are budget resources granted by the Budgetary Authority—i.e. budget resources which have been voted—the amount in the 1979 budget is different from the figure implemented as shown in Annex 12 (see p. 399). For the 1980 budget, on the other hand, the figures coincide, since Annex 12 for that year gives the figures for the budget adopted and not the budget implementation figures.

As we said earlier, the resources devoted to the management of the Community administrative machinery have grown considerably over the years, but at the same time their relative share in the budget has decreased.

Budget resources voted for the administrative organization of the European Communities

(million EUA)

	1979						1980					
	Commission	Parliament	Council	Court of Justice	Court of Auditors	Economic and Social Committee	Commission	Parliament	Council	Court of Justice	Court of Auditors	Economic and Social Committee
Staff (Title 1)	409.56	90.84	52.55	14.59	9.92	10.80	421.31	135.97	53.75	16.55	10.62	11.84
Operation (Chapters 20 to 24)	80.27	25.14	23.76	4.10	2.17	3.19	98.32	33.68	27.27	4.06	2.12	5.18
Committees (Chapter 25)	12.10	0.13	5.15	0.10	0.01	2.22	12.02	0.18	4.54	0.12	0.02	2.56
Studies (Chapter 26)	15.00	0.11	0.17	0.00	0.10	0.01	16.04	0.02	0.15	0.00	0.05	0.02
Administrative machinery (Total)	516.93	116.22	81.63	18.79	12.20	16.22	547.69	169.85	85.71	20.73	12.81	19.60
Subsidies Chapter 28	43.92	0.00	0.00	0.00	0.00	0.00	48.77	0.00	0.00	0.00	0.00	0.00
Chapter 29	2.20	1.65	0.03	0.02	0.00	0.00	2.39	2.14	0.03	0.02	0.00	0.00
Publications	11.95	4.02	2.55	0.69	0.11	0.33	14.40	4.65	2.90	0.92	0.23	0.36
Information	9.60	2.84	0.00	0.04	0.00	0.01	9.82	0.76	0.00	0.04	0.00	0.01
Total Titles 1 + 2	584.60	124.73	84.21	19.54	12.31	16.56	623.07	177.40	88.64	21.71	13.04	19.97
Chapter 40	721.13	—	—	—	—	—	789.15	—	—	—	—	—

Some figures for the expenditure of the Commission (see Annex 12, p. 396) will illustrate this fact, taking three reference dates: 1952 (year when the ECSC started), 1968 (first year following the merging of the three Executives) and 1979 (last year completed when this book was written). The operating expenditure of all the Community institutions rose from 4.6 to 91.8 m u.a. and then to 784.9 m EUA; it therefore multiplied by 171 between 1952 and 1979, whereas total expenditure had multiplied by 3 290. The relative share of administrative expenditure dropped from 100% in 1952 to 46.8% in 1958 (year when the EEC and Euratom started), and then to 27.2% (first year of payments under the EAGGF), falling to 6.8% (in 1968) and remaining below this figure subsequently (5.2% in 1979).

While the ECSC and Euratom have always had operational expenditure, the EEC had until 1965, when the EAGGF was launched, only administrative expenditure, except that for the former Social Fund after 1961. Gradually the operational expenditure grew and the proportion of administrative expenditure in total Community expenditure continually fell, stabilizing in the last few years.

In 1979 the administrative expenditure was 555.2 m EUA for the Commission and 229.7 m EUA for the other institutions: namely 115.5 m EUA for Parliament, 87.7 m EUA for the Council (including the expenditure of the Economic and Social Committee), 16.9 m EUA for the Court of Justice and 9.6 m EUA for the Court of Auditors. To this has to be added the administrative expenditure of the European Association for Cooperation: 3.6 m EUA charged to the budget for that of the headquarters and for the delegations in the southern Mediterranean countries and 34.6 m EUA charged against the appropriations of the EDF (delegations to the ACP States), namely 38.2 m EUA. Altogether, therefore, a sum of 823.1 m EUA.

The lump sum repayment of 10% in favour of the Member States amounts to 733.6 m EUA (12.5 thereof covered in 1980), which is not inconsiderable and brings the administrative expenditure, in the broad sense of the term, to 1 556.7 m EUA.

B—Location of expenditure on the administrative organization of the Community

The calculations done by the Commission for the European Councils in Dublin in 1979 and in Luxembourg in 1980, and revised in March 1980, show the breakdown of the expenditure on the administrative machinery of the Community to be:

Location of expenditure on the administrative organization of the European Community

(%)

B	DK	D	F	IRL	I	L	NL	UK	Subtotal	Other	Total
					Implementation in 1979						
66.6	—	0.7	—	0.2	0.6	31.5	0.3	0.1	100	—	100
					Estimates for 1980						
62.2	0.1	1.8	1.0	0.5	1.0	31.7	0.7	0.5	99.5	0.5	100

In fact, the operating expenditure contained in Aggregate No V (see p. 333) was broken down roughly as follows per Member State:

(i) expenditure on administrative machinery of the Commission, on the basis of recent information given by the accounts, according to places of work;
(ii) European Schools, Berlin Centre and Dublin Foundation;
(iii) Council: all expenditure attributed on a lump sum basis to Belgium;
(iv) European Parliament, Court of Justice and Court of Auditors: attributed mainly to Luxembourg.

This expenditure is concentrated in Belgium and Luxembourg because the provisional places of work of the Community institutions are located in these two countries.

*
* *

The expenditure on the administrative machinery of the European Communities was therefore 3 757.6 m u.a. from 1952 to 1979 (see p. 399), i.e. 6.3% of the total expenditure under the budget; about two-thirds of this amount were staff costs. In 1980 the Communities employed about 18 000 people. Because these figures are unknown even to enlightened public opinion, the spontaneous reaction has been to complain about excessive European bureaucracy, shameless waste, the spread of Parkinson's law. The real facts are quite different, but Europe's image has suffered. The staff of the European Communities actually represent about 0.1% of the staff employed by the national public authorities of the nine Member States, while the Community's budget resources correspond to about 2% of the national budget resources. It is unwise to conclude too much from a comparison of these two percentages, since the basic data are not comparable. Taken together, however, they show how wrong is the criticism directed against Community administration.

In conclusion, our finding must be that the European Communities have a substantial modern and high-grade administrative machine. The quality of the staff in particular should be emphasized. Administrations which can call upon the services of such highly-qualified staff in such numbers are rare anywhere in the world. Attention should also be drawn to the considerable number of people actually working for Europe throughout the Community. The Community institutions are also trying to make more use of national civil servants or even people from the private or para-public sector, by paying for their services in the former case or for their work in the latter, not wishing all those who are working for Europe to be directly in the service of the Community nor to be assembled in a vast European version of the 'District of Columbia'.

Footnotes to Chapter XV

[1] Application of the provisional twelfths system following the rejection of the budget on 13 December 1979 created serious difficulties for Parliament itself. The figure for appropriations for 1979, which was in fact the maximum, had been opened to cover for six months smaller allowances for 198 Members and not 410. Since Parliament did not wish to ask for additional provisional twelfths, it only paid out 60% of the allowances due.

[2] In 1978, for example, the Commission arranged the transfer of 379 staff (137 of Category A, 106 B's, and 136 C's) which shows that a considerable effort was made. In 1979 the figures were: 373 staff (141 of Category A, 116 B's, 115 C's and 1 D).

[3] The establishment plans show that the higher posts represent small percentages:
(a) with the exception of the LA posts, the total of other posts (16 763 minus 2 155) amounts to 14 608. The 721 senior posts (A/1, A/2, A/3) thus represent only 4.9% of the total;

(b) of all the 2 155 LA posts, the 65 LA/3s thus only represent 3.0%;

(c) of the total of 16 763 posts, 786 (721+65) A/1, A/2, A/3 and LA/3 posts thus represent 4.7%.

[4] To be precise, in 1980 this figure was 1 816, i.e. 193 officials and 276 local staff (both shown in the table on p. 310), 433 in the delegations and press offices, 1 250 in the EAC (see p. 282) and 97 in the eight delegations in the southern Mediterranean countries.

[5] Parliament is, it is true, prepared to consider the requests for staff of the Commission or other institutions (Court of Justice, Court of Auditors and Economic and Social Committee); Parliament is sometimes even more generous than the Council. However, in the end it only granted part of the increases requested (51.4% as against 32.7% by the Council for the Commission in the 1978 budget, and 84% as against 38.7% by the Council in 1979). In the latter case its plans, however, failed because of the budget crisis of December 1978 (see p. 45). In 1977 and 1980 Parliament even supported the Council's figure (+56% for 1977 and 34.5% for 1980).

Conclusion to Part Three

Between 1952 and 1979, the European Communities spent some 77 000 m u.a. and lent a further 19 000 m u.a. or so, making a total of around 100 000 m u.a. in all.[1] Over the years, their financial resources have been consolidated and expanded, while the number of operations has increased and diversified. Credit for this is due to the institutions, to the Commission as initiator and the Council and the European Parliament (collectively known as the Budgetary Authority) as decision-makers. The Council was, for a long time, the sole holder of budget powers but has shared them with the European Parliament since 1971, thus giving the budget a new dimension. The success of this partnership is undeniable.

In just over a quarter of a century, the Community institutions have succeeded in creating an entire system of public finance. With the peoples and governments of the Nine they have erected one of the central pillars of the edifice known as the European Community.

The figures set out in Annexes 11 to 13 (pp. 389 to 400) show *how much the financial resources of the European Communities have increased.* Between 1954, the year in which the public finances of the ECSC took off, and 1960, when the EEC and Euratom were getting under way, non-repayable expenditure went up by a factor of 2.3; by 1968, the year of the merger of the Executives, this factor had increased to 31.4; by 1972, the last year before the three Communities were enlarged through the accession of three new Member States, spending had increased by a factor of 65; by 1973, the first year of the enlarged Community, the factor was 92.5 and by 1979, the last year for which final expenditure was known at the time of writing, it was 291. Over the same period, the funds borrowed increased by a factor of 192. Since enlargement, the general budget of the European Communities has expanded faster than the Member States' budgets, though not at a steady rate.

There is still, despite the efforts of the Commission and the European Parliament, *an imbalance in the distribution of this spending*; the guarantee side of the agricultural policy continues to absorb almost 70% of the funds available, while other Community policies, i.e. concerning internal development, energy, research and cooperation with non-member countries, only receive a very small slice of the cake. The sums devoted to the Community's internal administrative machinery remain marginal. This imbalance in the amounts channelled to the various Community policies is accentuated by the actual payments made against budget appropriations. Although overall cancellations of appropriations amount to less than 10%, the appropriations spent on a linear monthly basis (for the EAGGF Guarantee Section and the running of the administration) are much less affected than the appropriations of the Funds with a structural purpose. The actual amounts devoted to these Funds therefore make up, at present at least, an even smaller proportion than the Budgetary Authority wanted. This unfortunate situation is a product of the great complexity of the financial machinery created by the Community and the problems the national governments have in taking advantage of it.

A third feature of Europe's finances is the *diversity of ways in which the Community policies with financial implications are implemented.* The activities of the European Communities may be direct, that is either undertaken by the Community itself or totally financed by it. Otherwise they are indirect, meaning they are carried out in collaboration with a public or private body and the Community contributes part of the finance. The Communities can also use their tax revenue to finance their own activities or make grants-in-aid, or they can borrow money for onlending. The table below is an attempt to summarize, in a compressed and readily graspable way, the points made throughout Part Three of the book using the classification of the IMF manual of government finance statistics.

The table shows that while direct action projects are few in number, they account for 80% of total non-repayable expenditure; this is because agricultural market guarantees are the Community's responsibility and they make up the bulk of the total. Spending on direct-action projects, involving as it does a transfer of responsibilities from the national to the Community level, is a reflection of the progress made in terms of economic, financial and human resources. Indirect action projects, on the other hand, are numerous but only repre-

Operations undertaken by the European Communities

Type of activity	IMF classification		Type of Community operation		Percentage contribution[1]		
	Category	Heading	Grants	Loans	100%	50% or more	Under 50%
Direct action[1]	1	General public services (general admin.[1]) (International development aid)	Institutions of the European Communities		×		
			Cooperation with associated countries (EDF)	Cooperation with developing countries (EDF and EIB)	×		
			Cooperation with non-member countries	Cooperation with non-member countries (EEC and EIB)	×		
	8	Economic services	EAGGF guarantee		×		
			JRC		×		
Indirect action	1	International development aid	Cooperation with non-associated developing countries				×
	3	Education	European Schools			×	
			Education programme				×
	4	Public health	ECSC research			×	
	5	Social welfare	Coordination			×	
			Anti-poverty campaign			×	
	6	Housing	Pilot schemes	Workers' housing (ECSC)		×	×

[1] The percentage contribution shown is that of the Community for those operations which it finances. This qualifying remark does not apply either to the EAGGF Guarantee Section, which finances everything connected with market policy, or to spending on general administration.

Type of activity	IMF classification		Type of Community operation		Percentage contribution[1]		
	Category	Heading	Grants	Loans	100%	50% or more	Under 50%
Indirect action	7	Culture	Studies, research				X
	8	Economic services	Energy				X
			Coking coal				X
			Hydrocarbons (EEC)	Hydrocarbons (EEC)			X
			Uranium				X
			EAGGF guidance			X	X
			Social Fund			X	
			Regional Fund	Regional development (EIB)			X
			Data processing				X
				Infrastructure (EIB)			X
			Transport (studies)				X
			Euratom research			X	
			ECSC research			X	
				Nuclear power stations (Euratom)			X
				Conversion and investment (ECSC)			X
	9	Other	Exceptional aid (e.g. Friuli)				X
				Balance-of-payments support (EEC)			X
			Financial mechanism			X	X

[1] The percentage contribution shown is that of the Community for those operations which it finances. This qualifying remark does not apply either to the EAGGF Guarantee Section, which finances everything connected with market policy, or to spending on general administration.

sent 20% of total expenditure. They will no doubt expand since the Community is rarely prepared to cover the whole cost of new schemes, that is to say to maintain an open-ended commitment whereby applicants can draw on the resources without limit. The own resources system, as it is at present or is likely to develop, will inevitably prevent such open-ended commitments becoming the general rule. Where most of its operations are concerned, the European Community will continue to be able to do no more than help finance projects within the limits of the budget allocations, without any obligation to exceed these limits, with the aim of supporting certain Community policies financially while ensuring solidarity between Member States in the context of sound financial management.

It will be noticed in the table that Category 2 is missing; this covers defence spending, on which the European Communities cannot have any say even allowing for Article 235 of the EEC Treaty. Nor should this particularly glaring omission hide the fact that the Community's powers are very limited, and budget funds—where they are available—very small, as regards Categories 3 (Education), 4 (Public health), 5 (Social welfare), 6 (Housing and public services) and 7 (Other social and public services). Indeed, a resemblance between the key fields of responsibility and operation of the European Community and those of a national government is only really to be found in Category 1 (General services), if law and

331

order is excluded, and Category 8 (Economic services) which is precisely the field of activity the European Communities were set up to cover. Category 9 (Non-attributable and other expenditure) is a substantial catch-all in the case of the Communities because it covers items not provided for in the Treaties but which have been necessitated by the realities of life as a Community.

The Community's responsibilities can only be widened if responsibilities assumed hitherto by national governments are transferred to it. Like any. federal or confederal system past or present, the Community can only have powers which are conferred on it. The expansion of Community activities, in terms of both quality and quantity, thus depends on the will of the peoples and politicians of the Member States to embark on the road to European Union by increasing the scope of Community activities and the resources to be devoted to them.

Since mid-1979, attention has focused on the question of *where Community funds are spent*—much to the regret of the Commission, which has always regarded this as an unsatisfactory and even dangerous approach as it can only provide an incomplete picture of what the Community is seeking to achieve. The figures on which the next table is based are those which the Commission used for the reference papers it submitted to the European Council meetings in Dublin in November 1979 and Luxembourg in April 1980. The percentages taken from this material for the purpose of this book are presented on the author's own responsibility. The table shows that expenditure under the Community budget is as unique in structure as the revenue discussed earlier (see p. 128). For the pattern to be properly understood, it is necessary to look at it by aggregates.

The first aggregate to be considered is spending on agricultural market guarantees (see p. 192), whereby negative MCAs paid in the exporting countries are credited to the importing countries. It should be recalled that expenditure on agricultural market guarantees accounts for about 70% of the total and is based on the principle of Community financial solidarity rather than the redistribution of resources among the Member States. However, as the geographical distribution of this spending to a great extent determines the pattern of spending as a whole under the Community budget, it has an effect which is quite distinctive, difficult to control and decisive.

The second aggregate is considerably smaller and consists of spending for structural purposes; we have referred to it already as expenditure on the internal development of the Community (EAGGF Guidance Section, the Regional Fund, the Social Fund, aid in the context of the EMS (see p. 239)). This accounts for only 10 to 12% of the total because disbursements lag behind commitments.

The third aggregate groups together all the other intervention spending, i.e. on research, energy and industrial schemes (see p. 269). It accounts for only 2% of total expenditure.

The fourth is the sum of repayments of all kinds to the Member States, such as the lump-sum repayment for the collection of own resources (see p. 306), the financial mechanism (see p. 124) and so on. This accounts for 5 to 5.6%.

The fifth aggregate covers the cost of running the various Community institutions (see p. 325), and accounts for 5 to 6% of the total.

The sixth, finally, lumps together spending on cooperation with non-member countries (food and other aid, described in Chapter XIV) and items which cannot be attributed for lack of reliable figures (accounting for less than 0.5%).

This short review of the six aggregates makes it clear that one can leave out the fifth in considering where Community funds are spent. Spending on running costs is not of direct benefit to the Member States, representing as it does amounts spent on administering and

Where Community funds were spent in 1979 (outturn) and 1980 (estimated)

(%)

Aggregate		B	DK	D	F	IRL	I	L	NL	UK	Total	% of total
I	1979	7.2	6.1	22.4	21.7	4.5	15.6	0.1	13.6	8.8	100	72.5
Guarantee	1980	6.2	6.4	24.4	21.8	4.5	16.9	0.2	13.5	6.1	100	70.7
II												
Internal	1979	1.5	2.4	14.0	17.3	9.8	26.4	0.1	2.7	25.8	100	11.3
development	1980	1.9	2.3	12.3	16.0	11.4	32.6	0.1	2.4	21.0	100	8.9
III												
Other	1979	9.1	0.7	17.1	12.8	0.5	33.0	0.1	7.2	19.5	100	1.8
intervention	1980	8.5	0.6	18.3	14.8	0.4	27.0	0.1	8.3	20.2	98.2	2.6
IV	1979	7.9	2.0	26.6	13.3	0.8	13.0	0.1	11.5	24.8	100	5.0
Repayment	1980	7.1	2.1	25.7	13.3	0.9	12.1	0.1	10.3	28.4	100	5.6
V	1979	66.6	–	0.7	–	0.2	0.6	31.5	0.3	0.1	100	4.7
Administration	1980	62.2	0.1	1.8	1.0	0.5	1.0	31.7	0.7	0.5	99.5	6
VI												
Non-member												
countries and	1979											4.7
other	1980											6.2
Overall	1979	9.1	4.8	19.5	18.6	4.4	15.5	1.6	10.9	10.9	95.3	100
average %	1980	9.0	4.8	20.3	18.0	4.3	16.3	2.1	10.6	8.3	93.7	100
I to IV	1979	6.6	5.3	21.5	20.5	4.9	17.1	0.1	12.0	12.0	100	91.6
%	1980	6.0	5.5	23.1	20.5	4.8	18.5	0.2	12.0	9.4	100	87.8

staffing the Community institutions, although it is a positive factor in balance-of-payments terms and as regards economic activity in the Member States where the institutions are sited. The sixth aggregate can also be discounted since the aid in question leaves the Community and is by definition not intended for one of its members.[2]

The table allows a number of interesting conclusions to be made. The first concerns spending on agricultural guarantees. In 1979, the Federal Republic of Germany had a 22.4% share, France 21.7% and Italy 15.6%, while the United Kingdom only received 8.8%, that is, less than the Netherlands with 13.6%. It is even possible that in 1980 the United Kingdom will receive only 6.1%. The level is so low because of Britain's share of total Community output (10 to 11% of the products subject to a common price system). Its domestic production is insufficient to meet the country's own food requirements. The possible drop from 8.8% to 6.1% is explained by the fall in high negative MCAs (see p. 177). In structural terms therefore, the British share in guarantee spending is likely to remain very much below that of the other Member States such as Belgium, Denmark, Ireland, Italy and the Netherlands. The second conclusion to be drawn is that the three least prosperous countries in the Community received a considerable amount of the expenditure on internal development in 1979 and 1980: Italy (26.4% and 32.6%), the United Kingdom (25.8% and 21%) and Ireland (9.8% and 11.4%). Their combined share in 1979 was 62%, and this will probably rise to 65% in 1980 because of the increase in Italy's share. The third conclusion is that the United Kingdom only benefits to a small extent from Community spending as a whole, and this has led it to request extra spending specifically in the UK.

The pattern of Community expenditure is accordingly very uneven and only partly controllable. Guarantee spending in respect of agricultural markets is determined automatically by

333

the CAP machinery, in which the idea of redistribution plays no role at all, and it is only in the case of spending for structural purposes that the Community institutions can channel funds from the richer countries to the less prosperous. This means that the Community authorities have to reconcile four requirements in 1980. They must control agricultural guarantee spending, increase the funds available for structural purposes, avoid too great an imbalance in the geographical spread of expenditure and keep total spending within the limits of the Community's own resources. This is like asking them to square the circle.

It should also be emphasized that the *enlargement of the Community southwards will be a severe test of European solidarity*. The Europe of the Community is already out of balance and will be even more so once it incorporates countries whose average living standards are lower than the average among the Nine. An additional effort will have to be made by the richest Member States. It is worth repeating here a point made throughout Part Three, which is that Community disbursements in the form of grants-in-aid are based on the principle that both parties contribute. In other words, except in the case of direct-action projects, the Community only makes a contribution if the Member States participate financially themselves. Community support takes the form of conditional grants, meaning that Community commitments are only disbursed if the Member States have financed the operations in question according to rules laid down by the Community. Payments made at the end of the day are therefore based on the actual costs incurred, and this calls for extremely rigorous and inevitably long drawn-out pre-auditing (internal audit) and post-auditing (external audit). Expansion of Community activities in the social, regional, energy and industrial fields would entail stepping up the amount of auditing, a price which in the long run might seem out of proportion to the effect achieved by these payments which, given the present state of budget resources, are only marginal substitutes for or additions to national support. It may turn out to be a better idea, particularly in view of enlargement, to abandon the principle of meeting actual costs and to turn structural appropriations into a means of redistributing the Community's funds from the 'rich' to the 'poor', with the sole condition that proof must be given that operations supported by the Community actually have been carried out by the competent authorities in the Member States. Since it is possible that the ECU will become the base unit for Community financial operations, with values that change every day in terms of each national currency, there will probably be pressure for a simpler form of Community aid. The amount due, in ECU, could be paid out in national currency whatever the actual cost of an operation in that currency on condition that schemes are actually carried through.

To conclude, it should be said that, although *borrowing/lending activities* remain comparatively limited, they already cover such key sectors as economic services, international development aid and balance-of-payments support. There is reason to think that the Community will want to expand these activities. Very soon, it may seem preferable to make repayable loans (possibly at reduced interest rates) than grants-in-aid in a number of fields, particularly where the internal development of the Community is concerned and especially at a time when the Community's own resources are close to being fully stretched. Grants-in-aid would become less predominant, while the case for simplifying the method of paying them would be stronger. The present reluctance on the part of the Community will probably be nothing more than a passing phenomenon, and there is likely to be growing awareness of the value of shifting responsibility to the agencies carrying out projects by granting them loans rather than feather-bedding them with outright grants, especially if there is also a greater desire to improve the transfer of resources.

General conclusion

The first point to be made is that the two Community budgets are still comparatively small. In 1979 they amounted to only 0.8% of the Community's GDP and 2.8% of all the national budgets put together. Even if the European Communities had exploited the full potential of their own resources, bringing the percentage to around 3%, this would still have been negligible compared with the corresponding percentage for federations such as Australia (50%), Canada (50%), the Federal Republic of Germany (60%) and the United States of America (61%). Of course the above figures are hardly surprising since it cannot be claimed that the European Community is a fully-fledged federation. In any case, it has been in existence for a much shorter time than the four federations referred to.

The MacDougall Report, drawn up at the Commission's request in 1977, indicates that this situation is likely to persist for some time yet.[3] It states that, as far as European public finance is concerned, the Community will not be able to attain, in the next few years, a degree of integration comparable with that achieved by the federations mentioned and that major changes in the political, monetary and budgetary fields will have to take place before it can become a Union. The report suggests that the Community should devote 5 to 10% of its GDP to public spending rather than the current 0.8%. It envisages a first stage of pre-federal integration which would pre-suppose new departures in the political structure of the Community, in particular direct general elections to the European Parliament. Within this framework, the Community's public expenditure could be increased to 2 or 2.5% of GDP. The report goes on to propose[4] that the Community should increase its development aid, both regional and international, in certain fields within a range of 2 000 to 4 000 m EUA, whereby the net cost of this additional expenditure would not be more than a 1% increase in Community GDP if account is taken of the cost reductions that a common market is likely to bring in the areas of agriculture, industry and technology.

In absolute terms, however, the two Community budgets are not insignificant and invite comparison with the three smallest national budgets, being 13 times the volume of Luxembourg's budget, three times larger than Ireland's and 94% the size of Denmark's. At the same time, they are equivalent to 13% of the British budget.

The Community's financial resources are therefore too small to be able to play a counter-cyclical role, for example in combating inflation and unemployment which are at present the main concerns of governments in all the Member States. Nevertheless, since two-thirds of non-repayable disbursements are for agriculture (in market guarantees) with the aim of maintaining farmers' incomes and preventing agricultural prices from rising excessively, they do contribute towards fighting unemployment and inflation. Moreover, it must be recognized that the Community's financial resources are beginning to constitute a real factor in structural change. The fact is that Europe's financial instruments should be used primarily to support Community policies, to provide the basis for solidarity among the Member States and to ensure that Community resources are employed rationally.[5]

Solidarity among the Member States is an objective publicly embraced by all, but the theory of fair shares has long been lurking in the background, if not indeed more openly in the backrooms of power. Yet in all of 20 years this question never really arose, except as regards Euratom. The EEC and ECSC functioned without the member governments being unduly concerned about totting up their contributions and returns, though they sometimes exercised self-restraint to avoid excessive imbalances. Application of the Treaties brought about a degree of economic integration in the member countries, and to some extent social integration too. Trade expanded. GDP grew, with fluctuations from country to country it is true, but at unprecedented rates. There was hope of seeing the Economic Community become a Political Community. As a result of the convictions of a number of people, coupled with a high level of economic growth, the Community's finances were in good shape, and the road to a united Europe seemed the best or indeed the only possible solution.

Then came scepticism because of the difficulty of transforming the economic entity into a political one. Difficulties arose with enlargement, inflation and unemployment loomed large and rising energy prices took their toll. The Community spirit eroded, purely national concerns came more and more to the fore. Europe's finances inevitably suffered as a result and became something of a disappointment. Without sound European policies it was difficult for Europe's finances to prosper.

The European Council meeting in Bremen in July 1978 was the turning point. The political will expressed there to establish a European Monetary System (EMS) was translated in practical details at the European Council in Brussels in December 1978. The desire to create a zone of monetary stability in Europe logically entails attempting to bring rates of inflation into line at the lowest possible level. However, although the convergence of inflation rates at a moderate level is the surest guarantee of exchange-rate stability and balance-of-payments equilibrium, it has to be part of a wider strategy that also covers other major economic and social goals, in particular sustained growth permitting a gradual return to full employment, the alignment of living standards and reduction in regional disparities. This strategy entails measures designed to allow the less-prosperous economies to join and stay in the EMS, in other words a transfer of resources. Concurrent studies were called for. They did not progress as quickly as intended, and have in fact unearthed a new problem. It was not the question of a fair return this time but the opposite. The studies showed that a viable monetary system cannot be achieved unless there is some convergence of economies, in other words unless there is a considerable sustained effort to establish balance within the Community at regional level in order to help the less-prosperous Member States, i.e. those whose *per capita* GDP is below the Community average: the United Kingdom (76%), Italy (62%) and Ireland (49%). The Community became a melting pot of ideas, the question being whether the existing machinery provided scope for large transfers of resources. As far as lending operations were concerned (EIB, ECSC, Euratom and recently the EEC), opinions differed over whether a genuine transfer effect was achieved, as the reduced interest system was only just getting off the ground and the sums involved have to be paid back. Some said there was no permanent transfer of resources while others maintained that loans facilitate lasting improvements in structural terms. As to grants, it was held by some that there was no way of measuring their impact. Others felt that Community spending should be considered as a whole, since expenditure for structural purposes partly offset the effects of other spending; this led to arguments over net contributions to the budget and the overall position of each country.

This discussion was completely transformed, however, following the request from the United Kingdom and Italy, formally submitted at the European Council meeting in

Strasbourg on 21 and 22 June 1979, for a reference paper describing the financial consequences of applying the budget arrangements on the situation in each Member State, especially in 1979 and 1980 (see Annex 3, p. 356). Instead of convergence, the watchword
was now balances and net balances, in other words the net profit or loss when a Member
State's contribution is compared with the Community's spending in that country. A report
was drawn up for the European Council in Dublin on 29 and 30 November 1979 and updated for the European Council in Luxembourg on 27 and 28 April 1980. This analysis,
undertaken by the Community, much to the chagrin of the Commission,[6] testified, by the
very fact that it was thought necessary, to a deterioration in the Community spirit. The bitter debates on the subject concentrated attention on the question of balancing the books,
disregarding all the other aspects of European integration in terms of political, economic
and human gains. The table below is based on the figures submitted to the two European
Council meetings and summarizes—in a form for which the author takes sole
responsibility—the results of applying the budget arrangements.

What do the figures in the table show?

First of all, Her Majesty's Government would appear to be right in saying the United
Kingdom is a major net contributor now that the own-resources arrangements are applied
in full. This is serious for the simple reason that the arrangements are genuinely organized
on a Community basis ('communautaire' in Brussels jargon), so the situation is bound to
persist, because it is built-in, for many years to come. Since the own-resources regime cannot be permanently undermined by a financial mechanism entailing substantial and continuing refunds, the system can only be brought back onto an even keel via the expenditure
side. So, in order to give the United Kingdom a bigger share of Community spending, the
section of the budget devoted to structural expenditure has to be increased, but without en-
dangering the agricultural guarantee policy. The only way to satisfy both these conditions is
to step up budget spending and, by implication, budget receipts. This entails transferring
more financial resources from the Member States to the Community. Moreover, the Italian
Government's call for a restructuring of the budget to make it more balanced can also only
be met by stepping up expenditure.

Community budget arrangements for 1979 and 1980

(%)

	B	DK	D	F	IRL	I	L	NL	UK	Total
					Outturn for 1979					
Budget contribution[1]	6.7	2.5	30.7	20.1	0.7	12.5	0.1	9.4	17.5	100
Spending in each State[2]	6.6	5.3	21.5	20.5	4.9	17.1	0.1	12.0	12.0	100
Difference	−0.1	+3.0	−9.2	+0.4	+4.2	+4.6	0	+2.6	−5.5	0
					Estimates for 1980[3]					
Budget contribution[1]	6.1	2.4	29.8	19.1	0.9	12.0	0.1	8.6	20.9	100
Spending in each State[2]	6.0	5.5	23.1	20.5	4.8	18.5	0.2	12.0	9.4	100
Difference	−0.1	+3.1	−6.7	+1.4	+3.9	+6.5	+0.1	+3.4	−11.5	0

[1] Percentages given in Chapter VII (see p. 128).
[2] Percentages given in the Conclusion to Part Three (see p. 333).
[3] Prior to the decision on the 'British problem' on 30 May 1980.

Secondly, in spite of the Federal Republic of Germany's increasing benefits from the EAGGF Guarantee Section, she is still a net contributor. The Federal Government has conceded this fact and is not kicking up a fuss about it. It has accepted the role of 'Zahlmeister' (paymaster in military parlance), particularly after it ceased to be the main contributor. The United Kingdom, on the other hand, has protested and regards the budget system as inequitable in itself and an unsatisfactory and unsound basis on which to finance the Community's common policies. Her partners have agreed and recognized, to quote the conclusions of the Paris Summit of 10 December 1974, that 'if unacceptable situations were to arise, the very life of the Community would make it imperative for the institutions to find equitable solutions' (see Annex 3, p. 351). Despite the setbacks at the European Council meetings in Dublin in November 1979 and Luxembourg in April 1980, but also as a result of them, the Council arrived at a solution to the 'British problem' for the years 1980, 1981 and 1982 on 30 May 1980. This involves large refunds[7] to the United Kingdom under the financial mechanism (see. p. 126) plus the financing of supplementary measures (see p. 222), but it does not clear up the essential problem at the heart of the crisis. It may well be things will never be quite the same as before.[8]

However, leaving aside this recent departure which may lead to the Community giving up or at least watering down the central principles on which it is currently based (and some of which concern us here, such as the question of independent revenue, financial solidarity, harmonious economic development), *two main directions for the future, one in the financial sector proper and the other on the institutional side*, should be examined.

Where Community public finance is concerned, the most urgent problem of the moment is the impending and certain exhaustion of the Community's own resources. The nearer this time comes, the more difficult the position of the Budgetary Authority is becoming. The Council can only cut agricultural guarantee spending with great difficulty, while the European Parliament is not willing to stop the growth of non-compulsory expenditure. In these circumstances, a solution (or solutions) must inevitably be found. One of these, adopted in 1979, is not to include what constitutes none the less Community expenditure in the budget at all, as in the case of the EDF. Another would be to remove some items of Community spending completely or partially from the budget, such as certain agricultural expenditure, but it is obvious that this approach would get neither a unanimous vote in the Council nor a majority in the Parliament. A third possibility would be to resurrect Article 200 of the EEC Treaty, since there are those who claim it was not rendered null and void by the Decision of 21 April 1970 and that therefore the system of financial contributions from Member States automatically comes back into effect if this is essential in order to finance Community activities because the own resources provided by the 1970 Decision are inadequate. Yet clearly this would be a political solution, implying agreement on the basic principle and approval of a new formula for calculating each country's contribution, and the Council would have to take both decisions unanimously, doubtless causing strained relations with member governments and difficulties with the European Parliament. The price would be worth paying to achieve a more 'communautaire' result. This brief resumé of three possible answers will have demonstrated that none of them is satisfactory and that the Community spirit calls for further independent revenue to finance Community activities. Although three of the member governments are at present firmly opposed to the prospect of additional own resources, there are grounds for thinking that this opposition may weaken eventually in the face of rising difficulties. It is the contention of the author that the right moment to take this step would be the enlargement of the Community to include Spain and Portugal. The accession of the former in particular will raise particularly acute problems with regard to economic convergence, solidarity among the Member States and the financial transfers needed to further the development of the less prosperous economies. As things have turned out, above all as a result of the Council's Decision of 30 May 1980 on the 'British problem', the time when further own resources become absolutely necessary and the date of Spain's accession are not going to coincide. If the two deadlines had come more or less at the same time, it would have been possible to combine approval of a new decision on own resources with the new act of accession. This would have entailed considerable political advantages for the Member States. But since the two dates will not coincide,[9] the own resources question remains a problem and some simplified, stop-gap solution may have to be considered, such as a small customs duty on energy.

At the institutional level, the Community has—in the final analysis—evolved in much the same way as the centralized or federal nation States. Power has been won through the right to raise taxes and approve the budget. To be sure the European Parliament does not at present possess anything like budgetary powers, but the use it has made of its budgetary prerogatives has turned it into an institution on a par with the others. The elections in June 1979 increased public awareness of the Community's financial problems, and the discussion over the budget is now undergoing a change in emphasis. The Council, for its part, has the task of resolving the issue of imbalance in the budget arrangements, so as to transcend the differing interests of the Member States; this gives a genuinely political dimension to its budget deliberations. As to the Commission, it is required more than ever to play the role of a partner supplying ideas, sound advice and impetus. The Community's financial system in its present form is one of the foundations for the perpetuation and development of the Community. The resources which the Community has at its disposal, the principle of solidarity which, when all is said and done, is one of the system's essential attributes, and the system's potential, could all be used to persuade the peoples, parliaments and governments of the Nine, as well as the Community institutions, to make the European Community more 'communautaire'.

Footnotes to the Conclusion to Part Three and the General conclusion

[1] These figures are equivalent to about UKL 58 thousand million or IRL 65 thousand million, though it should be pointed out that the purchasing power of the different units of account involved has varied considerably over the years. Consequently, the conversion made understates the actual position quite considerably.

[2] One particularly significant example of the difficulty of attributing expenditure to a specific Member State may be cited. When a product is exported, its Community price cannot be regarded, for accounting purposes, as a profit for the exporting country but only the refund paid to make it easier to sell it on an external market since this refund is financed from the Community budget (see p. 172). If the same product is donated as food aid, it would be misleading to attribute the value of the aid, which is equal to the Community price, to the exporting Member State. However, this is exactly what happens when balance-of-payments calculations are made (see footnote 6 below). In its report for the European Council meeting in Dublin in November 1979, therefore, the Commission did not include spending on aid to non-member countries in its calculations.

[3] The Commission asked a group of experts chaired by Sir Donald MacDougall, Chief Economic Adviser to the Confederation of British Industry, to draw up a report on the role of public finance in European integration. The MacDougall Report was completed in April 1977 and published in the Commission's economic and financial studies series (No A13).

[4] The proposals made in the MacDougall Report were:
(a) greater EEC involvement in labour market policies;
(b) establishment of a Community unemployment fund;
(c) a limited budget equalization scheme for the weaker Member States, say up to 65% of the Community average;

(d) a convergence fund aimed at preventing increasing divergences of the weaker Member States' economies away from the rest during recessions;

(e) a 10 000 m EUA programme to reduce disparities in living standards between Member States to about 10% compared with 40% at present.

⁵ In the Commission's report of 25 June 1975 on European Union (see Supplement 5/75—Bull. EC), which was to help Mr Tindemans in drawing up a report he himself was to give to the European Council on 2 April 1976 (see Supplement 1/76—Bull. EC), it was stated: 'The sums earmarked in the Community budget have been relatively small, and their actual utilization is largely determined by built-in mechanisms ... A more rational idea would be to provide the Union with a larger budget which was sufficiently flexible to allow of prompter responses to changes in the needs of the Union as a whole, both in respect of structures (the energy crisis is a good example of this requirement) and in relation to overall demand management. The budget could be used to influence economic trends in this way either by direct intervention measures, or by the Union granting Member States loans or subsidies linked to compliance with the objectives of the Union's policies. The Union's budget would thus play an important role in transferring resources between the economies and in redistributing them between social groups so as to eliminate imbalances. However, the Union's budget will probably continue to be primarily an instrument of structural policy, and its role in current economic activity will at first be extremely limited ... The role of the Union's budget as an instrument of general economic policy would of course be strengthened if ... quite new categories of expenditure could be included (e.g. infrastructure programmes, certain social security expenditure, unemployment insurance, etc.) ...

Transforming the role of the Union's budget in this way will also mean refining the system of own resources by creating a European tax system which would be activated by a decision of the institutions of the Union. As the measures of financial intervention by the Union are expanded, so too will the present range of sources for financing its budget have to be broadened ... A European tax system with a more varied range of instruments could also become an additional means of achieving redistribution so as to assist the most needy regions and social groups. As regards other revenue, the Union will have to be able to raise loans on the capital markets (particularly for investment and infrastructure expenditure of common interest). Hence the Union budget would constitute an instrument which, when combined with the instruments of monetary policy, would enable action to be taken not only to improve structures but also, to some extent at least, to influence short-term economic trends.'

⁶ Until November 1978, the Commission had always been against publishing information on financial flows between the Member States, since figures of this kind give a false impression of each country's individual efforts towards achieving Community goals and of the economic benefits which they derive from it. The Commission has always thought that working out fair returns for each Member State does nothing to help create a spirit of cooperation within the Community. However, finding that the Press and some Members of the European Parliament were at times miscalculating the impact of the Community budget on the various member countries, it felt that the time had come to disclose the figures. These were assembled on the basis of Council Regulation (EEC) No 1172/76 on the creation of the financial mechanism, in which the calculation of net transfers is based on purely financial transfers for accounting purposes and not on economic impact (see the answers to European Parliament Written Questions Nos 604/78 and 607/78 in OJ C 28 of 31.1.1979 and Written Question No 50/79 in OJ C 164 of 2.7.1979).

This exercise was based solely on payments balances between the Community and the Member States and contained some imperfections, so the Community used an entirely different analysis in its reference paper on budgetary questions of 12 September 1979 for its report to the European Council meeting in Dublin on 29 and 30 November 1979.

⁷ The solution to the 'British problem', adopted by the Council on 30 May 1980, covers the years 1980, 1981 and 1982. It is based on the principle of a net contribution which the United Kingdom must pay. This works as follows:

For 1980 Britain's net contribution to the European Communities' general budget is reduced to 609 m EUA, compared with the Commission's estimate of 1 784 m EUA based on the budget for 1980 which had not yet been adopted. This net contribution assumes that no new repayments are made. It should be pointed out that the financial mechanism introduced under the Regulation of 17 May 1976 could not be used.

This arrangement means that the British Government's partners accepted the idea that there should as a general rule be a broad balance between the United Kingdom's payments by way of own resources and the sums spent in the United Kingdom by the Community. The UK's net contribution, i.e. the difference between these two figures, is reduced to a third of what it would have been. The other eight partners thus have to make up this difference, a total of 1 175 m EUA.

If the contribution exceeds 1 784 m EUA, the extra amount will be split between the UK and its partners even more favourably: the UK bearing 25% and the other eight countries 75%. It will not be easy to determine the net contribution because the figure of 1 784 m EUA was a forecast made almost a year before the end of the financial year in question on the basis of a budget not adopted until much later. Some implicit assumptions were made in calculating the figure, too, and agreement will have to be reached on them.

The payments made to the UK are straightforward repayments (under the financial mechanism, see p. 124) which the British Government can use as it sees fit, and financial support under a Community Regulation (special supplementary measures, see p. 222).

The figure of 609 m EUA to be borne by the British Government was arrived at on the basis of political considerations.

For 1981 the United Kingdom's net contribution is set at 730 m EUA, compared with the 2 140 m EUA it would have been without further action being taken; this would have been an increase of 19.9% (or 121 m EUA) over 1980, the percentage by which 2 140 m EUA exceeds 1 784 m EUA.

If the United Kingdom's net contribution goes above 2 140 m EUA, a sharply decreasing coefficient in the UK's favour comes into play. It must bear all of the increase between 730 and 750 m EUA, 50% between 750 and 850 m EUA and 25% beyond 850 m EUA. The balance in the latter two cases is financed by the other partners in addition to the 1 410 m EUA they already have to bear.

For 1982, no figures have been laid down because it is impossible to forecast amounts which are anything like realistic. Instead it has been agreed that the Commission will put forward proposals to the Council on the lines of the solution for 1980 and 1981 if structural changes cannot resolve the problem (see footnote 30, p. 245).

Conclusions: Three conclusions can be drawn from the Council's deliberations:
 (i) The United Kingdom's net contribution has been reduced by 2 585 m EUA for 1980 and 1981.
 (ii) The new measures are to be carried out in the context of the Community's present own resources, that is within the limit of the 1% of VAT. There is some ambiguity as to how long the Council expects the situation to continue, which is just as well since it looks as if the decisions taken on 30 May 1980 will mean that the 1% ceiling will be reached in 1981.
 (iii) The Community will have to resolve the 'British problem' by making structural changes. The development of Community policies must not call into question the common financial responsibility for these policies, which are financed from the Community's own resources or the basic principles of the common agricultural policy. In addition, taking account of the situations and interests of all Member States, a recurrence of unacceptable situations for any of them must not be allowed to occur. The following is a quote from the Council's conclusions on this subject: 'It is important for the future well-being of the Community that day-to-day decisions and policy-making should function effectively and this particularly during the period when the review provided for is under way. With this objective in mind all Member States undertake to do their best to ensure that Community decisions are taken expeditiously and in particular that decisions on agricultural price fixing are taken in time for the next marketing year' (see footnote 30, p. 245).

Follow-up: On 12 June 1980, the Commission submitted a proposal for an EEC Regulation establishing supplementary measures in favour of the United Kingdom (OJ C 169 of 9.7.1980) as well as a proposal for a Regulation amending Regulation (EEC) No 1172/76 of 17 May 1976 setting up a financial mechanism (OJ C 171 of 11.7.1980).

The agreement of 30 May 1980 will have the following financial repercussions. The 1175 m EUA for 1980 will be financed in 1981 as follows (approximate figures): Federal Republic of Germany 466 m EUA, France 351 m EUA, Italy 155 m EUA, Netherlands 86 m EUA, Belgium 65 m EUA, Denmark 37 m EUA, Ireland 12 m EUA and Luxembourg 3 m EUA. The sum of 1 410 m EUA for 1981 will be spread in 1982 as follows (approximate figures): Federal Republic of Germany 545 m EUA, France, 427 m EUA, Italy 220 m EUA, Netherlands 90 m EUA, Belgium 74 m EUA, Denmark 38 m EUA, Ireland 13 m EUA and Luxembourg 3 m EUA. The major net contributors under the present budget arrangements will therefore be the Federal Republic of Germany, the United Kingdom and France, in that order.

[8] During the European Parliament debate on 8 July 1980 on the Council's declaration on Luxembourg's presidency, Mr Thorn, in his capacity as Council President, said: 'I should like to issue a solemn warning to those who favour going back to square one, a hypothetical idea which would seem to entail building new policies on the ruins of Community policies developed over two decades which have served us well. The cost of these principles should undoubtedly be re-examined in the light of criteria perhaps better suited to changing circumstances, and to new preoccupations, but the principles on which they are based must not be called into question. Otherwise there would be little hope of seeing genuinely Community policies taking over from the old ones.... As regards the budget and the restructuring of policies, I would remind you that in the views I have expressed this morning and this afternoon, the budget is regarded as a tool for implementing policies and not for formulating them. This is why I see impending danger if we put all our policy options in one basket, restrict them, confine them to the area of the budget discussions.... The budget, as you yourselves have proved, can provide impetus, direction. But on the pretext of providing impetus, we should not run the risk of inhibiting the smooth running of the Community.... If Community solidarity was abandoned, or watered

down, that would mark the end of Community policies, we would be left with the *quid pro quo* mentality.... I reject any policy based on fair returns but, just as firmly, I believe that unless we remedy the present overall imbalance in our policies, it will prevent the formulation of new policies, however vital these might be to further development.' (Mr Thorn's words are given here in an unofficial translation, the official version not being available at time of going to press.)

[9] On 21 July 1980, at the fourth negotiating conference on the accession of Spain to the European Communities, the Community stated that extensive preparatory work, which had already started among the Nine on the subject of agriculture and would soon begin on the subject of fisheries, was needed so that it could define its position. The problems are indeed considerable, and raise questions concerning olive oil (whether there should be a tax or not), fruit and vegetables and wine, as well as the changes to be made to the CAP as regards Mediterranean products.

Annexes

Correct protocol is to list the Member States of the European Communities in the alphabetical order of their names in the various national languages. The sequence is therefore Belgique/België, Danmark, Deutschland, France, Ireland, Italia, Luxembourg, Nederland, United Kingdom (Article 2 of the Merger Treaty as amended by Article 11 of the Act of Accession of 22 January 1972).

From 1 January 1981, Greece will come between the Federal Republic of Germany and France (Article 11 of the Act of Accession of 28 May 1979).

343

Member States of the European Community in relation to each other

Selected figures on the Community of Nine (in 1980)

(%)

Country	Popula-tion	GDP	Contribution to the budget			Category A staff at the Commission on 1 January 1980	Weighted votes in	
			Original own resources	VAT	Total		Council	European Parliament
Belgium	3.8	4.4	7.56	4.54	6.17	13.5	8.6	5.8
Denmark	2.0	2.5	2.16	2.62	2.38	3.0	5.2	3.9
FR of Germany	23.5	30.5	27.26	32.80	29.81	19.0	17.2	19.8
France	20.6	24.1	14.09	24.67	18.96	20.2	17.2	19.8
Ireland	1.3	0.6	0.93	0.86	0.90	2.9	5.2	3.6
Italy	21.9	14.0	12.76	10.90	11.90	17.4	17.2	19.8
Luxembourg	0.1	0.2	0.05	0.20	0.12	2.9	3.6	1.4
Netherlands	5.4	6.0	10.92	6.05	8.68	6.0	8.6	6.1
United Kingdom	21.4	17.8	24.27	17.36	21.08	14.5	17.2	19.8
Total	100	100	100	100	100	99.4	100	100

To substantiate the remark made on the first page of the introduction, it is worth listing Community and non-Community countries according to GDP at 1975 market prices in million US dollars (World Bank figures): 1. United States of America (1 519 890), 2. USSR (649 470), 3. Japan (496 260), 4. *Federal Republic of Germany* (412 480), 5. China (315 250), 6. *France* (314 080), 7. *United Kingdom* (211 700), 8. Canada (158 100), 9. *Italy* (156 590), 10. Brazil (110 130), 11. Spain (97 140), 14. *Netherlands* (78 550), 19. *Belgium* (61 470), 26. *Denmark* (34 350), *Ireland* (7 470), *Luxembourg* (2 150).

The Community budget compared with the GDP's and national budgets in the Community of Nine

Year	In 1 000 million	Community GDP	Member States' budgets (central government)	General budget of the Community	General budget as % of	
					GDP	Member States' budgets
1	2	3	4	5	6=5:3	7=5:4
1973	u.a.	868	228	4.6	0.53	2.0
1974	u.a.	983	268	5.0	0.51	1.9
1975	u.a.	1 111	337	6.2	0.55	1.8
1976	u.a.	1 282	388	8.0	0.62	2.1
1977	u.a.	1 489	443	9.6	0.66	2.2
	EUA	1 405	404	9.6	0.69	2.4
1978	EUA	1 554	470	12.2	0.78	2.6
1979	EUA	1 744	524	14.5	0.83	2.8
1980	EUA	1 958	595	14.7	0.75	2.5

The figures in columns 3 and 4 are estimates for 1979 and forecasts for 1980.

345

Selected national and Community indicators for the Community of Nine in 1979

Country	Per capita GDP		Per capita disbursements		National budget in 1 000 m EUA
	EUA	Relative to the average	National budget	Community budget	
Belgium	8 305	124	2 944	94	29
Denmark	9 235	138	3 007	66	15.4
FR of Germany	9 024	135	2 462	69	151
France	7 773	116	1 776	51	95
Italy	4 153	62	1 422	30	81
Ireland	3 299	49	1 486	32	5
Luxembourg	8 380	125	3 073	53	1.1
Netherlands	7 824	117	2 565	92	36
United Kingdom	5 098	76	1 986	54	111
Community average	6 696	100	2 014	55	

Reminder	Total of national budgets	524.5
	Community budget	14.5

1. *Sources*:
   Population data are based on Eurostat (Cronos).
   Gross domestic product data are based on Eurostat (Cronos).
   National budget data are from Commission departments.
   Community budget disbursements are taken from the 1977 revenue and expenditure accounts.
2. Rates for converting between EUA and national currencies are 1979 averages in all cases.
NB: *Per capita* GDP is calculated at current prices and exchange rates. If the figures were based on current purchasing power prices and parities they would show less of a spread and be more in line with the living standards in each country (see p. 200); however, this method is used by the Community only for calculating the salaries of European officials (see p. 308).
Also note that the Community still uses gross domestic products (GDP) alongside gross national products (GNP), e.g. for financial contributions (see p. 377) and the financial mechanism in its original form (see p. 124).

Selected data for the Community of Twelve

Country	Population %	GDP %	Weighted votes in		Per capita GDP	
			Council %	European Parliament %	In EUA	Relative to the average
Belgium	3.1	4.3	6.6	4.6	7 536	139
Denmark	1.6	2.6	3.9	3.2	8 603	159
FR of Germany	19.4	29.4	13.2	15.7	8 187	151
France	16.9	21.7	13.2	15.7	6 959	129
Ireland	1.0	0.6	3.9	2.9	2 892	54
Italy	18.0	12.0	13.2	15.7	3 605	67
Luxembourg	0.1	0.2	2.5	1.2	7 694	142
Netherlands	4.4	6.0	6.6	4.9	7 370	136
United Kingdom	17.7	14.2	13.2	15.7	4 348	80
Total (Nine)	82.2	91.0	76.3	79.6		
Greece	3.0	1.4	6.6	4.6	2 587	48
Spain	11.7	6.8	10.5	11.2	3 150	58
Portugal	3.1	0.8	6.6	4.6	1 431	27
Total (Twelve)	100	100	100	100		
Average (Twelve)					5 400	100

Population and GDP data are 1978 figures.
The figures given in Article 148 of the EEC Treaty and Article 118 of the Euratom Treaty apply to voting in the Council and those given in the Act of 20 September 1976 on direct elections to the European Parliament apply to voting in Parliament in the Community of Nine. Those given in the Commission's 'fresco' of 20 April 1978 (see Annex 16) apply to voting in the Community of Twelve.

346

Data on the institutions

A—Voting rules

Voting rules in the Council

(Article 148 of the EEC Treaty, Article 118 of the Euratom Treaty and Article 28 of the ECSC Treaty)

	B	DK	D	GR	F	IRL	I	L	NL	UK	Qualified majority
Community of Six:											
Administrative budget	2		4		4		4	1	2		12
Social Fund budget	8		32		32		20	1	7		67
Research budget	9		30		30		23	1	7		67
Community of Nine:											
General budget	5	3	10		10	3	10	2	5	10	41
Community of Ten:											
General budget	5	3	10	5	10	3	10	2	5	10	45

The rules for voting by qualified majority which apply to the budget also apply to other matters under the provisions of the EEC and Euratom Treaties. If the vote is on a Commission proposal, the 41 (45) votes in favour must include the votes cast by at least six Member States.

The ECSC Treaty provides for majorities which give particular weight to the Member States which each produce at least one-eighth of the total value of the Community's coal and steel output (the Federal Republic of Germany, France and the United Kingdom).

Voting rules in the European Parliament

The European Parliament votes on budget matters as follows:
(a) by 'a majority of its members' (for amendments to the budget on first reading, see p. 7);
(b) by 'an absolute majority of the votes cast' (for proposed modifications on first reading, see p. 6);
(c) by 'a majority of its members and three-fifths of the votes cast' (for amendments to the budget on

final reading, see p. 7, and for the new rate of increase of non-compulsory expenditure, see p. 122);
(d) by 'a majority of its members and two-thirds of the votes cast' (to reject the budget, see p. 9, or to pass censure, see p. x).

Before the direct elections, the European Parliament was able to assemble a majority of its members (i.e. 100) after Article 203 of the EEC Treaty and the corresponding articles of the other Treaties came into force (see p. 6) on all but one occasion, the vote on amending budget No 2/77. This was a remarkable achievement, so much so that, on 25 October 1978, Parliament took advantage of the presence of its members in Luxembourg for the vote on the first reading of the budget for 1979 to pass amendments to its rules of procedure, which require the same quorum. Several months had elapsed without it being able to adopt these changes for lack of a sufficient majority. This example more than any other illustrates how much importance Parliament attaches to its budget powers.

After the direct elections, the European Parliament has also been able to assemble a majority of its members (now 206). When the budget was thrown out on 13 December 1979, for instance, there were 352 members voting.

347

B—National and political make-up of the European Parliament, its Committee on Budgets and its Committee on Budgetary Control

The three following tables summarize the national and political make-up of the European Parliament and the two committees whose terms of reference cover Community finance matters. The initials and names of the various political groups are:

S —Socialist Group

EPP —Group of the European People's Party (Christian-Democratic Group before the direct elections)

ED —European Democratic Group (Conservative Group before the direct elections)

COM —Communist Group

L —Liberal and Democratic Group

EPD —Group of European Progressive Democrats

Others —In particular the Group for the Technical Coordination and Defence of Independent Groups and Members (since the direct elections)

Political and national make-up of the European Parliament before (1) and after (2) direct elections

Member State	S		EPP		L		ED		COM		EPD		Others		Total	
	(1)	(2)	(1)	(2)	(1)	(2)	(1)	(2)	(1)	(2)	(1)	(2)	(1)	(2)	(1)	(2)
Belgium	5	7	7	10	2	4								3	14	24
Denmark	4	4			1	3	2	3	1	1	2	1		4	10	16
FR of Germany	15	35	18	42	3	4									36	81
France	10	22	3	8	9	17			5	19	9	15			36	81
Ireland	1	4	3	4							6	5		2	10	15
Italy	5	13	15	30	2	5			12	24			2	9	36	81
Luxembourg	2	1	2	3	2	2									6	6
Netherlands	6	9	5	10	3	4								2	14	25
United Kingdom	18	18			1		16					1	1	1	36	81
Total	66	113	53	107	23	39	18	3	18	44	17	22	3	21	198	410

Column headings: *Political groups in order of size (2)*

Political and national make-up of the European Parliaments' Committee on Budgets before (1) and after (2) direct elections

Member State	S		EPP		ED		COM		L		EPD		Others		Total	
	(1)	(2)	(1)	(2)	(1)	(2)	(1)	(2)	(1)	(2)	(1)	(2)	(1)	(2)	(1)	(2)
Belgium	1	1													1	1
Denmark	1	1					1	1	1					1	3	3
FR of Germany	3	3	5	4					1						9	7
France	1	2	1	1				1	2	2	2	1			6	7
Ireland		1	1	1							1	1			2	3
Italy	1	1	1	3			2	2							4	6
Luxembourg	1								1						2	0
Netherlands	1	1	1	1						1					2	3
United Kingdom	3	1			3	6									6	7
Total	12	11	9	10	3	6	3	4	5	3	3	2	0	1	35	37

Column headings: *Political groups in order of size (2)*

Political and national make-up of the European Parliament's Committee on Budgetary Control before (1) and after (2) direct elections

Member State	Political groups in order of size (2)															
	S		EPP		ED		COM		L		EPD		Others		Total	
	(1)	(2)	(1)	(2)	(1)	(2)	(1)	(2)	(1)	(2)	(1)	(2)	(1)	(2)	(1)	(2)
Belgium		1														1
Denmark								1		1						2
FR of Germany	1	2	1	2					1	2					3	6
France		1		2							1	1			1	4
Ireland		1		1												2
Italy		1		2			1	1						1	1	5
Luxembourg	1														1	0
Netherlands		1	1	1											1	2
United Kingdom	1	1			1	4									2	5
Total	3	8	2	8	1	4	1	2	1	3	1	1	0	1	9	27

NB: The title of this table has been simplified for the sake of convenience. In fact the Committee on Budgetary Control has only existed since the direct elections were held (see p. 99); previously there was a Control Subcommittee under the Committee on Budgets.

ANNEX 3

European Summits and European Councils

In 1969 the Heads of State or Government of the Member States of the Community decided to hold regular meetings—called European Summits until 1974 and European Councils thereafter (see p. ix). A frequent topic of discussion at these meetings has been Europe's finances. Seventeen of these meetings touched on this matter between 1969 and summer 1980.

The Hague Summit
(1 and 2 December 1969)

Own resources: 'As regards the completion of the Communities, the Heads of State or Government have reaffirmed the will of their governments to pass from the transitional period to the final stage of the European Community and, accordingly, to lay down a definitive financial arrangement for the common agricultural policy by the end of 1969.

They agree to replace gradually, within the framework of this financial arrangement, the contributions of member countries by the Community's own resources, taking into account all the interests concerned, with the object of achieving in due course the integral financing of the Communities' budgets in accordance with the procedure provided for in Article 201 of the Treaty establishing the EEC and of strengthening the budgetary powers of the European Parliament' (point 5 of the Final Communiqué).

Cost of the agricultural policy: 'They have asked the governments to continue without delay, within the Council, the efforts already made to ensure a better control of the market by a policy of agricultural production making it possible to limit the burden on budgets' (point 6).

Financial arrangement: 'The acceptance of a financial arrangement for the final stage does not exclude its adaptation by unanimous vote in an enlarged Community, on condition that the principles of this arrangement are not watered down' (point 7).

Technology: 'As regards the technological activity of the Community, they reaffirmed their readiness to continue more intensively the activities of the Community with a view to coordinating and promoting industrial research and development in the principle pacemaking sectors, in particular by means of common programmes, and to supply the financial means for the purpose' (point 9).

Paris Summit
(19 to 21 October 1972)

Regional Fund: 'The Heads of State or Government agreed that a high priority should be given to the aim of correcting, in the Community, the structural and regional imbalances which might affect the attainment of economic and monetary union.

The Heads of State or Government invite the Commission to prepare without delay a report analysing the regional problems which arise in the enlarged Community and to put forward appropriate proposals.

From now on they undertake to coordinate their regional policies. Desirous of directing that effort towards finding a Community solution to regional problems, they invite the Community institutions to create a Regional Development Fund. This will be set up before 31 December 1973, and will be financed, from the beginning of the second phase of economic and monetary union, from the Community's own resources. Intervention by the Fund in coordination with national aids should permit, progressively with the attainment of economic and monetary union, the correction of the main regional imbalances in the enlarged Community and particularly those resulting from the preponderance of agriculture and from industrial change and structural underemployment' (point 5 of the Final Communiqué).

Social policy: 'The Heads of State or Government emphasized that they attached as much importance to vigorous action in the social field as to the attainment of economic and monetary union. They thought it essential to ensure the increasing involvement of labour and management in the economic and social decisions of the Community. They invited the institutions, after consulting labour and management, to draw up, between now and 1 January 1974, a programme of action providing for concrete measures and the corresponding resources, particularly in the framework of the Social Fund, based on the suggestions made in the course of the Conference by Heads of State or Government and by the Commission' (point 6).

Reinforcement of institutions: 'They were agreed in thinking that, for the purpose in particular of carrying out the tasks laid down in the different programmes of action, it was desirable to make the widest possible use of all the provisions of the Treaties, including Article 235 of the EEC Treaty' (end of point 15).

Copenhagen Summit
(14 and 15 December 1973)

The Heads of State or Government agreed:

Regional Fund: 'That the Regional Development Fund should be established on 1 January 1974. As an expression of their positive attitude to the establishment of the Fund, they agreed to recommend to their Foreign Ministers that the Council of the European Communities at its next session shall take the necessary decisions concerning the size and the distribution of the Fund and the criteria for the Fund's operations' (point 7, third paragraph, of the Communication from the Presidency).

Court of Auditors and Parliament's budgetary powers: 'They agreed to make the functioning of the Community's institutions more effective by improving cooperation between the Council, the Commission and the Parliament, by a more rapid procedure for the settlement of questions submitted to the Community authorities and by reinforcing its financial control, involving, *inter alia,* the establishment of an independent Court of Auditors for the Community and the strengthening of the role of the European Parliament in budgetary matters' (point 7, fifth paragraph).

Energy: 'The Heads of State or Government have considered the question of energy in a separate paper, attached to this Declaration' (point 8).

'The Heads of State or Government considered that the situation produced by the energy crisis is a threat to the world economy as a whole, affecting not only developed but also developing countries. A prolonged scarcity of energy resources would have grave effects on production, employment and balances of payments within the Community.

The Heads of State or Government therefore agreed on the necessity for the Community of taking immediate and effective action along the following lines.

They asked the Council to adopt provisions to ensure that all Member States introduce on a concerted and equitable basis measures to limit energy consumption.

With a view to securing the energy supplies of the Community the Council will adopt a comprehensive Community programme on alternative sources of energy. This programme will be designed to promote a diversification of supplies by developing existing resources, accelerating research into new sources of energy and creating new capacities of production notably a European capacity for enrichment of uranium, seeking the concerted, harmonious development of existing projects' (Annex to the Communication from the Presidency).

Paris Summit
(9 and 10 December 1974)

The Commission's management powers: 'Moreover, they agree on the advantage of making use of the provisions of the Treaty of Rome whereby the powers of implementation and management arising out of Community rules may be conferred on the Commission' (point 8 of the Final Communiqué).

Regional Fund: 'The Fund will be endowed with 300 m u.a. in 1975, with 500 m u.a. for each of the years 1976 and 1977, i.e. 1 300 m u.a., for a trial period of three years' (point 23).

'This total sum of 1 300 m u.a. will be financed up to a level of 150 m u.a. by as yet unused EAGGF (Guidance Section) appropriations.

The resources of the Fund will be divided along the lines envisaged by the Commission:

Belgium	1.5%
Denmark	1.3%
France	15.0%
Ireland	6.0%
Italy	40.0%
Luxembourg	0.1%
Netherlands	1.7%
Federal Republic of Germany	6.4%
United Kingdom	28.0%

Ireland will in addition be given another 6 m u.a. which will come from a reduction in the shares of the other Member States with the exception of Italy' (point 24).

Social Fund: 'When the time is ripe, the Council of the Community will consider, in the light of experience and with due regard to the problem of the regions and categories of workers most affected by employment difficulties, whether and to what extent it will be necessary to increase the resources of the Social Fund' (point 26).

Financial mechanism: 'The Heads of State or Government recall the statement made during the accession negotiations by the Community to the effect that "if unacceptable situations were to arise, the very life of the Community would make it imperative for the institutions to find equitable solutions"' (point 35).

'They confirm that the system of own resources represents one of the fundamental elements of the economic integration of the Community' (point 36).

'They invite the institutions of the Community (the Council and the Commission) to set up as soon as possible a correcting mechanism of a general application which, in the framework of the system of own resources and in harmony with its normal functioning, based on objective criteria and taking into consideration in particular the suggestions made to this effect by the British Government, could prevent during the period of convergence of the economies of the Member States, the possible development of situations unacceptable for a Member State and incompatible with the smooth working of the Community' (point 37).

First European Council
(Dublin, 10 and 11 March 1975)

Financial mechanism: 'The Heads of State or Government meeting in Council agreed on the correcting mechanism described in the Commission Communication entitled "Unacceptable situation and correcting mechanism", subject to the following provisions:
(1) The criteria concerning the balance-of-payments deficit and the two-thirds ceiling are dropped.
(2) The following provisions will be incorporated into the agreed mechanism:
   (a) The correcting mechanism shall be subject to a ceiling of 250 m u.a. However, as soon as the size of the Community budget exceeds 8 000 m u.a., the ceiling shall be fixed at an amount representing 3% of total budget expenditure;
   (b) When a moving average drawn up over 3 years indicates that the balance of payments on current account of the country in question is in surplus, the correction shall only affect any difference between the amount of its VAT payments and the figure which would result from its relative share in the Community GNP' (point I of the Summary of Decisions).

Third European Council
(Rome, 1 and 2 December 1975)

The Court of Auditors, Parliament's budgetary powers, the Budget Commissioner, the Joint Council and the EUA: 'The European Council carried out a thorough examination of the problems connected with the supervision of Community expenditure and the Community's budget policy.

The Council agreed on the need for more effective financial control over Community expenditure and stated that it was in favour of the suggestions made by the Heads of Government of the United Kingdom, the Federal Republic of Germany and Ireland and the proposals from the Commission being examined expeditiously.

The President of the Council and the President of the Commission were invited to make contact with the President of the European Parliament with a view to examining the role which that institution might play in controlling Community expenditure by means of a committee or subcommittee.

The Heads of State of Government agreed to make every effort to ensure the early completion of the procedure for the ratification of the Treaty setting up a European Court of Auditors signed on 22 July last in Brussels, with a view to enabling the Court to commence activities during 1976.

The European Council noted with satisfaction the information communicated by the President of the Commission regarding the strengthening which had already taken place in the powers of the Member of the Commission responsible for the budget, without prejudice, however, to the principle of the collective responsibility of the Commission as laid down in the Treaties.

With reference to the agreement reached at Villa Marlia and formally adopted by the Council meeting in Brussels on 5 and 6 November regarding the annual joint meeting of Ministers for Foreign Affairs and Ministers for Finance to carry out an overall assessment of Community budget problems, the European Council considers that discussions at such meetings should concentrate on general Community policy, ensure greater consistency as regards decisions on policies to be followed and budget decisions and allow better distribution of Community resources to be achieved by means of the gradual introduction of multiannual expenditure forecasts. The discussion relating to next year should take place, on the basis of a Commission Communication, before the end of April.

The European Council noted the Commission's intention to submit to the Council proposals concerning the use of the European unit of account in the Community budget' (pp. 2 and 3 of the Conclusions of the Presidency on the Community budget and financing).

Energy: 'The Commission will submit proposals and the Council will decide as soon as possible on appropriate mechanisms to protect existing supplies and ensure the development of alternative sources of Community energy, on reasonable economic terms, and to encourage conservation in the use of energy' (p. 7 of the Conclusions of the Presidency on the Conference on International Economic Cooperation).

Sixth European Council
(The Hague, 29 and
30 November 1976)

Coordination of financial instruments: 'The European Council took note of the fact that the Commission had already taken action of its own to ensure a greater degree of coordination between the existing Funds (Social, Regional, Agricultural) and of the Community's statement that it would be submitting proposals to the Council in early 1977 for the purpose of ensuring greater cohesion in the operations of those Funds' (point 1 of the Conclusions of the Presidency).

Seventh European Council
(Rome, 25 and 26 March 1977)

Employment, convergence and financial instruments: 'The European Council further agreed in particular to seek action at the Community level in three directions: firstly to promote measures to help resolve specific labour market problems, especially in improving training and employment opportunities for young people and women: secondly to encourage higher levels of investment in the Member States: and thirdly to halt divergence and promote convergence in their economic performance. To this end, the European Council invites on the one hand the Commission, in particular by the better use of Community instruments, and on the other hand the Board of Governors of the European Investment Bank to seek ways of improving the effectiveness of their activities' (point I.A.3. of the Conclusions of the Presidency).

Ninth European Council
(Brussels, 5 and 6 December 1977)

New Community Instrument (NCI): 'The European Council declared itself in favour of the development of the Community's financial means by approving the principle of the establishment, on an experimental basis, of a new instrument for Community lending and borrowing, the loans being managed by the European Investment Bank. It instructed the Council (Ministers for Financial and Economic Affairs) to examine the proposal which the Commission would make on this subject' (point I.4.c. of the Conclusions of the Presidency).

Common agricultural policy: 'The European Council took note of the problems raised by monetary compensatory amounts in the context of the agricultural policy, as regards their financial effects and their impact on the unity of the market. Between now and March 1978 it expects the Council to re-examine these problems on the basis of proposals from the Commission' (point I.5., second paragraph).

European unit of account (EUA): 'The EUA will be used in the budget of the European Communities from 1 January 1978' (point II). The rest of this statement is reproduced in full in Annex 10, p. 381.

Regional Fund: 'The European Council agreed:
(1) On three-year planning of the European Regional Development Fund, as follows:
1978: 580 m EUA ⎫
1979: 620 m EUA ⎬ Total 1 850 m EUA.
1980: 650 m EUA ⎭
(2) To grant France, for the benefit of the French Overseas Departments, a 2% increase in its national quota, to be deducted from the quotas of the other Member States.
(3) To instruct the Council to settle the other outstanding points, including the establishment of a non-quota section' (point III).

Tenth European Council
(Copenhagen, 7 and 8 April 1978)

New Community Instrument (NCI): 'The European Council considers it essential for the Community to achieve an annual growth rate of 4.5% by the middle of 1979.

With this in mind the Community will in the coming months assess the effects of present national economic policies and on this basis define the need for—and in appropriate cases—the margin of manoeuvre open to Member States for coordinated additional measures designed to achieve the necessary growth within the Community.

During the same period the Community will, through common measures, support the action of Member States and make better use of existing common facilities to alleviate present restraints on Member States' possibilities for action. In this connection the European Council referred to the new Community loan facility. It also invited the Governing Board of the EIB to adopt at its meetings in June a decision to double the capital of the Bank' (point I of the Conclusions of the Presidency).

Eleventh European Council
(Bremen, 6 and 7 July 1978)

EUA and monetary policy: 'Following the discussions in Copenhagen on 7 April 1978 the European Council has discussed the scheme for the creation of closer monetary cooperation (European Monetary System) leading to a zone of monetary stability in Europe, which has been introduced by members of the European Council. The European Council regards such a zone as a highly desirable objective. The European Council envisages a durable and effective scheme' (point I.2 of the Conclusions of the Presidency).

(Annex):
'1. In terms of exchange-rate management the European Monetary System (EMS) will be at least as strict as the "snake". In the initial stages of its operation and for a limited period of time member countries currently not participating in the snake may opt for somewhat wider margins around central rates. In principle, interventions will be in the currencies of participating countries. Changes in central rates will be subject to mutual consent. Non-member countries with particularly strong economic and financial ties with the Community may become associate members of the system. The European currency unit (ECU)[1] will be at the centre of the system; in particular, it will be used as a means of settlement between EEC monetary authorities.
2. An initial supply of ECUs (for use among Com-

---
[1] The ECU has the same definition as the European unit of account.

353

munity central banks) will be created against deposit of US dollars and gold on the one hand (e.g. 20% of the stock currently held by member central banks) and member currencies on the other hand in an amount of a comparable order of magnitude.

The use of ECUs created against member currencies will be subject to conditions varying with the amount and the maturity; due account will be given to the need for substantial short-term facilities (up to one year).

3. Participating countries will coordinate their exchange-rate policies *vis-à-vis* third countries. To this end, they will intensify the consultations in the appropriate bodies and between central banks participating in the scheme. Ways to coordinate dollar interventions should be sought which avoid simultaneous reserve interventions. Central banks buying dollars will deposit a fraction (say 20%) and receive ECUs in return; likewise, central banks selling dollars will receive a fraction (say 20%) against ECUs.

4. Not later than two years after the start of the scheme, the existing arrangements and institutions will be consolidated in a European Monetary Fund.[1]

5. A system of closer monetary cooperation will only be successful if participating countries pursue policies conducive to greater stability at home and abroad; this applies to deficit and surplus countries alike' (point IV).

Social Fund: 'The European Council confirms its view that improving the employment situation by means of increased growth is a crucial objective of the Community.

It notes that the Community is already providing considerable assistance through the European Social Fund and the European Regional Fund. It calls upon the Council of Ministers of Labour and Social Affairs to decide on measures to combat youth unemployment within the framework of the European Social Fund so that such measures can come into force on 1 January 1979' (point I.3).

Twelfth European Council (Brussels, 4 and 5 December 1978)

European Monetary System (EMS): 'In Bremen we discussed a "scheme for the creation of closer monetary cooperation leading to a zone of monetary stability in Europe". We regarded such a zone "as a highly desirable objective" and envisaged "a durable and effective scheme".

Today, after careful examination of the preparatory work done by the Council and other Community bodies, we are agreed as follows:

---

[1] The European Monetary Fund (EMF) will take the place of the European Monetary Cooperation Fund (EMCF).

A European Monetary System (EMS) will be set up on 1 January 1979.

We are firmly resolved to ensure the lasting success of the EMS by policies conducive to greater stability at home and abroad for both deficit and surplus countries.

We remain firmly resolved to consolidate, not later than two years after the start of the scheme, into a final system the provisions and procedures thus created. This system will entail the creation of the European Monetary Fund as announced in the conclusions of the European Council meeting at Bremen on 6 and 7 July 1978, as well as the full utilization of the ECU as a reserve asset and a means of settlement. It will be based on adequate legislation at the Community as well as the national level.

The ECU and its functions: A European currency unit (ECU) will be at the centre of the EMS. The value and the composition of the ECU will be identical with the value of the EUA at the outset of the system.

The ECU will be used:

(a) as the denominator (*numéraire*) for the exchange rate mechanism;

(b) as the basis for a divergence indicator;

(c) as the denominator for operations in both the intervention and the credit mechanism;

(d) as a means of settlement between monetary authorities of the European Community.

The weights of currencies in the ECU will be re-examined and if necessary revised within six months of the entry into force of the system and thereafter every five years or, on request, if the weight of any currency has changed by 25%.

Revisions have to be mutually accepted; they will, by themselves, not modify the external value of the ECU. They will be made in line with underlying economic criteria.

Measures designed to strengthen the economies of the less-prosperous Member States participating in the European Monetary System

1. We stress that, within the context of a broadly-based strategy aimed at improving the prospects of economic development and based on symmetrical rights and obligations of all participants, the most important concern should be to enhance the convergence of economic policies towards greater stability. We request the Council (Economic and Finance Ministers) to strengthen its procedures for coordination in order to improve that convergence.

2. We are aware that the convergence of economic policies and of economic performance will not be easy to achieve. Therefore, steps must be taken to strengthen the economic potential of the less-prosperous countries of the Community. This is primarily the responsibility of the Member States concerned. Community measures can and should serve a supporting role.

3. The European Council agrees that in the context of the European Monetary System, the following measures in favour of the less prosperous Member States effectively and fully participating in the exchange rate and intervention mechanisms will be taken.

3.1. The European Council requests the Community institutions, through the new financial instrument and the European Investment Bank, to make available for a period of 5 years loans of up to 1 000 m EUA per year to these countries on special conditions.

3.2. The European Council requests the Commission to submit a proposal to provide interest rate subsidies of 3% for these loans, with the following elements: The total cost of this measure, divided into annual tranches of 200 m EUA each over a period of 5 years shall not exceed 1 000 m EUA.

3.3. Any less-prosperous Member State which subsequently effectively and fully participates in the mechanisms would have the right of access to this facility within the financial limits mentioned above. Member States not participating effectively and fully in the mechanisms will not contribute to the financing of the scheme.

3.4. The funds thus provided are to be concentrated on the financing of selected infrastructure projects and programmes, with the understanding that any direct or indirect distortion of the competitive position of specific industries within Member States will have to be avoided.

3.5. The European Council requests the Council (Economics and Finance Ministers) to take a decision on the abovementioned proposals in good time so that the relevant measures can become effective on 1 April 1979 at the latest. There should be a review at the end of the initial phase of the EMS.

4. The European Council requests the Commission to study the relationship between greater convergence in the economic performance of the Member States and the utilization of Community instruments, in particular the Funds which aim at reducing structural imbalances. The results of these studies will be discussed at the next European Council.'

Common agricultural policy: 'The European Council considers that the introduction of the EMS should not of itself result in any changes in the situation obtaining prior to 1 January 1979 regarding the expression in national currencies of agricultural prices, monetary compensatory amounts and all other amounts fixed for the purposes of the common agricultural policy.

The European Council stresses the importance of henceforth avoiding the creation of permanent MCAs and progressively reducing present MCAs in order to re-establish the unity of prices under the common agricultural policy, giving also due consideration to prices policy' (Resolution of the European Council).

Thirteenth European Council (Paris, 12 and 13 March 1979)

Social Fund: 'The European Council devoted a large part of its proceedings to the employment situation and social policy. It acknowledged that priority should be given to improving the employment situation, which continues to give rise to concern.

The European Council confirmed the importance it attaches to improving youth employment and its wish that the Council keep the new aids from the Social Fund in favour of this category under review. It instructed the Council to study the following measures which should help, along with others, to improve the employment situation.

To make training better adapted to employment by developing staggered training schemes, i.e. by coupling practical training obtained through the exercise of an occupation at the place of work with theoretical training in a training establishment, body or department;
...

The European Council stressed the importance of the social measures taken by the Community in favour of workers in the iron and steel industry and other sectors in difficulty.

The European Council requested the Commission to continue its efforts to improve the effectiveness of the European Social Fund's action by directing its assistance more selectively in order to meet the current employment difficulties better.

The Council also noted the importance of a coordinated contribution by the various Community financial instruments to the intensification of the fight against unemployment' (third, fourth, fifth and sixth paragraphs of point II of the Conclusions of the Presidency).

Energy: 'The Community and the Member States will step up their efforts to make the best possible use of Community hydrocarbon and coal resources. The programmes for the production of electricity from nuclear sources must be strengthened and speeded up whenever conditions so permit; the use of solar and geothermal energy must likewise be further developed.

With regard to energy saving, the new measures taken at national or Community level must not adversely affect the level of economic activity in the Member States and will therefore be aimed particularly at the consumption of energy by government departments and public authorities, heating of business and residential premises and at a more rational use of energy by motor vehicles.

The Council will adopt the necessary provisions at Community level to pursue the development of oil technologies, promote the use of coal and nuclear energy and make use of new sources of energy through an increased research and development effort and through demonstration projects.

As regards energy saving, the Council will carry out the desired harmonization and will determine any additional means of intervention which might be applied at Community level' (second, third, fourth and sixth paragraphs of point III.2).

European Monetary System and convergence of economies: 'The implementation of the EMS, which will constitute an important contribution towards the development of stable and lasting growth in the Community, must be supported by increased convergence of the economic policies and performances of the Member States.

The European Council had an exchange of views on the means for arriving at improved convergence.

It emphasized the need for the Community institutions to ensure more efficient use of the existing instruments in order to attain this objective.

It invited the Council and the Commission to examine in depth how the Community could make a greater contribution, by means of all its policies taken as a whole, to achieving greater convergence of the economies of the Member States and to reduce the disparities between them' (first, fourth, fifth and sixth paragraphs of point IV).

Common agricultural policy: 'The European Council had a detailed exchange of views on the common agricultural policy, in the light of a Communication from the Commission. In confirmed the importance which it attaches to the fundamental objectives of this policy, which is one of the achievements in the construction of Europe.

It noted that growing imbalances on agricultural markets have led to an increase in expenditure on agricultural support.

It considered that a prices policy suited to the situation and a search for measures adapted to each type of production are likely to correct the imbalances which have become apparent on certain markets and to avoid the build-up of surpluses.

The European Council expressed its interest in the improvement of the agricultural structures policy, particularly in favour of the least-favoured regions of the Community, and invited the Commission to submit additional proposals in this sector.

Also, with a view to enlargement, the Council hoped that the efforts to improve structures undertaken in favour of the Mediterranean regions would be continued so that the interests of all agricultural producers in the Community received equal consideration.

The European Council invited the Council (Ministers for Agriculture) to examine those improvements which are necessary for the proper functioning of the common agricultural policy with due regard to the objectives laid down in the Treaty of Rome' (point V).

Fourteenth European Council (Strasbourg, 21 and 22 June 1979)

Energy: 'The Council also expresses its resolve to continue and step up this effort to limit oil consumption and, through energy saving, the development of indigenous production and the progressive use of alternative energy, to maintain Community imports between 1980 and 1985 at an annual level not higher than that for 1978.

So that these efforts may continue in consonance with the growth of their economies, the Community and the Member States will continue and extend the redeployment of energy which has already begun. This redeployment will be based on the strengthening of the energy-saving measures already under way and be such as to enlist the use of nuclear energy, coal and, as soon as possible, other alternative sources of energy.

In view of the necessary change in oil imports, the use of coal in power stations must be stepped up without delay; its use in industry must also be encouraged. Special attention will be given to technological programmes to devise new processes for the extraction, transport and processing of coal.

The European Council notes that the situation calls for national and Community research and development efforts in the energy sector to be stepped up by coordinating national action and joint programmes so that more tangible prospects may shortly be found for the economical use of new resources, especially solar and geothermal energy. Like nuclear energy, these "clean" forms of energy will contribute to halting the build-up in the atmosphere of carbon dioxide caused by the use of fossil fuels.

Such research will also be directed at promoting new techniques for the use of conventional resources and achieving energy savings' (Chapter III of the Conclusions of the Presidency).

Convergence of Member States' economic performances and European public finances: 'The European Council noted the report submitted to it by the Council (Economic and Financial Affairs) on the convergence of Member States' economic performances.

Following comments from a number of delegations, it asked the Commission to submit to the Council a reference paper describing the financial consequences of applying the budgetary system on the situation in each Member State, especially in 1979 and 1980. The study will have to take into account the economic, financial and social effects of each Member State's participation in the Community and the Community nature of the components contributing to the formation of own resources. For 1980, it will take account of the agricultural prices for the 1979/80 marketing year.

The Commission will at the same time examine the conditions under which the corrective mechanism decided on in 1975 can play its part in 1980 and the extent to which it fulfils the objectives assigned to it.

The Commission will submit its study to the Council so as to enable the Member States to give their opinions and present their requests in concrete form. In the light of the debate and of any guidelines which may emerge from the Council, the Commission will present proposals sufficiently early to enable decisions to be taken at the next meeting of the European Council' (Chapter IV).

Fifteenth European Council (Dublin, 29 and 30 November 1979)

Convergence and budgetary questions: 'The European Council held an exchange of views on convergence and budgetary questions. They re-affirmed the conclusions reached at their meetings in Brussels and Paris that achievement of the convergence of economic performances requires measures for which the Member States concerned are primarily responsible, that Community policies can and must play a supporting role within the framework of increased solidarity and that steps must be taken to strengthen the economic potential of the less-prosperous countries of the Community.

To these ends, the European Council expressed its determination to promote the adoption of measures to improve the working of Community policies, to reinforce those policies most likely to favour the harmonious growth of the economies of the Member States and to reduce the disparities between these economies. It further declared the need, particularly with a view to the enlargement of the Community and necessary provisions for Mediterranean agriculture, to strengthen Community action in the structural field.

The European Council has carried out a thorough examination of the problem of the British contribution to the Community budget.

It was agreed that the Commission's proposals concerning the adaptation of the financial mechanism could constitute a useful basis for a solution which would respect Community achievements and solidarity. This solution should not result in raising the 1% VAT cciling.

In addition, the Commission is requested to pursue the examination of proposals for developing supplementary Community measures within the United Kingdom which will contribute to greater economic convergence, and which will also lead to a greater participation by the United Kingdom in Community expenditure.

The Commission is asked to make proposals which will enable the Council of Ministers to pursue the search for appropriate solutions to be reached at the next meeting of the European Council. The President of the Council will convene the European Council as soon as the conditions for such a meeting have been fulfilled' (Conclusions of the Presidency).

Sixteenth European Council (Luxembourg, 27 and 28 April 1980)

European Monetary System: 'The European Council pointed out that a reduction in economic disparities and the strengthening of the weaker economies were prerequisites for the development of the European Monetary System.

The European Council took note of the progress of studies concerning transition to the second stage of the System, confirmed its resolve to see the Community progress towards the objective of monetary integration and invited the relevant Community bodies to press ahead with work in order to move on to the institutional stage, involving definition of the ECU's role and the creation of the European Monetary Fund.'

Energy: 'These structural changes could be speeded up by support at Community level, for a set period and subject to the financial constraints which the Community sets itself. The European Council invited the Council of Ministers to consider as a matter of urgency the steps proposed by the Commission to stimulate the development of a coherent energy policy within the Community' (Conclusions of the Presidency).

Convergence and budgetary questions: No Communiqué was issued on this aspect since the European Council failed to reach agreement.

Seventeenth European Council (Venice, 12 and 13 June 1980)

Brussels Compromise of 30 May: 'The conclusions reached on 29 and 30 May by the Council of Ministers of the Community were noted with satisfaction. These conclusions enabled a solution to be found to the problem of the United Kingdom's contribution to the Community budget, led to an agreement on 1980/81 farm prices and on the sheepmeat problem and defined the guidelines for a comprehensive common fisheries policy. The outcome of these discussions has led, *inter alia*, to finalization of the 1980 budget, thereby normalizing the working of the Community.

A key feature of the agreements thus reached is the Community's commitment to implement structural changes which, by ensuring a more balanced development of common policies, based on respect for their fundamental principles, and by preventing the recurrence of unacceptable situations, will enable each Member State to become more closely identified with Community objectives and with the deepening process of European integration.

This commitment is a fundamental prerequisite, especially bearing in mind the prospect of enlargement, if the Community is to be able to meet its internal and international responsibilities authoritatively and effectively; to respond to the expectations of the citizens of Europe with ever closer solidarity between Member States in the various sectors of political, economic and social activity; to promote greater convergence and the harmonious development of their economies, help to reduce the disparities between the various regions and the ground to be made up by the less well-off; in short, to attain in full the objectives enshrined in the Treaties in total compliance with the ideals underlying the grand design of European unification' (point I of the Summary by the Presidency).

*
* *

This is not an exhaustive list. Other European Summits and European Councils have discussed questions indirectly concerning Europe's finances, but have not been included here at the risk of drawing out what is already a lengthy account. Two facts will strike the reader. Firstly, a whole range of subjects from the important to the trivial are referred to or raised by the Council itself. Secondly, it deals with them or is forced to deal with them in very different ways: sometimes laying down guidelines or expressing its wishes and sometimes even specifying the very last detail. This makes it difficult to judge how effective the Council is. What is, however, undeniable is that it had to be created and that it has now become the Community's leading institution. Shortly before the European Council on 27 and 28 April, President Giscard d'Estaing made the following comment in *Le Figaro* of 11 April: 'The European Council is moving further and further away from its true objective. My intention in suggesting its creation was that it should give European leaders an opportunity to discuss international affairs from the European viewpoint and to provide the necessary stimulus for action to be taken by the Community institutions but not that it should supplant other Community institutions in the performance of their normal duties.'

The trend in appropriations included in preliminary draft budgets and budgets since 1974

The figures in the following table show the trend in the appropriations entered in the general budget in the last six years. The term 'final budget' refers to the ordinary budget plus any supplementary budgets up to and including 1979; i.e. there is no reference to budget implementation as in Annex 12 (pp. 393 to 399).

It can be seen from this table that the Commission has each year tried to reduce the share of the EAGGF Guarantee Section in its preliminary draft budget for the following financial year, while in the budget as finally adopted this expenditure accounted for an increasing share of the total except in 1978 and 1979.

The preparatory procedure for the 1980 budget has confirmed this pattern. In the preliminary draft budget submitted on 15 June 1979, the Commission proposed a ratio of EAGGF Guarantee Section to other expenditure of 59.9% to 40.1%. As a result of the agricultural price decisions for the 1979-80 marketing year and related measures adopted on 22 June 1979 in opposition to its own proposal (see pp. 171 and 183), the Commission was obliged to modify its initial preliminary draft so as to ensure that sufficient appropriations were available. Consequently, the ratio became 62.6% to 37.4%.

By substantially reducing non-compulsory expenditure during its second reading of the budget on 23 November 1979, the Council changed the ratio of EAGGF Guarantee Section expenditure to other expenditure to 67.2% to 32.8%. This new ratio became one of the reasons for the rejection on 13 December 1979 of the draft budget by the European Parliament, whose aim was to bring agricultural spending within bounds and to increase the non-compulsory expenditure.

In its new budget proposal of 29 February 1980, the Commission fixed the ratio of EAGGF Guarantee Section expenditure to other expenditure at 63.3% to 36.7%. This ratio was incorporated in the ordinary budget for 1980.

The trend in appropriations included in the preliminary draft budgets and budgets since 1974
for all the institutions of the European Communities
Since the application of Article 203 of the EEC Treaty, taking as a basis appropriations for commitments
(whether differentiated or not)

| | u.a. | | | | | | EUA | |
	Final budget 1974	Preliminary draft 1975	Final budget 1975	Preliminary draft 1976	Final budget 1976	Preliminary draft 1977	Final budget 1977
Total figures	5 225.0	6 955.7	6 268.3	8 058.0	8 470.6	10 121.1	10 267.9
		+33.12%		+28.55%		+19.49%	
			+19.97%		+35.13%		+21.22%
Of which								
EAGGF Guarantee Section	3 513.1	67.2	3 972.1	57.1	4 240.5	67.6	5 160.3	64.—	5 835.3	68.9	6 628.4	65.5	7 125.3
Other	1 711.9	32.8	2 983.6	42.9	2 027.8	32.4	2 897.7	36.—	2 635.3	31.1	3 492.7	34.5	3 142.6
	5 225.0	100.—	6 955.7	100.—	6 268.3	100.—	8 058.0	100.—	8 470.6	100.—	10 121.1	100.—	10 267.9	1
Of which								
Compulsory expenditure	4 496.9	86.1	5 298.6	76.2	5 243.4	83.7	6 252.1	77.6	6 991.8	82.5	7 981.5	78.9	8 365.2
		+17.83%		+19.24%		+14.16%	
			+16.60%		+33.34%		+19.64%
	728.1	13.9	1 657.1	23.8	1 024.9	16.3	1 805.9	22.4	1 478.8	17.5	2 139.6	21.1	1 902.7
Non-compulsory expenditure		+127.59%		+76.20%		+44.68%	
			+40.80%		+44.29%		+28.67%
		100.—		100.—		100.—		100.—		100.—		100.—		1

EUA

Preliminary draft 1978	Final budget 1978	Preliminary draft 1979	Final budget 1979	Preliminary draft 1980	Final budget 1980	Preliminary draft 1981
151.1	12 702.9	14 869.2	15 423.3	17 915.3	17 318.9	21 731.8
8.08%	+23.71%	+17.05%	+21.42%	+16%		+25.48%

3.4	63.7	8 695.3	68.5	9 718.1	65.4	10 384.1	67.3	11 212.9	62.6	11 485.5	66.3	12 941.5	59.6
7.7	36.3	4 007.6	31.5	5 151.1	34.6	5 039.2	32.7	6 702.4	37.4	5 833.4	33.7	8 790.3	40.4
.1	100.—	12 702.9	100.—	14 869.2	100.—	15 423.3	100.—	17 915.3	100.—	17 318.9	100.—	21 731.8	100.—

5.3	79.4	10 356.—	81.5	11 743.2	79.—	12 254.4	79.5	13 350.4	74.5	13 149.—	75.9	16 643.4	76.6
5%		+23.80%		+13.40%		+18.33%		+8.94%		+26.58%			

.8	20.6	2 346.9	18.5	3 126.0	21.—	3 168.9	20.5	4 564.9	25.5	4 169.9	24.1	5 088.4	23.4
3%		+23.35%		+33.20%		+35.02%		+44.05%		+31.59%		+22.03%	
	100.—		100.—		100.—		100.—		100.—		100.—		100.—

The work of the 'Conciliation Committee'

The origin of this liaison body involving the Council, Parliament and the Commission has already been described (see p. 10). Here we discuss what the Conciliation Committee has done, or what it has not done, since the signing of the Joint Declaration of 4 March 1975.

A—Regulations submitted to the 'Conciliation Committee' (in chronological order)

WORK COMPLETED

1. *Regional Fund* (1975-76-77)—The first meeting of the Conciliation Committee took place on 4 March 1975 to discuss the new proposals for regulations and decisions on the regional policy. In view of the circumstances which gave rise to the conciliation procedure, this was a hurried meeting, and the results were not very conclusive, the Council maintaining its position in every respect (Council Regulation (EEC) No 724/75 of 18 March 1975[1]) (see p. 218).

2. *JET*—Some attempt was made at conciliation on JET, the Presidents of the Council and Parliament meeting on 19 April 1977 (see footnote 13, p. 271).

3. *The Financial Regulation applicable to the general budget*—The text of this document prompted the first real round of conciliation meetings. At the time, the Council was in the habit of:
(a) adopting a 'common position', a kind of properly-worded and fully-motivated draft decision;
(b) forwarding this to the European Parliament as a basis for the conciliation meeting;
(c) amending it or not, depending on the outcome of the conciliation meeting; and
(d) adopting and publishing its Decision very soon afterwards.

This would be an excellent procedure were the delegations to the Council not inclined to choose the lowest common denominator for the 'common position'.

The Conciliation Committee met on 7 November, 22 November and 7 December 1977 to discuss the changes to be made to the Financial Regulation. The delegation from the European Parliament, actively encouraged by its rapporteur, Mr Michael Shaw (UK, Conservative), managed to get the Council to bring its views nearer to those of Parliament in many instances and thus obtained a considerable departure from the Council's 'common position' of 17 May 1977 (resulting in the Financial Regulation of 21 December 1977[2]).

The points made by Parliament in presenting these views concerned:
(i) the fixing of the budget nomenclature during the budgetary procedure (Article 15(3));
(ii) the division of appropriations into commitment appropriations and payment appropriations to be adopted during the budgetary procedure (Article 1(4));
(iii) borrowing and lending activities to be included in the budget (Articles 12 and 15); but Parliament did not obtain the form of budget entry that it wanted;
(iv) power to be granted to Parliament to authorize transfers in respect of non-compulsory expenditure (Article 21);
(v) the European Parliament to be informed in respect of preliminary draft budgets (Articles 11 and 12);
(vi) remarks of a non-binding character to be included, but an entry to be made in the minutes of the Council meeting of 21 December 1977, in respect of Article (16)(2)(b) stating that such remarks may contain conditions governing the execution of the expenditure;
(vii) EAGGF Guarantee Section expenditure: the Commission may request the European Parliament's opinion if there is a danger that the planned measures would give rise to costs appreciably in excess of the appropriations entered in a specific chapter (statement included in the minutes of the Council meeting of 21 December 1977 in respect of Article 96).

However, Parliament did not win its case (see p. 37) on the question of supplementary budgets (Article 1(5)), the power to authorize the carry-over of appropriations from one year to another (Article 6), the

---

[1] See OJ L 73 of 21.3.1973.

[2] See OJ L 356 of 31.12.1977 (30 pages).

budget of borrowing and lending operations (referred to above) and auditing (Title VI). But it did ratify the results of this conciliation, i.e. the compromise reached on the Financial Regulation as a whole, in its Resolution of 13 December 1977.

Furthermore, during this conciliation procedure, the Council and Parliament agreed to apply the provisions of Article 203 of the EEC Treaty separately to commitment appropriations and payment appropriations.

4. *New Community Instrument* (NCI)—The Conciliation Committee met on 19 June, 18 September and 16 October 1978 to discuss the Council's 'common position' of 22 May 1978. Parliament's delegation, with the active encouragement of its rapporteur, Mr Altiero Spinelli (Italian, Communist; a former Member of the Commission), obtained two concessions from the Council, which are apparent from the two texts adopted:[1]
(i) sharing of powers in the administration of the NCI between the Commission and the EIB (Article 5): the Council agreed that the two should consult each other on and both sign loan applications; the EIB/Commission joint decision-making system replaces decision-making exclusively by the Bank, which is what the Council originally wanted;
(ii) experimental or definitive nature of the new financing instrument: reconsideration once one of the following two conditions has been satisfied: commitment of 800 m EUA or the expiry of a two-year period.

On the other hand, as regards the more general question of the entry in the budget of borrowing and lending operations, the Council and Parliament declared that borrowing and lending operations effected through the New Community Instrument would be subject to the general regulations. This implies that as soon as the legislative procedure for amending the Financial Regulation of the Communities, based on the proposal from the Commission on the introduction of a capital budget (see p. 63), already approved by the European Parliament, has been completed, these regulations will apply to the New Community Instrument.

5. *Regional Fund*—The Conciliation Committee met on 24 July and 17 October 1978; its work was continued by means of an exchange of letters and by meetings of Parliament's delegation on its own. Compared with the Council's 'common position' of 27 June 1978, Parliament's delegation obtained the following concessions:
(i) flexibility in the utilization of resources in the non-quota section: the rule that the unexpended balance of these resources revert to · the quota section will apply not to each financial year, but

to the whole three-year period (1978, 1979 and 1980);
(ii) flexibility in the utilization of quota resources: the utilization of national quotas may be the subject of flexible interpretation, in the sense that the Commission may consider each national quota as applying for the three-year period, rather than for one year only;
(iii) changes in the Fund Committee's procedures for approving aid. The Committee must deliver its opinion within 30 days, and the Council must notify Parliament if the decision it takes differs from that proposed by the Commission;
(iv) the assurance that, when the Regulation is next reviewed, which must be before 1 January 1981, the Council will take particular account of the views expressed by Parliament.

In fact, the Council's 'common position' of 27 June 1978 ultimately became, without a change being made, the text of the Regulation adopted on 6 February 1979.[2] A record of the concessions made by the Council is to be found only in the minutes. In contrast, the following demands voiced by Parliament were not accepted:
(a) national quotas should be indicative and not fixed by the Regulation;
(b) as regards the non-quota section: the proportion of the total for which this section accounts should not be limited by the Regulation, but fixed during the budgetary procedure; the percentage for which the Regulation makes provision (5%) is far too small. Moreover, the Council's decisions on action covered by this section should be taken by a qualified majority;
(c) the maximum rate of intervention by the Fund for any particular infrastructure projects should be increased to 50% (from 40%), and priority regions for such intervention should be specified in the Regulation;
(d) the Regulation should not limit the total intervention for infrastructure projects to a proportion (70%) of the total of the Fund;
(e) the system of accelerated payments for which the Regulation provides should be replaced by the system of advances proposed by the Commission;
(f) the Fund Committee should play a purely consultative role.

WORK IN PROGRESS

6. *Financial cooperation with non-member countries*—Three similar texts exist:
(i) the Regulation on financial and technical aid to the non-associated developing countries;
(ii) the Regulation on the application of the financial protocols with Greece, Turkey and Portugal;
(iii) the Regulation on the application of the financial protocols with certain Mediterranean countries

---

[1] See OJ L 298 of 25.10.1978.

[2] See OJ L 35 of 9.2.1979.

(the Maghreb countries, the Mashreq countries, Malta and Cyprus).

Parliament requested conciliation for the first two of these Regulations (Opinions of 21 April 1977 and 11 May 1978), but did not explicitly do so in respect of the third. But the three texts are considered to be linked: all three have been the subject of 'common positions' of the Council; all three essentially pose the problem of the role of the committees in the decision-making process; in all three cases the Council intends to use the same solution, i.e. the solution which will be adopted for the Regulation of the non-associated developing countries, which is at present the subject of a conciliation procedure. The Conciliation Committee met on 19 September 1978 to discuss aid to non-associated developing countries. It dealt only with the question of the Commission's powers in the implementation of the budget. In a letter of 3 March 1980, the President of Parliament tried to relaunch the conciliation procedure with regard to this Regulation. The Council adopted a new common position which it sent to Parliament on 11 June 1980; in this the Council continues to take a much stricter line with regard to decisions on financing projects than the 'ERDF approach'. On 25 July, the President of Parliament proposed reopening the conciliation procedure in September.

7. *Application of the European unit of account to the acts of the institutions of the European Communities*—On 24 July 1978 the Council adopted a 'common position' and proposed to Parliament that the conciliation procedure should be opened. So far there have been no more than informal contacts between the departments of the Parliament and the Council to prepare the way for the conciliation procedure proper. The respective views of the two institutions differ very widely.

However, Article 15 of the proposed Regulation on the introduction of the EUA in the customs field has been considered separately (see footnote 19, p. 32).

8. *Financial Regulation applicable to the general budget*—As agreed by the institutions when the Financial Regulation of 21 December 1977 (see point 3 above) was adopted, on 15 June 1978 the Commission put forward a proposal for amendments to the Financial Regulation under three heads: research and investment appropriations, entry in the budget of borrowing and lending operations and the carry-over of appropriations. A conciliation meeting took place on 20 November 1978,[1] and then, on 12 December 1978, the Council adopted a 'revised common position' reflecting the Commission's proposals on research and investment appropriations, except where

they concerned the nature—indicative or mandatory—of the financial ceilings for research programmes. The position adopted on the carry-over of appropriations was substantially different. In contrast, no agreement was reached on the matter of entering borrowing and lending operations in the budget. The continuation of the procedure resulted in the formal adoption by the Council on 25 June 1979 of a Regulation on the first two aspects. On the other hand, in answer to the request for conciliation on the two aspects still outstanding, made by Parliament in its Opinion of 14 March 1979, the Council stated on 7 May 1979 that it had not yet drawn up a common position on these parts of the Commission's proposal and was not therefore yet in a position to open the conciliation procedure on this subject. The absence of a joint position within the Council thus means that for the moment the conciliation machinery is blocked.

9. *The Financial Regulation applicable to the general budget*—On 23 April 1979 the Commission put forward a second proposal for amendments to the Financial Regulation of 21 December 1977, seeking to do away with the 'additional period' (for the EAGGF) a significant derogation from the general budgetary procedure allowing the actual annual closure of the accounts to be deferred until 31 March, and to rearrange the deadlines applicable to the procedure for presenting and auditing the accounts. On 10 December 1979 the Commission presented a third proposal amending the Financial Regulation of 21 December 1977 on the use of the ECU in the general budget of the European Communities. This proposal was amended on 3 July 1980 in the light of the Opinion delivered by Parliament on 23 May 1980, in which Parliament 'calls for the opening of the conciliation procedure if the Council wishes to derogate from Parliament's proposal'. The Commission's proposal—in its present form—has been withdrawn.

B—Requests for the opening of the conciliation procedure not accepted by the Council

1. *Euratom loans*—On 29 March 1977 the Council adopted the decision empowering the Commission to contract Euratom loans, without in fact departing significantly from the Opinion delivered by Parliament on 19 June and requesting the opening of the conciliation procedure.

2. *Regulations on financial aids to demonstration projects in the field of energy saving and on financial support for projects to exploit alternative energy sources*—In its Opinion of 17 November 1977, Parliament endorsed the Commission's proposals and did

---

[1] After this meeting the Conciliation Committee did not meet again in 1979, and had not met by the end of the first half of 1980 when the finishing touches were being put to the manuscript of this book.

not formally request the opening of the conciliation procedure, but on 12 June 1978 the Council adopted the two Regulations in a form which differed substantially from the Commission's proposals (see p. 252).

Parliament then requested on 14 July 1978 that the conciliation procedure be opened in respect of these two Regulations.

On 10 October 1978 the Council informed Parliament that it had considered the two proposals for regulations at its meeting of 20 May 1978, taking particular account of the Opinion Parliament had delivered on 17 November 1977, and that it had adopted them at its meeting of 12 June 1978. In the circumstances the Council regretted that it was no longer possible to open the conciliation procedure.

The Council did, however, leave the door open by drawing Parliament's attention to the fact that, pursuant to the provisions of Article 10 of the first Regulation and Article 11 of the second, neither Regulation would enter into force until the Council adopted a further implementing regulation fixing, by a unanimous decision, the maximum amount of aid which might be granted under these two Regulations.

But this was not basically the problem as Parliament saw it: what it objected to was that, through Article 5(2) of the first Regulation and Article 6(2) of the second, the Council interferes in the decision-making machinery and, according to Parliament, violates Article 205 of the EEC Treaty. The problem is similar to that raised in respect of aid to the non-associated developing countries (see above).

On 9 April 1979 the Council adopted the two Regulations fixing the maximum amount of Community aid—along with three implementing regulations on specific energy sectors—after noting that the conciliation procedure was not applicable to them.

3. *Ninth VAT Directive*—In its Opinion of 16 June 1978 Parliament 'reserves the right to request that a conciliation procedure be initiated should the Council intend to depart from this opinion'. But on 26 June 1978 the Council adopted the directive without having forwarded a 'common position' to Parliament. In a statement included in the Council's minutes, the Commission regretted this absence of conciliation, but noted that the position adopted by the Council was essentially identical to the view expressed by Parliament and, given the urgency of the matter, therefore understood why the Council did not resort to this procedure.

4. *Financial participation by the Community in respect of the inspection and surveillance operations in the maritime waters of Denmark and Ireland*—The Council adopted the Decision on 25 July 1978 even though on 15 June 1978 Parliament had suggested various modifications and requested the opening of the conciliation procedure should the Council intend to depart from Parliament's Opinion.

5. *Amount allotted to the EAGGF Guidance Section*—On 15 December 1978 Parliament delivered two different Opinions on the Commission's proposal for a Regulation amending Regulation (EEC) No 729/70 concerning the amount allotted to the EAGGF Guidance Section: in one it 'supports the idea of placing a five-year ceiling on expenditure', in the other it 'confirms its opposition to a ceiling being placed by Regulation ...' and 'reserves the right to initiate the conciliation procedure'. The Regulation adopted by the Council on 8 May 1979 imposes a five-year ceiling, but is accompanied by the statement that the Council noted that the present Regulation does not prevent it from adopting, while respecting the applicable provisions, new Community decisions concerning common action relating to agricultural structures, and will ensure that the fixing of EAGGF Guidance Section expenditure by five-year periods does not affect the performance of the various Community operations and specifically those involving a multiannual financing commitment.

6. *Decision applying the decision on the New Community Instrument*—On 25 April 1979 Parliament adopted an Opinion in which it 'reserves the right to initiate the conciliation procedure' in this connection, the general question of the extent of the Budgetary Authority's powers over borrowing and lending operations being the subject of a further conciliation procedure on the Financial Regulation (see point A8 above). On 14 May 1979 the Council authorized the Commission, in application of the basic decision on the New Community Instrument (see point A4 above), to contract a first tranche of loans amounting to 500 m EUA. On 15 July 1980 the Council released 80% of the second tranche of loans amounting to 500 m EUA, the decision to release the remaining 20% still remaining conditional on the Council's consent to extend the scope of lending operations. In neither case was there any conciliation.

7. *Interest rebates for loans with a structural objective within the EMS*—Although Parliament reserved the right in its Opinion of 25 April 1979 to open the conciliation procedure, the Regulation fixing the amount of loans on which interest rebates might be paid and the amount of interest rebates to be charged to the Community budget was adopted by the Council on 3 August 1979 without arrangements being made for conciliation. However, the President-in-Office of the Council explained in a letter to the President of Parliament that this Regulation was not of a general nature, which is one of the conditions set out in the Joint Declaration for the application of the conciliation procedure.

C—Matters which might have been submitted to the 'Conciliation Committee' if Parliament had so wished

Although it had received a 'common position', Parliament did not request conciliation in two significant matters:

1. *Review of the Social Fund*—After a first meeting on 28 June 1977, the Council adopted 'common positions' on 28 October 1977 and forwarded them to Parliament on 10 November 1977 to initiate the conciliation procedure.

Although Parliament states in paragraph 14 of its Resolution of 12 May 1977 on the Commission's proposals that it 'agrees with the Commission that the nature of its proposals is such that if the Council intends to depart from the opinion of the European Parliament it will be necessary to open a conciliation procedure with the European Parliament', it decided on 16 December 1977 not to initiate the conciliation procedure on the various texts involved, considering that it had 'a prime interest in not delaying the introduction on 1 January 1978 of the compromise reached on the revision'.

The proposals were adopted by the Council on 20 December 1977 (see p. 206), the exception being the measures relating to the employment of young people. These measures, which had been announced in the form of 'conclusions' in the series of 'common positions' adopted by the Council on 10 November 1977, were the subject of a proposal from the Commission of 10 April 1978 and of an Opinion delivered by Parliament on 9 May 1978. It its Opinion Parliament did not request conciliation. As Parliament had moreover refrained from initiating the conciliation procedure for any of the 'common positions' of November 1977, the Council departments felt that there was no need for conciliation.

2. *Texts relating to VAT—Sixth VAT Directive*: In its Resolution of 20 April 1977 on the Commission's amended proposal, Parliament states, although it had not previously expressed a desire for the conciliation procedure to be applied, that it 'decides . . . not to request the opening of a conciliation procedure on the substance of the Sixth Directive so as not to delay implementation of the system of own resources'.

Regulations implementing the Decision of 21 April 1970 on own resources: In its Opinion of 16 June 1977, which concerned only the proposed VAT Regulation, Parliament requested the opening of a conciliation procedure.

In its Opinion of 14 October 1977 on the Commission's amended proposals for a VAT Regulation and a Regulation on 'other own resources', Parliament again reserved the right to request conciliation.

In its Resolution of 14 December 1977 on the joint position of the Council, Parliament 'declines, for the time being, to initiate the procedure for conciliation with the Council' since 'it is absolutely essential for the Regulations establishing the system of own resources and thus giving the Communities complete financial autonomy to be adopted by 1 January 1978'.

D—Striking cases where the opening of the conciliation procedure has not been requested

1. *System of Community financial aids designed to encourage the use of coal in power stations*—The Council has not yet adopted the Regulation. In its Opinion of 10 May 1977 Parliament does not mention conciliation.

2. *System of Community aid for financing cyclical stocks of hard coal, coke and patent fuel*—The Council has not yet adopted the Regulation. In its Opinion of 13 September 1977 Parliament did not request conciliation.

3. *Multiannual programme (1979-83) for the development of informatics*—The Council adopted the various texts relating to this programme on 11 September 1979, without Parliament having requested conciliation in its Opinion of 15 September 1977.

4. *Common policy in the field of science and technology*—The Council has not yet decided its position on the Commission's proposals. It its Opinion of 17 November 1977 Parliament did not request conciliation.

5. *Action programme for aeronautical research*—The Council has not yet acted on the Commission's proposals. It its Opinion of 17 January 1978 Parliament did not request conciliation.

6. *Financial measures for intra-Community trade in power-station coal*—The Council has not yet adopted a position on this operation. In its Opinion of 15 February 1979 Parliament did not request conciliation.

7. *Community aid for industrial restructuring and conversion operations*—The Council has not yet adopted this Regulation. In its Opinion of 26 April 1979 Parliament did not mention conciliation.

8. *Measures to be taken in the event of irregularities affecting own resources and the organization of an information system for the Commission in this field*—This proposal for a Regulation is still before the Council. In its Opinion of 11 May 1979 Parliament did not request conciliation.

9. *Joint programme of exchanges of young workers in the Community*—The Council adopted this programme on 16 July 1979. In its Opinion of 24 April 1979 Parliament did not envisage requesting conciliation.

E—Principal general questions or proposals before the Council in September 1980, on which Parliament has announced its intention of invoking the conciliation procedure

1. *Questions of institutional jurisdiction related to the Commission's powers with respect to the implementation of the budget (Article 205 of the EEC Treaty)*—In its Resolution of 17 March 1978 'on the European Parliament's guidelines for the budgetary and financial policy of the European Communities in 1979 (Part I)', Parliament calls for 'the initiation of a conciliation procedure, as promised by the Council during the procedure for establishing the 1978 budget in order to clarify the matter of institutional spheres of competence in connection with the Commission's unlimited power, under Article 205 of the EEC Treaty, in respect of the implementation of the budget, and to settle all related problems, in particular:

(i) the need for legislation in respect of the use of certain budgetary appropriations, which also covers the question of the legal nature of the "remarks" column,

(ii) the management committee procedure, and

(iii) the freezing of appropriations on the line.'

2. *Indicative nature of amounts included in the texts of Regulations*—In its Resolution of 16 March 1979 'on the European Parliament's guidelines for the budgetary policy of the Community for the 1980 financial year', Parliament 'recommends greater clarity in the separation of budgetary and legislative powers and recalls its proposal that a conciliation procedure be opened on the question of the indicative nature of the orders of magnitude and percentages in the texts of the Regulations'.

3. *Community financing of certain expenditure resulting from the implementation of the 1971 Food Aid Convention*—In its Opinions of 14 November 1978 and 16 March 1979, Parliament called for the opening of the conciliation procedure. It reiterated this request in its Opinion of 27 April 1979 on the regulations on food aid for 1979, in a letter from the President of Parliament to the President of the Council dated 15 May 1979, as also in its Opinion of 18 April 1980 on the rules governing food aid for 1980. The basic problem here is the same as that with aid to the non-associated developing countries (see point A6 above), i.e. the role to be played by the committee in the decision-making process.

4. *Support for joint hydrocarbon exploration projects*—It its Opinion of 9 May 1978, Parliament suggested major amendments regarding the power of decision on projects to which assistance was granted and called for the opening of the conciliation procedure. On 27 July 1978, the Commission modified its proposal to incorporate the amendments suggested by Parliament. On 24 May 1979, in view of the urgency of the matter, the Council adopted a Regulation concerning Community aid to a hydrocarbon exploration project in Greenland, without announcing its views on the basic proposal for a regulation. In a statement included in the minutes, however, the Council stated that the Commission's initial proposal was still being studied by the departments responsible, who were invited to continue their work with a view to arriving at a decision on the matter as quickly as possible.

5. *Establishment of an administrative tribunal of the European Communities*—In its Opinion of 25 April 1979, Parliament reserved the right to have recourse to the conciliation procedure should the Council intend departing in any significant way from the views expressed by Parliament.

6. *Convergence of the economic performances of the Member States*—On 15 November 1979, Parliament adopted a Resolution on the Commission's Communication entitled 'Convergence and budgetary questions', in which Parliament 'points out that no proposals of this kind can be adopted by the Council without the agreement of Parliament and stresses that the conciliation procedure is fully applicable in this matter'.

7. *Common agricultural policy*—In its Resolution of 11 May 1979 on general problems connected with the common agricultural policy, Parliament called for 'the deletion of the clause stipulating that the conciliation procedure with the Council can only be applied to general Community acts whose adoption is not necessitated by pre-existing acts'. Parliament was aware that 'this rules out conciliation, for example, on the annual farm price review'.

8. *Entry in the budget of the European Development Fund (EDF)*—Long an advocate of the inclusion in the general budget of the Communities of financial activities connected with the association with the ACP States, Parliament adopted on 12 March 1980 a Resolution in which it asks for 'a conciliation procedure to be opened immediately on the arrangements for this budgetization (of the Fifth EDF)'.

9. *Second application of the Decision on the New Community Instrument*—In its Opinion of 12 March 1980, Parliament 'reserves the right to initiate the conciliation procedure should the Council depart from this Opinion'.

**

One cannot escape the conclusion that to date the apparent potential of the conciliation procedure has not been fully exploited and that, in the form which it was given by the Joint Declaration of 4 March 1975, it is not always easy to initiate.

The procedure was successfully applied to the revision of the Financial Regulation of December 1977 (see point A3 above); it was also applied fairly successfully in the case of the basic decision on the New Community Instrument—and the revision of the texts relating to the Regional Fund (see points A4 and A5 above). On the other hand, it has long been in abeyance where cooperation with non-member countries and the modification of the Financial Regulation (see points A6 to A8 above) are concerned. In addition, the absence of a 'common position'—no deadline having been fixed for the adoption of this chief document in a procedure stemming from practical circumstances—precludes the initiation of conciliation.

The experience gained over a period of five years—in only one of which has the procedure been actively applied (November 1977 to November 1978)—enables us to make certain observations. It is clear that the initiative in asking for conciliation lies more with Parliament, since the procedure was established for its benefit. But the old Parliament did not make systematic use of the possibilities thus created, and the directly-elected Parliament has not yet really put this procedure to full use, despite the avowed intention of Mrs Veil, its President, in her inaugural statement on 18 July 1979 to make wide-scale use of this instrument, which 'should enable Parliament to participate effectively in the legislative decisions of the Communities'.

Caught between two conflicting requirements—its concern to exercise its powers to the full and its desire to avoid blocking the legislative process—Parliament has adopted a pragmatic approach in selecting matters for the application of the conciliation procedure (financial or political importance of the question, as Parliament sees it; the risk of serious differences with the Council, but also the will to come to an agreement with the Council, there thus being the chance of a compromise being reached).

Where the matter concerned is of a technical nature, e.g. the Financial Regulation, there seems to be a greater chance of agreement. This is doubtless due to the fact that not only are the political aspects less apparent in such cases: there is also a greater incentive in each institution to get things moving and the necessary action and the responsibilities are more clearly defined. In more complex cases, where more than one section in each institution has a say, it would seem that the organization and coordination problems raised by this new 'function' known as conciliation have not yet been entirely overcome. The financial element, which is common to all matters likely to be the subject of the conciliation procedure, might provide a logical solution to these problems.

Aware of the limitations of this procedure, Parliament has already envisaged ways of improving it, particularly in its Resolution of 25 October 1978 on the draft general budget of the European Communities for the financial year 1979, in its Resolution of 11 May 1979 on the common agricultural policy (see point E7), and in its Resolution of 7 November 1979 on the draft general budget for the financial year 1980, in which Parliament declared that it 'cannot tolerate unilateral decisions on financial matters being taken by the Council without the consent of Parliament and instructs its Committee on Budgets to make new proposals to strengthen the role of the European Parliament in the conciliation procedure, which has become unsatisfactory because the Council applies it more restrictively than intended or, on occasion, refuses to apply it at all'.

The Council is seeking ways of reformulating the process of conciliation.

In fact we have here the curious situation of two monologues rather than a dialogue, let alone a three-way conversation including the Commission too.

369

Units of account used by the European Communities

Units of account and national currencies

Currency	EUA/IMF parities	EUA on 2.11.1976	Green EUA on 2.11.1976	MCAs (%) on 2.11.1976	EUA on 1.2.1977	Percentage differences EUA/u.a.−IMF (in terms of national currency value) on 1.2.1977	EUA on 1.2.1978
	1	2	3	4	5	6:1/5	7
BFR/LFR	50	40.94	49.55	$\{$ +1.4[1] +2.0[2]	41.3	+21.1	40.1
DKR	7.5	6.54	7.89	0	6.60	+13.7	7.0
DM	3.66	2.67	3.48	$\{$ +9.3[1] +11.8[2]	2.69	+36.1	2.5
FF	5.55	5.53	5.63	−16.4	5.55	+0	5.8
LIT	625	959.5	963	$\{$ −17 −31.7[3]	986	−36.6	1 064.4
HFL	3.62	2.79	3.40	$\{$ +1.4[1] +2.0[2]	2.81	+28.7	2.7
UKL	$\}$ 0.41	0.70	0.57	−45.0	$\}$ 0.65	−36.0	0.6
IRL			0.64	$\{$ −29.3 −42.8[3]			

NB: Columns 2, 3 and 4 (values on 2 November 1976) were used because MCAs (monetary compensatory amounts, see p. 174) were then at their highest level;

Column 5 gives the rates used in the 1978 budget to convert EUA into national currencies and column 7 the rates used in the 1979 budget;

Column 8 gives the rates used in the 1980 budget to convert EUA into national currencies and column 12 those used in the 1981 budget. The representative (green) rates which are applied to most products are shown in columns 9 and 14.

A on 1979	Green EUA on 1.2.1979	MCAs (%) on 1.2.1979	Percentage differences EUA/green u.a. (in national currency value)	EUA on 1.2.1980	EUA on 1.7.1980	Green ECU on 1.7.1980	MCAs (%) on 1.7.1980	Percentage differences EUA/green ECU on 1.7.1980
	9	10	11:9/8	12	13	14	15	16:14/13
9.54	49.35	+3.3	+24.8	40.52	40.26	{ 40.73 40.52	+2.2[4] +1.9[5]	+1.2 +0.7
6.95	8.57	0	+23.3	7.80	7.81	7.72	0	−1.1
2.51	3.40	+10.8	+35.5	2.49	2.52	{ 2.78 2.75	+9.8[4] +8.8[5]	+10.5 +9.3
5.77	6.22	−10.6	+7.8	5.85	5.84	5.85	0	+1.6
5.2	1 154	−17.7	+1.7	1 154.4	1 201.1	{ 1 060.7[6] 1 157.8[5]	−9.5[6] −1.0[5]	−11.7 −3.6
2.71	3.40	+3.3	+25.5	2.76	2.76	{ 2.81 2.79	+2.2[4] +1.9[5]	+1.8 +1.3
	0.63	−28.2	−7.4	0.63	0.61	{ 0.59 0.62	−1.0[7] +1.7[2]	−2.9 +2.2
0.68								
	0.79	−3	+16.2	0.67	0.67	0.66	0	−1.8

[1] Milk, beef and veal, pigmeat and sugar.
[2] Other products.
[3] Wine.
[4] Milk and milk products.
[5] Most other products.
[6] Cereals, eggs, poultrymeat and wine.
[7] Cereals, eggs and poultrymeat.

Share of national currencies in the EUA basket

(%)

Currency	Basic weightings	Share on			
		28.6.1974	1.1.1976	1.1.1979	1.1.1980
	1	2	3	4	5
BFR	7.9	8.0	8.0	9.2	9.1
DKR	3.0	3.0	3.0	3.1	2.8
DM	27.3	26.8	27.1	33.0	33.4
FF	19.5	19.9	22.0	20.0	19.8
IRL	1.5	1.5	1.3	1.1	1.1
LIT	14.0	14.0	13.7	9.5	9.4
LFR	0.3	0.3	0.3	0.4	0.3
HFL	9.0	8.9	9.2	10.6	10.4
UKL	17.5	17.6	15.4	13.1	13.7
Total	100	100	100	100	100

The difference between the figures in column 1 and those in column 2 is due to the fact that column 2 uses the 28 June 1974 exchange rates whereas column 1 uses an average of the rates in April, May and June 1974.

Bodies involved with the budget

As the Community has developed it has become necessary to call on the help of a number of bodies to estimate or implement certain general-budget funds. They are grouped here to simplify matters. They are:
(a) committees which have an influence over what the authorizing authority (the Commission or persons to which it has delegated powers) does, and
(b) decentralized bodies subsidized by the Community (called 'Commission satellites' in Community jargon, meaning offshoots of the Commission).

I—Committees with budgetary powers

1. Reference system

A—Membership

The committees are of four types:
(1) Committees chaired by a representative of a Member State and consisting of representatives of the Member States and of the Commission;
(2) Committees chaired by a representative of the Commission and consisting of representatives of the Member States and, in some cases, the Commission;
(3) Committees chaired by a representative of the Commission and consisting of representatives of the Member States and of interested parties;
(4) Committees chaired by a representative of the Commission and consisting of representatives of interested parties.

B—Powers of committees responsible for estimating general budget expenditure

C—Powers of committees responsible for implementing the general budget (financing committees)

(individual aid decisions):
(1) Purely advisory committees;
(2) Committees which are kept informed of how the budget is being implemented but are not directly involved;
(3) Committees which are directly involved in the decision-making process (if they withhold their approval, the matter may be referred to the Council). See p. 77.

2. List of management committees

(a) Committees responsible for the general budget

1. *Revenue*—The Advisory Committee on Own Resources set up under Article 20 of Council Regulation (EEC, Euratom, ECSC) No 2891/77 of 19 December 1977:
(a) own resources in general (A2, B, C2);
(b) VAT own resources (A2, B, C3).
(It replaces the old Advisory Committee on Own Resources set up under Regulation No 2/71.)

2. *Determining the maximum rate of increase in non-compulsory expenditure*—The Economic Policy Committee set up under the Council Decision of 18 February 1974 following the amalgamation of the Conjunctural Policy Committee, the Budgetary Policy Committee, and the Medium-Term Economic Policy Committee (A1).

3. *Expenditure* (in the order in which they were set up):

(1) The European Social Fund (ESF) Committee set up under Article 124 of the EEC Treaty and Regulation (EEC) No 2396/71 of 8 November 1971 (Articles 9 and 10) (A3, B and C1).
Except as regards individual aid decisions, the Commission seeks the opinion of this Committee on proposals to act under Article 4 of the Decision of 1 February 1971, on all proposals it makes to the Council and on any Regulations bearing on the operation of the Fund.

(2) The Scientific and Technical Research Committee set up under Article 134 of the Euratom Treaty (A1 and B).

(3) The Administrative Commission on Social Security for Migrant Workers set up in 1958 under Regulation No 3 of 25 September 1958; Regulation No 3 was repealed by Regulation No 1408/71 of 14 June 1971, which confirmed the continued existence of the Commission and specified its powers. It is assisted by an Advisory Committee on Social Security for Migrant Workers and has a degree of independence in decision-making, (A1 and C2).

(4) The management committees for the common organizations of the agricultural markets set up under various Regulations, one for each common organization of the market (COM). They give opinions on all draft agricultural legislation

that may have financial implications. There are 19 such committees (A2 and C3).

(5) The Standing Committee on Agricultural Structures set up under the Council Decision of 4 December 1962 and Council Regulation (EEC) No 355/77 of 15 February 1977 on the coordination of agricultural structural policies (A2 and C3).

(6) The EAGGF (European Agricultural Guidance and Guarantee Fund) Committee set up under the Council Regulation of 5 February 1964. Amendments have since been made (A2, B and C3).

(7) The General Advisory Committee of the JRC set up under the Commission Decision of 13 January 1971. Its role is to help the Director-General for the JRC prepare draft programmes for the JRC's various fields of activity by giving its opinion on the draft programmes. Advisory Committees on Programme Management (ACPMs) set up under the Council Resolution of 18 July 1977, also make a contribution towards the successful implementation of Euratom programmes. Some 60 such committees have been set up under this Resolution in 18 areas of direct and indirect action. Concerted-action committees (COMACs) set up under the Council Decisions of 27 September 1977 and 13 February 1978, are also involved in this work (A1, B and C1).

(8) The Committee for Scientific and Technical Information and Documentation set up under the Council Resolution of 24 June 1971 (A3 and C1).

(9) The Consumers Consultative Committee set up under the Commission Decision of 25 September 1973 (A4 and C1).

(10) The Scientific and Technical Research Committee (CREST) set up under the Council Resolution of 14 January 1974 to promote the development of a common policy in the field of science and technology (A2 and B).

(11) The Energy Committee set up under the Council Decision of 30 January 1974 to coordinate the implementation by the Member States of energy policy measures adopted by the Community (A2). Its Chairman is the Member of the Commission with special responsibility for energy. It is likely to be asked to deal with a number of supplementary measures adopted under the plan proposed by the Commission on 12 June 1980 to resolve the United Kingdom problem.

(12) The Advisory Committee on Safety, Hygiene and Health Protection at Work set up under the Council Decision of 27 June 1974 (A3 and C1).

(13) The Regional Policy Committee set up under Article 1 of Council Decision 75/185/EEC of 18 March 1975 (A1, B and C1). It is likely to be asked to deal with a number of supplementary measures adopted under the plan proposed by the Commission on 12 June 1980, to resolve the United Kingdom problem.

(14) The ERDF (European Regional Development Fund) Committee set up under Article 11 of Regulation (EEC) No 724/75 of 18 March 1975 (A2 and C3).

(15) The Standing Committee for the Fishing Industry set up under Council Regulation (EEC) No 101/76 of 19 January 1976 (A2 and C3).

(16) The Education Committee set up under the Resolution adopted by the Council and Ministers of Education meeting in Council on 9 February 1976 (A1 and C2).

(17) The Transport Infrastructure Committee set up under the Council Decision of 20 February 1978 (A2 and C2).

(18) The Advisory Committee on the Management of Projects to Exploit Alternative Energy Sources set up under Council Regulation (EEC) No 1302/78 of 12 June 1978 (A2 and C3).

(19) The Advisory Committee on the Management of Energy-Saving Demonstration Projects set up under Council Regulation (EEC) No 1303/78 of 12 June 1978 (A2 and C3).

(20) The Advisory Committee for the Management and Coordination of Data-Processing Programmes set up under Council Decision 79/784/EEC of 11 September 1979 (A2 and C3).

(b) Committees responsible for the ECSC operational budget

(21) Technical research committees: the Coal Research Committee (CRC), and the Iron and Steel Technical Research Committee (TRC), each chaired by a Commission Director-General (A4, C1).

(22) Social research committees: research committees of scientific and technical experts, committees of government experts, and the Producers and Workers Committee on Industrial Safety and Medicine (A3, C1).

(23) The ECSC Consultative Committee set up under Article 18 of the ECSC Treaty. It is consulted by the High Authority (Commission) in the cases specified in the Treaty and on any other occasion when the High Authority (Commission) considers it appropriate that it should be consulted. The ECSC Treaty provides for consultation if the High Authority (Commission) wishes to grant aid towards research (Article 55(2)) or resettlement or wishes to grant subsidies (Article 56(2), subparagraph (a)). At present the Committee has 81 members, comprising equal numbers of producers, workers, consumers and dealers. Members are appointed by the Council, which has nominated the representative

producers and workers organizations who supply lists of candidates (two for each allocated to their organization). The present members have been appointed for two years until 15 October 1980 (A4, B and C1).

(c) EDF Committee

(24) The Committee for the Fifth European Development Fund set up under Article 17 of the Internal Agreement concluded between the nine Member States on the financing and administration of Community aid and signed on 20 November 1979 (A2). The votes of the Member States are weighted as follows (the figures in brackets relate to the Fourth EDF): Federal Republic of Germany 27 (25), France 24 (25), United Kingdom 17 (18), Netherlands 8 (8), Belgium 6 (6), Denmark 3 (3), Ireland 2 (2) and Luxembourg 1 (1). The Committee acts by a qualified majority of 69 votes and gives its opinion on financing proposals submitted by the Commission for projects or programmes to be financed by means of grants or special loans. If the Commission decides to depart from the opinion expressed by the Committee, or if a favourable opinion is not forthcoming, it must either withdraw its proposal or refer it as soon as possible to the Council, which will decide on the matter according to the voting rules which apply to the EDF Committee.

(d) Secretariat for these committees

The Commission's role in the operation of these committees is underlined by the fact that its staff provide their secretariat. The work is carried out by officials of the Directorates-General responsible, except in the case of the ECSC Consultative Committee, which, under its Rules of Procedure, has an independent secretariat of officials, itself linked to the Secretariat-General of the High Authority (Commission).

II—Decentralized bodies subsidized by the Community

Seven of the bodies subsidized by Community funds from the Commission budget in 1979 come under this heading (see p. 305). Only five are described below, as the other two (the European Communities Institute for Economic Analysis and Research and the European University Institute, Florence), are only allocated a token heading in the budget.

(25) The Euratom Supply Agency set up under Article 52 of the Euratom Treaty. It has legal personality and financial autonomy. The Agency's operating costs are subsidized by the Commission.

(26) The European Association for Cooperation (EAC) set up under the Belgian Royal Decree of 15 December 1964 as an international association under Belgian private law. It is managed by an Administrative Board consisting of Commission officials and is subsidized by the Commission.

(27) The Business Cooperation Centre set up under the Commission Decision of 21 June 1973. It receives an operating subsidy but does not have legal personality as it is part of the Commission.

Another body which, although it is part of the Commission, has a special status, is:

(28) The Office for Official Publications set up under Decision 69/13/Euratom, ECSC, EEC of 16 January 1969. Its statement of revenue and expenditure is annexed to the Commission section of the European Communities' general budget. Although it is subsidized by the Commission its Managing Board is composed of the Secretaries-General of all the Community institutions and quasi-institutions (Commission, European Parliament, Council, Court of Justice, Court of Auditors and Economic and Social Committee).

There are two other bodies which can be described as genuine satellites, or offshoots:

(29) The European Centre for the Development of Vocational Training set up under Council Regulation (EEC) No 337/75 of 10 February 1975. Its Management Board draws up an estimate of receipts and expenditure which it transmits to the Commission which has the power to amend it when entering the subsidy in its preliminary draft budget. The Board approves the estimate once the Budgetary Authority has determined the subsidy. The procedure for implementing this estimate is laid down in a special Financial Regulation (Council Regulation (EEC) No 1416/76 of 1 June 1976). The Centre has sole responsibility for implementing its budget.

(30) The European Foundation for the Improvement of Living and Working Conditions set up under Council Regulation (EEC) No 1365/75 of 26 May 1975. It is governed by provisions similar to those adopted for the Centre for the Development of Vocational Training (Council Regulation (EEC) No 1417/76 of 1 June 1976).

There is, finally, one body which is subsidized by the Commission to the tune of over 50% but is still more or less independent of the Commission:

(31) The European Schools (see p. 318) which are governed by a Board of Governors consisting of one representative from each Member State and the Commission. Its Chairman has an extended term of office and a very free hand.

ECSC levies paid between 1971 and 1980

For ease of comparison with the table in Annex 11 (see p. 390), the figures given in the following table only go back as far as 1971.[1]

---

[1] See *La Revue du Marché Commun* of December 1976 by the same author for the figures for 1952/53 to 1970 and the levy percentages (pp. 560 and 561 of the article entitled 'Histoire budgétaire de la CECA').

Every year the ECSC operational budget includes an estimate of revenue. The balance sheet drawn up in the following year shows the amount actually paid in levies.

The first table shows the levies actually paid between 1971 and 1979. These are compared with estimates—which we are unable to include here for shortage of space—in the second table.

ECSC levies paid

Member State	m IMF u.a.					m EUA				
Year	1971	1972	1973	1974	1975	1976	1977	1978	1979	Estimates 1980
Belgium	4.0	5.4	5.5	6.2	5.6	6.9	6.5	8.1	8.2	9.2
Denmark			0.2	0.2	0.2	0.4	0.4	0.5	0.5	0.6
FR of Germany	17.2	21.1	22.0	24.6	24.0	31.5	28.3	33.7	35.8	40.5
France	7.9	9.5	9.5	11.3	11.1	14.7	13.8	15.7	16.0	18.2
Ireland			0.1	0.1	0.1	0.1	0.1	0.1	0.1	0.1
Italy	5.7	7.4	7.4	9.7	10.1	13.1	13.1	14.4	14.3	16.2
Luxembourg	1.3	1.7	1.8	2.2	2.0	2.5	2.2	2.8	2.7	3.1
Netherlands	1.7	2.1	2.0	2.0	2.4	3.0	2.3	3.2	3.2	3.3
United Kingdom			14.4	13.3	14.7	20.3	20.1	22.3	22.4	25.5
Total	37.8	47.2	62.9	69.6	70.2	92.5	86.8	100.8	103.2	117.0
Percentage of levies	0.30	0.29	0.29	0.29	0.29	0.29	0.29	0.29	0.29	0.31

Percentage differences between estimates of ECSC levies and actual amounts paid

1971	1972	1973	1974	1975	1976	1977	1978	1979
Differences in relation to initial budget estimates								
−8.98	+13.76	−1.43	+0.40	−20.77	+2.90	−2.43	+0.77	+5.31
Differences in relation to amended estimates given in amending budgets								
		−7.51			−3.84		+6.55	

Financial contributions from the Member States (1958-74)

For 17 years the budget of the Brussels Communities (EEC and Euratom) was balanced by the provisions of financial contributions paid by the Member States.

A—Contribution scales

The scale for the apportionment of these contributions has varied both according to the expenditure to be financed, and also over time, as is shown by the following table.

Scales regulating contributions from the Member States in the Community of Six

Member State	EEC/Euratom	Social Fund	Euratom research	Agricultural policy	Agricultural policy	General budget	First EDF	Second EDF	Third EDF
	1	2	3	4	5	6	7	8	9
Belgium	7.9	8.8	9.9	7.95	8.25	6.8	12.04	9.45	8.89
FR of Germany	28.0	32.0	30.0	31.67	31.70	32.9	34.41	33.77	33.16
France	28.0	32.0	30.0	32.58	28.0	32.6	34.41	33.77	33.16
Italy	28.0	20.0	23.0	18.0	21.5	20.2	6.88	13.70	15.62
Luxembourg	0.2	0.2	0.2	0.22	0.2	0.2	0.22	0.27	0.28
Netherlands	7.9	7.0	6.9	9.58	10.35	7.3	12.04	9.04	8.89
Total	100	100	100	100	100	100	100	100	100

The table calls for the following comments on each scale.

Scale 1: Articles 200(1) of the EEC Treaty and 172(1) of the Euratom Treaty laid down a scale of contributions to the operating budgets of these two Communities. In laying down this scale, those who drafted the Treaties of Rome wished to take account of the Member States' capacity to pay and also of the presumed advantages to them of Community membership and of their mutually agreed respective weight in the two Communities' decision-making structures. This was the basic scale, and was determined by political considerations.

The Member States had to pay their contributions to the two budgets in accordance with this scale. To do this they had to enter the necessary appropriations as expenditure in their own budgets. Every change in the Community budget therefore had repercussions on national public expenditure. This system continued until 31 December 1974.

Scale 2: Article 200(2) of the EEC Treaty laid down a special scale, also politically determined, for the Social Fund. This was based on the Member States' capacity to pay and the desire to favour Italy.

Scale 3: Article 172(2) of the Euratom Treaty laid down a special scale for the research and investment budget based on Member States' capacity to pay— another politically determined scale.

Scales 4 and 5: Article 7 of Regulation No 25 of 4 April 1962 on the financing of the common agricultural policy provided that the revenue of the EAGGF during the first three years (1962-63, 1963-64, and 1964-65) should consist of financial contributions calculated, for part of the revenue, at 100, 90, and 80% respectively of Scale 1, and, for the remainder, in proportion to net imports by each Member State from non-member countries. This adjustment was approved by the Council unanimously in compliance with Article 200(3) of the EEC Treaty. Here, therefore, the scale is no longer determined purely by political factors.

Article 3 of Council Regulation No 130/66/EEC of 26 July 1966 established Scale 4 for the period 1965-66 and another scale (not shown in the table) for 1966-67. Article 11 of the same Regulation laid down a system for subsequent periods which foreshadowed the system of own resources, in that Member States had to pay contributions not simply according to an *ad hoc* scale but also in proportion to levies charged on imports from non-member countries.

Subsequently, other scales were established to take account of particular situations. Thus in the budget for the financial year 1970 the financial contributions were calculated according to six different scales, an incredible complication; the most recent was Scale 5 (Article 7 of Council Regulation (EEC) No 728/70 of 21 April 1970.

Scale 6: Article 3 of the Decision of 21 April 1970 on the replacement of financial contributions from Member States by the Communities' own resources established a general scale for contributions to balance the budget. This was the last politically determined scale to be applied by the Community of Six to the general budget of the Communities. It was amended by the Act of Accession and expired on 31 December 1974 (see p. 380).

Scales 7, 8 and 9: The scale for the First EDF was laid down by the Treaty of Rome itself and those for the Second and Third EDFs by the First and Second Yaoundé Conventions. The scales for the Fourth and Fifth EDFs are the last politically determined scales which still exist (see p. 380).

It is important to mention here that the Member States have always fulfilled their obligations and never failed to pay their contributions—which is not always the case in many international organizations. This is an example of the unique features of the European Communities. It must, however, be added that there have been hitches in contributions to the ECSC operational budget (see footnote 2, p. 118).

B—Paying over financial contributions

The Member States pay over the financial contributions provided for in Article 200(1) of the EEC Treaty to the Community in national currencies. Any available balances are deposited with the Treasuries of the Member States or bodies appointed by them. They may be invested on terms agreed between the Commission and the Member State concerned.

Gradual implementation of the own-resources system (1971-80)

An explanation of the legal aspects involved is followed by a quantitative description, which is itself divided into two parts.

A—Legal aspects of the introduction of own resources

The own-resources system as applied to the Community of Six (1971-77)

To mitigate the impact on national exchequers, particularly in the countries which are major importers, of transferring tax-raising powers to the Communities, the own-resources system was introduced by the Decision of 21 April 1970 gradually, over a period of seven years, but automatically, i.e. without any intervention by Community institutions, simply by applying the rules in question.

Stage One: 1971, 1972, 1973 and 1974 budgets

From 1 January 1971, the Community budget included the following revenue (Article 3 of the Decision of 21 April 1970):
(a) total revenue from agricultural levies, as was only right and proper, given that these are part of the common agricultural policy, which is itself financed in full from the Community budget;
(b) revenue from customs duties, the amount payable each year under this heading by each Member State corresponding to the difference between a reference amount and the amount made over to the Communities by way of agricultural levies. This reference amount was based on the grand total of agricultural levies and customs duties collected by each State, and was fixed at 50% of this total in 1971, 62.5% in 1972, 75% in 1973, 87% in 1974 and 100% from 1975, the aim being to avoid a sharp impact on the public finances of certain countries such as the Netherlands. The first table on p. 385 shows the amounts actually paid in these four years and the customs duties collected by the Member States, to illustrate the impact of this provision;

(c) financial contributions from Member States to bring the revenue and expenditure sides of the Community budget into balance, in other words to bridge the gap between total expenditure and total independent revenue. These contributions were calculated according to a system of politically agreed GNP based scales (see Scale 6 in the table in Annex 9, p. 377, for the Community of Six and the 1973-74 scale in the table in this Annex for the Community of Nine).

Throughout this period, the amount by which the proportionate or 'relative' share of each State within the overall total of these payments was allowed to vary from one year to the next was limited to 1% up and 1.5% down, 1970 being taken as the base year. This mechanism has been nicknamed the dynamic braking system.

Stage Two: 1975, 1976 and 1977 budgets

In this stage, without precluding other forms of revenue, the budget was now totally financed from the Communities' own resources, that is, agricultural levies, customs receipts, and VAT revenue (Article 4 of the Decision of 21 April 1970). Failure to achieve a uniform VAT tax base meant that financial contributions were still being paid during this period, but they were different from the financial contributions previously paid, because no political factor was involved. They depended purely on the relative share of each Member State in the aggregate GNP of the Community (see GNP-based scales in the table in this Annex).

The dynamic braking system remained in force, but the maximum rate of change was somewhat greater with a maximum 2% variation up or down. In 1976 (supplementary budget No 2/1976) this system produced a curious consequence. The limit of a 2% reduction in contributions meant that certain Member States, which would otherwise have paid even less, obliged them to pay over sums which carried Community revenue to a level higher than that of the expenditure needing to be financed (see p. 386).

Scales for contributions from the Member States in the Community of Nine

Scale	Budget scales				EDF scales		EIB scale[1, 2]
Member State	Scale for 1973-74[1]	GNP scales			4th EDF[1]	5th EDF[1, 2]	
		1975	1976	1977			
Belgium	5.28	4.11	4.07	4.14	6.25	5.90	5.85
Denmark	2.46	2.53	2.52	2.52	2.40	2.50	2.97
FR of Germany	25.53	29.87	29.58	28.60	25.95	28.30	22.22
France	25.30	22.99	23.05	23.29	25.95	25.60	22.22
Ireland	0.61	0.67	0.71	0.71	0.60	0.60	0.74
Italy	15.60	14.77	14.80	15.21	12.00	11.50	17.78
Luxembourg	0.16	0.16	0.16	0.17	0.20	0.20	0.15
Netherlands	5.66	5.26	5.32	5.32	7.95	7.40	5.85
United Kingdom	19.32	19.64	19.80	20.04	18.70	18.00	22.22
Total	100	100	100	100	100	100	100

[1] Political scale laid down by a Treaty or a Decision with equivalent effect:
  (a) for the budget: the Decision of 21 April 1970 on the Community's own resources (Article 3(2)), as amended by the Treaty of Accession (Article 129);
  (b) for the EDF: the first Lomé Convention which entered into force on 1 April 1976 and the Second Lomé Convention signed on 31 October 1979;
  (c) for the EIB: a Protocol to the EEC Treaty (Article 4), as amended by Protocol No 1 to the Treaty of Accession (Article 2).
[2] Scales still applied.

Conclusion: 1978 and later budgets

For the six founding members of the Community, Stage Three is marked by the full implementation of the own-resources system. The Community financial system is fully operational and applies equally to all, with no more use of the dynamic braking device.

The phasing out of this device, moreover, has made it possible to calculate Member States' payments in EUA (see p. 26).

The own-resources system as applied to the three new Member States (1973-79)

The accession of three new Member States was obviously a major factor in the negotiations, and subsequently posed an enormous problem for the Community institutions.

Since the introduction of the own-resources system for the Community of Six was already under way— 1973, when the three new Member States joined the Community, was the third year of a seven-year transitional period—the same system was chosen for the four prospective members, whose number fell to three after Norway pulled out.

Stage One: 1973, 1974, 1975, 1976 and 1977 budgets

The Act of Accession, which entered into force on 1 January 1973, specified in Articles 127 to 132 (the financial provisions), that the new Member States

were only required to pay a proportion of what they would have had to pay under the Decision of 21 April 1970. During a transitional period of five years, an 'abatement factor' was applied, whereby they were to pay only 45% in 1973, 56% in 1974, 67.5% in 1975, 79.5% in 1976 and 92% in 1977 of what they should have paid.

From 1 January 1978, when the own resources system became fully operational for the six original Member States, the full amounts were also due from the three new Member States, subject to special arrangements in 1978 and 1979.

Stage Two: 1978 and 1979 budgets

Article 131(1) of the Act of Accession stipulated that the relative shares of the three new Member States in 1978 were not to exceed two-fifths of the difference between the amount actually paid by the three new Member States in 1977 and what they should have paid if the dynamic brakes and abatement factor had not been applied. Article 131(2) required the Commission to carry out the calculations necessary for the application of this paragraph, and on 28 April 1976 the United Kingdom Government requested the Commission how it intended to make these calculations. In its reply of 21 September 1976, the Commission advocated that, as the budget unit of account (IMF u.a.) would be replaced by the EUA in 1978 and Article 131 would still apply in 1979, the relative shares for 1977 should be calculated in EUA so as to use comparable parameters. The relative share of the United Kingdom in 1977 would therefore be 12.27% compared with 19.24% in the budget adopted in u.a. It would have been 16.82% if the dynamic brakes and abatement factor had not been applied. The United Kingdom's relative share for 1978 would therefore be as follows:

(i) $(16.82-12.27)\frac{2}{5} = 1.82\%$.

(ii) $12.27\% + 1.82\% = 14.09\%$.

The foreseeable ceiling for the United Kingdom in 1980 would be 18.16%.

The Commission's approach was supported by the United Kingdom and Ireland but rejected by the German and other delegations, who suggested instead that the percentages arising from the situation in 1977 should be used without adjustment in 1978 and 1979. The explanation for this extremely complicated dispute is as follows: the Federal Government carried out calculations similar to those made by the Commission, based on the United Kingdom's relative share in the 1977 budget (19.24% on the basis of the IMF unit of account):

(i) Relative share without dynamic brakes and abatement factor = 25.43%.

(ii) $(25.43-19.24)\frac{2}{5} = 2.47\%$.

(iii) $19.24+2.47 = 21.72\%$.

Since this is more than the 18.16% ceiling for 1980, the effects of Article 131 of the Act of Accession would have been cancelled out.

To put it another way, with the Commission's working method, the change of unit of account would take place without affecting some Member States more than others, and the increase in the Irish and UK contributions would be gradual whereas with the German method these contributions would reach their ceiling as early as 1978. The Commission's method was realistic because it relied on percentages calculated on a single basis (the EUA). With this method the figure of 19.24% was converted into 12.27%. The German method, on the other hand, was formalistic, equating the figure of 19.24% calculated on the basis of the IMF unit of account with the figure of 18.16% calculated on the basis of the EUA. The Commission's approach was also consistent because in 1975 and 1976 it said that the change of unit of account proposed by the Federal Government would entail adjusting the percentages of the relative shares as restricted by the dynamic brakes. This would have meant amending the Decision of 21 April 1970 and fixing different basic relative shares, which was impracticable.

This is not just a theoretical argument, it has very real consequences. In 1978 (taking the draft budget regarded as adopted as the basis), the difference between the Commission's interpretation and the Federal Republic of Germany's interpretation was UKL 242.7 million for the United Kingdom (UKL

1 137.5 compared with UKL 1 380.2 million) and IRL 22.3 million for Ireland (IRL 42.7 million compared with IRL 65 million).

The Act of Accession clearly intended that the new Member States' contributions should be increased gradually over a transitional period of seven years. The Commission's method was the only one which would have ensured such a gradual increase. Its opponents took a completely different standpoint, arguing that prior to 1978 the United Kingdom had derived an advantage from the use of the obsolete IMF unit of account, and that this state of affairs should not be allowed to continue in 1978 and 1979.

Matters came to a head when the United Kingdom Government made it clear that it would oppose the introduction of the EUA in the 1978 budget if the Commission's interpretation was not accepted. The Council considered the matter sufficiently serious to refer it to the European Council. The solution agreed upon on 6 December 1977 was successful in that the European Council approved the introduction of the EUA in the 1978 budget but disappointing because full agreement could not be reached on the contributions of the three new Member States. The wording of the Conclusions of the European Council is a masterpiece of diplomacy allowing each Member State to choose the method it prefers, i.e. the one most advantageous to it. It reads as follows:

'1. The EUA will be introduced into the budget of the European Communities from 1 January 1978.

2. The budget will be adopted and implemented without regard to Article 131.

3. The necessary financial compensations for 1978 and 1979 under Article 131 will be made outside the framework of the budget on a quarterly basis.

4. The Commission will make the necessary calculations for each Member State in accordance with the interpretations of Article 131 which is most advantageous to that State.

5. These calculations will lead to a deficit to be financed from extra-budgetary payments by the Member States.

6. To establish its contribution to the financing of the abovementioned deficit, each Member State may choose one of the following scales:

(a) overall budget scale,

(b) VAT scale,

(c) 1976 GNP scale,

(d) proportional scale (relative share of each Member State resulting from the calculations referred to in point 4 above).'

On 10 October 1978, the Council agreed on the following additional measures:

(i) Any residual amount not covered as a result of the arrangements adopted by the European Council (points 4, 5 and 6 of the Conclusions) would have to be met by the Member States in proportion to their contributions under the previous arrangements. No Member State would, however, have to pay more than it would have done under the interpretation least advantageous to it. Any difference would be apportioned among the other Member States according to the same criteria.

(ii) All the necessary calculations would be made by the Commission and the Member States would be notified.

(iii) The financial compensation resulting from the apportionment of the residual amount would be made outside the budget on a quarterly basis. The Commission's revenue and expenditure accounts for 1978 and 1979 would hence be inaccurate as they would show revenue transactions from which the effects of applying Article 131 of the Act of Accession have been removed.

Financial compensation resulting from the application of Article 131 of the Act of Accession

(m EUA)

Member State	1978		1979	
	Debit	Credit	Debit	Credit
Belgium	34.1	—	40.7	—
Denmark	—	—	—	—
FR of Germany	210.2	—	165.1	—
France	130.3	—	163.0	—
Ireland	—	18.4	—	2.2
Italy	79.4	—	91.9	—
Luxembourg	0.9	—	0.5	—
Netherlands	44.9	—	53.9	—
United Kingdom	—	481.4	—	512.9
Total	499.8	499.8	515.1	515.1

Conclusion: Articles 127 to 132 of the Act of Accession turned out to be very advantageous for two of the new Member States. The table on pp. 386 and 387 shows quite clearly how gradually Ireland and the United Kingdom have come to pay their full shares in the financing of the budget from own resources (1980).

Article 131 of the Act of Accession has, however, been a source of regrettable dispute between Member States, because its application coincided with what should have been a welcome event—the transition from the budget unit of account (IMF unit of account) to the European unit of account (EUA). If these two events had not coincided there would probably not have been any disputes and the matter would not have been referred to the European Council in December 1977.

It makes one wonder whether the decisions taken on 30 May 1980 to solve the 'British problem' might be even more difficult to implement than the provisions of the 1972 Act of Accession were.

B—The own-resources system (1971-80) in figures

Five tables are given by way of illustration, accompanied by a few comments (the relevant article in the statement of revenue in the 1979 budget is given in brackets):

(i) Agricultural levies paid (Article 100);
(ii) Sugar levies paid (Articles 110, 111 and 112);
(iii) Customs duties paid (Article 120);
(iv) Financial contributions paid (Articles 500 and 510) and VAT (Article 130);
(v) Financing the general budget (last page of the statement of revenue).

It should be noted that the 1977 figures for agricultural levies, sugar levies and customs duties paid relate to January to October inclusive and not to a period of twelve months as in the case of the six previous years. The original own resources had to be paid to the European Communities from 1 January 1978 so that they would effectively be financially autonomous from that date. Since there is a time lag of two months between the establishment of own resources and their being made available (see p. 83), the own resources for November and December 1977 had to be attributed to the financial year 1978 thus reducing the total for the financial year 1977 accordingly. The approach used for revenue is thus based on the year of payment rather than the year of origin (see p. 74). In Community jargon the budget is a 'cash budget' as far as revenue is concerned.

General comments on the agricultural levies paid

The erratic trend in revenue from agricultural levies in previous years, illustrated by the following table, is due to many different factors (the weather, currency fluctuation, commercial factors), but primarily to the extremely wide fluctuations in world prices, especially for cereals, which account for most of the revenue from levies (between 70 and 80%). The other products on which levies are payable are dairy products, beef and veal, pigmeat, sugar, eggs and poultrymeat and olive oil.

Between 1968 and 1971 agricultural levies fell steadily from 810 m u.a. in 1968 to 776 m u.a. in 1969, 712 m u.a. in 1970 and 605 m u.a. in 1971, owing to the relative stability of world cereal prices during this period and a sharp drop in cereal imports from outside the Community between 1968 and 1970.

World prices jumped between 1971 and 1973/74 to levels exceeding Community threshold prices, particularly in 1974, causing export levies to be applied to prevent massive exports and excessive rises in internal prices. Export levies are own resources in the same way as import levies. It is not possible to make a breakdown between these two types of levy for all Member States.

Agricultural levies paid to the European Communities

Member State \\ Year	m IMF u.a.							m EUA			
	Outturn										Estimates
	1971	1972	1973	1974	1975	1976	1977	1977	1978	1979	1980
Belgium	68.0	52.7	22.2	10.4	50.7	121.3	181.1	221.5	184.5	229.7	198.3
FR of Germany	154.2	153.8	104.9	73.2	100.8	169.5	199.5	275.7	289.3	263.7	289.5
France	51.5	59.5	43.3	43.3	43.3	69.3	93.2	92.3	142.2	96.5	146.5
Italy	212.8	235.9	130.5	58.8	126.4	303.0	558.3	346.6	507.7	410.6	407.0
Luxembourg	0.1	0.1	0.1	0.1	0.1	0.1	0.1	0.1	0.2	0.1	0.2
Netherlands	117.9	115.8	81.5	22.7	105.1	253.5	258.1	333.7	395.3	313.2	283.3
Total (Six)	604.5	617.8	382.7	212.3	426.5	916.7	1 290.9	1 269.9	1 519.2	1 313.8	1 294.7
Denmark			1.2	1.4	1.7	8.9	17.1	18.7	9.8	8.0	14.6
Ireland			1.4	2.9	2.5	7.0	13.5	8.6	5.1	3.6	4.5
United Kingdom			26.1	38.4	79.7	102.6	255.3	162.7	338.6	353.2	405.4
Total (Nine)			411.4	255.0	510.4	1 035.2	1 576.1	1 459.9	1 672.7	1 678.5	1 719.2

Revenue from levies began to rise in 1975. Increases of 94% and 75% were recorded in 1976 and 1977 respectively, due to very poor cereal harvests in 1976, leading to exceptionally high imports, and due to an increase in the levy rate caused by a slump in world prices.

More revenue was collected from levies in 1978 than in 1977, despite an appreciable drop in cereal imports because there was a further increase in the levy rates.

In 1979, levy revenue was 10.4% down on the previous year owing to a further drop in imports caused by bumper Community harvests.

General comments on the sugar levies paid

Under the rules governing the common organization of the sugar market producers are required to pay production levies and storage levies. The variations in the amounts collected shown in the following table are due to the following factors: a widespread shortage of sugar between 1972-73 and 1974-75 caused world prices to rise, in some cases to above Community prices, and there were hardly any Community surpluses to be placed on the world market. Consequently, expenditure on refunds was very low or nil, as were the production levies. The Council was even forced to adopt a decision suspending the collection of these levies in 1975-76.

Community surpluses began to build up in 1976, however, as consumption failed to keep pace with production and world prices slipped back (in the face of relatively abundant production) amounting to only 63% of Community prices in September 1976.

Storage levies were hence higher in 1976 and production levies had to be brought in again. This accounts for the increase in Community revenue in 1976 (61.2%) and particularly in 1977 (57.5%) and 1978 (99.1%). The 14.5% rise in Community sugar production in 1979 again caused levies to rise.

Isoglucose levies: On 25 October 1978 the Court of Justice of the European Communities gave a judgment on the question of levies imposed by the Commission on isoglucose producers, having been requested to give a preliminary ruling by national courts to which the producers of this sugar substitute—who were opposed to these levies or wanted them to be repaid—had appealed. The Court was asked to give a ruling on the validity of Regulation (EEC) 1111/77 of 17 May 1977 introducing a levy on isoglucose production of 5 u.a. per 100 kg for the 1977/78 sugar year compared with 9.85 u.a. per 100 kg for sugar.

The Court, while not condemning the principle of the levy itself, ruled that the Regulation was invalid because it infringed the general principle of equality laid down by the Treaty. It considered that in calculating the amount to be paid by isoglucose producers the Commission had failed to take into account the fact that sugar producers can pass on to sugar beet producers 60% of the amount they pay. The Commission had thus overestimated the amount to be paid by isoglucose producers. The Court did not, however, uphold the other arguments put forward against the Regulation, in particular the argument that isoglucose is not an agricultural product and should not therefore be subject to the same rules as sugar. The Commission was only partly satisfied

Sugar[1] levies paid to the European Communities

Member State \ Year	m IMF u.a.							m EUA			Estimates
	Outturn										Estimates
	1971	1972	1973	1974	1975	1976	1977	1977	1978	1979	1980
Belgium	5.3	13.5	6.7	5.7	5.6	7.9	10.0	12.2	19.6	30.9	33.0
FR of Germany	27.6	57.0	25.7	19.5	21.3	26.6	51.2	70.8	144.7	146.3	140.9
France	63.2	88.3	43.3	21.5	27.6	43.0	51.1	50.6	117.5	152.3	170.6
Italy	8.8	12.9	11.4	13.5	11.7	24.8	47.7	29.6	46.0	45.9	60.7
Luxembourg	—	—	—	—	—	—	—	—	—	—	—
Netherlands	4.4	10.0	8.3	6.5	5.4	9.8	16.2	20.9	33.1	37.8	43.0
Total (Six)	109.3	181.7	95.3	66.7	71.6	112.2	176.3	184.1	361.0	413.2	448.2
Denmark			1.0	1.7	2.7	4.1	7.1	7.8	19.4	21.1	20.1
Ireland			0.1	1.1	1.4	2.6	3.8	2.4	3.6	4.6	5.4
United Kingdom			2.0	5.6	4.0	9.6	15.2	9.7	22.2	26.1	30.8
Total (Nine)			98.4	75.1	79.7	128.5	202.4	204.0	406.2	464.9	504.5

[1] Including isoglucose from 1980.

with the judgment. It welcomed the fact that it en- dorsed the basic principle involved and the desire to preserve the sugar sector, but it was disappointed that the Court ruled against the validity of the Regulation.

A new EEC Regulation (No 1293/79 of 25 June 1979) introduced new rules from the 1979/80 sugar year based on production quotas for isoglucose on the lines of those for sugar. This solution is in keeping with the suggestions made by the Court in its ruling.

Comments on fiscal duties treated as customs duties

The fiscal elements of customs duties levied by Ireland and the United Kingdom (fiscal duties) were treated as own resources in the same way as customs duties proper. Consequently, these countries' relative shares were covered solely by own resources (without the need for 'contributions'). In Ireland's case, fiscal duties were completely replaced by internal taxes on 1 January 1976, in accordance with Article 38 of the Act of Accession. The United Kingdom continued to apply them, but only on tobacco, from 1 January 1976 to 1 January 1978.

In 1975, the fiscal duties levied by Ireland and the United Kingdom represented some 88% of the total amount levied at borders. The United Kingdom's fiscal duties on tobacco represented around 70% of the total amount levied in 1977.

General comments on the revenue from customs duties

Receipts from customs duties are the result of apply- ing the Common Customs Tariff to the customs value of imported goods. If tariff rates are kept constant an increase in the value of imports should produce a proportionate increase in customs receipts. If the rates drop, customs revenue, far from falling, may well rise as import trade is created or deflected. Customs revenue in fact comes from imports of chemicals, machinery and transport equipment and certain other types of manufactured goods, and it should be pointed out that customs duties are imposed as a means of protecting trade rather than a source of own resources. Over the years the Community has negotiated many different types of tariff reductions within GATT or bilaterally:

(a) gradual abolition of duties after the accession of the three new Member States in 1973;

(b) reductions negotiated under association agree- ments of the 'customs union' type (Greece and Turkey) or 'free trade area' type (ACP, EFTA, Finland, Morocco, Tunisia, Algeria, Malta and Cyprus);

(c) reductions negotiated under preferential trading agreements (Spain, Israel, Lebanon, Syria, Jordan, etc.);

(d) generalized preference tariffs.

The financial contributions required to balance the budget from 1 January 1975—as it had proved impossible to make VAT an own resource—were based on GNP. Article 23 of Council Regulation (EEC, Euratom, ECSC) No 2/71 of 2 January 1971 defines the gross national product (GNP) at market prices (Article 23(6)(a)) and specifies that it is to be established in units of account at the parities declared to the International Monetary Fund and is to corres- pond to the arithmetic average for the first three years

Customs duties paid to the European Communities

Member State \ Year	m IMF u.a. Outturn							m EUA Outturn			Estimates
	1971	1972	1973	1974	1975	1976	1977	1977	1978	1979	1980
Belgium	48.8	87.2	146.9	199.3	211.9	242.2	209.5	256.2	295.7	335.7	366.0
FR of Germany	277.0	410.9	600.7	768.7	870.2	990.9	840.0	1 160.9	1 378.0	1 586.6	1 713.0
France	139.4	220.7	361.9	493.3	524.5	630.1	563.1	557.9	649.5	754.2	825.8
Italy	49.7	126.6	261.6	435.6	442.4	606.4	585.5	363.5	400.8	497.2	552.0
Luxembourg	2.0	2.7	2.9	4.4	3.4	3.2	2.5	3.1	3.5	3.8	4.0
Netherlands	65.4	109.3	190.8	268.7	293.3	323.0	290.3	375.3	444.3	485.6	536.0
Total payments (Six)	582.3	957.3	1 564.8	2 170.0	2 345.7	2 795.8	2 490.9	2 716.9	3 169.8	3 663.1	3 975.8
(Total customs duties)	(1 878.4)	(2 011.1)	(2 245.7)	(2 519.9)							
Denmark			36.4	49.5	68.0	100.7	96.5	105.6	107.9	124.3	135.0
Ireland			11.2	13.4	21.4	29.8	32.5	20.7	46.7	57.1	63.0
United Kingdom			374.4	504.7	716.0	1 138.1	1 307.3	833.3	1 066.5	1 344.6	1 473.0
Total payments (Three)			422.0	567.6	805.4	1 265.6	1 436.3	959.6	1 221.1	1 526.0	1 671.0
(Total customs duties)			(8 559.4)	(9 117.6)	(10 044.0)	(5 399.0)	(4 024.8)	(2 613.4)			
Total payments to Communities	582.3	957.3	1 986.8	2 737.6	3 151.0	4 064.5	3 927.2	3 676.5	4 390.9	5 189.1	5 667.8

of the five-year period preceding the financial year in question. This method of calculation based on parities declared to the IMF artificially inflated the GNP of Member States with depreciating currencies (the pound and the lira), causing these countries to contribute more to the Community budget. This is another example of how unrealistic these conversion rates were. In this case the effect is just the opposite of that observed elsewhere (see p. 25). From 1978, the GNP for each reference year has been established in EUA on the basis of the average EUA rate for the year in question (Article 13(3) of Council Regulation (EEC, Euratom, ECSC) No 2891/77 of 19 December 1977, OJ L 336 of 27.12.1977).

The GNP-based financial contributions had to be continued because of the saga of the Sixth VAT Directive which is briefly described below:

1. The Commission followed up the Council Deci-

Balancing the budget: VAT or financial contributions

Member State \ Year	m IMF u.a. Outturn							m EUA Outturn			Estimates
	1971	1972	1973	1974	1975	1976	1977	1977	1978	1979[1]	1980
Belgium	62.8	94.1	175.9	137.5	129.3	126.6	116.9	143.0	239.8	329.6	324.7
FR of Germany	303.9	336.3	650.3	554.8	662.2	920.8	1 028.2	1 420.7	1 716.1	(2 245.6)	2 345.2
France	301.2	462.6	726.1	630.3	750.6	909.8	954.1	945.3	1 275.4	1 720.4	1 764.3
Italy	186.6	264.4	513.3	405.7	449.9	382.4	176.8	109.8	700.3	747.7	779.3
Luxembourg	1.8	3.2	5.5	4.1	6.2	8.5	9.3	11.4	9.5	(14.9)	14.4
Netherlands	67.4	76.0	173.8	154.3	124.5	88.6	136.9	177.0	320.4	453.6	433.0
Total (Six)	923.8	1 236.6	2 244.9	1 886.7	2 122.7	2 436.7	2 422.2	2 807.2	4 261.5	5 511.7	5 660.9
Denmark			12.6	17.3	29.3	45.4	72.3	79.1	138.2	183.9	187.7
Ireland			–	–	–	–	–	–	32.2	(41.6)	61.3
United Kingdom			–	–	–	–	–	–	897.7	1 302.6	1 241.1
Total (Nine)			2 257.5	1 904.0	2 152.0	2 482.1	2 494.5	2 886.3	5 329.6	7 039.8	7 151.0

[1] The 1979 budget was balanced by means of VAT own resources in the case of Belgium, Denmark, France, Italy, the Netherlands and the United Kingdom and by means of financial contributions in the case of the other three Member States which did not apply the Sixth VAT Directive until 1 January 1980.

Financing the general budget
Contributions from the Member States

Member State	Reference year (1970)	Own resources+political scale[1] 1971	1972	1973	1974	Own res[...] 1975
Belgium	8.26	8.34	8.27	7.36	7.10	6.7
Denmark				1.12	1.41	1.7
FR of Germany	31.39	31.70	32.02	29.04	28.48	28.0
France	28.08	27.93	27.75	24.77	23.98	22.8
Ireland				0.28	0.35	0.4
Italy	21.68	21.53	21.36	19.03	18.38	17.4
Luxembourg	0.20	0.20	0.20	0.18	0.17	0.1
Netherlands	10.20	10.30	10.40	9.44	9.09	8.9
United Kingdom				8.78	11.04	13.5
Total	100	100	100	100	100	100
Amount in m u.a. and m EUA		2 219.9	2 993.4	4 583.9	4 971.5	5 893.1

[1] The political scales and GNP scale for each Member State are given on p. 380.
[2] The reason why this total exceeds 100% is explained on p. 379.

sion of 21 April 1970 and the two Directives of 11 April 1967—which laid the foundations for a common VAT system but left open a number of important questions concerning the scope of the tax—by submitting to the Council on 29 June 1973 a proposal for a Sixth Directive on the harmonization of Member States' legislation concerning turnover taxes (common system of value-added tax: uniform basis of assessment). This was published in Supplement 11/73—Bull. EC.

2. On 14 March 1974 the European Parliament put forward a number of amendments to the Commission's original proposal, with the comment that this European tax law was rather too ambitious, went further than necessary for the purpose of independent Community revenues, and was in fact aimed at the harmonization of Member States taxation systems. Parliament pointed out that Member States should not need to increase their national VAT rates to cover Community expenditure since they would be making a saving by ceasing to pay financial contributions.

3. The Commission amended its proposal on 12 August 1974 in the light of Parliament's Opinion.

4. The deadline of 1 January 1975 set in Article 4 of the Decision of 21 April 1970 was not met, and a German proposal made in June 1974 to calculate the uniform VAT assessment basis according to national accounting data (i.e. without harmonizing Member States' legislation) was rejected (although the final solution in fact bears quite a resemblance to this proposal), so Article 4(3) of the Decision of 21 April 1970 which stipulates that 'the financial contribution of each Member State to the budget of the Communities shall be determined according to the proportion of its gross national product to the sum total of the gross national products of the Member States' came into play. The budget thus continued to be financed by contributions from the Member States and not from tax revenue.

5. The Council failed to reach any agreement at a succession of meetings.

6. At its meeting in Luxembourg on 5 April 1976 the Joint Council of Foreign Affairs and Finance Ministers agreed to take steps to ensure that the Directive would be adopted in time for it to be applied from 1 January 1978.

7. On 29 March 1977, the Council adopted a joint position which it forwarded to Parliament.

8. Parliament, on 20 April 1977, decided to dispense with the conciliation procedure to allow the Sixth Directive to enter into force without further delay.

9. On 17 May 1977 the Council adopted the Sixth Directive (OJ L 145 of 13.6.1977).

10. On 25 May 1978, the Commission proposed, in view of the circumstances, that entry into force be postponed from 1 January 1978 to 1 January 1979.

11. On 26 June 1978, the Council adopted the Ninth Directive which postponed by one year the date of entry into force.

12. As a result of long delays in the application of the Sixth Directive by the Member States (see footnote 6, p. 134), VAT did not become a fully-fledged source of budget revenue until the 1980 budget.

scale¹		Own resources				Fully operational own-resources system
976	1977	1978	1979	1978³	1979³	1980⁴
6.69	6.31	6.18	6.44	6.47	6.72	6.13
2.08	2.35	2.29	2.35	2.29	2.35	2.38
27.48	25.84	29.39	29.52	31.14	30.66	29.84
21.54	20.26	18.20	18.95	19.29	20.08	19.13
0.51	0.61	0.73	0.74	0.58	0.73	0.89
17.17	16.69	13.79	11.84	14.45	12.48	11.96
0.15	0.15	0.11	0.13	0.12	0.13	0.12
8.80	8.55	9.94	8.98	10.31	9.35	8.61
16.30	19.24	19.37	21.06	15.36	17.49	20.94
00.52²	100	100	100	100	100	100
10.3	8 200.2	12 003.9	14 372.4	12 003.9	14 372.4	15 042.5

³ After application of Article 131 of the Act of Accession (see pp. 380 to 382 and in particular the table in which are shown the adjustments made between the Member States outside the budget in 1978 and 1979). The percentage for 1979 has already been given on p. 128.
⁴ These are the percentages in the budget and not those given in the revenue and expenditure accounts as in the case of the other years. The difference is, however, negligible as a general rule.

C—Differences between own-resources estimates and actual revenue (1971-79)

Each year a revenue estimate is included in the statement of revenue in the general budget. The Commission draws up the revenue and expenditure account on 1 June of the year following the financial year in question. It shows the actual budget revenue.

The preceding tables show actual revenue between 1971 and 1979. In the following table the outturn for each type of own resource other than VAT is given in relation to the estimates.

In accordance with Article 10(1) of Regulation No 2892/77 of 19 December 1977, the six Member States applying the Sixth Directive in 1979 forwarded to the Commission details of the final amount of their assessment bases for VAT own resources for 1979 in July 1980. For these six Member States, 1% of the VAT assessment basis, converted into EUA at the budget rates, is about 340 m EUA (5.66%) more than the amount estimated for 1979 (6 008 m EUA).

Percentage differences between own-resources estimates and actual revenue *(Estimates = 100)*

		1971	1972	1973	1974	1975	1976	1977	1978	1979
		Difference in relation to initial budget estimate								
Agricultural levies		80.5	82.5	74.7	84.5	120.4	164.5	158.2	111.1	98.4
Sugar levies		108.0	97.1	104.5	49.3	74.6	118.5	147.1	109.0	99.6
Customs duties		119.3	104.5	102.5	110.0	94.4	114.3	100.0	90.9	107.3
	Total	96.7	94.9	96.6	104.2	96.7	121.8	118.4	96.8	106.0
		Difference in relation to amended estimates in supplementary budgets								
Agricultural levies				96.1		128.9	148.4			
Sugar levies				97.1			136.6			101.1
Customs duties				97.4	92.7	98.7	97.9			102.8
	Total			97.3	95.2	104.0	110.0			101.7

Implementation of the European Communities' budgets, 1971-80 (revenue)

We have chosen the period 1971-80 because the general budget was not financed by own resources until 1971. The ECSC operational budget has been funded by own resources since 1952-53, but we have only given the figures for 1971-80 (10 years exactly).

General budget

Under Council Regulation No 2891/77 of 19 December 1977 implementing the Decision of 21 April 1970 on the replacement of financial contributions from Member States by the Communities' own resources, revenue must cover:
(i) payments made in the relevant financial year, and
(ii) carry-overs to the following year (see p. 74).

However, a sum equivalent to the amounts cancelled against appropriations carried over from the previous year is deducted from these amounts. This applies for the period 1971-79. The figures given for 1980 are the estimates in the budget adopted on 9 July 1980.

The figures under Heading 6 (Miscellaneous) for 1975, 1976 and 1977 are higher than for the earlier years, mainly because of exchange-rate gains (250 m u.a. in 1975, 204 m u.a. in 1976 and 135 m u.a. in 1977). The figure for 1977 (192 m u.a.) includes 40.5 m u.a. by way of surplus revenue from 1976, and that for 1979 (107.6 m EUA) includes 41.6 m EUA by way of surplus revenue from 1978.

Consequently they do not tally exactly with figures given for expenditure for which we have followed the 'year of commitment' approach (see p. 74) which alone gives a true reflection of the situation as regards the budget.

ECSC operational budget

Bearing in mind our earlier remarks we would add that revenue in the period 1952-79 totalled 1 823.70 m EUA (1 256.1 m EUA from levies, 49 m EUA from payments by the three new Member States between 1973 and 1975, 375 m EUA from revenue from own funds, 17.1 m EUA from fines and various sums recovered, 56 m EUA from *ad hoc* payments by Member States and a 70.51 m EUA balance from borrowing/lending operations). For accounting purposes the following must be added to this figure: 509 m EUA (cancellations of provisions for operational and administrative expenditure), 11.9 m EUA (cancellations of capital provisions and 63 m EUA (revaluation of assets and liabilities), bringing the total to 2 407.6 m EUA.

The figures under Heading 10 (Miscellaneous) for 1978, 1979 and 1980 show a sharp increase compared with earlier years. They are *ad hoc* payments from Member States to enable the ECSC to cover the additional requirements caused by the crisis in the steel industry (see pp. 116 and 117).

We should finally point out that we have had to deduct the ECSC payments made to the general budget to cover its administrative costs (Heading 3) from the Community's total receipts because this is an item of expenditure in the ECSC operational budget which is met by ECSC levies.

Unit of account

The unit of account used for the ECSC operational budget has not always been the same as that used for the general budget. The ECSC operational budget used to use a parity unit of account (revalued in 1974 and 1975) and adopted the EUA in 1976.

Extreme caution should be exercised when using these tables, because the figures they contain relate to current units of account—whose equivalent value in national currencies varies with time—added together. They do, however, tally with the European Communities' revenue and expenditure accounts.

Implementation of the European Communities' budget (revenue)

	1971	1972	1973	1974
		m IMF u.		
A—General budget	Transitional system (1st stage)			
1. Traditional own resources				
1.1 Agricultural levies	604.5	617.8	411.3	255.C
1.2 Sugar contributions	109.3	181.7	99.0	75.|
1.3 Customs duties	582.3	957.3	1 986.3	2 737.6
Total	1 296.1	1 756.8	2 496.6	3 067.1
2. Value-added tax				
3. ECSC payments	18.0	18.0	18.0	18.0
4. Deductions from staff pay	13.1	15.5	19.6	24.8
5. Financial contributions				
5.1 For balancing the budget	923.8	1 236.6	2 257.5	1 904.0
5.2 Euratom complementary programmes	26.0	27.0	10.4	10.0
Total	949.8	1 263.6	2 267.9	1 914.0
6. Miscellaneous	12.4	20.5	9.9	12.3
Total A	2 289.4	3 074.4	4 812.0	5 036.8
B—ECSC operational budget	m IMF u.a.			Revalue
7. Levies				
7.1 Coal levies	6.5	7.5	12.1	11.4
7.2 Steel levies	31.3	39.7	50.8	58.2
Total	37.8	47.2	62.9	69.6
8. Acceding States' contributions			19.2	15.9
9. Revenue from own funds	14.2	13.0	18.7	32.9
10. Miscellaneous	0.1	0.3	0.9	
11. Cancelled provisions				
(a) Capital				
(b) Operational expenditure	5.4	0.6	12.1	6..
12. Revaluation of assets and liabilities	0.4		6.5	
Total B	i 57.9	61.1	120.3	124.6
m IMF u.a. and m EUA Grand total A+B—3	2 329.3	3 117.5	4 914.3	5 143.4

| 1975 | 1976 | 1977 | m EUA | | | Total |
			1978	1979	1980	1971-79
Transitional system (2nd stage)			Fully operational system			
510.4	1 035.2	1 576.1	1 872.7	1 678.6	1 719.2	8 561.6
79.7	128.5	202.4	410.6	464.9	504.5	1 751.2
151.0	4 064.5	3 927.2	4 390.9	5 189.1	5 667.8	26 986.2
741.1	5 228.2	5 705.7	6 674.2	7 332.6	7 891.5	37 299.0
				4 737.7	7 151.0	4 737.7
18.0	18.0	18.0	5.0	5.0	5.0	136.0
29.0	33.0	65.8	95.6	107.9	121.9	404.3
152.0	2 482.1	2 494.5	5 329.7	2 302.1	—	21 082.3
12.6	8.8	8.7	10.6	10.9	12.8	125.0
164.6	2 490.9	2 503.2	5 340.3	2 313.0	12.8	21 207.3
260.9	223.1	192.0	66.6	107.6	500.8	905.3
213.6	7 993.2	8 484.7	12 181.7	14 603.8	15 683.0	64 689.6
MF u.a.	m EUA					
12.5	18.0	20.2	21.9	23.9	27.0	134.0
57.7	74.6	66.6	78.9	79.3	90.0	537.1
70.2	92.6	86.8	100.8	103.2	117.0	671.1
13.9						49.0
27.8	29.7	32.4	36.1	36.4	40.0	241.2
0.5	0.4	0.1	28.0	28.8	43.0	59.1
42.7	75.4	89.1	115.6	125.5	120.0	472.6
34.4	11.4	—	—	—	—	52.7
89.5	209.5	208.4	280.5	293.9	320.0	1 545.7
85.1	8 184.7	8 675.1	12 457.2	14 892.7	15 998.0	66 099.3

Implementation of the European Communities' budgets, 1952-80 (expenditure)

General

The following table summarizes, for the period 1952-80, figures taken from:

(a) in the case of ECSC expenditure: the annual balance sheets (see p. 88) as regards provisions. Provisions subsequently cancelled have been deducted (1952-79 column);

(b) in the case of EEC and Euratom expenditure: the revenue and expenditure accounts drawn up under Article 73(1) of the Financial Regulation. The figures are the actual amounts paid in the financial year in question and in the following financial year (to which appropriations may be carried over) to meet commitments entered into during earlier financial years. However, the 1974 figure for the new Social Fund reflects payments made during two subsequent years pursuant to a special arrangement authorizing the carrying over of appropriations for two years (1975 and 1976) instead of just one;

(c) in the case of EDF expenditure: the payments recorded in the annual accounts.

The amounts shown in the table for 1979 are provisional since, at the time of writing, the exact amount of payments made against carry-overs was not known. The amounts given for the 1980 budget are even less likely to reflect actual expenditure than the figures for 1979 as it will not be known until 31 December 1981 how much will be spent in 1980. The small increase in appropriations in 1977 compared with 1976 is due to the fairly general introduction of differentiated appropriations in that year; as a result only the payment appropriations are entered as expenditure.

General budget

The figures for agriculture include *EAGGF Guarantee Section* expenditure over 13 months in the 1972 column and over 11 months in the 1973 column. This oddity is a consequence of the enlargement of the Communities.

The *EAGGF Guidance Section* figures include only payments made during the year in which commitments were entered into and the first subsequent year

to which appropriations may be carried over, in order to maintain consistency in the table, since this is the rule that applies to all the other expenditure. It should be borne in mind, however, that as this Fund's appropriations, prior to 1977, could be carried over indefinitely, total payments before 1980 amount to 2 038 m u.a. rather than the figure of 1 314 m u.a. included in the 54 740 m u.a. for the common agricultural policy.

Euratom research expenditure for the period 1968-70 is shown in the horizontal column for historical reasons, since, although the general budget already existed then, research and investment appropriations were put in a separate budget of their own until the Treaty of 21 April 1970 provided otherwise. Expenditure for these and earlier financial years has not, however, been given a separate total in the vertical totals column (1952-79) but included in the total for the energy and industrial policy/Euratom to show the total volume of expenditure in this sector, research expenditure having been financed by the general budget since 1971. The administrative expenditure of the Euratom Commission, mainly for its Brussels headquarters before the Executives merged, is included in the total for Commission administrative expenditure.

ECSC operational budget

The ECSC's administrative expenditure amounts to 347.2 m u.a. However, this expenditure has been covered by the general budget since 1968. A payment of 18 m u.a. each year from 1968 to 1977 and 5 m u.a. from 1978 to 1980 has been made from the ECSC operational budget to cover it. These amounts therefore appear as revenue in the general budget (see p. 390, line A3). To avoid making administrative expenditure appear greater than it is by counting the annual payments twice (190 m u.a. for the period 1968-79), the appropriate amounts have been subtracted from the amounts shown in the totals 1, 5 and 7 in the last column of the table on p. 399 where total expenditure between 1952 and 1979 is shown.

It should also be pointed out that the ECSC budget total given in the expenditure table may not tally exactly for each year with total B for the ECSC budget in the revenue table (e.g. for 1976 the figures are 208.3 m u.a. and 209.5 m u.a. respectively), since any deficit or surplus for a particular year is entered as an unallocated balance in the balance sheet. Over the years the figures offset each other.

Between 1952 and 1979 surpluses totalled 53.1 m EUA and deficits amounted to 52.5 m EUA.

The table (on p. 399) shows the following expenditure amounts up to 1979: 342.2 m EUA (actually 338.1 m EUA as 4.1 m EUA were cancelled) for administrative expenditure by the High Authority (Commission) and 45.3 m EUA for administrative expenditure by other Community institutions before the merger, 1 090.7 m EUA for operational expenditure (not 1 618.1 m EUA as 504.8 m EUA were cancelled and 22.6 m EUA concern a revaluation of liabilities) and 389.4 m EUA by way of capitalization (not 401.3 m EUA as 11.9 m EUA were cancelled). On 31 December 1979 the ECSC's capital consisted of a guarantee fund of 230 m EUA, a special reserve of 140 m EUA and a former pension fund of 41.06 m EUA (of which only 7.82 m EUA from levies and contributions from acceding countries, most of it (24.51 m EUA) being employers' and employees' contributions).

The 1 090.7 m EUA of operational expenditure can be broken down as follows: 605 m EUA for social and regional policy (see p. 232), 422.09 m EUA for energy and industrial policy (see p. 268) and 63 m EUA for miscellaneous expenditure (financial costs, adjustment of parities and provisions for future years).

Administrative expenditure of all the institutions

The administrative expenditure of all the institutions totalled 4 534.4 m EUA in the period 1952-79 of which 3 249.8 m EUA for the Commission (EEC and Euratom Commissions from 1958 to 1967 and the Single Commission from 1968 to 1979), 152.2 m EUA for the ECSC High Authority and 1 132.4 m EUA for other institutions.

It should finally be noted that since in the case of the general budget, and its predecessors (EEC and ECSC budgets), revenue and expenditure must be in balance, total expenditure matches total revenue.[1]

Explanatory notes on the use of the EUA in the general budget in 1978

The transition from the u.a. to EUA could not be made simply by substituting, say, 1 EUA for 1 u.a., without running the risk of having insufficient or excessive funds, depending on the sector concerned. In its preliminary draft budget for 1978, the Commission

therefore worked out five transition coefficients for the appropriations in the 1977 budget as a means of comparing the 1978 and 1977 budgets and to ensure that the Community remained financially solvent:

Coefficient No 1: appropriations spent primarily in Belgian francs. Virtually all the appropriations in Titles 1 (Staff) and 2 (Administrative expenditure) and a large proportion of headings in Title 9 (Development cooperation) come into the category. In this case, the coefficient is 1 u.a. = 1.21 EUA.

Coefficient No 2: Miscellaneous appropriations spent in all the basket currencies. The EAGGF Guidance Section (Title 8), cooperation between the national employment services (Item 3051), consumer protection studies (Item 3550) and schemes concerning developing countries carried out by non-governmental organizations (Article 945) come into this category. In this case, it was thought that the increases (expenditure in strong currencies) would be more or less offset by the decreases (expenditure in weak currencies). The comparison of 1977 and 1978 appropriations was therefore made on the basis of 1 u.a. = 1 EUA.

Coefficient No 3: Certain minor appropriations spent in a specified currency. Some contributions to international agreements or the like (e.g. Items 2980 and 3103, Article 940, etc.), where it is known that the money in question will be spent in a specified currency, come into this category. In this case, the relevant conversion rate was used.

Coefficient No 4: Titles 6 and 7 (EAGGF Guarantee Section). These are special cases, since the existence of a 'dual exchange rate' entry obviated the need for calculations for each heading, as it covered the difference between payments at the representative rates and the charges in u.a. in 1977 and in EUA in 1978. There was therefore no need to work out a specific coefficient as the structure of the budget nomenclature allowed such a comparison to be made.

Coefficient No 5: Fields in which appropriations are spent primarily in certain basket currencies. For the purposes of comparison, the Commission worked out an *ad hoc* coefficient in relation to the composition of the expenditure based on the latest breakdown of 1976 expenditure. In the case of the Regional Fund (expenditure on the basis of quotas set by Regulation) the coefficient was 1 u.a. = 0.796 EUA (500 m u.a. = 398 m EUA) since the recipients were mainly countries with weak currencies. In the case of the Social Fund the coefficient was 1 u.a. = 0.815 EUA and for research and investment appropriations 1 u.a. = 0.99 EUA.

Using these rates, so that the EUA could be used in the 1978 budget, entailed recalculating the 1977 budget for comparison purposes. The final totals were very similar: 10 353 738 996 u.a. and 10 267 894 300 EUA (99.2%) in the case of appropriations for commitments and 9 584 257 659 u.a. and 9 599 865 100 EUA (100.2%) in the case of appropriations for payments.

---

[1] For more details see the author's article 'L'histoire budgétaire des Communautés européennes' published in French in the December 1976 and January and February 1977 issues of the *Revue du Marché Commun*.

Final remarks

We have used the traditional policy-by-policy breakdown for general budget expenditure in the table covering the period 1968-80 (agricultural policy, social policy, regional policy, energy and industrial policy, cooperation policy, repayments to Member States and miscellaneous). In this new edition we have, however, adopted a more up-to-date approach which is starting to gain ground, of making a distinction between agricultural guarantee policy and the Community's internal development policy, covering agricultural structures (EAGGF Guidance Section), social policy and regional policy. Hence Chapters XI and XII do not tally exactly with the table· which is in line with official Community documents. The comments made on p. 393 about the EAGGF Guidance Section clearly demonstrate what a small role it plays in agricultural policy which is primarily a market support policy. ·

Implementation of the European Communities' budgets (expenditure) and of the EDF

Period		ECSC alone					
ECSC financial years		1952/53	53/54	54/55	55/56	56/57	57/5
EEC/Euratom financial years							
ECSC (High Authority) Administrative expenditure Operational expenditure Capital		3.3 — —	5.0 8.2 36.6	5.3 11.8 40.7	6.3 4.1 28.4	7.6 13.8 8.5	9. 25. 5.
1.	Total	3.3	49.8	57.8	38.8	29.9	40.
EEC (Commission) Administrative expenditure Social policy Agricultural policy							
2.	Total						
Euratom (Commission) Administrative expenditure Research policy							
3.	Total						
Parliament 4. ECSC contribution 5. EEC/Euratom contribution		0.6 —	0.9 —	1.1 —	1.3 —	1.3 —	1. —
	Total	0.6	0.9	1.1	1.3	1.3	1.
Council 6. ECSC contribution 7. EEC/Euratom contribution		0.3 —	0.6 —	0.6 —	0.7 —	0.7 —	0. —
	Total	0.3	0.6	0.6	0.7	0.7	0.
Court of Justice 8. ECSC contribution 9. EEC/Euratom contribution		0.4 —	0.7 —	0.6 —	0.6 —	0.7 —	0. —
	Total	0.4	0.7	0.6	0.6	0.7	0.
Other institutions—Total 10. ECSC = 4+6+8 11. EEC+Euratom = 5+7+9		1.3	2.2	2.3	2.6	2.7	3
12.	Total = 10+11	1.3	2.2	2.3	2.6	2.7	3
13.	Total ECSC = 1+10	4.6	52.0	60.1	41.4	32.6	43
14.	Total EEC/Euratom = 2+3+11						
15.	Budgets—Total = 13+14	4.6	52.0	60.1	41.4	32.6	43
16.	EDF 1 EDF 2						
17.	Grand total = 15+16	4.6	52.0	60.1	41.4	32.6	43

	Three independent executives									Total
9	59/60	60/61	61/62	62/63	63/64	64/65	65/66	66/67	1967	1952 to 1967
8	1959	1960	1961	1962	1963	1964	1965	1966	1967	
0	9.3	9.8	10.8	11.2	12.1	13.6	14.6	15.7	8.1	152.2
7	30.7	23.5	26.5	13.6	21.9	18.7	37.3	28.1	10.4	295.8
9	2.6	7.6	10.3	8.3	8.0	7.3	7.9	7.4	1.1	186.2
	42.6	40.9	47.6	33.1	42.0	39.6	59.8	51.2	19.6	634.2
7	13.5	16.2	19.4	22.8	27.6	31.0	34.1	41.6	42.8	253.7
	—	—	8.6	11.3	4.6	7.2	3.0	18.4	20.0	73.1
							30.3	55.0	401.6	486.9
7	13.5	16.2	28.0	34.1	32.2	38.2	67.4	115.0	464.4	813.7
	2.5	5.4	5.4	5.4	6.6	7.7	8.7	9.5	10.3	63.9
	6.0	0.4	1.5	49.4	78.1	92.4	111.3	119.7	119.2	579.3
	8.5	5.8	6.9	54.8	84.7	100.1	120.0	129.2	129.5	643.2
	1.1	1.1	1.4	1.6	1.6	1.8	1.9	2.1	1.5	21.4
	2.2	2.2	2.8	3.2	3.2	3.6	3.8	4.2	4.8	31.2
	3.3	3.3	4.2	4.8	4.8	5.4	5.7	6.3	6.3	52.6
	0.7	0.7	0.9	1.3	1.4	1.5	1.7	2.0	1.5	15.9
	1.8	2.2	2.6	3.6	3.7	4.2	4.6	5.1	5.9	34.9
	2.5	2.9	3.5	4.9	5.1	5.7	6.3	7.1	7.4	50.8
	0.3	0.3	0.3	0.4	0.4	0.4	0.5	0.5	0.5	8.0
	0.6	0.6	0.6	0.6	0.7	0.8	0.8	0.9	1.0	6.8
	0.9	0.9	0.9	1.0	1.1	1.2	1.3	1.4	1.5	14.8
	2.1	2.1	2.6	3.3	3.4	3.7	4.1	4.6	3.5	45.3
	4.6	5.0	6.0	7.4	7.6	8.6	9.2	10.2	11.7	72.9
	6.7	7.1	8.6	10.7	11.0	12.3	13.3	14.8	15.2	118.2
	44.7	43.0	50.2	36.4	45.4	43.3	63.9	55.8	23.1	679.5
	25.6	27.0	40.9	96.3	124.5	146.9	196.6	254.4	605.6	1 529.8
	71.3	70.0	91.1	132.7	169.9	190.2	260.5	310.2	628.7	2 209.3
		3.4	15.8	53.3	65.3	83.4	84.8	76.7	61.7	444.4
							21.9	31.6	42.9	96.4
	71.3	73.4	106.9	186.0	235.2	273.6	367.2	418.5	733.3	2 750.1

Implementation of the European Communities' budgets (expenditure) and of the EDF (*continued*)

Period		Period of the three merged Executives in the Community of Six				
Year	Carryovers 1952-67	1968	1969	1970	1971	197:
ECSC						
Administrative expenditure	152.2	18.0	18.0	18.0	18.0	18
Operational expenditure	295.8	21.2	40.7	56.2	37.4	43
Capital	186.2	2.2	6.8	0.9	2.0	—
ECSC budget—Total	634.2	41.4	65.5	75.1	57.4	6
1. Total less administrative expenditure 1968-80	634.2	23.4	47.5	57.1	39.3	43
General budget						
Commission admin. expenditure	{253.7					
Agricultural policy	63.9	73.8	83.4	92.9	108.1	135
Social policy	486.9	1 295.6	1 675.1	3 166.8	1 817.5	2 540
Regional policy	73.1	26.1	20.6	37.7	57.0	84
Energy and industrial policy						
Euratom					64.0	7:
Other		—	0.1	1.0	0.9	
Cooperation policy		1.0	1.0	1.0	—	70
Repayments to Member States					129.6	17:
Miscellaneous						
2. Total	877.6	1 396.5	1 780.2	3 299.4	2 177.1	3 08:
Parliament	52.6	7.7	8.5	9.2	10.9	1
Council	50.8	8.7	9.7	11.0	16.6	2
Court of Justice	14.8	1.6	1.8	2.2	2.5	
Court of Auditors						
3. Other institutions—Total	118.2	18.0	20.0	22.4	30.0	3
Euratom (research)	579.3	73.4	59.2	63.4		
4. General budget—Total = 2+3	1 575.1	1 487.9	1 859.4	3 385.2	2 207.1	3 12:
5. European Communities' budget—Total = 1+4	2 209.3	1 511.3	1 906.9	3 442.3	2 246.4	3 16
EDF 1	444.4	38.6	25.6	16.1	11.4	1
6. EDF 2	96.4	67.9	89.4	129.5	120.5	7
EDF 3					22.5	4
EDF 4						
7. Grand total = 5+6	2 750.1	1 617.8	2 021.9	3 587.9	2 400.8	3 29

	The Community of Nine								Total
73	1974	1975	1976	1977	1978	1979	1980		1952-79
8.0	18.0	18.0	18.0	18.0	5.0	5.0	5.0		342.2
36.9	92.1	127.4	158.9	154.1	241.5	262.4	284.5		1 618.3
15.0	15.0	45.3	31.4	36.3	28.2	32.0	30.5		401.3
9.9	125.1	190.7	208.3	208.4	274.7	299.4	320.0		2 361.8
2.0	107.1	172.7	190.3	190.4	269.7	294.4	315.0		2 171.8
1.0	231.9	272.3	323.5	369.6	495.5	555.2	623.1		3 249.8
27.1	3 499.0	4 406.5	5 755.4	6 704.0	9 026.6	10 739.4	11 878.3		54.740.3
9.6	245.2	154.7	222.8	186.6	555.6	552.4	402.4		2 466.1
		150.0	300.0	400.0	525.0	699.0	603.0		2 074.0
8.8	83.0	95.7	110.7	150.6	208.0	217.0	276.7		1 848.3
1.3	27.4	20.2	16.5	30.2	58.9	77.9	102.8		235.5
1.1	357.9	250.9	202.8	194.1	313.2	541.2	641.6		1 995.1
9.7	306.8	374.1	523.7	568.9	667.9	766.5	834.5		3 762.9
8.6	4 751.2	5 724.4	7 455.4	8 603.9	11 850.7	14 148.6	15.362.4		70 372.0
2.6	31.7	39.1	45.3	60.1	88.8	115.5	177.4		506.2
8.4	36.6	45.3	53.0	60.7	80.5	87.7	108.6		510.9
5.6	6.9	8.1	9.1	10.8	14.7	16.9	21.7		98.2
				0.4	7.1	9.6	13.0		17.1
6.6	75.2	92.5	107.4	132.0	191.1	229.7	320.7		1 132.4
5.2	4 826.4	5 816.9	7 562.8	8 736.0	12 041.8	14 378.4	15 683.1		71 504.4
7.2	4 933.5	5 989.6	7 753.1	8 926.4	12 311.5	14 672.6	15 998.1		73 676.2
9.9	5.5	2.4	2.9	0.5	0.8	0.4	—		568.6
9.4	25.9	23.4	17.2	16.3	7.9	4.1	—		726.5
8.5	140.6	182.7	131.0	79.8	66.0	37.5	35.0		801.4
			97.5	148.1	326.3	420.3	522.5		992.2
5.0	5 105.5	6 198.1	8 001.7	9 171.1	12 712.5	15 135.0	16 555.6		76 764.9

Resources collected by the European Communities, 1952-79

European Community borrowings 1952-79

(m u.a. and m EUA)

Year \ Institution	ECSC	EIB	Euratom	EEC	Total
1952	0				0
1953	0				0
1954	100.0				100.0
1955	16.4				16.4
1956	12.7				12.7
1957	37.0				37.0
1958	50.0	0	0		50.0
1959	0	0	0		0
1960	35.0	0	0		35.0
1961	23.3	21.4	0		44.7
1962	69.8	32.3	0		102.1
1963	33.2	35.2	4.5		72.9
1964	127.8	66.8	8.0		202.6
1965	54.3	65.0	11.0		130.3
1966	103.0	138.5	13.7		255.2
1967	58.0	194.5	2.6		255.1
1968	108.0	212.5	0		320.5
1969	64.0	146.0	0		210.0
1970	60.0	168.9	0		228.9
1971	105.3	412.9	0.6		518.8
1972	200.4	479.5	0		679.9
1973	259.4	612.3	0		871.7
1974	477.8	825.5	0		1 303.3
1975	877.0	830.7	0		1 707.7
1976	956.0	748.9	0	1 017.0	2 721.9
1977	729.4	1.161.5	72.9	518.0	2 481.8
1978	1 068.7	1 949.7	72.3	0	3 090.7
1979	956.8	2 481.2	166.4	178.1	3 782.5
Total	6 583.3	10 583.3	352	1 713.1	19 231.7

The amounts shown are from the relevant annual revenue and expenditure accounts and balance sheets of the institutions or organs of the European Communities, so cross-reference between this book and the documents in question is possible if the reader so desires.

It should, however, be pointed out that the ECSC's latest financial balance sheets contain figures in units of account which have been recalculated using the rates for converting national currencies into EUA obtaining at a particular date. In the latest balance sheet available (for 1979) they were converted at the 31 December 1979 EUA conversion rate, giving 6 505.88 m EUA in total borrowings compared with the figure of 6 583.3 m u.a. given in the table.

The figures for the EIB's borrowing/lending activities since 1958 have, on the other hand, been worked out on the basis of the official parities from 1958 to

1971, the central rates in 1972, conversion rates adjusted for statistical purposes to the actual conversion rates in 1973 and the conversion rates described above from 1974. These two factors and the effects of price movements over the 20-year period diminish the value of these figures.

Loans raised by the European Communities between 1952 and 1979 totalled 19 231.7 m u.a. (10 583.3 by the EIB, 6 583.3 by the ECSC, 352 by Euratom and 1 713.1 by the EEC).

In 1979 borrowings amounted to 3 782.5 m EUA (2 481.2 m EUA by the EIB, 956.8 m EUA by the ECSC, 166.4 m EUA by Euratom and 178.1 m EUA by the EEC). Clearly there has been a large increase in the Communities' borrowing/lending activities, which are outside the budget framework. NCI loans raised (178.1 m EUA) resulted in on-lending totalling 277 m EUA in 1979. For technical reasons new loans had to be raised at the beginning of 1980 to cover all these on-lending operations.

Statement of subscriptions to the capital of the Bank since 1958

(m u.a.)

	Belgium	Denmark	FR of Germany	France	Ireland	Italy	Luxembourg	Netherlands	United Kingdom	Total
Initial subscription										
Subscribed capital	86.5	—	300.0	300.0	—	240.0	2.0	71.5	—	1 000.0
Paid-in capital	21.625	—	75.0	75.0	—	60.0	0.5	17.875	—	250.0
Decision of 26 April 1971										
Subscribed capital	129.75	—	450.0	450.0	—	360.0	3.0	107.25	—	1 500.0
Paid-in capital	25.95	—	90.0	90.0	—	72.0	0.6	21.45	—	300.0
Enlargement of the Community (1 January 1973)										
Subscribed capital	118.5	60.0	450.0	450.0	15.0	360.0	3.0	118.5	450.0	2 025.0
Paid-in capital	23.7	12.0	90.0	90.0	3.0	72.0	0.6	23.7	90.0	405.0
Decision of 10 July 1975										
Subscribed capital	207.375	105.0	787.5	787.5	26.25	630.0	5.25	207.375	787.5	3 543.750
Called capital (paid in and due to be paid in)	32.5875	16.5	123.75	123.75	4.125	99.0	0.825	32.5875	123.75	556.275
Decision of 19 June 1978										
Subscribed capital	414.75	210.0	1 575.0	1 575.0	52.5	1 260.0	10.5	414.75	1 575.0	7 087.5[1]
Called capital (paid in and due to be paid in)[2]	53.325	27.0	202.5	202.5	6.75	162.0	1.35	53.325	202.5	911.25
Percentage breakdown by Member State	5.85	2.96	22.22	22.22	0.74	17.78	0.15	5.25	22.22	100.0

N.B. 'Decision' means a decision of the Board of Governors.

[1] Under the Accession Treaty for Greece the Bank's capital will again be increased and Greece will subscribe 112.5 m u.a. of which 14.465 m u.a. will be paid between 1981 and 1983.

[2] Under the Decision of 19 June 1978 on the increase in the Bank's capital, 10% of this increase (354 375 000 u.a.) must be paid by the Member States in eight six-monthly instalments, payable on 30 April and 31 October of each year in the period 1980 to 1983. The Board of Directors may require the balance of the subscribed capital to be paid to such extent as may be required for the Bank to meet its obligations towards those who have made loans to it (Article 5(3) of the EIB's Statute).

Structure of the departments of the Commission, Council and Parliament of the European Communities

A—The Commission's central departments

The following table shows how the Commission's central departments are organized and how many top posts there are in each department.

'Top posts' means:

(i) A/1 Director-General posts (of which there are 23) which are not included in the table since there is only one post in this grade in each Directorate-General.

(ii) A/2 Director posts (of which 20 are A/1 (personal) and generally involve the duties of deputy Director-General) or A/2 Chief Adviser posts not involving administrative tasks and often given on a personal basis. The 13 'Chefs de cabinet' to the Members of the Commission (temporary A/2 posts) are not included here.

(iii) A/3 Head of Division posts (some of which are on a personal basis) and A/5-4 Head of Specialized Department posts (directly responsible to a Director). Deputy 'Chefs de cabinet' to the Members of the Commission (temporary A/3 posts) are also left out.

The names of the people in these posts are published in the Directory of the Commission of the European Communities.

External departments are not included in the table either.

The following symbols are used in relation to the Directorates-General and Departments:

a = responsible for administering a large volume of budget appropriations but not exceeding 25 m EUA;

A = responsible for administering appropriations exceeding 25 m EUA, usually operational appropriations;

G = general terms of reference;
S = specific terms of reference.

B—The Council's General Secretariat

The Council's General Secretariat is organized as follows.

In addition to the General Secretary's Private Office, the General Secretariat has seven Directorates-General: Legal Department; Administration and Budget (with two Directorates); Agricultural, Regional and Social Policies and Education (with three Directorates); Domestic Market, Industrial Policy, Intellectual Property, Transport, Environment, Consumer Protection, Right of Establishment and Services (with three Directorates); Company Law, Public Contracts, Iron and Steel Industry, Science, Technology and Energy (with two Directorates); External Relations and Relations with Associated States (with three Directorates); Economic, Financial, Parliamentary and Institutional Affairs, Information, Documentation and Publications (with three Directorates).

C—Parliament's Secretariat-General

Parliament's Secretariat-General consists of the Secretary-General's Office and five Directorates-General: Sessional and General Services (with three Directorates); Committees and Interparliamentary Delegations (with three Directorates); Information and Public Relations (with two Directorates); Administration, Personnel and Finance (with four Directorates); and Research and Documentation (with two Directorates). The Political Groups also have secretariats.

Directorates-General and other departments

No	Title	Director or Chief Adviser	Head of Division or of Specialized Department	Terms of reference		Administration of appropriations		Reference see page
	Directorates-General							
	Secretariat-General	6	9	G			a	315
	Legal Service	11	18	G				315
I	External Relations	13	22		S		a	298
II	Economic and Financial Affairs	8	27	G	S			
III	Internal Market and Industrial Affairs	11	33		S		a	257
IV	Competition	4	22	G				
V	Employment and Social Affairs	7	28	G	S	A		210, 231
VI	Agriculture	12	30		S	A		186, 216
VII	Transport	3	12		S			
VIII	Development	9	30		S	A		282, 293, 298
IX	Personnel and Administration	6	48	G		A		306, 315
X	Spokesman's Group and DG for Information	2	25	G			a	
XII	Research, Science and Education	8	20		S	A		264
XIII	Information Market and Innovation	2	9	G			a	266
XIV	Fisheries	2	5		S	A		186
XV	Financial Institutions and Taxation	3	7		S			
XVI	Regional Policy	3	7		S	A		226
XVII	Energy	7	17		S	A		254, 257
XVIII	Credit and Investments	2	5		S		a	index
XIX	Budgets	3	15	G				index
XX	Financial Control	1	9	G				index
	Statistical Office	6	27	G			a	
	Joint Research Centre	11	49		S	A		260, 264
	Other departments							
	Customs Union Service	3	9		S			
	Environment and Consumer Protection Service	2	10		S		a	231
	Euratom Supply Agency	1			S			index
	Security Office	1		G				
	Office for Official Publications	1	4	G			a	index

Assumptions about the outlook for the budget in the period 1981-83

In the preliminary draft budget for 1981 submitted on 1 September 1980, the Commission included assumptions or projections for the period 1981-83 (rather than the usual three-year forecasts). It did so because the situation was particularly difficult for the following reasons:

(a) the Community's own resources will soon be exhausted;

(b) a mandate had been given to the Commission on 30 May 1980 to put forward proposals for restructuring the Community budget to ensure that unacceptable situations do not recur for any Member State (see footnote 7 on p. 340);

(c) a political awareness of the need to contain EAGGF Guarantee Section expenditure had emerged;

(d) there was a desire to increase the role of the Community budget in the efforts to achieve economic convergence within the Community;

(e) a major new item of expenditure had emerged as a result of the decisions taken on 30 May 1980—payments to the United Kingdom of around two-thirds of its scheduled net contributions in 1980 and 1981;

(f) the second enlargement gets under way with the accession of Greece in 1981.

The following table, for which I accept sole responsibility, presents the projections in the form of alternatives which reflect varying degrees of success in the containment of agricultural spending and different rates of increase in expenditure on structural policies in the widest sense (i.e. including energy, industry, research and transport).

Assumption 1 is based on the hypothesis that agricultural spending will be contained: i.e. very small price increases for dairy products and a moderate increase (compared with an inflation rate of 8% per year) for other products. A number of containment measures would be applied, relating primarily to dairy products and sugar, following the guidelines given by the Council (Agriculture) on 30 May 1980. Dairy farmers would be required to shoulder a greater proportion of the cost of surpluses by paying an additional co-responsibility levy. For sugar, the cost of disposing of surplus Community sugar would be borne by the manufacturers, as a limit would be imposed on the quantities guaranteed. Monetary

compensatory amounts would also be gradually removed, and there would be no exceptional general economic fluctuations. According to this assumption, EAGGF Guarantee Section spending would increase from 13 000 m EUA in 1981 to 15 900 m EUA in 1983, in other words by some 10% a year; this could be more or less matched by an increase in own resources within the 1% limit. It is only a modest increase, but it would not allow the proportion of spending in other sectors to be increased.

Would it be possible to envisage containing expenditure even more stringently, e.g. by keeping EAGGF Guarantee Section spending constant in real terms? Additional measures are undoubtedly conceivable. The system of unlimited guarantees to producers and permanent intervention on home markets could be adjusted, as was the case in the sugar and dairy sectors. The political obstacles, however, are great. There is, therefore, little point in examining how a tighter rein might be kept on spending than in Assumption 1, but it is essential to explore the consequences of not containing spending as severely as under that assumption.

Until this year, the multiannual forecasts included a high assumption based on a continuation of the rate of increase in expenditure of recent years (23% a year between 1975 and 1979). The general climate has changed and this possibility can be discounted. Assumption 2 thus reflects a partial containment of expenditure: prices of dairy products rising at the same—but fairly low—rate as that of other products, no additional containment measures and no exceptional fluctuations in the general economic situation. On this assumption, spending would rise from 13 000 m EUA in 1981 to around 17 400 m EUA in 1983 (an average increase of about 16% with the rate of increase from 1982 to 1983 being slightly higher than the rate of growth in the GDP). If farm prices were to increase at a faster rate—i.e. keep pace with the general level of prices—the cost in 1983 would be 1 000 m EUA more.

As things now stand and without anticipating what the proposals on the restructuring of the budget may be, the Community's interests would be best served by a scenario combining effectual containment of agricultural expenditure with a dynamic development of structural policies. There is every reason to think that the budget should in fact be restructured along these lines.

This would entail combining the level of expenditure on agricultural policy under Assumption 1 with the level of expenditure on structural policies under Assumption 2. This scenario would constitute quite a change in the structure of the budget, because even under Assumption 1 on its own the respective proportions of agricultural guarantee expenditure and structural expenditure would be 61.6% and 20.3% as early as 1982.

It should be pointed out that the expenditure figures given in the table relate to appropriations for payments covered by revenue from the Community's own resources. However, in terms of appropriations for commitments, the figures are 60% and 21.9% respectively for guarantee and structural policy spending in 1982 under Assumption 1.

As far as structural funds are concerned, under Assumptions 1 and 2, 1 800 and 2 000 m EUA might be allotted to the Regional Fund, 1 120 and 1 250 m EUA to the Social Fund and 750 and 750 m EUA to the EAGGF Guidance Section in terms of appropriations for commitments.

The United Kingdom is due to receive repayments of 1 175 m EUA for 1980 and 1 410 m EUA for 1981. It should be noted that (a) these amounts will be entered in the budget of the following financial year, less any advances, and (b) they are net amounts, i.e. the United Kingdom does not have to finance its own repayments. In the 1981 budget, therefore, 469 m EUA will be entered under the financial mechanism and 1 075 million EUA under supplementary measures giving a total of 1 544 m EUA (1 175 m EUA in net terms and an advance of 100 m EUA); in the 1982 budget 467 m EUA will appear under the financial mechanism and 1 165 m EUA under supplementary measures giving a total of 1 632 m EUA (1 130 m EUA in net terms, i.e. 1 410 m EUA minus 100 m EUA).

It is impossible to make a meaningful forecast of the amounts which will be in the 1983 budget under these heads, so no figures are given, and no totals can be indicated.

As the total expenditure proposed in the preliminary draft budget for 1981 is approaching the current own resources ceiling, the chances are that, on the basis of the information now available, this ceiling will be exceeded in 1982, whatever combination of assumptions are made about the various blocks of budget expenditure. It remains to be seen whether the Community will be able politically to effect a restructuring of the budget quickly enough to avoid exceeding the 1% VAT ceiling. It is also open to speculation whether the Community will wish to continue the existing own resources arrangements beyond 1981.

405

Budget outlook

Budget for 1980, preliminary draft budget for 1981, assumptions for 1982 and 1983

(m EUA)

Heading	Appropriations for payments					
	1980	1981	1982		1983	
			Assumption 1	Assumption 2	Assumption 1	Assumption 2
A—Expenditure						
1. Agriculture and fisheries						
EAGGF Guarantee Section	11 485.5	12 941.5	14 500	15 600	15 900	17 400
EAGGF Guidance Section	317.2	490.1	700		735	
Fisheries and marine policy	64.1	69.1	127		150	
Other (Chapter 31)	11.5	13.6	16		18	
Agriculture/fisheries—Total	11 878.3	13 514.3	15 343	16 443	16 803	18 303
2. Social policy	402.4	743	1 240	1 300	1 550	1 690
2a. of which: Social Fund	(374.3)	(710)	(1 200)	(1 250)	(1 500)	(1 640)
3. Regional policy	403	770	1 450	1 500	1 700	1 900
4. EMS interest subsidies	200	200	200		200	
5. Supplementary measures (UK)	—	1 075	1 165		?	
6. Energy, research and investment, industry and transport	379.5	376.5	450	500	500	600
7. Development cooperation	641.6	748.3	850		1 000	
8. Administrative expenditure	623.1	737	840		930	
9. Repayments to Member States						
10% (Chapter 40)	789.1	874.4	940		1 015	
Financial mechanism (Chapter 41)	—	469	467		?	
UK—EMS (Article 571)	45.4	44.8	47		47	
Greece (Articles 490 and 491)	-—	133.9	113		60	
Repayments—Total	834.5	1 522.4	1 567		?	
10. Commission total	15 362.4	19.687.0	23 105	24 365	?	?
11. Other institutions	320.7	364	413		463	
12. Enlargement (Spain and Portugal)						
13. Grand total (rounded-off)	15 683.1	20 051.0	23 520	24 780	?	?
B—Resources						
1. Miscellaneous revenue	632.5	166	180		200	
2. Customs duties	5 667.8	6 274	6 700		7 150	
3. Agricultural and sugar levies	2 223.7	2 473	2 700		3 000	
4. Amount to be covered by VAT	7 159.1	11 138.0	13 940	15 200		
5. Total	15 683.1	20 051.0	23 520	24 780	?	?
6. 1% of VAT assessment basis	9 910	11 705	13 090		14 675	
7. Resources within 1% VAT limit	18 434	20 618	22 670		25 025	
8. Difference (B.7)—(A.13)	+2 750.9	+565[1]	−850	−2 110	?	?
9. VAT percentage (B.4): (B.6)	0.72	0.95	1.07	1.16	?	?

[1] In 1981, Greece will pay GNP-based contributions and 70% of any additional GDP payment will have to be reimbursed, so the actual margin for 1981 is only 553 m EUA.

Some thoughts on the second enlargement of the Community (to include Greece, Portugal and Spain)

What legal and practical implications does enlargement of the Community entail? Article 237 of the EEC Treaty, Article 205 of the Euratom Treaty and Article 98 of the ECSC Treaty lay down the following procedure:

(a) 'Any European State may apply to become a member of the Community. It shall address its application to the Council ...'.[1]

(b) (The Council) '... after obtaining the opinion of the Commission'.[2]

(c) 'Shall act unanimously'.[3]

(d) 'The conditions of admission and the adjustments (to the Treaties) necessitated thereby shall be the subject of an agreement between the Member States and the applicant State. This agreement shall be submitted for ratification by all the Contracting States in accordance with their respective constitutional requirements' (the latter clause does not appear in the Euratom Treaty).[4]

This is not the place to go into all the problems involved in enlarging the Community from nine to twelve Member States, but three financial aspects deserve our attention. Let us begin by looking at what the Commission had to say in its 'fresco' on the enlargement of the Community dated 20 April 1978:[5]

'When Greece, Portugal and Spain, newly emerging as democratic States after a long period of dictatorship, asked to be admitted to the Community, they were making a commitment which is primarily a political one. Their choice is doubly significant, both reflecting the concern of these three new democracies for their own consolidation and protection against the return of dictatorship and constituting an act of faith in a united Europe, which demonstrates that the ideas inspiring the creation of the Community have lost none of their vigour or relevance. The three countries have entrusted the Community with a political

responsibility which it cannot refuse, except at the price of denying the principles in which it is itself grounded. These principles are enshrined in the preamble to the EEC Treaty, where the founders of the Community, "being resolved ... to preserve and strengthen peace and liberty, (called) upon the other peoples of Europe who share their ideal to join in their efforts".

The Heads of State or Government have recently solemnly proclaimed their faith in this ideal, which requires the Community to give a positive answer to the applicant countries.'

A—The effect of enlargement on the finances of Europe

Calculations made by the Commission in 1978

In an analysis of the economic and sectoral aspects of the enlargement of the Community dated 20 April 1978,[6] the Commission asked 'what would be the expenditure and resources of the Community in the event of full integration of the applicant countries?'. First of all, in the light of the information available and the complexity of the possible hypotheses, the Commission decided to simulate the theoretical case of full integration of the new members as from 1978, and full application of the existing policies, instruments, aids, premiums, etc. The Commission's calculations did not take account of the possible impact of monetary compensatory amounts (see p. 177) on the budget and could not incorporate the potential dynamic effects of applying Community policies, particularly as regards agriculture, in the three countries. It seemed probable that the impact on the budget of applying the common agricultural policy would increase after a while, but at that stage it was impossible to make an accurate estimate.

The figures given in the following tables reflect a static situation at the start of the enlargement process and would therefore more than likely turn out to be higher in reality.

---

[1] Greece applied for membership on 12 June 1975, Portugal on 28 March 1977 and Spain on 26 July 1977.

[2] The Commission gave its views on Greece's application on 29 January 1976 (see Supplement 2/76—Bull. EC) on Portugal's application on 19 May 1978 (see Supplement 5/78—Bull. EC) and on Spain's application on 29 November 1978 (see Supplement 9/78—Bull. EC).

[3] Negotiations with a view to accession began on 27 July 1976 in the case of Greece, on 17 October 1978 in the case of Portugal and on 5 February 1979 in the case of Spain.

[4] The Act of Accession for Greece was signed in Athens on 28 May 1979 (OJ L 291 of 19.11.1979).

[5] Published in Supplement No 1/78—Bull. EC.

[6] Published in Supplement No 3/78—Bull. EC.

Assumed expenditure 1978

(m EUA)

	Community of Nine	Greece	Spain	Portugal	Three applicant countries	Community of Twelve (in very round figures)
EAGGF Guarantee Section	8 666	400	600	100-150	1 100-1 150 or more In round figures 1 000-1 500	9 700-10 200
EAGGF Guidance Section	473	100	200-250	50-100	350-450	800-900
Social Fund	570	20-50	80-120	90-130	190-300	750-900
Regional Fund	581	105	190	125	420	1 000
Other areas excluding the 10% lump sum refund	1 382	50	200	50	300	1 600-1 700
Total excluding 10% refund	11 672	In round figures 700	In round figures 1 250-1 350	In round figures 400-560	2 300-2 900	14 300 ± 700
10% refund	690	20	60	10	In round figures 100	800
Total	12 362	700-750	1 300-1 400	400-600	2 400-3 000	15 000

Assumed resources 1978

(m EUA)

	Community of Nine	Greece	Spain	Portugal	Three applicant countries	Community of Twelve
Customs duties (1)	4 833	100 ± 20	350 + 50	30 ± 10	480 ± 80	
Agricultural levies and sugar levies (2)	2 063	100 ± 20	275 ± 50	75 ± 15	450 ± 85	
VAT:						
(a) 1% (3)	8 290	170	610	110	890	
(b) Community of Nine 1978 rate: 0.6429% (4)	5 330	—	—	—	—	
(c) Community of Twelve rate: 0.75% (5)	6 380	130	470	85	685	
Miscellaneous revenue (6)	136	—	—	—	—	
Total with: (a) 1% VAT (1+2+3+6)	15 322	370	1 235	215	1·820[1]	In round figures 17 000
(b) 0.6429% VAT: Community of Nine 1978 rate (1+2+4+6)	12 362	—	—	—	—	—
(c) 0.75% VAT: Community of Twelve rate (1+2+5+6)	13 412	330	1 100	190	1 610	In round figures 15 000

[1] Converted for the three new Member States at the rate of 1 January 1978. At the rate of 1 January 1977 used for the 1978 budget and for the Community of Nine column, the total for the three new Member States would be 2 300 m EUA instead of 1 820 m EUA, i.e. about 25% higher.

Assumed net financial impact 1978

(m EUA)

	Community of Nine	Greece	Spain	Portugal	Three applicant countries	Community of Twelve
Expenditure	12 362	700-750	1 300-1 400	400-600	2 700 ±300	In round figures 15 000
Resources	13 400	330	1 100	200	approx. 1 600	In round figures 15 000
Balance	+1 000	approx. −400	approx. −200/300	−200/400	approx. −1 000	0

The last table is a summary of the general budget of the Communities, and shows that the three applicant countries together would have received a transfer of some 1 000 m EUA from the present Community of Nine. In relative terms, this transfer would have been comparatively large in the case of Greece and Portugal but small in the case of Spain. Taking the high assumption, the net balance as a percentage of GDP would have been 2.3% for Greece, 3.3% for Portugal and 0.4% for Spain. For Greece and Portugal these net percentage balances would have represented between 10% and 15% of their annual investment.

The ECSC operational budget (which would probably increase by 6%) and borrowing/lending operations (which are at present held in a legal straightjacket which would have to be relaxed), not to mention short-term monetary support and medium-term financial assistance (between 1 000 and 2 500 m EUA), have been left out in this analysis.

Using very rough hypotheses, therefore, the simulation exercise carried out for 1978 indicates that if the applicant countries had been full members of the Community, they could have benefited from a net flow of around 1 000 m EUA by way of transfers via the Community budget and 500 m EUA by way of loans.

These figures are based on an interesting but rather contrived hypothesis. There are two basic principles which must be upheld:
(a) The Community's acquired rights regarding its own resources must be respected, i.e. the arrangements must be applied in full by the new Member States, to avoid a repetition of the transitional period which the Community went through from 1971 to 1979. This will mean that:
　(i) the budgets of the three new Member States will have to be supported to offset an immediate and entire loss of revenue in respect of customs duties, levies and VAT (GNP);
　(ii) no new Member State should pay more than it receives;
　(iii) the arrangements to be set up should not have any unexpected side-effects.

(b) Assistance in the form of loans or grants, depending on the economic situation in each country, will have to be given to the three new Member States to help finance structural changes during the transitional period, in order to avoid imbalance within the Community. Grants would doubtless have to be made conditional on their being used for projects of Community interest, perhaps on a progressive basis, e.g. 20% of the grants conditional in the first year and 100% conditional in the last year. It would also be desirable to increase the rate of assistance from existing instruments, in some cases to 100%.

Updating the hypotheses and calculations worked out in 1978

The following new factors have emerged since the Commission's paper of 20 April 1978.

Greek accession—With the signing of the Act of Accession for Greece and in anticipation of its entry into the Community on 1 January 1981, detailed new financial provisions have been worked out. Transitional measures have been adopted with regard to revenue (see p. 127). On the expenditure side, Greece's quota in the Regional Fund has been valued at around 17% (14.5% of the total quota section of the Fund), and approximately 15% of Social Fund expenditure will be in Greece. Considering the time it will take for Community mechanisms to start operating, Greece should have a net inflow of 80 m EUA in 1981 and 220 m EUA in 1982 (0.5% to 1% of the budget according to the multiannual estimates for 1980-82 adopted on 15 June 1979).

Spanish accession—A further analysis of the financial consequences of Spanish accession made in the first half of 1980 shows that EAGGF Guarantee Section expenditure in Spain could be as much as 1 300 m EUA (based on 1980) compared with 600 m EUA (based on 1978). This difference highlights the need to revise estimates to take account of price rises, new factors and/or any change in the method used, as can be seen below:

409

(a) If the statistics are updated on the basis of the 1978 method, the extra cost will be around 770 m EUA (i.e. an increase of just over 25%), which is more or less in line with the rate of increase in agricultural spending between 1978 and 1979 (approximately 23%).

(b) A new factor which has to be taken into account is the effect of new legislation (concerning fruit and vegetables and olive oil); this will result in an increase of 210 m EUA in Spain's case, giving a total static cost of 980 m EUA.

(c) The method has been changed to take account of dynamic effects; these result in an increase of 320 m EUA, making a total of 1 300 m EUA.

B—Institutional arrangements in the enlarged Community

This is another aspect of enlargement which concerns the Community's finances and hence merits a brief review.

The Commission's thoughts in 1978

The Commission's thoughts on this matter in 1978[1] are set out below:

(a) *Use of the qualified majority*—The Commission recommends that use be made in practice of the possibility of majority voting in the cases already laid down by the Treaties but also that the Treaties should be amended to enable greater use to be made of majority voting. The Commission has no intention of reviving an old quarrel which resulted in the Luxembourg Compromise of January 1966. It merely wishes to endorse the approach of the Heads of State or Government who at the Paris Summit at the end of 1974 saw the necessity for abandoning the practice of making all decisions conditional on the unanimous agreement of the Member States. The Commission takes the view that unanimous voting is warranted on important political matters, even if a majority decision is legally possible, and that majority voting should in some cases be used even where the Treaties do not provide for it. The main criterion for deciding whether voting should be unanimous or not should hence be the political importance of the decision in question and whether it effects the essential interests of Member States.

As far as the finances of Europe are concerned, examples of cases where the Commission considers majority voting could be used are the adjustment or suspension of customs duties (Article 28 of the EEC Treaty), financial and accounting rules (Article 209 of the EEC Treaty and Article 183 of the Euratom Treaty) and the establishment of Euratom multiannual research programmes (Article 7 of the Euratom Treaty).

(b) *The European Commission's management and executive powers*—The Commission feels that the Council does not make adequate use of the possibility offered by the EEC and Euratom Treaties to confer management and executive powers on it. It has already indicated to the Council, in a working paper, the fields in which it might be given these powers. Article 155 (fourth indent of the EEC Treaty and Article 124 (fourth indent) of the Euratom Treaty could be altered in such a way that the Commission would exercise these powers unless the Council decided otherwise. This would introduce into the Community legal order a way of operating the merits of which have been acknowledged, while still allowing the Council to take a decision itself whenever it considered a matter to be politically sensitive. The procedure to be used could be based on the arrangements already in force in many fields, whereby committees of Member States' representatives assist the Commission and controversial matters are referred to the Council.

(c) *Greater flexibility in the choice of legal instruments for Community legislation*—In addition to these two basic changes the Commission proposes that there should be greater flexibility in choosing between a Regulation, Directive or Decision to implement provisions of the Treaties. In several instances, the EEC Treaty prescribes the exclusive use of one instrument, e.g. the Directive for the harmonization of legislation (Article 100), right of establishment (Articles 56 and 57), etc. Directives are, however, often so detailed that the national authorities (and the national parliaments where it is up to them to enact the necessary implementing measures) have virtually no leeway even on small details (see footnote 6 on p. 134). This generates hostility, frequently leading to—often long—delays in the translation of directives into national law, and hence it is a complicated matter to check that national provisions conform to the Community Directives.

The Commission therefore recommends that the Treaty should be amended to give the Community legislative authority the right to choose the legal instrument to be used in each case. The Commission takes the view that secondary Community legislation need not be uniform. On the contrary, different cases should be handled in different ways to avoid discrimination.

(d) *Changes in the composition of the institutions and weightings*—The increase in the number of Member States will automatically entail changes in the composition of the institutions. The general rule is likely to be the one which now applies, i.e. all the Member States must be represented in every institution. They are likely to continue to be weighted according to the criteria used so far, which are based on population

---

[1] See Supplement No 2/76—Bull. EC (Enlargement of the Community—Transitional period and institutional implications).

and political considerations. There is no golden rule, but generally speaking, Greece and Portugal are likely to occupy much the same position as Belgium and the Netherlands whereas Spain should lie somewhere between this group and the Big Four (France, Germany, Italy and the United Kingdom).

This would give the following result:
(i) *European Parliament*: Greece and Portugal would have 24 members each (like Belgium) and Spain 58 (compared with 81 for the Big Four). The total number of Members of the European Parliament would thus rise from 410 to 516.[1]
(ii) *Weighting of votes within the Council*: Greece and Portugal would have five votes each (like Belgium and the Netherlands) and Spain eight (compared with ten for the Big Four). This would give a total voting strength of 76 and the number of votes required for a qualified majority would be 51.[1] Council decisions which do not have to be taken on a Commission proposal would require at least eight out of the twelve countries to vote in favour. The majority for certain decisions under the ECSC Treaty would be increased to five-sixths.
(iii) *Commission*: The Commission takes a more cautious approach, envisaging various formulas: one possibility favourably received by the Ministers of Foreign Affairs at an informal meeting at Leeds Castle is that the Commission would consist of one Member from each Member State. The Commission feels, however, that this would raise a number of practical problems in view of the increased work-load entailed by an enlarged Community.
(iv) *Court of Justice*: The number of judges would be raised to 13 (an odd number to avoid tied votes).
(v) *Court of Auditors*: One new Member from each new Member State.
(vi) *Economic and Social Committee*: Greece and Portugal would have 12 seats (like Belgium and the Netherlands) and Spain 18.

The Act of Accession for Greece of 28 May 1979

The composition of the institutions is laid down as follows in the Act of Accession signed in Athens:
(i) *European Parliament*: Greece will have 24 members and the number of representatives from the other countries will remain the same. The total number of Members of the European Parliament will thus rise from 410 to 434.
(ii) *Weighting of votes within the Council*: Greece will have five votes, the weightings for the other countries remaining unchanged. Total voting strength will thus be 63, the number of votes required for a qualified majority being 45. Council decisions which do not have to be taken on a

proposal from the Commission will require six of the ten members to vote in favour (no change compared with the present situation). The majority required for certain decisions under the ECSC Treaty will be nine-tenths (see Annex 2, p. 347).
(iii) *Commission*: The Commission will consist of 14 Members, including one new member of Greek nationality.
(iv) *Court of Justice*: The number of judges will be increased by one (to 10).
(v) *Court of Auditors*: Its Members will be 10 in number.
(vi) *Economic and Social Committee*: Greece will have 12 seats. Total seats will thus amount to 156.

C—How enlargement will affect the budget problems apparent in mid-1980

The second enlargement will have the following effects on the budget.

Greece and the 1981 budget

The 1981 budget will be the first budget for a Community with ten members. In its preliminary draft budget for 1981, the Commission has of course allowed for the amounts to be paid by Greece under the head of own resources and for the total amounts to be spent in Greece.

Payments by Greece are scheduled as follows: customs duties 90 m EUA, agricultural levies 90 m EUA, sugar levies 7.4 m EUA (giving a total of 187.4 m EUA) plus a GDP-based financial contribution of 18 m EUA giving a total of 368 m EUA.

Expenditure will be as follows: EAGGF Guarantee Section (a very large amount), Regional Fund (230 m EUA in commitment appropriations[2] and 45 m EUA in payment appropriations), Social Fund and EAGGF Guidance Section (not insignificant amounts in both cases), and various specific measures. Greece will also receive a 10% lump-sum repayment of own resources (19 m EUA), a 70% refund of its financial contribution (126 m EUA) and, according to the Commission's proposal, a refund of its contribution towards measures to assist the United Kingdom.

All in all, therefore, in 1981 Greece should receive more than she pays in, even if only the payments to be made are taken into consideration and not the commitments to be entered into.

There are no plans as yet for Greece to join the European Monetary System and so Greece will receive a

---

[1] These figures are given in Annex 1.

[2] Greece's quota in the Regional Fund is to be 15%, and the quotas of the other Member States will be reduced accordingly.

special repayment, like the United Kingdom. Greece will therefore be entitled to four repayments.

Turning to the question of recruiting staff, the plan is that Greece will provide 4% of the Commission staff. One A/1, four A/2 and twelve A/3 posts will be filled by Greek nationals. These top posts will be from the existing establishment plan, so the Budgetary Authority will not be asked to create new posts.

Compared with the full integration scenario described above (see p. 408), these figures show that the impact of Greek accession will be small in the first year. This is hardly surprising.

How Portugal will affect the 1980, 1981 and 1982 budgets

On 12 June, to help prepare Portugal for accession to the Community, the Commission proposed Community aid totalling 350 m EUA between 1980 and 1982, one-third in the form of repayable loans from the own resources of the European Investment Bank, attracting 3% interest subsidies by way of non-repayable aid from the Community budget. The Council agreed in principle to this proposal on 22 July.

Official sources used

1. The Treaties establishing the European Communities and secondary legislation.[1,2]
2. The ECSC, EEC, Euratom and European Communities' budgets.[1,2]
3. The annual General Reports of the Commission of the European Communities.[2]
4. The Social Reports published in conjunction with the annual General Reports of the Commission of the European Communities.[2]
5. The Annual Reports of the European Investment Bank.[3]
6. The Bulletins issued each month by the Commission of the European Communities and the Supplements thereto.[2]
7. The revenue and expenditure accounts of the European Communities.[4]
8. The ECSC's balance sheets.
9. The EAGGF Reports (that for 1979 is the 9th), Social Fund Reports (that for 1979 is the 8th), Regional Fund Reports (that for 1979 is the 5th) and the Reports on Euratom's borrowing and lending activities (that for 1979 is the 2nd) and interest subsidies on certain EMS loans (that for 1979 is the 1st).[4]

---

[1] Published in the *Official Journal of the European Communities* in the six official Community languages (Danish, Dutch, English, French, German and Italian), detailed references being given at the appropriate points in the book.

[2] Obtainable from:

Ireland

Government Publications

Sales Office
G.P.O. Arcade
Dublin 1
or by post from
Stationery Office
Dublin 4
Tel. 789644

United Kingdom

H.M. Stationery Office

P.O. Box 569
London SE1 9NH
Tel. (01) 928 6977, ext. 365
National Giro Account 582-1002

United States of America

European Community Information Service

2100 M Street, N.W.
Suite 707
Washington, D.C. 20037
Tel. (202) 862 9500

[3] Obtainable from the institution concerned.

[4] Obtainable from the Commission of the European Communities, Division IX/C/1, Rue de la Loi 200, 1049 Brussels, Belgium.

Index

The figures in bold indicate the main page references for the subject matter concerned which may cover several subsequent pages.

B

Balance between revenue and expenditure? 24

Balance of payments: 144, 333

Basket unit of account (see European unit of account)

Binding (force of remarks): 56

Blockage (freezing of appropriations under a particular heading): 73

Borrowing/lending (operations): vii, xi, 21, 61

British problem: xii, 135, 337, 339, 341

Brussels Compromise (30 May 1980): 126, 182, 223, 338, 341, 357

Budget Commissioner: 2, **38**, 44, 71, 81, 102

Budget Committee (Council): 43, 46, 322

Budget crisis from December 1978 to April 1979: xi, 9, 41, **45**, 48, 146, 222

Budget item: 53, 56, 70

Budget nomenclature: **56**, 61

Budget power (see Budgetary Authority) **46**

Budget timetable: **42**, 48, 184

Budget trade-offs: 37, **40**

Budget transparency: 58, 59

Budgetary Authority: **x**, xi, **1**, 4, 47, 57, 65, 313

Budgetary conciliation: 8, **44**

Budgetary Executive: 57, **69, 77**

Budgetary monitoring: **83**

Budgetary procedure: 42, 48

Budgetary system (arrangements): 129, 130

Business Cooperation Centre: **257**, 305

Butter (exports, Russian butter): 197

C

Cancellation of commitments (ECSC): 87, 90, 117

Carrying-over (of appropriations): 74

Cash (budget): 382

Ceiling on expenditure: 47

Censure motion: x, 12, 100, 105, 181, 197

Chapter (of the budget): 24, 53, 56, 76

Chapter 100 (of the budget) for provisional expenditure: 57, 70, **73**

Charge on transactions of the Supply Agency: 21

Cheysson Fund: 288

CIRCE: 321

Coal (aid to): 71, **248**, 251

Coking coal (ECSC aid to): 248, 268

Commission: ix, 310, 324

Commission's new budget proposal (of 25 February 1980): 51

Commitment appropriations: 45, **60**

Commitments budget: 50

Committee: **373**

Committee on Budgets (Parliament): 43, 90, 102, 133, 177, 348

Committee on Budgetary Control (Parliament): **99**, 349

Committee of the Four Presidents (ECSC): 2

Common organization of agricultural markets (COM): **168**, 190

Community borrowing: **144**

Community farm prices: 170

Community institutions: ix

Community loans: 61, 147

Community preference (agriculture): 168

Como (Case): 84, 91

Compensatory aid (agriculture): **173**, 190

Compulsory and non-compulsory expenditure: 7, 35, **40**, 50, 184, 209, 215, 225, 231, 253, 257, 292, 296

Concerted action: 258

Conciliation Committee (see Legislative conciliation)

Containment (of agricultural policy): 182

Contingencies (appropriations for): 59

Control subcommittee (Parliament): **98**, 349

Convergence (of the economies): vii, **199**

Cooperation (political ... with non-member countries): 59, **273**

Copenhagen Summit (14 and 15 December 1973): 8, 94, 218, **351**

Co-responsibility (tax, principle): **181**

Council: ix, 1, 43, 311, 324, 363, 402

Court of Auditors: **x, 93**, 303, 311, 324

Court of Justice: **x**, 303, 311, 324

Currency snake: 25, 31

Customs duties (customs field): 32, 34, 83, **120**, 128, **384**

Cyprus (aid to): 295

D

Dash: 57

Data processing: 305

Data processing (programme in the field of): 256

Decision of 8 April 1965 (places of work): 138, 153, 317

Decision of 21 April 1970: 5, 22, 33, 37, **111**, 115, **119**

Deductions from the remuneration of officials: 130

Deficiency payments: 169, **195**

419

Inflation (rate): 34, 123, 200

Information (expenditure): 305

Integrated action: 238

Interest (rate): 140, 156

Interest charged: 89

Interest rebates (subsidies): 41, 76, 127, **145**, 158, 202, **222**, 301

Interest rebates (subsidies) (ECSC): 88, 140, 223

Interinstitutional Dialogue: 49

Internal audit/control: **82**, 95, 88, 91, 188, 211, 227, 254, 293, 323

Internal development of the Community (policy to further the...): **199**

International Monetary Fund (IMF): 25, 330

Investment budget (ECSC): 65

Irregularities: 188

Israel (aid to): 295

J

Jet: **262**

Joint approach/guidelines (Council): 363

Joint Council (of Foreign Affairs and Finance Ministers): **48**, 51, 103, 131, 133, 196

Joint Declaration (Council): 11

Joint Research Centre (JRC): 35, 80, 258, **260**, 268, 393

Joint Undertaking: 262

L

Language (problem): 317

Legislative conciliation: **10**, 46, 60, **363**

Legislative power: 12, **46**

Lending (see Borrowing/lending operations)

Letter of amendment (to the preliminary draft budget): 35

Loans (building... for European civil servants): 71

Lomé Convention: 26, 27, **276**, **278**, 282

Luxembourg Agreement (of 29 January 1966): 4, 410

M

Maghreb (aid to the... countries): 295

Making available (own resources): 83

Malt (affair): 106

Malta (aid to): 295

Management Committees (common organization of markets): **78**, 186, 373

Marathon (farm): 170

Mashreq (aid to the... countries): 295

Maximum rate of increase in non-compulsory expenditure (and new rate): 35, 39, 40, 44, 122, 347

Mediterranean (aid to the... countries): **294**

Merger Treaty of 8 April 1965 (Brussels): ix, 11, 20, 24, 69

Milk (market for... and milk products): **180**

Million units of account (m EUA): xi

Minority for acceptance: 7, 13

Miscellaneous revenue: 130

Monetary compensatory amounts: **174**

Multinational estimates: 37, 404

N

National constitutional rules: x, 5, 122, 185, 281

Negative expenditure: 76, 186

Net contributor: 337, 338

New Community Instrument (NCI): **157**, 202, 236, 369

New energy sources: 78, 80, 252

New rate of increase in non-compulsory expenditure: 123, 347

Non-assignment: 22

Non-associated developing countries (aid to): 57, 71, **289**

Non-governmental organizations carrying out measures to assist developing countries (aid to NGOs): 57, 71, 288

Non-recoverable expenditure: 76

O

Office for Official Publications of the European Communities: 17, 305, **321**

Open-ended commitment (see Expenditure based on...)

Open transfer: **73**

Operating (expenditure): 59, 80, **303**, 324, 394

Overall assessment of Community budget problems: **48**, 52

Overall operational reserve: 24, 31

Overseas Countries and Territories (OCT): 274, 276, 279

Overseas Departments: 219, 275, 276

Own funds (ECSC): **137**

Own resources: 5, 22, 35, **83**, 133, 185

Spain: 407

Special Committee of Inquiry: 188, 197

Special reserve (ECSC): 138

Specific (*ad hoc*) action ('action ponctuelle'): **71**

Specification: 23

Stabex: 99, 277, 278

Staff (expenditure): 59, **303,** 324, 394

Staff Regulations: 306

Statement of expenditure (general budget): **55**

Statement of revenue (general budget): **61**

Storage (of agricultural products): 172

Structural funds: (see Social Fund, Regional Fund, European Agricultural Guidance and Guarantee Fund (Guidance Section))

Structure (of the general budget): **53,** 185, 209, 216, 226, 254, 264, 292, 296, 303

Structure (of the ECSC operational budget): 64

Subsidized housing (ECSC): 208

Sugar (ACP/India Protocol): 173, 280

Summits: vii, ix, 350

Supplementary budget: 37, 63, 73, 184, 197

Supplementary measures to assist the United Kingdom: 41, 222, 341

Supplementary staff: 319

Supply Agency: 21, **249,** 270, 305

Surplus available: 85, 92, 130

T

Token entry: 57, 62, 63

Tranche: 47

Transfer (of appropriations): 72

Transport: 256

Treaty of 21 April 1970 (Luxembourg): x, **4,** 5, 11

Treaty of 22 July 1975 (Brussels): x, 8, 10, **93**

Turkey: 295

U

Unanimously: 3

Unavoidable expenditure: 35, 42, 73, 87, 179, 204, 211

Unity (comprehensiveness): 19

Universality (non-assignment of revenue): 21

Updated parity unit of account: 25

UNRWA (see Refugees)

Uranium (aid to ... prospecting): 57, 249

V

VAT (percentage): 5, 8, 34, 84, 120, **121,** 386, 387

W

Welfare (or lack of it) 36, 202, 291

World farm prices: 34, 120, 169

Y

Yaoundé Convention: **275**

Year of origin approach: **74,** 389

Year of payment approach: 74, 382

Yugoslavia: 295

This book is to be returned on or before
the last date stamped below.